Essentials in Petri Nets: Information Technology and Computers

Essentials in Petri Nets: Information Technology and Computers

Edited by **Ruth Hinrichs**

Clanrye International

New Jersey

Published by Clanrye International,
55 Van Reypen Street,
Jersey City, NJ 07306, USA
www.clanryeinternational.com

Essentials in Petri Nets: Information Technology and Computers
Edited by Ruth Hinrichs

International Standard Book Number: 978-1-63240-228-8 (Hardback)

Printed in the United States of America.

Contents

Preface

This book concentrates on the applications of Petri Nets in computer science. Petri Nets are graphical and mathematical tools, and the synchronism of executed actions is the natural phenomenon because of which Petri Nets are considered as mathematical tools for modeling synchronous systems. The primary idea of this theory was modified by several researchers according to their needs, owing to the odd "flexibility" of this theory. This area has great influence on our lives and our world. This theory is still developing and some directions of investigations are also encompassed in this book. Some flourishing facts regarding the application of Petri Nets in the public domain are also covered including the in-depth study and control of public bicycle sharing systems. The book displays the results of research works done with the help of Petri Nets in science centers across the globe.

This book is a comprehensive compilation of works of different researchers from varied parts of the world. It includes valuable experiences of the researchers with the sole objective of providing the readers (learners) with a proper knowledge of the concerned field. This book will be beneficial in evoking inspiration and enhancing the knowledge of the interested readers.

In the end, I would like to extend my heartiest thanks to the authors who worked with great determination on their chapters. I also appreciate the publisher's support in the course of the book. I would also like to deeply acknowledge my family who stood by me as a source of inspiration during the project.

Editor

Section 1

Computer Science

Chapter 1

Sequential Object Petri Nets and the Modeling of Multithreading Object-Oriented Programming Systems

Ivo Martiník

Additional information is available at the end of the chapter

1. Introduction

Sequential object Petri nets are the newly introduced class of Petri nets, whose definition is the main topics of this article; they feature certain original concepts and can be successfully used at a design, modeling and verification of multithreading object-oriented programming systems executing in highly-parallel or distributed environment. In this article basic characteristics of sequential object Petri nets are very briefly presented including possibilities in their definition of newly introduced tokens as non-empty finite recursive sequences over the set of non-negative integer numbers, functionalities of multiarcs and the mechanism of the firing of transitions. These properties significantly increase modeling capabilities of this class of Petri nets at the modeling of multithreading object-oriented programming systems. Sequential object Petri nets can be used also in the area of recursive algorithms modeling and they are also the initial step to explicitly represent paradigms of functional programming. The fusion of object-oriented and functional programming enables to express new kinds of programming patterns and component abstractions.

The theory of sequential object Petri nets proceeds from the theories of various types of Petri nets, starting with Place/Transition nets (Diaz, 2009) and their sub-classes, followed by High-Level nets (Jensen & Rozenberg, 1991), (Reisig, 2009) such as Predicate-Transition nets and Coloured nets (Jensen & Kristensen, 2009), enabling to model apart from the management structure of the system even data processing, and in connection with modeling of object-oriented programming systems it is Object nets (Agha et. al., 2001), (Köhler & Rölke, 2007), which are being studied lately. But practical usability of Petri nets (in their original form) in the role of the parallel programming language is mainly impeded by the static nature of their structure. They are missing standard mechanisms for description of methods alone, programming modules, classes, data types, hierarchical structures, etc.

Positive characteristics of Petri nets demonstrate only in not too much large-scale modules at high abstraction level. That is why Petri nets are often understood as the theoretical abstract module only, whose applicability for design, analysis and verification of extensive programming systems is limited. Therefore, this article briefly describes a special class of sequential object Petri nets and its possibilities of multithreading object-oriented programming systems modeling, which eliminates the stated shortcomings required for design, analysis and verification of these systems in several directions.

This chapter is arranged into the following sections: in the section 2 is described the term of the sequence over the finite set and its properties which denominates the class of the sequential object Petri nets; section 3 explains the base term of this chapter, ie. sequential object Petri net and its properties; section 4 explains in details implementation of the mechanism of firing of transitions in a sequential object Petri net; section 5 then discusses the area of object-oriented programming systems and their representation by the sequential object Petri nets; section 6 explains the example of simple class hierarchy represented by the sequential object Petri net and it is inspired by the several base classes of the Java programming language class hierarchy. Finally, the section 7 gives the conclusions of the research to conclude the chapter.

2. Sequences and their properties

Prior to the formal introduction of the term of sequential object Petri net, we present the definition of sequence over the finite set from which the denomination of this class of Petri nets has been derived. $\mathbf{N}$ denotes the set of all natural numbers, $\mathbf{N_0}$ the set of all non-negative integer numbers, $P(A)$ denotes the family of all the subsets of given set A.

Let A be a non-empty set. By the (non-empty finite) **sequence** σ over the set A we understand a mapping $\sigma: \{1, 2, \ldots, n\} \rightarrow A$, where $n \in \mathbf{N}$. Mapping $\varepsilon: \emptyset \rightarrow A$ is called the **empty sequence** over the set A. We usually represent the sequence $\sigma: \{1, 2, \ldots, n\} \rightarrow A$ by the notation $\sigma = <a_1, a_2, \ldots, a_n>$ of the elements of the set A, where $a_i = \sigma(i)$ for $1 \leq i \leq n$. We also consider any element of the set A as the sequence over the set A, ie. mapping $\sigma:\{1\} \rightarrow A$. Empty sequence $\varepsilon: \emptyset \rightarrow A$ over the set A we usually represent by the notation $\varepsilon = <>$. We denote the set of all **finite non-empty** sequences over the set A by the notation A_{SQ}, the set of all **finite** (and possible empty) sequences over the set A by the notation A_{ESQ}.

Note also, that the set A can be any non-empty set, which means that it can be also the non-empty set of sequences over some non-empty set B, ie. $A = B_{ESQ}$. Thus member of the sequence over the set B_{ESQ} can be then another sequence over the set B. This fact thus also similarly allows sequences over the sets $(B_{ESQ})_{ESQ}$, $((B_{ESQ})_{ESQ})_{ESQ}$, etc. The term of sequence over some non-empty set has thus **recursive character** and every such sequence can consists from **subsequences** consisting from subsequences etc. We denote the set of all **finite non-empty** sequences without the empty subsequences over the union of sets A, A_{SQ}, $(A_{SQ})_{SQ}$, $((A_{SQ})_{SQ})_{SQ}$, … by the notation A_{RQ}, the set of all **finite** (and possible empty or with empty subsequences) sequences over the union of sets A, A_{ESQ}, $(A_{ESQ})_{ESQ}$, $((A_{ESQ})_{ESQ})_{ESQ}$, … by the notation A_{ERQ}.

The **length of the sequence** $\sigma = <a_1, a_2, \ldots, a_n>$, where $\sigma \in A_{ERQ}$, $n \in \mathbf{N}$, is equal to the natural number n, the length of the empty sequence ε is equal to the number 0. The length of the sequence σ we represent by the notation $length(\sigma)$, or $@\sigma$, the set of all the elements of the sequence σ we represent by the notation $elem(\sigma)$, ie. $elem(\sigma) = \{a_i \mid a_i = \sigma(i) \text{ for } 1 \le i \le n\}$, $elem(\varepsilon) = \varnothing$. The **subsequences of the sequence** σ is the mapping $subsq$: $A_{ERQ} \to P(A_{ERQ})$, such that for $\forall i, 1 \le i \le n$: $((\sigma \in subsq(\sigma)) \vee (((a_i == \varepsilon) \vee (a_i \in A)) \Rightarrow a_i \in subsq(\sigma)) \vee (((a_i != \varepsilon) \wedge (a_i \notin A)) \Rightarrow ((a_i \in subsq(\sigma)) \wedge (subsq(a_i) \in subsq(\sigma)))$. The **members of the sequence** σ is the mapping $memb$: $A_{ERQ} \to P(A)$, so that $memb(\sigma) = \{a \mid (a \in subsq(\sigma)) \wedge (a \in A)\}$, $memb(\varepsilon) = \varnothing$.

If $\sigma = <a_1, a_2, \ldots, a_n>$ and $\tau = <b_1, b_2, \ldots, b_m>$ are the finite sequences, where $\sigma \in A_{ERQ}$, $\tau \in A_{ERQ}$, $n \in \mathbf{N}$, $m \in \mathbf{N}$, then by the **concatenation of the sequences** σ and τ, denoted by $\sigma\tau$, we understand the finite sequence $\sigma\tau = <a_1, a_2, \ldots, a_n, b_1, b_2, \ldots, b_m>$ and its length is equal to $n + m$. We say, that the sequences σ and τ are **equal**, denoted by $\sigma == \tau$, if the following is simultaneously true: $(n = m) \wedge (\forall i, 1 \le i \le n$: $(((a_i = \varepsilon) \wedge (b_i = \varepsilon)) \vee ((a_i \in A) \wedge (b_i \in A) \wedge (a_i = b_i)) \vee ((a_i \neq \varepsilon) \wedge (b_i \neq \varepsilon) \wedge (a_i \notin A) \wedge (b_i \notin A) \wedge (a_i == b_i))))$.

If, for instance, $\tau \in A_{ERQ}$, $\tau = <<a, <a, b>>, <a, <c>, b>, <>>$, then $length(\tau) = 3$, $elem(\tau) = \{<a, <a, b>>, <a, <c>, b>, <>\}$, $subsq(\tau) = \{<<a, <a, b>>, <a, <c>, b>, <>>, <a, <a, b>>, <a, <c>, b>, <a, b>, <a>, <b>, <c>, <>\}$ and $memb(\tau) = \{a, b, c\}$.

When operating with sequences, notation in the form of $n^*(\sigma)$ can be utilized, where $\sigma \in A_{ERQ}$, $n \in \mathbf{N}$. Informally, that notation expresses sequence consisting of n concatenations of the sequence σ. If, for example $A = \mathbf{N}_0$, $\sigma = <1, 2>$, then notation $3^*(\sigma)$ represents the sequence $3^*(<1, 2>) == <1, 2><1, 2><1, 2> == <1, 2, 1, 2, 1, 2>$.

Multiset M over a non-empty set S is a function m: $S \to \mathbf{N}_0$. By the non-negative number $m(a) \in \mathbf{N}_0$, $a \in S$, we denote the number of occurrences of the element a in the multiset m. We usually represent the multiset m by the formal sum $\sum_{a \in S} m(a)`a$. By S_{MS} we denote the set of all non-empty multisets over the set S, by S_{EMS} we denote the set of all multisets over the set S.

IDENT denotes the set of all **identifiers** and it is understood to be a set of non-empty finite sequences over the set of all letters of the selected national alphabet and the set of all decadic digits that starts with a letter. Identifiers are recorded in a way usual for standard programming languages. Examples of correctly formed identifiers for example involve the *thread*, *var22*, *αβχδ*, etc. On the contrary, for example sequences *2main*, *first goal*, *_input*, are not identifiers. Moreover is it true, that if $ID_1, ID_2, \ldots, ID_n \in$ ***IDENT***, where $n \in \mathbf{N}$, $n > 1$, then we call the sequence in the form $ID_1.ID_2. \ldots .ID_n$ **compound identifier** (i.e. for example the sequence *Main.Thread.Variable1* is a compound identifier). ***#IDENT*** set is understood to be the set of all non-empty finite sequences in the form #A, where A ∈ ***IDENT***. Then, elements of ***#IDENT*** set for example include sequences *#thread*, *#var22*, *#αβχδ*, etc.

The set $(\mathbf{N}_0)_{RQ}$ we will denote by the symbol ***Tokens***. The set ***ArcSeq*** (*arc sequences*) is defined by the following:

i. if $x \in$ (***IDENT*** ∪ ***#IDENT***), then $<x> \in$ ***ArcSeq***,
ii. if $x \in$ ***Tokens***, then $x \in$ ***ArcSeq***,

iii. if $x \in$ ***ArcSeq***, then $\langle x \rangle \in$ ***ArcSeq*** and also $\langle length(x) \rangle \in$ ***ArcSeq***,
iv. if $x \in$ ***ArcSeq*** and $y \in$ ***ArcSeq***, then $xy \in$ ***ArcSeq***,
v. if $n \in$ (***IDENT*** $\cup$ **N**) and $x \in$ ***ArcSeq***, then $n^*(x) \in$ ***ArcSeq***.

The elements of ***Tokens*** set for example involve sequences <1>, <22, <0, 0>>, <<3, 2>, <4, <7, 8>>>, etc.). The set of arc sequences ***ArcSeq*** is, informally said, the set of **non-empty final recursive sequences** over the set (***IDENT*** $\cup$ ***#IDENT*** $\cup$ ***Tokens***) which do not contain empty subsequences and which can contain as their members even selected operations over those recursive sequences, between which is the determination of the recursive sequence length and concatenation of recursive sequences. So examples of elements of the set ***ArcSeq*** can be sequences <a, b, 1>, <#s, @(s), <1, <2, 3>>>, <a, thread, a*(<thread>), <1, 0>>, etc.

Let $AS \in$ ***ArcSeq***, $AS = \langle a_1, a_2, \ldots, a_n \rangle$, where $n \in$ **N**. Then the mapping *variables*: ***ArcSeq*** $\rightarrow$ *P*(***IDENT*** $\cup$ ***#IDENT*** $\cup$ $\mathbf{N_0}$) is defined so that for $\forall AS \in$ ***ArcSeq*** $\forall i$, $1 \le i \le n$:

i. if $a_i \in$ (***IDENT*** $\cup$ **#IDENT**), then $a_i \in variables(AS)$,
ii. if $a_i \in$ ***Tokens***, then $memb(a_i) \subseteq variables(AS)$,
iii. if $a_i = \langle x \rangle$, where $x \in$ ***ArcSeq***, then $variables(x) \subseteq variables(AS)$,
iv. if $a_i = length(x)$, where $x \in$ ***ArcSeq***, then $variables(x) \subseteq variables(AS)$,
v. if $a_i = xy$, where $x \in$ ***ArcSeq*** and $y \in$ ***ArcSeq***, then $(variables(x) \subseteq variables(AS)) \wedge (variables(y) \subseteq variables(AS))$,
vi. if $a_i = n^*(x)$, where $n \in$ (***IDENT*** $\cup$ **N**) and $x \in$ ***ArcSeq***, then $(n \in variables(AS)) \wedge (variables(x) \subseteq variables(AS))$.

Thus mapping *variables* assigns to each arc sequence $AS \in$ ***ArcSeq***, $AS = \langle a_1, a_2, \ldots, a_n \rangle$, where $n \in$ **N**, the set of members from the sets ***IDENT***, ***#IDENT*** a $\mathbf{N_0}$ contained in it. The set of *variables*(*AS*) associated with a particular arc *AS* will be identified in the text by the term **variables of the arc sequence *AS***. So if for example *AS* = <a, thread, a*(<thread>), <1, 0>>, then *variables*(*AS*) = {a, thread, 1, 0}.

3. Sequential object Petri nets and their properties

Sequential Object Petri Net is an ordered pair $SOPN = (\Sigma, PN)$, where

i. Σ is a finite non-empty set of **pages,**
ii. *PN* is a **page number function**, $PN: \Sigma \rightarrow$ **N**, that is injective.

By elements of the finite non-empty set Σ of pages we routinely mark identifiers from the set ***IDENT***. Injective function *PN* of numbering of pages of the net assigns to each page of sequential object Petri net *SOPN* the unique natural number within the net.

Let $SOPN = (\Sigma, PN)$ is a sequential object Petri net. **Page** of the sequential object Petri net *SOPN* is an ordered touple $PG = (P, IP, OP, T, A, MA, IOPN, AF, MAF, TP, IPF, OPF, SP, IF)$, $PG \in \Sigma$, where:

i. *P* is a finite set of **places**,
ii. *IP* is a finite set of **input places**, $P \cap IP = \emptyset$,

iii. OP is a finite set of **output places**, $P \cap OP = \emptyset$,
iv. T is a finite set of **transitions**, $(P \cup IP \cup OP) \cap T = \emptyset$,
v. A is a finite set of **arcs**, $A \subseteq ((P \cup IP) \times T) \cup (T \times (P \cup OP))$,
vi. MA is a finite set of **multiarcs**, $MA \subseteq ((P \cup IP) \times T) \cup (T \times (P \cup OP))$, $A \cap MA = \emptyset$,
vii. $IOPN$ is a function of **input and output place numbers**, $IOPN$: $(IP \cup OP) \rightarrow \mathbf{N}$, that is injective,
viii. AF is an **arc function**, AF: $(A \cup MA) \rightarrow \boldsymbol{ArcSeq}$,
ix. MAF is a **multiarc function**, MAF: $MA \rightarrow \boldsymbol{ArcSeq}$,
x. TP is a function of **transition priorities**, TP: $T \rightarrow \mathbf{N}$,
xi. IPF is an **input place function** of multiarcs, IPF: $(T \times (P \cup OP)) \rightarrow AIP$, where $(T \times (P \cup OP)) \subseteq MA$, $AIP = \{p \mid \exists \gamma \in \Sigma: p \in IP \in \gamma\}$,
xii. OPF is an **output place function** of multiarcs, OPF: $((P \cup IP) \times T) \rightarrow AOP$, where $((P \cup IP) \times T) \subseteq MA$, $AOP = \{p \mid \exists \gamma \in \Sigma: p \in OP \in \gamma\}$,
xiii. SP is a finite set of **subpages**, $SP \subseteq \Sigma$,
xiv. IF is an **initialization function**, IF: $(P \cup IP \cup OP) \rightarrow \boldsymbol{Tokens}_{\mathbf{EMS}}$.

The finite set of places P is used for expressing of conditions of a modeled programming system and in the net layout we notate them with circles. IP is a finite set of input places of the net page representing its input interface. Additionally, no input place of the net page can be identical with any of its places. Input places are represented in the page layout with circles of highlighted upper semicircle. Then, OP is a finite set of output places of the net page representing its output interface. Additionally, no output place of the net page can be identical with any of its places. The definition admits even such possibility that the selected input place is identical with any of output places of the given net page. Output places are represented in the net page layout with circles of highlighted lower semicircle.

Likewise the finite set of transitions T is used for describing events in the programming system and we notate them with rectangles. That set is disjoint with the set of places P of the given net page. A is the finite set of arcs being principally oriented while connecting the place with transition or transition with place and in the layout of net we represent them by oriented arrows drawn in full line. It is worth considering that none of output arcs of any transition can be associated with any input place of the net page, and none of input arcs of any transition can be associated with any output place of the net page. MA is finite set of multiarcs, newly introduced type of arc in sequential object Petri nets. Functionalities of multiarc are used for the modeling of synchronous and asynchronous calling of methods in the given programming system and they follow the principles of the multiarcs in the bi-relational P/T Petri nets (Martiník, 2011). Multiarcs are represented in layouts of the net with oriented arrows drawn with dash line. The set of arcs of the given page is disjoint with the set of its multiarcs, hence it is not allowed the existence of the ordered pair (*place, transition*) or (*transition, place*) connected by both types of oriented arcs.

$IOPN$ function of the identification of input and output places of the net page assigns to each input and output place of the particular net page unique natural number which is used at the implementation of mechanism of execution of transitions associated with multiarcs of the net page. With each arc or multiarc of the net page is associated the value of its arc function *AF*, which assigns to each arc or multiarc (one) **arc sequence**, i.e. the element of ***ArcSeq*** set. With each multiarc of the net page is additionally associated the value of its multiarc function *MAF*, which assigns to each such multiarc (one) **arc sequence**, i.e. the element of ***ArcSeq*** set. The layout of the net page shows values of *AF* and *MAF* functions associated with particular multiarc in the form *AF* | *MAF*. With all transitions of the net page are associated values of their functions of transition priorities *TP* assigning each transition with (the only) value of such transition priority, which is the value of a certain natural number. If the value of function of transition priorities is not explicitly indicated in the net layout with the particular transition, we assign it to the value of natural number 1.

The input place function of multiarcs *IPF* assigns each multiarc of the net page connecting ordered pair (*transition, place*) a certain **input place of the selected net page.** The definition admits even the possibility of assigning the selected multiarc of the particular net page with some of the input places of the same net page (ie. it is allowed to model recursive methods). The particular input place p of the selected net page γ ($\gamma \in \Sigma$) is in the layout of network identified by ordered pair of natural numbers ($PN(\gamma)$, $IOPN(\gamma.p)$), where the first member of the pair indicates the value of page number function *PN* and the second member of the pair identifies the selected input place p on the net page γ with the particular value of function *IOPN*. We present this ordered pair in layouts of net pages usually in the form $PN(\gamma).IOPN(\gamma.p)$. The output place function of multiarcs *OPF* assigns each multiarc of the net page connecting the ordered pair (*place, transition*) with a certain **output place of the selected net page.** The definition again admits the possibility of assigning to the selected multiarc of the given net page some of the output places of the same net page. The particular output place p of the selected net page γ is marked in a similar way as in case of the function *IPF*.

A part of each net page can be the finite set *SP* of its subpages, which are by themselves the net pages (i.e. elements of the set Σ). Initialization function *IF* assigns each place including input and output places of the net page with a **multiset of tokens.** That function is also identified in literature as M_0. We routinely mark identifiers from the set ***IDENT*** by elements of the set of places, input places, output places and transitions.

Figure 1 shows the sequential object Petri net *SOPN* = (Σ, *PN*), where Σ = {**Main, Sub**}, *PN* = {(**Main,** 1), (**Sub,** 2)}. Net page of this sequential object Petri net **Main** = (*P, IP, OP, T, A, MA, IOPN, AF, MAF, AP, IPF, OPF, SP, IF*), where *P* = {**P1, P2**}, *IP* = {**in**}, *OP* = {**In**}, *T* = {**T1, T2**}, *A* = {(**in, T1**), (**P1, T1**), (**T2, In**)}, *MA* = {(**T1, P2**), (**P2, T2**)}, *IOPN* = {(**in**, 1), (**In**, 2)}, *AF* = {((**in, T1**), <a>), ((**P1, T1**), <b, 1>), ((**T1, P2**), <a>), ((**P2, T2**), <a>), ((**T2, In**), <b>)}, *MAF* = {((**P2, T2**), <b>), ((**T1, P2**), <b,1>)}, *TP* = {(**T1**, 1), (**T2**, 1)}, *IPF* = {((**T1, P2**), (2.1))}, *OPF* = {((**P2, T2**), (2.2))}, *SP* = ∅, *IF* = {(**in**, 1`<1>), (**P1**, ∅), (**P2**, ∅), (**In**, ∅)}. Net page **Sub** = (*P, IP, OP, T, A, MA, IOPN, AF, MAF, AP, IPF, OPF, SP, IF*), where *P* = ∅, *IP* = {**start**}, *OP* = {**Start**}, *T* = {**T1**}, *A* = {(**start, T1**), (**T1, Start**)}, *MA* = ∅, *IOPN* = {(**start**, 1), (**Start**, 2)}, *AF* = {((**start, T1**), <c, 1>), ((**T1, Start**), <c>)}, *MAF* = ∅, *TP* = {(**T1**, 1)}, *IPF* = ∅, *OPF* = ∅, *SP* = ∅, *IF* = {(**start**, ∅), (**Start**, 1`<3>)}.

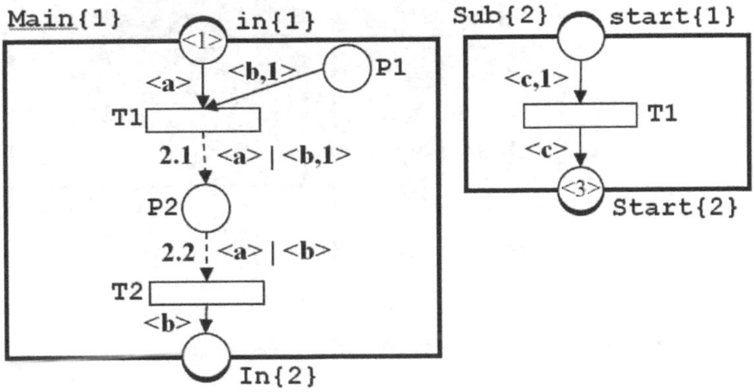

Figure 1. Sequential object Petri net

If **page_identifier** is the identifier of the selected net page and **element_identifier** is the identifier of a place, input place, output place or transition of the net page, we call the compound identifier in the form **page_identifier.element_identifier** so called **distinguished identifier of the element of net page**, which uniquely identifies it within the given sequential object Petri net. Designs of distinguished identifiers of subpages of the net and of its elements can be also executed for cases of sub subpages of the net pages, etc.

For the sake of better transparency we will not indicate in layouts of nets explicit values of page number function *PN*, and explicit values of function of input and output place numbers *IOPN* of identification of input and output places of individual net pages any more. Moreover, we will not indicate values of functions *IPF* and *OPF* of particular multiarcs in the form of **a.b** pair of natural numbers, but in the form of the pair of identifiers **page.ioplace**, where **page** $\in \Sigma$ is the net page and **ioplace** $\in$ *IP* $\in$ **page**, perhaps **ioplace** $\in$ *OP* $\in$ **page** is particular input, or output place of the net page while it holds that **a** = *PN*(**page**) and **b** = *IOPN*(**page.ioplace**).

Layouts of sequential object Petri nets are usually further adjusted in the sense of notations of declarations of headings of methods and their calling within the text of the program, similarly as shown in Figure 2. Here, identifiers of input and output places of the net pages are complemented by (informative) notation of the shape of tokens, which are accepted by those input and output places (see the notation of the input places **Main.in<a>, Sub.start<c, 1>** and of the output places **Main.In<b>, Sub.Start<c>**). We will not record values of functions *AF* and *MAF* in the form of the ordered pair separated by | line any more. The value of the arc function *AF* is indicated separately and the value of the multiarc function *MAF* is indicated behind the value of the input place function *IPF* on the net page, perhaps with a value of the output place function *OPF* of particular multiarc (see notation **Sub.start<b, 1>** and **Sub.Start<b>** of the net page **Main**) in the sense of declaration of calling of methods with the entry of values of input parameters or output values of these methods.

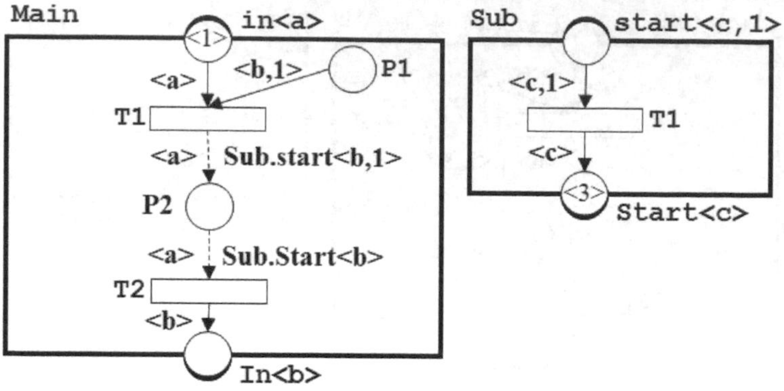

Figure 2. Sequential object Petri net

Let $SOPN = (\Sigma, PN)$ is a sequential object Petri net, $PG \in \Sigma$ is its net page. By the marking M of the net page PG we understand the mapping M: $(P \cup IP \cup OP) \rightarrow \boldsymbol{Tokens}_{\mathrm{EMS}}$, where $P \in PG$, $IP \in PG$, $OP \in PG$. By the marking of the net $SOPN$ we understand the marking of all its net pages.

Let $SOPN = (\Sigma, PN)$ is a sequential object Petri net, $PG \in \Sigma$ is its page. Then:

i. by $InputArcs(x)$ we denote the set of all input arcs of selected place, output place or transition x, ie. $\forall\ x \in (P \cup OP \cup T) \in PG$: $InputArcs(x) = \{a \in A \mid \exists\ y \in (P \cup IP \cup T): a = (y, x)\}$.
ii. by $InputMultiArcs(x)$ we denote the set of all input multiarcs of selected place, output place or transition x, ie. $\forall\ x \in (P \cup OP \cup T) \in PG$: $InputMultiArcs(x) = \{a \in MA \mid \exists\ y \in (P \cup IP \cup T): a = (y, x)\}$.
iii. by $InputNodes(x)$ we denote the set of all input nodes of selected place, output place or transition x, ie. $\forall\ x \in (P \cup OP \cup T) \in PG$: $InputNodes(x) = \{y \in (P \cup IP \cup T) \mid \exists\ a \in (A \cup MA): a = (y, x)\}$. We denote the set $InputNodes(x)$ by $\bullet x$.
iv. by $OutputNodes(x)$ we denote the set of all output nodes of selected place, input place or transition x, ie. $\forall\ x \in (P \cup IP \cup T) \in PG$: $OutputNodes(x) = \{y \in (P \cup OP \cup T) \mid \exists\ a \in (A \cup MA): a = (x, y)\}$. We denote the set $OutputNodes(x)$ by $x\bullet$.
v. by $TransitionInputVariables(x)$ we denote the set of all variables included in the values of arc functions AF (resp. multiarc functions MAF) of all the input arcs and multiarcs of the transition x, ie.$\forall\ x \in T \in PG$: $TransitionInputVariables(x) = \{v \mid ((v \in variables(AF(y)) \vee (v \in variables(MAF(y))) \wedge ((y \in InputArcs(x)) \vee (y \in InputMultiArcs(x)))\}$.

4. Firing of transitions in sequential object Petri nets

An important term used at the implementation of the mechanism of firing of transitions in a sequential object Petri net is the term of **binding of the arc sequence** contained in the value of AF, or MAF, function of the particular arc, or multiarc, to the token found at a certain marking of the net page in the place associated with this arc (for short, we will refer to that in the text also as **binding of token**).

Let $T \in$ ***Tokens***, $T = <t_1, t_2, \ldots, t_n>$, where $n \in$ **N**, $AS \in$ ***ArcSeq***. We denote, that there exists **input binding of the arc sequence** *AS* to the token *T*, if there exists mapping *InputBind*: $AS \to T$ that satifies the following:

i. If $AS = <a_1, a_2, \ldots, a_n>$, where $a_1, a_2, \ldots, a_n \in$ (***IDENT*** $\cup$ ***#IDENT*** $\cup$ $\mathbf{N_0}$), then:
a. if $a_i \in$ (***IDENT*** $\cup$ ***#IDENT***) for $1 \le i \le n$, then $InputBind(a_i) = t_i$,
b. if $a_i \in \mathbf{N_0}$ for $1 \le i \le n$, then $(InputBind(a_i) = t_i) \wedge (a_i = t_i)$,
c. $\forall\, u \in variables(AS)\ \forall\, v \in variables(AS)$: $((u = v) \Rightarrow (InputBind(u) == InputBind(v)))$.
ii. If $AS = <a_1, a_2, \ldots, a_{k-1}, a_k, a_{k+1}, \ldots, a_m>$, where $m < n$, $1 \le k \le m$, $a_k \in$ ***#IDENT***, $a_1, \ldots, a_{k-1}, a_{k+1}, \ldots, a_m \in$ (***IDENT*** $\cup$ $\mathbf{N_0}$), $m \in$ **N**, then:
a. $InputBind(a_k) = <t_k, t_{k+1}, \ldots, t_{k+n-m}>$,
b. if $a_i \in$ ***IDENT*** for $1 \le i \le k\text{-}1$, then $InputBind(a_i) = t_i$,
c. if $a_i \in$ ***IDENT*** for $k+1 \le i \le m$, then $InputBind(a_i) = t_{n-m+i}$,
d. if $a_i \in \mathbf{N_0}$ for $1 \le i \le k\text{-}1$, then $(InputBind(a_i) = t_i) \wedge (a_i = t_i)$,
e. if $a_i \in \mathbf{N_0}$ for $k+1 \le i \le m$, then $(InputBind(a_i) = t_{n-m+i}) \wedge (a_i = t_{n-m+i})$,
f. $\forall\, u \in variables(AS)\ \forall\, v \in variables(AS)$: $((u = v) \Rightarrow (InputBind(u) == InputBind(v)))$.
iii. In other case the mapping *InputBind* is not defined.

Then, input binding of the arc sequence *AS* to the token *T* via mapping *InputBind*: $AS \to T$ can be successfully realized in the following two cases:

i. Arc sequence is in the form $AS = <a_1, a_2, \ldots, a_n>$, where $n \in$ **N**, i.e. it holds that ***length*(AS)** = ***length*(T) = *n***, while generally **more than one** of elements $a_1, a_2, \ldots, a_n$ of that sequence can be the element of the set ***#IDENT***. Then, at the input binding of the arc sequence *AS* to the token *T* we execute, informally said, binding of mutually corresponding elements of sequences according to their order. If an element a_i of the arc sequence *AS* is a nonnegative integer, then such element must be bound to single-element t_i of token *T*, where $1 \le i \le n$, which is also nonnegative integer and the value of both those numbers must be identical. If *u* and *v* are two identical variables of the arc sequence *AS*, then the values of elements of the token *T* bound to them must be identical. Figure 3 shows a very simple example of input binding of the arc sequence *AS* = <1, a, a, #c, 3> to the token *T* = <1, 10, 10, 2, 3>:

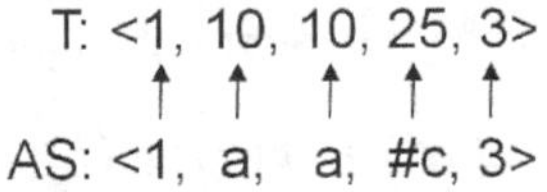

Figure 3. Binding of arc sequence to token

ii. Arc sequence is in the form $AS = <a_1, a_2, \ldots, a_{k-1}, a_k, a_{k+1}, \ldots, a_m>$, where $m \in$ **N**, holds that ***length*(AS) < *length*(T)**, i.e. $m < n$, and at the same time just a single element $a_k \in$ ***#IDENT***, where $1 \le k \le m$. Then, that only element a_k is bound to the **sequence** $<t_k, t_{k+1}, \ldots, t_{k+n-m}>$ of elements of the token *T*. In binding of other elements of the sequence *AS* the same rules hold as it was in the case of (i). An example of that type of binding of the arc sequence *AS* = <x, #y, 5, z> (and thus element $a_2 \in$ ***#IDENT***) to the token *T* = <4, 8, 10, 2, 5, 19> is shown in Figure 4.

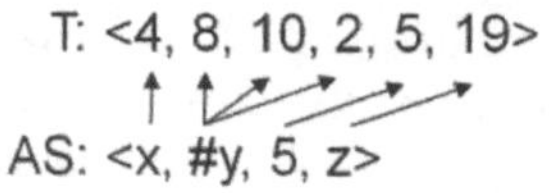

Figure 4. Binding of arc sequence to token

Next examples of the arc sequences binding to tokens in a sequential object Petri net involve:

- arc sequence <a, a, 1> can be successfully bound to token <2, 2, 1>, where *InputBind*(a) = 2, *InputBind*(1) = 1,
- arc sequence <a, a, 1> cannot be successfully bound to token <1, 2, 3> (it would hold that *InputBind*(a) = 1 and *InputBind*(a) = 2),
- arc sequence <#x> can be successfully bound to token <1, 2, 3>, where *InputBind*(#x) = <1, 2, 3>,
- arc sequence <x, #y> can be successfully bound to token <1, 2, 3>, where *InputBind*(x) = 1, *InputBind*(#y) = <2, 3>,
- arc sequence <x, y> can be successfully bound to token <<1, 2>, <3, 3>>, where *InputBind*(x) = <1, 2>, *InputBind*(y) = <3, 3>,
- arc sequence <x, #y> can be successfully bound to token <<1, 2>, <3, 3>, 4>, where *InputBind*(x) = <1, 2>, *InputBind*(#y) = <<3, 3>, 4>.

Let $SOPN = (\Sigma, PN)$ is a sequential object Petri net, $PG \in \Sigma$ is a net page, $t \in T$ is a transition of the net page PG, $p \in \bullet t \in (P \cup IP)$ is a place or input place of the net page PG, $q \in t\bullet \in (P \cup OP)$ is a place or output place of the net page PG, M is a marking of the net $SOPN$. Transition t is ***enabled*** in the marking M of the net $SOPN$, if:

i. $\forall\ (p, t) \in (InputArcs(t) \cup InputMultiArcs(t))\ \exists\ InputBind{:}\ AF(p, t) \rightarrow e$, where $e \in M(p)$,
ii. $\forall\ (p, t) \in InputMultiArcs(t)\ \exists\ InputBind{:}\ MAF(p, t) \rightarrow e$, where $e \in M(OPF(p, t))$,
iii. $\forall\ u \in TransitionInputVariables(t)\ \forall\ v \in TransitionInputVariables(t)$:

$$((u = v) \Rightarrow (InputBind(u) == InputBind(v))).$$

If transition t is enabled in the marking M of the net $SOPN$, we record that fact symbolically in the form of *t **en** M*.

Let $AS = \langle a_1, a_2, \ldots, a_n\rangle \in \mathbf{ArcSeq}$, $n \in \mathbf{N}$. If transition t is ***enabled*** in the marking M of the net $SOPN$, then we say, that there exists partial mapping $OutputBind$: $\mathbf{ArcSeq} \rightarrow \mathbf{Tokens}$, if

$$OutputBind(AS) = OB(a_1)\ OB(a_2)\ \ldots\ OB(a_n)$$

where OB: $\mathbf{ArcSeq} \rightarrow \mathbf{Tokens}$ and $\forall i,\ 1 \le i \le n$:

a. $OB(a_i) = \langle InputBind(a_i)\rangle$, if $a_i \in \mathbf{IDENT}$,
b. $OB(a_i) = InputBind(a_i)$, if $a_i \in \mathbf{\#IDENT}$,
c. $OB(a_i) = a_i$, if $a_i \in \mathbf{Tokens}$,
d. $OB(a_i) = \langle OB(x)\rangle$, if $a_i = \langle x\rangle$, where $x \in \mathbf{ArcSeq}$,
e. $OB(a_i) = \langle @(OB(x))\rangle$, if $a_i = @(x)$, where $x \in \mathbf{ArcSeq}$,
f. $OB(a_i) = OB(b_1)\ OB(b_2)\ \ldots\ OB(b_k)$, if $a_i = b_1\ b_2 \ldots b_k$, where $b_1, b_2, \ldots, b_k \in \mathbf{ArcSeq}$, $k \in \mathbf{N}$,
g. $OB(a_i) = OB(b)^*(OB(x))$, if $a_i = b^*(x)$, where $b \in (\mathbf{IDENT} \cup \mathbf{N_0})$, $x \in \mathbf{ArcSeq}$.

Thus transition *t* on the net page *PG* of the net *SOPN* is ***enabled***, if the following is satisfied:

i. for all the input arcs (*p*, *t*), resp. input multiarcs (*p*, *t*), of the transition *t* there exists input binding of the value of the arc function *AF*(*p*, *t*) to some token *e* in the place *p* of the marking *M*,
ii. for all the input multiarcs (*p*, *t*) of the transition *t* there exists input binding of the value of the multiarc function *MAF*(*p*, *t*) to some token *e* in the output place of the net page that is given by the value of the output place function *OPF* of the multiarc (*p*, *t*) in the net marking *M*,
iii. if *u* and *v* are two equal variables of the set *TransitionInputVariables*(*t*), then the values of elements (resp. subsequences) bound by them in the frame of mapping *InputBind* must be equal.

Figure 5 shows the fragment of sequential object Petri net in its marking *M* and the construction of the mapping *InputBind*: *AF*(**P1**, **T1**) → <2, 0>, where <2, 0> ∈ *M*(**P1**) and *InputBind*: *AF*(**P2**, **T1**) → <1, 1, 1>, where <1, 1, 1> ∈ *M*(**P2**). It is easily to find that transition **T1** is enabled.

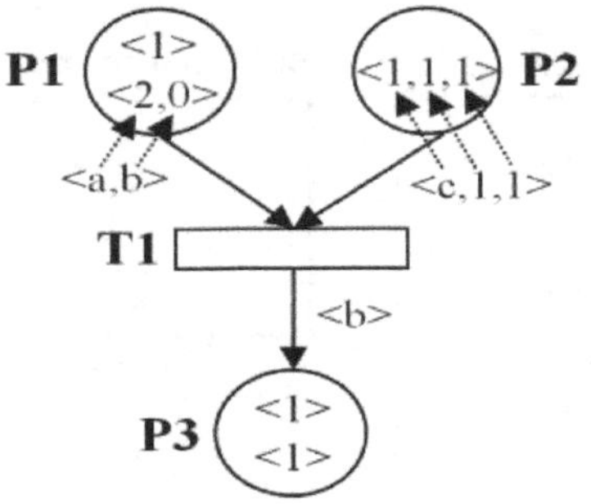

Figure 5. Mapping *InputBind* in sequential object Petri net

Partial mapping *OutputBind*: ***ArcSeq*** → ***Tokens*** is for the given transition *t* of the net page realized only in case that the transition *t* is enabled in the marking *M* of the net. Hence, partial mapping *OutputBind* assigns the selected arc sequence *AS* the **token**, being the element of the set of all ***Tokens*** (i.e. that token is not generally located in any of places of the net *SOPN* in its current marking *M*). The definition assumes that arc sequence *AS* is generally in the form $AS = \langle a_1, a_2, \ldots, a_n \rangle$, $n \in \mathbf{N}$. The value $OutputBind(\langle a_1, a_2, \ldots, a_n \rangle)$, which is generally the element of the set ***Tokens***, is given by concatenation of sequences in the form $OB(a_1)\ OB(a_2) \ldots OB(a_n)$, while individual values $OB(a_i)$ are for $1 \le i \le n$ determined according to specified rules.

Regarding recursive nature of the partial mapping *OutputBind* we will include several examples of binding of the arc sequences to elements of the set ***Tokens***. Let us assume in all cases that a certain sequential object Petri net *SOPN* is given containing the transition **T**, whose set of input variables *TransitionInputVariables*(**T**) = {a, b, c, x, #x} and in certain marking *M* of the net *SOPN* there exists binding of those input variables given as follows: *InputBind*(a) = 10, *InputBind*(b) = 2, *InputBind*(c) = <<1, 1>, 3>, *InputBind*(x) = <1, 2, 3>, *InputBind*(#x) = <1, 2, 3>. In the following examples we will investigate values of partial mapping *OutputBind* applied to various values of the arc sequence *AS*.

- if *AS* = <a>, then *OutputBind*(<a>) = *OB*(a) = <*InputBind*(a)> = <10>.
- if *AS* = <c, 1>, then *OutputBind*(<c, 1>) = *OB*(c) *OB*(1) = <*InputBind*(c)><1> = <<<1, 1>, 3>><1> = <<<1, 1>, 3>, 1>.
- if *AS* = <x, a, 5>, then *OutputBind*(<x, a, 5>) = *OB*(x) *OB*(a) *OB*(5) = <*InputBind*(x)><*InputBind*(a)><5> = <<1, 2, 3>><10><5> = <<1, 2, 3>, 10, 5>.
- if *AS* = <#x, a, 5>, then *OutputBind*(<#x, a, 5>) = *OB*(#x) *OB*(a) *OB*(5) = *InputBind*(#x)<*InputBind*(a)><5> = <1, 2, 3><10><5> = <1, 2, 3, 10, 5>.
- if *AS* = <b*(#x)>, then *OutputBind*(<b*(#x)>) = *OB*(b*(#x)) = *OB*(b)*(*OB*(#x)) = *InputBind*(b)*(*InputBind*(#x)) = 2*(<1, 2, 3>) = <1, 2, 3><1, 2, 3> = <1, 2, 3, 1, 2, 3>.
- if *AS* = <@(<x, a, 5>)>, then *OutputBind*(<@(<x, a, 5>)>) = <*OB*(@(<x, a, 5>))> = <@(*OB*(x) *OB*(a) *OB*(5))> = <@(<*InputBind*(x)><*InputBind*(a)>*OB*(5))> = <@(<<1, 2, 3>><10><5>)> = <@(<<1, 2, 3>, 10, 5>)> = <3>.

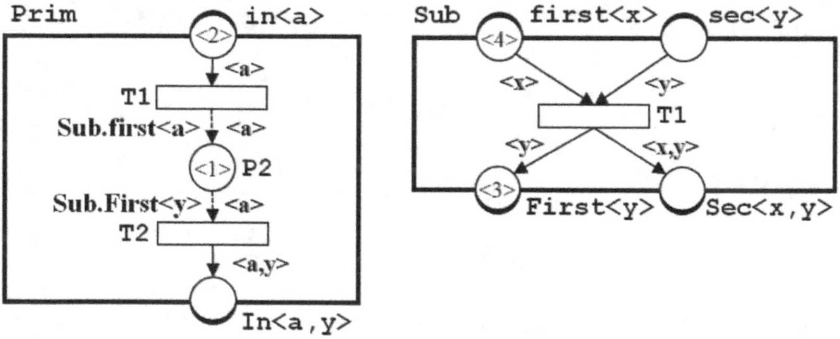

Figure 6. Marking of sequential object Petri net

Figure 6 shows the net pages **Prim** and **Sub** of a certain sequential object Petri net in their marking *M* and we are interested, if there exists input binding of transition variables associated with the transitions **Prim.T1** and **Prim.T2**. With the transition **Prim.T1** is associated one input arc (**Prim.in, Prim.T1**) whose value of the arc function *AF*(**Prim.in, Prim.T1**) = <a>, and thus the set *TransitionInputVariables*(**Prim.T1**) = {a}. We can easily determine that for the input arc (**Prim.in, Prim.T1**) there exists mapping *InputBind*: <a> → <2>, and thus holds that *InputBind*(a) = 2. With the transition **Prim.T2** is associated one input multiarc (**Prim.P2, Prim.T2**) whose value of arc function *AF*(**Prim.P2, Prim.T2**) = <a>, the value of multiarc function *MAF*(**Prim.P2, Prim.T2**) = <y> and thus the set *TransitionInputVariables*(**Prim.T2**) = {a, y}. And again, we can easily determine that for the input multiarc (**Prim.P2, Prim.T2**) there exists mapping *InputBind*: <a> → <1>, and thus holds that *InputBind*(a) = 1. With that input multiarc it is also necessary to determine the mapping *InputBind*: *MAF*(**Prim.P2, Prim.T2**) → e, where $e \in M(OPF(\mathbf{Prim.P2, Prim.T2}))$. The value of the output place function *OPF*(**Prim.P2**, **Prim.T2**) = **Sub.First**, whose marking *M*(**Sub.First**) = 1\`<3>. So we investigate, if there exists mapping *InputBind*: <y> → <3>. We can easily determine that the mapping exists and it holds that *InputBind*(y) = 3. Generally, for the transition **Prim.T2** holds that *InputBind*(a) = 1 and *InputBind*(y) = 3.

So it can be stated that for both transitions **Prim.T1** a **Prim.T2** exist particular input bindings of all the transition input variables associated with their input arcs and thus, both transitions are enabled. We are further interested, if there exists the mapping *OutputBind* of the values of functions *AF* and *MAF* associated with output arcs (or multiarcs) of both transitions. With transition **Prim.T1** is associated the only output multiarc (**Prim.T1, Prim.P2**) whose value of the arc function *AF*(**Prim.T1, Prim.P2**) = <a> and the value of the multiarc function *MAF*(**Prim.T1, Prim.P2**) = <a>. So we can easily find out that *OutputBind*(<a>) = <2>. With the transition **Prim.T2** is associated the only output arc (**Prim.T2, Prim.In**) whose value of the arc function *AF*(**Prim.T2, Prim.In**) = <a, y>. So again, we can easily find out that *OutputBind*(<a, y>) = <1, 3>.

Let *SOPN* = (*Σ, PN*) is a sequential object Petri net, $PG \in \Sigma$ is a net page, $t \in T$ is a transition of the net page *PG*, *M* is a marking of the net *SOPN*.

i. If the transition *t* is enabled in the marking *M*, then we obtain by its **firing** marking *M'* of the net *SOPN*, defined as follows:

$M'(p) = M(p) \setminus InputBind(AF(p, t))$, if $(p \in \bullet t) \wedge ((p, t) \in (A \cup MA)) \wedge (\exists\, InputBind: AF(p, t) \rightarrow e, e \in M(p))$,

$M'(p) = M(p) \cup OutputBind(AF(t, p))$, if $(p \in t\bullet) \wedge ((t, p) \in (A \cup MA))$,

$M'(q) = M(q) \setminus InputBind(MAF(p, t))$, if $(p \in \bullet t) \wedge ((p, t) \in MA) \wedge (q = OPF(p, t)) \wedge (\exists\, InputBind: MAF(p, t) \rightarrow e, e \in M(OPF(p, t)))$,

$M'(q) = M(q) \cup OutputBind(MAF(t, p))$, if $(p \in t\bullet) \wedge ((t, p) \in MA) \wedge (q = IPF(t, p))$.

$M'(p) = M(p)$, otherwise.

ii. Firing of transition $t \in T$, which will change the marking *M* of the sequential object Petri net *SOPN* into the marking *M'*, is symbolically denoted as $M\ [\, t \,\rangle\, M'$.

iii. Step is understood as firing of non-empty subset from the set of enabled transitions in the given marking *M* of the sequential object Petri net *SOPN*. Step Y which will the marking *M* into the marking *M'* is symbolically denoted as $M\ [\, Y \,\rangle\, M'$.

iv. Let step *Y* be enabled at the marking *M* of the net *SOPN*. If $t_1, t_2 \in Y$ and $t_1 \neq t_2$, we say then that transitions t_1 a t_2 are **concurrently enabled** and that fact is symbolically denoted in the form of $\{t_1, t_2\}$ ***en*** *M*.

Firing of transition will result in the new marking of given sequential object Petri net, which we will obtain as follows:

- from each input place *p* of the fired transition *t* we will remove the (unique) token in the marking *M*, which is bound to the value of the arc function *AF*(*p, t*),
- to each output place *p* of the fired transition *t* we will add up the (unique) token which is the value of partial function *OutputBind*(*AF*(*t, p*)),

- from each output place of page q, being the value of function OPF of the input multiarc (p, t) of the fired transition t, we will remove the (unique) token in the marking M, bound to the value of the multiarc function $MAF(p, t)$,
- to each input place of page q, being the value of function IPF of the output multiarc (t, p) of fired transition t, we will add up the (unique) token being the value of partial function $OutputBind(MAF(t, p))$,
- in all the remaining places of the net we will leave their original marking.

Figure 6 shows the net pages **Prim** and **Sub** of a certain sequential object Petri net in its marking M. From previous text we know that transitions **Prim.T1** and **Prim.T2** are **concurrently enabled.** Hence, firing of transition **Prim.T1** consists in:

- removing token <2> from the input place **Prim.in**,
- adding token <2> to the place **Prim.P2**,
- adding token <2> to the input place **Sub.first**.

Hence, firing of transition **Prim.T2** consists in:

- removing token <1> from the place **Prim.P2**,
- removing token <3> from the output place **Sub.First**,
- adding token <1, 3> to the output place **Prim.In**.

Marking M′ of the net after concurrent firing of transitions **Prim.T1** and **Prim.T2** is shown in Figure 7.

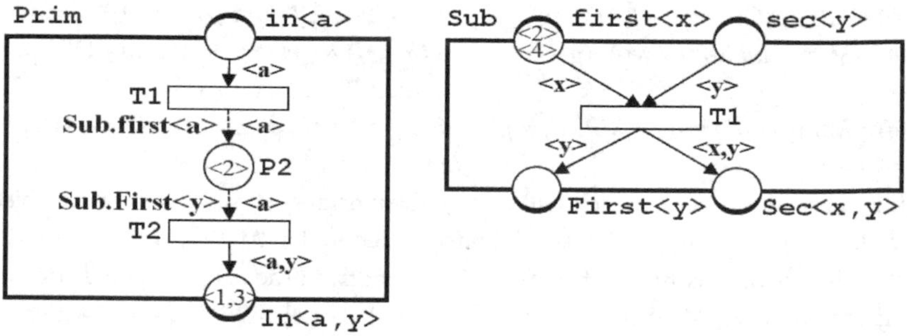

Figure 7. Firing of transitions in sequential object Petri net

Relatively complicated mechanism of firing of transitions in sequential object Petri nets can be better explained by notional substituting of all the multiarcs of the net by standard arcs, which can be realized as follows:

- if p is place and t transition of the given net page and (p, t) its multiarc whose value of arc function equals to $AF(p, t)$, the value of output place function equals to $OPF(p, t)$ and the value of multiarc function equals to $MAF(p, t)$, we substitute this multiarc by notional pair of the following standard arcs:
  - by the arc (p, t) with the value of the arc function equal to $AF(p, t)$,
  - by the arc $(OPF(p, t), t)$ with the value of the arc function equal to $MAF(p, t)$.

- if p is place and t transition of the given net page and (t, p) its multiarc whose value of arc function equals to $AF(t, p)$, the value of input place function equals to $IPF(t, p)$ and the value of multiarc function equals to $MAF(t, p)$, we substitute that multiarc with notional pair of the following standard arcs:
    - by the arc (t, p) with the value of the arc function equal to $AF(t, p)$,
    - by the arc $(t, IPF(t, p))$ with the value of the arc function equal to $MAF(t, p)$.

That notional substitution of multiarcs in the previous net is shown in Figure 8 where:

- multiarc (**Prim.T1, Prim.P2**) was substituted by the following pair of arcs:
    - the arc (**Prim.T1, Prim.P2**) with the value of the arc function *AF* equal to <a>,
    - the arc (**Prim.T1, Sub.first**) with the value of the arc function *AF* equal to <a>,
- multiarc (**Prim.P2, Prim.T2**) was substituted by the following pair of arcs:
    - the arc (**Prim.P2, Prim.T2**) with the value of the arc function *AF* equal to <a>,
    - the arc (**Sub.First, Prim.T2**) with the value of the arc function *AF* equal to <y>.

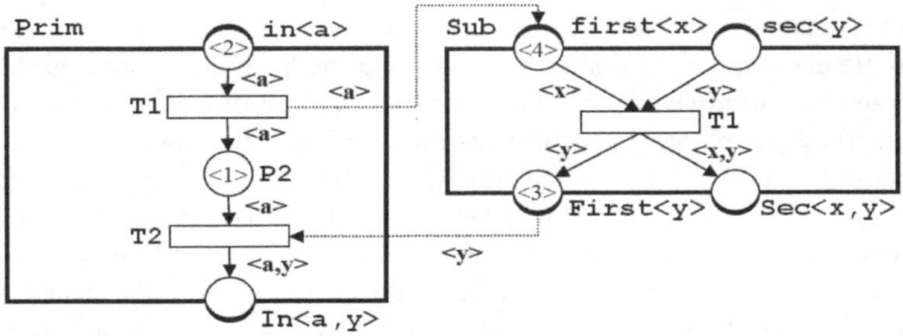

Figure 8. Substitution of multiarcs in sequential object Petri net

When enabling individual steps of the sequential object Petri net, so called *conflicts* can originate in certain markings of the net (or *conflict transitions*). At the enabling of transitions t_1 and t_2 of the given net and its marking M the conflict occurs, if both transitions t_1 and t_2 have at least one input place, each of t_1 and t_2 transitions is individually enabled in the marking M of the net, but t_1 and t_2 transitions are not in that marking M concurrently enabled, i.e. enabling of one of them will prevent enabling the other. The term of conflict transitions can be obviously easily generalized for the case of finite set $t_1, t_2, \ldots, t_n$ ($n \in \mathbf{N}$) of transitions of the given net.

A typical example of the conflict at enabling transitions in the particular marking of the net is shown in Figure 9, where transitions **T1** and **T2** of the net have a common input place **P1**, both are enabled (particular binding of tokens can be easily found), but not concurrently enabled, i.e. enabling of the transition **T1** will disable enabling of the transition **T2** and vice versa. When solving conflicts at enabling of transitions in sequential Petri nets we will therefore follow the rule which determines, informally said, that from the set of conflict transitions at the given binding of tokens the one will be enabled, whose value of transition priority function *TP* is the highest. If such transition from the set of conflict transitions does not exist, the given conflict would have to be solved by other means. In our studied example will be then on the basis of that rule the transition **T2** enabled (because $TP(\mathbf{T1}) = 1$ and $TP(\mathbf{T2}) = 2$).

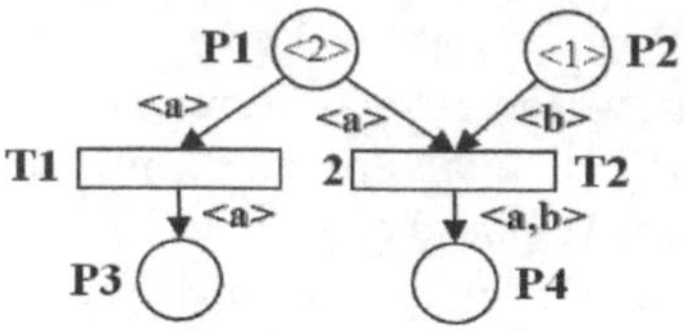

Figure 9. Conflict transitions in sequential object Petri net

5. Object-oriented programming systems and their representation by the sequential object Petri nets

This section deals with main principles applied at modeling of multithreading object-oriented programming systems with the sequential object Petri nets. All program listings are developed in the Java programming language (Goetz et. al, 2006), (Lea, 1999), (Subramaniam, 2011).

Each declared class of the object–oriented programming system is in the sequential object Petri net represented by a net page containing declared data items and methods. Their declarations are made by using elements of the net page. Individual input places of the net page then represent input points of static and non-static methods as a part of the class declaration, and output places of the net page then represent their output points. Input and output places of the net page are associated with identifiers of the particular method whose input and output point they represent while each method has one input and output place. In so doing, we abide to the convention whereby input place identifier of the particular method starts with a small letter and identifier of the output place of the same method with a capital letter. In order to differentiate graphically in layouts of the net declaration of static methods from non-static methods on a given net page, we demarcate identifiers of input and output places of the net page representing input and output points of static methods with the square brackets. Moreover, it is possible on the net page via a position of input and output places in its layout represent visibility of *public, protected* and *private* type of individual declared methods thus implementing the characteristic of encapsulation of the object-oriented programming.

Figure 10 illustrates the net page representing the following declaration of the class **Sys**:

```
public class Sys {
  public static void compute() { ... }
  protected void run() { ... }
  private void init() { ... }
}
```

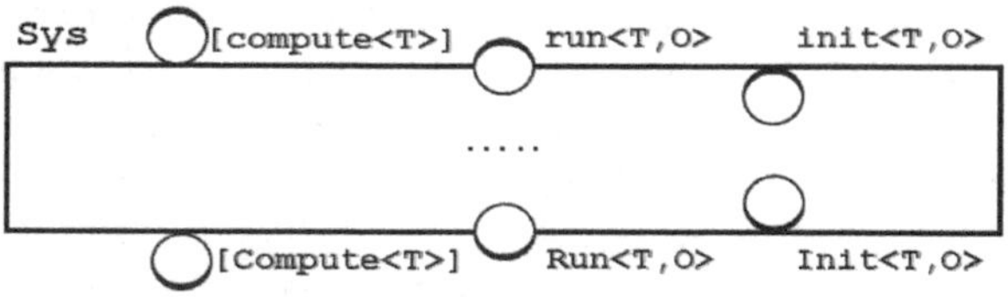

Figure 10. Net page representing declaration of class **Sys**

Static and non-static data items are on the net pages represented in the form of **tokens** in the given net marking, i.e. by elements of the set ***Tokens***. When representing values of static and non-static data items being the elements of particular tokens of the net, it is for example possible to proceed as follows:

- If the data type of the particular data item is a non-negative integer (*int*), its actual value equals to that non-negative integer.
- If the data type of the particular data item is *boolean*, we represent the truth value *false* most frequently with constant 0 and the truth value *true* with constant 1, while in layouts of the net we are also using symbolic values *false* and *true*.
- If the data type of the particular data item is *char*, whose value is the element of the set contained in the code table given by the Unicode standard, we represent its value corresponding to the value of the symbol code given in the Unicode Standard, i.e. the letter 'A' can be represented by the value 65. In order to make again layouts of nets more readable, the element of token can be entered as the particular symbol bounded by apostrophes, i.e. instead of token <65> we will indicate in layouts of nets token <'A'>.
- If the data type of the particular data item is *string*, whose value is text string, the values can be represented by sequences of codes of symbols according to the Unicode standard. Again, for better transparency of notations, it is possible to use instead of codes of symbols directly the sequence of symbols bounded by apostrophes, i.e. in layouts of nets represent data items of the data type *string* with the tokens of <'H', 'e', 'l', 'l', 'o'> shape, or to bound sequence of symbols of the string with quotation marks, i.e. to note the tokens in the form of <"Hello">.
- Data items whose data type are numbers with floating decimal point (*float, double*), or other numerical data type being the superset of the set of non-negative integer numbers, it is not possible to declare it directly on the basis of the stated definition of the sequential object Petri net. If a need emerges to operate with those numerical sets during simulation of multithreading object-oriented programming system, it is always easy to extend in this sense the definition of the token, arc sequence and other particular definitions, in order to ensure the support of those numerical sets (e.g. it is possible to define the token of sequential object Petri net as the finite non-empty sequence over the set of real numbers $\boldsymbol{R}$, etc.).
- In the case of data items whose data type is the pointer to instance of class, we represent their values with natural numbers. Each instance of the class has at its creation allocated unique natural number expressing its address within the programming heap. Number 0 than represents the value of pointer *null*.

Static data items are usually represented in layouts of nets with the tokens containing only their actual values. Non-static data items are usually represented by tokens containing both the value of pointer to a given instance of the class in which the particular data item is declared, and its actual value according to particular data type. So if within the declaration of the class First for example the following data items are declared:

```
public class First {
  private static boolean  indicator = true;
  private char status = 'a';
}
```

then, the static data item **indicator** can be represented by the token **<true>** and the non-static data item **status** by the token **<11, 'a'>**, where numerical value **11** represents the value of the pointer to the particular instance of class.

The dynamic creation of the instance of the class is not in the sequential object Petri net realized by the creation of a new instance of the particular net page representing declaration of the given class, but by creation of all the tokens representing non-static data items of the declared class. At the same time, each such token contains (usually as its first element) the value of the pointer to the newly created class instance. The fact, that during dynamic creation of instances of classes it is not necessary to create instances of net pages, dramatically simplifies its analysis.

All methods represented by elements of the net pages are executed by the programming threads. Each such programming thread is represented by the particular instance of class (usually by the class **Thread**). Thus, the token accepted by the input place of the net page must contain the pointer for particular programming thread realizing execution of the given method, while that pointer is within arc sequences of the net represented by default by some of the identifiers **T**, **U**, **V**, etc. By the element of the token accepted by the input place of the page representing the input point of some of the non-static methods must be then the pointer of the particular instance of class whose non-static method is (i.e. pointer **this**). That pointer is then within the arc sequences of the net standardly represented by the identifier **O** (while indeed, within representation of static methods that pointer cannot be used). When entering identifiers of static and non-static data items, parameters and local variables of methods, we use by default in layouts of the net so called Hungarian notations, where the first letter (or the first part) of identifier expresses its data type. For identification of standard data types we use the acronym **i** even for data type *int*, **b** for *boolean*, **c** for *char*, **s** for *string* and **p** for *pointer*. Hence for example the identifier **sName** within the arc sequence represents the variable of the data type *string* with the identifier **name**.

Figure 11 shows the net page representing the declaration of the following class **Obj** in its marking *M*:

```
public class Obj {
  private char val = 'a';
  public synchronized char getVal() { return value; }
  public synchronized void setVal(char value) { this.val = value; }
}
```

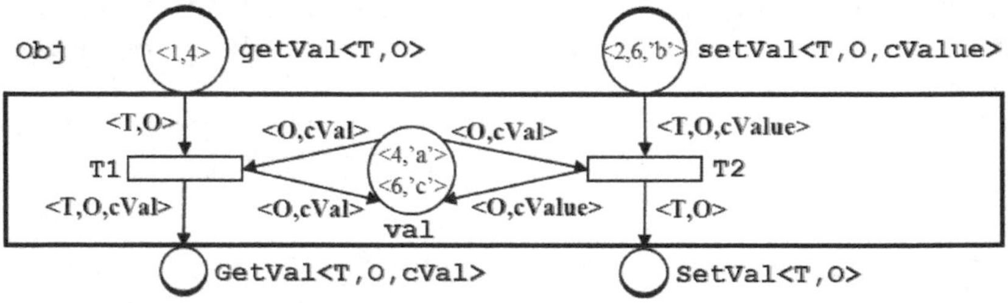

Figure 11. Net page representing declaration of class **Obj**

The current notation of that net page suggests, that within the program execution modeled by that net two instances of the class **Obj** have been already created, as in the place **Obj.val** appear tokens **<4, 'a'>** a **<6, 'c'>**, where the first element of each of those tokens is the pointer to the instance of the class **Obj** and second the actual value of the non-static data item **val** of the data type *char*. The non-static method **getVal** will be executed above the instance of class with the pointer **4** by the programming thread with the pointer equal to the value **1**, the non-static method **setVal** will be executed above the instance of the class with the pointer **6** by the programming thread with the pointer equal to the value **2**, while the value of method parameter **value** equals to character **'b'**. The shape of the net demonstrates, that over the selected instance of the class can be concurrently executed with any programming thread maximum one of **getVal** or **setVal** methods.

Additionally, in layouts of nets can be simply represented the relation of a simple inheritance between two declared classes. The identifier of the net page representing the class declaration being superclass of the given class, we indicate in the layout of the given net page of the class in its left bottom corner. If that identifier of the net page of the superclass is not explicitly indicated in the layout of the net, we consider the given class to be implicitly subclass of the top class in the hierarchy of classes created on the basis of relation of simple inheritance of classes (e.g. within the hierarchy of classes of the Java programming language it is the class **java.lang.Object**).

With the inheritance relation of classes is organically connected even the term of polymorphism of the object-oriented programming and the possibility of declaration of so called virtual methods. Figure 12 shows two net pages out of which the first represents declaration of the class **Object** and the second declaration of the class **System**, being subclass of the class **Object**. Within the class **Object** is also declared virtual method with the head **public int hashCode()**, which is in the declaration of the class **System** overwritten with the virtual method of identical method head. Input and output places of net pages **Object** and **System**, which appertain to input and output points of both virtual methods are indicated in the net layout by default while in the case of declaration of the virtual methods it is necessary that **all input places representing the input point of the given virtual method had assigned on all the net pages containing the declaration of this method the identical value of *IOPN* function and all output places representing the output point of the given virtual method had assigned on all relevant net pages the identical value of *IOPN* function** (see Figure 12).

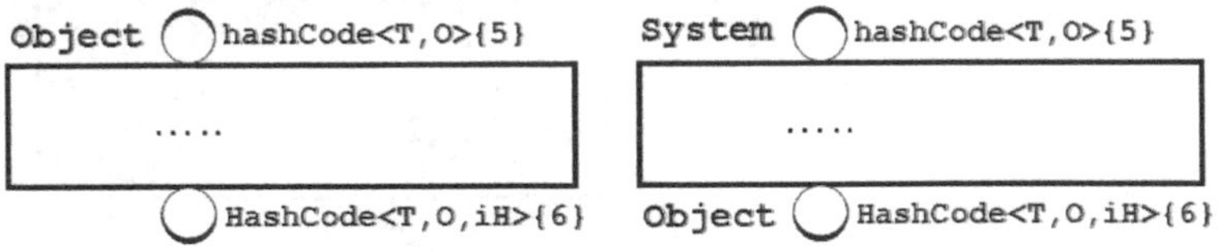

Figure 12. Virtual methods representation in sequential object Petri net

Next example demonstrates representation of classes containing declaration of virtual and abstract methods. **Virt** and **Add** classes are declared as follows:

```
public abstract class Virt {
  public abstract int compute(int a, int b);
  public int make(int a, int b)  { return compute(a, b); }
}

public class Add extends Virt {
  public int compute(int a, int b) { return (a + b); }
}
```

The **Virt** class is an abstract class with the declared abstract method **compute**. That method is called as a part of the declared method **make** of the **Virt** class. The method **compute** is then overwritten at the level of declaration of the class **Add**, being the subclass of the class **Virt**. The net page representing the declaration of the class **Virt** is shown in Figure 13. Abstract method **compute** is represented only by a pair of the input place **Virt.compute** and the output place **Virt.Compute**. Regarding the fact that it is also declaration of the virtual method, the selection of function *IOPN* values is important (i.e. in our case *IOPN*(**Virt.compute**) = 1 and *IOPN*(**Virt.Compute**) = 2). The key element of the net page is the manner of calling of the virtual method **compute** represented by the multiarc (**Virt.T1**, **Virt.P1**) and its value of input place function *IPF*, the multiarc (**Virt.P1**, **Virt.T2**) and its value of output place function *OPF*. The value of input place function *IPF* of the multiarc (**Virt.T1**, **Virt.P1**) is in the form of **O.compute** (more precisely in the **O.1** form), where identifier **O** represents the pointer of particular instance of non-abstract subclass of class **Virt**, whose non-static method **compute** is executed. The value of identifier **O** is in our case non-constant, ie. generalized at the realization of steps, and depends on binding of the specific token to the arc sequence in the form **<T, O, iA, iB>**, which shares in the given identification of the net execution of transition **Virt.T1**. According to the numerical value bound to identifier **O** the particular net page net will be determined whose value of the function *PN* of numbering net pages is identical with the numerical value bound to the identifier **O**. Then on this net page the input place with the value of *IOPN* function equal to number **1** will be selected (representing the input point of the virtual method **compute**), into which the particular token in the form **<T, O, iA, iB>** will be placed.

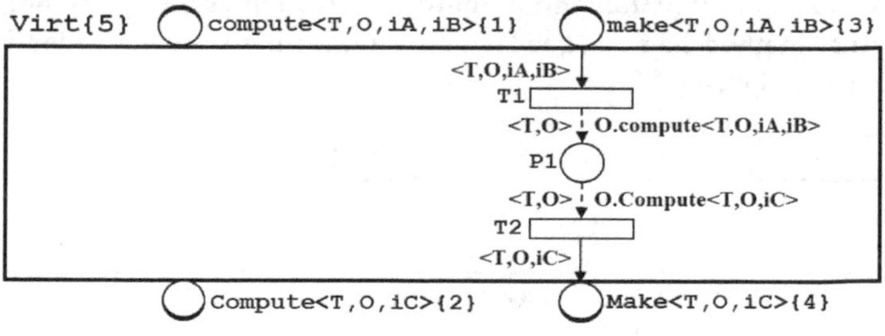

Figure 13. Polymorphism representation in sequential object Petri net

Net page representing the declaration of the class **Add**, being the subclass of the class **Virt**, is shown in Figure 14. In the class **Add** is declared the only non-static virtual method

compute, which overwrites the abstract method **compute** declared in the body of the class **Virt**. Thus, on the grounds of that fact it is necessary to correctly assign values of *IOPN* function (in our case *IOPN*(**Add.compute**) = 1 and *IOPN*(**Add.Compute**) = 2). An interesting detail of this net page is the way of determination of the addition of integral values bound to variables **iA** and **iB** of the arc sequence of the arc (**Add.compute, Add.T1**). The expression in the form **@(iA*<0>iB*<0>)** represents length of the sequence formed by concatenation of two sequences: first sequence containing in total **iA** of numbers **0** and the second sequence containing in total **iB** numbers **0** (in this case, it is worth mentioning, that e.g. via the expression in the form **@(iA*(iB*<0>))** product of integral values of variables **iA** a **iB** can be determined).

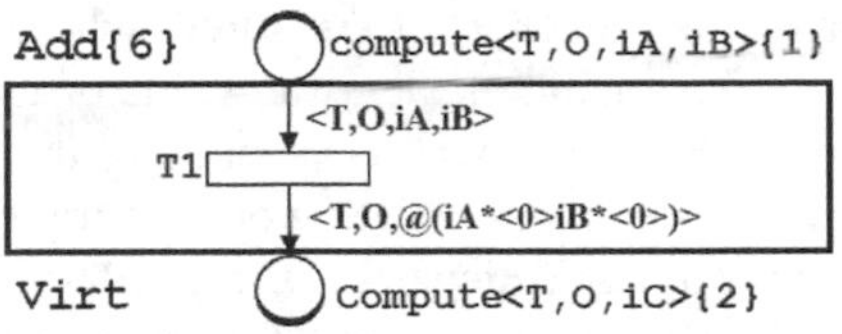

Figure 14. Polymorphism representation in sequential object Petri net

Next generalization of the form of functions *IPF* and *OPF* associated with multiarcs is possible within the sequential object Petri nets to implement the explicit support of the mechanism of **first order and higher order functions** known from functional programming (ie. given method can take another methods as parameters and return the method as the return value). Figure 15 shows the net page of the class **Func** containing declaration of method **call**. Arc sequence of the token accepted by the input place of that method contains a variable **mO**, the value of which is the value of the function *PN* for the net page with the input place **make** and output place **Make**, which are represented by particular integral values of the function *IOPN*. Values of functions *MAF* of multiarcs of the net in the form **mO.make** and **mO.Make**, whose all components are variables and whose values are not determined until particular arc sequence is bound to token of the net, provide general mechanism for the possibility of declaration of first order and higher order functions.

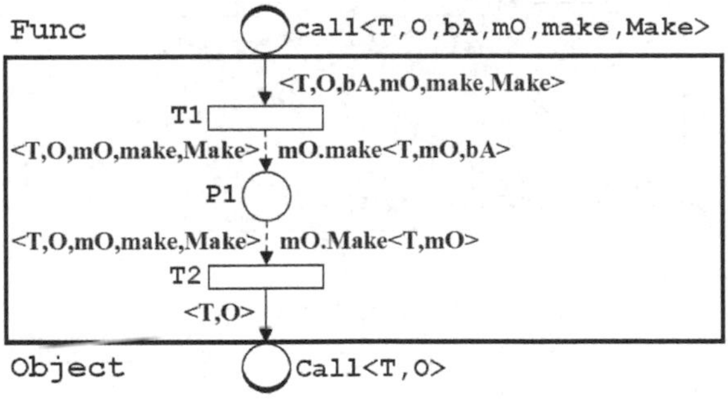

Figure 15. Higher order function representation in sequential object Petri net

Example of recursive method represented by the net page can be seen on Figure 16. This static recursive method **fact** of the class **Integer** implements calculation of the value of factorial function whose parameter is a certain natural number **n**. Recursive algorithm for calculation of factorial of the integer value **n** in the Java programming language is represented by the following listing:

```
public class Integer {
  public static int fact(int n) {
    if (n == 1) return 1;
    else return (n * fact(n – 1));
}
```

If the value of the parameter **iN** equals to number 1, the transition **Integer.T4** is enabled and in the output place **Integer.Fact** the token **<T, 1>** is stored, whose first element **T** represents the programming thread and the second element the value of factorial of number 1. If the value of number **iN** is greater than number 1, by enabling the transition **Integer.T2** that number **iN** is substituted by the sequence consisting of **iN** numbers 0, which is then used at recursive call modeled by the multiarc (**Integer.T3**, **Integer.P2**), whose enabling will always result in elimination of one element of that sequence. The programming stack which is used at realization of recursive procedure of the algorithm is represented by the token in the place **Integer.P3** in the form of the sequence **<T, ..., iN-2, iN-1, iN>**. At the moment where the sequence composed from 0 numerals contains after the series of recursive calls of algorithm one element (i.e. it is necessary to determine the value of factorial of number 1 within the stop condition of algorithm), the transition **Integer.T4** is enabled and the value of factorial of number 1 is represented in token **<T, 1>** located in the output place **Integer.Fact**. Then, by repeatedly enabling the transition **Integer.T5** and finally the transition **Integer.T6** the return from recursion is implemented with the gradual calculation of the value of factorial function, which is represented in the token of the form **<T, @(iM*(iF*0))>**. Following completion of the process of reverse return of recursion in the output place **Integer.Fact** the token in the form **<T, iF>** is stored, whose second element represents the value of factorial of the natural number **iN**.

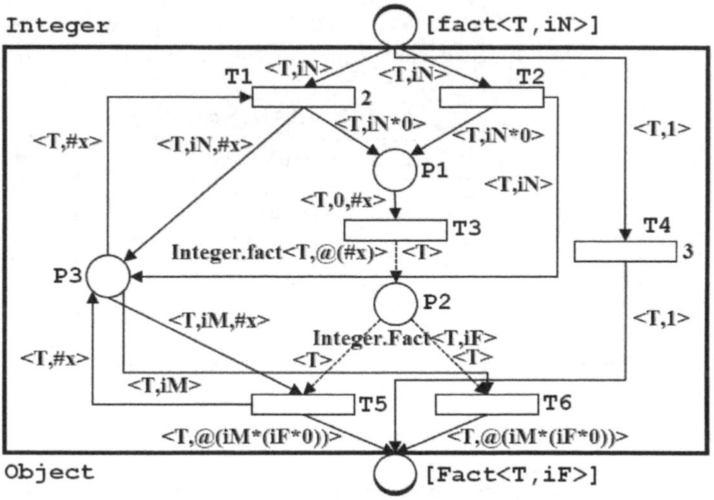

Figure 16. Recursive function representation in sequential object Petri net

Moreover, in the sequential object Petri nets can be simply represented declarations of inner classes of the selected class via subpages of the net page. So if for example the class **Obj** which within its declaration contains declaration of its own inner class **InnerObj**, that declaration can be represented by the subpage **InnerObj** of the page **Obj** (see Figure 17)

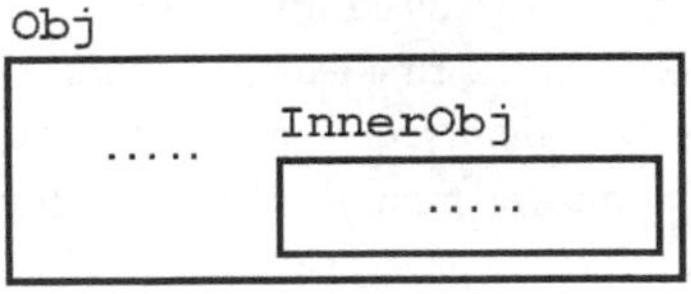

Figure 17. Inner class declaration representation in sequential object Petri net

The representation of declared interfaces, which can contain only declarations of headings of publicly accessible abstract methods, is also easy. Figure 18 shows the representation of interface ***Runnable*** (identifiers of interface we indicate in layouts of the net with spaced letters) containing declaration of the method with the head **public abstract void run()**.

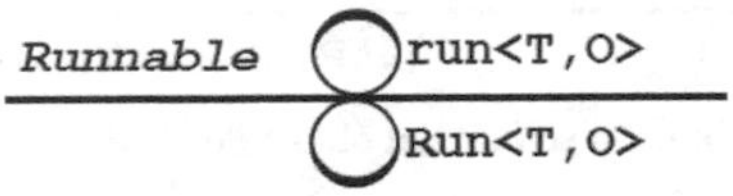

Figure 18. Interface declaration in sequential object Petri net

6. Example of simple class hierarchy represented by sequential object Petri net

In this section we will demonstrate how simple hierarchy of the classes via sequential object Petri nets is built. The model of those examples involve selected classes contained in standard library of classes of the Java programming language. (e.g. classes **java.lang.Object**, **java.lang.Thread**, etc.). For better visibility of layouts we usually present individual declared methods in separate figures representing individual parts of the particular net page (while naturally places and transitions of the net which appear in individual parts of the net page and have identical identifiers, always represent the same place or transition of the total page of the net). Thus, top of our hierarchy of classes will be the class **Object**, whose declaration made in the Java programming language is the following:

```
public class Object {
  private Object monitor;
  private Thread thread;
  private Vector<Thread> = new Vector<Thread>;
  private synchronized static int getPointer() { ... }
  public Object() { ... }
  protected void finalize() { ... }
  public void lock() { ... }
  public void unlock() { ... }
```

```
  public void wait() { ... }
  public void notify() { ... }
}
```

The static method **getPointer** (see Figure 19) can be executed by the only one programming thread only and it is determined for assigning unique integral values of pointers to individual instances of the classes. At the first execution of the method the integral value 1 is returned in variable **P** (because *InputBind*(#p) = 0 a @(#p) = @(<0>) = 1), in the place **Object.P1** is then stored the token **<0, 0>**, and at next execution of the method is in the variable **P** returned the value 2, etc.

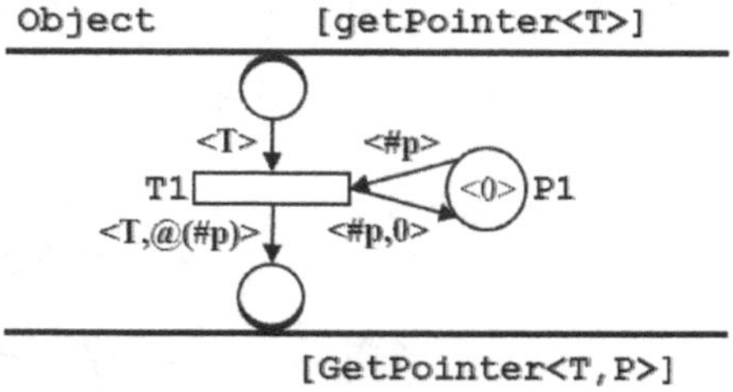

Figure 19. Declaration of class **Object** in sequential object Petri net

Within the declaration of the constructor of the object of the class **Object** (see Figure 20) is by the programming thread firstly obtained the value of the pointer for a newly created object by calling the method **getPointer**, that value is then stored to the variable **O** and the value of non-static data item **monitor** representing the monitor of particular instance of the class is then stored in the form of the token **<O>** in the place **Object.monitor.** The destructor of the object represented by the method **finalize** will then mainly ensure cancellation of the monitor of the object represented by the token **<O>** in the place **Object.monitor.**

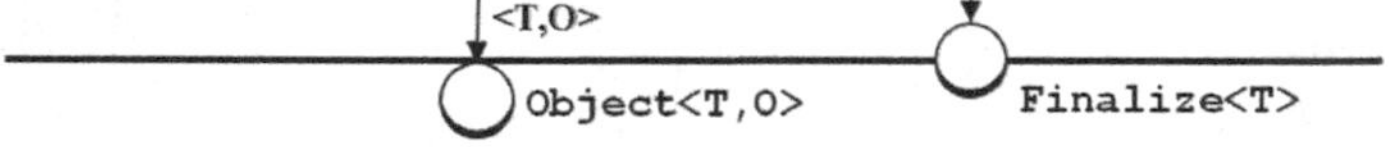

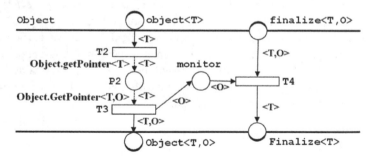

Figure 20. Declaration of class **Object** in sequential object Petri net

Entry into the critical section of the object (i.e. execution of the non-static method with the modifier **synchronized**) is conditioned by getting the object monitor with the particular programming thread. As a part of the execution of the method **lock** the programming thread **T** can respectively allocate the object monitor with the value of the pointer **O**, (i.e. the token **<O>** in the place **Object.monitor**) and then enter into the critical section of the object while the programming thread is permitted to enter the critical section of the same object several times in sequence. First entry of the programming thread **T** into the critical section of the object **O** is realized by execution of the transition **Object.T5**. Pointer to the programming thread, which successfully obtained the object monitor, is then stored in the variable **thread** (i.e. the token **<T, O, 1>** is located in the place **Object.thread**). At repeated entry of the programming thread into the critical sections of the object **O** the transition **Object.T6** is executed and particular token in the place **Object.thread** is added with the next element which is the number **1** (i.e. at second entry of the thread **T** into the critical section of the object **O** is in the place **Object.thread** stored the token **<T, O, 1, 1>**, at the third entry the token **<T, O, 1, 1, 1>**, etc). Deal location of the object monitor and initialization of its critical section is then realized by execution of the non-static method **unlock**, whose functionalities are inverse to functionalities of the method **lock** (see Figure 21).

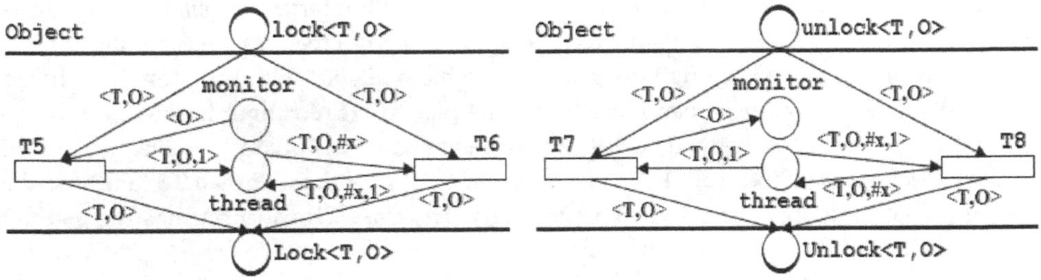

Figure 21. Declaration of class **Object** in sequential object Petri net

Method **wait** causes the current thread **T** to wait until another thread invokes the **notify** method for the object **O**. The current thread **T** must own the monitor of the object **O**. The thread releases ownership of this monitor and waits in the place **Object.pool** until another thread notifies threads waiting on the object's monitor to wake up through a call to the notify method. The thread **T** then waits in the place **Object.P3** until it can re-obtain ownership of the object monitor and resumes execution (see Figure 22).

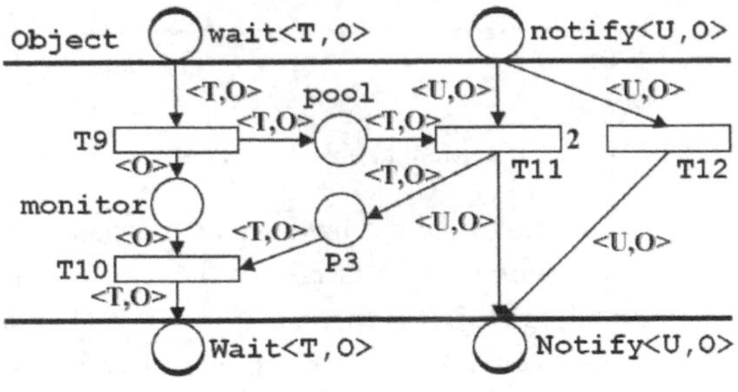

Figure 22. Declaration of class **Object** in sequential object Petri net

Next declared class in our hierarchy will be the class **Thread** representing the programming thread, which is the subclass of the class **Object** and it also implements the interface ***Runnable*** (see Figure 23). Its declaration in the Java programming language is as follows:

```
public class Thread extends Object implements Runnable {
  private Runnable runnable;
  public Thread(Runnable run) { ... }
  protected void finalize() { ... }
  public void start() { ... }
  public void run() { ... }
}
```

The method **Thread** is the constructor of the object which during its execution firstly invokes the construction of the instance of the class **Object**, that is the superclass of the class **Thread**, which in the variable value **U** returns the pointer to the newly created programming thread. In the place **Thread.runnable** (i.e. in the value of the variable **runnable**) is then stored the token **<U, pRun>**, where the value of the variable **pRun** contains the pointer to the class instance implementing the interface ***Runnable*** (see Figure 18) whose method **run** will be then executed by the newly created programming thread. That will be implemented through execution of the method **start** with programming thread T. The token **<U, pRun, 0>** is then located into the place **Thread.runnable** representing the fact that the execution of the method **pRun.run** was initiated. Its invocation itself is realized by asynchronous method call by the firing of the transition **Thread.T3** and by the mechanism of multiarc (**Thread.T3**, **Thread.Start**). The class **Thread** itself has the method **run** implemented the easiest possible way.

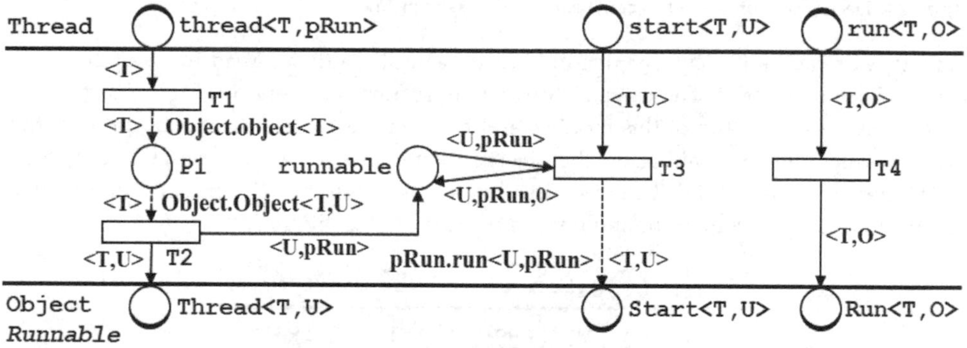

Figure 23. Declaration of class **Thread** in sequential object Petri net

As a part of execution of the destructor of the instance of the class **Thread**, i.e. the method **finalize** (see Figure 24), the particular token is removed from the place **Thread.runnable** and the destructor of the superclass **Object** is then executed. If in the place **Thread.runnable** is the token of the form **<U, pRun>**, the programming thread is not active to obeyed destruction and the transition **Thread.T7** can be fired. If, on the contrary, in the place **Thread.runnable** is the token in the form **<U, pRun, 0>**, the programming thread is active and the execution of the destructor must be delayed until the completion of the activities of this thread (i.e. returning of the thread **U** after executing the method **pRun.run** ensured by the mechanism of the multiarc (**Thread.finalize**, **Thread.T8**)).

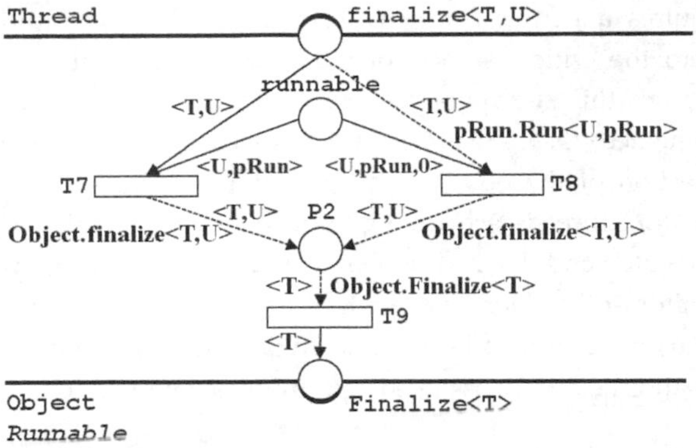

Figure 24. Declaration of class **Thread** in sequential object Petri net

Next declared class in our hierarchy will be the class **Semaphore** representing a counting semaphore. Conceptually, a semaphore maintains a set of permits. Method **down** blocks if necessary until a permit is available, and then takes it. Method **up** adds a permit, potentially releasing a blocking acquirer. However, no actual permit objects are used and the **Semaphore** just keeps a count of the number available and acts accordingly. Declaration of the class in the Java programming language is the following:

```
public class Semaphore extends Object {
  private int value = 1;
  public Semaphore() { ... }
  protected void finalize() { ... }
  public synchronized void down() { ... }
  public synchronized void up() { ... }
}
```

The constructor of the object, i.e. the method **Semaphore**, following execution of the constructor of the instance of the superclass **Object** will store in the place **Semaphore.value** the token **<O, 1>** representing the initial value of the data item value of the class instance **O**. As a part of the execution of the destructor of the instance of the class **Semaphore**, i.e. of the method **finalize**, that token is removed from the place **Semaphore.value** and then the destructor of the superclass **Object** is executed (see Figure 25).

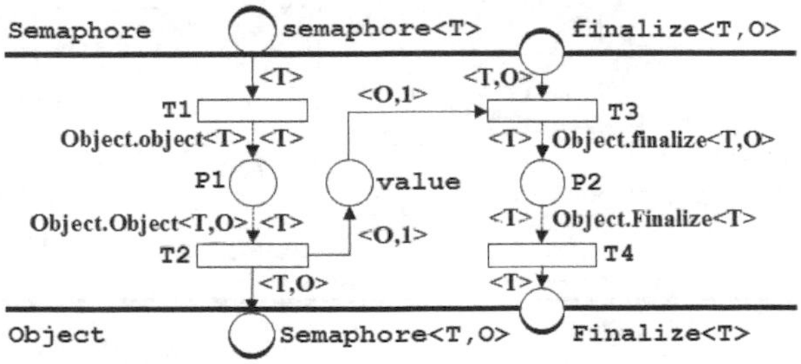

Figure 25. Declaration of class **Semaphore** in sequential object Petri net

Method **down** acquires a permit from this semaphore, blocking until one is available. Following entry into the critical section of the object instance the programming thread acquires a permit from this semaphore (ie. token in the place **Semaphore.value** can be bound to the arc sequence **<O, 1, #x>** after at least one execution of the method **up**) and will leave the critical section of the object. If no permit is available then the current thread becomes disabled for thread scheduling purposes and waits (i.e. the transition **Semaphore.T7** is executed and the method **Object.wait** is invoked, the programming thread will release the monitor of the object in order to enable execution of the method **up** by other programming thread) until some other thread invokes the **up** method for this semaphore and the current thread is next to be assigned a permit (see Figure 26).

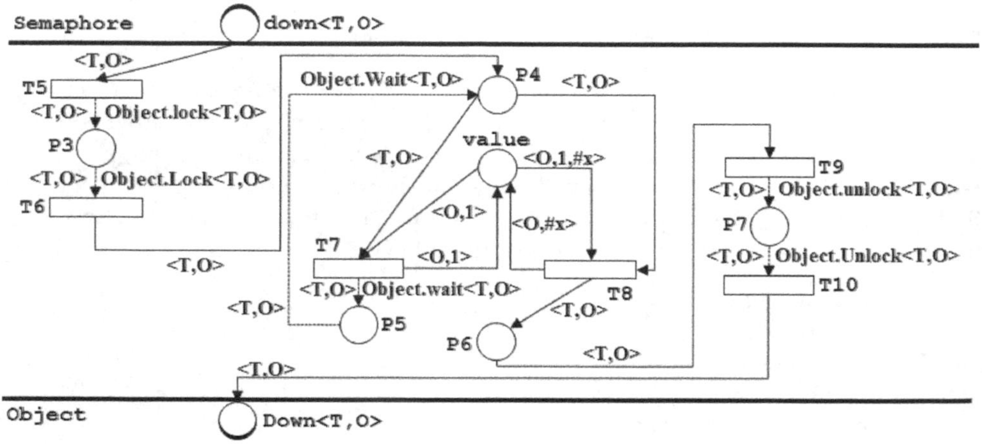

Figure 26. Declaration of class **Semaphore** in sequential object Petri net

Method **up** releases a permit, increasing the number of available permits by one. If any threads are trying to acquire a permit, then one is selected and given the permit that was just released. That thread is (re)enabled for thread scheduling purposes (see Figure 27).

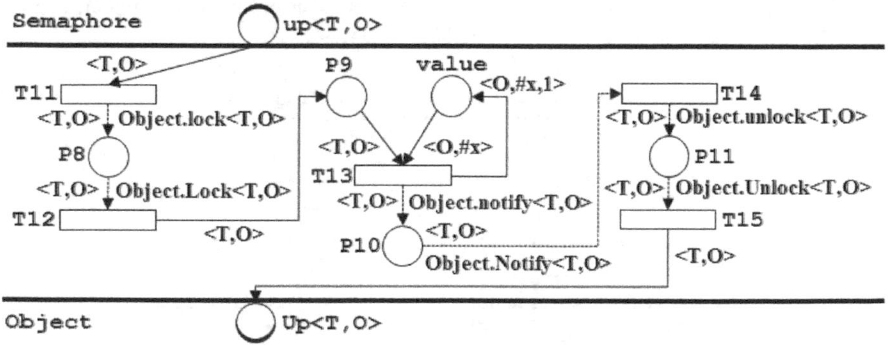

Figure 27. Declaration of class **Semaphore** in sequential object Petri net

7. Conclusion

Sequential object Petri nets represent an interesting class in the area of object Petri net classes, which can be applied at design, modeling, analysis and verification of generally distributed multithreading object-oriented programming systems. A newly introduced term of token as finite non-empty recursive sequence over the set of non-negative integer numbers, functionalities of multiarcs and the mechanism of the firing of transitions do not increase demands on performance of analysis of characteristics, as seen in other classes of high-level or colored Petri Nets.

Functional programming is one of the most important paradigms of programming that looks back on a long history. The recent interest in functional programming started as a response to the growing pervasiveness of concurrency as a way of scaling horizontally. Multithreaded programming is difficult to do well in practice and functional programming offers (in many ways) better strategies than object-oriented programming for writing robust, concurrent software. Functional programming is generally regarded a paradigm of programming that can be applied in many languages - even those that were not originally intended to be used with that paradigm. Like the name implies, it focuses on the application of functions. Functional programmers use functions as building blocks to create new functions and the function is the main construct that architecture is built from. Several programming languages (like Scala, C#, Java, Delphi, etc) are a blend of object-oriented and functional programming concepts in a statically typed language in the present time. The fusion of object-oriented and functional programming makes it possible to express new kinds of programming patterns and component abstractions. It also leads to a legible and concise programming style. Sequential object Petri nets then also fully support design, modeling, analysis and verification of programming systems based on this fusion of object-oriented and functional programming paradigms.

Author details

Ivo Martiník
VŠB-Technical University of Ostrava, Czech Republic

Acknowledgement

This paper has been elaborated in the framework of the IT4Innovations Centre of Excellence project, reg. no. CZ.1.05/1.1.00/02.0070 supported by Operational Programme 'Research and Development for Innovations' funded by Structural Funds of the European Union and state budget of the Czech Republic.

8. References

Agha, G. A.; Cinindio, F. & Rozenberg, G. (2001). *Concurrent Object-Oriented Programming and Petri Nets: Advances in Petri Nets*. Springer, ISBN 978-3-540-41942-6, Berlin, Germany

Diaz, M. (2009). *Petri Nets: Fundamental Models, Verification and Applications*, John Willey & Sons, ISTE Ltd., ISBN: 978-0-470-39430-4, London, United Kingdom

Goetz, B.; Peierls, T., Bloch, J.; Bowbeer, J.; Holmes, D. & Lea, D. (2006). *Java Concurrency in Practice*, Addison-Wesley, ISBN 978-0321349606, Reading, United Kingdom

Jensen, K.; Kristensen, L. M. (2009). *Coloured Petri Nets: Modelling and Validation of Concurrent Systems*, Springer, ISBN 978-3-642-00283-0, Berlin, Germany

Jensen, K.; Rozenberg, G. (1991). *High-Level Petri Nets: Theory and Application*, Springer, ISBN 3-540-54125-x, London, United Kingdom

Köhler, M.; Rölke, H. (2007). Web Services Orchestration with Super-Dual Object Nets, *ICATPN 2007, Lecture Notes in Computer Science 4546*, Springer-Verlag, pp. 263–280, ISBN 978-3-540-73093-4

Lea, D. (1999). *Concurrent Programming in Java, Second Edition*, Addison-Wesley, ISBN 0-201-31009-0, Reading, United Kingdom

Martiník, I. Bi-relational P/T Petri Nets and the Modeling of Multithreading Object-oriented Programming Systems, *Communications in Computer and Information Science.* 188 CCIS (Part 1), (July 2011), pp. 222-236. ISSN 1865-0929

Reisig, W. (2009). *Elements of Distributed Algorithms*, Springer, ISBN 3-540-62752-9, Berlin, Germany

Subramaniam, V. (2011). *Programming Concurrency on the JVM: Mastering Synchronization, STM and Actors*, Pragmatic Bookshelf, ISBN 978-1934356760, Dallas, USA

Chapter 2

Performance Evaluation of Distributed System Using SPN

Razib Hayat Khan, Poul E. Heegaard and Kazi Wali Ullah

Additional information is available at the end of the chapter

1. Introduction

Distributed system poses one of the main streams of information and communication technology arena with immense complexity. Designing and implementation of such complex systems are always an intricate endeavour. Likewise, performance evaluation is also a great concern of such complex system to evaluate whether the system meets the performance related system requirements. Hence, modeling plays an important role in the whole design process of the system for qualitative and quantitative analysis. However, in a distributed system, system functional behavior is normally distributed among several objects. The overall behavior of the system is composed of the partial behavior of the distributed objects of the system. So it is indispensable to capture the functional behavior of the distributed objects for appropriate analysis to evaluate the performance related factors of the overall system. We therefore adopt UML collaboration and activity oriented approach as UML is the most widely used modeling language which models both the system requirements and qualitative behavior through different notations. Collaboration and activity diagram are utilized to demonstrate the overall system behavior by defining both the structure of the partial object behavior as well as the interaction between them as reusable specification building blocks and later on, this UML specification style is applied to generate the SPN model by our performance modeling framework. UML collaboration and activity provides a tremendous modeling framework containing several interesting properties. Firstly, collaborations and activity model the concept of service provided by the system very nicely. They define structure of partial object behavior, the collaboration roles and enable a precise definition of the overall system behavior. They also delineate the way to compose the services by means of collaboration and role bindings [12].

Considering system execution architecture to specify the deployment of the service components is realized by the UML deployment diagram. Abstract view of the system execution architecture captured by the UML deployment diagram defines the execution architecture of the system by identifying the system components and the assignment of software artifacts to those identified system components. Considering the system architecture to generate the performance model resolves the bottleneck of system performance by finding a better allocation of service components to the physical nodes. This needs for an efficient approach to deploy the service components on the available hosts of distributed environment to achieve preferably high performance and low cost levels. The most basic example in this regard is to choose better deployment architectures by considering only the latency of the service. The easiest way to satisfy the latency requirements is to identify and deploy the service components that require the highest volume of interaction onto the same resource or to choose resources that are connected by the links with sufficiently high capacity [12].

It is indispensable to extend the UML model to incorporate the performance-related quality of service (QoS) information to allow modeling and evaluating the properties of a system like throughput, utilization and mean response time. So the UML models are annotated according to the *UML profile for MARTE: Modeling & Analysis of Real-Time Embedded Systems* to include quantitative system parameters [1]. Thus, it helps to maintain consistency between system design and implementation with respect to requirement specifications.

Markov models, stochastic process algebras, SPN (Stochastic Petri Net) are popular and much studied analytical approaches to conduct performance modeling and evaluation. Among all of them, we will focus on the SPN as the performance model generated by our framework due to its increasingly popular formalisms for describing and analyzing systems, its modeling generality, its ability to capture complex system behavior concisely, its ability to preserve the original architecture of the system, to allow marking dependency firing rates & reward rates defined at the net level, to facilitate any modification according to the feedback from performance evaluation and above all, the existence of analysis tools.

Several approaches have been followed to generate the performance model from system design specification. Lopez-Grao *et al.*, described a conversion method from annotated UML activity diagram to stochastic petrinet model [2]. Distefano *et al.*, proposed a possible solution to address software performance engineering that evolves through system specification using an augmented UML notation, creation of an intermediate performance context model, generation of an equivalent stochastic petri net model whose analytical solution provides the required performance measures [3]. D'Ambrogio proposed a framework for transforming source software models into target performance models by the use of meta-modeling techniques for defining the abstract syntax of models, the interrelationships between model elements and the model transformation rules [4]. Trowitzsch and Zimmermann proposed the modeling of technical systems and their behavior by means of UML and for the resulting models, a transformation into a Stochastic Petri Net was established [13]. Abdullatif and Pooly presented a method for providing computer support for extracting Markov chains from a performance annotated UML sequence diagram [14]. However, most existing approaches do not highlight more on the issue of how to optimally conduct the system modeling and performance evaluation. The approach presented here is the first known attempt that introduces a new specification style utilizing UML behavioral diagrams as reusable specification building block which is later on used for generating performance model to produce performance prediction result at early stage of the system development process. Building blocks describe the local behavior of several components and the interaction between them. This provides the advantage of reusability of building blocks, since solution that requires the cooperation of several components may be reused within one self-contained, encapsulated building block. In addition, the resulting deployment mapping provided by our approach has great impact with respect to QoS provided by the system. Our aim here is to deal with vector of QoS properties rather than restricting it in one dimension. Our presented deployment logic is surely able to handle any properties of the service, as long as we can provide a cost function for the specific property. The cost function defined here is flexible enough to keep pace with the changing size of search space of available host in the execution environment to ensure an efficient deployment of service components. Furthermore, we aim to be able to aid the deployment of several different services at the same time using the same framework. The novelty of our approach also reflected in showing the optimality of our solution with respect to both deployment logic and evaluation of performance metrics.

The objective of the chapter is to provide an extensive performance modeling framework that provides a translation process to generate SPN performance model from system design specification captured by the UML behavioral diagram and solves the model for relevant performance metrics to demonstrate performance prediction results at early stage of the system development life cycle. To incorporate the cost function to draw relation between service component and available physical resources permit us to identify an efficient deployment mapping in a fully distributed manner. The work presented here is the extension of our previous work described in [5, 6, 7, 12] where we present our framework with respect to the execution of single and multiple collaborative sessions and to consider alternatives system architecture candidates to describe system functional behavior and later on to evaluate the performance factors. The chapter is organized as follows: section 2 describes the performance evaluation of distributed system where the requirements of the successful performance evaluation are mentioned, section 3 introduces our performance modeling framework in details by considering the requirements outlined in the previous section, section 4 shows the applicability of our performance modeling framework with respect to performance modeling of a distributed system, and section 5 mentions the concluding remarks with future directions.

2. Performance evaluation of distributed software system

Performance evaluation is an integral part of any distributed software system which gives an indication of whether the system will meet non functional properties, once system built. The evaluation can be done in one of the two stages of the software development process:

1. Evaluation can be conducted at the early stage of the software development process
2. Evaluation can be done when the development process is completed.

Conducting the performance evaluation in any of the two stages has some merits and demerits. Early assessment of performance evaluation allows system designer predicting the system response in order to meet the non functional requirements before the system being built. This in turn guides the system designer about the system development process in right manner which thus increases the productivity and quality in accordance with the reduction in cost. But conducting performance evaluation in the early stage of the software development process is challenging because of the absence of the real system in hand. So predication in advance not always guides the system designer in right way. Modeling system functional behavior perfectly works as a catalyst to successfully conduct the system performance evaluation. System functional behavior is disseminated across several components that are physically distributed which increases the complexity in developing distributed software systems. Perfect modeling of distributed system functional behavior is realized by capturing the local behavior of the system components and also the interaction among them. It is very difficult to achieve these tasks in correct way when development of system is limited in the laboratory where modeling will be done by generating case study or scenario.

Conducting performance evaluation after the system development process being completed is less challenging than the former case. It is possible to retrieve the real system response in order to meet the system non functional requirements as the real system is already implemented. So the designer can get a real understanding about the correct status of the development process to know whether the system can meet the non functional requirements and end user's expectation. If the system fails to satisfy non functional requirements and can't meet the end user expectation, the only alternative is to rethink about the system design process. Any change in the system design process can cause the modification in the system development process. In worst case the development process might start from the beginning which in turn costs a lot.

In order to conduct the performance evaluation of distributed software system, the decision is not only influenced by when the evaluation should be performed but also other factors like which evaluation technique is appropriate and reasonable. There are mainly two evaluation techniques:

1. Simulation based evaluation
2. Analytic solution

Simulation based solution of the actual implementation gives a better assessment of the performance evaluation of the system. Simulation based solution gives the freedom to build the system arbitrary detailed and there is no restriction on building the simulation model of the real system [8]. Thus, it allows modeling and evaluating the system performance in a flexible way. But to develop the simulation model is not an easy task and sometimes it is error-prone. Implementing a complex system is usually a time-consuming, expensive task and needs experience [8]; mastering to handle this complexity is driven by the gaining vast knowledge in simulation language and how to apply this language to build and present the logic behind the complex distributed system to capture system functional behavior properly for conducting performance evaluation.

Analytical solution is another way to conduct the performance evaluation of the complex distributed software system. Presence of well established mathematical formula for analytical methods makes it popular to the scientific community to obtain the performance evaluation of the systems. This method of finding solution is more acceptable than simulation based evaluation because of the direct applicability of the mathematical formula and the availability of evaluation tools. Another advantage of using analytic model is the rapid development of model for performance evaluation of large and multifaceted system using the formalisms of analytical methods. However, sometimes such analytical models can usually be constructed by placing some structural restrictions and assumptions on the original system model based on the explicit modeling formalism which has been selected; the reason is that analytical models have a limited expressiveness in some cases to capture the complex system behavior. While it is sometimes doable to simplify the model of the system in order to make it analytically tractable, there are many cases in which the significant aspects of the system can not be effectively represented into the analytical model for performance evaluation [8].

In this chapter we particularly focus on the performance evaluation of the distributed software system at the early stage of the system development process using analytical models. The requirements for performance evaluation of distributed software system are not only influenced by the question of when to conduct the evaluation and which method is appropriate for the obtaining performance results but also driven by the other requirements such as:

1. Need for an efficient approach that will help to model the system functional behavior in a way that can reflect real system behavior so that performance evaluation can be meaningful afterwards.
2. Deployment mapping is an integral part of the distributed software system development process which is defined by the assignment of software components in the physical resources that are distributed. For large and complex system it requires an efficient approach for handling the deployment mapping so that it can also ensure the efficiency with respect to performance evaluation.
3. Model that captures the system functional behavior will be used as an input model for developing the analytical model. So we need a mechanism that can also include the performance parameters to the input models for conducting the successful evaluation.
4. Need for a scalable and efficient approach to establish the correspondence between the input model that will be utilized to capture the system functional behavior and the output model that will be used to conduct the performance evaluation of the distributed software system.
5. At last, developing a tool based support for the whole process of performance evaluation considering above requirements which can ensure the rapid development, evaluation and user friendliness.

The following Figure 1 mentions the requirements or factors that we need to consider for the successful performance evaluation of the distributed software systems. In order to capture all the above mentioned factors, it needs an efficient approach or developing a framework that will allow rapid and successful performance evaluation of distributed software system which at the end reflects the aim of this chapter.

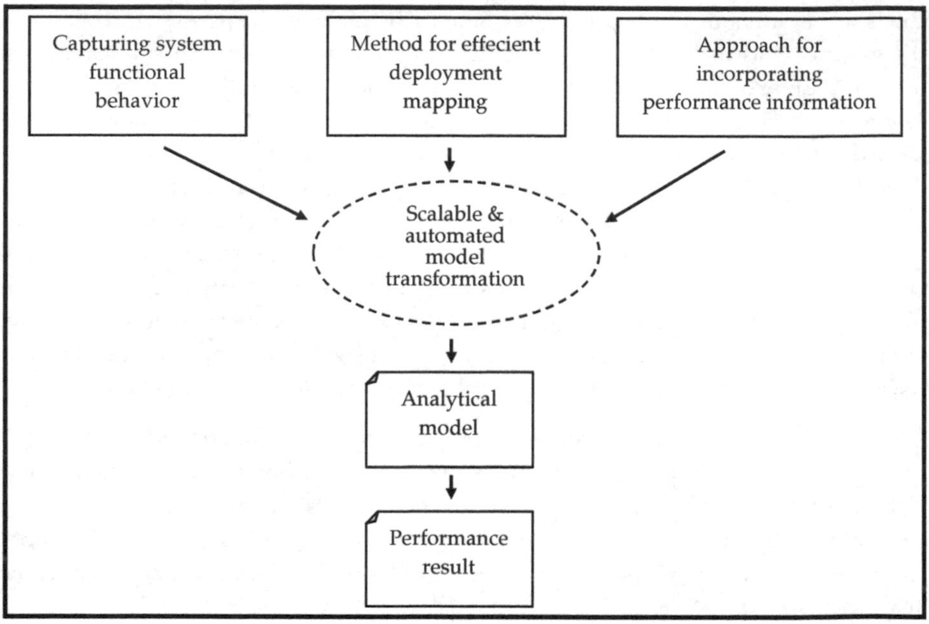

Figure 1. Performance modeling framework

3. Performance modeling framework

We already mentioned our main objective in the previous section that will be presented broadly in this section. In order to achieve the main objective, we need to follow an engineering approach that will accelerate the distributed software system development process. We also need to define the method that will be accounted for evaluating the system performance. We limit ourselves to methods targeting system development process using the standards of UML (Unified Modeling Languages) [9]. In the evaluation side we limit ourselves to methods that will analytically solve our problem using the technique SPN (Stochastic Petri Nets). This section mainly presents these two main techniques and also focuses on their properties that will be utilized to design our performance modeling framework.

3.1. Capturing system functional behavior

We use UML collaboration as main specification unit to specify system functional behavior. The UML standard focuses in particular on the structural aspects of UML collaborations. UML does not, however, elaborate detailed semantics of the behavioral implications of the structural composition. Collaborations are intended as a context in which behaviors may be defined. Compared to the other uses of collaborations, and what we need, this is an obvious shortcoming. We will later see how a combination of collaborations with activities may solve this problem [9].

Collaboration is an illustration of the relationship and interaction among software objects in the UML. Objects are shown as rectangles with naming label inside. The relationships between the objects are shown as line connecting the rectangles [11]. As a representative example, we introduce a scenario description utilizing UML collaboration 2. Several users equipped with cell phone or smart phone want to receive weather information of their current location using his/her hand held device. The user request is first transferred to authentication server through base transceiver station to ensure the authenticity of the user. Thereafter, the request of the legitimate user is transferred to the location server to retrieve the location information of the user. The location information is then transferred to weather server for retrieving the weather information according to the location of the user. Figure 2 defines this scenario as UML 2 collaboration. Participants in the system are users, mobile terminals, base transceiver stations, authentication servers, location servers, weather servers which are represented by the collaboration roles user, MT, BTS, AuS, LS, and WS. The users are the part of the environment and therefore labeled as <<external>>.The default multiplicity of the users, mobile terminals, base transceiver stations, authentication servers, location servers, weather servers are one to many, which are denoted by (1..*). The interactions between the collaboration roles are represented by the collaboration such as mobile terminal and BTS interact through *t: transfer*, BTS and authentication server, location server, weather server interact successively through *a: authenticate, l: request location info, w: request weather info*, while the user interacts with the mobile terminal by collaboration *g: generate request* [6].

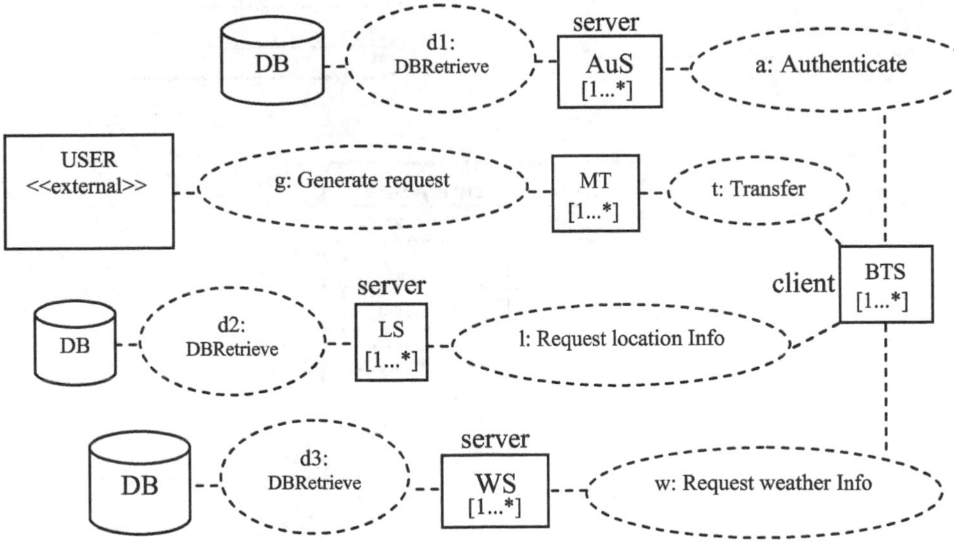

Figure 2. Collaboration diagram

The specifications for collaborations are given as coherent, self-contained reusable building blocks. The internal behavior of building block is described by the UML activity. It is declared as the classifier behavior of the collaboration and has one activity partition for each collaboration role in the structural description [6]. For each collaboration, the activity declares a corresponding call behavior action refereeing to the activities of the employed building blocks. Depending on the number of participants, connectivity to other blocks and level of decomposition, we distinguish three different kinds of building blocks [10]:

1. The most general building block is collaboration with two participants providing functionality that is intended to be composed with other functionality. We refer to such a building block as service collaboration.
2. Building blocks that involve only local behavior of one participant are referred to as activity blocks. They are represented by activities.
3. A special building block is system collaboration, which is collaboration on the highest composition level. In contrast to a service, a system is closed and cannot be composed with other building blocks.

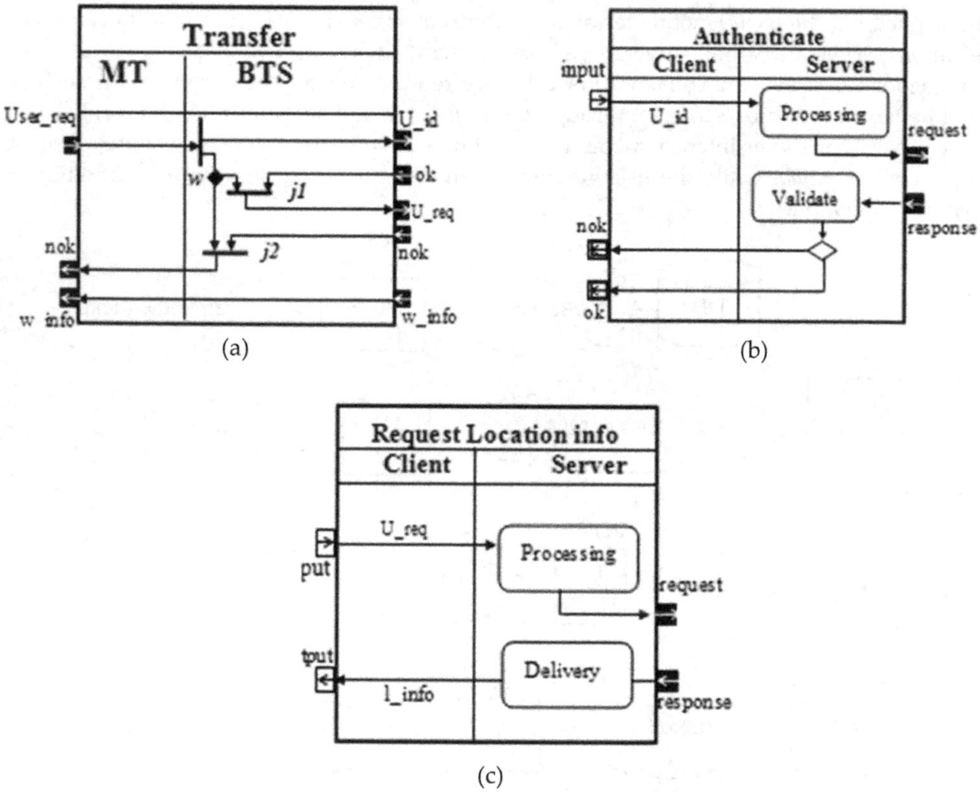

Figure 3. Activity diagram for expressing the internal behavior of collaboration

Hereby collaborations of Figure 2 are modeled by a call behavior action referring to the activity describing the behavior of the corresponding collaboration [10]. Activity diagram presents complete behavior in a quite compact form and may define connections to other behaviors via input and output pins [6]. Here we specify the behavior of one user request to show how the request is generated from his/her mobile terminal and served by the BTS, authentication server, location server and weather server and later on, compose this behavior to show how the requests will be processed by the BTS, authentication servers, location servers and weather servers so that the overall system behavior can be delineated. The activity *transfer* describes the behavior of the corresponding collaboration shown in Figure 3 (a). It has one partition for each collaboration role: mobile terminal (MT) and base transceiver station (BTS). Activities base their semantics on token flow [1]. The system starts by placing a token in the initial node of the mobile terminal when one request is generated by the user through his/her mobile terminal. The token is then transferred to the BTS where it moves through the fork node generating two flows. One flow places a token in the waiting decision node *w* which is the extension of a decision node with the difference that it may hold a token similar to an initial node, as defined in [1]. *w* is used in combination with join nodes *j1* and *j2* to explicitly model the acceptance or rejection of the user request based on the user authenticity. The other flow is forwarded as input to the authentication server to check whether the user is legitimate to generate service request. If the user is legitimate to generate the request a token is offered to the join node *j1*. If *w* still has its token *j1* can fire which emits a token which then forwarded to the location server for further processing. If the user is not legitimate to generate the request, a token is offered to the join node *j2*. If *w* still has its token *j2* can fire notifying the user upon the cancellation of request and then terminates the activity.

In order to validate the user identity (mobile number in this case) provided by a user who requests for service, BTS participates in the collaboration *authenticate* together with the authentication server. This is specified by collaboration *a: authenticate* where BTS plays the role of client and the authentication server plays the role of server. The behavior of the collaboration defined by the UML activity which is divided into two partitions, one for each collaboration role: client & server shown in Figure 3(b). The activity is started on the client side, when user id is provided as parameter *u_id* at the input pin. The input is then directly sent to the server, where it is converted into a database request in the call behavior action *processing*. Thereafter, it is the task of the collaboration between the server and the database to provide the stored user information. In order to get the information, the request leaves the activity *authenticate* and the server waits for the reception of the response. This is modeled with the input and output pins *request* and *response*. Depending on the validity of the user id, the server may decide to report *ok* or *nok* (not ok) to the client by the call behavior action *validate*. The result is then forwarded to the corresponding output pin in the client side and the activity is terminated. The semantics of all the pins are given in [12]. Likewise, we can describe the behavior of collaboration *l: Request Location info* (shown in Figure 3(c)) and w: *Request Weather info* through activity partition of client and server where BTS plays the role of client and location server and weather server play the role of server to deliver the requested information to the user through his/her mobile terminal.

The collaborative building blocks with help of activities specify overall system functional behavior which is introduced in Figure 4 for our scenario. For specifying detail behavior, UML collaborations and activities are used complementary to each other; UML collaborations focus on the role binding and structural aspect, while UML activities complement this by covering also the behavioral aspect for composition. For this purpose, call behavior actions are used. Each sub-service is represented by a call behavior action referring to the respective activity of the building blocks. Each call behavior action represents an instance of a building block. For each activity parameter node of the referred activity, a call behavior action declares a corresponding pin. Pins have the same symbol as activity parameter nodes to represent them on the frame of a call behavior action. Arbitrary logic between pins may be used to synchronize the building block events and transfer data between them. By connecting the individual input and output pins of the call behavior actions, the events occurring in different collaborations can be coupled with each other. There are different kinds of pins described as follows [10]:

1. Starting pins activate the building block, which is the precondition of any internal behavior.
2. Streaming pin may pass tokens throughout the active phase of the building block.
3. Terminating pins mark the end of the block's behavior. If collaboration is started and terminated via several alternative pins, they must belong to different parameter sets. This is visualized in UML diagram by an additional box around the corresponding node.

Figure 4 shows the activity diagram for our system to highlight the overall behavior of the system by composing all the building blocks. The initial node (·) marks the starting of the activity. The activity is started on the client side. When a user service request is generated via mobile terminal, *g: Generate request* will transfer the user service request as parameter *u_req* to the BTS via collaboration *t: Transfer*. Once the request arrived at the BTS the user id as parameter *u_id* is transferred to the authentication server to check whether the user is authentic to accept the service and the activity is represented by *a: authenticate*. The activity *authenticate* initiates a database request, modeled by collaboration *d1: DBRetrieve* and terminates with one of the alternative results *ok* or *nok*. After arriving the positive response at the BTS, request for location information is forwarded to the location server represented by activity *Request location info*. Location server makes a database request which is modeled by *d1: DBRetrieve* and terminates with result *l_info* (Location information). After getting the location information, request for weather information according to user current location is forwarded by the BTS to the weather server represented by activity *Request weather info*. Weather server makes a database request which is modeled by *d2: DBRetrieve* and terminates with result *w_info* (Weather information). After that, the final result is transferred to the user hand held device by BTS via activity *t: Transfer*. But if the user is failed to prove his/her identity then immediately a *nok* is sent to the user's hand held device.

So far, we introduced the system functional behavior with respect to specific example. Now we would like to introduce the specification in more generalized way. For example, the

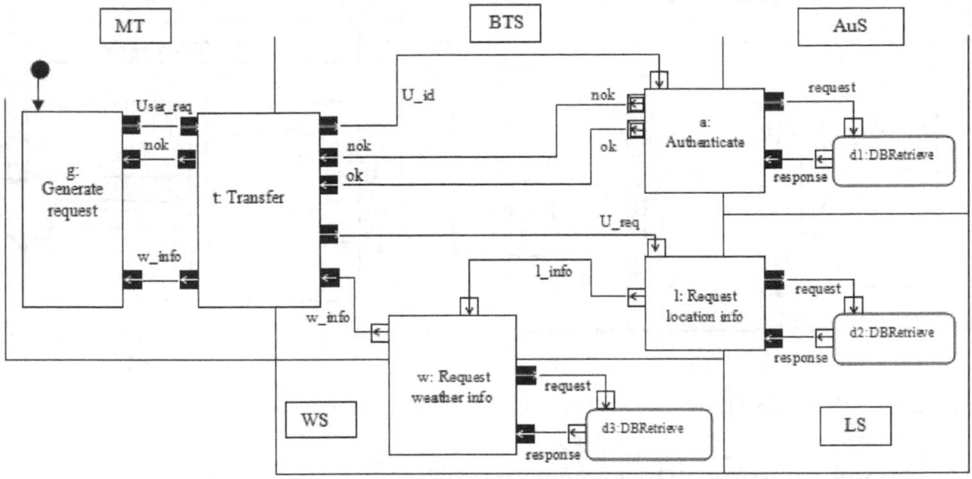

Figure 4. Activity diagram for detail system behavior

general structure of the building block *t* is given in Figure 5 where it only declares the participants A and B as collaboration roles and the connection between them is defined as collaboration use t_x (x=1…n_{AB} (number of collaborations between collaboration roles A and B)). The internal behavior of the same building block is shown in Figure 6(b). The activity $transfer_{ij}$ (*where ij = AB*) describes the behavior of the corresponding collaboration. It has one activity partition for each collaboration role: A and B. Activities base their semantics on token flow [1]. The activity starts by placing a token when there is a response (indicated by the streaming pin *res*) to transfer by either participant A or B. After completion of the processing by the collaboration role A and B the token is transferred from the participant A to participant B and from participant B to Participant A which is represented by the call behavior action *forward.*

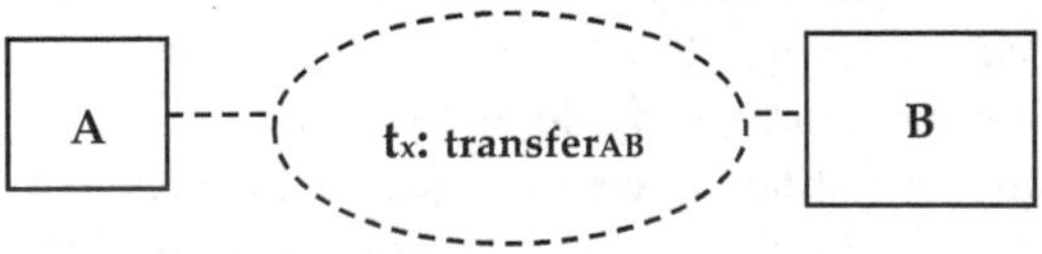

Figure 5. Collaboration diagram in generalized way

The detailed behavior of collaboration is given in following Figure 6(a). The initial node (·) indicates the starting of the activity. The activity is started at the same time from each participant A and B. After being activated, each participant starts its processing of the request which is mentioned by call behavior action P_i (Processing$_i$, where i = A, B). Completions of the processing by the participants are mentioned by the call behavior action d_i (Processing_done$_i$, i = A, B). After completion of the processing, the responses are delivered to the corresponding participants indicated by the streaming pin *res*. The response of the collaboration role A will be forwarded to B and vice versa which is mentioned by collaboration *t: transfer$_{ij}$* (where ij = AB).

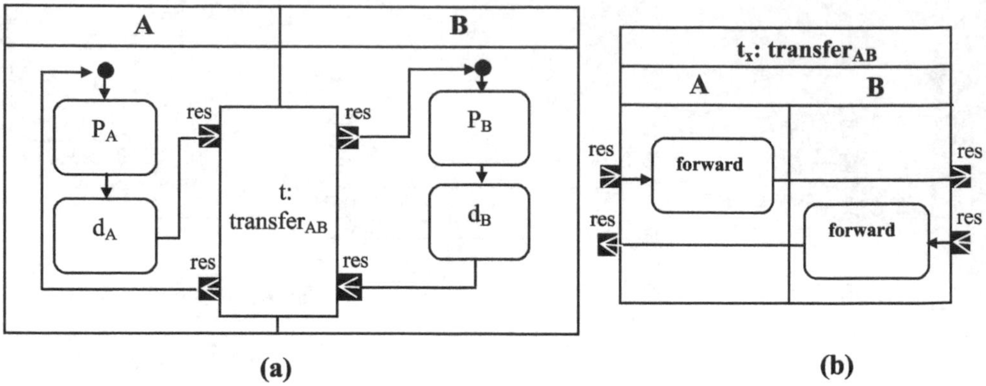

Figure 6. (a) Detail behavior of collaborative building block (b). Internal behavior of collaboration

3.2. Method for efficient Deployment mapping

Deployment diagram can be used to define the execution architecture of the system by identifying the system physical components and the assignment of software artifacts to those identified physical components [11]. After designing the deployment diagram the relation between system component and collaboration will be delineated to describe the service delivered by the system. The service is delivered by the joint behavior of the system components which may be physically distributed. The necessary partial behavior of the component used to realize the collaboration is represented by the collaboration role. In this way, it is possible to expose direct mapping between the collaboration roles to the system components to show the probable deployment of service components to the physical nodes of the system [6].

We consider two design alternatives of system architecture captured by UML deployment diagram to demonstrate the relationship between collaboration and system component for the scenario mentioned in Figure 2. For our defined scenario the identified system components by the 1st variation of deployment diagram are Mobile terminal, Base transceiver station, Authentication server, Location server and Weather server. After designing the deployment diagram the relationship between system component and collaboration will be delineated to describe the service delivered by the system. The service is delivered by the joint behavior of system components which may be physically distributed. The necessary partial behavior of the components used to realize the collaboration is represented by the collaboration role. Behavior of the components Mobile terminal, Base transceiver station, Authentication server, Location server, Weather server are represented by the collaboration roles MT, BTS, AuS, LS & WS to utilize the collaboration *t: transfer, a: authenticate, l: request location info, w: request weather info*. Here it is one to one mapping between system component & collaboration role shown in Figure 7(a).

We consider other variation of deployment diagram for mentioned scenario. In this variation of deployment diagram the identified system components are mobile terminal,

Base transceiver station, application server. In this case, the behavior of the components Mobile terminal and Base transceiver station is represented by the collaboration roles MT and BTS to utilize the collaboration *t: transfer* and the behavior of the component application behavior is represented jointly by the collaboration role AuS, LS and WS to utilize the collaboration *a: authenticate, l: request location info, w: request weather info*. In second case, the mapping between system component & collaboration role is generalized into one to many relations mentioned in Figure 7(b).

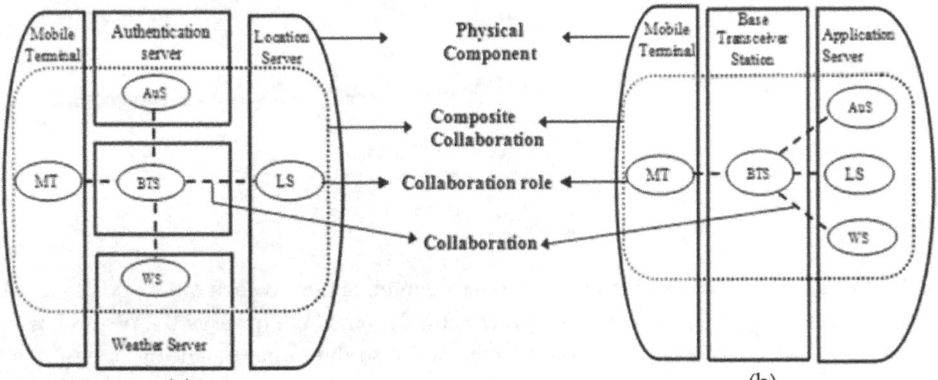

Figure 7. UML deployment diagram with service components deployment mapping

For large and complex system, conducting the deployment mapping is not straight forward like the previous cases. The deployment mapping has implication with respect to satisfying the non functional properties of the system. So we need for an approach that will be apposite for conducting the deployment mapping for complex system considering constraints and capabilities of the system components. We introduce our approach by considering the system as collection of N interconnected nodes. Our objective is to find a deployment mapping for this execution environment for a set of service components C available for deployment that comprises the service. Deployment mapping M can be defined as $(M : C \rightarrow N)$ between a numbers of service components instances c, onto nodes n mentioned in Figure 8. A components $c_i \in C$ can be a client process or a service process, while a node, $n \in N$ is a physical resource. Generally, nodes can have different responsibilities, such as providing services (*S1*), relaying traffic (*R1*), accommodating clients (*C1*), or a mixture of these (*SC1*). Components can communicate via a set of collaborations. We consider 3 types of requirements in the deployment problem where the term cost is introduced to capture several non-functional requirements those are later on utilized to conduct performance evaluation of the systems:

1. Components have execution costs
2. Collaborations have communication costs and costs for running of background process known as overhead cost
3. Some of the components can be restricted in the deployment mapping to specific nodes which are called bound components.

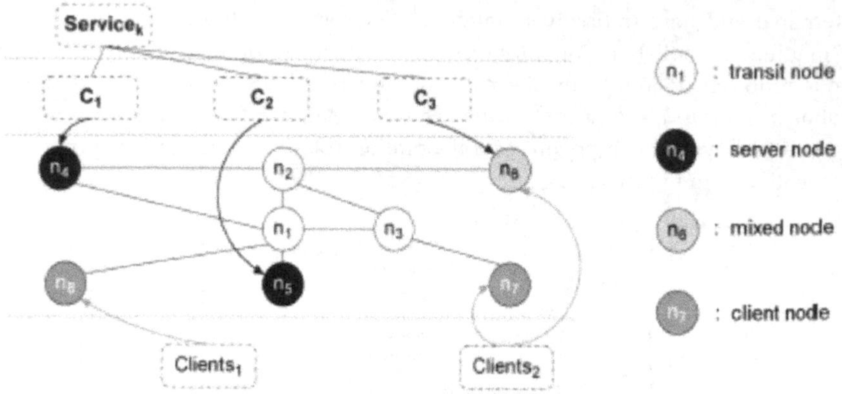

Figure 8. Service component mapping example

Furthermore, we consider identical nodes that are interconnected each other and are capable of hosting components with unlimited processing demand. We observe the processing cost that nodes impose while host the components and also the target balancing of cost among the nodes available in the network. Communication costs are considered if collaboration between two components happens remotely, i.e. it happens between two nodes [15]. In other words, if two components are placed onto the same node the communication cost between them will not be considered. The cost for executing the background process for conducting the communication between the collaboration roles is always considerable no matter whether the collaboration roles deploy on the same or different nodes. Using the above specified input, the deployment logic provides an optimal deployment architecture taking into account the QoS requirements for the components providing the specified services. We then define the objective of the deployment logic as obtaining an efficient (low-cost, if possible optimum) mapping of components onto the nodes that satisfies the requirements in reasonable time. The deployment logic providing optimal deployment architecture is guided by the cost function F(M). The cost function is designed here to reflect the goal of balancing the execution cost and minimizing the communications cost. This is in turn utilized to achieve reduced task turnaround time by maximizing the utilization of resources while minimizing any communication between processing nodes. That will offer a high system throughput, taking into account the expected execution and inter-node communication requirements of the service components on the given hardware architecture. The evaluation of cost function F(M) is mainly influenced by our way of service definition. Service is defined in our approach as a collaboration of total E components labeled as c_i (where i = 1.... E) to be deployed and total K collaborations between them labeled as k_j, (where j = 1 ... K). The execution cost of each service component can be labeled as f_{c_i}; the communication cost between the service components is labeled as f_{k_j} and the cost for executing the background process for conducting the communication between the service components is labeled as f_{B_j}. Accordingly, we only observe the total cost ($\hat{l}_n$, n = 1... X) ofa given deployment mapping at each node where X defines the total number of physical nodes available in the execution environment. We will strive for an optimal solution of equally distributed cost among the processing nodes and the lowest cost possible, while taking into account the execution cost fc_i, i = 1….E, communication cost fk_j, j = 1….K and cost for executing the background process fB_j, j = 1….k. fc_i, fk_j and fB_j are derived from the service specification, thus the offered execution cost can be calculated as $\sum_{i=1}^{|E|} fc_i$. This way, the logic can be aware of the target cost T [15]:

$$T = \frac{1}{|X|} \sum_{i=1}^{|E|} fc_i \tag{1}$$

To cater for the communication cost fk_j, of the collaboration k_j in the service, the function $q_0(M, c)$ is defined first [15]:

$$q_0(M,c) = \{n \in N \mid \exists (c \to n) \in M\} \tag{2}$$

This means that $q_0(M,c)$ returns the node n that hosts components in the list mapping M. Let collaboration $k_j = (c_1, c_2)$. The communication cost of k_j is 0 if components c_1 and c_2 are collocated, i.e. $q_0(M,c_1) = q_0(M,c_2)$, and the cost is fk_j if components are otherwise (i.e. the collaboration is remote). Using an indicator function I(x), which is 1 if x is true and 0 otherwise, this expressed as $I(q_0(M,c_1) \neq q_0(M,c_2)) = 1$, if the collaboration is remote and 0 otherwise. In order to determine which collaboration k_j is remote, the set of mapping M is used. Given the indicator function, the overall communication cost of service, $F_k(M)$, is the sum [15]:

$$F_k(M) = \sum_{j=1}^{|k|} I\left(q_0(M, K_{j,1}) \neq q_0(M, K_{j,2})\right) \cdot fk_j \tag{3}$$

Given a mapping M = $\{m_n\}$ (where m_n is the set of components at node n & $n \in$ N) the total load can be obtained as $\hat{l}_n = \sum_{c_i \in m_n} fc_i$. Furthermore the overall cost function F(M) becomes (where I_j = 1, if k_j external or 0 if k_j internal to a node) [15]:

$$F(M) = \sum_{n=1}^{|N|} |\hat{l}_n - T| + F_k(M) + \sum_{j=1}^{|k|} fB_j \tag{4}$$

3.3. Approach for incorporating performance information

UML is no doubt a well established language for modeling system functional behavior. But UML has lacking of incorporating non functional parameters in the model while specifying the functional behavior of any system. This needs for an approach or specification to incorporate the performance parameters in the UML for quantitative analysis. That's why we use a specification called the *UML profile for MARTE* for Modeling and Analysis of Real-Time and Embedded systems, provides support for specification, design, and verification/validation stages [1]. This new profile is intended to replace the existing UML Profile for Schedulability, Performance and Time. This specification of a UML profile adds capabilities to UML for model-driven development of Real Time and Embedded Systems (RTES) [1].

MARTE defines foundations for model-based descriptions of real time and embedded systems. These core concepts are then refined for both modeling and analyzing concerns. Modeling parts provides support required from specification to detailed design of real-time and embedded characteristics of systems. MARTE concerns also model-based analysis. In this sense, the intent is not to define new techniques for analyzing real-time and embedded systems, but to support them. Hence, it provides facilities to annotate models with information required to perform specific analysis. Especially, MARTE focuses on performance and schedulability analysis. But it defines also a general analysis framework that intends to refine/specialize any other kind of analysis. Among others, the benefits of using this profile are thus [1]:

1. Providing a common way of modeling both hardware and software aspects of an RTES in order to improve communication between developers.
2. Enabling interoperability between development tools used for specification, design, verification, code generation, etc.
3. Fostering the construction of models that may be used to make quantitative predictions regarding real-time and embedded features of systems taking into account both hardware and software characteristics.

We apply several stereotypes of MARTE that permit us to map model elements into the semantics of an analysis domain such as schedulability, and give values for properties that are needed in order to carry out the analysis [1]. Specific tagged values are also applied. Tagged values are a kind of value slots associated with attributes of specific UML stereotypes [1]. In order to annotate the UML diagram we use several stereotypes and tag values according to the UML profile for MARTE. The stereotypes are the following [1]:

1. *saStep* is a kind of step that begins and ends when decisions about the allocation of system resources are made.
2. *ComputingResource* represents either virtual or physical processing devices capable of storing and executing program code. Hence its fundamental service is to compute.
3. *Scheduler* is defined a kind of ResourceBroker that brings access to its brokered ProcessingResource or resources following a certain scheduling policy mentioned by tag value *schedPolicy*. The ResourceBroker is a kind of resource that is responsible for allocation and de-allocation of a set of resource instances (or their services) to clients according to a specific access control policy [1].

The tagged values are the following [1]:

1. *execTime*: The duration of the execution time is mentioned by the tagged value *execTime* which is the average time in our case. The execution cost of service component is expressed by this tagged value in the annotated UML model that is later on used by the performance model to conduct the performance evaluation.

2. *deadline* defines the maximum time bound on the completion of the particular execution segment that must be met. The overhead cost and communication cost between the service components are specified by this tagged value in the annotated UML model that is later on used as well by the performance model to conduct the performance evaluation.

3.4. Scalable and automated model transformation

We already mentioned that SPN model will be generated as analytical model from the UML specification style to conduct the performance evaluation. This needs for an efficient, scalable and automated approach to conduct the model transformation for large, complex and multifaceted distributed system. In this literature, the approach for efficient model transformation is realized by producing model transformation rules that can be applied in generalized way for various application domains. As we generate SPN model as analytical model we will give a brief introduction about SPN model. SPN model has the following elements: Finite set of the places (drawn as circles), finite set of the transition defined as either timed transition (drawn as thick transparent bar) or immediate transition (drawn as thin black bar), set of arcs connecting places and transition, multiplicity associated with the arcs, marking that denotes the number of token in each place. SPN model is mentioned formally by the 6-tuple $\{\mathbf{\Phi}, \mathbf{T}, \mathbf{A}, \mathbf{K}, \mathbf{N}, \mathbf{m_0}\}$:

$\mathbf{\Phi}$ = Finite set of the places

$\mathbf{T}$ = Finite set of the transition

$\mathbf{A} \subseteq \{\Phi \times T\} \cup \{T \times \Phi\}$ is a set of arcs connecting Φ and T

$\mathbf{K}: T \rightarrow \{\text{Timed (time>0), Immediate (time = 0)}\}$ specifies the type of the each transition

$\mathbf{N}: A \rightarrow \{1, 2, 3\ldots\}$ is the multiplicity associated with the arcs in A

$\mathbf{m}: \Phi \rightarrow \{0, 1, 2\ldots\}$ is the marking that denotes the number of tokens for each place in Φ. The initial marking is denoted as $\mathbf{m_0}$.

By utilizing the above formal representation of the SPN model, we initiate the model transformation rules that will generate SPN model from UML collaboration and activity oriented approach that captures the system functional behavior. The model transformation rules are the following:

Rule 1: The SPN model of a collaboration role is represented by the 6-tuple in the following way:

$\mathbf{\Phi} = \{P_i, d_i\}$

$\mathbf{T} = \{\text{do, exit}\}$

$\mathbf{A} = \{\{(P_i \times do) \cup (do \times d_i)\}, \{(d_i \times exit) \cup (exit \times P_i)\}\}$

$\mathbf{K} = (do \rightarrow \text{Timed}, exit \rightarrow \text{Immediate})$

$\mathbf{N} = \{(P_i \times do) \rightarrow 1, (do \times d_i) \rightarrow 1, (d_i \times exit) \rightarrow 1, (exit \times P_i) \rightarrow 1\}$

$\mathbf{m_0} = \{(P_i \rightarrow 1\}, (d_i \rightarrow 0)\}$

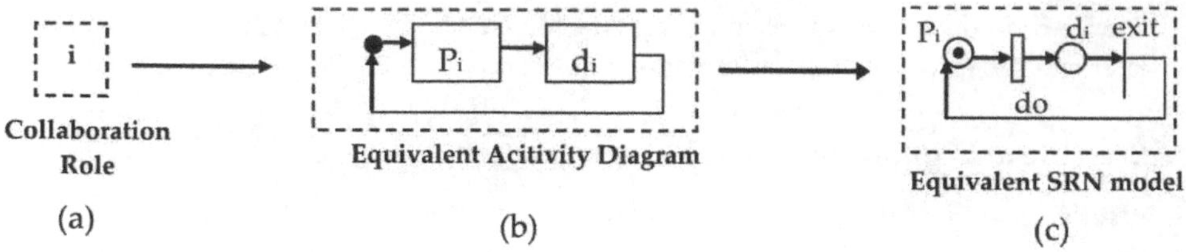

Figure 9. Model transformation rule 1

SPN model of a collaboration role is mentioned in Figure 9 (where P_i = Processing of ith collaboration role and d_i = Processing done of the ith collaboration role).

Rule 2: When the collaboration role of a building block deploys onto a physical node the equivalent SPN model is represented by 6-tuple in following way:

$\mathbf{\Phi} = \{P_i, d_i, PP_n\}$

$\mathbf{T} = \{do, exit\}$

$\mathbf{A} = \{\{(P_i \times do) \cup (do \times d_i)\}, \{(PP_n \times do) \cup (do \times PP_n)\}, \{(d_i \times exit) \cup (exit \times P_i)\}\}$

$\mathbf{K} = (do \rightarrow Timed, exit \rightarrow Immediate)$

$\mathbf{N} = \{(P_i \times do) \rightarrow 1, (do \times d_i) \rightarrow 1, (PP_n \times do) \rightarrow 1, (do \times PP_n) \rightarrow 1 (d_i \times exit) \rightarrow 1, (exit \times P_i) \rightarrow 1\}$

$\mathbf{m_o} = \{(P_i \rightarrow 1\}, (d_i \rightarrow 0), (PP_n \rightarrow q)\}$

Initially place PP_n contains **q** (where integer **q** > 0) tokens which define the upper bound of the execution of the process in parallel by a physical node *n* and the timed transition *do* will fire only when there is a token available in both the place P_i and PP_n. The place PP_n will again get back it's token after firing of the timed transition *do* indicating that the node is ready to execute other processes deployed on that physical node. The equivalent SPN model when a collaboration role deploy on a physical node is mentioned in Figure 10:

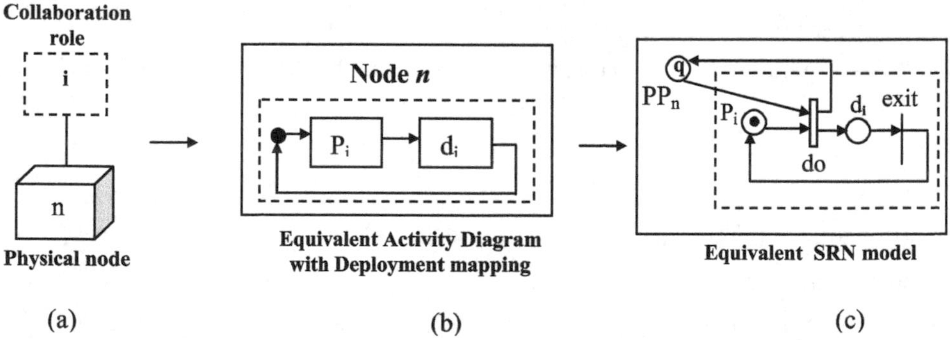

Figure 10. Model transformation rule 2

Rule 3: The SPN model of a collaboration where collaboration connects only two collaboration roles those deploy on the same physical node can be represented by the 6-tuple in the following way in Figure 11:

$\mathbf{\Phi} = \{P_i, d_i, P_j, d_j\ PP_n\}$

$\mathbf{T} = \{do_i, do_j, t_{ij}\}$

$\mathbf{A} = \{(P_i \times do_i) \cup (do_i \times d_i), (PP_n \times do_i) \cup (do_i \times PP_n), (d_i \times t_{ij}) \cup (t_{ij} \times P_i), (P_j \times do_j) \cup (do_j \times d_j), (PP_n \times do_j) \cup (do_j \times PP_n), (d_j \times t_{ij}) \cup (t_{ij} \times P_j)\}$

$\mathbf{K} = \{(do_i, do_j, t_{ij}) \rightarrow \text{Timed}\}$

$\mathbf{N} = \{((P_i \times do_i), (do_i \times d_i), (PP_n \times do_i), (do_i \times PP_n), (d_i \times t_{ij}), (t_{ij} \times P_i), (P_j \times do_j), (do_{ij} \times d_j), (PP_n \times do_j), (do_j \times PP_n), (d_j \times t_{ij}), (t_{ij} \times P_j)) \rightarrow 1\}$

$\mathbf{m_0} = \{(P_i \rightarrow 1), (d_i \rightarrow 0), (P_j \rightarrow 1)\ (d_j \rightarrow 0), (PP_n \rightarrow q)\}$

Here timed transition $\mathbf{t_{ij}}$ in the SPN model is only realized by the overhead cost as service components *i* and *j* deploy on the same physical node which makes the communication cost = 0.

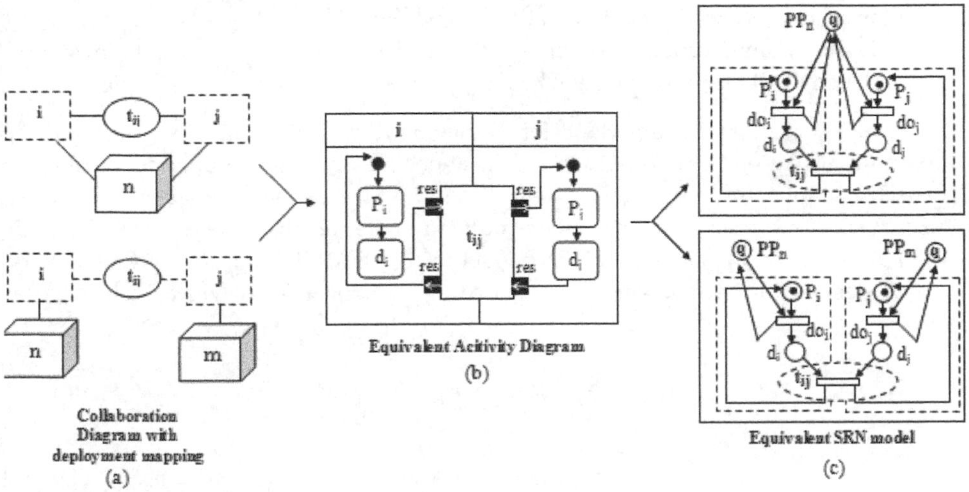

Figure 11. Model transformation rule 3

The SPN model of a collaboration where collaboration connects only two collaboration roles those deploy on the different physical node can be represented by the 6-tuple in the following way in Figure 11:

$\mathbf{\Phi} = \{P_i, d_i, P_j, d_j\ PP_n, PP_m\}$

$\mathbf{T} = \{do_i, do_j, t_{ij}\}$

$\mathbf{A} = \{(P_i \times do_i) \cup (do_i \times d_i), (PP_n \times do_i) \cup (do_i \times PP_n), (d_i \times t_{ij}) \cup (t_{ij} \times P_i), (P_j \times do_j) \cup (do_j \times d_j), (PP_m \times do_j) \cup (do_j \times PP_m), (d_j \times t_{ij}) \cup (t_{ij} \times P_j)\}$

$\mathbf{K} = \{(do_i, do_j, t_{ij}) \rightarrow \text{Timed}\}$

$\mathbf{N} = \{((P_i \times do_i), (do_i \times d_i), (PP_n \times do_i), (do_i \times PP_n), (d_i \times t_{ij}), (t_{ij} \times P_i), (P_j \times do_j), (do_{ij} \times d_j), (PP_m \times do_j), (do_j \times PP_m), (d_j \times t_{ij}), (t_{ij} \times P_j)) \rightarrow 1\}$

$\mathbf{m_o} = \{(P_i \rightarrow 1), (d_i \rightarrow 0), (P_j \rightarrow 1), (d_j \rightarrow 0), (PP_n \rightarrow q), (PP_m \rightarrow q)\}$

Here timed transition $\mathbf{t_{ij}}$ in the SPN model is realized by both the overhead cost and communication cost as service components *i* and *j* deploy on the different physical node.

3.5. Performance model Evaluation

We focus on measuring the throughput of the system from the developed SPN model. We are interested in throughput calculation as a measure of job that a system can process in a given time period which in turn justify the efficiency of our deployment logic mentioned in section 3.2 in accordance with system performance evaluation. Before deriving formula for throughput estimation, we consider several assumptions that will allow us to determine the parameters necessary for the throughput calculation of our system.

1. Executions of the processes occur independently each other.
2. All the communications occur in parallel.
3. Finally the communications between interconnected nodes will be started following the completion of all the processing and communication inside each physical node.

The above assumption is important for retrieving the parameters necessary for the throughput calculation from our system specification. We define the throughput as function of expected number of jobs in the system, E(N) and cost of the network, C_Net which defines the time required to complete the expected number of jobs in the system. The value of E(N) is calculated by solving the SPN model using SHARPE [16]. Cost of the network, C_Net is defined in the following: First the cost of a subnet (Csn) will be calculated as follows:

$$Csn_x = \sum_{i=1}^{|m|} fc_i + \max\left\{ f_{B_j} \right\} + F_k(M)$$

$$= \sum_{i=1}^{|m|} fc_i + \max\left\{ f_{B_j} \right\} \qquad (5)$$

Here:

- Csn_x = cost of the xth subnet (where x = 1….n; n is the total number of subnet that comprises the network)
- fc_i = execution cost of the ith process of the xth subnet
- m = total number of service components deployed on the xth subnet
- f_{Bj} = overhead cost of collaboration j (where j =1….n; n is the total number of collaboration in the xth subnet)
- f_{kj} = communication cost of collaboration j (where j =1….n; n is the total number of collaboration in the xth subnet)

- $F_k(M) = 0$ (defined in section 3.2.); as in this case processes connected by the collaboration deploy on the same physical node

Now we evaluate the cost between each pair of subnet with respect to the subnet's own processing cost, overhead cost and the cost associated with the communication with other subnet in the network.

$$Csnp_x = \left\{\max\left(Csn_i, Csn_j\right)\right\} + f_{B_j} + F_k(M)\} \tag{6}$$

Here:

- $Csnp_y$ = cost of the yth subnet pair (y = 1….n; n is the total number of subnet pair in the network where each subnet pair corresponds between two subnets)
- Csn_i, Csn_i = cost of the ith and j[th] subnet (where (i, j) ϵ x and i≠j)
- $F_k(M) = 1$ (defined in section 3.2.2); as in this case processes connected by the collaboration deploy on the different physical nodes

$$C\_Net = \max\left\{Csnp_1, \ldots, \ldots, Csnp_n\right\} \tag{7}$$

$$Throughput = \frac{E(N)}{C\_Net} \tag{8}$$

4. Case study

As a representative example, we consider the scenario dealing with heuristically clustering of modules and assignment of clusters to nodes [15, 17]. This scenario is sufficiently complex to show the applicability of our performance modeling framework. The problem is defined in our approach as a service of collaboration of $E = 10$ components or collaboration roles (labeled $C_1 \ldots C_{10}$) to be deployed and $K = 14$ collaborations between them depicted in Figure 12. We consider three types of requirements in this specification. Besides the execution cost, communication cost and overhead cost, we have a restriction on components C_2, C_7, C_9 regarding their location. They must be bound to nodes n_2, n_1, n_3, respectively. The internal behavior of the collaboration K_i of our example scenario is realized by the call behavior action through same UML activity diagram mentioned in Figure 6(b). The detail behavior of the collaboration role C is realized through same UML activity diagram already illustrated in Figure 6(a). However, there is no behavior modeled in detail, only that collaboration between processes deployed on different physical nodes. The UML collaboration diagram can be modeled by the activity that may model the detail behavior but the level of details must be selected with care in order for the model to scale while generating the performance model.

In this example, the target environment consists only of $N = 3$ identical, interconnected nodes with a single provided property, namely processing power and with infinite communication capacities depicted in Figure 13. The optimal deployment mapping can be observed in Table. 1. The lowest possible deployment cost, according to equation (4) is 17 + 100 + 70 = 187 [15, 17].

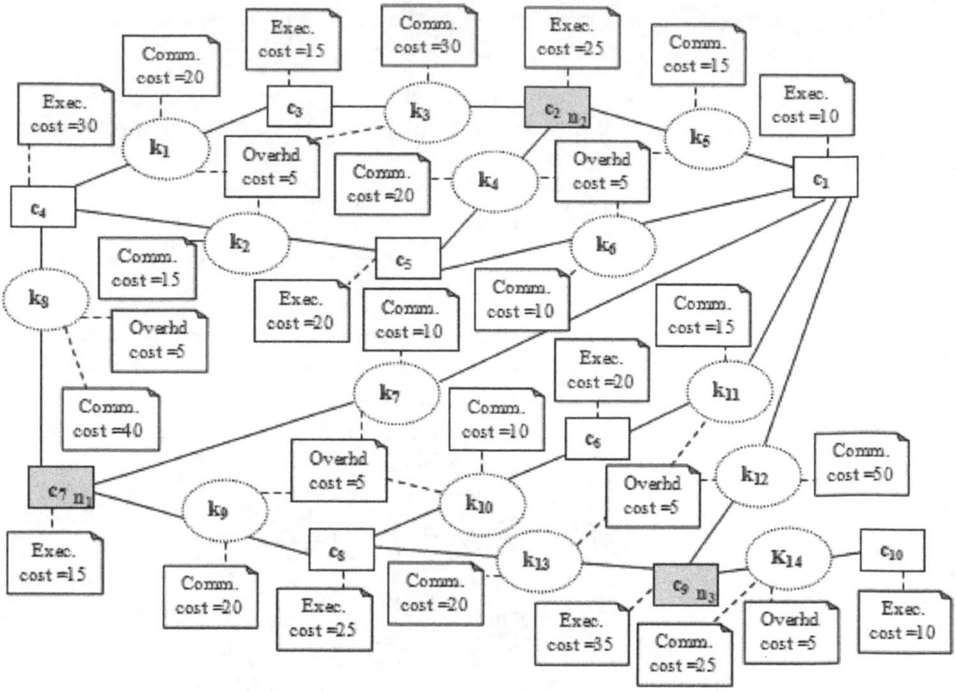

Figure 12. Collaborations and components in the example scenario

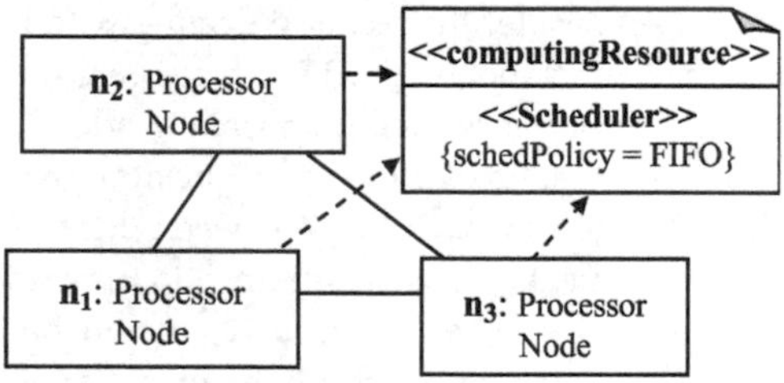

Figure 13. The target network of hosts

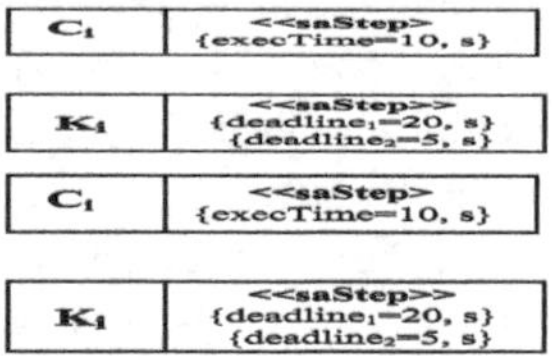

Figure 14. Annotated UML model

In order to annotate the UML diagram in Figure 12 and 13 we use the stereotypes *saStep, computingResource, scheduler* and the tag values *execTime, deadline* and *schedPolicy* which are already described in section 3.3. Collaboration K_i is associated with two instances of *deadline*

(Figure 14) as collaborations in example scenario are associated with two kinds of cost: communication cost and overhead cost.

Node	Components	$\hat{l}_n$	$\lvert \hat{l}_n - T \rvert$	Internal collaborations
n_1	c_4, c_7, c_8	70	2	k_8, k_9
n_2	c_2, c_3, c_5	60	8	k_3, k_4
n_3	c_1, c_6, c_9, c_{10}	75	7	k_{11}, k_{12}, k_{14}
			17	100
$\sum$ cost			117	

Table 1. Optimal deployment mapping in the example scenario [15, 17]

By considering the above deployment mapping and the transformation rules, the corresponding SPN model of our example scenario is depicted in Figure 15. Figure 15 sketches the resulting SPN model by illustrating details of all the places and transitions. According to the transformation rule 1, each collaboration role is defined by the two places P_i and d_i and the passing of token from place P_i to d_i is realized by the timed transition t_i

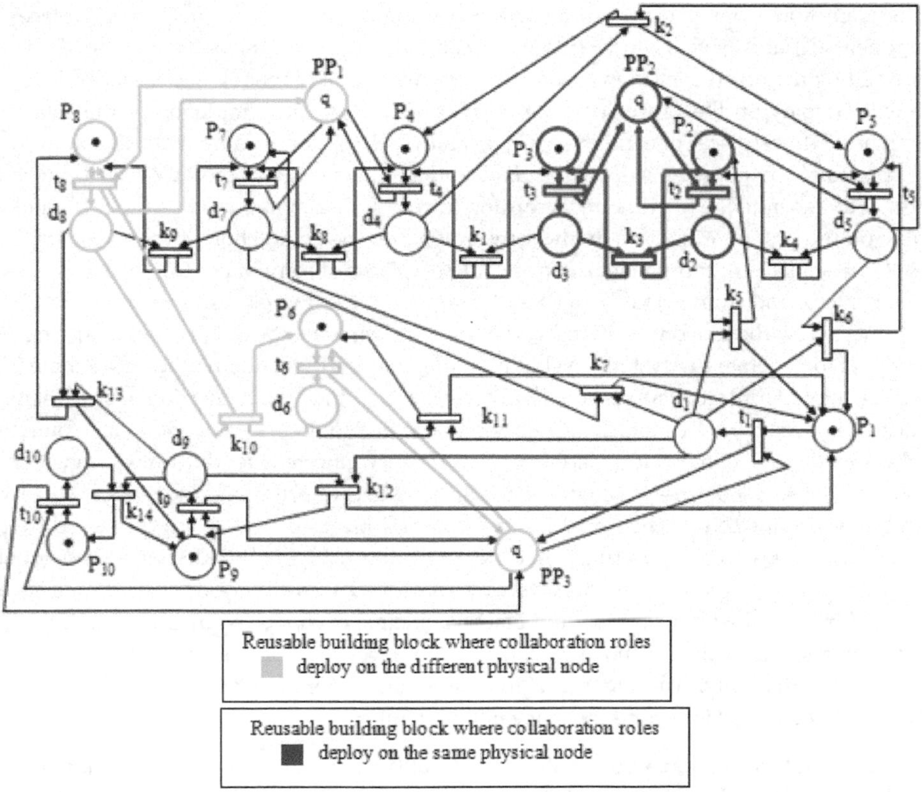

Figure 15. SPN model of our example scenario

which is derived from the annotated UML model. Initially, there will be a token from place P_1 to P_{10}. According to rule 2, in order to define the upper bound of the execution of parallel processes by a network node, we introduce three places PP_1, PP_2 and PP_3 in the SPN model for the corresponding three physical nodes and initially, these three places will contain q ($q > 0$) tokens where q will define the maximum number of the process that will be handled in parallel by a physical node at certain time. In order to ensure the upper bound of the parallel processing of a network node n_1, we introduce arcs from place PP_1 to transition t_4, t_7 and t_8. That means, components C_4, C_7 and C_8 can start their processing if there is token available in place PP_1 as the firing of transitions t_4, t_7 and t_8 not only depend on the availability of the token in the place P_4, P_7 and P_8 but also depend on the availability of the token in the place PP_1. Likewise, to ensure the upper bound of the parallel processing of a network node n_2 and n_3, we introduce arcs from place PP_2 to transition t_2, t_3 and t_5 and from place PP_3 to transition t_1, t_6, t_9, t_{10}.

For generating the SPN model from annotated UML model, firstly, we will consider the collaboration roles deploy on the processor node n_1 which are C_4, C_7 and C_8. Here components C_7 connects to C_4 and C_8. The communication cost between the components is zero but there is still cost for execution of the background process. So according to rule 3, after the completion of the transition from place P_7 to d_7 (places of component C_7), from P_4 to d_4 (places of component C_4) and from P_8 to d_8 (places of component C_8) the places d_7, d_4 and d_7, d_8 are connected by the timed transition k_8 and k_9 to generate the SPN model. Collaboration roles C_2, C_3 and C_5 deploy on the processor node n_2. Likewise, after the completion of the transition from place P_2 to d_2 (places of component C_2), from P_3 to d_3 (places of component C_3) and from P_5 to d_5 (places of component C_5) the places d_2, d_3 and d_2, d_5 are connected by the timed transition k_3 and k_4 to generate the SPN model according to rule 3. Collaboration roles C_6, C_1, C_9 and C_{10} deploy on the processor node n_3. In the same way, after the completion of the transition from place P_1 to d_1 (places of component C_1), from P_6 to d_6 (places of component C_6), P_9 to d_9 (places of component C_9) and from P_{10} to d_{10} (places of component C_{10}) the places d_1, d_6; d_1, d_9 and d_9, d_{10} are connected by the timed transition k_{11}, k_{12} and K_{14} to generate the SPN model following rule 3. In order to generate the system level SPN model we need to combine the entire three SPN model generated for three processor nodes by considering the interconnection among them. In order to compose the SPN models of processor node n_1 and n_2, places d_4 and d_3 are connected by the timed transition k_1 and places d_4 and d_5 are connected by the timed transition k_2 according to rule 3. Likewise, to compose the SPN models of processor node n_2 and n_3, places d_2 and d_1 are connected by the timed transition k_5 and places d_5 and d_1 are connected by the timed transition k_6 according to rule 3. In order to compose the SPN models of processor node n_1 and n_3, places d_7 and d_1 are connected by the timed transition k_7, places d_8 and d_6 are connected by the timed transition k_{10} and places d_8 and d_9 are connected by the timed transition k_{13} according to rule 3. By the above way, the system level SPN model is derived and all these are done automatically. The algorithm for automatic generation of SPN model from the annotated UML model is beyond the scope of this chapter.

The throughput calculation according to equation (8) for the different deployment mapping including the optimal deployment mapping is shown in Table 2. The optimal deployment mapping presented in Table 1 (first entry) also ensures the optimality in case of throughput calculation though we present here the throughput calculation of some of the deployment mappings of the software artifacts but obviously, the approach presented here confirms the optimality.

Deployment Mapping			Possible total cost	Throughput
n_1	n_2	n_3		
$\{c_4, c_7, c_8\}$	$\{c_2, c_3, c_5\}$	$\{c_1, c_6, c_9, c_{10}\}$	*187 (min)*	*0.0663 (max)*
$\{c_4, c_7\}$,	$\{c_2, c_3, c_5, c_6,\}$	$\{c_1, c_8, c_9, c_{10}\}$	232	0.0603
$\{c_4, c_6, c_7, c_8\}$	$\{c_2, c_3, c_5\}$	$\{c_1, c_9, c_{10}\}$	218	0.0575
$\{c_5, c_7, c_8\}$	$\{c_2, c_3, c_4\}$	$\{c_1, c_6, c_9, c_{10}\}$	227	0.0574
$\{c_1, c_6, c_7, c_8\}$	$\{c_2, c_3, c_4\}$	$\{c_5, c_9, c_{10}\}$	247	0.0545
$\{c_3, c_7, c_8\}$	$\{c_2, c_4, c_5\}$	$\{c_1, c_6, c_9, c_{10}\}$	252	0.0538
$\{c_4, c_7, c_8\}$	$\{c_1, c_2, c_3, c_5\}$	$\{c_6, c_9, c_{10}\}$	217	0.0532
$\{c_1, c_6, c_7, c_8\}$	$\{c_2, c_3, c_5\}$	$\{c_4, c_9, c_{10}\}\}$	257	0.052
$\{c_3, c_6, c_7, c_8\}$	$\{c_1, c_2, c_4, c_5\}$,	$\{c_9, c_{10}\}$	302	0.0469
$\{c_6, c_7, c_8\}$	$\{c_1, c_2, c_4, c_5\}$	$\{c_3, c_9, c_{10}\}\}$	288	0.0464

Table 2. Deployment mapping in the example scenario along with throughput

5. Conclusion

The contribution of this chapter is to develop a framework that focuses on the performance evaluation of the distributed system using SPN model. The developed framework recognizes the fact of rapid and efficient way of capturing the system dynamics utilizing reusable specification of software components that has been utilized to generate SPN performance model. The deployment logic presented here, is applied to provide the optimal, initial mapping of components to hosts, i.e. the network is considered rather static. Performance related QoS information is taken into account and included in the SPN model with equivalent timing and probabilistic assumption for enabling the evaluation of performance prediction result of the system at the early stage of the system development process. However, our eventual goal is to develop support for run-time redeployment of components, this way keeping the service within an allowed region of parameters defined by the requirements. Our modeling framework support that, our logic will be a prominent candidate for a robust and adaptive service execution platform for assessing a deployment of service components on an existing physical topology. Future work includes providing a tool based support of the developed performance modeling framework.

Author details

Razib Hayat Khan and Poul E. Heegaard
Norwegian University of Science & Technology, Trondheim, Norway

Kazi Wali Ullah
Aalto University, Helsinki, Finland

6. References

[1] OMG 2009, "UML Profile for MARTE: Modeling & Analysis of Real-Time Embedded Systems", V – 1.0

[2] J. P. Lopez, J. Merseguer, and J. Campos, "From UML Activity Diagrams to SPN: Application to Software Performance Engineering", Workshop on Software & Performance, ACM SIGSOFT software engineering notes, pp. 25-36, NY, 2004

[3] S. Distefano,M. Scarpa, and A. Puliafito, "Software Performance Analysis in UML Models", Workshop on Techniques Methodologies and Tools for Performance Evaluation of Complex Systems, Vol. 2005, pp. 115-125, 2005

[4] A. D'Ambrogio, "A Model Transformation Framework for the Automated Building of Performance Models from UML Models", Workshop on Software & Performance, ACM SIGSOFT software engineering notes, NY, 2005

[5] R H Khan, P E Heegaard, "Translation from UML to SPN model: A Performance Modeling Framework", EUNICE, pp. 270-271, LNCS, Springer, 2010

[6] R H Khan, P E Heegaard, "Translation from UML to SPN model: A Performance Modeling Framework for Managing Behavior of Multiple Collaborative Sessions & Instances" ICCDA, pp. V5-72-V5-80, IEEE computer Society, China, 2010

[7] R H Khan, P E Heegaard, " A Performance Modeling Framework Incorporating Cost Efficient Deployment of Collaborating Components" ICSTE, pp. V1-340-V1-349, IEEE computer Society, San Juan, USA, 2010

[8] Moreno Marzolla, "Simulation-based Performance Modeling of UML Software Architectures", PhD thesis, Universit`a Ca' Foscari di Venezia, 2004

[9] Frank Kræmer, "Engineering System: A Compositional and Mode-Driven Method Based on Collaborative Building block", PhD Thesis, NTNU, Trondheim, Norway, 2008

[10] F. A. Kramer, R. Bræk, P. Herrmann, "Synthesizes Components with Sessions from Collaboration-oriented Service Specifications", Proceedings of SDL, V-4745, LNCS, Springer, 2007.

[11] OMG UML Superstructure, Version-2.2

[12] R H Khan, P E Heegaard, "A Performance Modeling Framework Incorporating Cost Efficient Deployment of Multiple Collaborating Instances" ICSECS, pp. 31-45, Springer, 2011

[13] J. Trowitzsch, A. Zimmermann, "Using UML State Machines and Petri Nets for the Quantitative Investigation of ETCS", Valuetools, 2006

[14] Abdullatif, R. Pooly, "A Computer Assisted State Marking Method for Extracting Performance Models from Design Models", International Journal of Simulation, Vol. 8, No. 3, pp. 36-46, 2008

[15] Mate J Csorba, "Cost Efficient Deployment of Distributed Software Services", PhD Thesis, NTNU, Norway, 2011

[16] K. S. Trivedi and R Sahner, "Symbolic Hierarchical Automated Reliability / Performance Evaluator (SHARPE)", Duke University, NC, 2002

[17] Efe, K., "Heuristic Models of Task Assignment Scheduling in Distributed Systems", Computer, 1982

Chapter 3

Fluid Stochastic Petri Nets: From Fluid Atoms in ILP Processor Pipelines to Fluid Atoms in P2P Streaming Networks

Pece Mitrevski and Zoran Kotevski

Additional information is available at the end of the chapter

1. Introduction

Fluid models have been used and investigated in queuing theory [1]. Recently, the concept of fluid models was used in the context of Stochastic Petri Nets, referred to as *Fluid Stochastic Petri Nets* (FSPNs) [2-6]. In FSPNs, the fluid variables are represented by fluid places, which can hold fluid rather than discrete tokens. Transition firings are determined by both discrete and fluid places, and fluid flow is permitted through the enabled timed transitions in the Petri Net. By associating exponentially distributed or zero firing time with transitions, the differential equations for the underlying stochastic process can be derived. The dynamics of an FSPN are described by a system of first-order hyperbolic *partial differential equations* (PDEs) combined with initial and boundary equations. The general system of PDEs may be solved by a standard discretization approach. In [6], the problem of immediate transitions has also been addressed in relation to the fluid levels, by allowing fluid places to be connected to immediate transitions. The transportation of fluid in zero time is described by appropriately chosen boundary conditions.

In a typical multiple-issue processor, instructions flow through pipeline and pass through separate pipeline stages connected by buffers. An open multi-chain queuing network can present this organization, with each stage being a service center with a limited buffer size. Considering a machine that employs multiple execution units capable to execute large number of instructions in parallel, the service and storage requirements of each individual instruction are small compared to the total volume of the instruction stream. Individual instructions may then be regarded as *atoms of a fluid* flowing through the pipeline. The objective of this approach is to approximate large buffer levels by continuous fluid levels and decrease state-space complexity. Thus, in the first part of this chapter, we employ an analytical model based on FSPNs, derive the state equations for the underlying stochastic process and present performance evaluation results to illustrate its usage in deriving measures of interest. The attempt to capture the dynamic behavior of an ILP processor with aggressive use of prediction techniques and speculative execution is a rare example that demonstrates the usage of this recently introduced formalism in modeling actual systems. Moreover, we take into consideration numerical transient analysis and present numerical solution of a FSPN with more than three fluid places. Both the application of finite-difference approximations for the partial derivatives [7,8], as well as the discrete-event simulation of the proposed FSPN model [9,10], allow for the evaluation of a number of performance measures and lead to numerous conclusions regarding the performance impact of predictions and speculative execution with varying parameters of both the microarchitecture and the operational environment. The numerical solution makes possible the probabilistic analysis of the dynamic behavior, whereas the advantage of the discrete-event simulation is the much faster generation of performance evaluation results. Since the modeling framework is implementation-independent, it can be used to estimate the performance potential of branch and value prediction, as well as to assess the operational environment influence on the performance of ILP processors with much more aggressive, wider instruction issue.

Another challenging task in the application of FSPNs is the modeling and performance analysis of *Peer-to-Peer* (P2P) live video streaming systems. Web locations offering live video content increasingly attract more and more visitors, which, if the system is based on the client/server architecture, leads to sustainability issues when clients rise above the upload capabilities of the streaming servers. Since IP Multicast failed to satisfy the requirements of an affordable, large scale live video streaming, in the last decade the science community intensively works in the field of P2P networking technologies for live video broadcast. P2P live video streaming is a relatively new paradigm that aims for streaming live video content to a large number of clients with low cost. Even though many such applications already exist, these systems are still in their early stages and prior to creation of such a system it is necessary to analyze performance via representative model that provides significant insight into the system's behavior. Nevertheless, modeling and performance analysis of P2P live video streaming systems is a complex combinatorial problem, which requires addressing many properties and issues of such systems. Inspired by several research articles concerned with modeling of their behavior, in the second part of this chapter, we present how FSPNs can be used for modeling and performance analysis of a mesh based P2P live video streaming system. We adopt fluid flow to represent bits as *atoms of a fluid* that travel through fluid pipes (network infrastructure). If we represent peers with discrete tokens and video bits as fluid, then we have numerous possibilities to evaluate the performance of the system. The developed model is simple and quite flexible, providing performance evaluation of a system that accounts for a number of system features, such as: network topology, peer churn, scalability, peer average group size, peer upload bandwidth heterogeneity, video buffering, control traffic overhead and admission control for lesser contributing peers. In this particular case, discrete-event simulation (DES) is carried out using SimPy (http://simpy.sourceforge.net) – an object-oriented, process-based discrete-event simulation language based on standard Python (http://www.python.org), which provides the modeler with components of a simulation model including processes (for active components) and resources (for passive components) and provides monitor variables to aid in gathering statistics.

2. Part A: Fluid atoms in ILP processor pipelines

Most of the recent microprocessor architectures assume *sequential programs* as input and use a *parallel execution* model. The hardware is expected to extract the parallelism out of the instruction stream at run-time. The efficiency is highly dependent on both the hardware mechanisms and the program characteristics, i.e. the *instruction-level parallelism* (ILP) the programs exhibit. Many ILP processors *speculatively* execute control-dependent instructions before resolving the branch outcome. They rely upon *branch prediction* in order to tolerate the effect of *control dependences.* A branch predictor uses the current fetch address to predict whether a branch will be fetched in the current cycle, whether that branch will be taken or not, and what the target address of the branch is. The predictor uses this information to decide where to fetch from in the next cycle. Since the branch execution penalty is only seen if the branch was mispredicted, a highly accurate branch predictor is a very important mechanism for reducing the branch penalty in a high performance ILP processor.

A variety of branch prediction schemes have been explored [11] – they range between *fixed, static displacement-based, static with profiling,* and various dynamic schemes, like *Branch History Table with n-bit counters, Branch Target Address Cache, Branch Target Instruction Cache, mixed, two-level adaptive, hybrid,* etc. Some research studies have also proposed concepts to implement high-bandwidth instruction fetch engines based on *multiple branch prediction.* Such concepts include *trace cache* [12] or the more conventional *multiple-block fetching* [13].

On the other hand, given that a majority of static instructions exhibit very little variations in values that they produce/consume during the course of a program's execution [14], *data dependences* can be eliminated at run-time by predicting the outcome values of instructions (*value prediction*) and by executing the true data dependent instructions. In general, the outcome value of an instruction can be assigned to registers, memory locations, condition codes, etc. The execution is *speculative,* as it is not assured that instructions were fed with correct input values. Since the correctness of execution must be maintained, speculatively executed instructions retire only if the prediction was proven correct – otherwise, they are discarded.

Several architectures have been proposed for value prediction [15] – *last value predictor, stride predictor, context predictors* and *hybrid approaches* in order to get good accuracy over a set of programs due to the different data value locality characteristics that can be exploited only by different schemes. Based on instruction type, value prediction is sometimes identified as prediction of the outcome of *arithmetic instructions* only, and the prediction of the outcome of *memory access instructions* as a different class, referred to as *memory prediction.*

2.1. Model definition

A model should always have a form that is more concise and closer to a designer's intuition about what a model should look like. In the case of a processor pipeline, the simplest description would be that the instructions flow and pass through separate pipeline stages connected by buffers. Control dependences stall the inflow of useful instructions (fluid) into the pipeline, whereas true data dependences decrease the aperture of the pipeline and the outflow rate. The buffer levels always vary and affect both the inflow and outflow rates. Branch prediction techniques tend to eliminate stalls in the inflow, while value prediction techniques help keeping outflow rate as high as possible.

Representing the dynamic behavior of systems subject to randomness or variability is the main concern of *stochastic modeling*. It relies on the use of random variables and their distribution functions [16]. We assume that the distribution of the time between two consecutive occurrences of branch instructions in the fluid stream is exponential with rate λ. The rate depends on the instruction fetch bandwidth, as well as the program's average *basic block size*. Branches vary widely in their dynamic behavior, and predictors that work well on one type of branches may not work as well on others. A set of hard-to-predict branches that comprise a fundamental limit to traditional branch predictors can always be identified [17]. We assume that there are two classes: *easy-to-predict* and *hard-to-predict branches*, and the expected branch prediction accuracy is higher for the first, and lower for the second. The probabilities to classify a branch as either easy- or hard-to-predict depend on the program characteristics.

When the instruction fetch rate is low, a significant portion of data dependences span across instructions that are fetched consecutively [18]. As a result, these instructions (a producer-consumer pair) will eventually initiate their execution in a sequential manner. In this case, the prediction becomes useless due to the availability of the consumer's input value. Hence, in each cycle, an important factor is the number of instructions that consume results of *simultaneously* initiated producer instructions. We assume that the distribution of the time between two consecutive occurrences of consuming instructions in the fluid stream is exponential with rate μ. The rate depends on the number of instructions that simultaneously initiate execution at a functional unit, as well as the program's average *dynamic instruction distance*. We assume that there are two classes of consuming instructions: (1) instructions that consume *easy-to-predict values* and (2) instructions that consume *hard-to-predict values*. The expected value prediction accuracy is higher for the first and lower for the second. The probability to classify a value as either easy- or hard-to-predict depends on the program's characteristics, similarly to the branch classification.

The set of programs executed on the machine represent the *input space*. Programs with different characteristics are executed randomly and independently according to the *operational profile*. We partition the input space by grouping programs that exhibit as nearly as possible homogenous behavior into *program classes*. Since there are a finite number of partitions (classes), the upper limits of λ and μ, as well as the probabilities to classify a branch/value as either easy- or hard-to-predict are considered to be discrete random variables and have different values for different program classes.

2.2. FSPN representation

We assume that the pipeline is organized in four stages: Fetch, Decode/Issue, Execute and Commit. Fluid places P_{IC}, P_{IB}, $P_{RS/LSQ}$, P_{ROB}, P_{RR}, P_{EX} and P_{REG}, depicted by means of two concentric circles (Figure 1), represent buffers between pipeline stages: *instruction cache, instruction buffer, reservation stations and load/store queue, reorder buffer, rename registers, instructions that have completed execution* and *architectural registers*. Five of them have limited capacities: Z_{IBmax}, $Z_{RS/LSQmax}$, Z_{RRmax}, Z_{ROBmax} and Z_{EXmax}. We prohibit both an overflow and a negative level in a fluid place. The fluid place P_{TIME} has the function of an hourglass: it is constantly filled at rate 1 up to the level 1 and then flushed out, which corresponds to the machine clock cycle. $Z_{TIME}(t)$ denotes the fluid level in P_{TIME} at time t. Fluid arcs are drawn as double arrows to suggest a pipe. Flow rates are piecewise constant, i.e. take different values at the beginning of each cycle and are limited by the fetch/issue width of the machine (W). Rates depend on the vector of fluid levels $\mathbf{Z}(t)$ and change when T_{CLOCK} fires and the fluid in P_{TIME} is flushed out. The flush out arc is drawn as thick single arrow.

Let $Z_{IC_0}, Z_{IB_0}, Z_{RS/LSQ_0}, Z_{RR_0}, Z_{ROB_0}$ and Z_{EX_0} be the fluid levels at the beginning of the clock cycle, i.e. $Z_{IC_0} = Z_{IC}(t_0)$, $Z_{IB_0} = Z_{IB}(t_0)$, $Z_{RS/LSQ_0} = Z_{RS/LSQ}(t_0)$, $Z_{RR_0} = Z_{RR}(t_0)$, $Z_{ROB_0} = Z_{ROB}(t_0)$ and $Z_{EX_0} = Z_{EX}(t_0)$, where $t_0 = \lfloor t \rfloor$ and $Z_{TIME}(t_0) = 0$.

A high-bandwidth instruction fetch mechanism fetches up to W instructions per cycle and places them in the instruction buffer. The fetch rate is given by:

$$r_{FETCH} = \min(Z_{IB_{max}} - Z_{IB_0} + r_{ISSUE}, Z_{IC_0}, W) \quad (1)$$

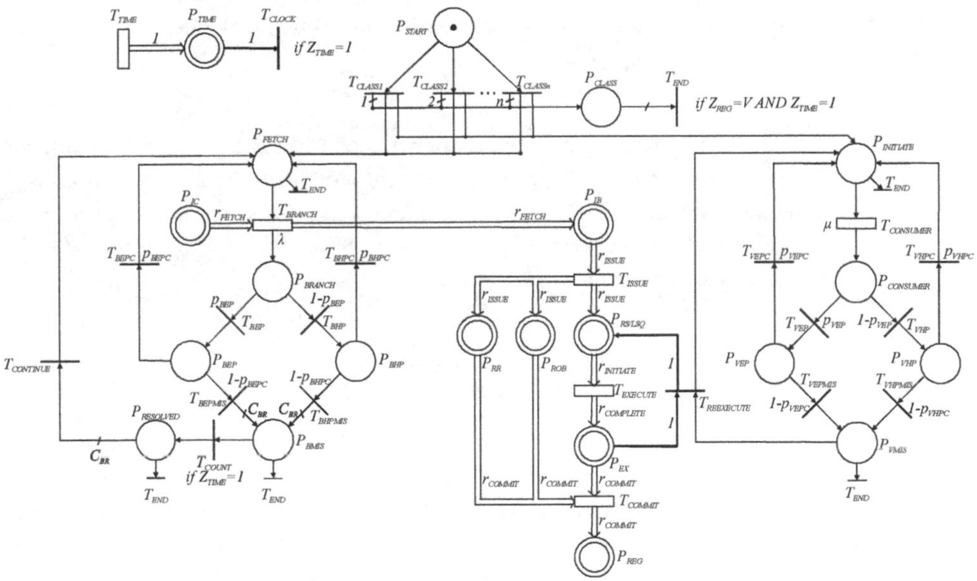

Figure 1. A Fluid Stochastic Petri Net model of an ILP processor

In the case of a branch misprediction, the fetch unit is effectively stalled and no useful instructions are added to the buffer. Instruction cache misses are ignored.

Instruction issue tries to send W instructions to the appropriate reservation stations or the load/store queue on every clock cycle. Rename registers are allocated to hold the results of the instructions and reorder buffer entries are allocated to ensure in-order completion. Among the instructions that initiate execution in the same cycle, speculatively executed consuming instructions are forced to retain their reservation stations. As a result, the issue rate is given by:

$$r_{ISSUE} = \min(Z_{RR\max} - Z_{RR0} + r_{COMMIT}, Z_{ROB\max} - Z_{ROB0} + r_{COMMIT}, Z_{RS/LSQ\max} - Z_{RS/LSQ0}, Z_{IB0}, W) \quad (2)$$

Up to W instructions are *in execution* at the same time. With the assumptions that functional units are always available and out-of-order execution is allowed, the instructions *initiate* and *complete* execution with rate:

$$r_{INITIATE} = r_{COMPLETE} = \min(Z_{RS/LSQ_0}, W) \quad (3)$$

During the execute stage, the instructions first check to see if their source operands are available (predicted or computed). For simplicity, we assume that the execution latency of each instruction is a single cycle. Instructions execute and forward their own results back to subsequent instructions that might be waiting for them (no result forwarding delay). Every reference to memory is present in the first-level cache. With the last assumption, we eliminate the effect of the memory hierarchy.

The instructions that have completed execution are ready to move to the last stage. Up to W instructions may commit per cycle. The results in the rename registers are written into the register file and the rename registers and reorder buffer entries freed. Hence:

$$r_{COMMIT} = \min(Z_{EX_0}, W) \quad (4)$$

In order to capture the relative occurrence frequencies of different program classes, we introduce a set of weighted immediate transitions in the Petri Net. Each program class is assigned an immediate transition T_{CLASS_i} with weight w_{CLASS_i}. The operational profile is a set of weights. The probability of firing the immediate transition T_{CLASS_i} represents the probability of occurrence of a class i program, given by:

$$\widehat{w}_{T_{CLASS_i}} = \frac{w_{T_{CLASS_i}}}{\sum_{k=1}^{n} w_{T_{CLASS_k}}} \quad (5)$$

A token in P_{START} denotes that a new execution is about to begin. The process of firing one of the immediate transitions randomly chooses a program from one of the classes. The firing of transition T_{CLASS_i} puts i tokens in place P_{CLASS}, which identify the class. At the same time instant, tokens occur in places P_{FETCH} and $P_{INITIATE}$, while the fluid place P_{IC} is filled with fluid with volume V_i equivalent to the total number of useful instructions (*program volume*).

Firing of exponential transition T_{BRANCH} corresponds to a branch instruction occurrence. The parameter λ changes at the beginning of each clock cycle and formally depends on both the number of tokens in P_{CLASS} and the fetch rate:

$$\lambda = f(\# P_{CLASS}) \frac{r_{FETCH}}{W} = f(i) \frac{r_{FETCH}}{W} = \lambda_i \frac{r_{FETCH}}{W} \tag{6}$$

where λ_i is its upper limit for a given program class i at maximum fetch rate ($r_{FETCH}=W$). The branch is classified as easy-to-predict with probability p_{BEP}, or hard-to-predict with probability $1-p_{BEP}$. In either case, it is correctly predicted with probability p_{BEPC} (p_{BHPC}), or mispredicted with probability $1-p_{BEPC}$ ($1-p_{BHPC}$). These probabilities are included in the FSPN model as weights assigned to immediate transitions T_{BEP}, T_{BHP}, T_{BEPC}, T_{BHPC}, T_{BEPMIS} and T_{BHPMIS}, respectively. This approach is known as *synthetic branch prediction.* Branch mispredictions stall the fluid inflow for as many cycles as necessary to resolve the branch (C_{BR} tokens in place P_{BMIS}). Usually, a branch is not resolved until its execution stage (C_{BR}=3). With several consecutive firings of T_{CLOCK}, these tokens are consumed one at a time and moved to $P_{RESOLVED}$. As soon as the branch is resolved, transition $T_{CONTINUE}$ fires, a token appears in place P_{FETCH} and the inflow resumes.

Similar to this, firing of exponential transition $T_{CONSUMER}$ corresponds to the occurrence of a consuming instruction among the instructions that initiated execution. The parameter μ changes at the beginning of each clock cycle and formally depends on both the number of tokens in P_{CLASS} and the initiation rate:

$$\mu = g(\# P_{CLASS}) \frac{r_{INITIATE}}{W} = g(i) \frac{r_{INITIATE}}{W} = \mu_i \frac{r_{INITIATE}}{W} \tag{7}$$

where μ_i is its upper limit for a given program class i when maximum possible number of instructions simultaneously initiate execution ($r_{INITIATE}=W$). The consumed value is classified as easy-to-predict with probability p_{VEP}, or hard-to-predict with probability $1-p_{VEP}$. In either case, it is correctly predicted with probability p_{VEPC} (p_{VHPC}), or mispredicted with probability $1-p_{VEPC}$ ($1-p_{VHPC}$). These probabilities are included in the FSPN model as weights assigned to immediate transitions T_{VEP}, T_{VHP}, T_{VEPC}, T_{VHPC}, T_{VEPMIS} and T_{VHPMIS}, respectively. Whenever a misprediction occurs (token in place P_{VMIS}), the consuming instruction has to be *rescheduled* for execution. The firing of immediate transition $T_{REEXECUTE}$ causes transportation of fluid in zero time. Fluid jumps have deterministic height of 1 (one instruction) and take place when the fluid levels in P_{RS} and P_{EX} satisfy the condition $Z_{RS}(t) \le Z_{RS_{max}} - 1$ and $Z_{EX}(t) \ge 1$. Jumps that would go beyond the boundaries cannot be carried out. The arcs connecting fluid places and immediate transitions are drawn as thick single arrows. The fluid flow terminates at the end of the cycle when all the fluid places except P_{REG} are empty and T_{END} fires.

2.3. Derivation of state equations

When executing a class i program, the nodes m_i of the reachability graph (Figure 2) consist of all the tangible discrete markings, as well as those in which the enabling of immediate transitions depends on fluid levels and cannot be eliminated, since they are of mixed tangible/vanishing type (Table 1). It is important to note that the number of discrete markings does not depend on the machine width in any way.

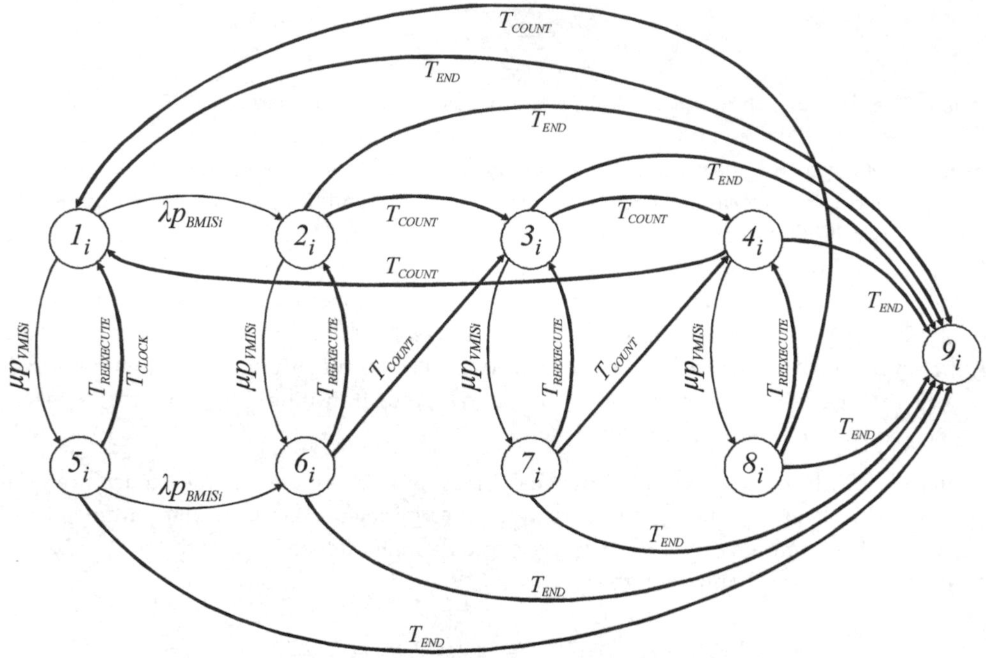

Figure 2. Reachability graph of the FSPN model

Number of tokens / Marking (m_i)	$\#P_{FETCH}$	$\#P_{BMIS}$	$\#P_{INITIATE}$	$\#P_{VMIS}$
1_i	1	0	1	0
2_i	0	3	1	0
3_i	0	2	1	0
4_i	0	1	1	0
5_i	1	0	0	1
6_i	0	3	0	1
7_i	0	2	0	1
8_i	0	1	0	1
9_i	0	0	0	0

Table 1. Discrete markings of the FSPN model (C_{BR}=3)

A vector of fluid levels supplements discrete markings. It gives rise to a stochastic process in continuous time with continuous state space. The total amount of fluid contained in P_{IC}, P_{IB}, $P_{RS/LSQ}$, P_{EX} and P_{REG} is always equal to V_i, and the amount of fluid contained in P_{RR} (as well as

P_{ROB}) is equal to the total amount of fluid in $P_{RS/LSQ}$ and P_{EX}. Therefore, only the fluid levels $Z_{IB}(t)$, $Z_{RS/LSQ}(t)$, $Z_{EX}(t)$ and $Z_{REG}(t)$ are identified as four supplementary variables (components of the fluid vector $\mathbf{Z}(t)$), which provide a full description of each state.

The instantaneous rates at which fluid builds in each fluid place are collected in diagonal matrices:

$$\begin{aligned}
&\mathbf{R}_{IB} = \mathbf{diag}\left(r_{FETCH} - r_{ISSUE}, -r_{ISSUE}, -r_{ISSUE}, -r_{ISSUE}, r_{FETCH} - r_{ISSUE}, -r_{ISSUE}, -r_{ISSUE}, -r_{ISSUE}, 0\right)\\
&\mathbf{R}_{RS/LSQ} = \mathbf{diag}\left(r_{ISSUE} - r_{INITIATE}, \ldots, r_{ISSUE} - r_{INITIATE}, 0\right)\\
&\mathbf{R}_{EX} = \mathbf{diag}\left(r_{COMPLETE} - r_{COMMIT}, \ldots, r_{COMPLETE} - r_{COMMIT}, 0\right)\\
&\mathbf{R}_{REG} = \mathbf{diag}\left(r_{COMMIT}, \ldots, r_{COMMIT}, 0\right)
\end{aligned} \tag{8}$$

The matrix of *transition rates* of exponential transitions causing the state changes is:

$$\mathbf{Q}_i = \begin{bmatrix}
-(\lambda p_{BMIS_i} + \mu p_{VMIS_i}) & \lambda p_{BMIS_i} & 0 & 0 & \mu p_{VMIS_i} & 0 & 0 & 0 & 0\\
0 & -\mu p_{VMIS_i} & 0 & 0 & 0 & \mu p_{VMIS_i} & 0 & 0 & 0\\
0 & 0 & -\mu p_{VMIS_i} & 0 & 0 & 0 & \mu p_{VMIS_i} & 0 & 0\\
0 & 0 & 0 & -\mu p_{VMIS_i} & 0 & 0 & 0 & \mu p_{VMIS_i} & 0\\
0 & 0 & 0 & 0 & -\lambda p_{BMIS_i} & \lambda p_{BMIS_i} & 0 & 0 & 0\\
0 & 0 & 0 & 0 & 0 & 0 & 0 & 0 & 0\\
0 & 0 & 0 & 0 & 0 & 0 & 0 & 0 & 0\\
0 & 0 & 0 & 0 & 0 & 0 & 0 & 0 & 0\\
0 & 0 & 0 & 0 & 0 & 0 & 0 & 0 & 0
\end{bmatrix}$$

where:

$$\begin{aligned}
&p_{BMIS_i} = p_{BEP_i}\left(1 - p_{BEPC}\right) + \left(1 - p_{BEP_i}\right)\left(1 - p_{BHPC}\right)\\
&\text{and}\\
&p_{VMIS_i} = p_{VEP_i}\left(1 - p_{VEPC}\right) + \left(1 - p_{VEP_i}\right)\left(1 - p_{VHPC}\right)
\end{aligned} \tag{9}$$

Let π_{m_i} be an abbreviation for the *volume density* $\pi_{m_i}(t, z_{IB}, z_{RS/LSQ}, z_{EX}, z_{REG})$ that is the transient probability of being in discrete marking m_i at time t, with fluid levels in an infinitesimal environment around $\mathbf{z} = [z_{IB} \quad z_{RS/LSQ} \quad z_{EX} \quad z_{REG}]$. If $\boldsymbol{\pi}_i = [\pi_{1_i} \quad \pi_{2_i} \quad \ldots \quad \pi_{9_i}]$, according to [4-6] the evolution of the process is described by a coupled system of nine *partial differential equations* in four continuous dimensions plus time:

$$\frac{\partial \boldsymbol{\pi}_i}{\partial t} + \frac{\partial(\boldsymbol{\pi}_i \cdot \mathbf{R}_{IB})}{\partial z_{IB}} + \frac{\partial(\boldsymbol{\pi}_i \cdot \mathbf{R}_{RS/LSQ})}{\partial z_{RS/LSQ}} + \frac{\partial(\boldsymbol{\pi}_i \cdot \mathbf{R}_{EX})}{\partial z_{EX}} + \frac{\partial(\boldsymbol{\pi}_i \cdot \mathbf{R}_{REG})}{\partial z_{REG}} = \boldsymbol{\pi}_i \cdot \mathbf{Q}_i \tag{10}$$

If $\mathbf{z}_0 = \begin{bmatrix}0 & 0 & 0 & 0\end{bmatrix}$ is the vector of initial fluid levels, the *initial conditions* are:

$$\begin{aligned}
&\pi_{1_i}(0, \mathbf{z}) = \delta(\mathbf{z} - \mathbf{z}_0)\\
&\pi_{m_i}(0, \mathbf{z}) = 0 \quad (2 \le m \le 9)
\end{aligned} \tag{11}$$

Since fluid jumps shift probability mass along the continuous axes (in addition to discrete state change), firing of transition $T_{REEXECUTE}$ at time t can be seen as a *jump* to another location in the four-dimensional hypercube defined by the components of the fluid vector. It can be described by the following *boundary conditions*:

$$
\begin{aligned}
&\pi_{1_i}(t^+, z_{IB}, z_{RS/LSQ}+1, z_{EX}-1, z_{REG}) = \pi_{1_i}(t^-, z_{IB}, z_{RS/LSQ}+1, z_{EX}-1, z_{REG}) + \pi_{5_i}(t^-, z_{IB}, z_{RS/LSQ}, z_{EX}, z_{REG})\\
&\pi_{2_i}(t^+, z_{IB}, z_{RS/LSQ}+1, z_{EX}-1, z_{REG}) = \pi_{2_i}(t^-, z_{IB}, z_{RS/LSQ}+1, z_{EX}-1, z_{REG}) + \pi_{6_i}(t^-, z_{IB}, z_{RS/LSQ}, z_{EX}, z_{REG})\\
&\pi_{3_i}(t^+, z_{IB}, z_{RS/LSQ}+1, z_{EX}-1, z_{REG}) = \pi_{3_i}(t^-, z_{IB}, z_{RS/LSQ}+1, z_{EX}-1, z_{REG}) + \pi_{7_i}(t^-, z_{IB}, z_{RS/LSQ}, z_{EX}, z_{REG})\\
&\pi_{4_i}(t^+, z_{IB}, z_{RS/LSQ}+1, z_{EX}-1, z_{REG}) = \pi_{4_i}(t^-, z_{IB}, z_{RS/LSQ}+1, z_{EX}-1, z_{REG}) + \pi_{8_i}(t^-, z_{IB}, z_{RS/LSQ}, z_{EX}, z_{REG})\\
&\pi_{m_i}(t^+, z_{IB}, z_{RS/LSQ}, z_{EX}, z_{REG}) = 0 \quad (\text{if } z_{RS/LSQ} \le Z_{RS/LSQ_{\max}}-1,\ z_{EX} \ge 1,\ 5 \le m \le 8)
\end{aligned}
\tag{12}
$$

The firing of transitions T_{CLOCK} and T_{COUNT} at time t_0 causes switching from one discrete marking to another. Therefore:

$$
\begin{aligned}
\pi_{1_i}(t_0^+, z_{IB}, z_{RS/LSQ}, z_{EX}, z_{REG}) &= \pi_{1_i}(t_0^-, z_{IB}, z_{RS/LSQ}, z_{EX}, z_{REG}) + \pi_{4_i}(t_0^-, z_{IB}, z_{RS/LSQ}, z_{EX}, z_{REG}) +\\
&\quad + \pi_{5_i}(t_0^-, z_{IB}, z_{RS/LSQ}, z_{EX}, z_{REG}) + \pi_{8_i}(t_0^-, z_{IB}, z_{RS/LSQ}, z_{EX}, z_{REG})\\
\pi_{4_i}(t_0^+, z_{IB}, z_{RS/LSQ}, z_{EX}, z_{REG}) &= \pi_{3_i}(t_0^-, z_{IB}, z_{RS/LSQ}, z_{EX}, z_{REG}) + \pi_{7_i}(t_0^-, z_{IB}, z_{RS/LSQ}, z_{EX}, z_{REG})\\
\pi_{3_i}(t_0^+, z_{IB}, z_{RS/LSQ}, z_{EX}, z_{REG}) &= \pi_{2_i}(t_0^-, z_{IB}, z_{RS/LSQ}, z_{EX}, z_{REG}) + \pi_{6_i}(t_0^-, z_{IB}, z_{RS/LSQ}, z_{EX}, z_{REG})\\
\pi_{m_i}(t_0^+, z_{IB}, z_{RS/LSQ}, z_{EX}, z_{REG}) &= 0 \quad (m \in \{2,5,6,7,8\})
\end{aligned}
\tag{13}
$$

Similarly, the firing of transition T_{END} when all the fluid places except P_{REG} are empty, causes switching from any discrete marking to 9_i:

$$
\pi_{9_i}(t_0^+, 0,0,0,V_i) = \sum_{m=1}^{9} \pi_{m_i}(t_0^-, 0,0,0,V_i) \qquad \pi_{m_i}(t_0^+, 0,0,0,V_i) = 0 \quad (m \le 8) \tag{14}
$$

The *probability mass conservation law* is used as a normalization condition. It corresponds to the condition that the sum of all state probabilities must equal one. Since no particle can pass beyond barriers, the sum of integrals of the volume densities over the definition range evaluates to one:

$$
\sum_{m=1}^{9} \int_0^{Z_{IB_{\max}}} \int_0^{Z_{RS/LSQ_{\max}}} \int_0^{Z_{EX_{\max}}} \int_0^{V_i} \pi_{m_i}(t, z_{IB}, z_{RS/LSQ}, z_{EX}, z_{REG})\, dz_{IB}\, dz_{RS/LSQ}\, dz_{EX}\, dz_{REG} = 1 \tag{15}
$$

Let $M_i(t)$ be the state of the discrete marking process at time t. The *probabilities of the discrete markings* are obtained by integrating volume densities:

$$
\Pr\{M_i(t) = m_i\} = \int_0^{Z_{IB_{MAX}}} \int_0^{Z_{RS/LSQ_{MAX}}} \int_0^{Z_{EX_{MAX}}} \int_0^{V_i} \pi_{m_i}(t, z_{IB}, z_{RS/LSQ}, z_{EX}, z_{REG})\, dz_{IB}\, dz_{RS/LSQ}\, dz_{EX}\, dz_{REG} \quad (m \le 9) \tag{16}
$$

The *fluid levels* at the beginning of each clock cycle are computed as follows:

$$Z_{IB_0} = E\left(Z_{IB}(t_0)\right) = \int_0^{Z_{IB_{max}}} z_{IB} \underbrace{\left(\int_0^{Z_{RS/LSQ_{max}}} \int_0^{Z_{EX_{max}}} \int_0^{V_i} \left(\sum_{m=1}^{9} \pi_{m_i}(t_0, z_{IB}, z_{RS/LSQ}, z_{EX}, z_{REG}) \right) dz_{RS/LSQ} dz_{EX} dz_{REG} \right)}_{\text{marginal density for } Z_{IB}} dz_{IB}$$

$$Z_{RS/LSQ_0} = E\left(Z_{RS/LSQ}(t_0)\right) = \int_0^{Z_{RS/LSQ_{max}}} z_{RS/LSQ} \underbrace{\left(\int_0^{Z_{IB_{max}}} \int_0^{Z_{EX_{max}}} \int_0^{V_i} \left(\sum_{m=1}^{9} \pi_{m_i}(t_0, z_{IB}, z_{RS/LSQ}, z_{EX}, z_{REG}) \right) dz_{IB} dz_{EX} dz_{REG} \right)}_{\text{marginal density for } Z_{RS/LSQ}} dz_{RS/LSQ} \tag{17}$$

$$Z_{EX_0} = E\left(Z_{EX}(t_0)\right) = \int_0^{Z_{EX_{max}}} z_{EX} \underbrace{\left(\int_0^{Z_{IB_{max}}} \int_0^{Z_{RS/LSQ_{max}}} \int_0^{V_i} \left(\sum_{m=1}^{9} \pi_{m_i}(t_0, z_{IB}, z_{RS/LSQ}, z_{EX}, z_{REG}) \right) dz_{IB} dz_{RS/LSQ} dz_{REG} \right)}_{\text{marginal density for } Z_{EX}} dz_{EX}$$

$$Z_{REG_0} = E\left(Z_{REG}(t_0)\right) = \int_0^{V_i} z_{REG} \underbrace{\left(\int_0^{Z_{IB_{max}}} \int_0^{Z_{RS/LSQ_{max}}} \int_0^{Z_{EX_{max}}} \left(\sum_{m=1}^{9} \pi_{m_i}(t_0, z_{IB}, z_{RS/LSQ}, z_{EX}, z_{REG}) \right) dz_{IB} dz_{RS/LSQ} dz_{EX} \right)}_{\text{marginal density for } Z_{REG}} dz_{REG}$$

$Z_{IC_0} = V_i - (Z_{IB_0} + Z_{RS/LSQ_0} + Z_{EX_0} + Z_{REG_0})$ and $Z_{RR_0} = Z_{ROB_0} = Z_{RS/LSQ_0} + Z_{EX_0}$.

Finally, the flow rates and the parameters λ and μ are computed as indicated by Eqs. 1-4, 6 and 7, respectively.

2.4. Performance measures

Let τ be a random variable representing the time to absorb into $A = \{m_i \,|\, \pi_{m_i}(t,0,0,0,V_i) = 1\}$. The *distribution of the execution time* of a program with volume V_i is:

$$F_{t_{EX_i}}(t) = \Pr\{\tau \le t \wedge M_i(t) \in A\} = \Pr\{M_i(t) = 9_i\} =$$
$$= \int_0^{Z_{IB_{MAX}}} \int_0^{Z_{RS/LSQ_{MAX}}} \int_0^{Z_{EX_{MAX}}} \int_0^{V_i} \pi_{9_i}\left(t, z_{IB}, z_{RS/LSQ}, z_{EX}, z_{REG}\right) dz_{IB} dz_{RS/LSQ} dz_{EX} dz_{REG} = \pi_{9_i}(t,0,0,0,V_i) \tag{18}$$

with *mean execution time*:

$$t_{EX_i} = \int_0^{\infty} \left(1 - F_{t_{EX_i}}(t)\right) dt \tag{19}$$

Consequently, the *sustained number of instructions per cycle* (*IPC*) is given by:

$$IPC_i = V_i / t_{EX_i} \tag{20}$$

When the input space is partitioned, *IPC* is the ratio between the average volume and the average execution time of all the programs of different classes, as indicated by the operational profile:

$$IPC = \sum_{k=1}^{n} V_k \varpi_{T_{CLASS_k}} \Big/ \sum_{k=1}^{n} t_{EX_k} \varpi_{T_{CLASS_k}} \tag{21}$$

The sum of probabilities of the discrete markings that do not carry a token in place *P_{FETCH}* gives the *probability of a stall* in the instruction fetch unit at time *t*:

$$P_{STALL_i}(t) = \Pr\{M_i(t) \neq 1_i \wedge M_i(t) \neq 5_i\} = \\ = \sum_{\substack{m\neq 1\\ m\neq 5}} \int_0^{Z_{IB_{MAX}}} \int_0^{Z_{RS/LSQ_{MAX}}} \int_0^{Z_{EX_{MAX}}} \int_0^{V_i} \pi_{m_i}\left(t, z_{IB}, z_{RS/LSQ}, z_{EX}, z_{REG}\right) dz_{IB} dz_{RS/LSQ} dz_{EX} dz_{REG} \quad (22)$$

Because of the discrete nature of pipelining, additional attention should be given to the probability that no useful instructions will be added to the instruction buffer in the cycle beginning at time t_0 (complete stall in the instruction fetch unit that can lead to an effectively empty instruction buffer) due to branch misprediction. It can be obtained by summing up the probabilities of the discrete markings that still carry one or more tokens in place P_{BMIS} immediately after firing of T_{CLOCK}:

$$P_{NO\_FETCH_i}(t_0) = \Pr\{M_i(t_0) = 3_i \vee M_i(t_0) = 4_i\} = \\ = \sum_{m=3}^{4} \int_0^{Z_{IB_{MAX}}} \int_0^{Z_{RS/LSQ_{MAX}}} \int_0^{Z_{EX_{MAX}}} \int_0^{V_i} \pi_{m_i}\left(t_0, z_{IB}, z_{RS/LSQ}, z_{EX}, z_{REG}\right) dz_{IB} dz_{RS/LSQ} dz_{EX} dz_{REG} \quad (23)$$

In addition, the *execution efficiency* is introduced, taken as a ratio between the number of useful instructions and the total number of instructions executed during the course of a program's execution:

$$\eta_{EX_i} = \frac{V_i}{V_i + \begin{pmatrix} \text{instructions reexecuted} \\ \text{due to value misprediction} \end{pmatrix}} \approx \frac{V_i}{V_i + \overline{\mu} \cdot p_{VMIS_i} \cdot t_{EX_i}} = \frac{1}{1 + \dfrac{\mu_i \cdot \overline{r}_{INITIATE_i} \cdot p_{VMIS_i}}{W \cdot IPC_i}} \quad (24)$$

where $\overline{r}_{INITIATE}$ is the *average initiation rate.*

2.5. Numerical experiments and performance evaluation results

We have used *finite difference approximations* to replace the derivatives that appear in the PDEs: *forward* difference approximation for the time derivative and first-order *upwind* differencing for the space derivatives, in order to improve the stability of the method [7,8]:

$$\frac{\partial \pi_{m_i}(t, z_1, \ldots, z_n)}{\partial t} \approx \frac{\pi_{m_i}(t + \Delta t, z_1, \ldots, z_n) - \pi_{m_i}(t, z_1, \ldots, z_n)}{\Delta t} \\ r \frac{\partial \pi_{m_i}(t, z_1, \ldots, z_k, \ldots, z_n)}{\partial z_k} \approx r \cdot \operatorname{sgn}(r) \cdot \frac{\pi_{m_i}(t, z_1, \ldots, z_k, \ldots, z_n) - \pi_{m_i}(t, z_1, \ldots, z_k - \operatorname{sgn}(r)\Delta z_k, \ldots, z_n)}{\Delta z_k} \quad (25)$$

The explicit discretization of the right-hand-side coupling term allows the equations for each discrete state to be solved separately before going on to the next time step. The discretization is carried out on a hypercube of size $Z_{IB_{max}} \times Z_{RS/LSQ_{max}} \times Z_{EX_{max}} \times V_i$ with step size Δz in direction of z_{IB}, z_{RS}, z_{EX} and z_{REG}, and step size Δt in time. The computational complexity for the solution is

$$O\left(8 \cdot \frac{t}{\Delta t} \cdot \frac{Z_{IB_{\max}} \cdot Z_{RS/LSQ_{\max}} \cdot Z_{EX_{\max}} \cdot V_i}{\Delta z^4}\right) \text{ floating-point operations,}$$

since for each of $t/\Delta t$ time steps we must increment each solution value in the four-dimensional grid for eight of the nine discrete markings. The storage requirements of the algorithm are at least

$$8 \cdot \frac{Z_{IB_{\max}} \cdot Z_{RS/LSQ_{\max}} \cdot Z_{EX_{\max}} \cdot V}{\Delta z^4} \cdot 4 \text{ bytes,}$$

since for eight of nine discrete markings we must store a four-dimensional grid of floating-point numbers (solutions at successive time steps can be overwritten).

Unless indicated otherwise, $Z_{IB_{\max}} = W$, $Z_{RS/LSQ_{\max}} = Z_{RR_{\max}} = Z_{ROB_{\max}} = Z_{EX_{\max}} = 2W$ and $\Delta t = \Delta z/(n \cdot W)$, where n=4 is the number of continuous dimensions. With these capacities of fluid places, virtually all name dependences and structural conflicts are eliminated. Step size Δz is varied between $\Delta z = 1/2$ (coarser grid, usually when the prediction accuracy is high) and $\Delta z = 1/6$ (finer grid, usually when the prediction accuracy is low).

Considering a low-volume program (V_i=50 instructions) executed on a four-wide machine (W=4), we investigate:

- The influence of branch prediction accuracy on the distribution of the program's execution time, when value prediction is not involved (Figure 3a),
- The influence of branch prediction accuracy on the probability of a complete stall in the instruction fetch unit (Figure 3b), and
- The influence of value prediction accuracy on the distribution of the program's execution time, when *perfect* branch prediction is involved (Figure 4).

It is indisputably clear that both branch and value prediction accuracy improvements reduce the mean execution time of a program and increase performance. As an illustration, the size of the shaded area in Figure 3a is equal to the mean execution time when perfect branch prediction is involved, and IPC is computed as indicated by Eq. (20). In addition, looking at Figure 3b one can see that the probability of a complete stall in the instruction fetch unit, which can lead to an empty instruction buffer in the subsequent cycle, decreases with branch prediction accuracy improvement. As a result, both the utilization of the processor and the size of dynamic scheduling window increase as branch prediction accuracy increases.

The correctness of the discretization method is verified by comparing the numerical transient analysis results with the results obtained by discrete-event simulation, which is specifically implemented for this model and not for a general FSPN. The types of events that need to be scheduled in the event queue are either *transition firings* or the *hitting of a threshold* dependent on fluid levels. We have used a *Unif[0,1]* pseudo-random number generator to generate samples from the respective cumulative distribution functions and determine transition firing times via inversion of the *cdf* ("Golden Rule for Sampling"). Discrete-event simulation alone has been used to obtain performance evaluation results for wide machines with much more aggressive instruction issue (*W*>>1).

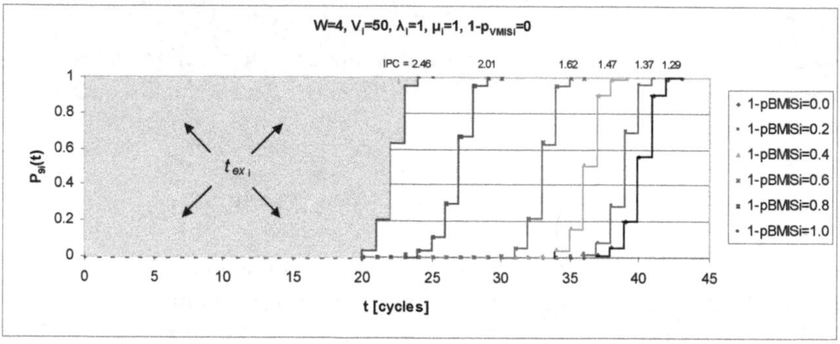

(a)

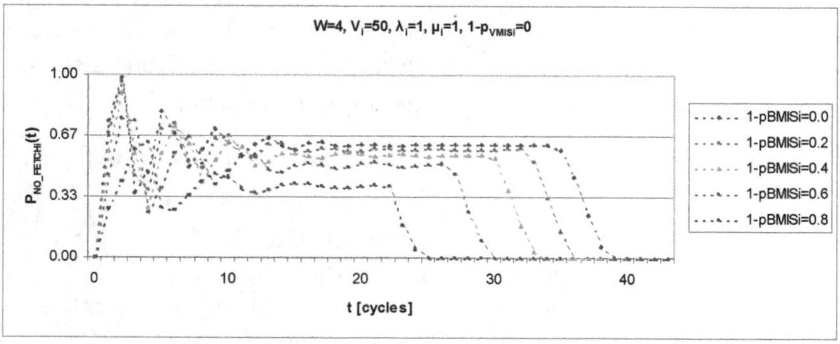

(b)

Figure 3. Influence of branch prediction accuracy on (a) the distribution of the program's execution time and (b) the probability of a complete stall in the instruction fetch unit

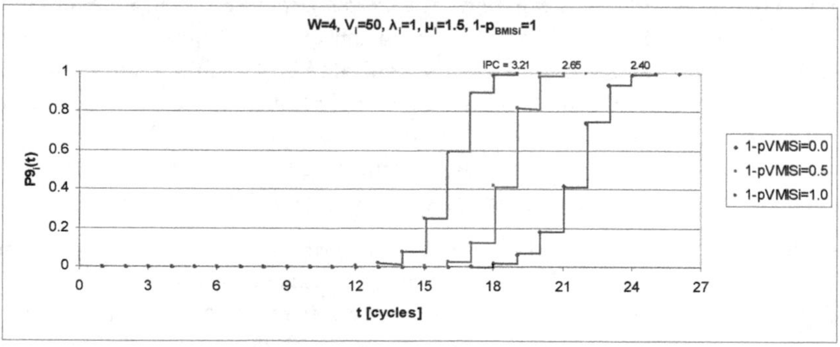

Figure 4. Influence of value prediction accuracy on the distribution of the program's execution time

It takes quite some effort to tune the numerical algorithm parameters appropriately, so that a sufficiently accurate approximation is obtained. Various discretization and convergence errors may cancel each other, so that sometimes a solution obtained on a coarse grid may agree better with the discrete-event simulation than a solution on a finer grid – which, by definition, should be more accurate. In Figures 5a-b, a comparison of discretization results and results obtained using discrete-event simulation for a four-wide machine is given. Furthermore, Figure 5c shows the performance of several machines with realistic predictors executing a program with an average basic block size of eight instructions, given that about 25% of the instructions that initiate execution in the same clock cycle are consuming instructions.

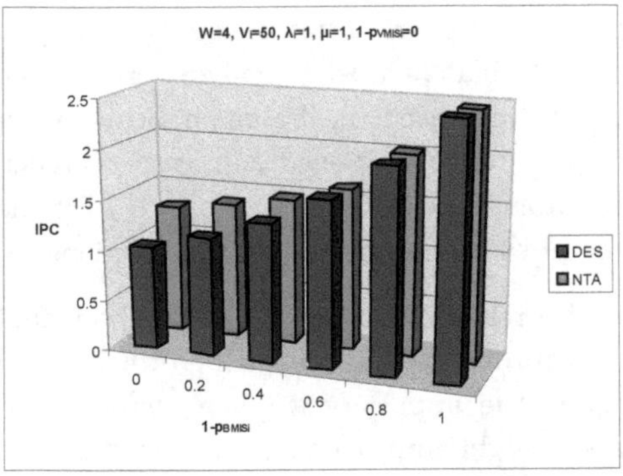

(a)

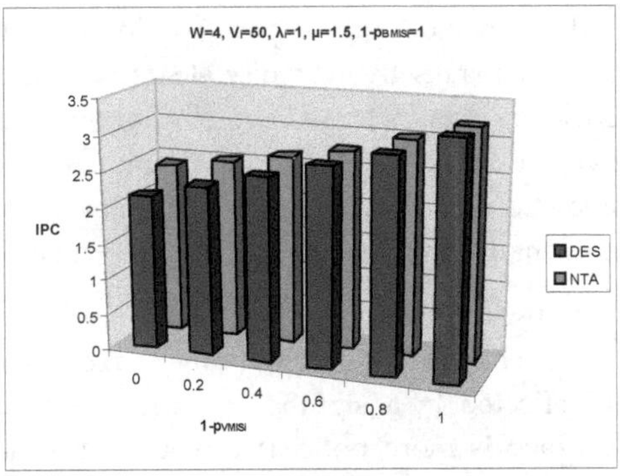

(b)

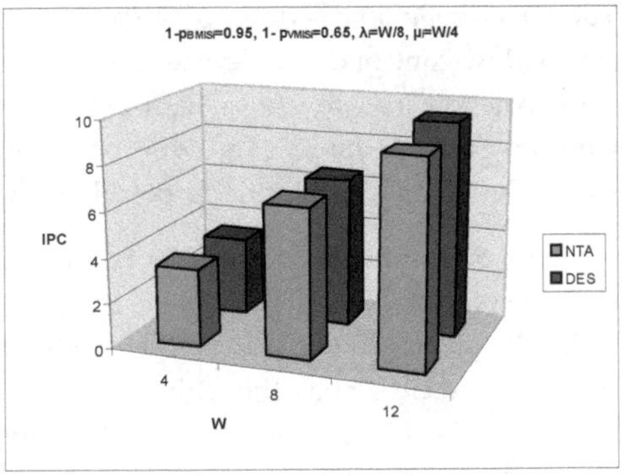

(c)

Figure 5. Comparison of numerical transient analysis results (NTA) and results given by discrete-event simulation (DES)

Since the conservation of probability mass is enforced, the differences between the numerical transient analysis and the discrete-event simulation results arise only from the improper distribution of the probability mass over the solution domain. Due to the inherent dissipation error of the first-order accurate numerical methods, the solution at successive time steps is more or less dissipated to neighboring grid nodes. The phenomenon is emphasized when the number of discrete state changes is increased owing to the larger number of mispredictions.

The results are satisfactorily close to each other, especially when the prediction accuracy is high, which is common in recent architectures. Yet, we believe that much work is still uncompleted and many questions are still open for further research in the field of development of strategies for reducing the amount of memory needed to represent the volume densities, as well as efficient discretization schemes for numerical transient analysis of general FSPNs. *Alternating direction implicit* (ADI) methods [19] in order to save memory, and parallelization of the numerical algorithms to reduce runtime have been suggested.

In the remainder of this part, we do not distinguish the numerical transient analysis results from the results given by discrete-event simulation of the FSPN model. Initially we analyze the efficiency of branch prediction by varying branch prediction accuracy. Value prediction is not involved at all. The speedup is computed by dividing the IPC achieved with certain branch prediction accuracy over the IPC achieved without branch prediction ($1-p_{BMIS_i}=0$). For the moment, the input space is not partitioned and program volume is set to V_i=10^6 instructions.

It is observed that, looking at Figures 6a-b, branch prediction curves have an exponential shape. Therefore, building branch predictors that improve the accuracy just a little bit may be reflected in a significant performance increase. The impact of a given increment in accuracy is more noticeable when it experiences a slight improvement beyond the 90%. Another conclusion drawn from these figures is that one can benefit most from branch prediction in programs with relatively short basic blocks (high λ_i / W) and which do not suffer excessively from true data dependences (low μ_i / W). When the ratio μ_i / W is high, true data dependences overshadow control dependences. As a result, the amount of ILP that is expected without value prediction in a machine with extremely aggressive instruction issue is far below the maximum possible value, even with perfect branch prediction. Value prediction has to be involved to go beyond the limits imposed by true data dependences.

Next, we analyze the efficiency of value prediction by varying value prediction accuracy (Figures 7a-b). The speedup is computed by dividing the IPC achieved with certain value prediction accuracy over the IPC achieved without value prediction ($1-p_{VMIS_i}=0$). With perfect branch prediction, it seems clear that the value prediction curves have a linear behavior. Therefore, it is worthwhile to build a predictor that significantly improves the accuracy. Only a small improvement on the value predictor accuracy has a little impact on ILP processor performance, regardless of the accuracy range. Another conclusion drawn from these figures is that the effect of value prediction is more noticeable when a significant number of instructions consume results of simultaneously initiated producer-instructions during execution (high μ_i / W), i.e. when true data dependences have a much higher influence on the program's total execution time.

Branch prediction has a very important influence on the benefits of value prediction. One can see that the performance increase is less significant when branch prediction is realistic.

Because mispredicted branches limit the number of useful instructions that enter the instruction window, the processor is able to provide almost the same number of instructions to leave the instruction window, even with lower value prediction accuracy. As a result, graphs tend to flatten out. Correct value predictions can only be exploited when the fetch rate is quite high, i.e. when mispredicted branches are infrequent. Branch misprediction becomes a more significant performance limitation with wider processors (Figure 7b).

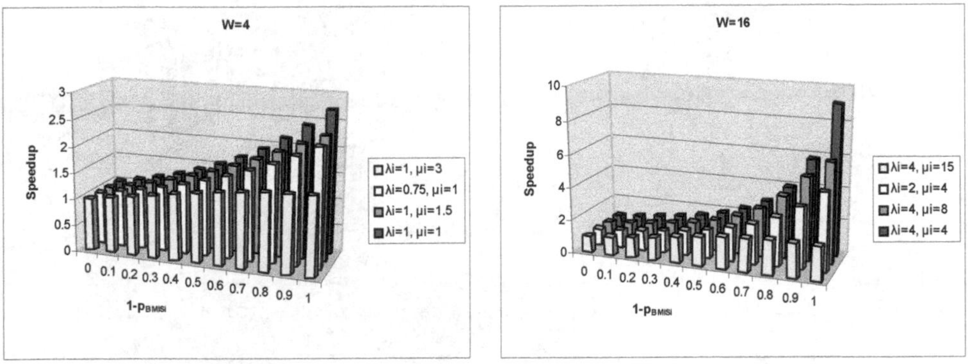

(a) (b)

Figure 6. Speedup achieved by branch prediction with varying accuracy

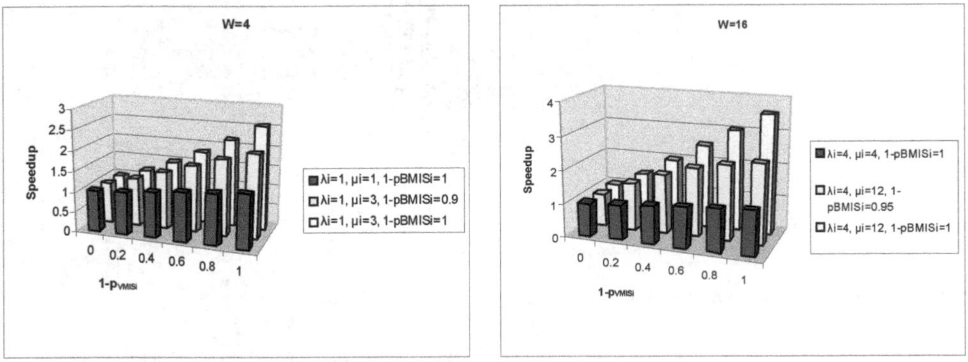

(a) (b)

Figure 7. Speedup achieved by value prediction with varying accuracy

In addition, we investigate branch and value prediction efficiency with varying machine width (Figures 8a-c). The speedup in this case is computed by dividing the IPC achieved in a machine over the IPC achieved in a *scalar* counterpart (W=1, μ_i=0). The speedup due to branch prediction is obviously higher in wider machines. With perfect branch prediction, the speedup unconditionally increases with the machine width. For a given width, the speedup is higher when there are a smaller number of consuming instructions (low μ_i / W). With realistic branch prediction, there is a threshold effect on the machine width. Below the threshold the speedup increases with the machine width, whereas above the threshold the speedup is close to a limit – machine width is by far larger than the average number of instructions provided by the fetch unit. The threshold decreases with increasing the number of mispredicted branches.

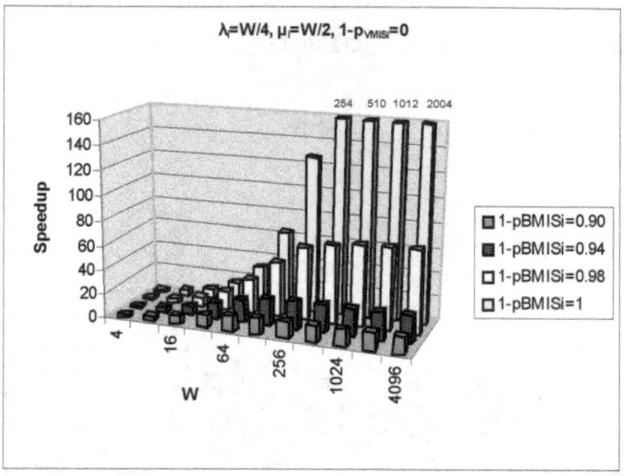

(a)

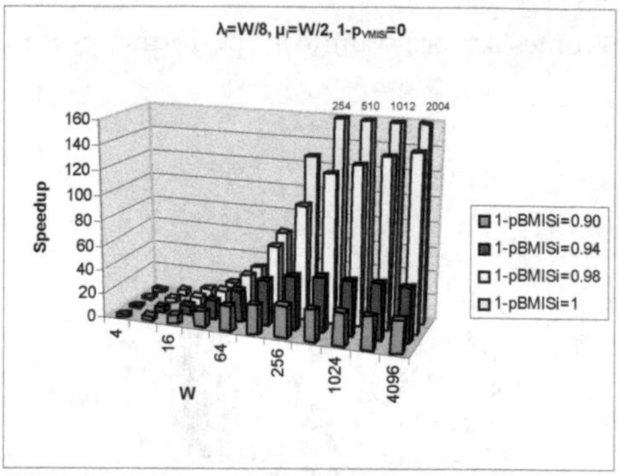

(b)

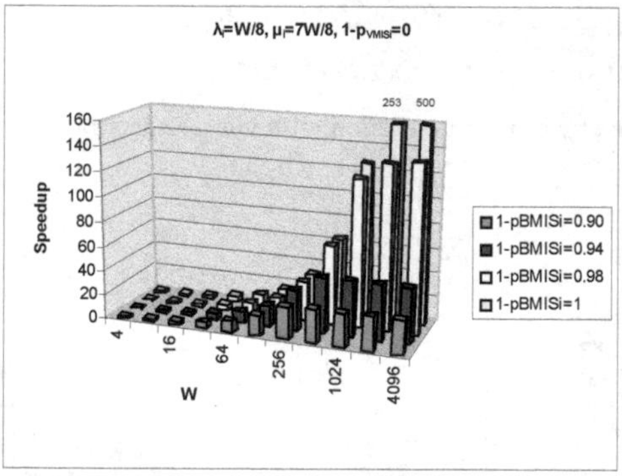

(c)

Figure 8. Speedup achieved by branch prediction with varying machine width

The maximum *additional speedup* that value prediction can provide is computed by dividing the IPC achieved with perfect value prediction over the IPC achieved without value prediction (Figures 9a-c). With perfect branch prediction, some true data dependences can always be eliminated, regardless of the machine width. Actually, the maximum additional speedup is predetermined by the ratio $W/(W-\mu_i)$. However, with realistic branch prediction, the additional speedup diminishes when the machine width is above a threshold value. It happens earlier when there are a smaller number of consuming instructions and/or a larger number of mispredicted branches. In either case, the number of independent instructions examined for simultaneous execution is sufficiently higher than the number of fetched instructions that enter the instruction window. Again, branch prediction becomes more important with wider processors.

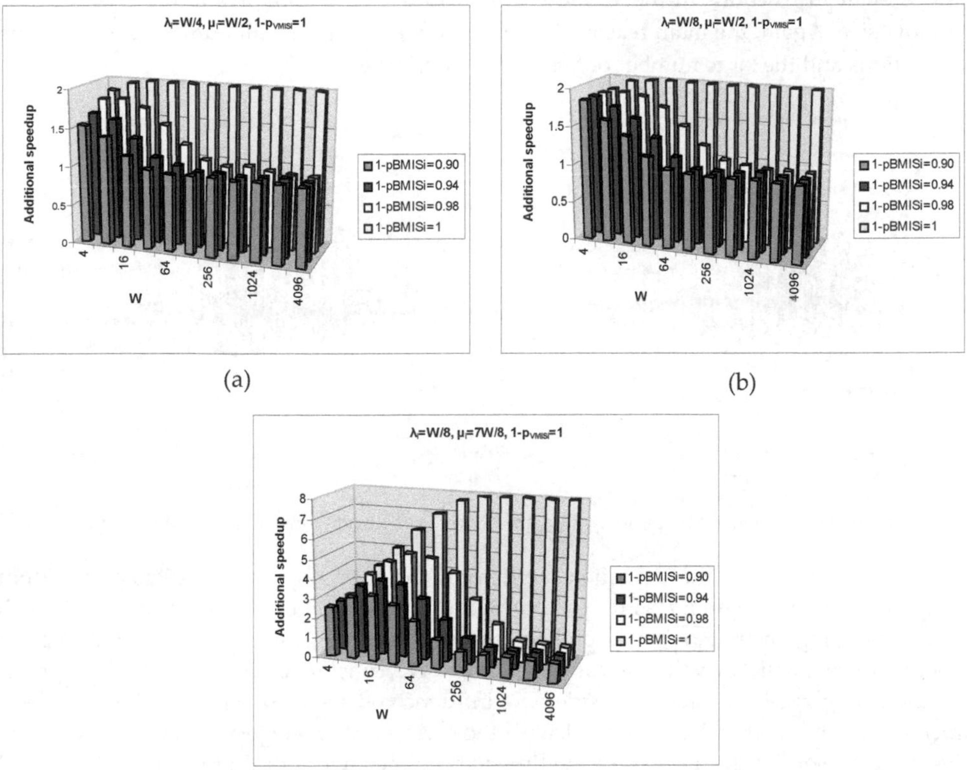

(c)

Figure 9. Additional speedup achieved by perfect value prediction with varying machine width

The rate at which consuming instructions occur depends on the initiation rate. Therefore, we also investigate the value prediction efficiency with varying instruction window size (varying capacity $Z_{RS/LSQ_{MAX}}$ of the fluid place $P_{RS/LSQ}$) (Figures 10a-b). The speedup is computed in the same way as in the previous instance. It increases with the instruction window size in [W, 2W], but the increase is more moderate when there are a smaller number of consuming instructions (low μ_i / W) and/or branch prediction is not perfect. As the instruction window grows larger, performance without value prediction saturates, as does the performance with perfect value prediction. The upper limit value emerges from the fact that in each cycle up to W new instructions may enter the fluid place $Z_{RS/LSQ_{MAX}}$ and up to W consuming instructions may be forced to retain their reservation stations. One should also note that the speedup for W>>1 and realistic branch prediction is almost constant with increasing instruction window size. Two scenarios arise in this case: (1) the number of consuming instructions is large – the speedup is constant but still noticeable as there are not enough independent instructions in the window without value prediction, and (2) the number of consuming instructions is small – there is no speedup as there are enough independent instructions in the window even without value prediction, regardless of the window size. Again, the main reasons for this behavior are the small number of consuming instructions and the large number of mispredicted branches.

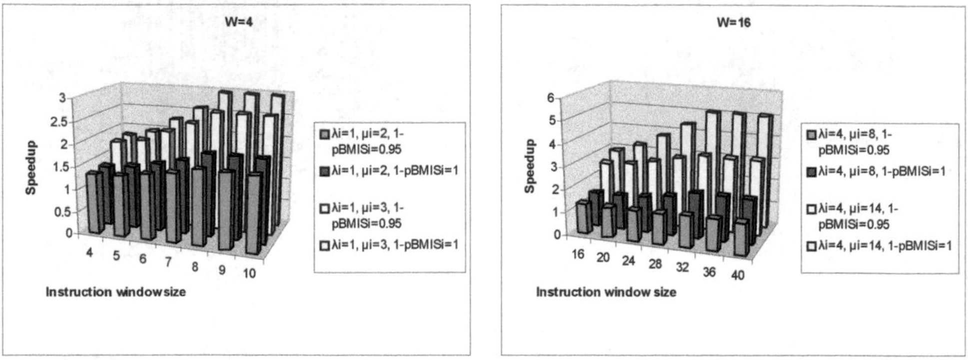

(a) (b)

Figure 10. Speedup achieved by perfect value prediction with varying instruction window size

In order to investigate the operational environment influence, we partitioned the input space into several program classes, each of them with at least one different aspect: branch rate, consuming instruction rate, probability to classify a branch as easy-to-predict or probability to classify a value as easy-to-predict. We concluded that the set of programs executed on a machine have a considerable influence on the *perceived IPC*. Since the term *program* may be interchangeably used with the term *instruction stream*, these observations give good reason for the analysis of the time varying behavior of programs in order to find simulation points in applications to achieve results representative of the program as a whole. From a user perspective, a machine with more sophisticated prediction mechanisms will not always lead to a higher *perceived performance* as compared to a machine with more modest prediction mechanisms but more favorable operational profile [20,21].

3. Part B: fluid atoms in P2P streaming networks

In P2P live streaming systems every user (peer) maintains connections with other peers and forms an application level *logical network* on top of the *physical network*. The video stream is divided in small pieces called *chunks* which are streamed from the source to the peers and every peer acts as a client as well as a server, forwarding the received video chunks to the next peer after some short buffering. The peers are usually organized in one of the two basic types of logical topologies: *tree* or *mesh*. Hence, the tree topology forms structured network of a single tree as in [22], or multiple multicast trees as in [23], while mesh topology is unstructured and does not form any firm logical construction, but organizes peers in *swarming* or gossiping-like environments, as in [24]. To make greater use of their complementary strengths, some protocols use combination of these two aspects, forming a hybrid network topology, such as [25]. Hence, members are free to join or leave the system at their own free will (*churn*), which leads to a certain user driven dynamics resulting in constant disruptions of the streaming data delivery. This peer churn has high influence on the quality of offered services, especially for P2P systems that offer live video broadcast. Also, P2P network members are heterogeneous in their upload bandwidth capabilities and provide quite different contribution to the overall system performance. Efficient construction of P2P live video streaming network requires data latency reduction as much as possible, in order to disseminate the content in a live manner. This latency is firstly introduced by network infrastructure latency presented as a sum of serialization latency, propagation delay, router processing delay and router queuing delay. The second type of delay is the initial start-up delay required for filling the peer's buffer prior to the start of the video play. The buffer is used for short term storage of video chunks which often arrive out of sequence in manner of order and/or time, and resolving this latency issue requires careful buffer modeling and management. Thus, buffer size requires precise dimensioning because even though larger buffers offer better sequence order or latency compensation, they introduce larger video playback delay. Contrary, small buffers offer smaller playback delay, but the system becomes more error prone. Also, since the connections between participating peers in these P2P logical networks are maintained by the means of control messages exchange, the buffer content (buffer map) is incorporated in these control messages and it is used for missing chunks acquisition. Chunk requesting and forwarding is controlled by a chunk scheduling algorithm, which is responsible for on-time chunk acquisition and delivery among the neighboring peers, which is usually based on the available content and bandwidth of the neighboring peers. A lot of research activities are strictly focused on designing better chunk scheduling algorithms [26,27] that present the great importance of carefully composed scheduling algorithm which can significantly compensate for churn or bandwidth/latency disruptions. Beside the basic coding schemes, in latest years an increasing number of P2P live streaming protocols use *Scalable Video Coding* (SVC) technologies. SVC is an emerging paradigm where the video stream is split in several sub-streams and each sub-stream contributes to one or more characteristics of video content in terms of temporal, spatial and SNR/quality scalability. Mainly, two different concepts of SVC are in greater use: *Layered Video Coding* (LVC) where the video stream is split in several dependently decodable sub-stream called *Layers,* and *Multiple Description Coding* (MDC) where the video stream is split in several independently decodable sub-stream called *Descriptions*. A number of P2P video streaming models use LVC [27] or MDC [23,28] and report promising results.

3.1. Model definition

As a base for our modeling we use the work in [29,30], where several important terms are defined. One of them is the maximum achievable rate that can be streamed to any individual peer at a given time, which is presented in Eq. (26).

$$r_{MAX} = \min\left\{ r_{SERVER}, \frac{r_{SERVER} + \sum_{i=1}^{n} r_{Pi}}{n} \right\} \tag{26}$$

where:
r_{MAX} – maximum achievable streaming rate
r_{SERVER} – upload rate of the server
r_{Pi} – upload rate of the ith peer
n – number of participating peers.

Clearly, r_{MAX} is a function of r_{SERVER}, r_{Pi} and n, i.e. $r_{MAX} = \phi(r_{SERVER}, r_P, n)$. This maximum achievable rate to a single peer is further referred to as the *fluid function*, or $\phi()$. The second important definition is of the term *Universal Streaming*. Universal Streaming refers to the streaming situations when each participating peer receives the video stream with bitrate no less than the video rate, and in [29] it is achievable if and only if:

$$\varphi() \geq r_{VIDEO} \tag{27}$$

where r_{VIDEO} is the rate of the streamed video content.

Hence, the performance measures of the system are easily obtained by calculating the *Probability for Universal Streaming* (P_{US}).

Now, we add one more parameter to the previously mentioned to fulfill the requirements of our model. We define the *stream function* $\psi()$ which, instead of the maximum, represents the *actual* streaming rate to any individual peer at any given time, and $\psi()$ satisfies:

$$\psi() \leq \varphi() \tag{28}$$

3.2. FSPN representation

The FSPN representation of the P2P live streaming system model that accounts for: network topology, peer churn, scalability, peer average group size, peer upload bandwidth heterogeneity, video buffering, control traffic overhead and admission control for lesser contributing peers, is given in Figure 11. We assume asymmetric network settings where peers have infinite download bandwidths, while stream delay, peer selection strategies and chunk size are not taken into account.

Similar as in [29] we assume two types of peers: high contributing peers (HP) with upload bitrate higher than the video rate, and low contributing peers (LP) with upload bitrate lower than the video rate. Different from the fluid function $\phi()$, beside the dependency to r_{SERVER}, r_P, and n, the stream function $\psi()$ depends on the level of fluid in the unique fluid place P_B as well:

$$\psi() = f\left(r_{SERVER}, \#P_{HP}, \#P_{LP}, r_{HP}, r_{LP}, Z_B\right) \tag{29}$$

where Z_B represents the level of fluid in P_B.

The FSPN model in Figure 11 comprises two main parts: the discrete part and the continuous (fluid) part of the net. Single line circles represent discrete places that can contain discrete tokens. The tokens, which represent peers, move via single line arcs to and

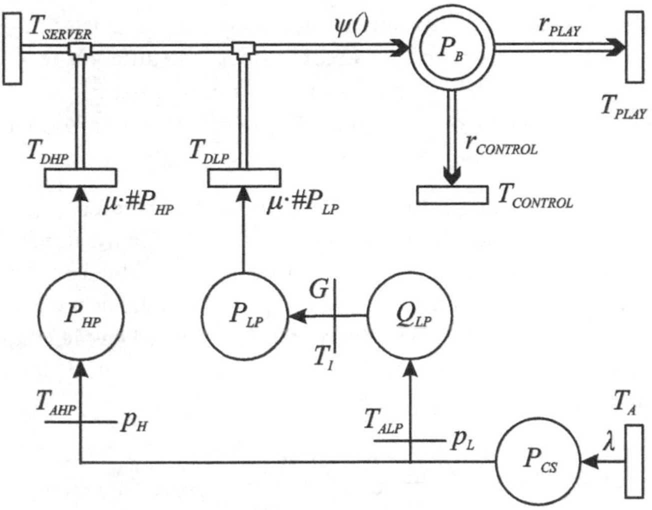

Figure 11. FSPN model of a P2P live video streaming system

out of the discrete places. Fluid arcs, through which fluid is pumped, are drawn as double lines to suggest a pipe. The fluid is pumped through fluid arcs and is streamed to and out of the unique fluid place P_B which represents a single peer buffer. The rectangles represent timed transitions with exponentially distributed firing times, and the thin short lines are immediate transitions. Peer arrival, in general, is described as a stochastic process with exponentially distributed interarrival times, with mean $1/\lambda$, where λ represents the arrival rate. We make another assumption that after joining the system peers' sojourn times (T) are also exponentially distributed. Clearly, since each peer is immediately served after joining the system, we have a queuing network model with an infinite number of servers and exponentially distributed joining and leaving rates. Hence, the mean service time T is equal to $1/\mu$, which transferred to FSPN notation leads to the definition of the departure rate as μ multiplied by the number of peers that are concurrently being served. Now, λ represents peer arrival in general, but the different types of peers do not share the same occurrence probability (p_H and p_L). This occurrence distribution is defined by immediate transitions T_{AHP} and T_{ALP} and their weight functions p_H and p_L. Hence, HP arrive with rate $\lambda_H = p_H \cdot \lambda$, and LP arrive with rate $\lambda_L = p_L \cdot \lambda$, where $p_H + p_L = 1$. In this particular case $p_H = p_L = 0.5$, but, if needed, these occurrence probabilities can be altered. This way the model with peer churn is represented by two independent $M/M/\infty$ Poisson processes, one for each of the different types of peers. The average number of peers that are concurrently being served defines the size of the system as a whole (S_{SIZE}) and is derived from the queuing theory:

$$S_{SIZE} = \lambda/\mu \tag{30}$$

T_A is a timed transition with exponentially distributed firing times that represents peer arrival, and upon firing (with rate λ) puts a token in P_{CS}. P_{CS} (representing the control server) checks the type of the token and immediately forwards it to one of the discrete places P_{HP} or Q_{LP} (P_{LP}). Places P_{HP} and P_{LP} accommodate the different types of peers in our P2P live streaming system model. Q_{LP} on the other hand, represents queuing station for the LP, which is connected to the place P_{LP} with the immediate transition T_I that is guarded by a *Guard function* G.

The Guard function G is a Boolean function whose values are based on a given condition. The expression of a given condition is the argument of the Guard function and serves as enabling condition for the transition T_I. If the argument of G evaluates to true, T_I is enabled. Otherwise, if the argument of G evaluates to false, T_I is disabled. For the model that does not take admission control into account G is always enabled, but when we want to evaluate the performance of a system that incorporates admission control we set the argument of the guard function as in Eq. (31):

$$G\left\{\frac{r_{SERVER}+\#P_{HP}\cdot r_{HP}+(\#P_{LP}+1)\cdot r_{LP}}{\#P_{HP}+\#P_{LP}}\geq r_{VIDEO}+r_{CONTROL}\right\} \tag{31}$$

Transitions T_{DHP} and T_{DLP} are enabled only when there are tokens in discrete places P_{HP} and P_{LP}. These are marking dependent transitions, which, when enabled, have exponentially distributed firing times with rate $\mu\cdot\#P_{HP}$ and $\mu\cdot\#P_{LP}$ respectively, where $\#P_{HP}$ and $\#P_{LP}$ represent the number of tokens in each discrete place. Upon firing they take one token out of the discrete place to which they are connected.

Concerning the fluid part of the model, we represent bits as atoms of fluid that travel through fluid pipes (network infrastructure) with rate dependent on the system's state (marking). Beside the stream function as a derivative of several parameters, we identify three separate fluid flows (streams) that travel through the network with different bitrates. The main video stream represents the video data that is streamed from the source to the peers that we refer to as the *video rate* (r_{VIDEO}). The second stream is the play stream which is the stream at which each peer plays the streamed video data, referred to as the *play rate* (r_{PLAY}), and the third stream is the control traffic overhead, referred to as *control rate* ($r_{CONTROL}$), which describes the exchange of control messages needed for the logical network construction and management. As mentioned earlier, transitions T_{DHP} and T_{DLP} are enabled only when there are tokens in discrete places P_{HP} and P_{LP} respectively and beside the fact that they consume tokens when firing, when enabled, they constantly pump fluid through the fluid arc to the fluid place. Flow rates of $\psi()$ are piecewise constant and depend on the number of tokens in the discrete places and their upload capabilities. Continuous place P_B represents single peer's buffer, which is constantly filled with rate $\psi()$ and drained with rate (r_{PLAY} + $r_{CONTROL}$). Z_B is the amount of fluid in P_B and Z_{BMAX} is the buffer's maximum capacity. Transition T_{SERVER} represents the functioning of the server, which is always enabled (except when there are no tokens in any of the discrete places) and constantly pumps fluid toward the continuous place P_B with maximum upload rate of r_{SERVER}. Transition T_{PLAY} represents the video play rate, which is also always enabled and constantly drains fluid from the continuous place P_B, with rate r_{PLAY}. $T_{CONTROL}$, that represents the exchange of control messages among neighboring peers, is the third transition that is always enabled, has the priority over T_{PLAY}, and constantly drains fluid from P_B with rate $r_{CONTROL}$. For further analysis we derived the rate of $r_{CONTROL}$ from [31] where it is declared that it *linearly* depends on the number of peers in the neighborhood, and for r_{VIDEO} of 128 kbps, the protocol overhead is 2% for a group of 64 users, which leads to a bitrate of 2.56 kbps. Thus, for our performance analysis we assume that peers are organized in neighborhoods with an average size of 60 members where $r_{CONTROL}$ is 2.4 kbps. For the sake of convenience and chart plotting we also define the average upload rate of the participating peers as $r_{AVERAGE}$, which is given in Eq. (32):

$$r_{AVERAGE} = \frac{\#P_{HP} * r_{HP} + \#P_{LP} * r_{LP}}{\#P_{HP} + \#P_{LP}} \tag{32}$$

Since in our model of a P2P live video streaming system we take in consideration $r_{CONTROL}$ as well, Universal Streaming is achievable if and only if:

$$\psi() \geq r_{VIDEO} + r_{CONTROL} \tag{33}$$

3.3. Discrete-event simulation

The FSPN model of a P2P live video streaming system accurately describes the behavior of the system, but suffers from state space explosion and therefore analytic/numeric solution is infeasible. Hence, we provide a solution to the presented model using *process-based discrete-event simulation* (DES) language. The simulations are performed using SimPy which is a DES package based on standard Python programming language. It is quite simple, but yet extremely powerful DES package that provides the modeler with simulation processes that can be used for active model components (such as customers, messages or vehicles), and resource facilities (resources, levels and stores) which are used for passive simulation components that form limited capacity congestion points like servers, counters, and tunnels. SimPy also provides monitor variables that help in gathering statistics, and the random variables are provided by the standard Python random module.

Now, although we deal with vast state space, we provide the solution by identifying four distinct cases of state types. These cases of state types are combination of states of the discrete part and the continuous part of the FSPN, and are presented in Table 2. Hence, the rates at which fluid builds up in the fluid place P_B, in each of these four cases, can be described with linear differential equations that are given in Eq. (34).

case 1	if	$Z_B = Z_{BMAX}$ and $\phi() \geq r_{VIDEO}+r_{CONTROL}$	then	$\psi() = r_{VIDEO}+r_{CONTROL}$ and $r_{PLAY} = r_{VIDEO}$
case 2	if	$0 < Z_B \leq Z_{BMAX}$ *and* $\phi() < r_{VIDEO}+r_{CONTROL}$	then	$\psi() = \phi()$ and $r_{PLAY} = r_{VIDEO}$
case 3	if	$0 \leq Z_{BUF} < Z_{BUFMAX}$ *and* $\phi() \geq r_{VIDEO}+r_{CONTROL}$	then	$\psi() = \phi()$ and $r_{PLAY} = r_{VIDEO}$
case 4	if	$Z_{BUF} = 0$ *and* $\phi() < r_{VIDEO}+r_{CONTROL}$	then	$\psi() = \phi()$ and $r_{PLAY} < r_{VIDEO}$

Table 2. Cases of state types

$$\frac{dZ_B(t)}{dt} = \begin{cases} 0 & case1, \\ \psi() - V_R - C_R & case2, \\ \psi() - V_R - C_R & case3, \\ 0 & case4. \end{cases} \quad (34)$$

In the next few lines (Table 3a-d) we briefly present the definitions of some of the the FSPN model components in SimPy syntax. Algorithm 1 presents the definition of SimPy processes for the different types of tokens. All the FSPN places (as well as r_{PLAY}) are defined as *resource facilities* of the type "Level" and are given in Algorithm 2. The formulation of a "Level" for representing the r_{PLAY} was enforced by the requirement for monitoring and modifying the r_{PLAY} at each instant of time. Algorithm 3 presents T_A combined with T_{AHP} and T_{ALP} where it is defined as two separate SimPy Proceses that independently generate two different types of token processes. Algorithm 4 represents the definition of transitions T_{DHP} and T_{DLP}.

Definition of HP token

```
class tokenHP (Process):
  def join (self):
    yield put, self, Php, 1
```

Definition of LP token with integrated Guard for T_I

```
class tokenLP (Process):
  def join (self):
    if (Php.amount + Plp.amount) == 0:
      yield put, self, Plp, 1
    else:
      yield put, self, Qlp, 1
      def GuardOFF():
            return (((Rserver + (Plp.amount + 1)*Rlp + Php.amount*Rhp)/((Plp.amount +
                  1) + Php.amount)) >= Rvideo + Rcontrol)
      while True:
        yield waituntil, self, GuardOFF
        yield get, self, Qlp, 1
        yield put, self, Plp, 1
        yield passivate, self
```

(a) Algorithm 1: Definition of tokens in SimPy

```
Pcs = Level (name = 'Control Server', initialBuffered=0, monitored = True)
Php = Level (name = 'Discrete Place Php', initialBuffered=0, monitored = True)
Plp = Level (name = 'Discrete Place Plp', initialBuffered=0, monitored = True)
```

Qlp = Level (name = 'Queuing Station', initialBuffered=0, monitored = True)
Pb = Level (name = 'Peer Buffer', initialBuffered=Zbmax, monitored = True)
Pplay = Level (name = 'Play rate', initialBuffered=Rvideo, monitored = True)

(b) Algorithm 2: Definition of FSPN places in SimPy

Transition T_A combined with T_{AHP}

```
class HPgenerator (Process):
  def generate (self, end):
    while now() < end:
      yield peerHP = tokenHP ()
      activate (peerHP, peerHP.join())
      yield hold, self, expovariate (pH * Lamda)
```

Transition T_A combined with T_{ALP}

```
class LPgenerator (Process):
  def generate (self, end):
    while now() < end:
      peerLP = tokenLP ()
      activate (peerLP, peerLP.join())
      yield hold, self, expovariate (pL * Lamda)
```

(c) Algorithm 3: Definition of transition T_A combined with T_{AHP} and T_{ALP}

Transition T_{DHP}

```
class HPdeparture (Process):
  def depart (self, end):
    def Condition():
        return (Php.amount > 0)
      while True:
        yield waituntil, self, Condition
        yield hold, self, expovariate (Mi * Php.amount)
        yield get, self, Php, 1
```

Transition T_{DLP}

```
class LPdeparture (Process):
  def depart (self, end):
    def Condition():
        return (Plp.amount > 0)
      while True:
        yield waituntil, self, Condition
        yield hold, self, expovariate (Mi * Plp.amount)
        yield get, self, Plp, 1
```

(d) Algorithm 4: Definition of transitions T_{DHP} and T_{DLP}

Table 3. Definitions of FSPN model components in SimPy

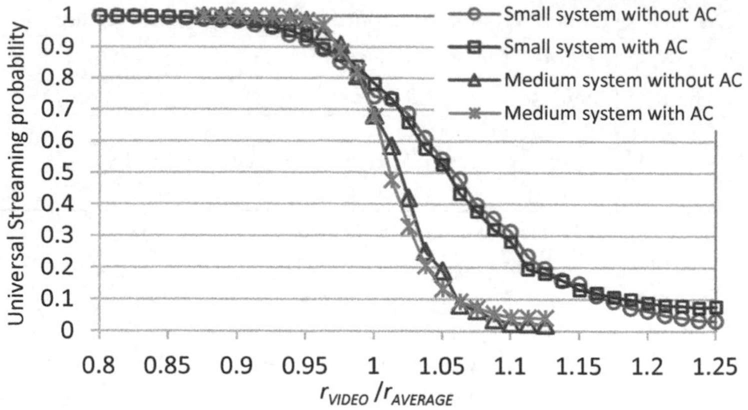

Figure 12. Performance of small and medium systems with and without AC

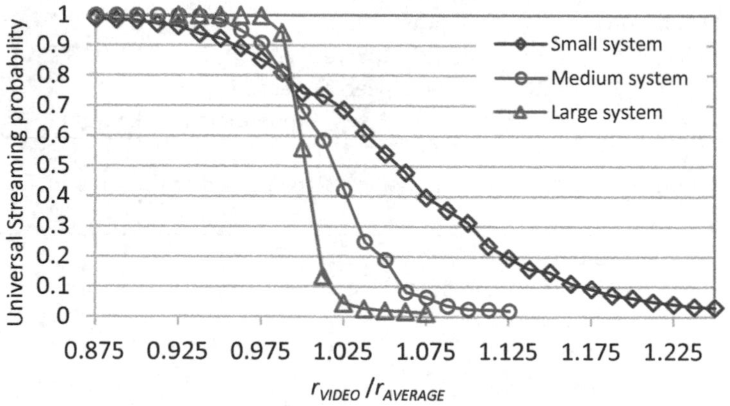

Figure 13. Performance in respect to system scaling

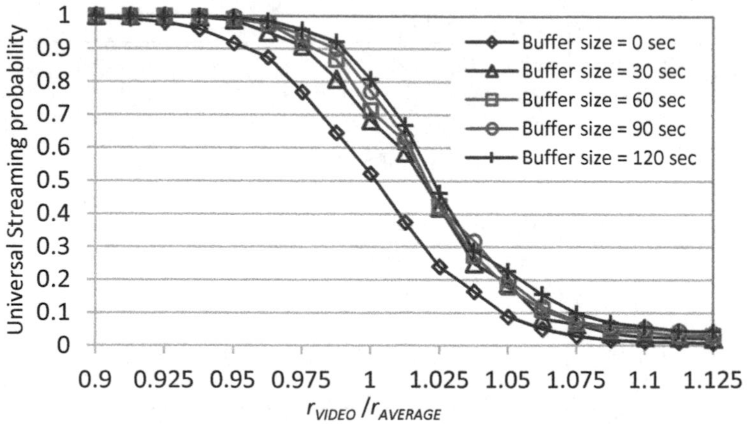

Figure 14. Buffer analysis of medium system without admission control

For simulating the fluid part of the FSPN, time discretization is applied where a SimPy "Stream Processs" checks the system state in small time intervals and consequently makes changes to the level of fluid in the fluid place P_B and r_{PLAY} according to Eq. (34). For gathering the results we use the frequency theory of probability where the probability for Universal Streaming is computed as the amount of time the system spends in Universal Streaming mode against the total simulation time.

3.4. Performance evaluation results and analysis

In this section we make a brief evaluation of three system sizes:

1. Small system with an average of 100 concurrent participating peers
2. Medium system with an average of 500 concurrent participating peers
3. Large system with an average of 5000 concurrent participating peers

The simulation scenario is as follows: $r_{SERVER} = (r_{VIDEO} + r_{CONTROL})*3$, upload bandwidth of HP is r_{HP} = 700kbps, upload bandwidth of LP is r_{LP} = 100kbps, and sojourn time T = 45 minutes. For gathering the performance results we vary the r_{VIDEO} and we plot the P_{US} against the quotient of $r_{VIDEO}/r_{AVERAGE}$, where $r_{AVERAGE}$ for this case is 400kbps. For calculating the P_{US} of a single scenario we calculate the average of 150 simulations for the small system, and an average of 75 simulations for the medium and large system, while each single simulation simulates 10 hours of system activity. Initial conditions are: $Z_{B0} = Z_{BMAX}$, where Z_{B0} is the amount of fluid in P_B in time $t_0 = 0$ and all discrete places are empty.

Comparison of performance of small and medium systems with and without AC is presented in Figure 12, from which an obvious conclusion is inferred that AC almost does not have any direct influence on the performance, but considering the incremented initial delay, incorporation of AC would only have a negative effect on the quality of offered services. Regarding the performance of the system in respect to system scaling, presented in Figure 13, it is obvious that scaling causes increase in performance, but only to a certain point after which performance steeply decreases. Fortunately, the performance decrease is in the region of under capacity which is usually avoided, so it can be concluded that larger systems perform better than smaller ones. Finally, Figure 14 shows that optimal buffer size is about 30 seconds of stored material, and larger buffers only slightly improve performance, but introduce quite large play out delay which leads to diminished quality of user experience.

4. Conclusion

In the first part of this chapter, we have introduced an implementation-independent analytical modeling approach to evaluate the performance impact of branch and value prediction in modern ILP processors, by varying several parameters of both the microarchitecture and the operational environment, like branch and value prediction accuracy, machine width, instruction window size and operational profile. The proposed analytical model is based on recently introduced Fluid Stochastic Petri Nets (FSPNs). We have also presented performance evaluation results in order to illustrate its usage in deriving measures of interest. Since the equations characterizing the evolution of FSPNs are a coupled system of partial differential equations, the numerical transient analysis poses some interesting challenges. Because of a mixed, discrete and continuous state space, another important avenue for the solution is the discrete-event simulation of the FSPN model. We believe that our stochastic modeling framework reveals considerable potential for further research in this area, needed to better understand speculation techniques in ILP processors and their performance potential under different scenarios.

In the second part of this chapter, we have shown how the FSPN formalism can be used to model P2P live video streaming systems. We have also presented a simulation solution method using process-based discrete-event simulation language whenever analytic/numeric solution becomes infeasible, that is usually a result of state space explosion. We managed to create a model that accounts for numerous features of such complex systems including: network topology, peer churn, scalability, average size of peers' neighborhoods, peer upload bandwidth heterogeneity and video buffering, among which control traffic overhead and admission control for lesser contributing peers are introduced for the first time.

Author details

Pece Mitrevski* and Zoran Kotevski
Faculty of Technical Sciences, University of St. Clement Ohridski, Bitola, Republic of Macedonia

5. References

[1] Rajan R (1995) General Fluid Models for Queuing Networks. PhD Thesis. University of Wisconsin - Madison.

[2] Gribaudo M, Sereno M, Bobbio A (1999) Fluid Stochastic Petri Nets: An extended Formalism to Include non-Markovian Models. Proc. 8th Int. Workshop on Petri Nets and Performance Models. Zaragoza.

[3] Gribaudo M, Sereno M, Horvath A, Bobbio A (2001) Fluid Stochastic Petri Nets Augmented with Flush-out Arcs: Modeling and Analysis. Kluwer Academic Publishers: Discrete Event Dynamic Systems. 11(1/2): 97-117.

[4] Horton G, Kulkarni V, Nicol D, Trivedi K (1998) Fluid Stochastic Petri Nets: Theory, Applications, and Solution. European Journal of Operations Research. 105(1): 184-201.

[5] Trivedi K, Kulkarni V (1993) FSPNs: Fluid Stochastic Petri Nets. In: M. Ajmone Marsan, editor. Lecture Notes in Computer Science: Proc. 14th Int. Conf. on Applications and Theory of Petri Nets. 691: 24-31.

[6] Wolter K, Horton G, German R (1996) Non-Markovian Fluid Stochastic Petri Nets. TU Berlin: TR 1996-13.

[7] Ferziger JH, Perić M (1997) Computational Methods for Fluid Dynamics. Springer-Verlag.

---

* Corresponding Author

[8] Hoffmann KA, Chiang ST (1993) Computational Fluid Dynamics for Engineers: Volume I & II. Engineering Education System.

[9] Ciardo G, Nicol D, Trivedi K (1997) Discrete-Event Simulation of FSPNs. Proc. 7th Int. Workshop on Petri Nets and performance Models (PNPM'97). Saint Malo. pp. 217-225.

[10] Gribaudo M, Sereno M (2000) Simulation of Fluid Stochastic Petri Nets. Proc. 8th Int. Symposium on Modeling, Analysis and Simulation of Computer and Telecommunication Systems. San Francisco. pp. 231-239.

[11] Chang PY, Hao E, Patt Y (1995) Alternative Implementations of Hybrid Branch Predictors. Proc. 28th Annual Int. Symposium on Microarchitecture. Ann Arbor. pp. 252-263.

[12] Rotenberg E, Bennett S, Smith J (1996) Trace Cache: a Low Latency Approach to High Bandwidt Instruction Fetching. Proc. 29th Annual Int. Symposium on Microarchitecture. Paris. pp. 24-35.

[13] Yeh TY, Marr D, Patt Y (1993) Increasing the Instruction Fetch Rate via Multiple Branch Prediction and a Branch Address Cache. Proc. Int. Conf. on Supercomputing. Tokyo. pp. 67-76.

[14] Lipasti M, Wilkerson C, Shen JP (1996) Value Locality and Load Value Prediction. Proc. 7th Int. Conf. on Architectural Support for Programming Languages and Operating Systems. Cambridge. pp. 138-147.

[15] Wang K, Franklin M (1997) Highly Accurate Data Value Prediction using Hybrid Predictors. Proc. 30th Annual Int. Symposium on Microarchitecture. Research Triangle Pk. pp. 281-290.

[16] Milton JS, Arnold JC (1990) Introduction to Probability and Statistics: Principles and Applications for Engineering and the Computing Sciences (2nd Edition). McGraw-Hill.

[17] Chang PY, Hao E, Yeh TY, Patt Y (1994) Branch Classificaion: a New Mechanism for Improving Branch Predictor Performance. Proc. 27th Annual Int. Symposium on Microarchitecture. San Jose. pp. 22-31.

[18] Gabbay F, Mendelson A (1998) The Effect of Instruction Fetch Bandwidth on Value Prediction. Proc. 25th Int. Symposium on Computer Architecture. Barcelona. pp. 272-281.

[19] Wolter K (1999) Performance and Dependability Modelling with Second Order Fluid Stochastic Petri Nets. PhD Thesis. TU Berlin.

[20] Mitrevski P, Gušev M (2003) On the Performance Potential of Speculative Execution Based on Branch and Value Prediction. Int. Scientific Journal Facta Universitatis. Series: Electronics and Energetics. 16(1): 83-91.

[21] Gušev M, Mitrevski P (2003) Modeling and Performance Evaluation of Branch and Value Prediction in ILP Processors. International Journal of Computer Mathematics. 80(1): 19-46.

[22] Tu X, Jin H, Liao X (2008) Nearcast: A Locality-Aware P2P Live Streaming Approach for Distance Education. ACM Transactions on Internet Technology. 8(2): Article No. 2.

[23] Zezza, S., Magli E, Olmo G, Grangetto M (2009) Seacast: A Protocol for Peer to Peer Video Streaming Supporting Multiple Description Coding. IEEE Int. Conf. on Multimedia and Expo. pp. 1586-1587.

[24] Covino F, Mecella M (2008) Design and Evaluation of a System for Mesh-based P2P Live Video Streaming. ACM Int. Conf. on Advances in Mobile Computing and Multimedia. pp. 287-290.

[25] Lu Z, Li Y, Wu J, Zhang SY, Zhong YP (2008) MultiPeerCast: A Tree-mesh-hybrid P2P Live Streaming Scheme Design and Implementation based on PeerCast. 10th IEEE Int. Conf. on High Performance Computing and Communications. pp. 714-719.

[26] Chen Z, Xue K, Hong P (2008) A Study on Reducing Chunk Scheduling Delay for Mesh-Based P2P Live Streaming. In: 7th IEEE Int. Conf. on Grid and Cooperative Computing, pp. 356-361.

[27] Xiao X, Shi Y, Gao Y (2008) On Optimal Scheduling for Layered Video Streaming in Heterogeneous Peer-to-Peer Networks. ACM Int. Conf. on Multimedia. pp. 785-788.

[28] Guo H, Lo KT (2008) Cooperative Media Data Streaming with Scalable Video Coding. IEEE Transactions on Knowledge and Data Engineering. 20(9): 1273-1281.

[29] Kumar R, Liu Y, Ross K (2007) Stochastic Fluid Theory for P2P Streaming Systems. IEEE INFOCOM. pp. 919–927.

[30] Kotevski Z, Mitrevski P (2011) A Modeling Framework for Performance Analysis of P2P Live Video Streaming Systems. In: Gušev M, Mitrevski P, editors. ICT Innovations 2010. Berlin Heidelberg: Springer Verlag. pp. 215-225.

[31] Chu Y, Rao SG, Seshan S, Zhang H (2000) A Case for End System Multicast. IEEE Journal on Selected Areas in Communications. 20(8): 1456–1471.

Chapter 4

State of the Art in Interactive Storytelling Technology: An Approach Based on Petri Nets

Hussein Karam Hussein Abd El-Sattar

Additional information is available at the end of the chapter

1. Introduction

Interactive Storytelling is one of most promising technologies for the development of new media and new forms of digital entertainment. Interactive Storytelling can be defined as the endeavour to develop new media in which the presentation of a narrative, and its evolution can be influenced, in real-time, by the user. In traditional forms of storytelling, a storyteller would present the scenario of a story to the audiences in a predefined way (also known as a plot), which limited the variation in character interactions and context. The story refers to the succession of actions that happen in the world represented by the narrative. The origin of computerized storytellers can be traced to the "story-generation system TALE-SPIN" (Meehan, J., 1981) which is the most popular generator of short tales. A scene of the storyline is composed of beats, where the term beat refers to the smallest unit of action that has its own complete shape. A beat is a dramatic action that occurs in a scene to achieve a narrative goal. It consists of

i. Pre-conditions, a list of predicates that need to be true for the beat to be selected;
ii. Post-conditions; a list of predicates that will be true as a consequence of firing the beat;
iii. Success and failure conditions, and
iv. A joint plan to be executed by the actors.

The growing interest in Interactive Storytelling as a Research topic and as a potential technology derives from the current competition between traditional and interactive digital media. Interactive Storytelling is of interest to broadcasters and computer game producers alike. In the former case, Interactive Storytelling will bring interactivity into traditional media, potentially revolutionizing the entertainment experience. In the latter, it would improve the narrative and "aesthetic" value of computer games, with the potential to develop new game genres and attract a wider audience. The term Interactive Storytelling is sometimes used in a broader sense in the field of new media, to reflect the fact that some interactive systems, like computer games, can be designed to reflect an underlying narrative, which is conveyed via the gameplay, often enhanced by animation cut scenes.

On the other hand, several years of research are establishing Petri nets (PN) (Tado, M., 1990; Peterson, J. L., 1997) and its extension High-level PN as a process modelling formalism for a variety of application domains. A high level PN is a Petri net extended with colour, time, and hierarchy (Jenson, K., 1997). The power of Petri nets lies in its formal semantics and non semantics properties. This chapter addresses a new application domain of PN for modeling game systems and game workflow control in the context of workflow management concept and game rules principles. It presents state-of-the-art results with respect to interactive storytelling and PN, and highlights some petri-net-based workflow tools for game design. This is done by proposing an integrated framework for deeply combining interactivity and narrative in computer games which is achieved by:

i. composing the game rules in the game's workflow environment by different triggers and effects, and
ii. separating the rules of the game environment into two parts: controllable rules, and uncontrollable rules. The controllable rules are the rules in which its template is directly related to the goal of the game, mainly as a feedback within the rule effects. The uncontrollable rules are the rules in which its template is independent from the game goal. The rule is then characterized by a trigger based on the computer game's input, and an effect targeting only the game elements.

Evaluation and performance results supported by some case study called crazy ball 2 are also demonstrated. Crazy ball 2 is a platform-type genre, much like the worldwide-known game Mario and the Konami's Castlevania series.

In the reminder of this chapter we will offer insights into how workflow management concepts can be jointly utilized with Petri nets (PN) for modeling game systems and game workflow control. To do this, we first introduces the problem statatment, prior research and objectives in section 2. Section 3, briefly summarizes the background and the basic terminology and notions that will be used throughout this chapter. Section 4 introduces the methodology used. Evaluation and practical performance results are discussed in Section 5. Sections 6 concludes this chapter and outlines some directions for future work.

2. Prior research, problem statement, and objectives

2.1. Prior research

Building interactive storytelling systems is gained a growing attention among a growing number of researchers from a huge diversity of discipline and orgins of expertise. As a result, many different approaches which differ on various dimensions and sometimes overlap are developed under the following four and some other research directions:

i. Generative computer graphics, animated storytelling for film production;
ii. Human-computer interaction (HCI);

iii. Computer game design, and
iv. Artificial intelligence.

Story plot and character(s) are the two most important element of a story. As a consequence, several approaches, at different levels of complexity, have been developed for representing plots in games, monitoring the course of the story and controlling stories in games and storytelling applications. These techniques are summarized as follows:

i. Planning techniques (Riedl, M. & Stern, A., 2006);
ii. Beat approach (Brom, et. al., 2007);
iii. Finite-state machines (Sheldon, L., 2004), and
iv. Petri nets (PN) (Delmas, G. et. al, 2007; Brom, C. & Abonyi, A. 2006; Karam, H., 2010).

Several years of research are establishing Petri nets (PN) and its extension High-level PN as a process modelling formalism for a variety of application domains, for instance: network protocols, logistics, scientific workflows and gaming theory. Their power lies in their formal semantics and non semantics properties. The main contribution of this chapter is to show how workflow management concepts can be jointly utilized with Petri nets (PN) for modeling game systems and game workflow control. This is done by composing the game rules in the game's workflow environment by different triggers and effects. The idea is derived from the study of PN, game theory, workflow management, story writting, AI, and cinematography in interactive storytelling. In this contribution, interactive storytelling is viewed as a hybrid form of game design and cinematic storytelling for entertainment applications among two skills: artistic and technical. Evaluation and performance results in terms of some case study called crazy ball 2 are also demonstrated. Crazy ball 2 is a platform-type genre, much like the worldwide-known game Mario and the Konami's Castlevania series.

2.2. Problem statement and objectives

Recently, interactive storytelling has become a major issue in video games development. Several categories of video games arose to either historical, editorial or narrative criteria. Within the field of Interactive Storytelling, interactive drama is a computer-based fiction where a user chooses most of the actions for the main character in a story. Interactive drama is the ultimate challenge of digital entertainment because it involves both the dynamic generation of narrative events and the integration of user inputs within the generation. This is a hard challenge, because it involves both the dynamic generation of narrative events and the integration of user inputs within the generation. Moreover, both Storytelling unfolding and player's interaction can't take place at the same time. The first relates to game designer's control of the game he/she has created as the second relates to player's control on the game he/she has bought. Each interactive drama needs a model of narrative. The challenge of interactive drama is to find a model suited to the interactive nature of computers. Interactive drama architecture has several key components: the environment, the player, the user, the writer, and the director. For successful interactive drama architecture, three requirements are necessary (Magerko, B. & Laird, J. 2003):

i. the balance between writer flexibility vs. user flexibility;
ii. temporal variability (i.e. allowing time to be the key variable for the flexibility in an interactive experience), and
iii. transparency (How do we encourage the User to follow a particular destiny without having him feel forced into it?).

Moreover, it is necessary to overcome two obstacles (Szilas, N., 2005): technical problem and conceptual problem. This chapter attempts to solve these problems by proposing an integrated framework for deeply combining interactivity and narrative in computer games. The approach is based on separating the actions of the system into two parts, the controllable and the controllable actions. The controllable actions are controllable by the system we model. The system can choose which and when to execute controllable actions. The controllable actions are not controllable by the system, but can occur whenever they are enabled. In this contribution, interactive drama is viewed as a hybrid form of game design and cinematic storytelling for entertainment applications among two skills: artistic and technical. The idea is derived from the study of interactive drama, Petri nets (PN), narrative structures in computer games and game workflow activity process. The main advantages of using PN are that it copes well with branching stories and can evolve in parallel in large virtual world. The proposed idea is supported by some case study called Crazy ball 2. Crazy ball 2 is a platform-type genre, much like the worldwide-known game Mario and the Konami's Castlevania series. It possesses many universally-shared game features such as Hit Points (HP), Game Over, Enemies, and Bosses. One of the advantages of the proposed computer game is the inclusion of the "Freestyle combat system", which allows the user to completely control the attacks of the player using a mouse. Moreover, it possesses a feature which is called an "even game", in which the game challenge level matches the skill of the human player.

3. Fundamentals and basic notions

3.1. Petri Nets

Petri nets are a "pinball game" for mathematicians (Tado, M., 1990; Peterson, J. L., 1997). It is a particular kind of directed graph, together with an initial state called the initial marking M_0. The underlying graph G of a PN is a directed, weighted, bipartite graph consisting of two kinds of nodes, called places (P) and transitions (T), where arcs are either from a place to a transition or from a transition to a place. N=(T,P,F) is called a net, iff

$$\begin{cases} (i) P \cap T = \emptyset, and \\ (ii) F \subseteq (P \times T) \cup (T \times P) \text{ is a binary relation} \end{cases} \quad (1)$$

Let N be a net and let $x \in (P \cup T)$, then

$$\begin{cases} {}^{\cdot}x = \{y|yFx\} \text{ is called the set of pre-conditions} \\ x^{\cdot} = \{y|xFy\} \text{ is called the set of post-conditions} \end{cases} \quad (2)$$

Formally, a Petri nets $PN = (N, M_0)$ consists of a structure N and an initial marking M_0, where:

i. N=(P,T,F,W) is a Petri nets structure,
ii. $P = \{p_1, p_2, \cdots, p_m\}$ is a finite set of m places,
iii. $T = \{t_1, t_2, \cdots, t_n\}$ is a finite set of n transitions,
iv. $F \subseteq (P \times T) \cup (T \times P)$ is a set of arcs with $P \cap T = \phi, P \cup T \neq \phi$.

Arcs are labeled with their weights (positive integers), where a k-weighted arc is interpreted as a set of k parallel arcs. Labels for unitary weight are usually omitted.

$$W : F \rightarrow \{1,2,3,\cdots\}$$

is a mapping which associates to each arc of the net its weight,

$$M_0 : P \rightarrow \{1,2,3,\cdots\}$$

is the initial marking representing the initial state of PN. The state of PN is described by means of the concepts of marking. A marking is a transition function that assigns to each place a nonnegative integer called a token. A token is the main information unit and a primitive concept of PN like places and transitions. If a sufficient number of tokens are contained in specific places, an action is triggered. After firing an action, the tokens that helped to fire this action are removed, and some new tokens are generated. Which tokens fire which action and which action generates tokens to which places is specified by the transition function. In graphical representation, places, transitions, tokens and transition function are represented by circles, rectangles or bars, pellets and arrows respectively. Table 1, illustrates such representations and its interpretations of a PN model. Figure 1 presents an example of a PN model with graphical and mathematical notations.

In modeling using PN, we regard the places as conditions, the transitions as events or actions, and a marking as triggers. A trigger can be associated with an action (action trigger) or a place (place trigger). A transition has a certain number of input and output places representing the pre-conditions and post-conditions of the event, respectively. The presence of a token in a place is interpreted as holding the truth of the condition associated with the place. In another interpretation, "k" tokens are put in a place to indicate that "k" data items or resources are available. Some typical interpretations of transitions and their inputs and outputs places are shown in Table 2.

PN Model	Graphical representations	Interpretations
Places	○	States/conditions
Transitions	▭	Events/actions
Tokens	●	Marks/States
Transition function	→	Triggers

Table 1. Graphical Representations and Interpretations of a PN Model.

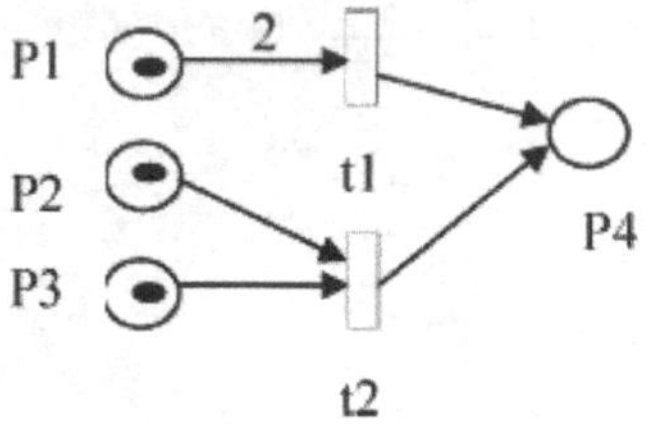

$P=\{P1,P2,P3,P4\}$,
$T=\{t1,t2\}$,
$F=\{(P1,t1),(P2,t2),(P3,t2),(t1,P4),(t2,P4)\}$,
$W(P1,t1)=2$,
$W(P2,t2)=W(P3,t2)=W(t1,P4)=W(t2,P4)=1$,
$M_0=[1\ \ 1\ \ 1\ \ 0]^T$.

Figure 1. An illustration example of a PN model with graphical notation (left), and mathematical notation (right).

Input Places	Transition	Output Places
Pre-conditions	Event	Post-conditions
Input data	Computation step	Output data
Conditions	Clause in logic	Conclusion(s)
Resources needed	Task/job/behavior	Resources released

Table 2. Some typical interpretations of transitions and places.

The dynamics of the net is described by moving tokens among places according to the transition firing rules or enabling test in marking. A transition t is said to be enabled if each input place P of t is marked with at least W (P, t) tokens, where W (P, t) is the weight of the arc from P to t. Once enabled, a transition will fire when its associated event occurs. A firing of an enabled transition t removes W (P, t) tokens from each input place P of t, and adds W (t, P) tokens to each output place P of t, where W (t, P) is the weight of the arc from t to P. Figure 2 demonstrates an example for the transition firing rules of a PN model shown in Figure 1. In the PN of Figure 2, only transition t2 is enabled; t1 is not enabled because it would require two tokens in P1 to fire, since W (P1, t1) =2. When t2 is fired, the tokens in P2 and P3 are removed and P4 receives one token (see Figure 2).

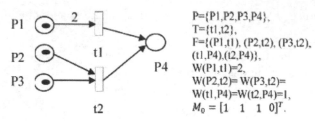

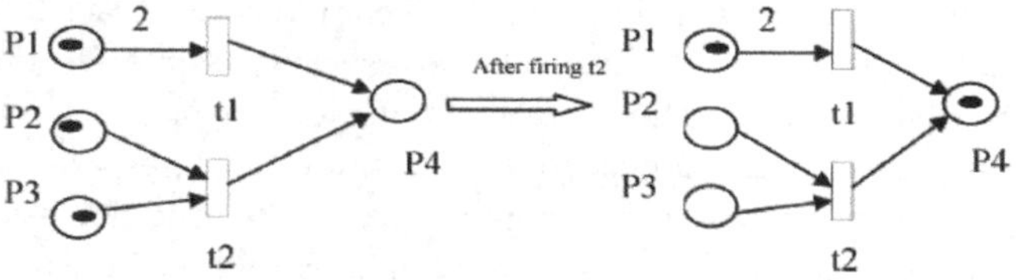

Figure 2. PN marking example before and after firing the enabled transition t2.

3.2. Workflow management concept

Workflows are gaining a lot of interest both in the business and scientific environments for automating the execution of complex IT processes. The term workflow management (WM) refers to the domain which focuses on the logistics of business processes (Van der Aalst, W., 1998). The goal of workflow management is to handle cases as efficiently and effectively as possible by the right resource (e.g. actor, person, participant, or application) at the right time. Workflows are case-based, i.e. every piece of work is executed for a specific case. The key concept of WM is task. A task is a piece of work to be done by one or more resources in a pre-determined time interval. A task item is a task that needs to be executed to handle a specific case. Task items are executed by resources. Synonyms for resource are actor or participant. A work item which is being executed by a specific resource is called an activity, which is an actual performance of a work item. The activity contains the rule entities to describe the conditions under which the activity may be fired. A workflow procedure defines a partial ordering of tasks to handle cases of a specific type. A workflow process definition comprises a workflow procedure, a set of resources and a strategy to map task items to resources. Figure 3 shows that a workflow has three dimensions: case, resource and process definition dimension. A number of dots shown represent either a work item (case+task) or an activity (case+task+resource). Note that, work items link cases and tasks. Activities link cases, tasks, and resources

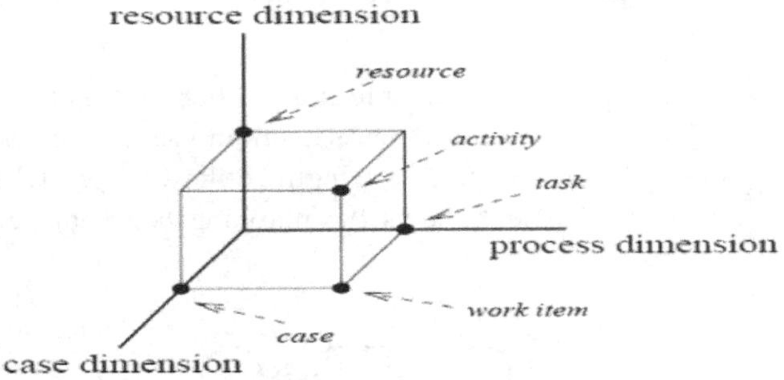

Figure 3. A three dimensional view of a workflow

A "workflow process definition" dimension specifies how the cases are routed along the tasks that need to be executed. Routing of cases describes the lifecycle of a case, i.e., which tasks need to be performed and in which order. Four types of routed are identified as shown in Figure 4: sequential (tasks are executed sequentially), parallel (task B and C are executed in parallel), conditional (either task B or C is executed), and iteration (multiple B's). These four routed types outlined the currently accepted narrative structures used in the creation of computer games (Mark Reidl, O., Michael R., 2005). For instance, linear narrative which corresponds to the sequential routing is a traditional form of narrative in which a sequence

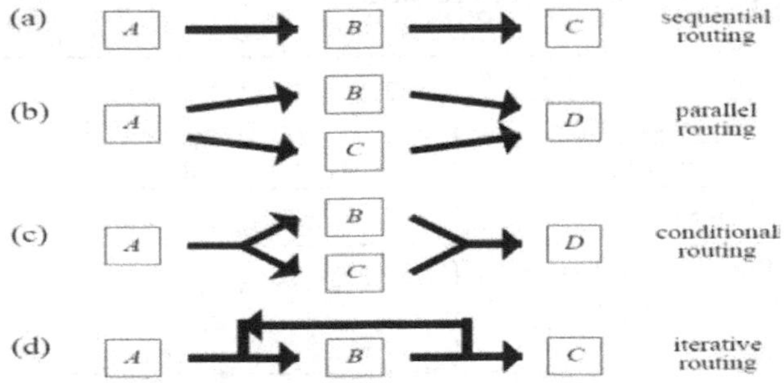

Figure 4. Four routing constructions demonstration.

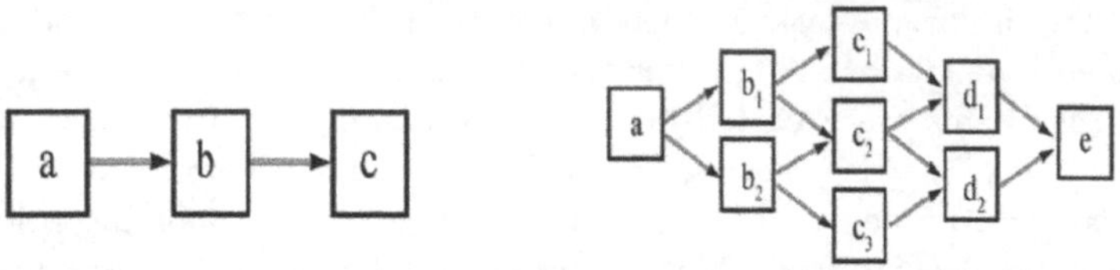

(a) Linear Narrative Progression (b) Branching Narrative Progression

Figure 5. An illustration for both linear and branching narrative progressions.

of events is narrated from beginning to ending without variation or possibility of a user altering the way in which the story unfolds or ends. Some computer games use branching narrative in which there are many points in the story at where some action or decision made by the user alters the way in which a narrative unfolds or ends. Both narratives are shown in Figures 5(a)-(b).

Since Petri Nets (PN) are a process modeling technique, then modeling a "workflow process definition" onto PN is straightforward: tasks, conditions, and cases are modeled by transitions, conditions and tokens respectively. Figure 6 shows how all these concepts can be mapped onto the Petri net. Table 3 shows the mapping between the workflow process definitions and PN terms.

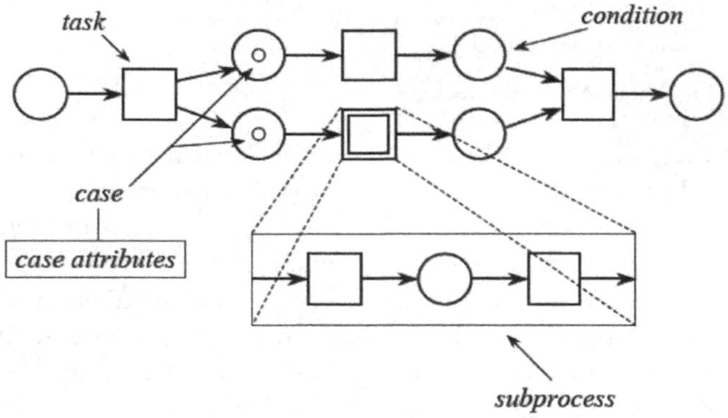

Figure 6. Mapping a process definition onto Petri nets.

Workflow Perspective	PN terms
Task execution	One or more transition
Work item	Transition being enabled
Activity	Firing of a transition
Data that flows between tasks/case attributes	Tokens
Conditions	Places

Table 3. Mapping Workflow process onto Petri nets (PN) terms.

4. Methodology

Computer games are defined as an activity with some rules engaged in for an outcome. Key components of games are goals, rules, challenge, and interactivity. Games are regarded in terms of three levels of temporal design, from simulation at the lowest time scale, through the design of game moves above the simulation level, to the structure of specific narrative patterns at the highest level. The methodology in our approach is based on the study of workflow process under these levels for the structural parts of a computer games and is shown in Figure 7.

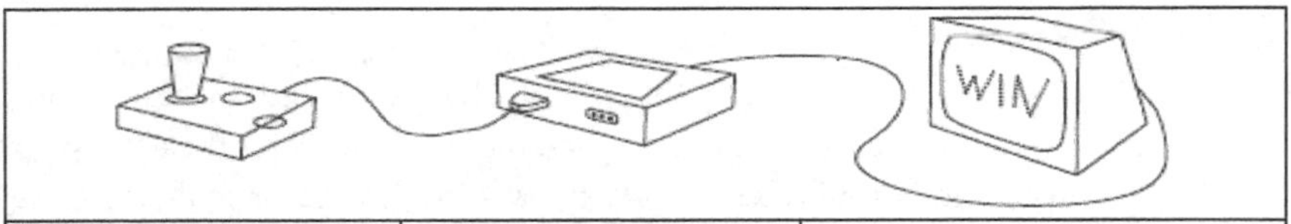

Input: Player pushes any buttons	Computing: the computer is thinking	Output: A "result" is displayed on the screen

Figure 7. The structural parts of computer games.

The diagram in Figure 7 is composed of three parts: the "Input" peripheral devices allowing the user to enter choices. These choices are then evaluated by the rules of the "Computing" part, in order to produce a "result". This result is finally communicated to the player through the "Output" device. Computer game development is a tremendous task that requires different roles for the storyteller and audience, and a lot of resources including: storytelling elements and elemental interplay. Storytelling elements includes: narrative, plot, and story. The interplay of elements in the game environment consists of: structure, theme and metaphor. The structure describes the influence of plot on narrative. Theme is the expression of the story within the plot. Metaphor is the means by which story is encoded within the narrative. From the technical point of view, game can be seen as a client-server application connected with some data. From the conceptual point of view for game representation and according to (Salen, K., Zimmerman, E., 2003), computer games are defined as an activity with some rules engaged in for an outcome. Therefore, there is a need to develop an integrated framework for deeply combining interactivity and narrative. As a sort for achieving this goal and under the study of workflow management concept, Figure 8 shows a design of a workflow activity process for the conceptual representation of computer games.

Figure 8 shows how the conceptual representation of a game can be modeled as a series of processes, where each process consists of some activities. Activity is a description of a piece of work that forms one logical step within a process. An activity has one or multiple roles, zero or multiple rules, zero or multiple event and one or more multiple data. Partial order relationships between activities (e.g. sequential, parallel, alternative and looped) are notated with the arc, which links the activity entity to itself. The activity also contains the rule entities to describe the conditions under which the activity may be fired. The rule is used to

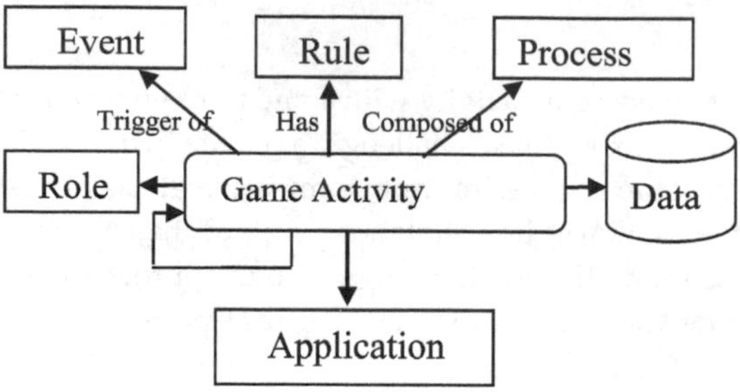

Figure 8. Game workflow activity process

describe logic conditions for executing activity and always related to case "data". The "application" entity extracts software tools, by which the role completes the activity, and the "data" depicts the input and output data of the activity. Since the game engine we are going to propose in this paper executes workflows represented in terms of PN. The classical structure of a PN model is formally defined by a set of places, a set of transitions and a set of arcs connecting places to transitions and vice versa. For the purpose of this chapter we extend the classical PN with features that make them more suitable for workflow representation given in terms of High level Petri nets (HLPN) workflow (Jenson, K., 1997). An HLPN is normally represented using a graphical form which allows visualization of system dynamics (flows of data and control). By using HLPN formalism it is possible to

i. formally represent the workflow state (and its evolution);
ii. formally describe both the control and the data flow, and
iii. deal with dynamic workflows.

An HLPN can be defined by the tuple: HLPN= (P, T, Type, Pre, Post, E, G, M_0), where

- P is a finite set of elements called places
- T is a finite set of elements called transitions
- "Type" is a function that assigns a type to places and expressions;
- $Pre \subseteq (P \times T)$ is the subset of arcs from places to transitions and $Post \subseteq (T \times P)$ is the set of arcs from transition to places
- E is an expression. It is defined from $(Pre \cup Post)$ into expressions. Expressions may comprise constants, variables (e.g. m,n) and functions (e.g. g(x)) which are types;
- G is the guard function, a Boolean expression inscribing a transition $(t \in T)$ (where Type(G(t))=Boolean);
- M_0 is the initial marking: a multi-set of tokens associated with the places

Now let us analyze the game workflow activity shown in Figure 8 in terms of HLPN and game components. Key components of games are goals, rules, challenge, and interactivity. Games takes place in a virtual universe and it is composed by several elements, where these elements are submitted to "rules", in accordance to the game. Since a workflow system is a reactive system, i.e. it is triggered by the environment. This means that, enabling of a task doesn't imply that the task will be directly executed. Therefore, the objective is to analyze the workflow management process of games rules and an attempt to classify them in terms of the game elements constitutes the game environment. By focusing on games as rules we means looking at games as reactive systems, both in the sense that the rules are inner structures that constitute the games and also in the sense that the rules schemas are analytic tools that mathematically dissects games. As a result, we found it is necessary for game developers to distinguish between the enabling of a task and the execution of a task. Since the enabling of a task does not imply that the task will be executed immediately, it is important to have this distinction. In order to have this distinction, we should consider triggering of tasks in the game's flow environment. A trigger is an external condition which leads to the execution of an enabled task. One way to perform this is to separate the rules of the game environment based on whether its template is direct or indirect related to the goal of the game into two parts: controllable rules, and uncontrollable rules. Controllable rules are the rules in which its template is directly related to the goal of the game, mainly as a feedback within the rule effects. In this case, the rule is characterized by a trigger based on the state of the game elements, and an effect linked to the computer game's output. The uncontrollable rules are the rules in which its template is independent from the game goal. The rule is then characterized by a trigger based on the computer game's input, and an effect targeting only the game elements. An example for the template is the one given by: "if player element collides with a hostile element, then there is a negative feedback towards the player element". The real power of separating these rules illustrates how the separation of them allow us to explicitly specify what parts of the model comprise the system and what parts comprise the environment. For this purpose we used four types of tasks:

i. automatic: a task is triggered the moment it is enabled (i.e. No trigger is required);
ii. user: a task is triggered by participant/actor;
iii. Message: an external event is required, and
iv. time: the task requires a time trigger.

An awareness of a narrative's time line is an important element to focus on when creating the environment for an audience's imagination. The triggering concept can be modeled in terms of HLPN for user task "A" as shown in Figure 9.

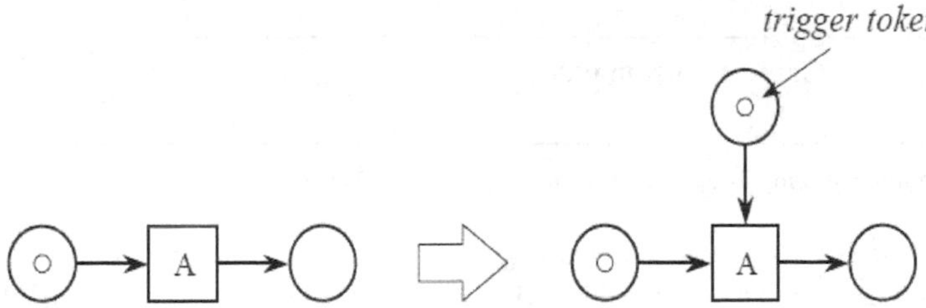

Figure 9. The triggering concept for user task called "A" workflow activity process

Since game is defined as an activity with some rules engaged in for an outcome. So, game activity can be represented now as: activity = task + case + (resource) + (trigger), where trigger is one of the previous mentioned tasks. This activity represents the actual execution of a task for a specific case. Now let us analyze the effects of trigger concept and game rules (controllable/uncontrollable) applied to the proposed case study game "crazy ball 2". Games takes place in a virtual universe and it is composed by several elements, where these elements are submitted to "rules", in accordance to the game. For example, table 4, shows some of the universe "elements" applied for the case study game "crazy ball 2" and its uses. These elements are submitted to different rules, for instance, "if the red ball element jumps towards the player, then it explodes on touch". By analyzing this rule, we realized that it is composed of two parts: (i) the "trigger": "if the red ball element jumps towards the player,", and (ii) the "effect(s)": "then it explodes on touch". In the same logic, the goal of a game can also be described and controlled by its rules.

Game Elements	Uses
	Used in the combat system to control the player using mouse and also used for the render that made the Game Over screen
	Used as a model for Bad Ball and Red Ball enemies.
	Used as the door object in the game's stage, it has an animation that allows the grey stone part to slide open upwards.
	Used as the model for the player's hit points (HP). Eight heart graphics models are used to display player's HP on the screen.
	Used as the Information Signs' object. The question mark has a rotation animation that is constantly active in the game.
	Used for setting the sword swing power (force) display
	Player control
	Game envirnoment

Table 4. Some game elements for the Crazy ball 2 game and its uses.

Now, the question is how can we construct game rules that include game goals? The answer to this question is derived from the study of both HLPN and game workflow activity process previously mentioned. As a result, we defined the "game elements" as "a canvas of rules", a diagram to follow in order to build a rule or a group of rules in a computer games. This is done by composing the game rules by different triggers and effects as shown in Figure 10. The game workflow activity engine forr crazy ball 2 is shown in Figure 11.

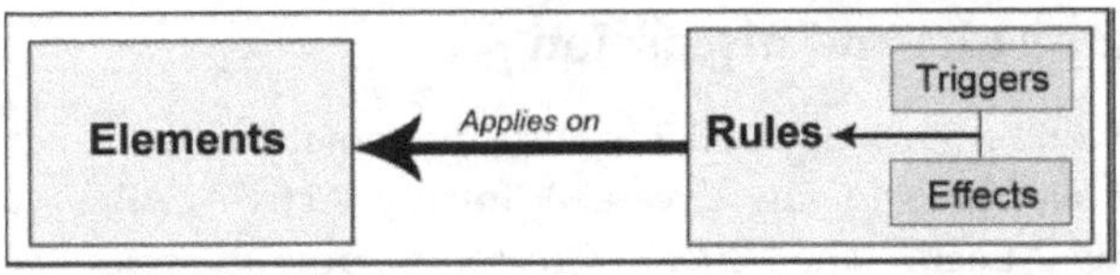

Figure 10. Game rules as a triggers and effects.

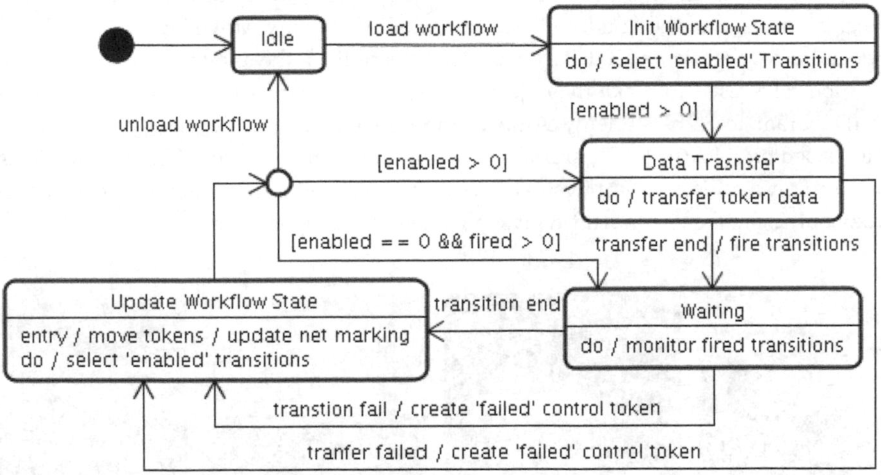

Figure 11. Game workflow activity engine

The following flowchart summarizes the idea, where T is a set of transition instances in the given HLPN, $T_{disabled}$ is a subset of T with elements having status disabled, and $T_{unknowns}$ is a subset of T with elements having status unknown

Step 1. (Initialization)

- $T_{disabled} \leftarrow \phi$
- $T_{unknowns} \leftarrow T$ and $count \leftarrow 0$

Step 2. (Loop)

- While ($T_{unknowns} \neq \phi$) do
  - $t_{candidate} \leftarrow$ (random element from $T_{unknowns}$)
  - Status $\leftarrow$ (try finding an enabled binding for $t_{candidate}$, make it occur and return occurred. Otherwise return enabling status)
- if (status = disabled) Then (move $T_{candidate}$ from $T_{unknowns}$ to $T_{disabled}$)
- else if status=occurred Then ($count \leftarrow count + 1$)
- $T_{dependents} \leftarrow (\{T_{candidate}\}^{\bullet})^{\bullet}$
- Move ($T_{dependents} \cap T_{disabled}$) from $T_{disabled}$ to $T_{unknowns}$
- End if ;
- End while

5. Experimental results and discussion

In the implementation of the Crazy ball 2 case study game, five game rules in terms of five modules are used namely: "Enemy Create", "Enemy Active", "Enemy Move", "Enemy effect", and "Enemy Attack". The "Enemy Create" module is basically used to create the desired enemy with some collection of predefined attributes and values. The "Enemy Move" module is used to move the enemy object based on its Move ID parameter. For instance, in the case of the "Bad Ball", enemy model, "Enemy Move" module will make it gain positive or negative speed based on the position of the player object. The "Enemy effect" module is used to make the object emit special effects or change colors based on its Effect ID parameter. The "Enemy Attack" module will make the enemy engages or do damage based on its Attack ID parameter. Finally, the "Enemy Active" module enables the enemy to receive collision and physics calculations. Figure 12 shows some screen shoots for the crazy ball 2 game environment with some enemies challenging modules.

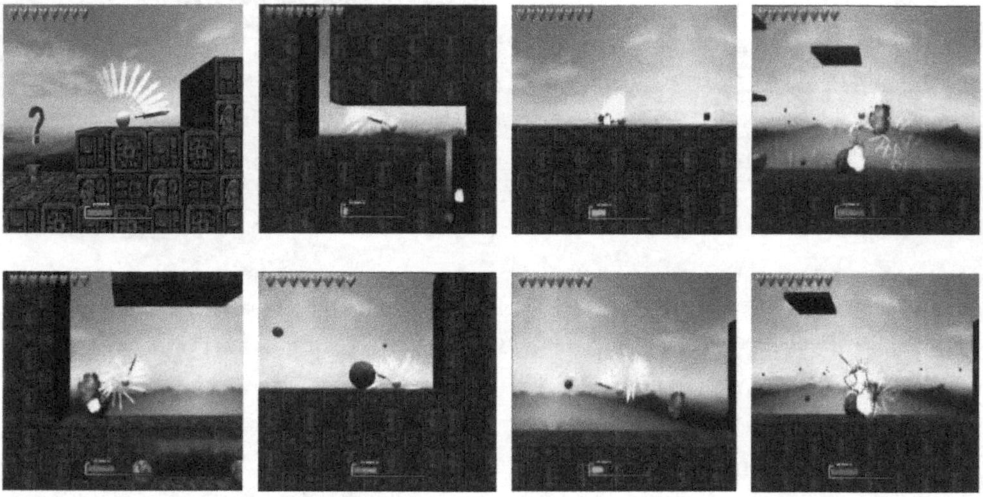

Figure 12. Screenshots for Crazy ball 2 game environment with some enemies challenging modules.

6. Conclusion and future work

This chapter attempts to overcome some problems which are encountered in the interactive drama systems as well as storytelling applications. This is achieved by proposing an integrated framework for deeply combining interactivity and narrative in computer games workflow. The idea is derived from the study of interactive drama, Petri nets (PN), narrative structures in computer games and game workflow activity process. The main contribution of this paper is to show how workflow management concepts can be jointly utilized with Petri nets (PN) for modeling game systems and game workflow control. The main advantages of using PN are that it copes well with branching stories and can evolve in parallel in large virtual world. The proposed idea is supported by some case study called Crazy ball 2. Further research effort is still needed for establishing more relationship between the game workflow activity process and other entertainment game applications with different graphics aspects, interfaces and contents.

Author details

Hussein Karam Hussein Abd El-Sattar
Ain Shams University, Faculty of Science, Mathematics & Computer Science Dept., Abbassia, Cairo, Egypt
Al-Yamamah University, CCIS, Riyadh, KSA

7. References

Brom, C.; Abonyi, A. (2006). Petri nets for game plot, *In Proc. of AISB*, Vol. 3, pp. 3-13, AISB press, 2006

Brom, C.; Sisler, V.; and Holan, T. (2007). Story manager in Europe 2045 uses Petri nets, Proceedings of the 4th International Conf. on Virtual Storytelling, LNCS 4871, pp. 38-50, Springer-verlag, 2007

Delmas, G.; Champagnat, R.; and Augeraud, M., (2007). Plot monitoring for interactive narrative games, *Proc. of ACE07*, Austria, pp. 17-20, 2007

Jenson, K. (1997). *Coloured Petri nets-based concepts, analysis methods and practical use* (2nd Edition), Springer-Verlage, New York, 1997

Karam, H., (2010). A new plot/character-based interactive system for story-based virtual reality applications, *International Journal of image and graphics*, Vol. 10, No. 1, 2010

Magerko, B.; Laird, J. (2003). Building interactive drama architecture, ACM SIGCHI International Conf. on Advances in Computer Entertainment technology, ACE 2003

Mark Reidl, O., Michael R. (2005). From linear story generation to branching story graphs, *American Association for AI*, 2005

Meehan, J. (1981). TALE_SPIN, Shank, R. C. and Riesbeck C. K. (Eds.), *Inside Computer Understanding: Five programs plus Miniatures* (Erlbaum, Hillsdale NJ), pp.197

Peterson, J. L. (1997). Petri Nets. ACM Computing Sueveys, Vol 9, No. 3, 1977

Riedl , M.; Stern, A., (2006). Believable agent and intelligent story adaptation for interactive storytelling, In Proc. of TIDSE, LNCS 4326, Springer-verlage, pp. 1-12, 2006

Salen, K., Zimmerman, E. (2003). *The rules of play*, MIT Press, 2003

Sheldon, L., (2004). *Character development and storytelling, Thompson course Technology, 2004.*

Szilas, N. (2005). The future of interactive drama, Proc. of IE2005, the Second Australian Conference on Interactive Entertainment, ISBN: 0-9751533-2-3, 2005

Tado, M. (1990). Petri Nets: Properties, Analysis and Applications. Proc. IEEE, 77, 1990

Van der Aalst, W. (1998). The application of petri nets to workflow management, the journal of Circuits, Systems and Computers 8, (1), pp. 21-66, 1998.

Chapter 5

Timed Petri Nets in Performance Exploration of Simultaneous Multithreading

Wlodek M. Zuberek

Additional information is available at the end of the chapter

1. Introduction

In modern computer systems, the performance of the whole system is increasingly often limited by the performance of its memory subsystem [1]. Due to continuous progress in manufacturing technologies, the performance of processors has been doubling every 18 months (the so–called Moore's law [2]), but the performance of memory chips has been improving only by 10% per year [1], creating a "performance gap" in matching processor's performance with the required memory bandwidth [3]. More detailed studies have shown that the number of processor cycles required to access main memory doubles approximately every six years [4]. In effect, it is becoming more and more often the case that the performance of applications depends on the performance of the system's memory hierarchy and it is not unusual that as much as 60% of time processors spend waiting for the completion of memory operations [4].

Memory hierarchies, and in particular multi–level cache memories, have been introduced to reduce the effective latency of memory accesses [5]. Cache memories provide efficient access to information when the information is available at lower levels of memory hierarchy; occasionally, however, long–latency memory operations are needed to transfer the information from the higher levels of memory hierarchy to the lower ones. Extensive research has focused on reducing and tolerating these large memory access latencies.

Techniques which tolerate long–latency memory accesses include out–of–order execution of instructions and instruction–level multithreading. The idea of out–of–order execution [1] is to execute, instead of waiting for the completion of a long–latency operation, instructions which (logically) follow the long–latency one, but which do not depend upon the result of this long–latency operation. Since out–of–order execution exploits instruction–level concurrency in the executed sequential instruction stream, it conveniently maintains code–base compatibility [6]. In effect, the instruction stream is dynamically decomposed into micro-threads, which are scheduled and synchronized at no cost in terms of executing additional instructions. Although this is desirable, speedups using out–of–order execution on superscalar pipelines are not so impressive, and it is difficult to obtain a speedup greater than 2 using 4 or 8-way superscalar issue [7]. Moreover, in modern processors, memory latencies are so long that out–of–order processors require very large instruction windows to tolerate them.

Although ultra–wide out-of-order superscalar processors were predicted as the architecture of one-billion-transistor chips, with a single 16 or 32-wide-issue processing core and huge branch predictors to sustain good instruction level parallelism, the industry has not been moving toward the wide–issue superscalar model [8]. Design complexity and power efficiency direct the industry toward narrow–issue, high–frequency cores and multithreaded processors. According to [6]: "Clearly something is very wrong with the out–of–order approach to concurrency if this extravagant consumption of on–chip resources is only providing a practical limit on speedup of about 2."

Instruction–level multithreading [9], [10], [1] is a technique of tolerating long–latency memory accesses by switching to another thread (if it is available for execution) rather than waiting for the completion of the long–latency operation. If different threads are associated with different sets of processor registers, switching from one thread to another (called "context switching") can be done very efficiently [11], in one or just a few processor cycles.

In simultaneous multithreading [12], [6] several threads can issue instructions at the same time. If a processor contains several functional units or it contains more than one instruction execution pipeline, the instructions can be issued simultaneously; if there is only one pipeline, only one instruction can be issued in each processor cycle, but the (simultaneous) threads complement each other in the sense that whenever one thread cannot issue an instruction (because of pipeline stalls or context switching), an instruction is issued from another thread, eliminating 'empty' instruction slots and increasing the overall performance of the processor.

Simultaneous multithreading combines hardware features of wide-issue superscalar processors and multithreaded processors [12]. From superscalar processors it inherits the ability to issue multiple instructions in each cycle; from multithreaded processors it takes hardware state for several threads. The result is a processor that can issue multiple instructions from multiple threads in each processor cycle, achieving better performance for a variety of workloads.

The main objective of this work is to study the performance of simultaneously multithreaded processors in order to determine how effective simultaneous multithreading can be. In particular, an indication is sought if simultaneous multithreading can overcome the out–of–order's "barrier" of the speedup (equal to 2 [13]). A timed Petri net [14] model of multithreaded processors at the instruction execution level is developed, and performance results for this model are obtained by event–driven simulation of the developed model. Since the model is rather simple, simulation results are verified (with respect to accuracy) by state–space–based performance analysis (for those combinations of modeling parameters for which the state space remains reasonably small).

Section 2 recalls basic concepts of timed Petri nets which are used in this study. A model of simultaneous multithreading, used for performance exploration, is presented in Section 3. Section 4 discusses the results obtained by event–driven simulation of the model introduced in Section 3. Section 5 contains concluding remarks including a short comparison of simulation and analytical results.

2. Timed Petri nets

A marked place/transition Petri net $\mathcal{M}$ is typically defined [15] [16] as $\mathcal{M} = (\mathcal{N}, m_0)$, where the structure $\mathcal{N}$ is a bipartite directed graph, $\mathcal{N} = (P, T, A)$, with a set of places P, a set of transitions T, a set of directed arcs A connecting places with transitions and transitions with places, $A \subseteq T \times P \cup P \times T$, and the initial marking function m_0 which assigns nonnegative numbers of tokens to places of the net, $m_0 : P \rightarrow \{0, 1, ...\}$. Marked nets can be equivalently defined as $\mathcal{M} = (P, T, A, m_0)$.

A place p is an input place of a transition t if the (directed) arc (p, t) is in the set A. A place is shared if it is an input place to more than one transition. If a net does not contain shared places, the net is (structurally) conflict–free, otherwise the net contains conflicts. The simplest case of conflicts is known as a free–choice (or generalized free–choice) structure; a shared place is (generalized) free–choice if all transitions sharing it have identical sets of input places. A net is free–choice if all its shared places are free–choice. The transitions sharing a free–choice place constitute a free–choice class of transitions. For each marking function, and each free–choice class of transitions, either all transitions in this class are enabled or none of them is. It is assumed that the selection of transitions for firing within each free–choice class is a random process which can be described by "choice probabilities" assigned to (free–choice) transitions. Moreover, it is usually assumed that the random variables describing choice probabilities in different free–choice classes are independent.

All places which are not conflict–free and not free–choice, are conflict places. Transitions sharing conflict places are (directly or indirectly) potentially in conflict (i.e., they are in conflict or not depending upon a marking function; for different marking functions the sets of transitions which are in conflict can be different). All transitions which are potentially is conflict constitute a conflict class. All conflict classes are disjoint. It is assumed that conflicts are resolved by random choices of occurrences among the conflicting transitions. These random choice are independent in different conflict classes.

In timed nets [14], occurrence times are associated with transitions, and transition occurrences are real–time events, i.e., tokens are removed from input places at the beginning of the occurrence period, and they are deposited to the output places at the end of this period. All occurrences of enabled transitions are initiated in the same instants of time in which the transitions become enabled (although some enabled transitions may not initiate their occurrences). If, during the occurrence period of a transition, the transition becomes enabled again, a new, independent occurrence can be initiated, which will overlap with the other occurrence(s). There is no limit on the number of simultaneous occurrences of the same transition (sometimes this is called infinite occurrence semantics). Similarly, if a transition is enabled "several times" (i.e., it remains enabled after initiating an occurrence), it may start several independent occurrences in the same time instant.

More formally, a timed Petri net is a triple, $\mathcal{T} = (\mathcal{M}, c, f)$, where $\mathcal{M}$ is a marked net, c is a choice function which assigns choice probabilities to free–choice classes of transitions or relative frequencies of occurrences to conflicting transitions (for non–conflict transitions c simply assigns 1.0), $c : T \rightarrow \mathbf{R}^{0,1}$, where $\mathbf{R}^{0,1}$ is the set of real numbers in the interval [0,1], and f is a timing function which assigns an (average) occurrence time to each transition of the net, $f : T \rightarrow \mathbf{R}^{+}$, where $\mathbf{R}^{+}$ is the set of nonnegative real numbers.

The occurrence times of transitions can be either deterministic or stochastic (i.e., described by some probability distribution function); in the first case, the corresponding timed nets are referred to as D–timed nets [18], in the second, for the (negative) exponential distribution of firing times, the nets are called M–timed nets (Markovian nets [17]). In both cases, the concepts of state and state transitions have been formally defined and used in the derivation of different performance characteristics of the model [14]. Only D–timed Petri nets are used in this paper.

The firing times of some transitions may be equal to zero, which means that the firings are instantaneous; all such transitions are called *immediate* while the other are called *timed*. Since the immediate transitions have no tangible effects on the (timed) behavior of the model, it is convenient to split the set of transitions into two parts, the set of immediate and the set of timed transitions, and to fire first the (enabled) immediate transitions; only when no more immediate transitions are enabled, the firings of (enabled) timed transitions are initiated (still in the same instant of time). It should be noted that such a convention effectively introduces the priority of immediate transitions over the timed ones, so the conflicts of immediate and timed transitions should be avoided. Consequently, the free–choice and conflict classes of transitions must be "uniform", i.e., all transitions in each such class must be either immediate or timed, but not both.

Performance analysis of net models can be based on their behavior (i.e., the set of reachable states) or on the structure of the net; the former is called *reachability analysis* and the latter – *structural analysis*. For reachability analysis, the state space of the analyzed model must be finite and reasonably small while for structural analysis the model must satisfy a number of structural conditions. However, since timed Petri net models are discrete–event systems, their analysis can also be based on discrete–event simulation, which imposes very few restrictions on the class of analyzed models. All performance characteristics of simultaneous multithreading presented in Section 4 are obtained by event–driven simulation [19] of timed Petri net models shown in the next section.

3. Models of simultaneous multithreading

A timed Petri net model of a simple multithreaded processor is shown in Fig.1 (as usually, timed transitions are represented by solid bars, and immediate ones, by thin bars).

For simplicity, Fig.1 shows only one level of memory; this simplification is removed further in this section.

Ready is a pool of available threads; it is assumed that the number of of threads is constant and does not change during program execution (this assumption is motivated by steady–state considerations). If the processor is idle (place *Next* is marked), one of available threads is selected for execution (transition *Tsel*). *Cont*, if marked, indicates that an instruction is ready to be issued to the execution pipeline. Instruction execution is modeled by transition *Trun* which represents the first stage of the execution pipeline. It is assumed that once the instruction enters the pipeline, it will progress through the stages and, eventually, leave the pipeline; since these pipeline implementation details are not important for performance analysis of the processor, they are not represented here.

Done is another free-choice place which determines if the current instruction performs a long–latency access to memory or not. If the current instruction is a non–long–latency one, *Tnxt* occurs (with the corresponding probability), and another instruction is fetched for issuing. *Pnxt* is a free-choice place with three possible outcomes: *Tst0* (with the choice probability p_{s0}) represents issuing an instruction without any further delay; *Tst1* (with the

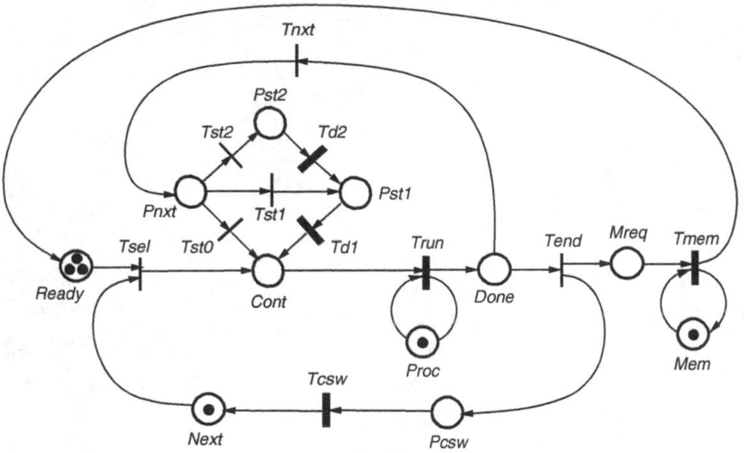

Figure 1. Petri net model of a multithreaded processor.

choice probability p_{s1}) represents a single-cycle pipeline stall (modeled by *Td1*), and *Tst2* (with the choice probability p_{s2}) represents a two–cycle pipeline stall (*Td2* and then *Td1*); other pipeline stalls could be represented in a similar way, if needed.

If long–latency operation is detected in the issued instruction, *Tend* initiates two concurrent actions: (i) context switching performed by enabling an occurrence of *Tcsw*, after which a new thread is selected for execution (if it is available), and (ii) a memory access request is entered into *Mreq*, the memory queue, and after accessing the memory (transition *Tmem*), the thread, suspended for the duration of memory access, becomes "ready" again and joins the pool of threads *Ready*. *Tmem* will typically represent a cache miss (with all its consequences); cache hits (at the first level cache memory) are not considered long-latency operations.

The choice probability associated with *Tend* determines the runlength of a thread, ℓ_t, i.e., the average number of instructions between two consecutive long–latency operations; if this choice probability is equal to 0.1, the runlength is equal to 10, if it is equal to 0.2, the runlength is 5, and so on.

Proc, which is connected to *Trun*, controls the number of pipelines. If the processor contains just one instruction execution pipeline, the initial marking assigns a single token to *Proc* as only one instruction can be issued in each processor cycle. In order to model a processor with two (identical) pipelines, two initial tokens are needed in *Proc*, and so on.

The number of memory ports, i.e., the number of simultaneous accesses to memory, is controlled by the initial marking of *Mem*; for a single port memory, the initial marking assigns just a single token to *Mem*, for dual-port memory, two tokens are assigned to *Mem*, and so on.

In a similar way, the number of simultaneous threads (or instruction issue units) is controlled by the initial marking of *Next*.

Memory hierarchy can be incorporated into the model shown in Fig.1 by refining the representation of memory. In particular, levels of memory hierarchy can be introduced by replacing the subnet *Tmem–Mem* by a number of subnets, each subnet for one level of the hierarchy, and adding a free–choice structure which randomly selects the submodel according

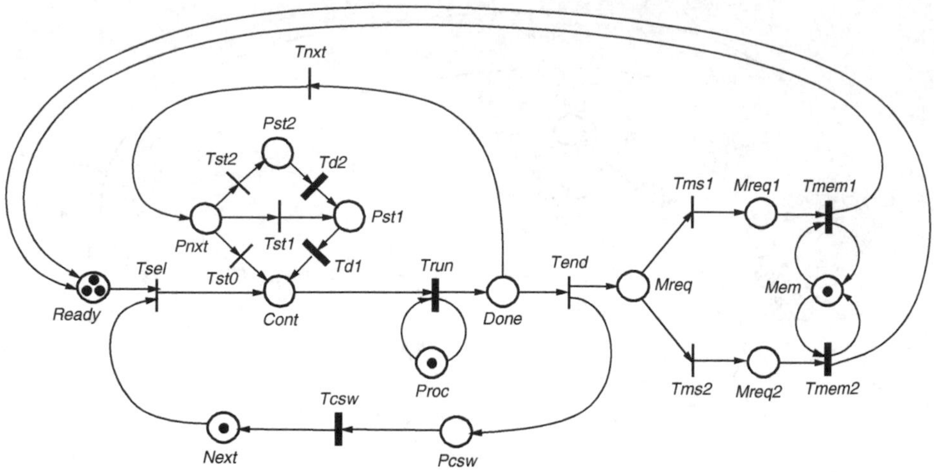

Figure 2. Petri net model of a multithreaded processor with a two–level memory.

to probabilities describing the use of the hierarchical memory. Such a refinement, for two levels of memory (in addition to the first-level cache), is shown in Fig.2, where *Mreq* is a free–choice place selecting either level–1 (submodel *Mem–Tmem1*) or level–2 (submodel *Mem–Tmem2*). More levels of memory can be easily added similarly, if needed.

The effects of memory hierarchy can be compared with a uniform, non–hierarchical memory by selecting the parameters in such a way that the average access time of the hierarchical model (Fig.2) is equal to the access time of the non–hierarchical model (Fig.1).

Processors with different numbers of instruction issue units and instruction execution pipelines can be described by a pair of numbers, the first number denoting the number of instruction issue units, and the second – the number of instruction execution pipelines. In this sense a 3-2 processor is a (multithreaded) processor with 3 instruction issue units and 2 instruction execution pipelines.

For convenience, all temporal properties are expressed in processor cycles, so, the occurrence times of *Trun*, *Td1* and *Td2* are all equal to 1 (processor cycle), the occurrence time of *Tcsw* is equal to the number of processor cycles needed for a context switch (which is equal to 1 for many of the following performance analyzes), and the occurrence time of *Tmem* is the average number of processor cycles needed for a long–latency access to memory.

The main modeling parameters and their typical values are shown in Table 1.

4. Performance exploration

The model developed in the previous section is evaluated for different combinations of modeling parameters. Performance results are obtained by event-driven simulation of timed Petri net models.

The utilization of the processor and memory, as a function of the number of available threads, for a 1-1 processor (i.e., a processor with a single instruction issue unit and a single instruction execution pipeline) is shown in Fig. 3.

symbol	*parameter*	*value*
n_t	number of available threads	1,...,10
n_p	number of execution pipelines	1,2,...
n_s	number of simultaneous threads	1,2,3,...
ℓ_t	thread runlength	10
t_m	average memory access time	5
t_{cs}	context switching time	1,3
p_{s1}	prob. of one–cycle pipeline stall	0.2
p_{s2}	prob. of two–cycle pipeline stall	0.1

Table 1. Simultaneous multithreading – modeling parameters and their typical values

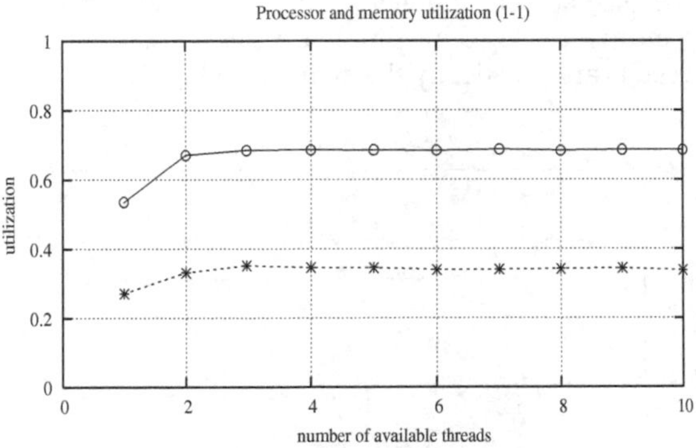

Figure 3. Processor (-o-) and memory (-x-) utilization for a 1-1 processor; $l_t = 10$, $t_m = 5$, $t_{cs} = 1$, $p_{s1} = 0.2$, $p_{s2} = 0.1$

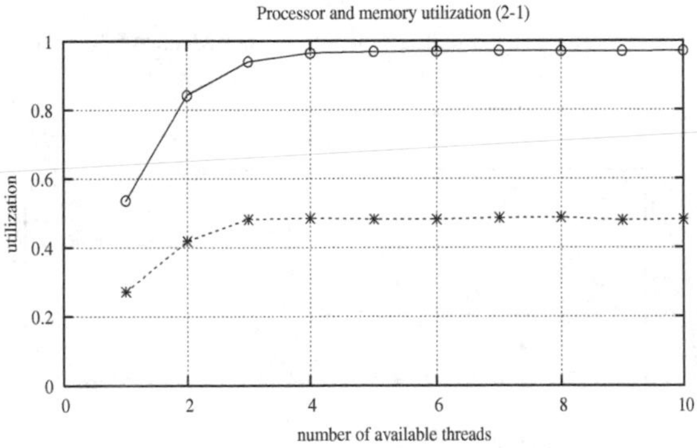

Figure 4. Processor (-o-) and memory (-x-) utilization for a 2-1 processor; $l_t = 10$, $t_m = 5$, $t_{cs} = 1$, $p_{s1} = 0.2$, $p_{s2} = 0.1$

The value of the processor utilization for $n_t = 1$ (i.e., for one thread) can be derived from the (average) number of unused instruction issuing slots. Since the probability of a single–cycle stall is 0.2, and probability of a two–cycle stall is 0.1, on average 40 % of issuing slots remain unused because of pipeline stalls (for all instructions except the first one in each thread). Processor utilization for one thread is thus $\ell_t/(\ell_t + (\ell_t - 1) * 0.4 + t_m) = 10/18.6 = 0.537$, which corresponds very well with Fig.3. For a large number of threads processor utilization is obtained similarly, but with the context switching time, t_{cs}, replacing t_m, so it is $\ell_t/(\ell_t + (\ell_t - 1) * 0.4 + t_{cs}) = 0.685$.

The utilization of the processor can be improved by introducing a second (simultaneous) thread which issues its instructions in the slots unused by the first slot. Fig.4 shows the utilization of the processor and memory for a 2-1 processor, i.e., a processor with two (simultaneous) threads (or two instruction issue units) and a single pipeline. The utilization of the processor is improved by almost 50 % and is within a few percent from its upper bound (of 100 %).

The influence of pipeline stalls (probabilities p_{s1} and p_{s2}) is shown in Fig.5 and Fig.6. Fig.5 shows that the performance actually depends upon the total number of stalls rather than specific values of p_{s1} and p_{s2}; in Fig.5 all pipeline stalls are single–cycle ones, so $p_{s1} = 0.4$ and $p_{s2} = 0$, and the results are practically the same as in Fig. 3.

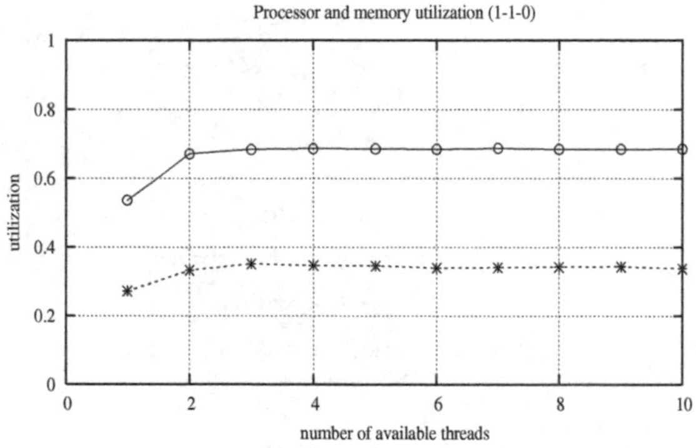

Figure 5. Processor (-o-) and memory (-x-) utilization for a 1-1 processor; $l_t = 10$, $t_m = 5$, $t_{cs} = 1$, $p_{s1} = 0.4$, $p_{s2} = 0$

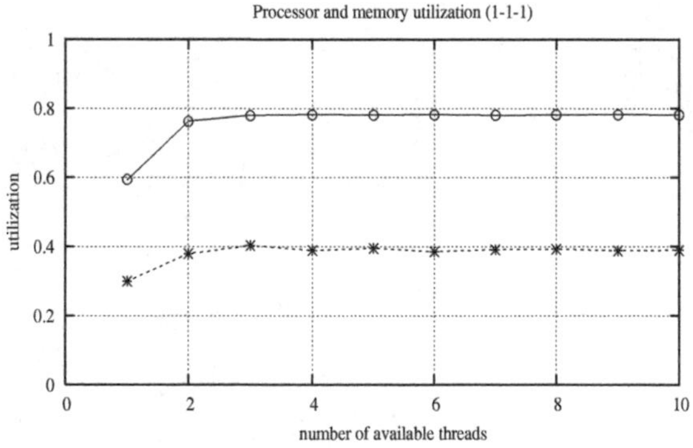

Figure 6. Processor (-o-) and memory (-x-) utilization for a 1-1 processor; $l_t = 10$, $t_m = 5$, $t_{cs} = 1$, $p_{s1} = 0.2$, $p_{s2} = 0$

Fig. 6 shows the utilizations of processor and memory for reduced probabilities of pipeline stalls, i.e., for $p_{s1} = 0.2$ and $p_{s2} = 0$. As is expected, the utilizations are higher than in Fig.3 and Fig.5.

A more realistic model of memory, that captures the idea of a two–level hierarchy, is shown in Fig.2. In order to compare the results of this model with Fig.3 and Fig.4, the parameters of the two–level memory are chosen in such a way that the average memory access time is equal to the memory access time in Fig.1 (where $t_m = 5$). Let the two levels of memory have access times equal to 4 and 20, respectively; then the choice probabilities are equal to 15/16 and 1/16 for level–1 and level–2, respectively, and the average access time is:

$$4 * \frac{15}{16} + 20 * \frac{1}{16} = 5.$$

The results for a 1-1 processor with a two–level memory are shown in Fig.7, and for a 2-1 processor in Fig.8.

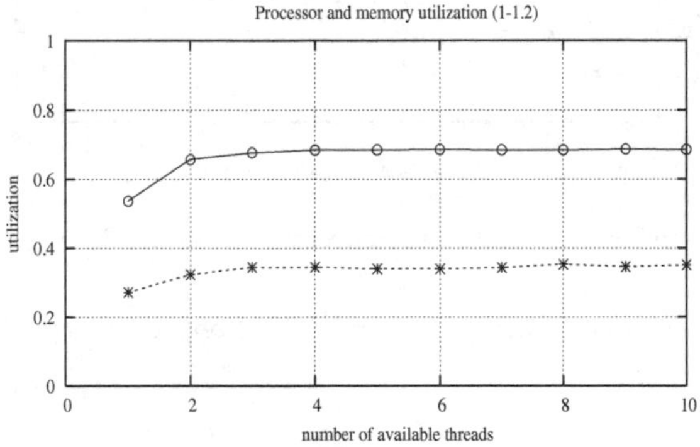

Figure 7. Processor (-o-) and memory (-x-) utilization for a 1-1 processor with 2-level memory; $l_t = 10$, $t_m = 4 + 20$, $t_{cs} = 1$, $p_{s1} = 0.2$, $p_{s2} = 0.1$

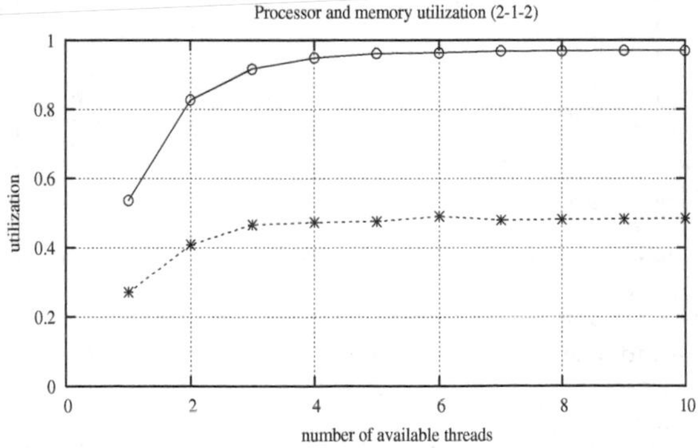

Figure 8. Processor (-o-) and memory (-x-) utilization for a 2-1 processor with 2-level memory; $l_t = 10$, $t_m = 4 + 20$, $t_{cs} = 1$, $p_{s1} = 0.2$, $p_{s2} = 0.1$

The results in Fig.7 and Fig.8 are practically the same as in Fig.3 and Fig.4. This is the reason that the remaining results are shown for (equivalent) one-level memory models; the multiple levels of memory hierarchy apparently have no significant effect on the performance results.

The effects of simultaneous multithreading in a more complex processor, e.g., a processor with two instruction issue units and two instruction execution pipelines, i.e., a 2-2 processor, can be obtained in a very similar way. The utilization of the processor (shown as the sum of the utilizations of both pipelines, with the values ranging from 0 to 2), is shown in Fig.9.

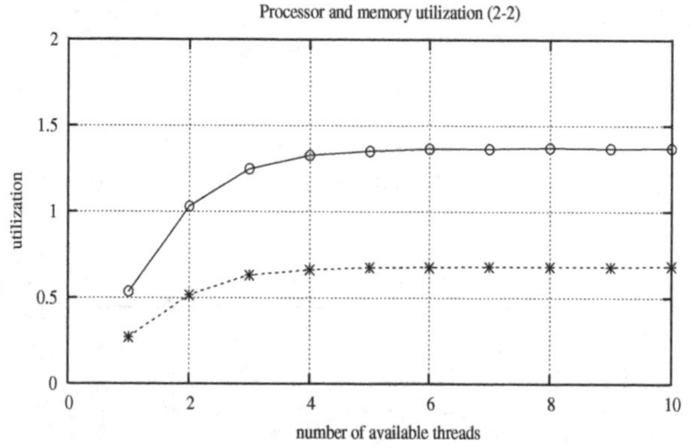

Figure 9. Processor (-o-) and memory (-x-) utilization for a 2-2 processor; $l_t = 10$, $t_m = 5$, $t_{cs} = 1$, $p_{s1} = 0.2$, $p_{s2} = 0.1$

When another instruction issue unit is added, the utilization increases by about 40 %, as shown in Fig.10.

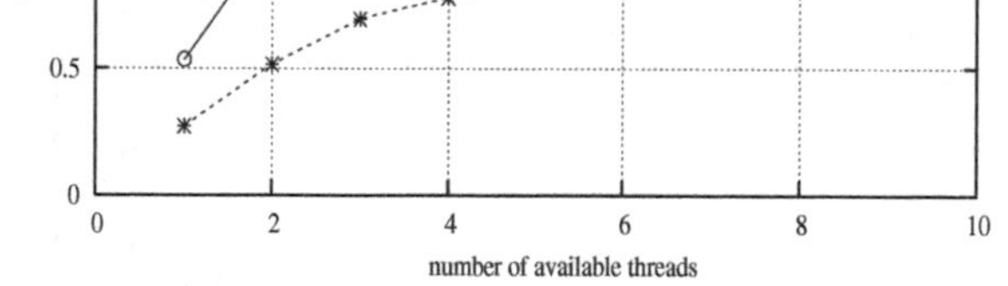

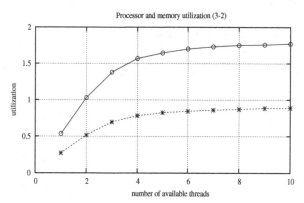

Figure 10. Processor (-o-) and memory (-x-) utilization for a 3-2 processor; $l_t = 10$, $t_m = 5$, $t_{cs} = 1$, $p_{s1} = 0.2$, $p_{s2} = 0.1$

Further increase of the number of the simultaneous threads (in a processor with 2 pipelines) can provide only small improvements of the performance because the utilizations of both, the processor and the memory, are quite close to their limits. The performance of the system can be improved by increasing the number of pipelines, but then the memory becomes the system bottleneck, so its performance also needs to be improved, for example, by introducing dual ports (which allow to handle two accesses at the same time). The performance of a 5-3 processor with a dual-port memory is shown in Fig.11 (the utilization of the processor is the sum of utilizations of its 3 pipelines, so it ranges from 0 to 3).

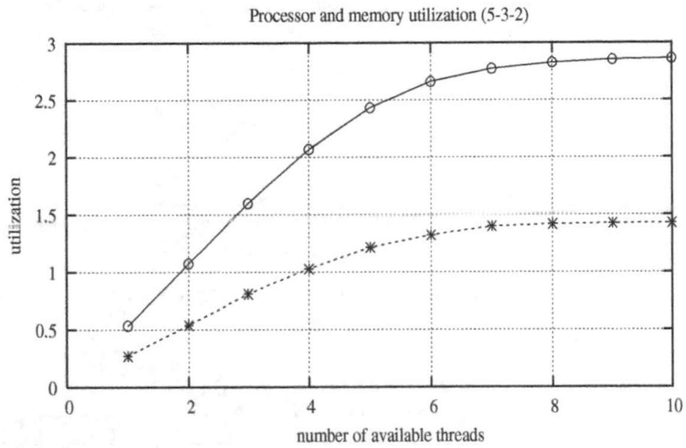

Figure 11. Processor (-o-) and memory (-x-) utilization for a 5-3 processor with dual–port memory; $l_t = 10$, $t_m = 5||2$, $t_{cs} = 1$, $p_{s1} = 0.2$, $p_{s2} = 0.1$

Fig.11 shows that for 3 pipelines and 5 simultaneous threads, the number of available threads greater than 6 provides the speedup that is almost equal to 3.

System bottlenecks can be identified by comparing service demands for different components of the system (in this case, the memory and the pipelines); the component with the maximum service demand is the bottleneck because it is the first component to reach its utilization limit and to prevent any increase of the overall performance. For a single runlength (of all simultaneous threads) the total service demand for memory is equal to $n_s * t_m$, while the service demand for each pipeline (assuming an ideal, uniform distribution of load over the pipelines) is equal to $n_s * \ell_t / n_p$. For a 4-2 processor, the service demands are equal (such a system is usually called "balanced"), so the utilizations of both, the processor and the memory, tend to their limits in a "synchronous" way. For a 5-3 processor with a dual-port memory, the service demand for the pipelines is greater than the service demand for memory, so the number of pipelines could be increased (by one pipeline); for more than 4 pipelines, the memory again becomes the bottleneck.

Simultaneous multithreading is quite flexible with respect to context switching times because the (simultaneous) threads fill the instruction issuing slots which normally would remain empty during context switching. Fig.12 shows the utilization of the processor and memory in a 1-1 processor with $t_{cs} = 3$, i.e., context switching time 3 times longer than in Fig.3. The reduction of the processor's utilization is more than 10 %, and is due to the additional 2 cycles of context switching which remain empty (out of 17 cycles, on average).

Fig.13 shows utilization of the processor and memory in a 2-1 processor, also for $t_{cs} = 3$. The reduction of utilization is much smaller in this case and is within 5 % (when compared with Fig.4).

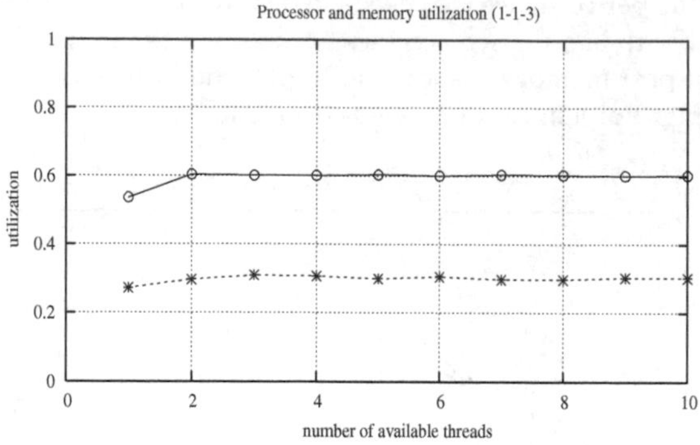

Figure 12. Processor (-o-) and memory (-x-) utilization for a 1-1 processor; $l_t = 10$, $t_m = 5$, $t_{cs} = 3$, $p_{s1} = 0.2$, $p_{s2} = 0.1$

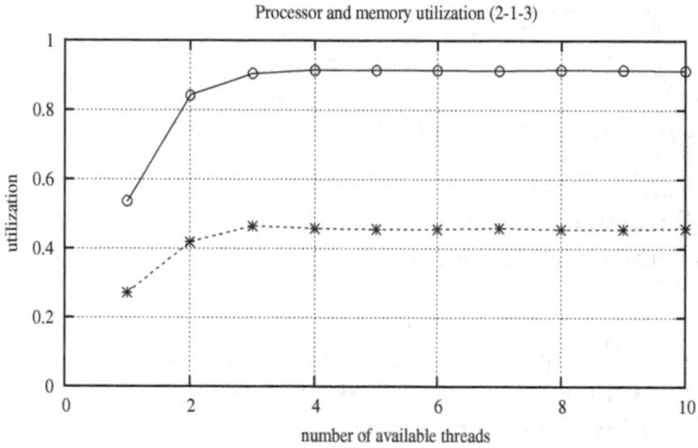

Figure 13. Processor (-o-) and memory (-x-) utilization for a 2-1 processor; $l_t = 10$, $t_m = 5$, $t_{cs} = 3$, $p_{s1} = 0.2$, $p_{s2} = 0.1$

5. Concluding remarks

Simultaneous multithreading discussed in this paper is used to increase the performance of processors by tolerating long–latency operations. Since the long–latency operations are playing increasingly important role in modern computer system, so is simultaneous multithreading. Its implementation as well as the required hardware resources are much simpler than in the case of out–of–order approach, and the resulting speedup scales well with the number of simultaneous threads. The main challenge of simultaneous multithreading is to balance the system by maintaining the right relationship between the number of simultaneous threads and the performance of the memory hierarchy.

All presented results indicate that the number of available threads, required for improved performance of the processor, is quite small, and is typically greater by 2 or 3 threads than the number of simultaneous threads. The results show that a larger number of available threads provides rather insignificant improvements of system's performance.

The presented models of multithreaded processors are quite simple, and for small values of modeling parameters (n_t, n_p, n_s) can be analyzed by the explorations of the state space. The following tables compare some results for the 1-1 processor and 3-2 processors:

n_t	*number of states*	*analytical utilization*	*simulated utilization*
1	11	0.538	0.536
2	52	0.670	0.671
3	102	0.684	0.685
4	152	0.685	0.686
5	202	0.685	0.686

Table 2. A comparison of simulation and analytical results for 1-1 processors.

n_t	*number of states*	*analytical utilization*	*simulated utilization*
1	11	0.538	0.536
2	80	1.030	1.031
3	264	1.384	1.381
4	555	1.568	1.568
5	951	1.655	1.647

Table 3. A comparison of simulation and analytical results for 3-2 processors.

The comparisons show that the results obtained by simulation of net models are very similar to the analytical results obtained from the analysis of states and state transitions.

A similar performance analysis of simultaneous multithreading, but using a slightly different model, was presented in [20]. All results presented there are very similar to results presented in this work which is an indication that the performance of simultaneous multithreaded systems is insensitive to (at least some) variations of implementation.

It should also be noted that the presented model is oversimplified with respect to the probabilities of pipeline stalls and does not take into account the dependence of stall probabilities on the history of instruction issuing. In fact, the model is "pessimistic" in this regard, and the predicted performance, presented in the paper, is worse than the expected performance of real systems. However, the simplification effects are not expected to be significant.

Acknowledgement

The Natural Sciences and Engineering Research Council of Canada partially supported this research through grant RGPIN-8222.

Author details

Wlodek M. Zuberek
Memorial University, St.John's, Canada,
University of Life Sciences, Warsaw, Poland

6. References

[1] Patterson, D.A., Hennessy, J.L. (2006). *Computer architecture – a quantitative approach* (4-th ed.); Morgan Kaufmann.

[2] Hamilton, S. (1999). "Taking Moore's law into the next century"; *IEEE Computer*, vol.32, no.1, pp.43-48.

[3] Wilkes, M.V. (2001). "The memory gap and the future of high-performance memories"; *ACM Architecture News*, vol.29, no.1, pp.2-7.

[4] Sinharoy B. (1997). "Optimized thread creation for processor multithreading"; *The Computer Journal*, vol.40, no.6, pp.388-400.

[5] Baer, J-L. (2010). *Microprocessor architecture: from simple pipelines to chip multiprocessors*; Cambridge University Press.

[6] Jesshope, C. (2003). "Multithreaded microprocessors – evolution or revolution"; in *Advances in Computer Systems Architecture* (LNCS 2823), pp.21-45.

[7] Tseng, J. & Asanovic, K. (2003). "Banked multiport register files for high–frequency superscalar microprocessor"; *Proc. 30-th Int. Annual Symp. on Computer Architecture*, San Diego, CA, pp.62-71.

[8] Burger, D. & Goodman, J.R. (2004). "Billion–transistor architectures: there and back again"; *IEEE Computer*, vol.37, no.3, pp.22-28.

[9] Byrd, G.T. & Holliday, M.A. (1995). "Multithreaded processor architecture"; *IEEE Spectrum*, vol.32, no.8, pp.38-46.

[10] Dennis, J.B. & Gao, G.R. (1994). "Multithreaded architectures: principles, projects, and issues"; in *Multithreaded Computer Architecture: a Summary of the State of the Art*, Kluwer Academic, pp.1-72.

[11] Ungerer, T., Robic, G. & Silc, J. (2002). "Multithreaded processors"; *The Computer Journal*, vol.43, no.3, pp.320-348.

[12] Eggers, S.J., Emer, J.S., Levy, H.M., Lo, J.L., Stamm, R.L. & Tullsen, D.M. (1997). "Simultaneous multithreading: a foundation for next-generation processors"; *IEEE Micro*, vol.17, no.5, pp.12-19.

[13] Mutlu, O., Stark, J., Wilkerson, C. & Patt, Y.N. (2003). "Runahead execution: an effective alternative to large instruction windows"; *IEEE Micro*, vol.23, no.6, pp.20-25.

[14] Zuberek, W.M. (1991). "Timed Petri nets – definitions, properties and applications"; *Microelectronics and Reliability* (Special Issue on Petri Nets and Related Graph Models), vol.31, no.4, pp.627-644.

[15] Murata, T. (1989). "Petri nets: properties, analysis, and applications"; *Proceedings of the IEEE*, vol.77, no.4, pp.541-580.

[16] Reisig, W. (1985). *Petri nets – an introduction* (EATCS Monographs on Theoretical Computer Science 4); Springer-Verlag.

[17] Zuberek, W.M. (1986). "M–timed Petri nets, priorities, preemptions, and performance evaluation of systems"; in *Advances in Petri Nets 1985* (LNCS 222), Springer-Verlag, pp.478-498.

[18] Zuberek, W.M. (1987). "D–timed Petri nets and modelling of timeouts and protocols"; *Transactions of the Society for Computer Simulation*, vol.4, no.4, pp.331-357.

[19] Zuberek, W.M. (1996). "Modeling using timed Petri nets – discrete–event simulation"; Technical Report #9602, Department of Computer Science, Memorial University, St. John's, Canada A1B 3X5.

[20] Zuberek, W.M. (2007). "Modeling and analysis of simultaneous multithreading"; *Proc. 14-th Int. Conf. on Analytical and Stochastic Modeling Techniques and Applications (ASMTA-07)*, a part of the *21-st European Conference on Modeling and Simulation (ECMS'07)*, Prague, Czech Republic, pp.115-120.

Chapter 6

Grammars Controlled by Petri Nets

J. Dassow, G. Mavlankulov, M. Othman, S. Turaev, M.H. Selamat and R. Stiebe

Additional information is available at the end of the chapter

1. Introduction

Formal language theory, introduced by Noam Chomsky in the 1950s as a tool for a description of natural languages [8–10], has also been widely involved in modeling and investigating phenomena appearing in computer science, artificial intelligence and other related fields because the symbolic representation of a modeled system in the form of strings makes its processes by information processing tools very easy: coding theory, cryptography, computation theory, computational linguistics, natural computing, and many other fields directly use sets of strings for the description and analysis of modeled systems. In formal language theory a model for a phenomenon is usually constructed by representing it as a set of words, i.e., a *language* over a certain alphabet, and defining a generative mechanism, i.e., a *grammar* which identifies exactly the words of this set. With respect to the forms of their rules, grammars and their languages are divided into four classes of *Chomsky hierarchy*: *recursively enumerable*, *context-sensitive*, *context-free* and *regular*.

Context-free grammars are the most investigated type of Chomsky hierarchy which, in addition, have good mathematical properties and are extensively used in many applications of formal languages. However, they cannot cover all aspects which occur in modeling of phenomena. On the other hand, context-sensitive grammars, the next level in Chomsky hierarchy, are too powerful to be used in applications of formal languages, and have bad features, for instance, for context-sensitive grammars, the emptiness problem is undecidable and the existing algorithms for the membership problem, thus for the parsing, have exponential complexities. Moreover, such concepts as a derivation tree, which is an important tool for the analysis of context-free languages, cannot be transformed to context-sensitive grammars. Therefore, it is of interest to consider "intermediate" grammars which are more powerful than context-free grammars and have similar properties. One type of such grammars, called *grammars with regulated rewriting* (*controlled* or *regulated grammars* for short), is defined by considering grammars with some additional mechanisms which extract some subset of the generated language in order to cover some aspects of modeled phenomena. Due to the variety of investigated practical and theoretical problems, different additional mechanisms to grammars can be considered. Since Abraham [1] first defined matrix grammars in 1965, several grammars with restrictions such as programmed, random context, valence grammars, and etc., have been introduced (see [16]). However, the rapid developments in present day technology, industry, medicine and other areas challenge to deal with more and more new and complex problems, and to look for new suitable tools for the modeling and investigation of these problems. *Petri net controlled grammars*, which introduce *concurrently parallel control mechanisms* in formal language theory, were proposed as a theoretical model for some problems appearing in systems biology and automated manufacturing systems (see [18–23, 56, 59–62]).

Petri nets, which are graphical and mathematical modeling tools applicable to many concurrent, asynchronous, distributed, parallel, nondeterministic and stochastic systems, have widely been used in the study of formal languages. One of the fundamental approaches in this area is to consider Petri nets as language generators. If the transitions in a Petri net are labeled with a set of (not necessary distinct) symbols, a sequence of transition firing generates a string of symbols. The set of strings generated by all possible firing sequences defines a language called a Petri net language, which can be used to model the flow of information and control of actions in a system. With different kinds of labeling functions and different kinds of final marking sets, various classes of Petri net languages were introduced and investigated by Hack [34] and Peterson [46]. The relationship between Petri net languages and formal languages were thoroughly investigated by Peterson in [47]. It was shown that all regular languages are Petri net languages and the family of Petri net languages are strictly included in the family of context-sensitive languages but some Petri net languages are not context-free and some context-free languages are not Petri net languages. It was also shown that the complement of a free Petri net language is context-free [12].

Another approach to the investigation of formal languages was considered by Crespi-Reghizzi and Mandrioli [11]. They noticed the similarity between the firing of a transition and application of a production rule in a derivation in which places are nonterminals and tokens are separate instances of the nonterminals. The major difference of this approach is the lack of ordering information in the Petri net contained in the sentential form of the derivation. To accommodate it, they defined the commutative grammars, which are isomorphic to Petri nets. In addition, they considered the relationship of Petri nets to matrix, scattered-context, nonterminal-bounded, derivation-bounded, equal-matrix and Szilard languages in [13].

The approach proposed by Crespi-Reghizzi and Mandrioli was used in the following works. By extending the type of Petri nets introduced in [11] with the places for the terminal symbols and arcs for the control of nonterminal occurrences in sentential forms, Marek and Češka showed that for every random-context grammar, an isomorphic Petri net can be constructed, where each derivation of the grammar is simulated by some occurrence sequence of transitions of the Petri net, and vice versa. In [39] the relationship between vector grammars and Petri nets was investigated, partially, hybrid Petri nets were introduced and the equality of the family of hybrid Petri net languages and the family of vector languages was shown. By reduction to Petri net reachability problems, Hauschildt and Jantzen [35] could solve a number of open problems in regulated rewriting systems, specifically, every matrix language without appearance checking over one letter alphabet is regular and the finiteness problem for the families of matrix and random context languages is decidable; In several papers [2, 14, 25], Petri nets are used as minimization techniques for context-free (graph) grammars. For instance, in [2], algorithms to eliminate erasing and unit (chain) rules, algorithms to remove useless rules using the Petri net concept are introduced.

Control by Petri nets has also been introduced and studied in automata theory [26–28, 38] and grammar systems theory [6].

In this chapter we summarize the recent obtained results on Petri net controlled grammars and propose new problems for further research.

In Section 2 we recall some basic concepts and results from the areas formal languages and Petri nets: strings, grammars, languages, Petri nets, Petri net languages and so on, which will be used in the next sections.

In Section 3 we define a *context-free Petri net* (a *cf Petri net* for short), where places correspond to nonterminals, transitions are the counterpart of the production rules, the tokens reflect the occurrences of symbols in the sentential form, and there is a one-to-one correspondence between the application of (sequence of) rules and the firing of (sequence of) transitions. Further, we introduce grammars controlled by k-Petri nets, i.e., cf Petri nets with additional k places, and studies the computational power and closure properties of families of languages generated by k-Petri net controlled grammars.

In Section 4 we consider a generalization of the k-Petri net controlled grammars: we associate an arbitrary place/ transition net with a context-free grammar and require that the sequence of applied rules corresponds to an occurrence sequence of transitions in the Petri net. With respect to different labeling strategies and different definitions of final marking sets, we define various classes of Petri net controlled grammars. Here we study the influence of the labeling functions and the effect of the final markings on the generative power.

It is known that many decision problems in formal language theory are equivalent to the reachability problem in Petri net theory, which has been shown that it is decidable, however, it has exponential time complexity. The result of this has been the definition of a number of structural subclasses of Petri nets with a smaller complexity and still adequate modeling power. Thus, it is interesting to consider grammars controlled by such kind of subclasses of Petri nets. In Section 5 we continue our study of arbitrary Petri net controlled grammars by restricting Petri nets to their structural subclasses, i.e., special Petri nets such as state machines, marked graphs, and free-choice nets, and so on.

In Section 6 we examine Petri net controlled grammars with respect to dynamical properties of Petri nets: we use (cf and arbitrary) Petri nets with place capacities. We also investigate capacity-bounded grammars which are counterparts of grammars controlled by Petri nets with place capacities.

In Section 7 we draw some general conclusions and present suggestions for further research.

2. Preliminaries

In this section we recall some prerequisites, by giving basic notions and notations of the theories formal languages, Petri nets and Petri net languages which are used in the next sections. The reader is referred to [16, 34, 36, 42, 45, 47, 50, 52] for further information.

2.1 General notions and notations

Throughout the chapter we use the following general notations. $\in$ denotes the membership of an element to a set while the negation of set membership is denoted by $\notin$. The inclusion is denoted by $\subseteq$ and the strict (proper) inclusion is denoted by $\subset$. The symbol $\emptyset$ denotes the empty set. The set of positive (non-negative) integers is denoted by $\mathbb{N}$ ($\mathbb{N}_0$). The set of integers is denoted by $\mathbb{Z}$. The power set of a set X is denoted by 2^X, while the cardinality of a set X is denoted by $|X|$.

Let Σ be an *alphabet* which is a finite nonempty set of symbols. A *string* (sometimes a *word*) over the alphabet Σ is a finite sequence of symbols from Σ. The *empty* string is denoted by λ. The *length* of a word w, denoted by $|w|$, is the number of occurrences of symbols in w. The number of occurrences of a symbol a in a string w is denoted by $|w|_a$. The set of all strings over the alphabet Σ is denoted by Σ^*. The set of nonempty strings over Σ is denoted by Σ^+, i.e., $\Sigma^+ = \Sigma^* - \{\lambda\}$. A subset of Σ^* is called a *language*. A language $L \in \Sigma^*$ is *λ-free* if $\lambda \notin L$. For two languages $L_1, L_2 \subseteq \Sigma^*$ the *operation shuffle* is defined by

$$\text{Shuf}(L_1, L_2) = \{u_1v_1u_2v_2\cdots u_nv_n \mid u_1u_2\cdots u_n \in L_1, v_1v_2\cdots v_n \in L_2, \\ u_i, v_i \in \Sigma^*, 1 \le i \le n\}$$

and for $L \subseteq \Sigma^*$, $\text{Shuf}^*(L) = \bigcup_{k\ge 1} \text{Shuf}^k(L)$ where

$$\text{Shuf}^1(L) = L \text{ and } \text{Shuf}^k(L) = \text{Shuf}(\text{Shuf}^{k-1}(L), L), k \ge 2.$$

2.2 Grammars

A *phrase structure* (*Chomsky*) grammar is a quadruple $G = (V, \Sigma, S, R)$ where V and Σ are two disjoint alphabets of *nonterminal* and *terminal* symbols, respectively, $S \in V$ is the *start symbol* and $R \subseteq (V \cup \Sigma)^*V(V \cup \Sigma)^* \times (V \cup \Sigma)^*$ is a finite set of (*production*) *rules*. Usually, a rule $(u, v) \in R$ is written in the form $u \to v$. A rule of the form $u \to \lambda$ is called an *erasing rule*.

A phrase structure grammar $G = (V, \Sigma, S, R)$ is called a *GS grammar* (a phrase structure grammar due to Ginsburg and Spanier [31]) if $R \subseteq V^+ \times (V \cup \Sigma)^*$.

The families of languages generated by GS grammars and by phrase structure grammars are denoted by **GS** and **RE**, respectively. It is well-known that the family **GS** is equal to the family **RE**.

A string $x \in (V \cup \Sigma)^*$ *directly derives* a string $y \in (V \cup \Sigma)^*$ in G, written as $x \Rightarrow y$ if and only if there is a rule $u \to v \in R$ such that $x = x_1ux_2$ and $y = x_1vx_2$ for some $x_1, x_2 \in (V \cup \Sigma)^*$. The reflexive and transitive closure of the relation $\Rightarrow$ is denoted by $\Rightarrow^*$. A derivation using the sequence of rules $\pi = r_1r_2\cdots r_k$, $r_i \in R$, $1 \le i \le k$, is denoted by $\overset{\pi}{\Rightarrow}$ or $\xRightarrow{r_1r_2\cdots r_k}$. The *language* generated by G, denoted by $L(G)$, is defined by $L(G) = \{w \in \Sigma^* \mid S \Rightarrow^* w\}$.

A phrase-structure grammar $G = (V, \Sigma, S, R)$ is called *context-sensitive* if each rule $u \to v \in R$ has $u = u_1Au_2$, $v = u_1xu_2$ for $u_1, u_2 \in (V \cup \Sigma)^*$, $A \in V$ and $x \in (V \cup \Sigma)^+$ (in context sensitive grammars $S \to \lambda$ is allowed, provided that S does not appear in the right-hand members of rules in R); *context-free* if each rule $u \to v \in R$ has $u \in V$; *linear* if each rule $u \to v \in R$ has $u \in V$ and $v \in \Sigma^* \cup \Sigma^*V\Sigma^*$; *regular* if each rule $u \to v \in R$ has $u \in V$ and $v \in \Sigma \cup \Sigma V$.

The families of languages generated by context-sensitive, context-free, linear and regular grammars are denoted by **CS**, **CF**, **LIN** and **REG**, respectively. Further we denote the family of finite languages by **FIN**. The next strict inclusions, named *Chomsky hierarchy*, hold (for details, see [52]):

Theorem 1. **FIN** $\subset$ **REG** $\subset$ **LIN** $\subset$ **CF** $\subset$ **CS** $\subset$ **RE**.

2.3 Regulated grammars

The idea of regulated rewriting consists of restricting the application of the rules in a context-free grammar in order to avoid some derivations and hence obtaining a subset of the context-free language generated in usual way. The computational power of some context-free grammars with regulated rewriting turns out to be greater than the power of context-free grammars.

A *regularly controlled grammar* is a quintuple $G = (V, \Sigma, S, R, K)$ where V, Σ, S, R are specified as in a context-free grammar and K is a regular set over R. The language generated by G consists of all words $w \in \Sigma^*$ such that there is a derivation $S \xrightarrow{r_1 r_2 \cdots r_n} w$ where $r_1 r_2 \cdots r_n \in K$.

A *matrix grammar* is a quadruple $G = (V, \Sigma, S, M)$ where V, Σ, S are defined as for a context-free grammar, M is a finite set of *matrices* which are finite strings over a set R of context-free rules (or finite sequences of context-free rules). The language generated by the grammar G is $L(G) = \{w \in \Sigma^* \mid S \stackrel{\pi}{\Rightarrow} w \text{ and } \pi \in M^*\}$.

A *vector grammar* is a quadruple $G = (V, \Sigma, S, M)$ whose components are defined as for a matrix grammar. The language generated by the grammar G is defined by

$$L(G) = \{w \in \Sigma^* \mid S \stackrel{\pi}{\Rightarrow} w \text{ and } \pi \in \text{Shuf}^*(M)\}.$$

An *additive valence grammar* is a quintuple $G = (V, \Sigma, S, R, v)$ where V, Σ, S, R are defined as for a context-free grammar and v is a mapping from R into $\mathbb{Z}$. The language generated by G consists of all strings $w \in \Sigma^*$ such that there is a derivation $S \xrightarrow{r_1 r_2 \cdots r_n} w$ where $\sum_{i=1}^{n} v(r_i) = 0$.

A *positive valence grammar* is a quintuple $G = (V, \Sigma, S, R, v)$ whose components are defined as for additive valence grammars. The language generated by G consists of all strings $w \in \Sigma^*$ such that there is a derivation $S \xrightarrow{r_1 r_2 \cdots r_n} w$ where $\sum_{i=1}^{n} v(r_i) = 0$ and for any $1 \leq j < n$, $\sum_{i=1}^{j} v(r_i) \geq 0$.

The families of languages generated by regularly controlled, matrix, vector, additive valence and positive valence grammars (with erasing rules) are denoted by **rC**, **MAT**, **VEC**, **aV**, **pV** ($\mathbf{rC}^\lambda$, $\mathbf{MAT}^\lambda$, $\mathbf{VEC}^\lambda$, $\mathbf{aV}^\lambda$, $\mathbf{pV}^\lambda$), respectively.

Theorem 2. *The following inclusions and equalities hold (for details, see [16]):*

$$(1)\ \mathbf{CF} \subset \mathbf{aV} = \mathbf{aV}^\lambda \subset \mathbf{MAT} = \mathbf{rC} = \mathbf{pV};$$

$$(2)\ \mathbf{MAT} \subseteq \mathbf{VEC} \subset \mathbf{CS};$$

$$(3)\ \mathbf{MAT} \subseteq \mathbf{MAT}^\lambda = \mathbf{rC}^\lambda = \mathbf{VEC}^\lambda = \mathbf{pV}^\lambda \subset \mathbf{RE}.$$

2.4 Petri nets

A *Petri net* (PN) is a construct $N = (P, T, F, \phi)$ where P and T are disjoint finite sets of *places* and *transitions*, respectively, $F \subseteq (P \times T) \cup (T \times P)$ is the set of *directed arcs*, $\phi : F \to \mathbb{N}$ is a *weight function*.

A Petri net can be represented by a bipartite directed graph with the node set $P \cup T$ where places are drawn as *circles*, transitions as *boxes* and arcs as *arrows*. The arrow representing an arc $(x, y) \in F$ is labeled with $\phi(x, y)$; if $\phi(x, y) = 1$, then the label is omitted.

An *ordinary net* (ON) is a Petri net $N = (P, T, F, \phi)$ where $\phi(x, y) = 1$ for all $(x, y) \in F$. We omit ϕ from the definition of an ordinary net, i.e., $N = (P, T, F)$.

A mapping $\mu : P \to \mathbb{N}_0$ is called a *marking*. For each place $p \in P$, $\mu(p)$ gives the number of *tokens* in p. Graphically, tokens are drawn as small solid *dots* inside circles. ${}^\bullet x = \{y \mid (y, x) \in F\}$ and $x^\bullet = \{y \mid (x, y) \in F\}$ are called *pre-* and *post-sets* of $x \in P \cup T$, respectively. For $t \in T$ ($p \in P$), the elements of ${}^\bullet t$ (${}^\bullet p$) are called *input* places (transitions) and the elements of $t^\bullet$ ($p^\bullet$) are called *output* places (transitions) of t (p).

A transition $t \in T$ is *enabled* by marking μ if and only if $\mu(p) \geq \phi(p, t)$ for all $p \in {}^\bullet t$. In this case t can *occur* (*fire*). Its occurrence transforms the marking μ into the marking μ' defined for each place $p \in P$ by $\mu'(p) = \mu(p) - \phi(p, t) + \phi(t, p)$. We write $\mu \xrightarrow{t} \mu'$ to indicate that the firing of t in μ leads to μ'. A marking μ is called *terminal* if in which no transition is enabled. A finite sequence $t_1 t_2 \cdots t_k$, $t_i \in T, 1 \leq i \leq k$, is called *an occurrence sequence* enabled at a marking μ and finished at a marking μ_k if there are markings $\mu_1, \mu_2, \ldots, \mu_{k-1}$ such that $\mu \xrightarrow{t_1} \mu_1 \xrightarrow{t_2} \ldots \xrightarrow{t_{k-1}} \mu_{k-1} \xrightarrow{t_k} \mu_k$. In short this sequence can be written as $\mu \xrightarrow{t_1 t_2 \cdots t_k} \mu_k$ or $\mu \xrightarrow{\nu} \mu_k$ where $\nu = t_1 t_2 \cdots t_k$. For each $1 \leq i \leq k$, marking μ_i is called *reachable* from marking μ. $\mathcal{R}(N, \mu)$ denotes the set of all reachable markings from a marking μ.

A *marked* Petri net is a system $N = (P, T, F, \phi, \iota)$ where (P, T, F, ϕ) is a Petri net, ι is the *initial marking*.

A Petri net *with final markings* is a construct $N = (P, T, F, \phi, \iota, M)$ where (P, T, F, ϕ, ι) is a marked Petri net and $M \subseteq \mathcal{R}(N, \iota)$ is set of markings which are called *final* markings. An occurrence sequence ν of transitions is called *successful* for M if it is enabled at the initial marking ι and finished at a final marking τ of M. If M is understood from the context, we say that ν is a successful occurrence sequence.

A Petri net N is said to be *k-bounded* if the number of tokens in each place does not exceed a finite number k for any marking reachable from the initial marking ι, i.e., $\mu(p) \leq k$ for all $p \in P$ and for all $\mu \in \mathcal{R}(N, \iota)$. A Petri net N is said to be *bounded* if it is k-bounded for some $k \geq 1$.

A Petri net with *place capacity* is a system $N = (P, T, F, \phi, \iota, \kappa)$ where (P, T, F, ϕ, ι) is a marked Petri net and $\kappa : P \to \mathbb{N}_0$ is a function assigning to each place a number of maximal admissible tokens. A marking μ of the net N is valid if $\mu(p) \leq \kappa(p)$, for each place $p \in P$. A transition $t \in T$ is *enabled* by a marking μ if additionally the successor marking is valid.

2.5 Special Petri nets

It is known that many decision problems are equivalent to the reachability problem [33], which has been shown to be decidable. However, it has exponential space complexity [40], thus from a practical point of view, Petri nets may be too powerful to be analyzed. The result of this has been the definition of a number of subclasses of Petri nets in order to find a subclass with a smaller complexity and still adequate modeling power for practical purposes. These subclasses are defined by restrictions on their structure intended to improve their analyzability. We consider the following main structural subclasses of Petri nets.

A *state machine* (SM) is an ordinary Petri net such that each transition has exactly one input place and exactly one output place, i.e., $|^{\bullet}t| = |t^{\bullet}| = 1$ for all $t \in T$. This means that there can not be concurrency but there can be conflict.

A *generalized state machine* (GSM) is an ordinary Petri net such that $|^{\bullet}t| \leq 1$ and $|t^{\bullet}| \leq 1$ for all $t \in T$.

A *marked graph* (MG) is an ordinary Petri net such that each place has exactly one input transition and exactly one output transition, i.e., $|^{\bullet}p| = |p^{\bullet}| = 1$ for all $p \in P$. This means that there can not be conflict but there can be concurrency.

A *generalized marked graph* (GMG) is an ordinary Petri net such that $|^{\bullet}p| \leq 1$ and $|p^{\bullet}| \leq 1$ for all $p \in P$.

A *casual net* (CN) is a generalized marked graph each subgraph of which is not a a cycle.

A *free-choice* net (FC) is an ordinary Petri net such every arc is either the only arc going from the place, or it is the only arc going to a transition, i.e., that if $p_1^{\bullet} \cap p_2^{\bullet} \neq \emptyset$ then $|p_1^{\bullet}| = |p_2^{\bullet}| = 1$ for all $p_1, p_2 \in P$. This means that there can be both concurrency and conflict but not the same time.

An *extended free-choice* net (EFC) is an ordinary Petri net such that if $p_1^{\bullet} \cap p_2^{\bullet} \neq \emptyset$ then $p_1^{\bullet} = p_2^{\bullet}$ for all $p_1, p_2 \in P$.

An *asymmetric choice net* (AC) is an ordinary Petri net such that if $p_1^{\bullet} \cap p_2^{\bullet} \neq \emptyset$ then $p_1^{\bullet} \subseteq p_2^{\bullet}$ or $p_1^{\bullet} \supseteq p_2^{\bullet}$ for all $p_1, p_2 \in P$. In asymmetric choice nets concurrency and conflict (in sum, confusion) may occur but not asymmetrically.

3. *k*-Petri net controlled grammars

Since a context-free grammar and its derivation process can also be described by a Petri net (see [11]), where places correspond to nonterminals, transitions are the counterpart of the production rules, and the tokens reflect the occurrences of symbols in the sentential form, and there is a one-to-one correspondence between the application of (sequence of) rules and the firing of (sequence of) transitions, it is a very natural and very easy idea to control the derivations in a context-free grammar by adding some features to the associated Petri net. In this section we introduce a Petri net associated with a context-free grammar (i.e., a *context-free Petri net*), construct Petri net control mechanisms from cf Petri nets by adding new places, and define the corresponding grammars, called *k-Petri net controlled grammars*.

The construction of the following type of Petri nets is based on the idea of using similarity between the firing of a transition and the application of a production rule in a derivation in which places are nonterminals and tokens are separate occurrences of nonterminals.

Definition 1. A *context-free Petri net* (in short, a *cf Petri net*) w.r.t. a context-free grammar $G = (V, \Sigma, S, R)$ is a septuple $N = (P, T, F, \phi, \beta, \gamma, \iota)$ where

- (P, T, F, ϕ) is a Petri net;
- labeling functions $\beta : P \to V$ and $\gamma : T \to R$ are bijections;
- there is an arc from place p to transition t if and only if $\gamma(t) = A \to \alpha$ and $\beta(p) = A$. The weight of the arc (p, t) is 1;

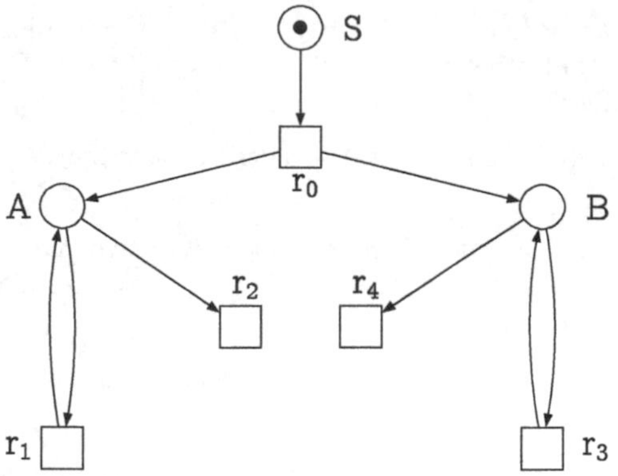

Figure 1. A cf Petri net N_1

- there is an arc from transition t to place p if and only if $\gamma(t) = A \to \alpha$ and $\beta(p) = x$ where $|\alpha|_x > 0$. The weight of the arc (t, p) is $|\alpha|_x$;
- the initial marking ι is defined by $\iota(\beta^{-1}(S)) = 1$ and $\iota(p) = 0$ for all $p \in P - \{\beta^{-1}(S)\}$.

Example 1. Let G_1 be a context-free grammar with the rules:

$$r_0 : S \to AB,\ r_1 : A \to aAb,\ r_2 : A \to ab,\ r_3 : B \to cB,\ r_4 : B \to c$$

(the other components of the grammar can be seen from these rules). Figure 1 illustrates a cf Petri net N_1 with respect to the grammar G_1. Obviously, $L(G_1) = \{a^n b^n c^m \mid n, m \geq 1\}$.

The following proposition shows the similarity between terminal derivations in a context-free grammar and successful occurrences of transitions in the corresponding cf Petri net.

Proposition 3. *Let $N = (P, T, F, \phi, \iota, \beta, \gamma)$ be the cf Petri net with respect to a context-free grammar $G = (V, \Sigma, S, R)$. Then $S \xRightarrow{r_1 r_2 \cdots r_n} w$, $w \in \Sigma^*$ is a derivation in G iff $t_1 t_2 \cdots t_n$, $\iota \xrightarrow{t_1 t_2 \cdots t_n} \mu_n$, is an occurrence sequence of transitions in N such that $\gamma(t_1 t_2 \cdots t_n) = r_1 r_2 \cdots r_n$ and $\mu_n(p) = 0$ for all $p \in P$.*

Now we define a *k-Petri net*, i.e., a cf Petri net with additional k places and additional arcs from/to these places to/from transitions of the net, the pre-sets and post-sets of the additional places are disjoint.

Definition 2. Let $G = (V, \Sigma, S, R)$ be a context-free grammar with its corresponding cf Petri net $N = (P, T, F, \phi, \beta, \gamma, \iota)$. Let k be a positive integer and let $Q = \{q_1, q_2, \ldots, q_k\}$ be a set of new places called *counters*. A *k-Petri net* is a construct $N_k = (P \cup Q, T, F \cup E, \varphi, \zeta, \gamma, \mu_0, \tau)$ where

- $E = \{(t, q_i) \mid t \in T_1^i, 1 \leq i \leq k\} \cup \{(q_i, t) \mid t \in T_2^i, 1 \leq i \leq k\}$ such that $T_1^i \subset T$ and $T_2^i \subset T$, $1 \leq i \leq k$ where $T_l^i \cap T_l^j = \emptyset$ for $1 \leq l \leq 2$, $T_1^i \cap T_2^j = \emptyset$ for $1 \leq i < j \leq k$ and $T_1^i = \emptyset$ if and only if $T_2^i = \emptyset$ for any $1 \leq i \leq k$.
- the weight function $\varphi(x, y)$ is defined by $\varphi(x, y) = \phi(x, y)$ if $(x, y) \in F$ and $\varphi(x, y) = 1$ if $(x, y) \in E$,

- the labeling function $\zeta : P \cup Q \to V \cup \{\lambda\}$ is defined by $\zeta(p) = \beta(p)$ if $p \in P$ and $\zeta(p) = \lambda$ if $p \in Q$,
- the initial marking μ_0 is defined by $\mu_0(\beta^{-1}(S)) = 1$ and $\mu_0(p) = 0$ for all $p \in P \cup Q - \{\beta^{-1}(S)\}$,
- τ is the final marking where $\tau(p) = 0$ for all $p \in P \cup Q$.

Definition 3. A *k-Petri net controlled grammar* (*k-PN controlled grammar* for short) is a quintuple $G = (V, \Sigma, S, R, N_k)$ where V, Σ, S, R are defined as for a context-free grammar and N_k is a k-PN with respect to the context-free grammar (V, Σ, S, R).

Definition 4. The *language* generated by a k-Petri net controlled grammar G consists of all strings $w \in \Sigma^*$ such that there is a derivation

$$S \xRightarrow{r_1 r_2 \cdots r_n} w \text{ where } t_1 t_2 \cdots t_n = \gamma^{-1}(r_1 r_2 \cdots r_n) \in T^*$$

is an occurrence sequence of the transitions of N_k enabled at the initial marking ι and finished at the final marking τ.

We denote the family of languages generated by k-PN controlled grammars (with erasing rules) by $\mathbf{PN}_k$ ($\mathbf{PN}_k^\lambda$), $k \geq 1$.

Example 2. Let G_2 be a 2-PN controlled grammar with the production rules:

$$\begin{array}{lll} r_0 : S \to A_1 B_1 A_2 B_2, & r_1 : A_1 \to a_1 A_1 b_1, & r_2 : A_1 \to a_1 b_1, \\ r_3 : B_1 \to c_1 B_1, & r_4 : B_1 \to c_1, & r_5 : A_2 \to a_2 A_2 b_2, \\ r_6 : A_2 \to a_2 b_2, & r_7 : B_2 \to c_2 B_2, & r_8 : B_2 \to c_2 \end{array}$$

and the corresponding 2-Petri net N_2 is given in Figure 2. Then it is easy to see that G_2 generates the language

$$L(G_2) = \{a_1^n b_1^n c_1^n a_2^m b_2^m c_2^m \mid n, m \geq 1\}.$$

Theorem 4. *The language*

$$L = \prod_{i=1}^{k+1} a_i^{n_i} b_i^{n_i} c_i^{n_i}$$

where $k \geq 1$ and $n_i \geq 1$, $1 \leq i \leq k+1$, cannot be generated by a k-PN controlled grammar.

The following theorem presents the relations of languages generated by k-Petri net controlled grammars to context-free, (positive) additive valence and vector languages.

Theorem 5.

$$\mathbf{CF} \subset \mathbf{PN}_1^{[\lambda]} \subseteq \mathbf{pV}^{[\lambda]}, \ \mathbf{aV}^{[\lambda]} \subset \mathbf{PN}_2^{[\lambda]} \text{ and } \mathbf{PN}_n^{[\lambda]} \subseteq \mathbf{VEC}^{[\lambda]}, n \geq 1.$$

The next theorem shows that the language families generated by k-Petri net controlled grammars form infinite hierarchy with respect to the numbers of additional places.

Theorem 6. *For $k \geq 1$, $\mathbf{PN}_k^{[\lambda]} \subset \mathbf{PN}_{k+1}^{[\lambda]}$.*

The closure properties of the language families generated by k-PN controlled grammars are given in the following theorem.

Theorem 7. *The family of languages $\mathbf{PN}_k$, $k \geq 1$, is closed under union, substitution, mirror image, intersection with regular languages and it is not closed under concatenation.*

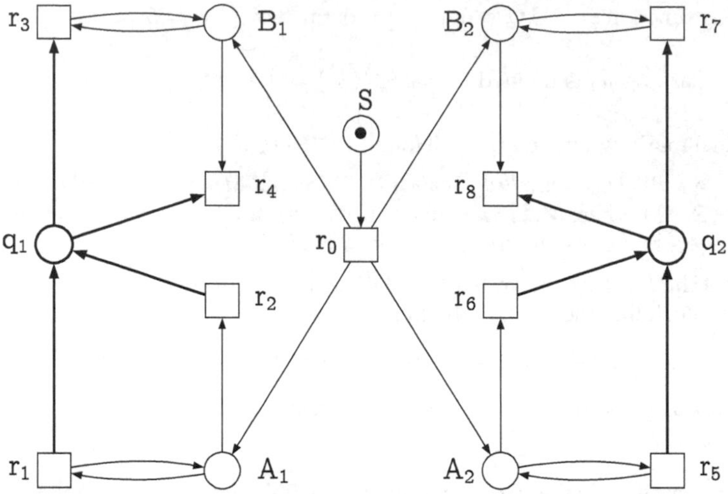

Figure 2. A 2-Petri net N_2

4. Arbitrary Petri net controlled grammars

In this section we consider a generalization of regularly controlled grammars: instead of a finite automaton we associate a Petri net with a context-free grammar and require that the sequence of applied rules corresponds to an occurrence sequence of the Petri net, i.e., to sequences of transitions which can be fired in succession. However, one has to decide what type of correspondence is used and what concept is taken as an equivalent of acceptance. Since the sets of occurrence sequences form the language of a Petri net, we choose the correspondence and the equivalent for acceptance according to the variations which are used in the theory of Petri net languages.

Therefore as correspondence we choose a bijection (between transitions and rules) or a coding (any transition is mapped to a rule) or a weak coding (any transition is mapped to a rule or the empty word) which agree with the classical three variants of Petri net languages (see e.g. [34, 57, 58]).

We consider two types of acceptance from the theory of Petri net languages: only those occurrence sequences belonging to the languages which transform the initial marking into a marking from a given finite set of markings or all occurrence sequences are taken (independent of the obtained marking). If we use only the occurrence sequence leading to a marking in a given finite set of markings we say that the Petri net controlled grammar is of t-type; if we consider all occurrence sequences, then the grammar is of r-type. We add a further type which can be considered as a complement of the t-type. Obviously, if we choose a finite set M of markings and require that the marking obtained after the application of the occurrence sequence is smaller than at least one marking of M (the order is componentwise), then we can choose another finite set M' of markings and require that the obtained marking belongs to M'. The complementary approach requires that the obtained marking is larger than at least one marking of the given set M. The corresponding class of Petri net controlled grammars is called of g-type. Therefore, we obtain nine classes of Petri net controlled grammars since we have three different types of correspondence and three types of the set of admitted occurrence sequences. These types of control are generalizations of those types of control considered in the previous chapter, too, where instead of arbitrary Petri nets only such Petri nets have been considered where the places and transitions correspond in a one-to-one manner to nonterminals and rules, respectively.

We now introduce the concept of control by an arbitrary Petri net.

Definition 5. An *arbitrary Petri net controlled grammar* is a tuple $G = (V, \Sigma, S, R, N, \gamma, M)$ where V, Σ, S, R are defined as for a context-free grammar and $N = (P, T, F, \varphi, \iota)$ is a (marked) Petri net, $\gamma : T \to R \cup \{\lambda\}$ is a transition labeling function and M is a set of final markings.

Definition 6. The *language* generated by a Petri net controlled grammar G, denoted by $L(G)$, consists of all strings $w \in \Sigma^*$ such that there is a derivation $S \xRightarrow{r_1 r_2 \cdots r_k} w \in \Sigma^*$ and an occurrence sequence $\nu = t_1 t_2 \cdots t_s$ which is successful for M such that $r_1 r_2 \cdots r_k = \gamma(t_1 t_2 \cdots t_s)$.

Example 3. Let $G_3 = (\{S, A, B, C\}, \{a, b, c\}, S, R, N_3, \gamma, M)$ be a Petri net controlled grammar where R consists of

$$S \to ABC,$$

$$A \to aA, \quad B \to bB, \quad C \to cC,$$

$$A \to a, \quad B \to b, \quad C \to c$$

and N_3 is illustrated in Figure 3. If M is the set of all reachable markings, then G_3 generates the language

$$L(G_3) = \{a^n b^m c^k \mid n \geq m \geq k \geq 1\}.$$

If $M = \{\mu\}$ with $\mu(p) = 0$ for all $p \in P$, then it generates the language

$$L(G_3) = \{a^n b^n c^n \mid n \geq 1\}.$$

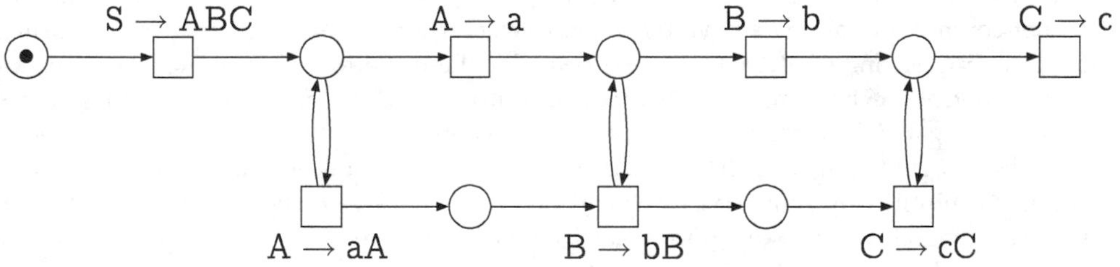

Figure 3. A labeled Petri net N_3

Different labeling strategies and different definitions of the set of final markings result in various types of Petri net controlled grammars. We consider the following types of Petri net controlled grammars.

Definition 7. A Petri net controlled grammar $G = (V, \Sigma, S, R, N, \gamma, M)$ is called *free* (abbreviated by f) if a different label is associated to each transition, and no transition is labeled with the empty string; λ-*free* (abbreviated by $-\lambda$) if no transition is labeled with the empty string; *extended* (abbreviated by λ) if no restriction is posed on the labeling function γ.

Definition 8. A Petri net controlled grammar $G = (V, \Sigma, S, R, N, \gamma, M)$ is called *r-type* if M is the set of all reachable markings from the initial marking ι, i.e., $M = \mathcal{R}(N, \iota)$; *t-type* if $M \subseteq \mathcal{R}(N, \iota)$ is a finite set; *g-type* if for a given finite set $M_0 \subseteq \mathcal{R}(N, \iota)$, M is the set of all markings such that for every marking $\mu \in M$ there is a marking $\mu' \in M_0$ such that $\mu \geq \mu'$.

We use the notation (x, y)-*PN controlled grammar* where $x \in \{f, -\lambda, \lambda\}$ shows the type of a labeling function and $y \in \{r, t, g\}$ shows the type of a set of final markings. We denote by $\mathbf{PN}(x, y)$ and $\mathbf{PN}^\lambda(x, y)$ the families of languages generated by (x, y)-PN controlled grammars without and with erasing rules, respectively, where $x \in \{f, -\lambda, \lambda\}$ and $y \in \{r, t, g\}$.

The following theorem shows that the labeling strategy does not effect on the generative capacity of arbitrary Petri net controlled grammars.

Theorem 8. *For* $y \in \{r, t, g\}$,

$$\mathbf{PN}^{[\lambda]}(f, y) = \mathbf{PN}^{[\lambda]}(-\lambda, y) = \mathbf{PN}^{[\lambda]}(\lambda, y).$$

Not surprisingly, arbitrary Petri net controlled grammars generate matrix languages. Moreover, in [65] it was proven that the erasing rules in arbitrary Petri net controlled grammars can be eliminated without effecting on the generative power of the grammars. If we take into consideration this result, we obtain the following inclusions and equalities:

Theorem 9. *For* $x \in \{f, -\lambda, \lambda\}$ *and* $y \in \{r, t, g\}$,

$$\mathbf{MAT} \subseteq \mathbf{PN}(x, r) = \mathbf{PN}(x, g) \subseteq \mathbf{PN}(x, t) = \mathbf{PN}^\lambda(x, y) = \mathbf{MAT}^\lambda.$$

5. Grammars controlled by special Petri nets

In the previous section we investigated arbitrary Petri net controlled grammars in dependence on the type of labeling functions and on the definitions of final markings, and showed that Petri net controlled grammars have the same power as some other regulating mechanisms such as matrices, finite automata. If we consider these matrices and finite automata in terms of control mechanisms, special types of matrices and special regular languages are widely investigated in literature, for instance, as control, simple matrices ([37]) or some subclasses of regular languages ([15, 17]) are considered. Thus, it is also natural to investigate grammars controlled by some special classes of Petri nets. We consider (generalized) state machines, (generalized) marked graphs, causal nets, (extended) free-choice nets, asymmetric choice nets and ordinary nets. Similarly to the general case we also investigate the effects of labeling policies and final markings to the computational power, and prove that the family of languages generated by (arbitrary) Petri net controlled grammars coincide with the family of languages generated by grammars controlled by free-choice nets.

Let $G = (V, \Sigma, S, R, N, \gamma, M)$ be an arbitrary Petri net controlled grammar. The grammar G is called a (generalized) state machine, (generalized) marked graph, causal net, (extended) free-choice net, asymmetric choice net or ordinary net controlled grammar if the net N is a (generalized) state machine, (generalized) marked graph, causal net, (extended) free-choice net, asymmetric choice net or ordinary net, respectively.

We also use a notation an (x,y)-(generalized) state machine, ((generalized) marked graph, causal net, (extended) free-choice net, asymmetric choice net and ordinary net) controlled grammar where $x \in \{f, -\lambda, \lambda\}$ shows the type of a labeling function γ and $y \in \{r,t,g\}$ shows the type of a set of final markings.

We denote the families of languages generated by grammars controlled by state machines, generalized state machines, marked graphs, generalize marked graphs, causal nets, free-choice nets, extended free-choice nets, asymmetric nets, ordinary nets and Petri nets

$$\mathbf{SM}^{[\lambda]}(x,y),\ \mathbf{GSM}^{[\lambda]}(x,y),\ \mathbf{MG}^{[\lambda]}(x,y),\ \mathbf{GMG}^{[\lambda]}(x,y),\ \mathbf{CN}^{[\lambda]}(x,y),$$
$$\mathbf{FC}^{[\lambda]}(x,y),\ \mathbf{EFC}^{[\lambda]}(x,y),\ \mathbf{AC}^{[\lambda]}(x,y),\ \mathbf{ON}^{[\lambda]}(x,y),\ \mathbf{PN}^{[\lambda]}(x,y)$$

where $x \in \{f, -\lambda, \lambda\}$ and $y \in \{r,t,g\}$.

The inclusion $\mathbf{X}(x,y) \subseteq \mathbf{X}^{\lambda}(x,y)$ immediately follows from the definition where

- $\mathbf{X} \in \{\mathbf{SM}, \mathbf{GSM}, \mathbf{MG}, \mathbf{GMG}, \mathbf{CN}, \mathbf{FC}, \mathbf{EFC}, \mathbf{AC}, \mathbf{ON}\}$,
- $x \in \{f, -\lambda, \lambda\}$ and $y \in \{r,t,g\}$.

Example 4. Let $G_4 = (\{S,A,B\}, \{a,b\}, S, R, N_4, \gamma, M)$ be a SM controlled grammar where R consists of

$$S \to AB,$$
$$A \to aA, \quad A \to bA, \quad A \to \lambda,$$
$$B \to aB, \quad B \to bB, \quad B \to \lambda,$$

the Petri net N_4 illustrated in Figure 4 is a labeled state machine and $M = \{\mu\}$ where $\mu(p_0) = 1$ and $\mu(p) = 0$ for all $p \in P - \{p_0\}$, then

$$L(G_4) = \{ww \mid w \in \{a,b\}^*\} \in \mathbf{SM}^{\lambda}(\lambda, t).$$

Example 5. Let $G_5 = (\{S,A,B\}, \{a,b\}, S, R, N_5, \gamma', M')$ be a MG controlled grammar where R is as for the grammar G_1 in Example 4, a labeled marked graph N_5 is illustrated in Figure 5 and $M' = \{\mu\}$ where $\mu(p) = 0$ for all $p \in P$. Then

$$L(G_5) = \{ww' \mid w \in \{a,b\}^* \text{ and } w' \in \text{Perm}(w)\} \in \mathbf{MG}^{\lambda}(\lambda, t).$$

We have the same result on the labeling strategies as that in the previous section: the labeling of transitions of special Petri nets do not effect on the generative powers of the families of languages generated by grammars controlled by these nets.

Theorem 10. *For* $\mathbf{X} \in \{\mathbf{SM}, \mathbf{GSM}, \mathbf{MG}, \mathbf{GMG}, \mathbf{CN}, \mathbf{FC}, \mathbf{EFC}, \mathbf{AC}, \mathbf{ON}\}$, *and* $y \in \{r,t,g\}$,

$$\mathbf{X}^{[\lambda]}(f,y) = \mathbf{X}^{[\lambda]}(-\lambda,y) = \mathbf{X}^{[\lambda]}(\lambda,y).$$

The following theorem shows the relations of families of languages generated by special Petri net controlled grammars.

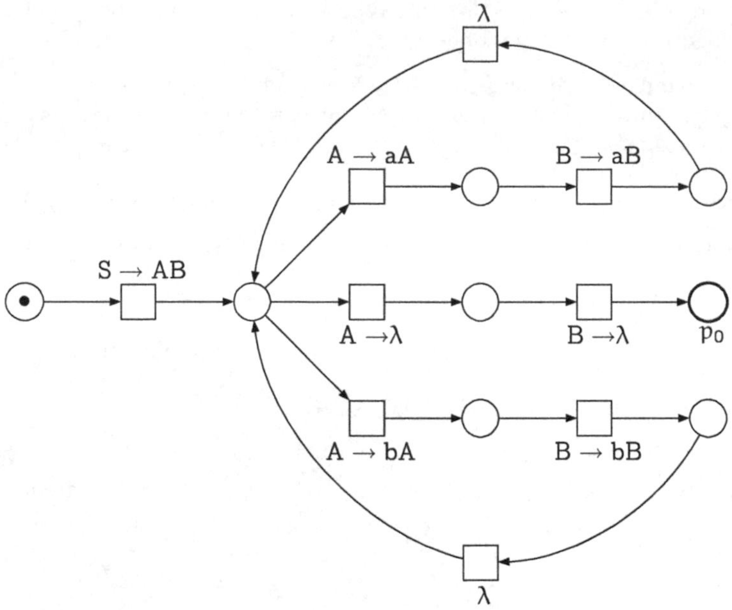

Figure 4. A labeled state machine N_4

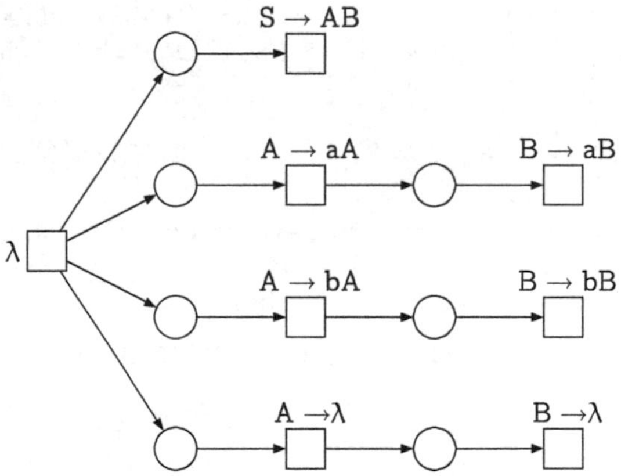

Figure 5. A labeled marked graph N_5

Theorem 11. *The following inclusions and equalities hold:*

$$(1)\ \mathbf{MG}^{[\lambda]}(x,y) = \mathbf{GMG}^{[\lambda]}(x,y) \text{ and } \mathbf{PN}(x,y') = \mathbf{X}(x,y'),$$

$$(2)\ \mathbf{CN}(x,y') \subseteq \mathbf{MG}(x,y') \subseteq \mathbf{PN}(x,y') \subseteq \mathbf{MAT}^{\lambda},$$

$$(3)\ \mathbf{MAT} \subseteq \mathbf{GSM}(x,y') \subseteq \mathbf{PN}(x,y') \subseteq \mathbf{MAT}^{\lambda},$$

$$(4)\ \mathbf{CF} \subset \mathbf{MAT} = \mathbf{SM}(x,y) \subseteq \mathbf{VEC} \subseteq \begin{cases} \mathbf{GSM}(x,t) \\ \mathbf{CN}(x,t) \subseteq \mathbf{MG}(x,t) \end{cases} \subseteq \mathbf{MAT}^{\lambda},$$

$$(5)\ \mathbf{MAT}^{\lambda} = \mathbf{PN}^{\lambda}(x,y) = \mathbf{PN}(x,t) = \mathbf{X}^{\lambda}(x,t) = \mathbf{Y}^{\lambda}(x,t) = \mathbf{Z}^{\lambda}(x,y),$$

where $x \in \{f,-\lambda,\lambda\}$, $y \in \{r,g,t\}$, $y' \in \{r,g\}$ *and* $\mathbf{X} \in \{\mathbf{FC},\mathbf{EFC},\mathbf{AC},\mathbf{ON}\}$, $\mathbf{Y} \in \{\mathbf{MG},\mathbf{GMG},\mathbf{CN}\}$, $\mathbf{Z} \in \{\mathbf{SM},\mathbf{GSM},\mathbf{FC},\mathbf{EFC},\mathbf{AC},\mathbf{ON}\}$.

6. Capacity-bounded grammars

In this section we continue the research in this direction by restricting to (context-free, extended or arbitrary) Petri nets with place capacities. Quite obviously, a context-free Petri net with place capacity regulates the defining grammar by permitting only those derivations where the number of each nonterminal in each sentential form is bounded by its capacity. Similar mechanisms have been introduced and investigated by several authors. Grammar with *finite index* (the index of a grammar is the maximal number of nonterminals simultaneously appearing in its complete derivations (considering the most economical derivations for each string)) were first considered by Brainerd [7]. *Nonterminal-bounded* grammars (a grammar a nonterminal-bounded if the total number of nonterminals in every sentential form does not exceed an upper bound) were introduced by Altman and Banerji in [3–5]. A "weak" variant of nonterminal-bounded grammars (only the complete derivations are required to be bounded) were defined by Moriya [44]. Ginsburg and Spanier introduced *derivation-bounded* languages in [32] (all strings which have complete derivation in a grammar G consisting of sentential forms each of which does not contain more than k nonterminals collected in the set $L_k(G)$). There it was shown that grammars regulated in this way generate the family of context-free languages of finite index, even if arbitrary nonterminal strings are allowed as left-hand sides of production rules. Finite index restrictions to regulated grammars have also been investigated [29, 30, 48, 49, 51, 53–55]. There it was shown that the families of most regulated languages are collapse.

In this section we show that capacity-bounded context-free grammars have a larger generative power than context-free grammars of finite index while the family of languages generated by capacity-bounded phrase structure grammars (due to Ginsburg and Spanier) and several families of languages generated by grammars controlled by extended cf Petri nets with place capacities coincide with the family of matrix languages of finite index.

We will now introduce capacity-bounded grammars and show some relations to similar concepts known from the literature.

Definition 9. A *capacity-bounded* grammar is a tuple $G = (V,\Sigma,S,R,\kappa)$ where $G' = (V,\Sigma,S,R)$ is a grammar and $\kappa : V \to \mathbb{N}$ is a capacity function. The derivation relation $\Rightarrow_G$ is defined as $\alpha \Rightarrow_G \beta$ iff $\alpha \Rightarrow_{G'} \beta$ and $|\alpha|_A \le \kappa(A)$ and $|\beta|_A \le \kappa(A)$, for all $A \in V$. The language of G is defined as $L(G) = \{w \in \Sigma^* \mid S \Rightarrow_G^* w\}$.

The families of languages generated by capacity-bounded GS grammars and by context-free capacity-bounded grammars are denoted by $\mathbf{GS}_{cb}$ and $\mathbf{CF}_{cb}$, respectively. The capacity function mapping each nonterminal to 1 is denoted by $\mathbf{1}$. The notions of finite index and bounded capacities can be extended to matrix, vector and semi-matrix grammars. The corresponding language families are denoted by

$$\mathbf{MAT}_{fin}^{[\lambda]}, \mathbf{VEC}_{fin}^{[\lambda]}, \mathbf{sMAT}_{fin}^{[\lambda]}, \mathbf{MAT}_{cb}^{[\lambda]}, \mathbf{VEC}_{cb}^{[\lambda]}.$$

Capacity-bounded grammars are very similar to derivation-bounded grammars, which were studied in [32]. A *derivation-bounded* grammar is a quintuple $G = (V, \Sigma, S, R, k)$ where $G' = (V, \Sigma, S, R)$ is a grammar and $k \in \mathbb{N}$ is a bound on the number of allowed nonterminals. The language of G contains all words $w \in L(G')$ that have a derivation $S \Rightarrow^* w$ such that $|\beta|_V \leq k$, for each sentential form β of the derivation.

Other related concepts are nonterminal-bounded grammars and grammars of finite index. A context-free grammar $G = (V, \Sigma, S, R)$ is *nonterminal-bounded* if $|\beta|_V \leq k$ for some fixed $k \in \mathbb{N}$ and all sentential forms β derivable in G. The *index* of a derivation in G is the maximal number of nonterminal symbols in its sentential forms. G is of *finite index* if every word in $L(G)$ has a derivation of index at most k for some fixed $k \in \mathbb{N}$. The family of context-free languages of finite index is denoted by $\mathbf{CF}_{fin}$.

Note that there is a subtle difference between the first two and the last two concepts. While context-free nonterminal-bounded and finite index grammars are just context-free grammars with a certain structural property (and generate context-free languages by definition), capacity-bounded and derivation-bounded grammars are special cases of *regulated rewriting* (and could therefore generate non-context-free languages). However, it has been shown that the family of derivation bounded languages is equal to $\mathbf{CF}_{fin}$, even if arbitrary grammars due to Ginsburg and Spanier are permitted [32]. We will now give an example of capacity-bounded grammars generating non-context-free languages.

Example 6. Let $G = (\{S, A, B, C, D, E, F\}, \{a, b, c\}, S, R, \mathbf{1})$ be the capacity-bounded grammar where R consists of the rules:

$$\begin{aligned}
&r_1 : S \to ABCD,\ r_2 : AB \to aEFb,\ r_3 : CD \to cAD,\ r_4 : EF \to EC,\\
&r_5 : EF \to FC,\quad r_6 : AD \to FD,\quad r_7 : AD \to ED,\quad r_8 : EC \to AB,\\
&r_9 : FD \to CD,\quad r_{10} : FC \to AF,\quad r_{11} : AF \to \lambda,\quad r_{12} : ED \to \lambda.
\end{aligned}$$

The possible derivations are exactly those of the form

$$\begin{aligned}
S &\xRightarrow{r_1} ABCD\\
&\xRightarrow{(r_2r_3r_4r_6r_8r_9)^n} a^nABb^nc^nCD\\
&\xRightarrow{r_2r_3} a^{n+1}EFb^{n+1}c^{n+1}AD\\
&\xRightarrow{r_5r_7} a^{n+1}FCb^{n+1}c^{n+1}ED\\
&\xRightarrow{r_{10}r_{11}r_{12}} a^nb^nc^n
\end{aligned}$$

(in the last phase, the sequences $r_{10}r_{12}r_{11}$ and $r_{12}r_{10}r_{11}$ could also be applied with the same result). Therefore,

$$L(G) = \{a^nb^nc^n \mid n \geq 1\}.$$

The above example shows that capacity-bounded grammars – in contrast to derivation bounded grammars – can generate non-context-free languages. Moreover, any context-free language generated by a grammar of G of finite index is also generated by the capacity-bounded grammar (G, κ) where κ is capacity function constantly k.

Let $\mathbf{CF}_{cb}^{1}$ and $\mathbf{GS}_{cb}^{1}$ be the language families generated by context-free and arbitrary grammars with capacity function **1**. Then,

Lemma 12. $\mathbf{CF}_{cb} = \mathbf{CF}_{cb}^{1}$ *and* $\mathbf{GS}_{cb} = \mathbf{GS}_{cb}^{1}$.

On the other hand, capacity-bounded GS grammars generate exactly the family of matrix languages of finite index. This is in contrast to derivation bounded grammars which generate only context-free languages of finite index [32].

Lemma 13. $\mathbf{GS}_{cb} = \mathbf{MAT}_{fin}$.

It turns out that capacity-bounded context-free grammars are strictly between context-free languages of finite index and matrix languages of finite index.

Theorem 14. $\mathbf{CF}_{fin} \subset \mathbf{CF}_{cb} \subset \mathbf{GS}_{cb} = \mathbf{MAT}_{fin}$.

The next theorem shows that the families of capacity bounded matrix and vector languages are exactly the family of matrix languages with finite index.

Theorem 15. $\mathbf{MAT}_{fin} = \mathbf{VEC}_{cb}^{[\lambda]} = \mathbf{MAT}_{cb}^{[\lambda]}$.

As regards closure properties, we remark that the constructions showing the closure of **CF** under homomorphisms, union, concatenation and Kleene closure can be easily extended to the case of capacity-bounded languages.

Theorem 16. $\mathbf{CF}_{cb}$ *is closed under homomorphisms, union, concatenation and Kleene closure.*

Regarding intersection with regular sets and inverse homomorphisms, we can show non-closure properties.

Theorem 17. $\mathbf{CF}_{cb}$ *is neither closed under intersection with regular sets nor under inverse homomorphisms.*

Control by Petri nets can in a natural way be adapted to Petri nets with place capacities. A context-free grammar is controlled by its context-free Petri net with place capacity by only allowing derivations that correspond to valid firing sequences respecting the capacity bounds. The (trivial) proof for the equivalence between context-free grammars and grammars controlled by cf Petri nets can be immediately transferred to context-free grammars and Petri nets with capacities:

Theorem 18. *Grammars controlled by context-free Petri nets with place capacity functions generate the family of capacity-bounded context-free languages.*

Let us now turn to grammars controlled by arbitrary Petri nets with capacities. Let $G = (V, \Sigma, S, R, N, \gamma, M)$ be an arbitrary Petri net controlled grammar. G is called a grammar controlled by an arbitrary Petri net with place capacity if N is a Petri net with place capacity. The families of languages generated by grammars controlled by arbitrary Petri nets with place capacities (with erasing rules) is denoted by $\mathbf{PN}_{cb}(x,y)$ ($\mathbf{PN}_{cb}^{\lambda}(x,y)$) where $x \in \{f, -\lambda, \lambda\}$ and $y \in \{r, t, g\}$.

The next statement indicates that the language generated by a grammar controlled by an arbitrary Petri net with place capacities iff it is generated by a matrix grammar (for details, see [56]).

Theorem 19. *For $x \in \{f, -\lambda, \lambda\}$ and $y \in \{r, t, g\}$,*

$$\mathbf{PN}_{cb}(x,y) = \mathbf{MAT} \subseteq \mathbf{PN}_{cb}^{\lambda}(x,y) = \mathbf{MAT}^{\lambda}.$$

We summarize our results in the following theorem.

Theorem 20. *The following inclusions and equalities hold:*

$$\begin{aligned} \mathbf{CF}_{fin} &\subset \mathbf{CF}_{cb} = \mathbf{CF}_{cb}^{1} \\ &\subset \mathbf{MAT}_{fin} = \mathbf{MAT}_{cb}^{[\lambda]} = \mathbf{VEC}_{cb}^{[\lambda]} = \mathbf{GS}_{cb} = \mathbf{GS}_{cb}^{1} \\ &\subset \mathbf{MAT} = \mathbf{PN}_{cb}(x,y) \subseteq \mathbf{MAT}^{\lambda} = \mathbf{PN}_{cb}^{\lambda}(x,y) \end{aligned}$$

where $x \in \{f, -\lambda, \lambda\}$ and $y \in \{r, t, g\}$.

7. Conclusions and future research

The chapter summarizes the recent results on Petri net controlled grammars presented in [18–23, 56, 59–62] and the close related topic: capacity-bounded grammars. Though the theme of regulated grammars is one of the classic topics in formal language theory, a Petri net controlled grammar is still interesting subject for the investigation for many reasons. On the one hand, this type of grammars can successfully be used in modeling new problems emerging in manufacturing systems, systems biology and other areas. On the other hand, the graphically illustrability, the ability to represent both a grammar and its control in one structure, and the possibility to unify different regulated rewritings make this formalization attractive for the study. Moreover, control by Petri nets introduces the concept of *concurrency* in regulated rewriting systems.

We should mention that there are some open problems, the study of which is of interest: one of them concerns to the classic open problem of the theory of regulated rewriting systems – the strictness of the inclusion $\mathbf{MAT} \subseteq \mathbf{MAT}^{\lambda}$. We showed that language families generated by (arbitrary) Petri net controlled grammars are between the families **MAT** and $\mathbf{MAT}^{\lambda}$. Moreover, the work [65] of G. Zetzsche shows that the erasing rules in Petri net controlled grammars with finite set of final markings can be eliminated without effecting on the generative power, which gives hope that one can solve this problem.

There is also another very interesting topic in this direction for the future study. If we notice the definitions of derivation-bounded [32] or nonterminal-bounded grammars [3–5] only nonterminal strings are allowed as left-hand sides of production rules. Here, an interesting question is emerged, what kind of languages can be generated if we derestrict this condition, i.e., allow any string in the left-hand side of the rules?

In all investigated types of Petri net controlled grammars, we only used the sequential firing mode of transitions. The consideration of simultaneous firing of transitions, another fundamental feature of Petri nets, opens a new direction for the future research: one can study *grammars controlled by Petri nets under parallel firing strategy*, which introduces concurrently parallelism in formal language theory.

Grammar systems can be considered as a formal model for a phenomenon of solving a given problem by dividing it into subproblems (grammars) to be solved by several parts in turn (CD grammar systems) or in parallel (PC grammar systems). The control of derivations in grammar systems also allows increasing computational power grammar systems. We can extend the regulation of a rule by a transition to the regulation a set of rules by a transition, which defines a new type of grammar systems: the firing of a transition allows applying several (assigned) rules in a derivation step parallelly and different modes.

In [19–22, 41, 62] it was shown that by adding places and arcs which satisfy some structural requirements one can generate well-known families of languages as random context languages, valence languages, vector languages and matrix languages. Thus, the control by Petri nets can be considered as a unifying approach to different types of control. On the other hand, Petri nets can be transformed into *occurrence nets*, i.e., usually an infinite, tree-like structure whose nodes have the same labels as those of the places and transitions of the Petri net preserving the relationship of adjacency, using *unfolding technique* introduced in [43] and given in [24] in detail under the name of *branching processes*. Any *finite initial* part, i.e., *prefix* of the occurrence net of a cf Petri net can be considered as a derivation tree for the corresponding context-free grammar as it has the same structure as a usual derivation tree, here we can also accept the rule of reading "leaf"-places with tokens from the left to the right as in usual derivation trees. We can also generalize this idea for regulated grammars considering prefixes of the occurrences nets obtained from cf Petri nets with additional places. Hence, we can take into consideration the grammar as well as its control, and construct (Petri net) derivation trees for regulated grammars, which help to construct effective parsing algorithms for regulated rewriting systems. Though the preliminary results (general parsing algorithms, Early-like parsing algorithm for deterministic extended context-free Petri net controlled grammars, etc.) were obtained in [63, 64], the problem of the development of the effective parsing algorithms for regulated grammars remain open.

Acknowledgements

This work has been supported by Ministry of Higher Education of Malaysia via Fundamental Research Grant Scheme FRGS /1/11/SG/UPM/01/1 and Universiti Putra Malaysia via RUGS 05-01-10-0896RU/F1.

Author details

Jürgen Dassow and Ralf Stiebe
Fakultät für Informatik, Otto-von-Guericke-Universität Magdeburg, Magdeburg, Germany

Gairatzhan Mavlankulov, Mohamed Othman, Mohd Hasan Selamat and Sherzod Turaev
Faculty of Computer Science and Information Technology, Universiti Putra Malaysia, UPM Serdang, Selangor, Malaysia

8. References

[1] Abraham, A. [1965]. Some questions of phrase-structure grammars, *Comput. Linguistics* 4: 61–70.

[2] Al-A'ali, M., Khan, A. & Al-Shamlan, N. [1996]. Simplification of context-free grammar through Petri net, *Computers and Structures* 58: 1055–1058.

[3] Altman, E. [1964]. The concept of finite representability, *Systems Research Center Report SRC 56-A-64-20*, Case Institute of Technology.

[4] Altman, E. & Banerji, R. [1965]. Some problems of finite representability, *Information and Control* 8: 251–263.

[5] Banerji, R. [1963]. Phrase structure languages, finite machines, and channel capacity, *Information and Control* 6: 153–162.

[6] Beek, M. t. & Kleijn, H. [2002]. Petri net control for grammar systems, *Formal and Natural Computing*, Vol. 2300 of *LNCS*, Springer, pp. 220–243.

[7] Brainerd, B. [1968]. An analog of a theorem about context-free languages, *Information and Control* 11: 561–567.

[8] Chomsky, N. [1956]. Three models for the description of languages, *IRE Trans. on Information Theory* 2(3): 113–124.

[9] Chomsky, N. [1957]. *Syntactic structure*, Mouton, Gravenhage.

[10] Chomsky, N. [1959]. On certain formal properties of grammars, *Information and Control* 2: 137–167.

[11] Crespi-Reghizzi, S. & Mandrioli, D. [1974]. Petri nets and commutative grammars, *Internal Report 74-5*, Laboraterio di Calcolatori, Instituto di Elettrotecnica ed Elettromca del Politecnico di Milano, Italy.

[12] Crespi-Reghizzi, S. & Mandrioli, D. [1975]. Properties of firing sequences, *Proc. MIT Conf. Petri Nets and Related Methods*, MIT, Cambridge, Mass., pp. 233–240.

[13] Crespi-Reghizzi, S. & Mandrioli, D. [1977]. Petri nets and Szilard languages, *Inform. and Control* 33: 177–192.

[14] Darondeau, P. [2001]. On the Petri net realization of context-free graphs, *Theor. Computer Sci.* 258: 573–598.

[15] Dassow, J. [1988]. Subregularly controlled derivations: Context-free case, *Rostock. Math. Kolloq.* 34: 61–70.

[16] Dassow, J. & Păun, G. [1989]. *Regulated rewriting in formal language theory*, Springer-Verlag, Berlin.

[17] Dassow, J. & Truthe, B. [2008]. Subregularly tree controlled grammars and languages, *in* E. Csuhaj-Varjú & Z. Esik (eds), *Proc. the 12th International Conference AFL 2008*, Balatonfured, Hungary, pp. 158–169.

[18] Dassow, J. & Turaev, S. [2008a]. Arbitrary Petri net controlled grammars, *in* G. Bel-Enguix & M. Jiménez-López (eds), *Linguistics and Formal Languages. Second International Workshop on Non-Classical Formal Languages In Linguistics, Tarragona, Spain*, pp. 27–39. ISBN 978-84-612-6451-3.

[19] Dassow, J. & Turaev, S. [2008b]. *k*-Petri net controlled grammars, *in* C. Martín-Vide, F. Otto & H. Fernau (eds), *Language and Automata Theory and Applications. Second*

International Conference, LATA 2008. Revised Papers, Vol. 5196 of *LNCS*, Springer, pp. 209–220.

[20] Dassow, J. & Turaev, S. [2009a]. Grammars controlled by special Petri nets, *in* A. Dediu, A.-M. Ionescu & C. Martín-Vide (eds), *Language and Automata Theory and Applications, Third International Conference, LATA 2009*, Vol. 5457 of *LNCS*, Springer, pp. 326–337.

[21] Dassow, J. & Turaev, S. [2009b]. Petri net controlled grammars: the case of special Petri nets, *Journal of Universal Computer Science* 15(14): 2808–2835.

[22] Dassow, J. & Turaev, S. [2009c]. Petri net controlled grammars: the power of labeling and final markings, *Romanian Jour. of Information Science and Technology* 12(2): 191–207.

[23] Dassow, J. & Turaev, S. [2010]. Petri net controlled grammars with a bounded number of additional places, *Acta Cybernetica* 19: 609–634.

[24] Engelfriet, J. [1991]. Branching processes of petri nets, *Acta Informatica* 28: 575–591.

[25] Erqing, X. [2004]. A Pr/T-Net model for context-free language parsing, *Fifth World Congress on Intelligent Control and Automation*, Vol. 3, pp. 1919–1922.

[26] Farwer, B., Jantzen, M., Kudlek, M., Rölke, H. & Zetzsche, G. [2008]. Petri net controlled finite automata, *Fundamenta Informaticae* 85(1-4): 111–121.

[27] Farwer, B., Kudlek, M. & Rölke, H. [2006]. Petri-net-controlled machine models, *Technical Report 274*, FBI-Bericht, Hamburg.

[28] Farwer, B., Kudlek, M. & Rölke, H. [2007]. Concurrent Turing machines, *Fundamenta Informaticae* 79(3-4): 303–317.

[29] Fernau, H. & Holzer, M. [1997]. Conditional context-free languages of finite index, *New Trends in Formal Languages – Control, Cooperation, and Combinatorics (to Jürgen Dassow on the occasion of his 50th birthday)*, Vol. 1218 of *LNCS*, pp. 10–26.

[30] Fernau, H. & Holzer, M. [2008]. Regulated finite index language families collapse, *Technical Report WSI-96-16*, Universität Türbingen, Wilhelm-Schickard-Institut für Informatik.

[31] Ginsburg, S. & Spanier, E. [1968a]. Contol sets on grammars, *Math. Syst. Th.* 2: 159–177.

[32] Ginsburg, S. & Spanier, E. [1968b]. Derivation bounded languages, *J. Comput. Syst. Sci.* 2: 228–250.

[33] Hack, M. [1975a]. *Decidablity questions for Petri nets*, PhD thesis, Dept. of Electrical Engineering, MIT.

[34] Hack, M. [1975b]. Petri net languages, *Computation Structures Group Memo, Project MAC 124*, MIT, Cambridge Mass.

[35] Hauschildt, D. & Jantzen, M. [1994]. Petri nets algorithms in the theory of matrix grammars, *Acta Informatica* 31: 719–728.

[36] Hopcroft, J. & Ullman, J. [1990]. *Introduction to automata theory, languages, and computation*, Addison-Wesley Longman Publishing Co., Inc.

[37] Ibarra, O. [1970]. Simple matrix grammars, *Inform. Control* 17: 359–394.

[38] Jantzen, M., Kudlek, M. & Zetzsche, G. [2008]. Language classes defined by concurrent finite automata, *Fundamenta Informaticae* 85(1-4): 267–280.

[39] Jiang, C. [1996]. Vector grammar and PN machine, *Sci. Chin. (Ser. A)* 24: 1315–1322.

[40] Liptop, R. [1976]. The reachability problem requires esponential space, *Technical Report 62*, Yale University.

[41] Marek, V. & Češka, M. [2001]. Petri nets and random-context grammars, *Proc. of the 35th Spring Conference: Modelling and Simulation of Systems*, MARQ Ostrava, Hardec nad Moravicí, pp. 145–152.

[42] Martín-Vide, C., Mitrana, V. & Păun, G. (eds) [2004]. *Formal languages and applications*, Springer-Verlag, Berlin.

[43] McMillan, K. [1995]. A technique of a state space search based on unfolding, *Formal Methods in System Design* 6(1): 45–65.

[44] Moriya, E. [1973]. Associate languages and derivational complexity of formal grammars and languages, *Information and Control* 22: 139–162.

[45] Murata, T. [1989]. Petri nets: Properties, analysis and applications, *Proceedings of the IEEE* 77(4): 541–580.

[46] Peterson, J. [1976]. Computation sequence sets, *J. Computer and System Sciences* 13: 1–24.

[47] Peterson, J. [1981]. *Petri net theory and modeling of systems*, Prentice-Hall, Englewood Cliffs, NJ.

[48] Păun, G. [1977]. On the index of grammars and languages, *Inf. Contr.* 35: 259–266.

[49] Păun, G. [1979]. On the family of finite index matrix languages, *JCSS* 18(3): 267–280.

[50] Reisig, W. & Rozenberg, G. (eds) [1998]. *Lectures on Petri Nets I: Basic Models*, Vol. 1491 of *LNCS*, Springer, Berlin.

[51] Rozenberg, G. [1976]. More on ET0L systems versus random context grammars, *IPL* 5(4): 102–106.

[52] Rozenberg, G. & Salomaa, A. (eds) [1997]. *Handbook of formal languages*, Vol. 1–3, Springer.

[53] Rozenberg, G. & Vermeir, D. [1978a]. On ET0L systems of finite index, *Inf. Contr.* 38: 103–133.

[54] Rozenberg, G. & Vermeir, D. [1978b]. On the effect of the finite index restriction on several families of grammars, *Inf. Contr.* 39: 284–302.

[55] Rozenberg, G. & Vermeir, D. [1978c]. On the effect of the finite index restriction on several families of grammars; Part 2: context dependent systems and grammars, *Foundations of Control Engineering* 3(3): 126–142.

[56] Selamat, M. & Turaev, S. [2010]. Grammars controlled by petri nets with place capacities, *2010 International Conference on Computer Research and Development*, pp. 51–55.

[57] Starke, P. [1978]. Free Petri net languages, *Mathematical Foundations of Computer Science 1978*, Vol. 64 of *LNCS*, Springer, Berlin, pp. 506–515.

[58] Starke, P. [1980]. *Petri-Netze*, Deutscher Verlag der Wissenschaften.

[59] Stiebe, R. & Turaev, S. [2009a]. Capacity bounded grammars, *Journal of Automata, Languages and Combinatorics* 15(1/2): 175–194.

[60] Stiebe, R. & Turaev, S. [2009b]. Capacity bounded grammars and Petri nets, *EPTCS* 3: 193–203.

[61] Stiebe, R. & Turaev, S. [2009c]. Capacity bounded grammars and Petri nets, *in* J. Dassow, G. Pighizzini & B. Truthe (eds), *Eleventh International Workshop on Descriptional Complexity of Formal Systems, Magdeburg, Germany*, pp. 247–258.

[62] Turaev, S. [2007]. Petri net controlled grammars, *Third Doctoral Workshop on Mathematical and Engineering Methods in Computer Science, MEMICS 2007*, Znojmo, Czechia, pp. 233–240. ISBN 978-80-7355-077-6.

[63] Turaev, S., Krassovitskiy, A., Othman, M. & Selamat, M. [2011]. Parsing algorithms for grammars with regulated rewriting, *in* A. Zaharim, K. Sopian, N. Mostorakis & V. Mladenov (eds), *Recent Researches in Applied Informatics and Remote Sensing. The 11th WSEAS International Conference on APPLIED COMPUTER SCIENCE*, pp. 103–109.

[64] Turaev, S., Krassovitskiy, A., Othman, M. & Selamat, M. [2012]. Parsing algorithms for regulated grammars, *Mathematical Models & Methods in Applied Science* . (to appear).

[65] Zetzsche, G. [2009]. Erasing in petri net languages and matrix grammars, *Proceedings of the 13th International Conference on Developments in Language Theory*, DLT '09, Springer-Verlag, Berlin, Heidelberg, pp. 490–501.

Chapter 7

A Petri Net-Based Approach to the Quantification of Data Center Dependability

Gustavo Callou, Paulo Maciel, Dietmar Tutsch, Julian Araújo,
João Ferreira and Rafael Souza

Additional information is available at the end of the chapter

1. Introduction

Data center availability and reliability have accomplished greater concern due to increased dependence on Internet services (e.g., Cloud computing paradigm, social networks and e-commerce). For companies that heavily depend on the Internet for their operations, service outages can be very expensive, easily running into millions of dollars per hour [15]. A widely used design principle in fault-tolerance is to introduce redundancy to enhance availability. However, since redundancy leads to additional use of resources and energy, it is expected to have a negative impact on sustainability and the associated cost.

Data center designers need to verify several trade-offs and select the feasible solution considering dependability metrics. In this context, formal models (e.g., Stochastic Petri nets and Reliability Block Diagrams) are important to provide estimates before implementing the data center system. Additionally, a growing concern of data center designers is related to the identification of components that may cause system failure as well as systems parts that must be improved before implementing the architecture.

In this work, we propose a set of formal models for quantifying dependability metrics for data center power infrastructures. The adopted approach takes into account a hybrid modeling technique that considers the advantages of both stochastic Petri nets (SPN) [22] and reliability block diagrams (RBD) [10] to evaluate system dependability. An integrated environment, namely, ASTRO [20] has been developed as one of the results of this work to automate dependability evaluation of data center architectures.

2. Preliminaries

This section briefly touches some fundamental concepts as a basis for a better understanding of this work.

2.1. Petri nets

Petri nets (PN) were introduced in 1962 by the PhD dissertation of Carl Adams Petri [16], at Technical University of Darmstandt, Germany. The original theory was developed as an approach to model and analyze communication systems. Petri Nets (PNs) [14] are a graphic and mathematical modeling tool that can be applied in several types of systems and allow the modeling of parallel, concurrent, asynchronous and non-deterministic systems. Since its seminal work, many representations and extensions have been proposed for allowing more concise descriptions and for representing systems feature not observed on the early models. Thus, the simple Petri net has subsequently been adapted and extended in several directions, in which timed, stochastic, high-level, object-oriented and coloured nets are a few examples of the proposed extensions.

2.2. Place-Transition nets

Place/Transition Petri nets are one of the most prominent and best studied class of Petri nets, and it is sometimes called just by Petri net (PN). A marked Place/Transition Petri net is a bipartite directed graph, usually defined as follows:

Definition 2.1. (Petri net) A Petri net [14] is a 5-tuple:

$$PN = (P, T, F, W, M_0)$$

where:

1. $P = \{p_1, p_2, ..., p_m\}$ is a finite set of places;
2. $T = \{t_1, t_2, ..., t_n\}$ is a finite set of transitions;
3. $F \subseteq (P \times T) \cup (T \times P)$ is a set of arcs (flow relation);
4. $W : F \rightarrow \{1, 2, 3, ...\}$ is a weight function;
5. $M_0 : P \rightarrow \{0, 1, 2, 3, ...\}$ is the initial marking;

This class of Petri net has two kinds of nodes, called places (P) represented by circles and transitions (T) represented by bars, such that $P \cap T =$ and $P \cup T \neq$. Figure 1 depicts the basic elements of a simple PN. The set of arcs F is used to denote the places connected to a transition (and vice-versa). W is a weight function for the set of arcs. In this case, each arc is said to have multiplicity k, where k represents the respective weight of the arc. Figure 2 shows multiple arcs connecting places and transitions in a compact way by a single arc labeling it with its weight or multiplicity k.

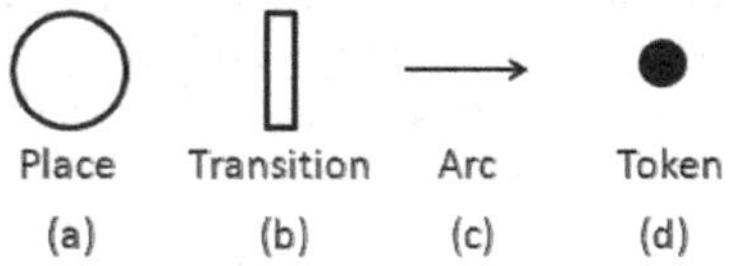

Figure 1. Petri net basic elements.

Places and transitions may have several interpretations. Using the concept of conditions and events, places represent conditions, and transitions represent events, such that, an event may have several pre-conditions and post-conditions. For more interpretations, Table 1 shows other meanings for places and transitions [14].

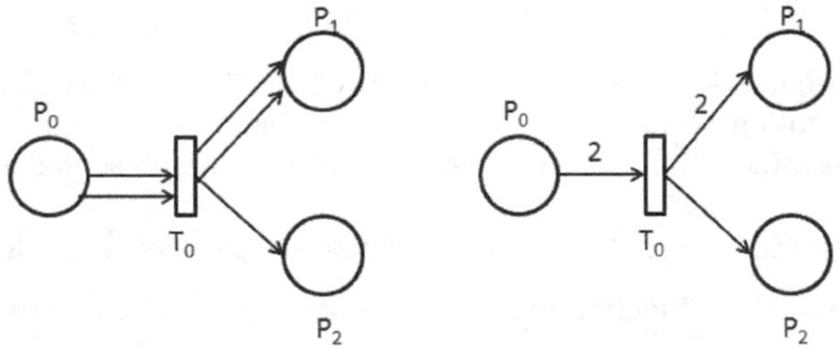

Figure 2. Compact representation of a PN

Input Places	Transitions	Output Places
pre-conditions	events	post-conditions
input data	computation step	output data
input signals	signal processor	output signals
resource needed	tasks	resource releasing
conditions	logical clauses	conclusions
buffers	processor	buffers

Table 1. Interpretation for places and transitions.

It is important to show that there are another way to represent PN's elements. As an example, the set of input and output places of transitions is shown in Definition 2.2. Similarly, the set of input and output transitions of determinate place is shown in Definition 2.3.

Definition 2.2. (Input and Output Transitions of a place) The set of input transitions (also called pre-set) of a place $p_i \in P$ is:

$$\text{label} = \bullet p_i = \{t_j \in T | (t_j, p_i) \in F\}.$$

and the set of output transitions (also called post-set) is:

$$\text{label} = p_i \bullet = \{t_j \in T | (p_i, t_j) \in F\}.$$

Definition 2.3. (Input and output places of a transition) The set of input places of a transition $t_j \in T$ is:

$$\text{label} = \bullet t_j = \{p_i \in P | (p_i, t_j) \in F\}.$$

and the set of output places of a transition $t_j \in T$ is:

$$\text{label} = t_j \bullet = \{p_i \in P | (t_j, p_i) \in F\}.$$

2.2.1. *Marked Petri nets*

A marking (also named token) has a primitive concept in PNs such as place and transitions. Markings are information attributed to places; the number and mark distributions consist of the net state in determined moment. The formal definitions are presented as follows.

Definition 2.4. (Marking) Considering the set of places P in a net N, the formal definition of marking is represented by a function that maps the set of places P into non negative integers $M : P \to \mathbb{N}$.

Definition 2.5. (Marking vector) Considering the set of places P in a net N, the marking can be defined as a vector $M = (M(p_1), ..., M(p_n))$, where $n = \#(P)$, $\forall p_i \in P \;/\; M(p_i) \in \mathbb{N}$. Thus, such vector gives the number of tokens in each place for the marking M_i.

Definition 2.6. (Marked net) A marked Petri net is defined by a tupla $NM = (N; M_0)$, where N is the net structure and M_0 is the initial marking.

A marked Petri net contains tokens, which reside in places, travel along arcs, and their flow through the net is regulated by transitions. A peculiar distribution (M) of the tokens in the places, represents a specific state of the system. These tokens are denoted by black dots inside the places as shown in Figure 1 (d).

2.2.2. *Transition enabling and firing*

The behavior of many systems can be described in terms of system states and their changes. In order to simulate the dynamic behavior of a system, a state (or marking) in a Petri net is changed according to the following firing rule:

1. A transition t is said to be enabled, if each input place p of t is marked with at least the number of tokens equal to the multiplicity of its arc connecting p with t. Adopting a mathematical notation, an enabled transition t for given marking m_i is denoted by $m_i[t>$, if $m_i(p_j) \geq W(p_j, t), \forall p_j \in P$.
2. An enabled transition may or may not fire (depending on whether or not the respective event takes place).
3. The firing of an enabled transition t removes tokens (equal to the multiplicity of the input arc) from each input place p, and adds tokens (equal to the multiplicity of the output arc) to each output place p'. Using a mathematical notation, the firing of a transition is represented by the equation $m_j(p) = m_i(p) - W(p,t) + W(t,p), \forall p \in P$. If a marking m_j is reachable from m_i by firing a transition t, it is denoted by $m_i[t > m_j$.

Figure 3 (a) shows the mathematical representation of a Petri net model with three places (p_0, p_1, p_2) and one transition (t_0). Besides, there is one arc connecting the place p_0 to the transition t_0 with weight two, one arc from the place p_1 to the transition t_0 with weight one, and one arc connecting the transition t_0 to the place p_2 with weight two. The initial marking (m_0) is represented by three tokens in the place p_0 and one token in the place p_1. Figure 3 (b) outlines its respective graphical representation, and Figure 3 (c) provides the same graphical representation after the firing of t_0. For this example, the set of reachable markings is m = $\{m_0 = (3,1,0), m_1 = (1,0,2)\}$. The marking m_1 was obtained by firing t_0, such that, $m_1(p_0)$ = 3 - 2 + 0, $m_1(p_1)$ = 1 - 1 + 0, and $m_1(p_2)$ = 0 - 0 + 2.

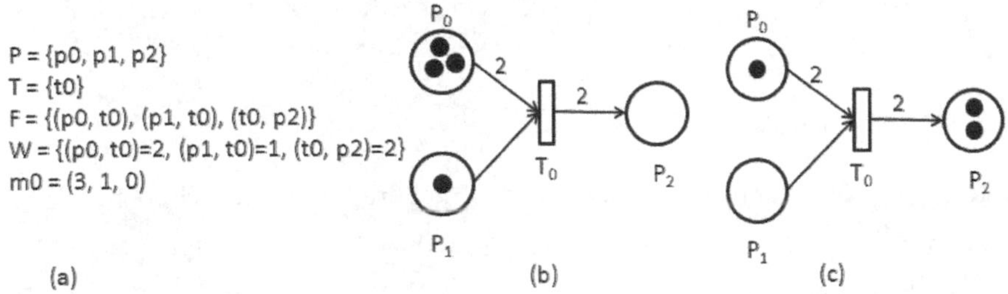

Figure 3. (a) Mathematical formalism; (b) Graphical representation before the firing of t_0; (c) Graphical representation after the firing of t_0.

There are two particular cases which the firing rule happens differently. The first one is a transition without any input place that is called as a *source* transition, and the other one is a transition without any output place, named *sink* transition. A *source* transition is unconditionally enabled, and the firing of a *sink* transition consumes tokens, but does not produce any. Figure 4 (a) shows a *source* transition, and Figure (b) 4 depicts a *sink* transition. In both, the markings are represented before and after their respective firing.

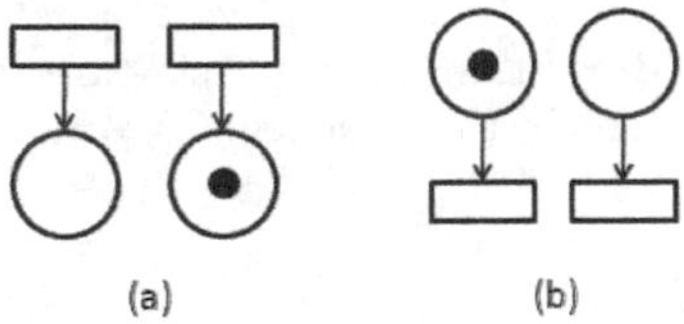

Figure 4. (a) *Source* transitions; (b) *Sink* transitions.

Definition 2.7. (Source transitions) A transition is said to be source if, and only if, $I(p,t) = 0$, $\forall p \in P$.

Definition 2.8. (Sink transitions) A transition is said to be sink if, and only if, $O(p,t) = 0$, $\forall p \in P$.

Definition 2.9. (Inhibitor arc) Originally not present in PN, the introduction of the concept of inhibitor arc increases the modeling power of PN, adding the ability of testing if a place does not have tokens. In the presence of an inhibitor arc, a transition is enabled to fire if each input place connected by a normal arc has a number of tokens equal to the arc weight, and if each input place connected by an inhibitor arc has no tokens. Figure 5 illustrates an inhibitor arc connecting the input place p_0 to the transition t_0, which is denoted by an arc finished with a small circle. In such Figure, the transition t_0 is enabled to fire.

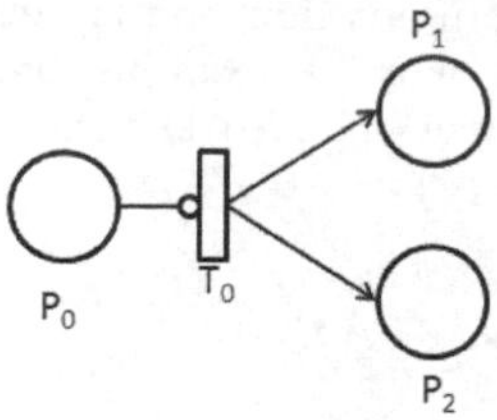

Figure 5. PN with an inhibitor arc.

Definition 2.10. (Pure net) A Petri net is said to be pure if it has no self-loops. A pair of a place p and transition t is called a self-loop if p is both an input and output place of t. Figure 6 shows a self-loop net.

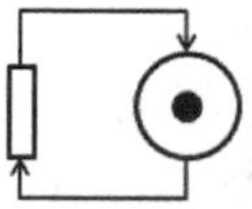

Figure 6. Self-Loop.

2.3. Elementary structures

Elementary nets are used as building blocks in the specification of more complex applications. Figure 7 shows five structures, namely, (a) sequence, (b) fork, (c) synchronization, (d) choice, and (e) merging.

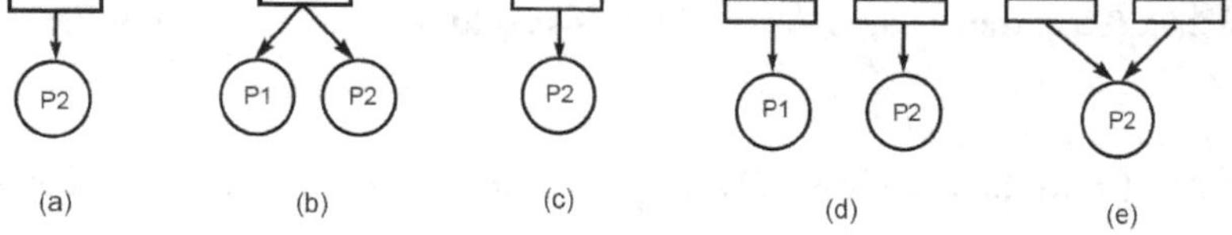

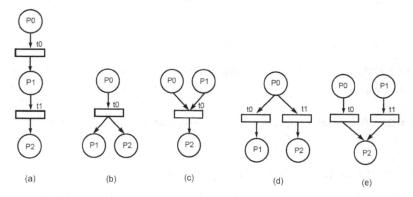

Figure 7. Elementary PN Structures.

Sequence

Sequence structure represents sequential execution of actions, provided that a condition is satisfied. After the firing of a transition, another transition is enabled to fire. Figure 7(a) depicts an example of this structure in which a mark in place p_0 enables the transition t_0. The firing of transition t_0 enables the transition t_1 (p_1 is marked).

Fork

Figure 7(b) shows an example of a fork structure that allows the creation of parallel processes.

Join

Generally, concurrent activities need to synchronize with each other. This net (Figure 7(c)) combines two or more nets, allowing that another process continues this execution only after the end of predecessor processes.

Choice

Figure 7(d) depicts a choice model, in which the firing of the transition $t0$ disables the transition t_1. This building block is suited for modeling if-then-else statement, for instance.

Merging

The merging is an elementary net that allows the enabling of the same transition by two or more processes. Figure 7(e) shows a net with two independent transitions (t_0 and t_1) that have an output place in common ($P2$). Therefore, firing of any of these two transitions, a condition is created (p_2 is marked) which allows the firing of another transition (not shown in the figure).

Confusions

The mixing between conflict and concurrency is called confusion. While conflict is a local phenomenon in the sense that only the pre-sets of the transitions with common input places are involved, confusion involves firing sequences. Figure 8 depicts two types of confusions: (a) symmetric confusion, where two transitions t_1 and t_3 are concurrent while each one is in conflict with transition t_2; and (b) asymmetric confusion, where t_1 is concurrent with t_2, but will be in conflict with t_3 if t_2 fires first.

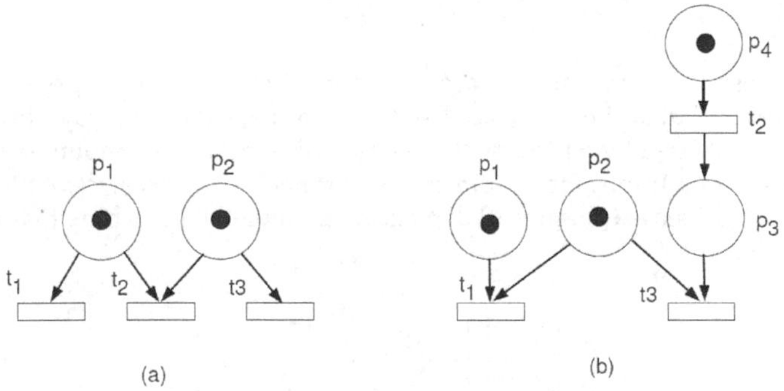

Figure 8. (a) symmetric confusion; (b) asymmetric confusion.

2.4. Petri nets modeling examples

In this section, several simple examples are given in order to introduce how to model some basic concepts such as parallel process and mutual exclusion in Petri nets.

Parallel processes

In order to represent parallel processes, a model may be obtained by composing the model for each individual process with a fork and synchronization models. Two transitions are said to be parallel (or concurrent), if they are causally independent, i.e., one transition may fire either before (or after) or in parallel with the other.

Figure 9 depicts an example of parallel process, where transitions t_1 and t_2 represent parallel activities. When transition t_0 fires, it creates marks in both output places (p_0 and p_1), representing a concurrency. When t_1 and t_2 are enabled for firing, each one may fire independently. The firing of t_3 depends on two pre-conditions, p_2 and p_3, implying that the system only continues if t_1 and t_2 have been fired.

Figure 9 presents a net in which each place has exactly one incoming arc and exactly one outgoing arc. Thus, such model represents a sub-class of Petri nets known as marked graphs. Marked graphs allow representation of concurrency but not decisions or conflicts.

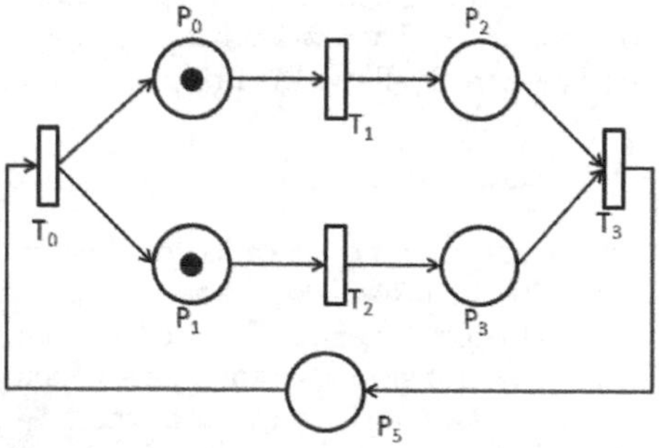

Figure 9. A Petri net representing parallel activities.

Mutual exclusion

The sharing of resources and/or data are common in many system applications, in which most of resources and data should be accessed in a mutual exclusive way. Resources (or data variable) may be modeled by a place with tokens representing the amount of resources. This place is seen as pre-conditions for all transitions that need such resource. After the use of one resource, it must be released. Figure 10 depicts an example of a machine that is accessed in a mutual exclusive way.

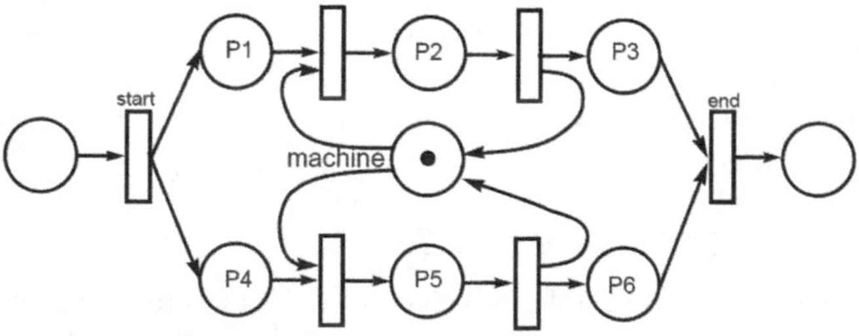

Figure 10. Mutual Exclusion.

Dataflow computation

Petri nets can be used to represent not only the control-flow but also the data-flow. The net shown in Figure 11 is a Petri net representation of a dataflow computation. A dataflow is characterized by the concurrent instruction execution (or transitions firing) as soon as the operands (pre-conditions) are available. In the Petri net representation, tokens may denote values of current data as well as the availability of data. The instructions are represented by transitions such as *Add* and *Subtract* that can be executed in parallel. After that, if the activity *Subtract* has computed a result different from zero, meaning that the pre-conditions to perform *divide* operation were satisfied. Afterwards, when the transition *divide* occur, the dataflow computation is completed.

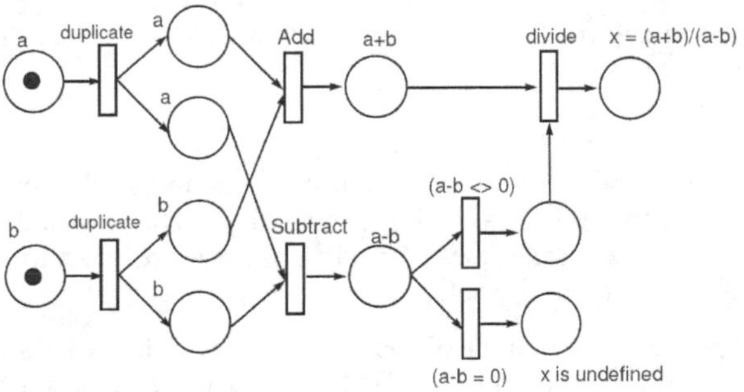

Figure 11. Dataflow example.

2.5. Petri nets properties

The PN properties allow a detailed analysis of the modeled system. For this, two types of properties have been considered in a Petri net model: behavioral and structural properties. Behavioral properties are those which depend on the initial marking. Structural properties, on the other hand, are those that are marking-independent.

2.5.1. *Behavioral properties*

This section, based on [14], describes some behavioral properties, since such properties are very important when analyzing a given system.

Reachability

The firing of an enabled transition changes the token marking in a Petri net, and a sequence of firings results in a sequence of markings. A marking M_n is said to be reachable from a marking M_0 if there exists a sequence of firings that transforms M_0 to M_n.

A firing (or occurrence) sequence is denoted by $\sigma = t_1, t_2, ..., t_n$. In this case, m_i is reachable from m_0 by σ, and it is denoted by $m_0[\sigma > m_i$. The set of all possible reachable markings from m_0 in a net (PN, m_0) is denoted by R(PN,m_0), or simply R(m_0). The set of all possible firing sequence from m_0 in a net (PN,m_0) is denoted by L(PN, m_0), or simply L(m_0).

Boundedness

A Petri net is said to be bounded if the number of tokens in each place does not exceed a finite number k for any marking reachable from M_0. In a formal way, $M(p) \leq k, \forall p \in P$ and $\forall M \in R(M_0)$.

Safe

When the number of tokens in each place does not exceed the number "1" (one), such Petri net is said to be safe. It is important to state that if a net is bounded or safe, it is guaranteed that there will be no overflows in any place, no matter the firing sequence adopted.

Deadlock freedom

A PN is said to be deadlock free if there is no reachable marking such that no transition is enabled.

Liveness

In an informal way, a Petri net is said to be live if it is guaranteed that no matter what firing sequence is chosen, it continues in deadlock-free operation. The formal definition, a Petri net (N,M_0) is said to be live if, no matter what marking has been reached from M_0, it is possible to ultimately fire any transition of the net.

Liveness is an ideal property for many real systems. However, it is very strong and too costly to verify. Thus, the liveness condition is relaxed in different levels. A transition *t* is said to be live at the following levels:

- L_0 Live (dead), if *t* can never be fired in any firing sequence in L(m_0), it is a dead transition.
- L_1-Live (potentially firable), if it can be fired at least once in some firing sequence in L(m_0).
- L_2-Live if, given any positive integer k, *t* can be fired at least k times in some firing sequence in L(m_0).
- L_3-Live if there is an infinite-length firing sequence in L(m_0) in which *t* is fired infinitely.
- L_4-Live (or simply live), if it is L1-Live for every marking m in R(m_0).

Persistence

A Petri net is said to be persistent if, for any two enabled transitions, the firing of one transition will not disable the other. Once a transition is enabled in a persistent net, it is continue to be enabled until it fires. Persistency is closed related to conflict-free nets. It is worth noting that all marked graph are persistent, but not all persistent nets are marked graphs. Persistence is a very important property when dealing with parallel system design and speed-independent asynchronous circuits.

2.5.2. Structural properties

Structural liveness

A PN *N* is said to be structurally live if there is a live initial marking for *N*.

Structural boundedness

A PN *N* is said to be structurally bounded if it is bounded for any finite initial marking M_0.

Structural conservativeness

A PN that provides a constant weighted sum of tokens for any reachable marking when considering any initial marking is said to be structural conservative.

Structural repetitiveness

A PN is classified as repetitive if there is an initial marking m_0 and an enabled firing sequence from m_0 such that every transition of the net is infinitely fired. On the other hand, if only some of these transitions are fired infinitely often in the sequence σ, this net is called partially repetitive.

Consistence

A net is classified as consistent if there is an initial marking m_0 and an enabled firing sequence from m_0 back to m_0 such that every transition of the net is fired at least once. If only some of these transitions are not fired in the sequence σ, this net is called partially consistent.

2.6. Stochastic Petri nets

Petri nets [17] are a classic tool for modeling and analyzing discrete event systems which are too complex to be described by automata or queueing models. Time (stochastic delays) and probabilistic choices are essential aspects for a performance evaluation model. We adopt the usual association of delays and weights with transitions [11] in this paper, and adopt the extended stochastic Petri net definition similar to [9]:

Let *SPN*= $(P, T, I, O, H, \Pi, G, M_0, Atts)$ be a stochastic Petri net, where

- $P = \{p_1, p_2, ..., p_n\}$ is the set of places, which may contain tokens and form the discrete state variables of a Petri net.
- $T = \{t_1, t_2, ..., t_m\}$ is the set of transitions, which model active components.
- $I \in (\mathbb{N}^n \rightarrow \mathbb{N})^{n \times m}$ is a matrix of marking-dependent multiplicities of input arcs, where i_{jk} entry of I gives the (possibly marking-dependent) arc multiplicity of input arcs from place p_j to transition t_k $[A \subseteq (P \times T) \cup (T \times P)$ — set of arcs$]$. A transition is only enabled if there are enough tokens in all input places.
- $O \in (\mathbb{N}^n \rightarrow \mathbb{N})^{n \times m}$ is a matrix of marking dependent multiplicities of output arcs, where o_{jk} entry of O specifies the possibly marking-dependent arc multiplicity of output arcs from transition t_j to place p_k. When a transition fires, it removes the number of tokens specified by the input arcs from input places, and adds the amount of tokens given by the output arcs to all output places.
- $H \in (\mathbb{N}^n \rightarrow \mathbb{N})^{n \times m}$ is a matrix of marking-dependent multiplicities describing the inhibitor arcs, where h_{jk} entry of H returns the possibly marking-dependent arc multiplicity of an inhibitor arc from place $p_j$to transition t_k. In the presence of an inhibitor arc, a transition is enabled to fire only if every place connected by an inhibitor arc contains fewer tokens than the multiplicity of the arc.
- $\Pi \in \mathbb{N}^m$ is a vector that assigns a priority level to each transition. Whenever there are several transitions fireable at one point in time, the one with the highest priority fires first and leads to a state change.

- $M_0 \in \mathbb{N}^n$ is a vector that contains the initial marking for each place (initial state).
- $Atts : (Dist, W, G, Policy, Concurrency)^m$ comprises a set of attributes for the m transitions, where
  - $Dist \in \mathbb{N}^m \rightarrow \mathcal{F}$ is a possibly marking dependent firing probability distribution function. In a stochastic timed Petri net, time has to elapse between the enabling and firing of a transition. The actual firing time is a random variable, for which the distribution is specified by $\mathcal{F}$. We differ between immediate transitions ($\mathcal{F} = 0$) and timed transitions, for which the domain of $\mathcal{F}$ is $(0, \infty)$.
  - $W \in \mathbb{R}^+$ is the weight function, that represents a firing weight w_t for immediate transitions or a rate λ_t for timed transitions. The latter is only meaningful for the standard case of timed transitions with exponentially distributed firing delays. For immediate transitions, the value specifies a relative probability to fire the transition when there are several immediate transitions enabled in a marking, and all have the same probability. A random choice is then applied using the probabilites w_t.
  - $G \in \mathbb{N}^n \rightarrow \{true, false\}$ is a function that assigns a guard condition related to place markings to each transition. Depending on the current marking, transitions may not fire (they are disabled) when the guard function returns false. This is an extension of inhibitor arcs.
  - $Policy \in \{prd, prs\}$ is the preemption policy (*prd — preemptive repeat different* means that when a preempted transition becomes enabled again the previously elapsed firing time is lost; *prs — preemptive resume*, in which the firing time related to a preempted transition is resumed when the transition becomes enabled again),
  - $Concurrency \in \{ss, is\}$ is the concurrency degree of transitions, where *ss* represents single server semantics and *is* depicts infinity server semantics in the same sense as in queueing models. Transitions with policy *is* can be understood as having an individual transition for each set of input tokens, all running in parallel.

In many circumstances, it might be suitable to represent the initial marking as a mapping from the set of places to natural numbers ($m_0 : P \rightarrow \mathbb{N}$), where $m_0(p_i)$ denotes the initial marking of place p_i. $m(p_i)$ denotes a reachable marking (reachable state) of place p_i. In this work, the notation $\#p_i$ has also been adopted for representing $m(p_i)$.

2.7. Dependability

Dependability of a computer system must be understood as the ability to deliver services with respect to some agreed-upon specifications of desired service that can be fully trusted [1, 13]. Indeed, dependability is related to disciplines such as fault tolerance and reliability. Reliability is the probability that the system will deliver a set of services for a given period of time, whereas a system is fault tolerant when it does not fail even when there are faulty components. Availability is also another important concept, which quantifies the mixed effect of both failure and repair process in a system. In general, availability and reliability are related concepts, but they differ in the sense that the former may consider maintenance of failed components [8] (e.g., a failed component is restored to a specified condition).

In many situations, modeling is the method of choice either because the system might not yet exist or due to the inherent complexity for creating specific scenarios under which the system should be evaluated. In a very broad sense, models for dependability evaluation can be classified as simulation and mathematical models. However, this does not mean that mathematical models cannot be simulated. Indeed, many mathematical models, besides being analytically tractable, may also be evaluated by simulation. Mathematical models can be characterized as being either state-based or non-state-based.

Dependability metrics (e.g., availability, reliability and downtime) might be calculated either by using RBD or SPN (to mention only the models adopted in this work). RBDs allow to one represent component networks and provide closed-form equations, so the results are usually obtained faster than using SPN simulation. Nevertheless, when faced with representing maintenance policies and redundant mechanisms, particularly those based on dynamic redundancy methods, such models experience drawbacks concerning the thorough handling of failures and repairing dependencies. On the other hand, state-based methods can easily consider those dependencies, so allowing the representation of complex redundant mechanisms as well as sophisticated maintenance policies. However, they suffer from the state-space explosion. Some of those formalism allow both numerical analysis and stochastic simulation, and SPN is one of the most prominent models of such class.

If one is interested in calculating the availability (A) of given device or system, he/she might need either the uptime and downtime or the time to failure (TTF) and time to repair (TTR). Considering that the uptime and downtime are not available, the later option is the mean. If the evaluator needs only the mean value, the metrics commonly adopted are Mean Time to Failure ($MTTF$) and Mean Time To Repair ($MTTR$) (other central values might also be adopted). However, if one is also interested in the availability variation, the standard deviation of time to failure ($sd(TTF)$), and the respective standard deviation of time to repair ($sd(TTR)$) allow one the estimate the availability variation.

The availability (A) is obtained by steady-state analysis or simulation, and the following equation expresses the relation concerning $MTTF$ and $MTTR$:

$$A = \frac{MTTF}{MTTF + MTTR} \tag{1}$$

Through transient analysis or simulation, the reliability (R) is obtained, and, then, the $MTTF$ can be calculated as well as the standard deviation of the Time To Failure (TTF):

$$MTTF = \int_0^\infty tf(t)dt = \int_0^\infty -\frac{dR(t)}{dt} tdt = \int_0^\infty R(t)dt \tag{2}$$

$$sd(TTF) = \sqrt{\int_0^\infty t^2 f(t)dt - (MTTF)^2} \tag{3}$$

Considering a given period t, $R(t)$ is the probability that the time to failure is greater than or equal to t. Regarding exponential failure distributions, reliability is computed as follows:

$$R(t) = exp\left[-\int_0^t \lambda(t')dt'\right] \tag{4}$$

where $\lambda(t')$ is the instantaneous failure rate.

One should bear in mind that, for computing reliability of a given system service, the repairing activity of the respective service must not be represented. Besides, taking into account $UA = 1 - A$ (unavailability) and Equation 1, the following equation is derived

$$MTTR = MTTF \times \frac{UA}{A} \tag{5}$$

As well, the standard deviation of the Time To Repair (TTR) can be calculated as follows:

$$sd(TTR) = sd(TTF) \times \frac{UA}{A} \tag{6}$$

Next, $\frac{MTTF}{sd(TTF)}$ (and $\frac{MTTR}{sd(TTR)}$) are computed for choosing the expolinomial distribution that best fits the TTF and TTR distributions [6, 22].

Figure 12 depicts the generic simple component model using SPN, which provides a high-level representation of a subsystem. One should notice the trapezoidal shape of transitions (high-level transition named s-transition). This shape means that the time distributions of such transitions are not exponentially distributed, instead they should be refined by subnets. The delay assigned to s-transition f is the TTF and the delay of s-transition r is the TTR. If the TTF and TTR are exponentially distributed, the shape of the transitions should be the regular one (white rectangles) and TTF and TTR should be summarized by the respective $MTTF$ and $MTTR$.

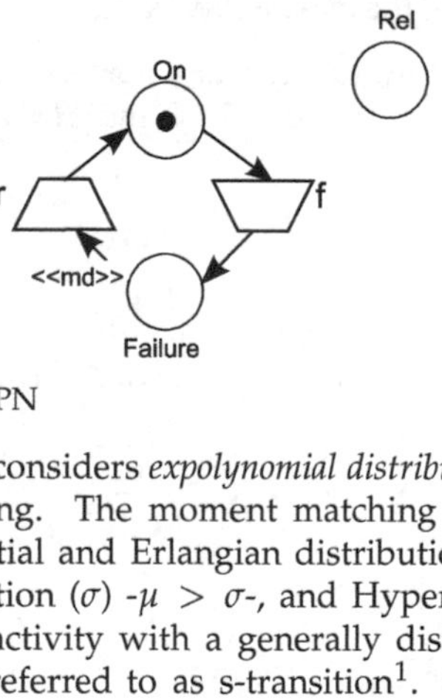

Figure 12. Generic simple model - SPN

A well-established method that considers *expolynomial distribution* random variables is based on distribution moment matching. The moment matching process presented in [6] takes into account that Hypoexponential and Erlangian distributions have the average delay (μ) greater than the standard-deviation (σ) -$\mu > \sigma$-, and Hyperexponential distributions have $\mu < \sigma$, in order to represent an activity with a generally distributed delay as an Erlangian or a Hyperexponential subnet referred to as s-transition[1]. One should note that in cases where these distributions have $\mu = \sigma$, they are, indeed, equivalent to an exponential distribution with parameter equal to $\frac{1}{\mu}$. Therefore, according to the coefficient of variation associated with an activity's delay, an appropriate s-transition implementation model could be chosen. For each s-transition implementation model (see Figure 13), a set of parameters should be configured for matching their first and second moments. In other words, an associated delay distribution (it might have been obtained by a measuring process) of the

[1] In this work, μ could be $MTTF$ or $MTTR$ and the σ could represent $sd(TTF)$ or $sd(TTR)$, for instance.

original activity is matched with the first and second moments of s-transition (*expolynomial distribution*). According to the aforementioned method, one activity with $\mu<\sigma$ is approximated by a two-phase Hyperexponential distribution with parameters

$$r_1 = \frac{2\mu^2}{(\mu^2+\sigma^2)}, \tag{7}$$

$$r_2 = 1 - r_1 \tag{8}$$

and

$$\lambda = \frac{2\mu}{(\mu^2+\sigma^2)}. \tag{9}$$

where λ is the rate associated to phase 1, r_1 is the probability of related to this phase, and r_2 is the probability assigned to phase 2. In this particular model, the rate assigned to phase 2 is assumed to be infinity, that is, the related average delay is zero.

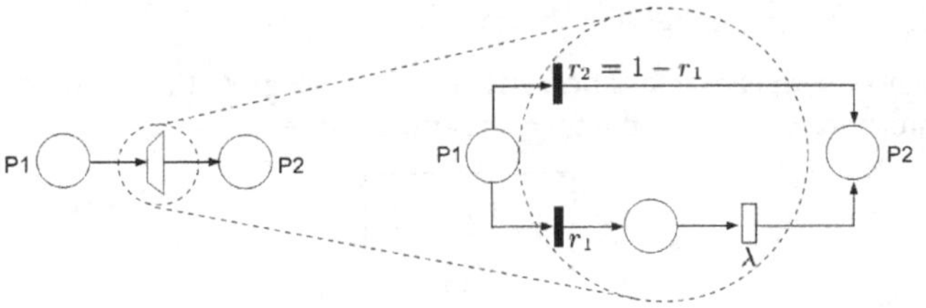

Figure 13. Hyperexponential Model

Activities with coefficients of variation less than one might be mapped either to Hypoexponential or Erlangian s-transi-
tions. If $\frac{\mu}{\sigma} \notin \mathbb{N}, \frac{\mu}{\sigma} \neq 1, (\mu, \sigma \neq 0)$, the respective activity is represented by a Hypoexponential distribution with parameters λ_1, λ_2(exponential rates); and γ, the integer representing the number of phases with rate equal to λ_2, whereas the number of phases with rate equal to λ_1 is one. In other words, the s-transition is represented by a subnet composed of two exponential and one immediate transitions. The average delay assigned to the exponential transition t_1 is equal to μ_1 ($\lambda_1 = 1/\mu_1$), and the respective average delay assigned to the exponential transition t_2 is $\mu_2(\lambda_2 = 1/\mu_2)$. γ is the integer value considered as the weight assigned to the output arc of transition t_1 as well as the input arc weight value of the immediate transition t_3 (see Figure 14). These parameters are calculated by the following expressions:

$$(\frac{\mu}{\sigma})^2 - 1 \leq \gamma < (\frac{\mu}{\sigma})^2, \tag{10}$$

$$\lambda_1 = \frac{1}{\mu_1} \; and \, _2 = \frac{1}{\mu_2}, \tag{11}$$

where

$$\mu_1 = \frac{\mu \pm \sqrt{\gamma(\gamma+1)\sigma^2 - \gamma\mu^2}}{\gamma+1}, \tag{12}$$

$$\mu_2 = \frac{\gamma\mu \mp \sqrt{\gamma(\gamma+1)\sigma^2 - \gamma\mu^2}}{\gamma+1} \tag{13}$$

If $\frac{\mu}{\sigma} \in \mathbb{N}, \frac{\mu}{\sigma} \neq 1, (\mu, \sigma \neq 0)$, an Erlangian s-transition with two parameters, $\gamma = (\frac{\mu}{\sigma})^2$ is an integer representing the number of phases of this distribution; and $\mu_1 = \mu/\gamma$, where $\mu_1(1/\lambda_1)$ is the average delay value of each phase. The Erlangian model is a particular case of a Hypoexponential model, in which each individual phase rate has the same value.

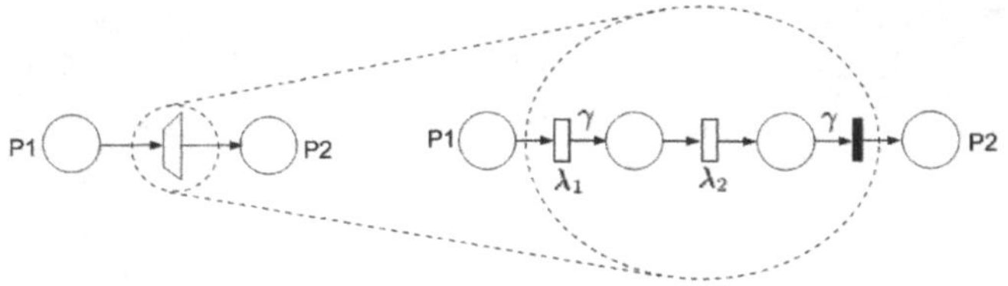

Figure 14. Hypoexponential Model

The reader should refer to [6] for details regarding the representation of expolinomial distributions using SPN. For the sake of simplicity, the SPN models presented in the next sections consider only exponential distributions.

Depending on the system characteristics, a RBD model (Figure 15) could be adopted instead of the SPN counterpart, whenever the former is more suitable.

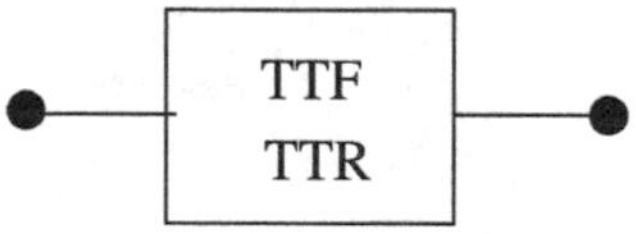

Figure 15. Generic simple model - RBD

3. Related works

In the last few years, some works have been developed to perform dependability analysis of data center systems [24][26][27]. Reliability (which encompasses both the durability of the data and its availability for access) correspond to the primary property that data center users desire [2], .

Robidoux [28] proposes Dynamic RBD (DRBD) model, an extension to RBD, which supports reliability analysis of systems with dependence relationships. The additional blocks (in relation to RBD) to model dependence, turned the DRBD model complex. The DRBD model is automatic converted to CPN model in order to perform behavior properties analysis which may certify the correctness of the model [18]. It seems that an interesting alternative would be to model the system directly using CPN or any other formalism (e.g., SPN) which is able to perform dependability analysis as well as to model dependencies between components.

Wei [25] presents an hierarchical method to model and analyze virtual data center (VDC). The approach combines the advances of both RBD and General SPN (GSPN) for quantifying availability and reliability. Data center power architectures are not the focus of their research and the proposed models are specific for modeling VDC.

Additionally, redundancies on components to increase system reliability are costly. [7] propose an approach for reliability evaluation and risk analysis of dynamic process systems using stochastic Petri nets.

Different from previous works, this paper proposes a set of models to the quantification of dependability metrics in the context of data center design. Furthermore, the adopted methodology for the quantification of those values takes into account a hybrid modeling approach, which utilizes RBD and SPN whenever they are best suited. The idea of mixing state (SPN) and non-state (RBD) based models is not new (e.g., [23]), but, as far as we are concerned, there is no similar work that applies such technique on the evaluation of data center infrastructures. Besides, a tool is proposed to automate several activities.

4. Dependability models

The following sections presents the adopted dependability models.

RBD Models

Reliability Block Diagram (RBD) [8] is a combinatorial model that was initially proposed as a technique for calculating reliability of systems using intuitive block diagrams. Such a technique has also been extended to calculate other dependability metrics, such as availability and maintainability [10]. Figure 16 depicts two examples, in which independent blocks are arranged through series (Figure 16(a)) and parallel (Figure 16(b)) compositions.

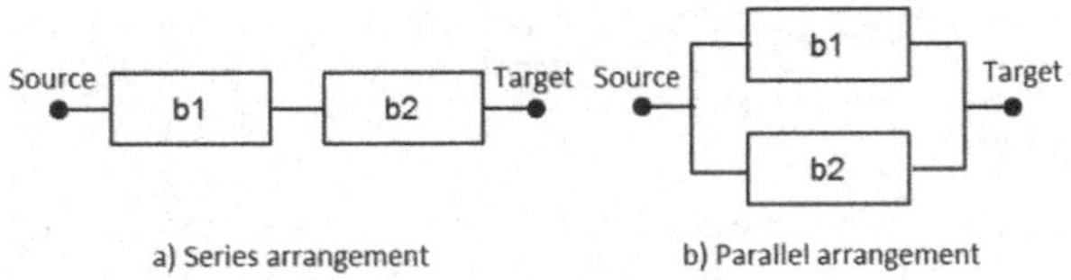

Figure 16. Reliability Block Diagram

In the series arrangement, if a single component fails, the whole system is no longer operational. Assuming a system with n independent components, the reliability (instantaneous availability or steady state availability) is obtained by

$$P_s = \prod_{i=1}^{n} P_i \tag{14}$$

where P_i is the reliability - $R_i(t)$ (instantaneous availability ($A_i(t)$) or steady state availability (A_i)) of block b_i.

For a parallel arrangement (see Figure 16(b)), if a single component is operational, the whole system is also operational. Assuming a system with n independent components, the reliability (instantaneous availability or steady state availability) is obtained by

$$P_p = 1 - \prod_{i=1}^{n}(1 - P_i) \tag{15}$$

where P_i is the reliability - $R_i(t)$ (instantaneous availability ($A_i(t)$) or steady state availability (A_i)) of block b_i.

A k-out-of-n system functions if and only if k or more of its n components are functioning. Let p be the success probability of each of those blocks. The system success probability (reliability or availability) is depicted by:

$$\Sigma_{i=k}^{n}\binom{n}{b}p^{k}(1-p)^{n-k} \tag{16}$$

For other examples and closed-form equations, the reader should refer to [10].

SPN Models

This section presents two proposed SPN building block for obtaining dependability metrics.

Simple Component. The simple component has two states: functioning or failed. To compute its availability, $MTTF$ and $MTTR$ should be represented. Figure 17 shows the SPN model of the "simple component", which has two parameters (not depicted in the figure), namely X_MTTF and X_MTTR, representing the delays associated to the transitions $X\_Failure$ and X_Repair, respectively.

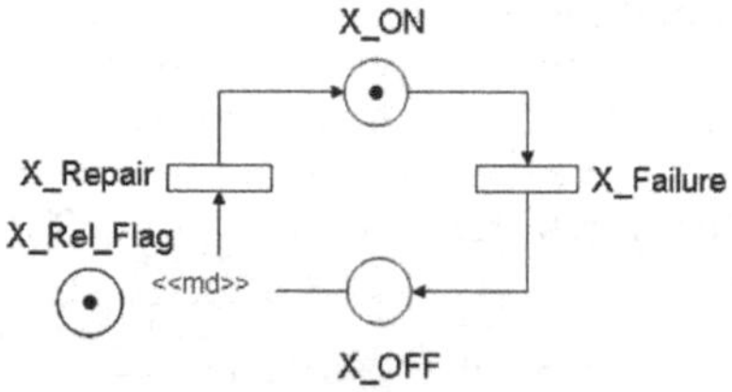

Figure 17. Simple component model

Places X_ON and X_OFF are the model component's activity and inactivity states, respectively. The simple component also includes an arc from X_OFF to X_Repair with multiplicity depending on place marking. The multiplicity is defined through the expression IF(#X_Rel_Flag = 1):2 ELSE 1, where place X_Rel_Flag models the evaluation of reliability/availability. Hence, if condition #X_Rel_Flag = 1 is true, then the evaluation refers to reliability. Otherwise, the evaluation concerns availability.

Besides, although simple component model has been presented using the exponential distribution, other expolinomial distributions that best fits the TTF and TTR may be adopted following the techniques presented in [22].

Cold standby. A cold standby redundant system is composed by a non-active spare module that waits to be activated when the main active module fails. Figure 18 depicts the SPN model of this system, which includes four places, namely X_ON, X_OFF, X_Spare1_ON, X_Spare1_OFF that represent the operational and failure states of both the main and spare modules, respectively. The spare module (Spare1) is initially deactivated, hence no tokens are initially stored in places X_Spare1_ON and X_Spare1_OFF. When the main module fails, the transition $X\_Activate\_Spare1$ is fired to activate the spare module.

Table 2 presents the attributes of each transition of the model. Once considering reliability evaluation (number of tokens (#) in the place X_Rel_Flag = 1), the X_Repair, $X\_Activate\_Spare1$ and X_Repair_Spare1 transitions receive a huge number (many times larger than the associated MTTF or MTActivate) to represent the absence of repair. The MTActivate corresponds to the mean time to activate the spare module. Besides, when considering reliability, the weight of the edge that connects the place X_Wait_Spare1 and the $X\_Activate\_Spare1$ transition is two; otherwise, it is one. Both availability and reliability may be computed by the probability $P\{\#X\_ON = 1 \text{ OR } \#X\_Spare1\_ON = 1\}$.

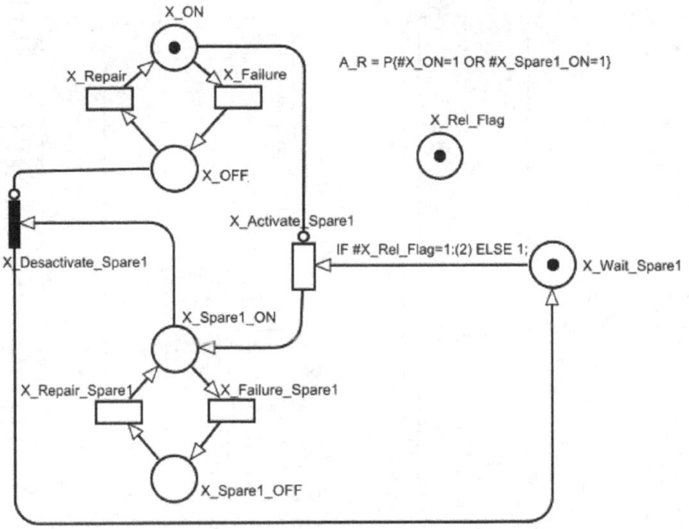

Figure 18. Cold standby model.

Transition	Priority	Delay or Weight
X_Failure	-	X_MTTF
X_Repair	-	IF #X_Rel_Flag=1:(10^{13} x X_MTTF) ELSE X_MTTR
X_Activate_Spare1	-	IF #X_Rel_Flag=1:(10^{13} x MTActivate) ELSE MTActivate
X_Failure_Spare1	-	X_MTTF_Spare1
X_Repair_Spare1	-	IF #X_Rel_Flag=1:(10^{13} x X_MTTF_Spare1) ELSE X_MTTR_Spare1
X_Desactivate_Spare1	1	1

Table 2. Cold standby model - Transition attributes.

5. Applications

This section focuses in presenting the applicability of the proposed models to perform dependability analysis of real-world data center power architectures (from HP Labs Palo Alto, U.S. [12]). The environment ASTRO was adopted to conduct the case study. ASTRO was validated through our previous work [5] [3] [4].

5.1. Architectures

Data center power infrastructure is responsible for providing uninterrupted, conditioned power at correct voltage and frequency to the IT equipments. Figure 19 (a) depicts a real-world power infrastructure. From the utility feed (i.e., AC Source), typically, the power goes through voltage panels, uninterruptible power supply (UPS) units, power distribution units (PDUs) (composed of transformers and electrical subpanels), junction boxes, and, finally, to rack PDUs (rack power distribution units). The power infrastructure fails (and, thus, the system) whenever both paths depicted in Figure 19 are not able to provide the power demanded (500 kW) by the IT components (50 racks). The reader should assume a path as a set of redundant interconnected components inside the power infrastructure. Another architecture is analyzed with an additional electricity generator (Figure 19 (b)) for supporting the system when both AC sources are not operational.

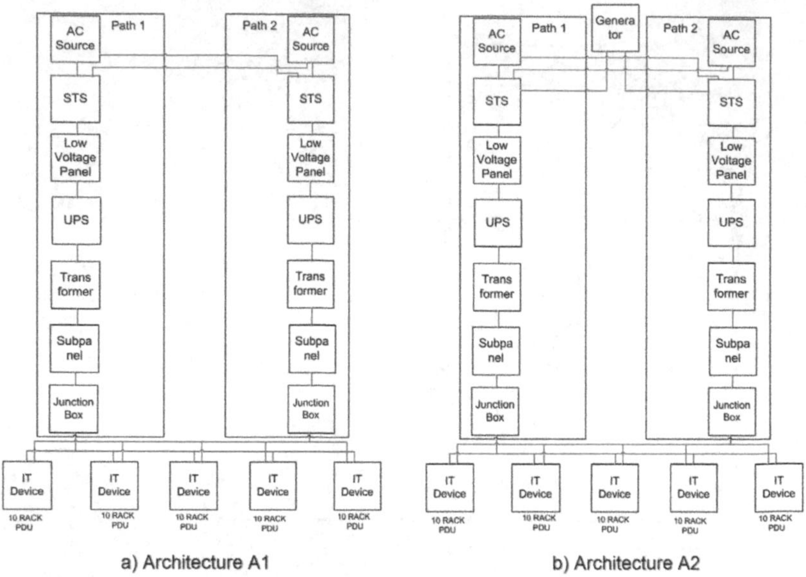

Figure 19. Data Center Power Architectures.

5.2. Models

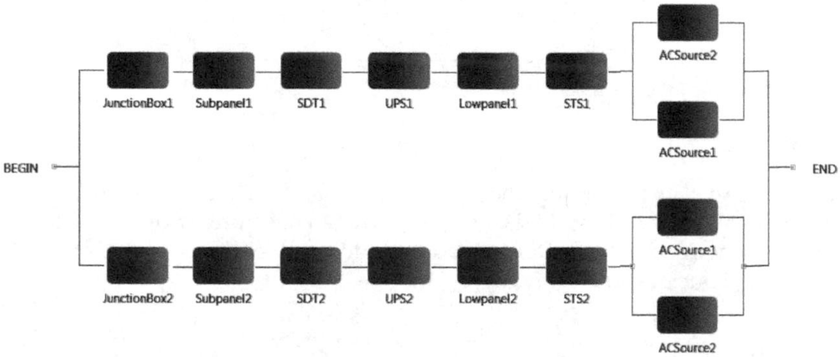

Figure 20. RBD of Architecture A1.

This work adopts a hierarchical methodology for conducting dependability evaluation of data center architectures. In general, the methodology aims at grouping related components in order to generate subsystem models, which are adopted to mitigate the complexity of the final system model evaluation. Thus, the final model is an approximation, but rather simpler, of a more intricate system model. One should bear in mind that the detailed model could be adopted instead, but at the expenses of complexity.

Following the adopted methodology, systems with no failure dependencies between components have been evaluated through RBD models. For instance, Figure 20 depicts the RBD model that represents the architecture A1.

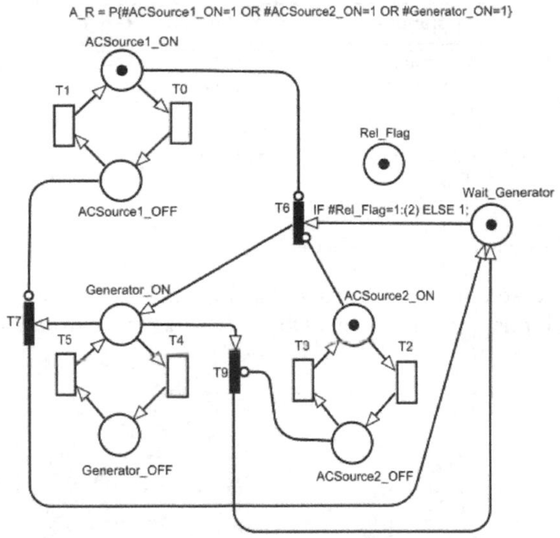

Figure 21. SPN of Architectures A2.

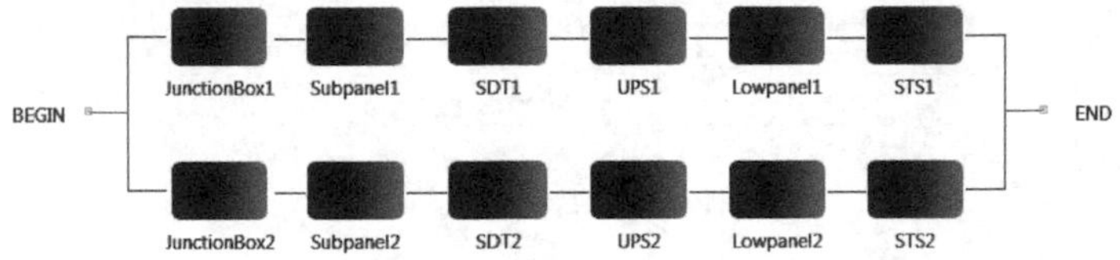

Figure 22. RBD of Architectures A2.

In architecture A2, the generator is only activated when both AC sources are not available. Therefore, a model that deal with dependencies must be adopted. Figure 21 shows the SPN model considering cold standby redundance to represent the subsystem composed of generator and two AC sources. Besides, we assume that UPS' batteries support the system during the generator activation. The reliability or availability is computed by the probability $P\{\#ACSource1\_ON = \text{OR } \#ACSource2\_ON = 1 \text{ OR } \#Generator\_ON = 1\}$.

The other components of the architecture A2 are modeled using RBD as shown in Figure 22. Once obtained the results of both models (RBD and the SPN model with dependencies), a RBD model with two blocks (considering the results of those models) in a serial arrangement is created. The RBD evaluation provides the dependability results of the architecture A2 system.

The adopted MTTF and MTTR values for the power devices were obtained from [21] [29] [19] and are shown in Table 3.

5.3. Results

Figure 23 depicts a graphical comparison between the reliability results (in number of 9's) of those two data center power architectures. The respective number of nines (-*log*[1 - A/100]) and the period of 8760 hours (1 year) are adopted. As the reader should note, the reliability of both architectures decreases when the time increases. Besides, it is also possible to notice that

Equipment	MTTF (hs)	MTTR (hs)
AC Source	4,380	8
Generator	2,190	8
STS	240,384	8
Subpanel	1,520,000	8
Transformer	1,412,908	8
UPS	250,000	8
Low Voltage Panel	1,520,000	8

Table 3. MTTF and MTTR values for power devices.

the generator has increased the reliability of the architecture A2. Considering the availability results, similar behavior happened. The availability has increased from 5.47 to 7.96 (in number of 9's).

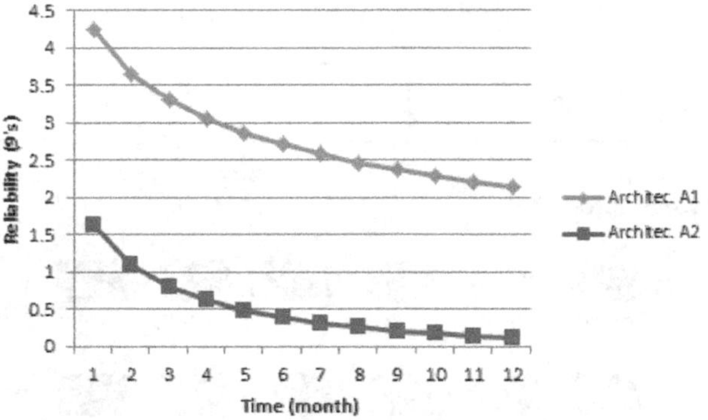

Figure 23. Reliability Comparison of Architectures A1 and A2.

6. Conclusion

This work considers the advantages of both Stochastic Petri Nets (SPN) and Reliability Block Diagrams (RBD) formalisms to analyze data center infrastructures. Such approach is supported by an integrated environment, ASTRO, which allows data center designers to estimate the dependability metrics before implementing the architectures. The methodology proposes that the system should be evaluated piecewisely to allow the composition of simpler models representing a data center infrastructure appropriately. Moreover, experiments demonstrate the feasibility of the environment, in which different architectures for a data center power infrastructures have been adopted.

Acknowledgments

The authors would like to thank CNPQ for financing the project (290018/2011-0) and supporting the development of this work.

Author details

Gustavo Callou, Paulo Maciel, Julian Araújo, João Ferreira and Rafael Souza
Informatics Center, Federal University of Pernambuco - Recife, Brazil

Dietmar Tutsch
Automation/Computer Science, University of Wuppertal, Wuppertal, Germany

7. References

[1] Avizienis, A., Laprie, J. & Randell, B. [2001]. Fundamental Concepts of Dependability, *Technical Report Series-University of Newcastle upon Tyne Computing Science* .

[2] Banerjee, P., Bash, C., Friedrich, R., Goldsack, P., Huberman, B. A., Manley, J., Patel, C., Ranganathan, P. & Veitch., A. [2011]. Everything as a service: Powering the new information economy, *IEEE Computer* pp. 36–43.

[3] Callou, G., Maciel, P., Magnani, F., Figueiredo, J., Sousa, E., Tavares, E., Silva, B., Neves, F. & Araujo, C. [2011]. Estimating sustainability impact, total cost of ownership and dependability metrics on data center infrastructures, *Sustainable Systems and Technology (ISSST), 2011 IEEE International Symposium on*, pp. 1 –6.

[4] Callou, G., Maciel, P., Tavares, E., Sousa, E., Silva, B., Figueiredo, J., Araujo, C., Magnani, F. & Neves, F. [2011]. Sustainability and dependability evaluation on data center architectures, *Systems, Man, and Cybernetics (SMC), 2011 IEEE International Conference on*, pp. 398 –403.

[5] Callou, G., Sousa, E., Maciel, P., Tavares, E., Silva, B., Figueirêdo, J., Araujo, C., Magnani, F. & Neves, F. [2011]. A formal approach to the quantification of sustainability and dependability metrics on data center infrastructures, *Proceedings of the 2011 Symposium on Theory of Modeling & Simulation: DEVS Integrative M&S Symposium*, TMS-DEVS '11, Society for Computer Simulation International, San Diego, CA, USA, pp. 274–281.
URL: *http://dl.acm.org/citation.cfm?id=2048476.2048512*

[6] Desrochers, A. & Al-Jaar, R. [1995]. *Applications of Petri Nets in Manufacturing Systems: Modeling, Control, and Performance Analysis*, IEEE Press.

[7] Dutuit, Y., Chātelet, E., Signoret, J. & Thomas, P. [1997]. Dependability modelling and evaluation by using stochastic Petri nets: application to two test cases, *Reliability Engineering & System Safety* 55(2): 117–124.

[8] Ebeling, C. [1997]. *An Introduction to Reliability and Maintainability Engineering*, Waveland Press.

[9] German, R. [2000]. *Performance Analysis of Communication Systems with Non-Markovian Stochastic Petri Nets*, John Wiley & Sons, Inc., New York, NY, USA.

[10] Kuo, W. & Zuo, M. J. [2003]. *Optimal Reliability Modeling - Principles and Applications*, Wiley.

[11] Marsan, M. A., Balbo, G., Conte, G., Donatelli, S. & Franceschinis, G. [1995]. *Modelling with Generalized Stochastic Petri Nets.*, John Wiley and Sons.

[12] Marwah, M., Maciel, P., Shah, A., Sharma, R., Christian, T., Almeida, V., Araújo, C., Souza, E., Callou, G., Silva, B., Galdino, S. & Pires, J. [2010]. Quantifying the sustainability impact of data center availability, *SIGMETRICS Perform. Eval. Rev.* 37: 64–68.
URL: *http://doi.acm.org/10.1145/1773394.1773405*

[13] Meyer, J. F. & Sanders, W. H. [1993]. Specification and construction of performability models., *Proceedings of the Second International Workshop on Performability Modeling of Computer and Communication Systems, Mont Saint-Michel, France.*

[14] Murata, T. [1989]. Petri nets: Properties, analysis and applications, *Proceedings of the IEEE* 77(4): 541 –580.

[15] Patterson, D. [2002]. A simple way to estimate the cost of downtime, *Proceedings of the 16th USENIX conference on System administration*, LISA '02, USENIX Association, Berkeley, CA, USA, pp. 185–188.
URL: *http://dl.acm.org/citation.cfm?id=1050517.1050538*

[16] Petri, C. A. [1962]. *Kommunikation mit Automaten*, PhD Dissertation, Darmstad University, Germany.

[17] Reisig, W. [1985]. *Petri nets: an introduction*, Springer-Verlag New York, Inc., New York, NY, USA.

[18] Robidoux, R., Xu, H., Member, S., Xing, L., Member, S. & Zhou, M. [2010]. Automated modeling of dynamic reliability block diagrams using colored petri nets, *IEEE Transactions on Systems, Man, and Cybernetics, Part A: Systems and Humans* 40(2): 337–351.

[19] *Service Level Agreement for Data Center Services* [2012]. http://www.earthlinkbusiness.com/_static/_files/_pdfs/legal/DataCenterServiceSLA.p

[20] Silva, B., Maciel, P., Tavares, E., Araujo, C., Callou, G., Sousa, E., Rosa, N., Marwah, M., Sharma, R., Shah, A., Christian, T. & Pires, J. [2010]. Astro: A tool for dependability evaluation of data center infrastructures, *Systems Man and Cybernetics (SMC), 2010 IEEE International Conference on*, pp. 783 –790.

[21] std., I. [1997]. *Gold Book 473 Design of Reliable Industrial and Commercial Power Systems*, IEEE.

[22] Trivedi, K. [2002]. *Probability and Statistics with Reliability, Queueing, and Computer Science Applications*, 2 edn, Wiley Interscience Publication.

[23] Trivedi, K. & et al [1994]. Reliability analysis techniques explored through a communication network example, *International Workshop on Computer-Aided Design, Test, and Evaluation for Dependability*.

[24] Vilkomir, S. A., Parnas, D. L., Mendiratta, V. B. & Murphy, E. [2006]. Segregated failures model for availability evaluation of fault-tolerant system, *ACSC '06: Proceedings of the 29th Australasian Computer Science Conference*, Australian Computer Society, Inc., Darlinghurst, Australia, Australia, pp. 55–61.

[25] Wei, B., Lin, C. & Kong, X. [2011]. Dependability modeling and analysis for the virtual data center of cloud computing, *High Performance Computing and Communications (HPCC), 2011 IEEE 13th International Conference on*, pp. 784 –789.

[26] Wiboonrat, M. [2008a]. An empirical study on data center system failure diagnosis, *Internet Monitoring and Protection, 2008. ICIMP '08. The Third International Conference on*, pp. 103 –108.

[27] Wiboonrat, M. [2008b]. Risk anatomy of data center power distribution systems, *ICSET'08*.

[28] Xu, H., Xing, L. & Robidoux, R. [2008]. Drbd: Dynamic reliability block diagrams for system reliability modeling, *International Journal of Computers and Applications* .

[29] Zhou, L. & Grover, W. [2005]. A theory for setting the "safety margin" on availability guarantees in an sla, *Design of Reliable Communication Networks, 2005. (DRCN 2005). Proceedings.5th International Workshop on*, p. 7 pp.

Chapter 8

Timed Petri Nets

José Reinaldo Silva and Pedro M. G. del Foyo

Additional information is available at the end of the chapter

1. Introduction

In the early 60's a young researcher in Darmstadt looked for a good representation for communicating systems processes that were mathematically sound and had, at the same time, a visual intuitive flavor. This event marked the beginning of a schematic approach that become very important to the modeling of distributed systems in several and distinct areas of knowledge, from Engineering to biologic systems. Carl Adam Petri presented in 1962 his PHD which included the first definition of what is called today a Petri Net. Since its creation Petri Nets evolved from a sound representation to discrete dynamic systems into a general schemata, capable to represent knowledge about processes and (discrete and distributed) systems according to their internal relations and not to their work domain. Among other advantages, that feature opens the possibility to reuse some experiences acquired in the design of known and well tested systems while treating new challenges.

In the conventional approach, the key issue for modeling is the partial ordering among constituent events and the properties that arise from the arrangement of state and transitions once some basic interpretation rules are preserved. Such representation can respond from several systems of practical use where the foundation for analysis is based in reachability and other property analysis. However, there are some cases where such approach is not enough to represent processes completely, for instance, when the assumption that all transitions can fire instantaneously is no longer a good approximation. In such cases a time delay can be associated to firing transitions. This is absolutely equivalent (in a broader sense) to say that firing pre-conditions must hold for a time delay before the firing is completed. The first approach is called T-time Petri Net and the second P-time Petri Nets.

Thus, what we have in conclusion is that even in a hypothesis that we should consider only firing pre-conditions[1] [31][19] a time delay is associated with a transition location and consequently to its firing. Several applications in manufacturing, business, workflow and

[1] In many text books and review articles the enabling condition is presented using only firing pre-conditions as a requirement. This can be justified since the use of this week firing condition is sufficient if a complete net, that is, that includes its dual part, is used

other processes can use this approach to represent processes in a more realistic way. It is also true tat even with a simple approach a strong representation power can be derived, including the possibility to make some direct performance analysis [29][42]. This is called a time slice or a time interval approach. In general, this augmented nets with time delay (P-time, T-time or even both) are called Timed Petri Nets[2].

There are also cases where it is necessary to use more than time delays. In such cases the time is among the variables that describes the state (a set of places in Petri Nets). Notice that raising the number of variables that characterize a state would make untreatable the enumeration of a net state space. Therefore, a more direct approach is adopted, where each transition is associated to a time interval t_{min} and t_{max} where the first would stand for the minimal waiting time since the enabling until a firing can occur. Similarly, t_{max} stands for the maximum waiting time allowed since enabling up to a firing.

If the time used in the model is a real number, then we call that a Time Petri Net. It should be also noticed that if $t_{min} = t_{max}$ the situation is reduced to the previous one where a deterministic time interval is associated to a transition. Thus, Time Petri Net is the more general model which can be used to model real time systems in several work domains, from electronic and mechatronic systems to logistic a business domains.

In this chapter we focus in the timed systems and its application which are briefly described in section 2. In section 3 we will present a perspective and demand for a framework to model, analysis and simulation of timed (and time) systems mentioning the open discussion about algorithms and approaches to represent the state space. That discussion will be oriented by the recent advances to establish a standard to Petri Nets in general that includes Timed and Time Petri Nets as a extension. Such standard is presented in ISO/IEC 15.909 proposal launched for the first time in 2004. A short presentation of what could be a general formalization to Time Petri Nets is done in section 4. Concluding remarks are in section 5.

2. A schematic description of time dependent systems

Petri Nets are an abstract formal model for describing and studying information processing systems that are characterized as being concurrent, asynchronous, distributed, parallel, non-deterministic and/or stochastic [31]. Since its creation the formalism has been extended by practitioners and theoreticians for dealing with complex systems attached to many application fields. One of those important extensions were proposed to deal with timed systems.

Among several proposed extensions to deal with time we detach two basic models: Ranchamdani's *Timed Petri nets* [34] and Merlin *Time Petri nets* [30]. These two temporal Petri net models are included in t-time nets because time inscriptions are always associated to transitions. Other time extensions have been published including some approaches where time is associated to places or even to both places and arcs (see [13] for a survey).

Formally, Petri Nets can defined as:

---

[2] Some authors also include another possibility where time is associated to the arcs, that is, to a pair (x, y) where $x, y \in X = S \subseteq T$ where S and T denotes the set of places and transitions, respectively.

Definition 1. [Petri Net] A Petri net structure is a directed weighted bipartite graph

$$N = (P, T, A, w)$$

where

P is the finite set of places, $P \neq \emptyset$

T is the finite set of transitions, $T \neq \emptyset$

$A \subseteq (P \times T) \cup (T \times P)$ is the set of arcs from places to transitions and from transitions to places

$w : A \rightarrow \{1, 2, 3, \ldots\}$ is the weight function on the arcs.

We will normally represent the set of places by $P = \{p_1, p_2, \ldots, p_n\}$ and the set of transitions $T = \{t_1, t_2, \ldots, t_m\}$ where $|P| = n$ and $|T| = m$ are the cardinality of the respective sets. A typical arc is of the form (p_i, t_j) or (t_j, p_i) according to arc direction, where its weight w is a positive integer greater than zero.

Definition 2. [Marked Petri Net] A marked Petri net is a five-tuple (P, T, A, w, M) where (P, T, A, w) is a Petri Net and M is a marking, defined as a mapping $M : P \rightarrow \mathbb{N}^+$

Thus, a marking is a row vector with $|P|$ elements. Figure 1 shows a possible marking for a simple Petri Net.

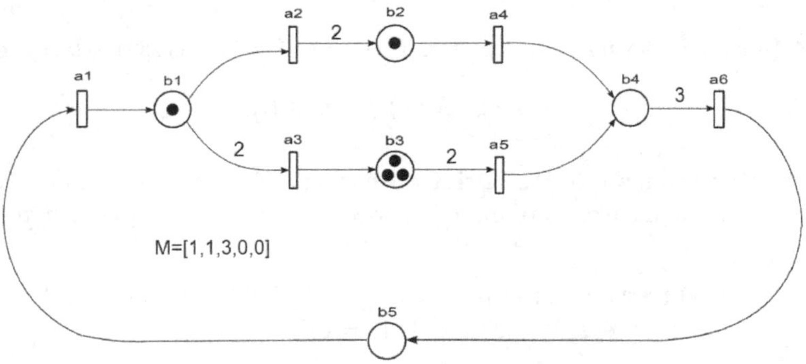

Figure 1. A marked Petri net and it respective marking vector M

The relational functions $Pre, Pos : P \times T \rightarrow \mathbb{N}$ are defined to obtain the number of tokens in places p_i, p_j which are preconditions or postconditions of a transition $t \in T$, that is, there exists arcs $(p_i, t), (p_j, t) \in A$ for the Pre function or $(t, p_i), (t, p_j) \in A$ for the Pos function. In Fig. 1 for instance we have $Pre(b1, a3) = 1$ and $Pos(b3, a3) = 3$.

Using Petri nets to model systems imply in associate net elements (places or transitions) to some components and actions of the modeled system, turning out in what is called "labeled" or "interpreted" nets. The evolution of marking in a labeled Petri nets describes the dynamic behavior of the modeled system.

We restrict the definition of Labeled Petri Net to associate labels only to events or actions similarly to the formalism of automata.

Definition 3. [Labeled Petri Net] A labeled Petri net is a seven-tuple

$$N = (P, T, A, w, E, l, M_0)$$

where

$$(P, T, A, w) \text{ is a Petri net structure}$$
$$E \subseteq \mathbb{P}(T) \ , E \neq \emptyset$$
$$l : T \rightarrow E \text{ is the transition labeling function}$$
$$M_0 : P \rightarrow \mathbb{N}^+ \text{ is the initial state of the net}$$

Labeled Petri Nets has been proved to be an efficient tool for the modeling, analysis and control of Discrete Event System (DES). Petri Nets is a good option to model these DES systems for wide set of applications, from manufacturing, traffic, batch chemical processes, to computer, communications, database and software systems [27]. From now on we shall refer to "labeled Petri nets" simply as "Petri nets".

The state transition mechanism in Petri nets is provided by moving tokens through the net and hence changing to a new state. When a transition is enabled, we say that it can fire or that it can occur.

Definition 4. [Enabled Transition] A transition $t_j \in T$ in a Petri net is said to be enabled if

$$\forall p \in P, \quad M(p) \geq Pre(p, t_j)$$

In other words, a transition t_j in the Petri net is enabled when the number of tokens in p is greater then or equal to the weight of the arc connecting p to t_j , for all places p that are input to transition t_j.

The set of all enabled transition at some marking M is defined as $enb(M)$. In Fig. 1 only transitions $a2$, $a4$ and $a5$ are enabled, then $enb(M) = \{a2, a4, a5\}$.

Definition 5. [State Transition] A Petri net evolves from a marking M to a marking M′ through the firing of a transition $t_f \in T$ only if $t_f \in enb(M)$. The new marking M′ can be obtained by

$$\forall p \in P | (p, t_f) \vee (t_f, p) \in A, M'(p) = M(p) - Pre(p, t_f) + Pos(p, t_f)$$

The reachable markings in a Petri net can be computed using an algebraic equation. Two incidence matrices must be defined (A^- for incoming arcs, and A^+ for outgoing arcs) and a firing vector u which is a (unimodular) row vector containing "1" in the corresponding position of the firing transition and "0" in all other positions.

The new marking can be obtained using the state equation:

$$M' = M + u(A^+ - A^-) \tag{1}$$

This formalism is sufficient to represent a great amount of dynamic discrete systems, based only in partial order sequence of transitions. However, "untimed"[3] Petri nets are not powerful enough to deal with performance evaluations, safety determination, or behavioral properties in systems where time appears as a quantifiable and continuous parameter.

Ramchandani's timed Petri nets were derived from Petri nets by associating a firing finite duration to each transition in the net. Timed Petri nets and related equivalent models have been used mainly to performance evaluation [7].

Definition 6. [Timed Petri Net] A timed Petri net is a six-tuple

$$N = (P, T, A, w, M_0, f)$$

where

(P, T, A, w, M_0) is a marked Petri net

$f : T \to \mathbb{R}^+$ is a firing time function that assigns a positive real number to each transition on the net

Therefore, the firing rule has to be modified in order to consider time elapses in the transition firing. If an enabled transition $t_j \in enb(M)$ then it will fire after $f(t_j)$ times units since it became enabled. The system state is not only determined by the net marking but also by a timer attached to every enabled transition in the net.

Definition 7. [Clock State] The clock state is a pair (M, V), where M is a marking and V is a clock valuation function, $V : enb(M) \to \mathbb{R}^+$

For a clock state (M, V) and $t \in enb(M)$, $V(t)$ is the value of the clock associated with a transition t. The initial clock state is $s_0 = (M_0, V_0)$ where $V_0(t) = f(t), \forall t \in enb(M_0)$.

Definition 8. [New Enabled Transition] A transition $t \in T$ is said new enabled, after firing transition t_f at marking M which leads to marking M', if it is enabled at marking M' and it was not enabled at M or, if it was enabled at M, it is the former fired transition t_f. Formally:

$$new(M') = \{t \in enb(M') | t = t_f \vee \exists p, \ (M'(p) - Pos(p, t_f)) \leq Pre(p, t)\}$$

We denote as $new(M')$ the set of transitions new enabled at marking M'.

The reachability graph of a timed Pedri net can be computed using the definition of firable transition, that is, those transitions that can be fired in a certain marking.

Definition 9. [Firable Transition] A transition $t_f \in T$ can fire in a marking M yielding a marking M' if:

$t_f \in enb(M)$

$V_M(t_f) \leq V_M(t_i) \ \forall t_i \in enb(M)$

[3] A Petri Net where there is no event depending directly or parametrically of the time

We denote as $\Upsilon(M)$ the set of transitions firable at a marking M. Assuming that the firing of transition t_f leads to a new marking M', we denote it as $(M, V_M) \xrightarrow{\tau} (M', V_{M'})$ where $\tau = V_M(t_f)$ is the time elapsed in state transition, M′ is computed using equation 1 and $V_{M'}$ is computed as follows:

$$V_{M'} = \begin{cases} f(t) & \text{se } t \in new(M'); \\ V_M(t) - \tau & \text{se } t \in enb(M') \setminus new(M') \end{cases}$$

The reachability tree can be built including all feasible firing sequences of the timed Petri net. Notice that in M_0 all transition are new enabled, $enb(M_0) = new(M_0)$. However, finite reachability trees can be built only for bounded Petri nets (see bounded property in [31], and an equivalent result for Time Petri in [6]).

Paths or runs in a reachability tree are sequences of state transitions in a timed Petri net. Then, the time elapsed in some path can be computed as the summation of all the elapsed times in the firing schedule. If a path $\omega = s_0 \xrightarrow{\tau_1} s_1 \xrightarrow{\tau_2} s_2 \xrightarrow{\tau_3} s_3$ exists, then the time elapsed between states s_0 and s_3 is $\tau = \tau_1 + \tau_2 + \tau_3$.

The reachabitity tree approach has been successfully used in communication protocols validation and in performance analyses [38, 45]. Moreover, these tests require known computation times for the tasks (often referred by WCET as "Worst Case Execution Time") or process durations. Besides the difficulty to measure or estimate such times, taking into consideration a deterministic time (even in the longest path) does not lead necessarily to the worst case [36].

More realistic analysis can be done on communication protocols using Merlin approach, since some network time durations or even software routines cannot be completed always in the same time [6, 30].

Merlin defined Time Petri Nets (TPN) as nets with a time interval associated to each transition. Assuming that a time interval $[a, b]$ $(a, b \in \mathbb{R}^+)$ is associated with a transition t_i, and that such transition has been enabled at a marking M_i and is being continuously enabled since then in all successive markings $M_{i+1}, \ldots, M_{i+k}$, we define:

- a $(0 \leq a)$, as the minimal time that transition t_i must remain continuously enabled, until it can fire. This time is also known as Early Firing Time (EFT)
- b $(0 \leq b \leq \infty)$, as the maximum time that transition can remain continuously enabled without fire. This time is also known as Latest Firing Time (LFT)

Times a and b for transition t_i are relative to the moment in which transition t_i became last enabled. If transition t_i became enabled at time τ, and remains continuously enabled at $\tau + a$ then it can be fired. After time $\tau + a$, transition t_i can remains continuously enabled without fire until $\tau + b$, in which it must be fired. Note that transitions with time intervals $[0, \infty]$ correspond to the classical "untimed" (no deterministic) Petri net behavior.

The firing semantic described here is called "strong semantic". There also exists a called "weak semantic" in which transitions must not necessarily be fired at its LFT, and after that time it can no longer be fired [35]. In this chapter we will used the strong semantic.

Time Petri nets then can model systems in which events has non-deterministic durations. State transitions in that kind of systems may occur not in an exact time but in some time interval. Real-time systems are examples of this kind of system.

Definition 10. [Time Petri Net] A time Petri net is a six-tuple

$$N = (P, T, A, w, M_0, I)$$

where

(P, T, A, w, M_0) is a marked Petri net

$I : T \to \{\mathbb{R}^+, \mathbb{R}^+ \cup \{\infty\}\}$ associates with each transition t an interval $[\downarrow I(t), \uparrow I(t)]$ called its static firing interval. The bounds of the time interval are also known as EFT and LFT respectively.

The enabling condition remains the same as in the timed Petri Net but the firing rule must be redefined. The possibility to fire in a time interval rather than an exact time lead to the existence of infinite clock states. Then, even for bounded Petri nets the state space will be infinite, turning intractable any analysis technique based on that model formalism. To overcome this problem, Berthomieu and Menasche [7] proposed a new definition for state.

Definition 11. [Interval State] A state in a TPN is a pair (M, θ) where

M is a marking

θ is a firing interval function $\theta : enb(M) \to \{\mathbb{R}^+, \mathbb{R}^+ \cup \{\infty\}\}$.

The firing interval associated with transition $t \in enb(M)$ is $\theta(t) = [\downarrow \theta(t), \uparrow \theta(t)]$.

Using that approach, a bounded TPN yields a finite number of states [6]. Note that each Interval state contains infinite clock states, then the new state definition allow us to group infinite clock states into one interval state satisfying the condition:

$$(M, V) \in (M', \theta) \text{ iff } (M = M') \land \forall t \in enb(M), \downarrow \theta(t) \leq f(t) - V(t) \leq \uparrow \theta(t)$$

An enumerative analysis technique was introduced in [7] based in what is called "state classes". An algorithm for enumeration of these state classes was proposed for bounded TPNs and then used to the analysis of system. Since then, many algorithm has been proposed to build system state space based on the state class approach [6, 9, 11, 17, 22, 44].

Definition 12. [Firable Transition] Assuming that transition $t_f \in T$ becomes enabled at time τ in state (M, θ), it is firable at time $\tau + \lambda$ iff:

$t_f \in enb(M)$: t_f is enabled at (M, θ).

$\forall t_i \in enb(M), \downarrow t_f \leq \lambda \leq min(\uparrow t_i)$

We denote as $\Upsilon(s)$ the set of transitions firable at state $s = (M, \theta)$ and as $(M, \theta) \xrightarrow{t_f, \lambda} (M', \theta')$ the behavior "transition t_f is firable from state (M, θ) at time λ and its firing leads to state (M', θ')"

The first condition is the usual one for Petri nets and the second results from the necessity of firing transitions according to their firing interval. According to the second condition, a transition t_f, enabled by a marking M at absolute time τ, could be fired at the firing time λ iff λ is not smaller than the EFT of t_f and not greater than the smallest of the LFT's of all the transitions enabled by marking M.

Each firable transition will have its own time interval in which it can be fired. That time depends of its EFT and of the time elapsed since it became last enabled, and of the time in which the rest of the the enabled transitions will reach its LFTs, also according to the time elapsed since each one became last enabled.

Definition 13. [State Class] A state class is a pair $C = (M, D)$ where:

M is a marking;

D is the firing domain of the class.

The state class marking is shared by all states in the class and the firing domain is defined as the union of the firing domains of all the states in the class. The domain D is a conjunction of atomic constraints of the form $(t - t' \prec c)$, $(t \prec c)$ or $(-t \prec c)$, where $c \in \mathbb{R} \cup \{\infty, -\infty\}$, $\prec \in \{=, \leq, \geq\}$ and $t, t' \in T$.

The domain of D is therefore convex and has a unique canonical form defined by:

$$\bigwedge_{(t,t') \in enb(M)^2} t - t' \leq Sup_D(t - t') \wedge \bigwedge_{(t \in enb(M))} t \leq Sup_D(t) \wedge -t \leq Sup_D(-t)$$

where $Sup_D(t - t')$, $Sup_D(t)$, and $Sup_D(-t)$ are respectively the supremum of $t - t'$, t, and $-t$ in the domain of D.

In [12] was proposed an implementation for the firing rule, which directly computes the canonical form of each reachable state class in $O(n^2)$. The firing sequences beginning at some state s_i has the form:

$$\omega = s_i \overset{t_1,[l_{i+1},u_{i+1}]}{\longrightarrow} s_{i+1} \overset{t_2,[l_{i+2},u_{i+2}]}{\longrightarrow} s_{i+2} \cdots s_{i+n-1} \overset{t_j,[l_{i+n},u_{i+n}]}{\longrightarrow} s_{i+n} \tag{2}$$

where the intervals $[l_n, u_n]$ for each t_n are respectively the minimum and maximum time in which the transition can fire.

Once the state space is built, different verifications can be done, including model-checking techniques which determine if some temporal formulas are true or false over the state space. There are severals tools that use such approach [8, 17, 20, 21, 44].

In the special case where EFT and LFT has the same value, the behavior of the TPN reproduce the one of timed Petri Nets. Note that in paths over the graph which is built using the timed Petri net firing rule, the elapsed time in state transitions is fixed while in the TPN it is a time interval. In timed Petri nets states are clock states while in TPN they are interval states or state classes that contain infinite clock states.

The Timed Automaton (TA) with guards [3] is an automaton to which is adjoined a set of continuous variables whose dynamical evolution is time-driven. This formalism has been used to modeling and to a formal verification of real-time systems with success. Some tools as KRONOS [16] and UPPAAL [28] are available for such purposes. The state space yielded using Timed Automaton with guards is quite similar of that of TPN regarding the differences on their constructions.

3. Towards a unified PN system framework

In spite of the great theoretical importance and applicability of Time (or Timed) Petri Nets the PN theory was develop since the early 60's in different directions, always seeking for a way to face combinatorial explosion or to approximate to Fuzzy Logic or object-oriented systems. Several extensions were developed to fit practical applications or to attend the need to treat a new class of distributed systems, such as real-time systems. The new century started with a good amount of work published in this area but also with some confusion about concepts and representations. On the other hand, the raising complexity of distributed systems demanded a unified approach that could handle from abstract models down to the split of these general schemas in programs addressed to specific devices. In fact, integrated and flexible systems depend on that capacity.

A ISO/IEC project were launched in the beginning of this century to provide a standard to Petri Nets: the ISO/IEC 15909. Briefly, this project consists of three phases, where the first one defined P/T nets and High Level Nets in a complementary view, that is, taken P/T nets as a reduced set of the High Level Nets (HLPNs) when we reduce the color set to only one type. That is equivalent to unfold the net. Therefore, the proposed standard provides a comprehensive documentation of the terminology, the semantical model and graphic notations for High-level Petri nets. It also describes different conformance levels. Technically, the part 1 of the standard provides mathematical definitions of High-level Petri Nets, called semantic model, and a graphical form, known as High-level Petri Net Graphs (HLPNGs), as well as its mapping to the semantic model [23, 24].

Similarly to other situations where advances in technology and engineering demands a standardization, the introduction of a Petri Net standard also put in check the capacity of exchanging models among different modeling environments and tools. Thus, a Petri Net Markup Language (PNML) was introduced as an interchange format for the Petri nets defined in part 1 of the standard [25]. That composes the Part 2 of the standard and was published in February 2011, after a great amount of discussion, defining a transfer format to support the exchange of High-level Petri Nets among different tool environments [24]. The standard defined also a transfer syntax for High-level Petri Net Graphs and its subclasses defined in the first part of the standard, capturing the essence of all kinds of colored, high-level and classic Petri nets.

Part 3 is of the standard is devoted to Petri nets extensions, including hierarchies, time and stochastic nets, and is still being discussed, with a estimated time to be launched in 2013. The main requirement is that extensions be built upon developments over the core model, providing a structured and sound description. That also would allow user defined extensions based on built-in extensions and would reduce the profusion of nets attached to application domains. At least two main advantages would come out from that:

- a simple, comprehensive and structured definition of PN which would make it easier the modeling and design of distributed systems;
- a wide range of possible applications will be using the same representation which facilitate the re-use of modeling inside work domains;
- the expansion of reusability to cases among different work domains, reinforcing the use of PNs as a general schema;
- the extension of the use of Petri Nets beyond the modeling phase of design, including requirements analysis and validation.

Thus, it is very important to insert Timed Petri Nets in the proper context of the net standard, and in the context of PN extensions. During the last years a design environment has been built, in parallel with our study of Timed nets and its application to the design of automated and real time systems: the General Hierarchical Enhanced Net System (GHENeSys), where timed Petri Nets were included in a complementary way. That is, the time definition - which could be a proposal to part 3 of the standard - is made associating to each transition (place) a time interval, as proposed by Merlin [30] to model dense time. In the special case of deterministic transition (place) time it suffices to make the interval collapse by making the extremes equal to the same constant. For the case of a deterministic time PN, this imply in modifying Definition 6 to have the mapping $f : T \to \{\mathbb{R}^+ \times \mathbb{R}^+ \cup \{\infty\}\}$.

Besides the time extension, GHENeSys is also a hierarchical, object-oriented net which has also the following extended elements:

- **Gates:** which stands for elements propagating only information and preserving the marking in its original place. It could be an enabling gate, that is, one that send information if is marked or an inhibitor gate, if propagates information when is not marked. Of course GHENeSys does not allow internal gates. Thus gates should have always an original place, a special place called pseudo-box.
- **Pseudo-boxes:** denotes an observable condition that is not controlled by the modeled system. During the course of the modeling pseudo-boxes could also stand for control information external to the hierarchical components and could be collapsed when components are put together. Thus, pseudo-boxes must be considered in the structure of the net but should not affect its properties or the rank of the incidence matrix.

The graphic representation of the elements followed the schema shown in the Fig. 2 bellow,

Since our focus in this work is time extensions we illustrate hierarchy with a simple example net shown in the Fig. 3 Notice that hierarchical elements are such that the border is composed of only place or transition elements and has a unique entrance element and a unique output element. Besides, we require that each hierarchical element be simply live, that is, there is at least one live path from the entrance to the output. This is called a proper element in the theory of structured systems.

Definition 14.[GHENeSys] GHENeSys is tuple $G = (L, A, F, K, \Pi, C_0, \tau)$ where (L, A, F, K, Π) represents a net structure, C_0 is a set of multisets representing the initial marking, and τ is a function that maps time intervals to each element of the net.

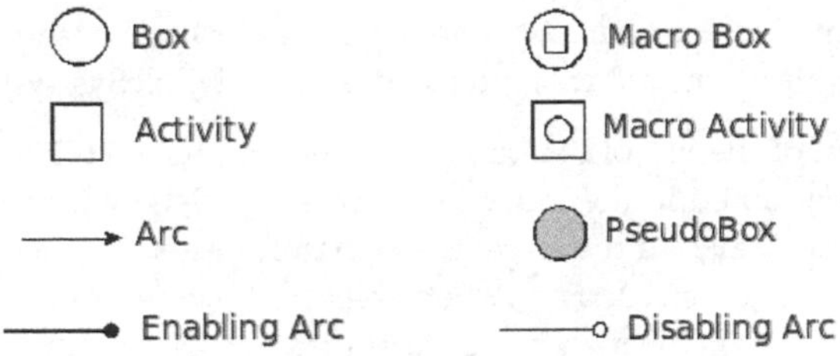

Figure 2. Graphic representation GHENeSys graphic elements.

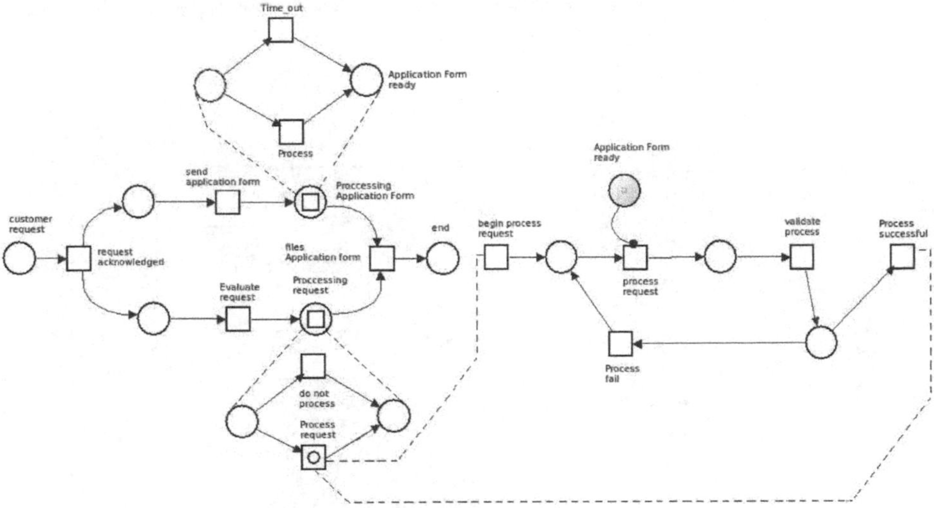

Figure 3. Example of hierarchical proper elements or macro-boxes and macro-transitions.

- $L = B \cup P$, are sets of places denoted by *Boxes* and *pseudo-boxes;*
- A is a set of activities;
- $F \subseteq (L \times A \rightarrow N) \cup (A \times L \rightarrow N)$ is the flux relation;
- $K : L \rightarrow N^+$ is a capacity function;
- $\Pi : (B \cup A) \rightarrow \{0, 1\}$ is a mapping that identifies the macro elements;
- $C_0 = \{(l, \sigma_j) | l \in L, \sigma_j \in R^+ \ |l| \leq K(l)\}$ is the marking of the initial state;
- $\tau : (B \cup A) \longrightarrow \{\mathbb{R}^+, \mathbb{R}^+ \cup \{\infty\}\}$ is a mapping that associates time intervals to each element of the net

3.1. A simple example of verification with GHENeSys

As mentioned before the main advantage of GHENeSys is to facilitate the verification of requirements and restrictions in the modeling and design of distributed systems. Therefore the environment should be able to related the elements and verify the interpretation of formulas that could involve deterministic time (explicitly or not). In the simple example that follow we show how this verification is performed in the GHENeSys system.

Besides the illustration of the use of deterministic time and the GHENeSys net, the example also shows a method adopted to the modeling with Petri Nets, which is based on eliciting requirements in UML and then (if the target is a dynamic system) transforming the semantic diagrams of UML in classic Petri Nets[4]. A Petri Net with some extensions is created in the GHENeSys which also allows the insertion of formulas in CTL that can be verified. Figure 4 [5] shows the UML class diagram to this problem. In a cycle time three drives come to the station which has only two independent pumps.

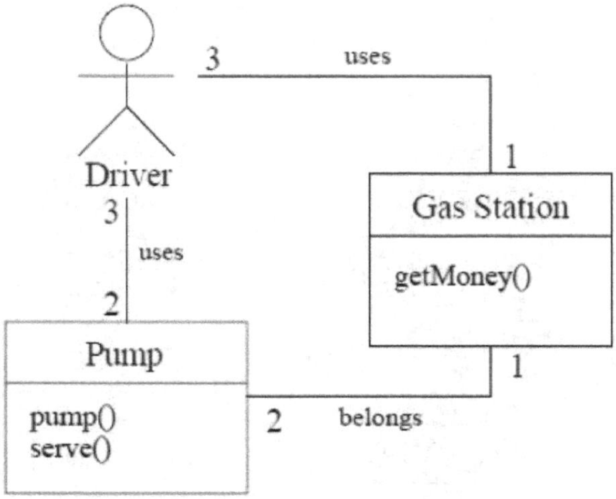

Figure 4. Class diagram to the problem of gas station.

In the gas station problem three different agents are identified: i) the gas station management who is responsible for charging the users, ii) the pumps that are supposed to serve gasoline to the costumers, and iii) the costumers, that is, drivers who are supposed to pay for a proper amount of gasoline and them help themselves. In this simple event we follow the model proposed in Baresi [5] where three drivers depends of only one cashier to pay for the gas and can use two different pumps to fill their cars. First of all we can guarantee that the proper process is followed and them we could insert a characteristic time in the basic operations. We used GHENeSys to provide the model using a classic P/T net. The resulting model is shown in the Fig. 5. This problem is to simple to use extensions but even in that case it would be possible to simply verify if the payment was done (using a gate) to enable the pump with the proper amount of gas instead or carrying the mark. For this problem it would be no significant difference in the size of the graph or in the resulting model.

The important feature here is to follow a modeling approach, which is implied in the steps described so far. Before modeling, requirements should be modeled in UML by semantic

[4] It would also be possible to synthesize a high level net, but this is not in the scope of the present work

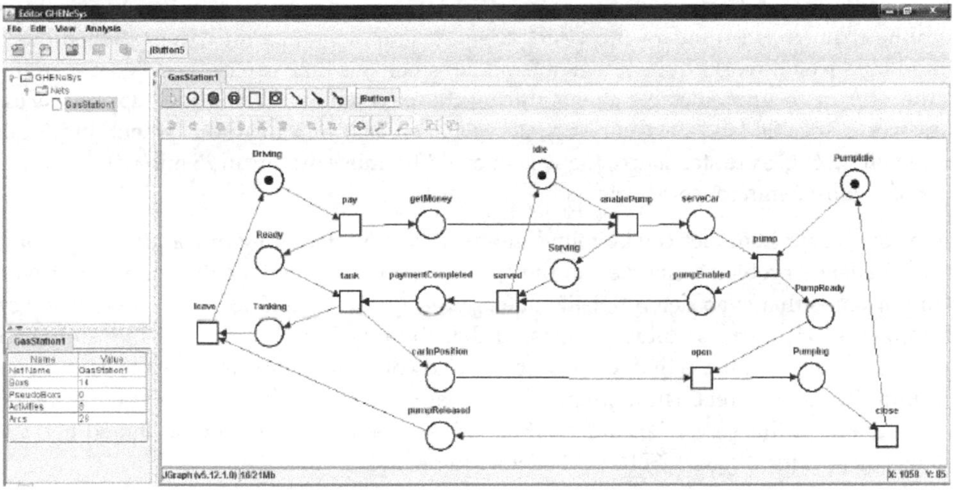

Figure 5. Classic model to the gas problem.

diagrams. There is a good discussion in the academy about the choice of the diagrams to each class of problem. Some authors prefer to go directly to SysML [4] while others just leave open the question about which diagrams should be used and invest in the analysis of this diagrams using Petri Nets [5, 10, 18, 39, 40].

Proceeding with our example let us suppose that we desire to verify some properties of the model such as

$$getMoney \longrightarrow \forall \diamond Pumping \tag{3}$$

$$\forall \Box (getMoney \longrightarrow \forall \diamond Pumping) \tag{4}$$

Using GHENeSys, formulas 3 and 4 can be evaluated by the Timed Petri Net modeling as we can see in the following.

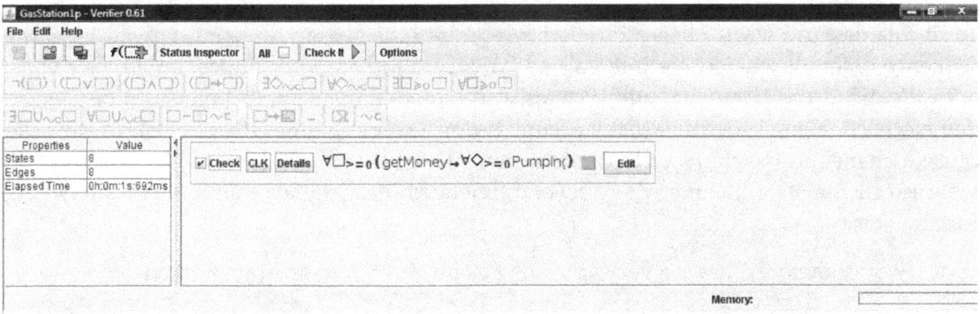

Figure 6. Sanpshot of the GHENeSys verifier for property 4.

The introduction of deterministic time (transition) would add more detail about the process, with the characteristic time for processing the payment or to fill a car. An organized queue would fail (even if works quite fine in the model) since this time can be modified depending of the user or to unpredictable events during the payment or during the supply process. However if specific (and deterministic)intervals such as 3 min for the payment and 5 min for the filling of gas are stablished, the system could handle 9 drivers in 25 min with a waiting time of at most 2 min for some drivers.

More convincing examples can be found in business, manufacturing or computer networks. More challenge problems emerged in the spatial applications or satellite control, but what is important is that even deterministic time approach can be used to solve a diversified set of problems. However, it could be stressed that the timed approach should be supported for tools and environments that rely in a sound and complementary approach to Timed Nets including Time Petri Nets. The approach shown here, inserted in the GHENeSys environment is exactly one of this cases. Besides, GHENeSys is an implementation of a unified net, that follows the specifications in ISO/IEC 15909 standard.

In the next section we go further in the discussion of using Petri Nets and specifically Timed Petri Nets to fit requirements that come in the new version of UML, which includes time diagrams and timelines.

4. PN as a general system representation framework

As pointed in the beginning of this work, Petri Nets has developed for the last fifty years to become a general schema for systems modeling.

In the previous section, we showed that a modeling discipline should be followed to achieve good results with Petri Nets formal representation, specially when time is an important variable to consider, either by deterministic time or using continuous dense time intervals. However, in the example above time does not appear explicitly at the beginning, since we started with the class diagram where there was no reference to duration time of the processes (supplying or payment). The problem them begins with a demand to a proper representation of time duration in UML that could later be transformed in a timed net.

To fit this demand UML 2.0 specification inserted an interaction diagram derived from the sequence diagram where time intervals or time duration are very important issues. Thus, once identified the actors and sub-systems in the model, their interaction could be viewed and modeled taking in account that it occurs during a running time where specific events can cause a change in the status of that interaction. Thus, the full relation can be described in what is called a state lifetime where several timelines show the evolution of the interacting components.

OMG (www.omg.org) shows a very appealing example of time diagram to model

In Figure 7 we can see a hierarchical superposition of levels and the action derived from the interaction between a user and a web system. Sub-systems invoked by this action and the time they spent to provide a proper action are explicitly depicted. As in the previous problem

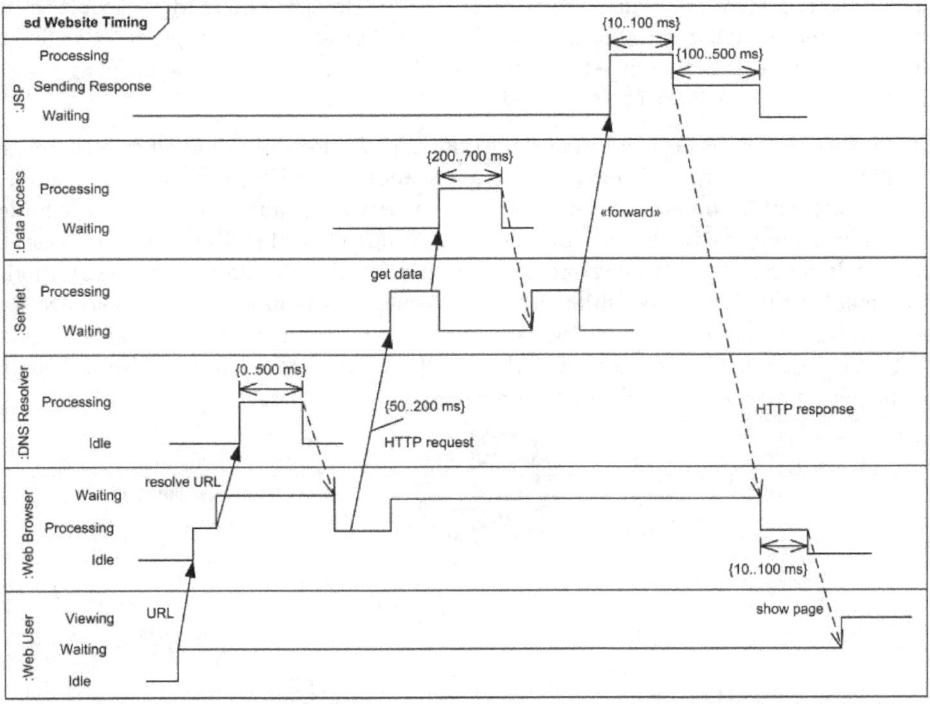

Figure 7. Time diagram for the web user latency.

of the gas station, the total time interval spent to serve one or nine users is the summation of the not superposed time intervals required for each dependent action.

Thus, the complete process would be to elicit the requirements using UML diagrams - including time diagrams - synthesize a Timed Petri Net from this model, and them perform the requirement analysis and final synthesis of a model for the problem. In fact, the final results for the example of the gas station were obtained following this approach.

Formally, the timelines are drawn according the behavior of *state variables*, defined in the following.

Definition 15.[State Variables] A state variable is a triple (V, T, D) where:

$V = v_i$ is a finite set of state values;

$T : V \to V$ specify each atomic transition or change in value.

$D : V \to \mathbb{N} \times \mathbb{N}$ is the time duration for each state value.

A timeline is the tracking of all changes in state value in a interval $[0, \tau)$ where τ is the observed time horizon. A timeline is said to be completely closed if the union of its not superposed values is exactly τ. In that case the transitions occur in deterministic time.

If the transitions occur in a time interval $[t_{min}, t_{max}]$ the timeline is said to be flexible. In this case we can represent the transition in a Timed Petri Net by an interval, as proposed in the first section. If we want to deal with deterministic time transition it is enough to make $t_{min} = t_{max}$ and the same net framework could be used.

Timeline models can be very useful in some critical problem applications such as intelligent planning and scheduling. Some of those applications could be used in spatial projects [14][5]. In other applications Petri Nets were used to perform requirements analysis including deterministic time, as in the one proposed by Vaquero et al.[40][41]. In that case the idea of solving real life planning problems starts with the elicitation and specification of requirements using UML, goes through the analysis of this requirements using Timed Petri Nets, synthesizes a model also in Petri Nets and finally uses a specific language, PDDL, to transfer the model to software planners which will provide the final result. Also, a modeling design environment were developed to perform this process[41][40].

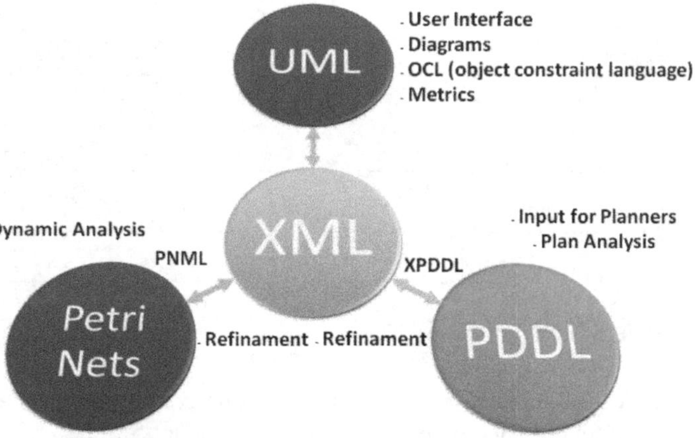

Figure 8. Language structure in itSIMPLE 3.1

A specific state lifetime were developed to model and analyze the timelines for the agents and objects that would compose the plan, as shown in Figure 8.

Based on this time diagram Petri Nets could be synthesized to make the proper validation of the model. It is important to notice that there are a large number of approaches and tools that claim to perform a good analysis of models directly associated to a planer software with good results. However, most of this systems address only model problems which are well behaved and/or have a limited size and complexity. When the challenge is to model a large system, such as the space project mentioned before or a port to get and deliver petroleum, the challenge could be too big to be faced by these proposals.

Therefore the combination UML/Timed Petri Nets could be successful in the modeling of large and complex problems also in the planning area, with the possibility to be applied in practice to real systems.

---

[5] See also the Mexar 2 Project and the use of intelligent software application in the link mexar.istc.cnr.it/mexar2.

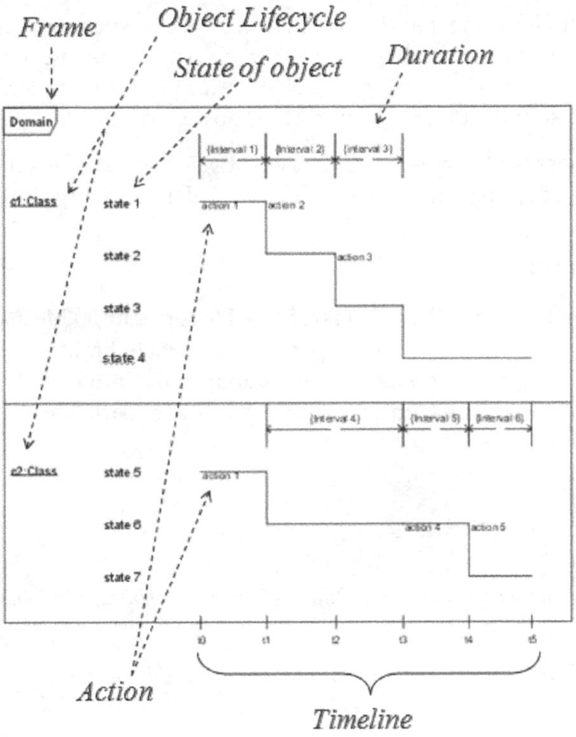

Figure 9. Time diagram in the itSIMPLE system.

5. Conclusions

In conclusion it is important to remark that the evolution of Petri Nets towards a formal representation, capable to treat complex systems should be based in two basis: the extension to model timed systems; and the development of a unified net that includes all extensions besides the timed approach - hierarchy, gates, not controled elements, always respecting the recent published ISO/IEC standard and its next release to appear in 2013. This is the fundamental concepts to have new environments that could support a complementary treatment of timed systems, that is, that could deal with deterministic timed net as well as with time PN in the same environment. That is the focus of the present work.

Besides, it would be advisable that the same environment could deal, also in a complementary way, with classic P/T nets as well as with high level (HLPN) nets or even with simetric nets, which is also part of the ISO/IEC standard. The novelty would be to use a unified net system as a platform to reach the further challenge which would be the introduction of abstract nets.

In what concerns the unified net to treat time intervals and dense time, we achieve a good point with the system GHENeSys where the present work focus most in the first part. However, in [17] a more detailed description of the state class algorithm is given and the basic concepts that lead to a modeling and simulation approach to dense time nets. Therefore the unification with timed PN is a promising result in the near future. Also the system GHENeSys is being developed to implement a unified net as we described above, dealing with P/T and HLPN in the same environment. That is a good combination, capable to model and simulate timed and time nets (in that case using model checking) in the same environment, with the advantage to have a sound and formal representation supporting all process.

Thus, it would be possible to have performance analysis that really fits the complexity of the problem addressed, adapting very easily to discrete or dense time approach.

Acknowledgements

The authors acknowledge to all members of the Design Lab in Mechatronic Department for their work who are present in every part of this article be in the background, in the implementation of tools, in the search for new applications in the analysis of the problems already solved. Particularly we thank the work of Gustavo Costa, Arianna Salmon and Jose Armando S. P. Miralles.

Author details

Silva, José Reinaldo
University of São Paulo, Mechatronics Department, Escola Politécnica, São Paulo, Brazil

Del Foyo, Pedro M. G.
Federal University of Pernambuco, Department of Mechanical Engineering, Recife, Brazil

6. References

[1] Aalst, W van der (2002) Workflow Management: Models, Methods, and Systems, MIT Press, 365 p.

[2] Aalst, W van der (2004) Business Process Management Demystified: A Tutorial on Models, Systems and Standards for Workflow Mangement , LNCS 3098 pp 1-65.

[3] Alur, R. and Dill, D. (1990) Automata for modeling real-time systems, *Lecture Notes in Computer Science* 443: 322–335.

[4] Andrade, E, Maciel, P, Callou, G, Nogueira, B, Araujo, C (2011) An Approach Based in Petri Nets for Requirements Analysis, in in Petri Nets Applications, Pauwel Pawlewski (ed.), InTech, 752 p.

[5] Baresi, L, Pezze, M (2001) Uniform Approaches to Graphical Process Specification Techniques, Electronic Notes in Theoretical Computer Science, vol. 44, pp. 107-119.

[6] Berthomieu, B. and Diaz, M. (1991). Modelling and verification of time dependent systems using time petri nets, *IEEE Trans. on Software Engineering* 17(3): 259–273.

[7] Berthomieu, B. and Menasche, M. (1983) . An enumerative approach for analyzing time Petri nets, *in* R. E. A. Mason (ed.), *Information Processing: proceedings of the IFIP congress 1983*, Vol. 9, Elsevier Science Publishers, Amsterdam, pp. 41–46.

[8] Berthomieu, B., Ribet, P. O. and Vernadat, F. (2004). The tool tina - construction of abstract state spaces for petri nets and time petri nets, *Int. J. Prod. res.* 42(14): 2741–2756.

[9] Berthomieu, B. and Vernadat, F. (2003). State class constructions for branching analysis of time petri nets, *Lecture Notes in Computer Science* 2619: 442–457.

[10] Bodbar, B, Giacomini, L, Holding, DJ (2000) UML and Petri Nets for the Design and Analysis of Distributed Systems, Proc. of the IEEE Int. Conf. on Control Applications, pp. 610-615.

[11] Boucheneb, H., Alger, U. and Berthelot, G. (1993) . Towards a simplified building of time petri nets reachability graph, *Proc. 5th International Workshop on Petri Nets and Performance Models*, Toulouse, France, pp. 46–55.

[12] Boucheneb, H. and Mullins, J. (2003). Analyse des réseaux temporels. calcul des classes en o(n2) et des temps de chemin en o(m x n), *Technique et Science Informatiques* 22(4): 435–459.

[13] Cerone, A. and Maggiolo-Schettini, A. (1999). Time-based expressivity of time petri nets for system specification, *Theoretical Computer Science* 216(1): 1–53.

[14] Cesta, A, Finzi, A, Fratini, S, Orlandini, A, Ronci, E (2010) Validation and verification issues in a temiline-bsed planning system, Knowledge Engineering Review, vol. 25, no. 3, pp. 299-318.

[15] Ciufudean C, Filote C (2010) Workflow Diagnosis Using Petri Net Charts, in Petri Nets Applications, Pauwel Pawlewski (ed.), InTech, 752 p.

[16] Daws, C., Olivero, A., Tripakis, S. and Yovine, S. (1995). The tool KRONOS, *Hybrid Systems III: Verification and Control*, Vol. 1066, Springer, Rutgers University, New Brunswick, NJ, USA, pp. 208–219.

[17] del Foyo, P. M. G. and Silva, J. R. (2011). Some issues in real-time systems verification using time petri nets, *Journal of the Braz. Soc. of Mech. Sci. & Eng.* XXXIII(4): 467–474.

[18] del Foyo, P. M. G., Salmon, A. Z. O., Silva, J. R. (2011) Requirements Analysis of Automated Projects Using UML/Petri Nets, Proc. of COBEM 2011.

[19] Girault, C, Valk, R (2003) Petri Nets for System Engineering, Springer, 607 p.

[20] Gardey, G., Lime, D., Magnin, M. and Roux, O. H. (2005). Romeo: A tool for analyzing time petri nets, *in* K. Etessami and S. Rajamani (eds), *CAV2005*, Vol. 3576, Springer-Verlag, pp. 418–423.

[21] Hadjidj, R. and Boucheneb, H. (2006). On-the-fly tctl model checking for time petri nets using state class graphs, *acsd* 0: 111–122.

[22] Hadjidj, R. and Boucheneb, H. (2008). Improving state class constructions for ctl* model checking of time petri nets, *STTT* 10(2): 167–184.

[23] ISO/IEC (2002) High-Level Petri Nets: Concepts, Definitions and Graphical Notation, International Standard Final Draft, ISO/IEC 15909.

[24] ISO/IEC (2005) Software and Systems Engineering - High-Level Petri Nets, Part 2: Transfer Format, International Standard WD ISO/IEC 15909.

[25] Kindler, E (2006) PNML: Concepts, Status and Future Directions, Invited paper, Proc. of EKA 2006, pp. 35-55.

[26] Kordic, V (ed.) (2008) Petri Nets: Theory and Applications, I-Tech Education and Pub, 208 p.

[27] Lafortune, S. and Cassandras, C. G. (2008). *Introduction to Discrete Event Systems*, second edn, Springer, 233 Spring Street, New York, NY 10013, USA.

[28] Larsen, K. G., Pettersson, P. and Yi, W. (2000). Uppaal - validation and verification of real time systems - status & developments.

[29] Marsan MA, Bobbio, A, Donatelli S (1998) Petri Nets in Performance Analysis: an Introduction, LNCS 1491, pp. 211-256.
[30] Merlin, P., Faber, D. (1976) Recoverability on communication protocols - implications of a theoretical study, IEEE Trans. on Communications, vol. 4, no. 9, pp. 1036-1043.
[31] Murata, T (1989) Petri Nets: Properties, Analysis and Applications, Proceedings of IEEE, vol. 77, pp 541-580.
[32] Patrice B (2010) A New Control Synthesis Approach of P-Time Petri Nets, in Petri Nets Applications, Pawel Pawlewski (ed.), InTech, 752 p.
[33] Pawlewski P (2010) Using Petri Nets to Model and Simulation Production Systems in Process Reengineering, in Petri Nets Applications, Pawel Pawlewski (ed.), InTech, 752 p.
[34] Ramchandani, C. (1973) Analysis of Asynchronous Concurrent Systems by Timed Petri Nets, PHD thesis, MIT, 220 p.
[35] Riviere, N., Valette, R., Pradin-Chezalviel, B. and Ups, I. A. . (2001). Reachability and temporal conflicts in t-time petri nets, *PNPM '01: Proceedings of the 9th international Workshop on Petri Nets and Performance Models (PNPM'01)*, IEEE Computer Society, Washington, DC, USA, p. 229.
[36] Roux, O. H. and Déplanche, A. M. (2002) . A T-time petri net extension for real time-task scheduling modeling, *European Journal of Automation* 36: 973–987.
[37] Salmon, A. Z. O., Miralles, J. A. S. P., del Foyo, P. M. G., Silva, J. R. (2011) Towards a Unified View of Modeling and Design with GHENeSys, Proc. of COBEM 2011.
[38] Sifakis, J. (1980). Performance evaluation of systems using nets, *Proceedings of the Advanced Course on General Net Theory of Processes and Systems*, Springer-Verlag, London, UK, pp. 307–319.
[39] Tierry-Mieg, Y, Hilah, L-M (2008) UML Behavioral Consistency Checking Using Instantiable Petri Nets, Workshop UML in Formal Methods, 10th. Int. Conf. on Formal Engineering Methods.
[40] Vaquero, T.S., Silva, J.R., Ferreira, M., Tonidandel, F., Bech, J.C. (2009) From Requirements and Analysis to PDDL in itSIMPLE 3.0, Proc. of Int. Conf. in Artificial Planning and Scheduling, AAAI.
[41] Vaquero, T.S., Silva, J.R., Bech, J.C. (2011) A Brief Review of Tools and Methods for Knowledge Engineering for Planning and Scheduling, Proc. of Int. Conf. in Artificial Planning and Scheduling, AAAI.
[42] Wang, J (1998) Timed Petri Nets: Theory and Applications, Kluwer Academic Pub. 281 p.
[43] Wang, J, Deng, Y, Xu, G (2000) Reachability Analysis of Real-time Systems Using Timed Petri Nets, IEEE Trans. on Syst. Man and Cybernetics, vol 30 no. 5, pp. 725-736.
[44] Yoneda, T. and Ryuba, H. (1998). CTL model checking of time petri nets using geometric regions, *IEICE Trans. on Information and Systems* E81-D(3): 297–396.
[45] Zuberek, W. M. (1980). Timed petri nets and preliminary performance evaluation, *ISCA '80: Proceedings of the 7th annual symposium on Computer Architecture*, ACM Press, New York, NY, USA, pp. 88–96.

Section 2

Theory

Chapter 9

Boolean Petri Nets

Sangita Kansal, Mukti Acharya and Gajendra Pratap Singh

Additional information is available at the end of the chapter

1. Introduction

Petri net is a graphical tool invented by Carl Adam Petri [13]. These are used for describing, designing and studying discrete event-driven dynamical systems that are characterized as being concurrent, asynchronous, distributed, parallel, random and/or nondeterministic. As a graphical tool, Petri net can be used for planning and designing a system with given objectives, more practically effective than flowcharts and block diagrams. As a mathematical tool, it enables one to set up state equations, algebraic equations and other mathematical models which govern the behavior of discrete dynamical systems. Still, there is a drawback inherent in representing discrete event-systems. They suffer from the state explosion problem as what will happen when a system is highly populated, i.e., initial state consists of a large number of places that are nonempty. This phenomenon may lead to an exponential growth of its reachability graph. This makes us to study the safe systems. The aim of this chapter is to present some basic results on 1-safe Petri nets that generate the elements of a Boolean hypercube as marking vectors. Complete Boolean hypercube is the most popular interconnection network with many attractive and well known properties such as regularity, symmetry, strong connectivity, embeddability, recursive construction, etc. For brevity, we shall call a 1-safe Petri net that generates all the binary n-vectors as marking vectors a *Boolean Petri net*. *Boolean Petri nets* are not only of theoretical interest but also are of practical importance, required in practice to construct control systems [1]. In this chapter, we will consider the problems of characterizing the class of Boolean Petri nets as also the class of *crisp* Boolean Petri nets, viz., the Boolean Petri nets that generate all the binary n-vectors exactly once. We show the existence of a disconnected Boolean Petri net whose reachability tree is homomorphic to the n-dimensional complete lattice L_n. Finally, we observe that characterizing a Boolean Petri net is rather intricate.

We begin by showing that a 1-safe *Star Petri net* S_n [5], with $|P| = n$ and $|T| = n+1$, having a central transition, is a Boolean Petri net; here, P is the set of its places and T is the set of its transitions. Often, it is desirable to have a crisp Boolean Petri net because one may possibly explore for existence of certain sequences of enabled transitions to fire toward initiating and completing a prescribed process that uses specified nodes of the Boolean lattice.

For example, in the design of generalized switches such as those used to control automatic machines [1], suppose that we have a sequence of n terminals each of which can be either at a prescribed low-voltage (denoted by zero '0') or at a prescribed high-voltage (denoted by unity, '1'). It is required to arrange them so that every one of the 2^n sequences of n bits, corresponding to the 2^n binary n-tuples, can appear on the terminals [1]. Now that Q_n, the binary n-cube, is known to be Hamiltonian (in the sense that there exists an all-vertex covering cycle) one can design a "Hamiltonian switch" using a crisp Boolean Petri net that triggers operation of a machine exactly once after 2^n successive switching moves along the prescribed Hamiltonian cycle in Q_n. The 'switch design' may be imagined to be an arbitrary connected graph of order 2^n, where connection between a pair (u,v) of nodes would mean that v is to be the terminal that needs to be turned on after the terminal corresponding to u (which may or may not be in an active state depending on the machine design). Therefore, a good characterization of such Boolean Petri nets is needed. This problem is still open. Many specific classes of such 1-safe Petri nets have been found [5–7]. Also, many fundamental issues regarding Boolean Petri nets emerge from this study.

2. Preliminaries

To keep this chapter self-contained as far as possible, we present some of the necessary definitions and concepts. For standard terminology and notation on Petri net theory and graph theory, we refer the reader to Peterson [12] and Harary [3], respectively. In this chapter, we shall adopt the definition of Jenson [4] for Petri nets:

Definition 1. *A Petri net is a 5-tuple* $C = (P, T, I^-, I^+, \mu^0)$, *where*

(a) P *is a nonempty set of 'places',*

(b) T *is a nonempty set of 'transitions',*

(c) $P \cap T = \emptyset$,

(d) $I^-, I^+ : P \times T \longrightarrow \mathbf{N}$, *where* $\mathbf{N}$ *is the set of nonnegative integers, are called the negative and the positive 'incidence functions' (or,'flow functions') respectively,*

(e) $\forall\, p \in P, \exists t \in T : I^-(p,t) \neq 0 \;\; or \;\; I^+(p,t) \neq 0$ *and*
$\forall t \in T, \exists p \in P : I^-(p,t) \neq 0 \;\; or \;\; I^+(p,t) \neq 0$,

(f) $\mu^0 : P \to \mathbf{N}$ *is the initial marking.*

In fact, $I^-(p,t)$ and $I^+(p,t)$ represent the number of arcs from p to t and t to p respectively, and some times referred to a 'flow relations'. I^-, I^+ and μ^0 can be viewed as matrices of size $|P| \times |T|$, $|P| \times |T|$ and $|P| \times 1$, respectively.

The quadruple (P, T, I^-, I^+) in the definition of the Petri net is called the *Petri net structure.* The *Petri net graph* is a representation of the Petri net structure, which is essentially a bipartite directed multigraph, in which any pair of symmetric arcs (p_i, t_j) and (t_j, p_i) is called a *self-loop.*

As in many standard books (e.g., see [14]), Petri net is a particular kind of directed graph [3], together with an initial marking μ^0. The underlying graph of a Petri net is a directed, weighted, bipartite graph consisting of two kinds of nodes, called places and transitions, where arcs are either from a place to a transition or from a transition to a place. No two of the same kind being adjacent. Hence, Petri nets have a well known graphical representation in which transitions are represented as boxes and places as circles with directed arcs interconnecting places and transitions, to represent the flow relations. The initial marking is represented by placing a token, shown as a black dot, in the circle representing a place p_i, whenever $\mu^0(p_i) = 1,\ 1 \leq i \leq n = |P|$. In general, a *marking* μ is a mapping $\mu : P \longrightarrow \mathbf{N}$. A marking μ can hence be represented as a vector $\mu \in \mathbf{N}^n$, $n = |P|$, such that the ith component of μ is the value $\mu(p_i)$, viz., the number of tokens placed at p_i.

Definition 2. *Let $C = (P, T, I^-, I^+, \mu)$ be a Petri net. A transition $t \in T$ is said to be enabled at μ if and only if $I^-(p,t) \leq \mu(p), \forall p \in P$. An enabled transition may or may not 'fire' (depending on whether or not the event actually takes place). After firing at μ, the new marking μ' is given by the rule*

$$\mu'(p) = \mu(p) - I^-(p,t) + I^+(p,t), \text{for all } p \in P.$$

We say that *t fires at μ* to yield μ' (or, that *t fires μ* to μ'), and we write $\mu \xrightarrow{t} \mu'$, whence μ' is said to be *directly reachable* from μ. Hence, it is clear, what is meant by a sequence like

$$\mu^0 \xrightarrow{t_1} \mu^1 \xrightarrow{t_2} \mu^2 \xrightarrow{t_3} \mu^3 \cdots \xrightarrow{t_k} \mu^k,$$

which simply represents the fact that the transitions

$$t_1, t_2, t_3, \ldots, t_k$$

have been successively fired to transform the *initial marking* μ^0 into the *terminal* marking μ^k. The whole of this sequence of transformations is also written in short as $\mu^0 \xrightarrow{\sigma} \mu^k$, where $\sigma = t_1, t_2, t_3, \ldots, t_k$ is called the corresponding *firing sequence*.

A marking μ is said to be *reachable from* μ^0, if there exists a firing sequence of transitions which successively fire to reach the state μ from μ^0. The set of all markings of a Petri net C reachable from a given marking μ is denoted by $M(C, \mu)$ and, together with the arcs of the form $\mu^i \xrightarrow{t_r} \mu^j$, represents what in standard terminology is called the *reachability graph* of the Petri net C, denoted by $R(C, \mu^0)$. In particular, if the reachability graph has no semicycle then it is called the *reachability tree* of the Petri net.

A place in a Petri net is *safe* if the number of tokens in that place never exceeds one. A Petri net is *safe* if all its places are safe.

The *preset* of a transition t is the set of all input places to t, i.e., $^\bullet t = \{p \in P : I^-(p,t) > 0\}$. The *postset* of t is the set of all output places from t, i.e., $t^\bullet = \{p \in P : I^+(p,t) > 0\}$. Similarly, p's preset and postset are $^\bullet p = \{t \in T : I^+(p,t) > 0\}$ and $p^\bullet = \{t \in T : I^-(p,t) > 0\}$, respectively.

Definition 3. *Let $C = (P, T, I^-, I^+, \mu^0)$ be a Petri net with $|P| = n$ and $|T| = m$, the incidence matrix $I = [a_{ij}]$ is an $n \times m$ matrix of integers and its entries are given by $a_{ij} = a_{ij}^+ - a_{ij}^-$ where $a_{ij}^+ = I^+(p_i, t_j)$ is the number of arcs from transition t_j to its output place p_i and $a_{ij}^- = I^-(p_i, t_j)$ is the number of arcs from place p_i to its output transition t_j i.e., in other words, $I = I^+ - I^-$.*

3. 1-safe star Petri net is Boolean

We shall now define *1-safe star* Petri net. The notion of a *star* is from graph theory (see [3]); it is the *complete bipartite graph* $K_{1,n}$ which consists of exactly one vertex c, called the *center*, joined by a single edge cv_i to the pendant vertex v_i (i.e. the degree of v_i is 1) for each $i \in \{1, 2, \ldots, n\}, n \geq 1$. A *1-safe star Petri net* S_n is obtained by *subdividing* every edge of the graph $K_{1,n}$, $n \geq 1$, so that every subdividing vertex is a place node and the original vertices of $K_{1,n}, n \geq 1$, are the $(n+1)$ transition nodes, $(n+1)^{th}$ being the central node. Further, every arc incident to the central node is directed towards it, and every arc incident to a pendent node is directed towards the pendent node (See Figure 1).

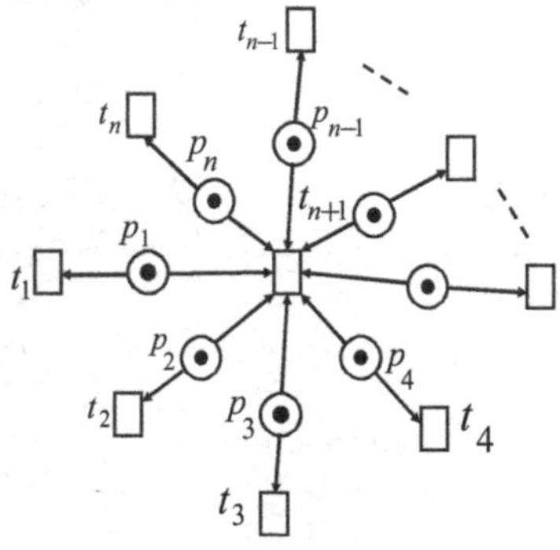

Figure 1. 1-safe star Petri net S_n

Theorem 1. *[5] The reachability tree of* S_n *with* $\mu_0 = (1, 1, 1, 1, \ldots, 1)$ *as the initial marking contains every binary n-vector* $(a_1, a_2, a_3, \ldots, a_n)$, $a_i \in \{0, 1\}$.

Proof. We shall prove this result by using the Principle of Mathematical Induction (PMI). Clearly, the reachability tree $R(S_1, \mu^0)$ of S_1 generates both the binary 1-vectors (1) and (0) as shown in Figure 2. Next, consider the 1-safe star Petri net S_2 as shown in Figure 3 and its reachability tree $R(S_2, \mu^0)$ displayed in Figure 4.

It is clear from Figure 4 that $R(S_2, \mu^0)$ has all the $4 = 2^2$, binary 2-vectors (a_1, a_2), $a_1, a_2 \in \{0, 1\}$. We can construct $R(S_2, \mu^0)$ from $R(S_1, \mu^0)$ as follows. Take two copies of $R(S_1, \mu^0)$. In the first copy, augment each vector of $R(S_1, \mu^0)$, by putting a 0 entry at the second position of every marking vector and denote the resulting labeled tree as $R_0(S_1, \mu^0)$. Similarly, in the second copy, augment each vector by putting 1 at the second position of every marking and let $R_1(S_1, \mu^0)$ be the resulting labeled tree (See Figure 5). Now, using the following steps we construct the reachability tree $R(S_2, \mu^0)$ of S_2 from $R_0(S_1, \mu^0)$ and $R_1(S_1, \mu^0)$.

1. Clearly, the set of binary 2-vectors in $R_0(S_1, \mu^0)$ is disjoint with the set of those appearing in $R_1(S_1, \mu^0)$ and together they contain all the binary 2-vectors.

2. In $R_0(S_1, \mu^0)$, transition t_2 does not satisfy the enabling condition, since $I^-(p_i, t) \leq \mu(p_i)$, for each $p_i \in S_1$ is violated. So, we can ignore this transition at this stage.

3. In $R_1(S_1, \mu^0)$, transition t_2 is enabled and the marking obtained after firing of t_2 is actually (1, 0) whereas the augmented vector attached to this node is (0,1). So, we concatenate

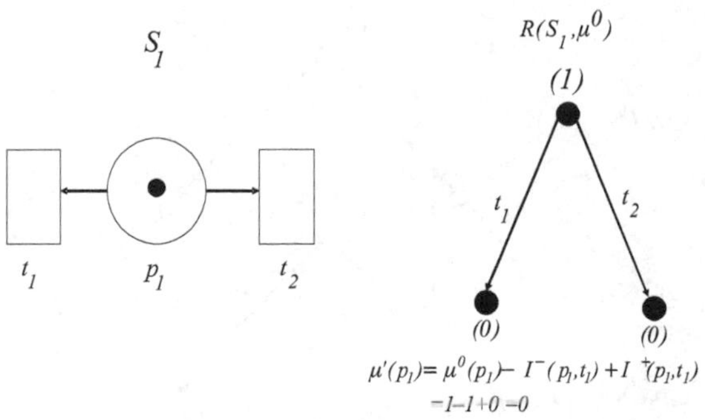

Figure 2. 1−safe star Petri net S_1 and $R(S_1, \mu^0)$

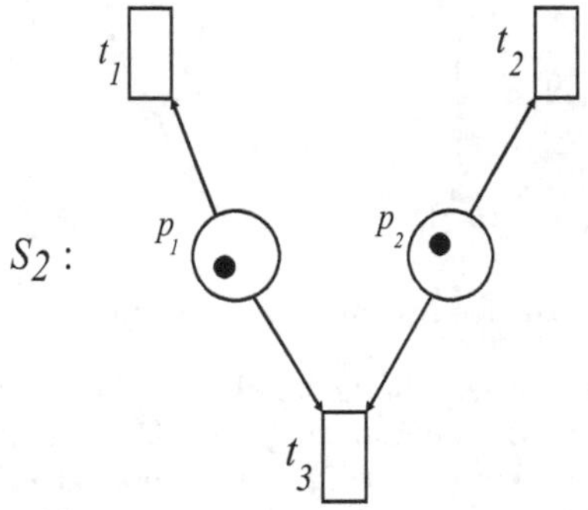

Figure 3. 1-safe star Petri net S_2

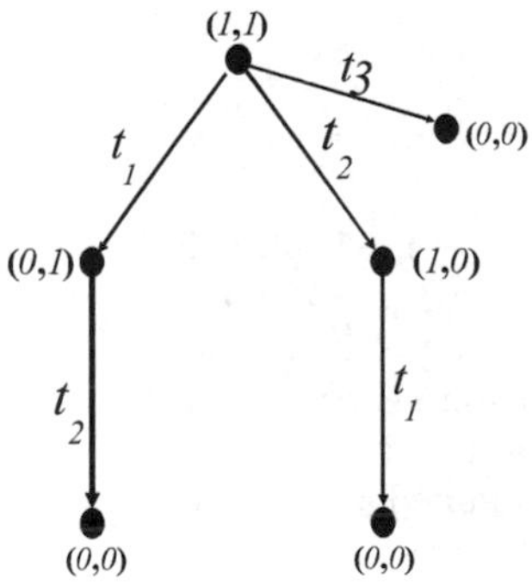

Figure 4. $R(S_2, \mu^0)$, $\mu^0 = (1,1)$

$R_0(S_1, \mu^0)$ by fusing the node labeled (1, 0) with the node labeled (0, 1) in $R_1(S_1, \mu^0)$ and replacing (0, 1) by the label (1, 0) which is the initial marking of $R_0(S_1, \mu^0)$.

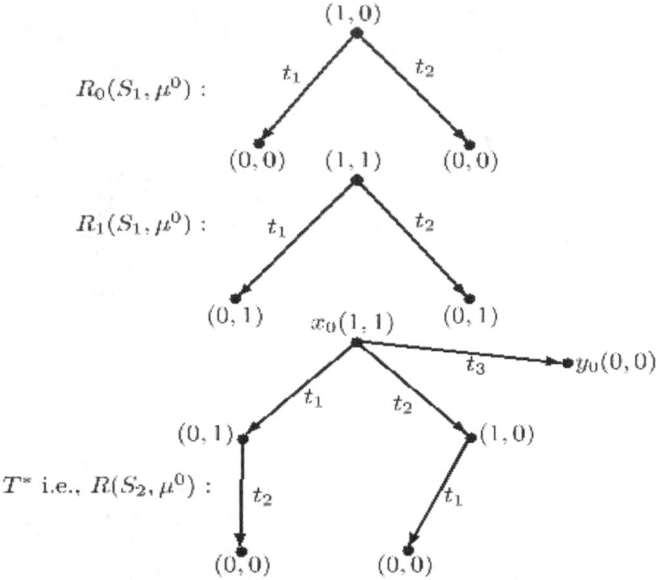

Figure 5. Augmented reachability trees and resulting labeled tree T^*

4. We then augment an extra pendent node labeled y_0 joined to the new root node x_0, labeled by the 2-vector (1, 1), by the new arc $(x_0,\ y_0)$ labeled as t_3 and complete this tree by firing transitions(s) at the marking vector(s) where nonzero components appear, till all the transitions become dead. Then the resulting labeled tree T^* is shown in Figure 5. This has all the binary 2-vectors as its node labels, possibly with repetitions. It remains to show that it is the reachability tree $R(S_2, \mu^0)$ of S_2 with 2-vector (1, 1) as its initial marking μ^0. For this, consider an arbitrary 2-vector $\mu = (a_1,\ 1)$, where $a_1 \in \{0, 1\}$. When transition t_2 is enabled, this yields

$$\mu'(p_i) = \mu(p_i) - I^-(p_i,\ t_2) + I^+(p_i,\ t_2)$$

$$= 1 - 1 + 0 = 0$$

Then, we get a new marking $\mu' = (a_1,\ 0)$, where $a_1 \in \{0,\ 1\}$. The marking μ' is found in $R_0(S_2,\ \mu^0)$. If all a_i's are zero then μ' is a dead marking. Hence, suppose some $a_i \neq 0$. In this case, t_i is enabled and in the next new marking μ'', the ith component is reduced to zero. Eventually, this process will lead to a dead marking. Further, the marking vectors of the form $\mu = (a_1,\ 0)$ are already obtained as a result of firing $t_1,\ t_2$, through some subsequences. Thus, T is indeed the reachability tree $R(S_2, \mu^0)$ of S_2.

Now, we assume that the result is true for all the 1-safe star Petri nets S_k having k places, $k \leq n$. We will prove the result for the 1-safe star Petri net S_{n+1} having $(n+1)$ places. For this purpose, consider two copies of the reachability tree $R(S_n, \mu^0)$ of S_n. In the first copy, we extend each vector by augmenting a 0 entry at the $(n+1)^{th}$ position and let $R_0(S_n,\ \mu^0)$ denote the resulting labeled tree. Next, in the second copy of $R(S_n, \mu^0)$, we augment the entry 1 to the $(n+1)^{th}$ position in every marking vector and let $R_1(S_n,\ \mu^0)$ be the resulting labeled tree. Hence, using the following steps we construct the reachability tree of the 1-safe star Petri net S_{n+1} having $(n+1)$ places.

1. Clearly, the set of binary $(n+1)$-vectors in $R_0(S_n, \ \mu^0)$ is disjoint with the set of those appearing in $R_1(S_n, \ \mu^0)$ and together they contain all the binary $(n+1)$-vectors.

2. In $R_0(S_n, \mu^0)$, transition t_{n+1} does not satisfy the enabling condition, $I^-(p_i, \ t) \leq \mu(p_i)$, for each $p_i \in S_n$. So, we can ignore this transition for the moment.

3. In $R_1(S_n, \ \mu^0)$, transition t_{n+1} is enabled and the marking obtained after firing of t_{n+1} is actually $(1, \ 1, \ldots, \ 0)$. So we concatenate $R_0(S_n, \ \mu^0)$ at this node with the $(n+1)$-vector $(0, \ 0, \ldots, \ 1)$ replaced by the actual marking $(1, \ 1, \ldots, \ 0)$ being the initial marking of $R_0(S_n, \ \mu^0)$.

4. We then augment an extra pendent node labeled y_0 joined to the new root node x_0, labeled by the $(n+1)$-vector $(1, \ 1, \ldots, \ 1)$ by the new arc $(x_0, \ y_0)$ labeled as t_{n+2} and complete this tree by firing transition(s) at the marking vector(s) where nonzero components appear, till all the transitions become dead. In this way, the tree T^* so obtained has all the binary $(n+1)$-vectors as its node labels, possibly with repetitions. It remains to show that T^* is indeed the reachability tree $R(S_{n+1}, \mu^0)$ of S_{n+1} with binary $(n+1)$-vector $(1, \ 1, \ 1, \ \ldots, \ 1)$ as its initial marking μ^0. For this, consider an arbitrary $(n+1)$-vector $\mu = (a_1, \ a_2, \ a_3, \ \ldots, \ a_n, \ 1)$, where $a_i \in \{0,1\}, \forall \ i$. When transition t_{n+1} is enabled, this yields

$$\mu'(p_i) = \mu(p_i) - I^-(p_i, \ t_{n+1}) + I^+(p_i, \ t_{n+1}) \ = 1 - 1 + 0 = 0$$

Then, we get a new marking $\mu' = (a_1, \ a_2, \ a_3, \ \ldots, \ a_n, \ 0)$, where $a_i \in \{0, \ 1\}$. The marking μ' is found in $R_0(S_{n+1}, \ \mu^0)$. If all a_i's are zero, then μ' is a dead marking. Hence, suppose some $a_i \neq 0$. In this case, t_i is enabled and in the next new marking μ'', the ith component is reduced to zero. Eventually, this process will lead to a dead marking. Further, the marking vectors of the form $\mu = (a_1, \ a_2, \ a_3, \ \ldots, \ a_n, 0)$ are already obtained as a result of firing $t_1, \ t_2, \ t_3, \ \ldots., \ t_n$ through some subsequences by virtue of the induction hypothesis. Thus, T^* is precisely the reachability tree $R(S_{n+1}, \ \mu^0)$ of S_{n+1}. Hence, the result follows by PMI. □

4. Some general questions and a necessary condition

The above theorem opens not only the general problem of determining all such Petri nets but also raises the question of determining such optimal Petri nets ; for example, one can ask

1. Precisely which Petri nets produce the set of all binary n-vectors with minimum repetitions?

2. Precisely which Petri nets produce all the binary n-vectors in the smallest possible number of steps? As pointed out, these questions could be quite important from practical application point of view.

3. Do there exist Petri nets that generate every binary n-vector exactly once?

4. Is it not possible to take any marking other than $(1,1,1,\cdots,1)$ as an initial marking for such a Petri net?

The following proposition and theorem answer the last two questions.

Proposition 1. *[6] If a Petri net is Boolean then $\mu^0(p) = 1, \forall p \in P$.*

Proof. Suppose $C = (P, T, I^-, I^+, \mu^0)$ is a Petri net which is Boolean and $\mu^0(p_i) \neq 1$ for some $p_i \in P$. By the definition of a Petri net, no place can be isolated. Therefore p_i has to be connected to some $t_i \in T$. Now, three cases arise for consideration:

Case-1: $p_i \in t_i^\bullet$,
Case-2: $p_i \in {}^\bullet t_i \cap t_i^\bullet$, and
Case-3: $p_i \in {}^\bullet t_i$

In Case 1, since the given Petri net C is safe, ${}^\bullet t_i \neq \emptyset$ [2]. Therefore, $\exists\, p_j \in {}^\bullet t_i$ for some $p_j \in P$. p_j will have either one token or no token. If p_j has one token then t_i is enabled and hence fires. After firing of t_i, p_j will have no token and p_i will receive one token. So, both the places cannot have one token simultaneously. Hence, we will not get the marking vector whose components are all equal to 1. Again, if p_j has no token then t_i cannot fire, whence p_i will never receive a token, which contradicts the assumption of the case.

Case 2 follows from the arguments given for Case 1 above since, in particular, $p_i \in t_i^\bullet$.

Also, in Case 3, as in the proof of Case 1 $p_i \in {}^\bullet t_i$ implies that we cannot have the marking vector whose components are all equal to 1.

Thus, if a Petri net generates all the binary n-vectors then $\mu^0(p_i) = 1\ \forall\, p_i \in P$. □

5. Crisp Petri nets

Theorem 2. *[6] There exists a 1-safe Petri net with the initial marking $\mu^0(p) = 1, \forall p \in P$ which generates each of the 2^n binary n-vectors*

$$(a_1, a_2, a_3, \cdots, a_n),\ a_i \in \{0, 1\},\ n = |P|,$$

as one of its marking vectors, exactly once.

Proof. We shall prove this result again by using the PMI on $n = |P|$.

For $n = 1$, we construct a Petri net C_1 as shown in Figure 6. In this Petri net C_1,

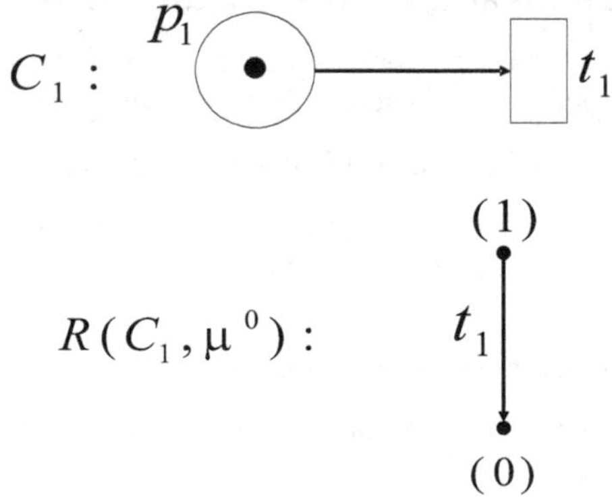

Figure 6. Petri net C_1 and $R(C_1, \mu^0)$

the total number of transitions $= 2^1 - 1 = 1$,

$|p_1^\bullet| = 2^1 - 1 = 1$,

$|{}^\bullet p_1| = 2^{1-1} - 1 = 0$,

$|{}^\bullet t_1| = 1$.

Total number of transitions whose post-sets having no element $= {}^1C_0 = 1$ and this transition is t_1. Clearly, $R(C_1, \mu^0)$ of C_1 generates both the binary 1-vectors (1) and (0) as shown in Figure 6 in the first step and after this step, transition becomes dead.

Next, for $n = 2$, the Petri net C_2 shown in Figure 7 has two places. In C_2, we have

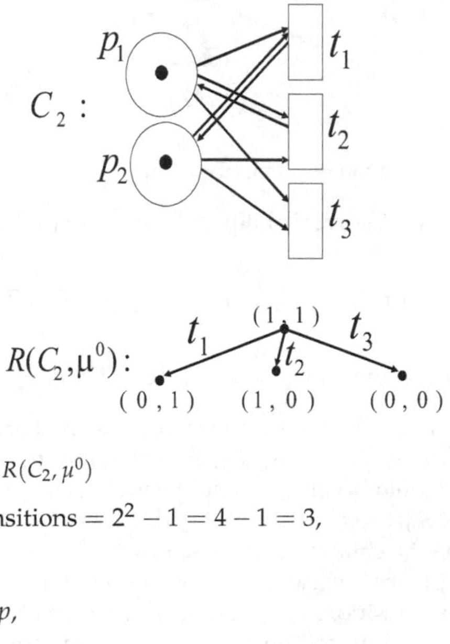

Figure 7. Petri net C_2 and $R(C_2, \mu^0)$

the total number of transitions $= 2^2 - 1 = 4 - 1 = 3$,

$|p^\bullet| = 2^2 - 1 = 3, \ \forall\, p$,

$|{}^\bullet p| = 2^{2-1} - 1 = 1, \ \forall\, p$,

$|{}^\bullet t| = 2, \ \forall\, t$.

The total number of transitions whose post-sets have one element $= {}^2C_1 = 2$ and these transitions are t_1, t_2.

The total number of transitions whose post-sets have no element $= {}^2C_0 = 1$ and this transition is t_3.

It is clear from Figure 7 that $R(C_2, \mu^0)$ has exactly $4 = 2^2$ binary 2-vectors (a_1, a_2), $a_1, a_2 \in \{0, 1\}$ in the first step and after this step, all the transitions become dead.

We can construct $R(C_2, \mu^0)$ from $R(C_1, \mu^0)$ as follows: Take two copies of $R(C_1, \mu^0)$. In the first copy, augment each vector of $R(C_1, \mu^0)$ by the adjunction of a '0' entry at the second coordinate of every marking vector and denote the resulting labeled tree as $R_0(C_1, \mu^0)$. Similarly, in the second copy, augment each vector by the adjunction of a '1' at the second coordinate of every marking vector and let $R_1(C_1, \mu^0)$ be the resulting labeled tree (see Figure 8). Now, using

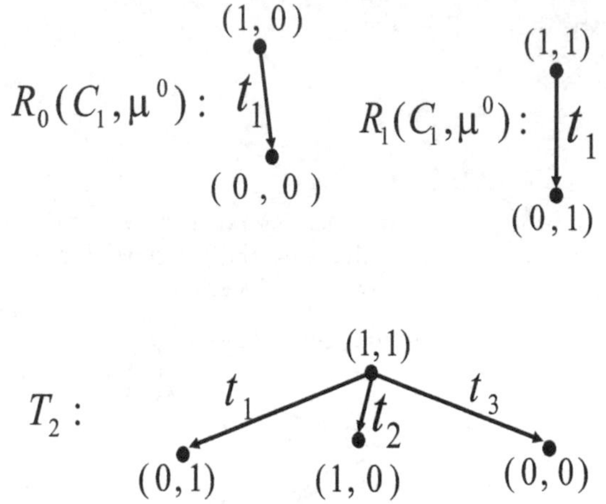

Figure 8. Augmented reachability trees and resulting labeled tree T_2

the following steps we construct the reachability tree $R(C_2, \mu^0)$ of C_2 from $R_0(C_1, \mu^0)$ and $R_1(C_1, \mu^0)$.

Step-1. Clearly, the binary 2-vectors in $R_0(C_1, \mu^0) \cup R_1(C_1, \mu^0)$ are all distinct and are exactly $2^2 = 4$ in number.

Step-2. In $R_0(C_1, \mu^0)$, none of the transitions t_j is enabled at $(1, 0)$.

Step-3. In $R_0(C_1, \mu^0)$, the root node $(1, 0)$ has the marking obtained after firing of transition t_2 in C_2. Hence, we join the root node $(1, 0)$ of $R_0(C_1, \mu^0)$ to the root node $(1, 1)$ of $R_1(C_1, \mu^0)$ by an arc labeled t_2 so that $(1, 0)$ would become the 'child node' obtained by firing t_2 in C_2. Next, we join the child node $(0, 0)$ of $R_0(C_1, \mu^0)$ to the root node $(1, 1)$ of $R_1(C_1, \mu^0)$ by an arc labeled t_3 so that $(0, 0)$ would become the child node obtained by firing t_3 in C_2. Then, the resulting labeled tree T_2 has exactly 2^2 binary 2-vectors as its set of nodes. T_2 is indeed the reachability tree of C_2 because in C_2 all the transitions t_1, t_2 and t_3 are enabled at the initial marking $(1, 1)$ and fire. Further, after firing of each transition, the new markings obtained by the rule

$$\mu'(p_i) = \mu^0(p_i) - I^-(p_i, t_j) + I^+(p_i, t_j)$$

are $(0, 1), (1, 0)$ and $(0, 0)$ respectively and no further firing takes place as the enabling condition fails to hold for these marking vectors; i.e., we get exactly $2^2 = 4$ binary 2-vectors in the first step only.

Next, suppose this result is true for $n = k$. That is, C_k is the 1-safe Petri net having k-places and $2^k - 1$ transitions $t_1, t_2, t_3, \cdots$, generating each of the 2^k binary k-vectors exactly once and having the structure as schematically shown in Figure 9 which has the following parameters:

$|p^\bullet| = 2^k - 1, \ \forall \ p,$
$|^\bullet p| = 2^{k-1} - 1, \ \forall \ p,$
$|^\bullet t| = k, \ \forall \ t.$

The total number of transitions whose post-sets have $k - 1$ elements $= {}^kC_{k-1} = {}^kC_1 = k$ and these transitions are $t_1, t_2, t_3, \cdots, t_k$.

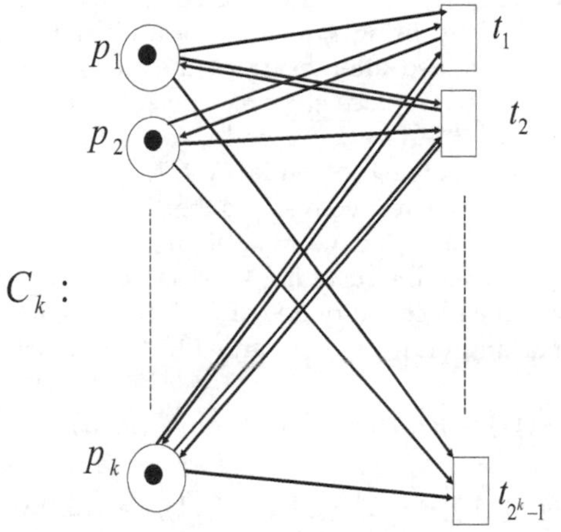

Figure 9. Petri net C_k for k places

The total number of transitions whose post-sets have $k-2$ elements $= {}^kC_{k-2} = {}^kC_2 = \frac{k(k-1)}{2}$ and these transitions are $t_{k+1}, t_{k+2}, t_{k+3}, \cdots, t_{\frac{k^2+k}{2}}$.

The total number of transitions whose post-sets have $k-3$ elements $= {}^kC_{k-3} = {}^kC_3 = \frac{k(k-1)(k-2)}{6}$ and these transitions are $t_{\frac{k^2+k+2}{2}}, t_{\frac{k^2+k+4}{2}}, t_{\frac{k^2+k+6}{2}}, \cdots, t_{\frac{k^3+5k}{6}}$.

$\vdots \quad \vdots \quad \vdots \quad \vdots \quad \vdots$

The total number of transitions whose post-sets have one element $= {}^kC_1 = k$ and these transitions are $t_{2^k-k-1}, t_{2^k-k}, t_{2^k-k+1}, \cdots, t_{2^k-2}$.

The total number of transitions whose post-sets have no element $= {}^kC_0 = 1$ and this transition is t_{2^k-1}.

We will now prove the result for the 1-safe Petri net C_{k+1} having $k+1$ places and $t_{2^{k+1}}-1$ transitions and having the structure shown schematically in **Figure-9**. For this purpose, take two copies of $R(C_k, \mu^0)$. In the first copy, augment each vector of $R(C_k, \mu^0)$ by the adjunction of a '0' entry at the $(k+1)^{th}$ coordinate of every marking vector and denote the resulting labeled tree as $R_0(C_k, \mu^0)$. Similarly, in the second copy, augment each vector by the adjunction of a '1' at the $(k+1)^{th}$ coordinate of every marking vector and let $R_1(C_k, \mu^0)$ be the resulting labeled tree. Now, using the following steps we construct the reachability tree $R(C_{k+1}, \mu^0)$ of C_{k+1} from $R_0(C_k, \mu^0)$ and $R_1(C_k, \mu^0)$.

Step-1. The induction hypothesis implies that the binary $(k+1)$-vectors in $R_0(C_k, \mu^0) \cup R_1(C_k, \mu^0)$ are all distinct and they are exactly $2^k + 2^k = 2^{k+1}$ in number.

Step-2. In $R_0(C_k, \mu^0)$, none of the transitions is enabled at $(1, 1, 1, \cdots, 0)$.

Step-3. In $R_0(C_k, \mu^0)$, the root node $(1, 1, 1, \cdots, 0)$ is the marking obtained after firing of transition t_{k+1} in C_{k+1}. Hence, we join the root node $(1, 1, 1, \cdots, 0)$ of $R_0(C_k, \mu^0)$ to the root node $(1,1,1,\cdots,1)$ of $R_1(C_k,\mu^0)$ by an arc labeled t_{k+1} so that $(1,1,1,\cdots,0)$ would become the child node obtained by firing t_{k+1} in C_{k+1} and in $R_1(C_k,\mu^0)$ the child node $(0,0,0,\cdots,1)$ is the marking obtained after firing of the transition t_{k+2} at the root node $(1,1,1,\cdots,1)$ of $R_1(C_k,\mu^0)$; so, we replace the arc labeled as t_{k+1} by t_{k+2} in $R_1(C_k,\mu^0)$. Next, we join the remaining $(2^{k+1}-1)-\overline{k+2}$ child nodes $(0,1,0,\cdots,0)$, $(1,0,0,\cdots,0)$, $\cdots,(0,0,0,\cdots,0)$ of $R_0(C_k,\mu^0)$ to the root node $(1,1,1,\cdots,1)$ of $R_1(C_k,\mu^0)$ by an arc each, labeled $t_{k+3},t_{k+4},t_{k+5},\cdots,t_{2^k-1}$ respectively, so that $(0,1,0,\cdots,0)$, $(1,0,0,\cdots,0)$, $\cdots$, $(0,0,0,\cdots,0)$ would become the marking vector obtained after firing of t_{k+3}, t_{k+4}, t_{k+5}, $\cdots$, t_{2^k-1} respectively in C_{k+1}. Then the resulting labeled tree T_{k+1} has exactly 2^{k+1} binary $(k+1)$-vectors. T_{k+1} is indeed the reachability tree of C_{k+1} because in C_{k+1} all the transitions are enabled at the initial marking $(1,1,1,\cdots,1)$ and fire. After firing, the new markings obtained by the rule

$$\mu'(p_i)=\mu^0(p_i)-I^-(p_i,t_j)+I^+(p_i,t_j)$$

are

$$(0,1,1,\cdots,1),(1,0,1,\cdots,1),(1,1,0,\cdots,1),\cdots,(0,0,0,\cdots,0)$$

respectively and no further firing takes place as the enabling condition fails to hold for these marking vectors; i.e., we get exactly 2^{k+1} binary $(k+1)$-vectors, each generated exactly once in the first step itself.

It is clear that the Petri net constructed above generates each of the 2^n binary n-vectors exactly once in the very first step and, hence, is the smallest number of steps because no firing will take place after that step.

Hence, the result follows by the PMI. □

Hence, we shall call a Boolean Petri net *crisp* if it generates every binary $n-$vector exactly once.

It may be observed from the above proof that the Petri net constructed therein yields all the binary n-vectors as marking vectors in the least possible number of steps. Such a Boolean Petri net will be called *optimal*.

6. Uniqueness of minimal crisp Petri net

The problem of characterizing 1-safe Petri nets generating all the 2^n binary n-vectors as marking vectors exactly once is an open problem [6]. We completely settle a part of this problem, viz., to determine minimal such Petri nets, 'minimal' in the sense that the depth of their reachability tree is minimum possible, where the *depth* of a rooted tree is defined as the maximum distance of any vertex in it from the root. In fact, we show here that such a 1-safe Petri net has a unique structure.

Theorem 3. *[8] The Petri net $C=(P,T,I^-,I^+,\mu^0)$ constructed in theorem 2 is the only minimal Crisp Petri net and the underlying graph of its reachability tree is isomorphic to the star $\downarrow K_{1,2^n-1}$, where '$\downarrow$' indicates the fact that arcs of the reachability tree of C are oriented downward from its root which is the center of $K_{1,2^n-1}$.*

Proof. The existence of C has already been established in Theorem 2. We will establish here the uniqueness of C. Suppose there exists a Petri net

$$C' = (P', T', I'^{-}, I'^{+}, \mu^0)$$

satisfying the hypothesis of the theorem. This implies, in particular that the reachability graph $R(C', \mu^0)$ of C' is isomorphic to the reachability graph $R(C, \mu^0)$ of C, i.e.,

$$R(C', \mu^0) \cong R(C, \mu^0) \cong\downarrow K_{1,2^n-1}.$$

Now, we need to show that $C' \cong C$.

Toward this end, define a map $\psi : P' \cup T' \longrightarrow P \cup T$ satisfying $\psi(p'_i) = p_i$ and $\psi(t'_i) = t_i$. Clearly, ψ is a bijection. We shall now show that it preserves the directed adjacency of C' onto C. For this, consider any isomorphism $\varphi : M(C', \mu^0) \longrightarrow M(C, \mu^0)$ from the reachability set $M(R(C', \mu^0))$ of C' onto the reachability set of C; this has the property that

$$(\mu^0, \mu^i) \in \mathcal{A}(R(C', \mu^0)) \Leftrightarrow (\varphi(\mu^0), \varphi(\mu^i)) \in \mathcal{A}(R(C, \mu^0)), \tag{1}$$

where $\mathcal{A}(D)$ denotes the set of arcs of any digraph D (in this case, D is the reachability graph of the corresponding Petri net).

Let (p'_i, t'_j) be an arc in C', we will show then that $(\psi(p'_i), \psi(t'_j))$ is an arc in C. Suppose, on the contrary $(\psi(p'_i), \psi(t'_j)) = (p_i, t_j)$ is not an arc in C. This implies in C that the marking vector μ^i whose i^{th} component is zero does not get generated by firing t_j or when $t_j^{\bullet} = \emptyset$ the marking vector obtained by firing t_j is repeated. The latter case does not arise due to the hypothesis that every marking vector is generated exactly once in C. But, then the former statement implies $\varphi(\mu^0)$ does not form the arc $(\varphi(\mu^0), \varphi(\mu^i))$ in $R(C, \mu^0)$ and hence, from (1), it follows that (μ^0, μ^i) does not form an arc in the reachability tree $R(C', \mu^0)$. This is a contradiction to our assumption that C' generates all the binary n-vectors exactly once. Similarly, one can arrive at a contradiction by assuming $(\psi(t'_j), \psi(p'_i))$ is not an arc in C. Thus, $C' \cong C$ follows, because the choice of the arcs (p'_i, t'_j) and (t'_j, p'_i) was arbitrary in each case. □

7. A Boolean Petri net whose reachability graph is homomorphic to the complete lattice

As mentioned already, Boolean Petri nets generating all the 2^n binary n-vectors as their marking vectors are not only of theoretical interest but also are of practical importance. We demonstrate the existence of a disconnected 1-safe Petri net whose reachability tree is homomorphic to the n-dimensional complete lattice L_n. This makes the problem of characterizing the crisp Boolean Petri nets appear quite intricate.

Definition 4. *Given any graph $G = (V, E)$, by a homomorphism of G we mean a partition $\{V_1, V_2, \ldots, V_t\}$ of its vertex-set $V(G) := V$ such that for any $i \in \{1, 2, \ldots, t\}$ no two distinct vertices in V_i are adjacent; in other words, V_i is an independent set of G. In general, given any partition $\pi = \{V_1, V_2, \ldots, V_t\}$ (not necessarily a homomorphism) of G, the partition graph with respect to π of G, denoted $\pi(G)$, is the graph whose vertex-set is π and any two vertices V_i and V_j are adjacent whenever there exist vertices $x \in V_i$ and $y \in V_j$ such that x and y are adjacent in G, that is, whenever, $xy \in E(G)$. If, in particular, π is a homomorphism then $\pi(G)$ is called a homomorphic image of G; further, a graph H is homomorphic to a graph G if there exists a homomorphism π of H such that $\pi(H) \cong G$ (read as "$\pi(H)$ is 'isomorphic to' G").*

Theorem 4. *[7] Let $C_n = (P, T, I^-, I^+, \mu^0)$ be the 1-safe Petri net consisting of n connected components, each isomorphic to $C^\star := \odot \longrightarrow \square$. Then the reachability tree of C_n is homomorphic to the n-dimensional complete lattice L_n.*

Proof. We prove this result by using the PMI on the number of connected components each isomorphic to $C^\star$.

Let $n = 1$. That is, C_1 has only one connected component $C^\star$, whence $C_1 = C^\star$. Then, the reachability tree of C_1 is the 1-dimensional complete lattice L_1, in which the direction of the 'link' (or, 'arc') $((1), (0))$ between the two 1-dimensional marking vectors (1) and (0) is shown as the 'vertical' one, as in Figure 10. The arc $((1), (0))$ in L_1, labeled as t_1, signifies the fact that the transition t_1 fires at (1), moving the only token out of the place p_1 resulting in the next state of the Petri net in which t_1 is 'dead' in the sense that it no longer fires at (0). Therefore, the next state of the Petri net C_1 is determined by the *zero vector* (0) as the marking vector of C_1. Thus, C_1 has just two states, viz., the 'active' one represented by the 1-dimensional 'unit vector' (1) and the 'dead' one represented by the 1-dimensional zero vector (0). Hence, the entire 'dynamics' of C_1 is completely represented by L_1. Next, consider $n = 2$. That is, we

Figure 10. Lattice L_1

have the 1-safe Petri net C_2, consisting of two connected components, each isomorphic to $C^\star$ as shown in Figure 11, along with its reachability tree (seen as a connected acyclic digraph) that is isomorphic to the 2-dimensional complete lattice L_2. In C_2, the transitions t_1 and t_2 are

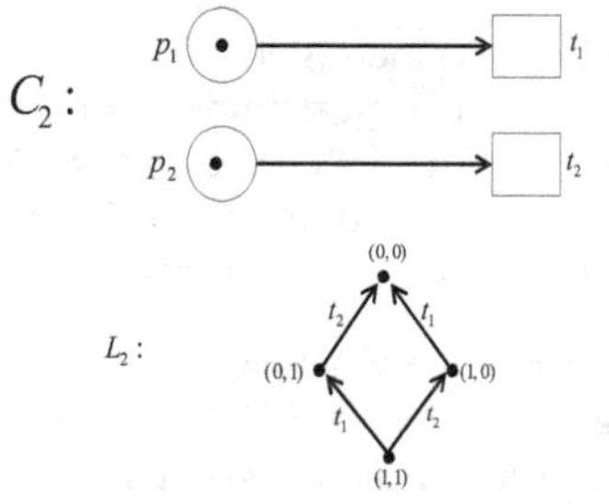

Figure 11. Petri net C_2 and its directed reachability tree L_2

both enabled. After firing t_1 and t_2 at the node $(1, 1)$ successively, in the first step, we get the marking vectors $(0, 1)$ and $(1, 0)$ respectively. Here, we fix the direction of t_2 to be 'orthogonal' to that of t_1 in L_2. Further, at $(0, 1)$ the transition t_2 is enabled, which fires in the same direction as in the first step giving the marking $(0,0)$. Subsequently, at $(1,0)$ transition t_1 is enabled, which fires in the same direction as in its previous step of firing giving the marking $(0,0)$. After this second step of firing, both the transitions t_1 and t_2 become dead at $(0,0)$. Thus, it is clear from Figure 11 that the reachability tree L_2 of C_2, seen as a connected acyclic digraph, has exactly $4 = 2^2$ binary vectors (a_1, a_2), $a_1, a_2 \in \{0,1\}$ as the marking vectors of C_2.

We can construct L_2 tactically from L_1 as follows.

Step1. Take two copies of L_1. In the first copy, augment each vector of L_1 by one extra coordinate position on the right by putting a 0 entry in that position and denote the resulting labeled copy of L_1 as L_1^0. Similarly, in the second copy, augment each vector by one extra coordinate position on the right by filling it with 1 and denote the resulting labeled copy of L_1 as L_1^1.

Step2. Take the union $L_1^0 \cup L_1^1$ and augment the new 'edges' (i.e., undirected line segments) joining those pairs of nodes whose marking vectors are at unit Hamming distance from each other. Direct each of these edges from the node, represented by its marking vector, at which t_2 fires to the node whose label (i.e., marking vector) gives the result of that firing. Accordingly, label each of such arcs by the label t_2.

Thus, the directed arcs labeled t_2 join every node of L_1^1 to exactly one node in L_1^0 in a bijective manner as shown in Figure 12. In this way, we see that the resulting discrete structure L_2^* has $4 = 2^2$ nodes which correspond to 2^2 binary vectors (a_1, a_2), $a_1, a_2 \in \{0,1\}$. Clearly, L_2^* is nothing but the reachability tree L_2 of C_2, seen as a connected acyclic digraph. Next, consider

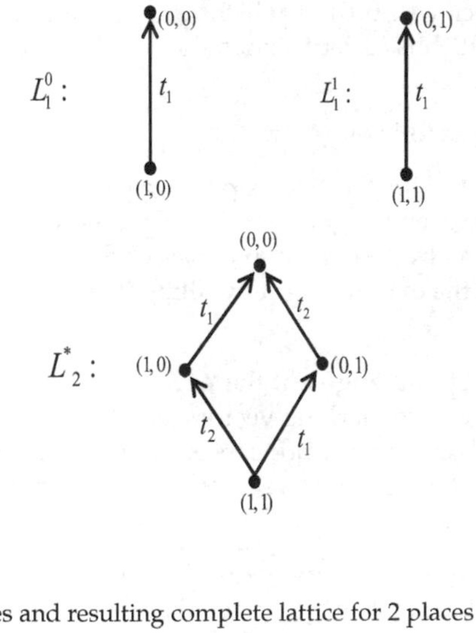

Figure 12. Augmented lattices and resulting complete lattice for 2 places

$n = 3$. That is, we have the 1-safe Petri net C_3 consisting of three connected components each isomorphic to C^* as shown in Figure 13. In C_3, all the three transitions t_1, t_2, t_3 are enabled. Hence, after firing the transitions t_1, t_2 and t_3 successively at $(1,1,1)$ we get the marking vectors $(0,1,1), (1,0,1)$ and $(1,1,0)$ respectively, in first step. Right here, we fix the directions of t_1, t_2 and t_3 so as to be orthogonal to each other. Further, at $(0,1,1)$ the transitions

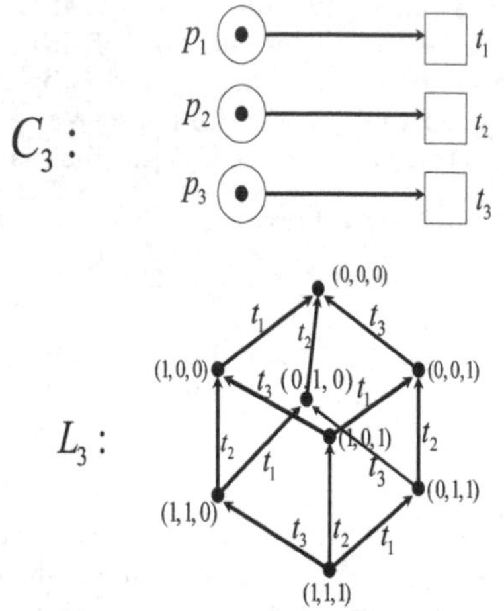

Figure 13. Petri net C_3 with 3 places and its complete lattice

t_2 and t_3 are enabled. After firing them successively we get the marking vectors $(0,0,1)$ and $(0,1,0)$, respectively. Subsequently, firing t_1 and t_3 at $(1,0,1)$ will give the marking vectors $(0,0,1)$ and $(1,0,0)$ respectively, whereas the firing of t_1 and t_2 at $(1,1,0)$ give the marking vectors $(0,1,0)$ and $(1,0,0)$. On continuing the process of firing in the next (i.e., the third) step we get the marking vector $(0,0,0)$ at which no transition is enabled. So, we have the reachability tree L_3 of C_3, which is isomorphic to the 3-dimensional complete lattice L_3, seen as a connected acyclic digraph.

We can construct L_3 from L_2 as follows.

Step1. Take two copies of L_2. In the first copy, augment each vector of L_2 by one extra coordinate position on the extreme right by putting a 0 entry in that position; denote the resulting labeled copy of L_2 as L_2^0. Similarly, in the second copy, augment each vector by one extra coordinate position on the extreme right by filling it with 1; denote the resulting labeled copy of L_2 as L_2^1.

Step2. Take the union $L_2^0 \cup L_2^1$ and augment the new 'edges' (i.e., undirected line segments) joining those pairs of nodes whose marking vectors are at unit Hamming distance from each other. Direct each of these edges from the node, represented by its marking vector, at which t_3 fires, to the node whose label (i.e., marking vector) gives the result of that firing. Accordingly, label each of such arcs by the label t_3.

Thus, the directed arcs labeled t_3 join every node of L_2^1 to exactly one node in L_2^0 in a bijective manner as shown in Figure 14. In this way, we see that the resulting discrete structure L_3^* has $8 = 2^3$ nodes which correspond to 2^3 binary vectors (a_1, a_2, a_3), $a_1, a_2, a_3 \in \{0,1\}$. Clearly, L_3^* is nothing but the reachability tree L_3 of C_3, seen as a connected acyclic digraph. Hence, let us assume that the result is true for $n = k$. That is, we have the 1-safe Petri net C_k consisting of k connected components each isomorphic to C^* and L_k is isomorphic to the reachability

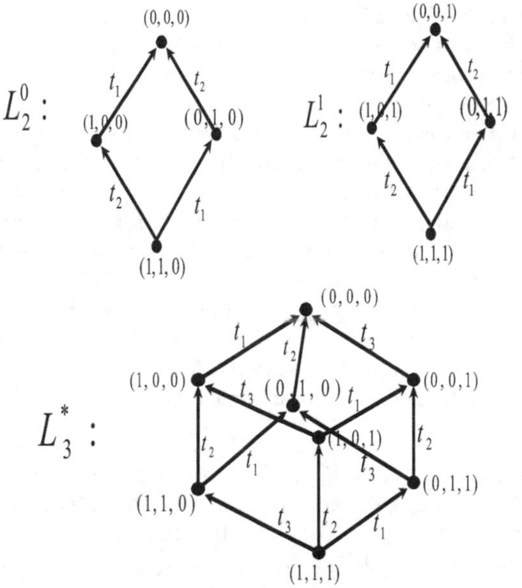

Figure 14. Augmented lattices and resulting complete lattice

tree of C_k, seen as a connected acyclic digraph. Now, we will prove that the result is true for $n = k + 1$.

Note that, in C_k, all the k transitions $t_1, t_2, \ldots, t_k$ are enabled at the k-dimensional unit vector $(1, 1, \ldots, 1)$.

Step1. Take two copies of L_k. In the first copy, augment each vector of L_k by one extra coordinate position on the extreme right by putting a 0 entry in that position; denote the resulting labeled copy of L_k as L_k^0. Similarly, in the second copy, augment each vector by one extra coordinate position on the extreme right by filling it with 1; denote the resulting labeled copy of L_k as L_k^1.

Step2. Take the union $L_k^0 \cup L_k^1$ and augment the new 'edges' (i.e., undirected line segments) joining those pairs of nodes whose marking vectors are at unit Hamming distance from each other. Direct each of these edges from the node, represented by its marking vector, at which t_{k+1} fires, to the node whose label (i.e., marking vector) gives the result of that firing. Accordingly, label each of such arcs by the label t_{k+1}.

It is now enough to show that L_{k+1} is indeed isomorphic to the reachability tree of C_{k+1}, seen as a connected acyclic digraph. Towards this end, consider the sets $A_0 = \{(a_1, a_2, \ldots, a_{k+1}) : a_{k+1} = 0\}$ and $A_1 = \{(a_1, a_2, \ldots, a_{k+1}) : a_{k+1} = 1\}$ Clearly, the subdigraph induced by A_0 is 'label-isomorphic' to L_k^0 whose nodes are labeled by the 2^k $(k+1)$-dimensional vectors in A_0 and the subdigraph induced by A_1 is 'label-isomorphic' to L_k^1 whose nodes are labeled by the 2^k $(k+1)$-dimensional vectors in A_1. Every arc in $L_k^0 \cup L_k^1$ is labeled by one of the transitions $t_1, t_2, \ldots, t_k$ in such a way that for any two indices $i, j \in \{1, 2, \ldots, k\}$ t_i and t_j are in orthogonal or parallel directions in each of L_k^0 and L_k^1 according to whether $i \neq j$ or $i = j$, thus, by Step 1 and the induction hypothesis, each of the $k2^{k-1}$ arcs in L_k^0 (respectively, in L_k^1) represents one of the transitions $t_1, t_2, \ldots, t_k$ fired in accordance with the firing rule, yielding the next state marking vector from its previous state marking vector that is at unit Hamming distance from the former. Now, by Step 2, the edges joining those pairs of nodes whose marking vectors are at unit Hamming distance from each other are directed in such a way that each of the resulting arcs represents the firing of a new transition t_{k+1} at the node, represented by its marking vector in the reachability tree of C_{k+1}, yielding the node of the reachability tree of C_{k+1} whose label (i.e., marking vector) gives the result of that firing. Accordingly, label each of such arcs by the label t_{k+1}. Since no two marking vectors in A_0 or in A_1 are interconnected by an arc labeled t_{k+1} in the above scheme, it follows that every arc labeled t_{k+1} has its initial node in A_1 and terminal node in A_0, signifying the fact that t_{k+1} fires at its initial node in A_1 and yields the next state marking vector that belongs to A_0. Further, no two of these arcs have a common node (whence we say that they are *independent*). Also, every node in A_1 is joined to a unique node in A_0 at Hamming distance one by an arc labeled t_{k+1} in a bijective way and, therefore, the number of such arcs is 2^k.

Next, consider the node labeled $(0,0,\ldots,0)$ in L_{k+1}. The only arcs incoming at this node are from the nodes that are at unit Hamming distance from it, viz., those that are labeled by the elementary coordinate vectors $(1,0,0,\ldots,0)$, $(0,1,0,\ldots,0)$, $(0,0,1,\ldots,0)$, $\ldots$, $(0,0,0,\ldots,1)$ and, hence, the corresponding arcs are labeled $t_1, t_2, \ldots, t_k, t_{k+1}$. Consequently, all these transitions become dead at the node labeled by the $(k+1)$-dimensional zero vector $(0,0,\ldots,0)$ as its marking vector.

The foregoing arguments imply that L_{k+1} indeed represents the reachability tree of C_{k+1}, being a connected acyclic digraph, invoking the PMI.

Now, for any arbitrary positive integer n, construct the partition π_H of the reachability tree $R(C_n, \mu^0)$ by defining its 'parts' (which are subsets of the nodes of $R(C_n, \mu^0)$) by letting $V_0 = \{(1,1,\ldots,1)\}$ and $V_i = \{(a_1, a_2, \ldots, a_n) : d_H((1,1,\ldots,1),(a_1,a_2,\ldots,a_n)) = i\}$, for each $i \in \{1,2,\ldots,n\}$, where $d_H(A,B)$ denotes the Hamming distance between the vectors A and B of the same dimension. Clearly, $|V_i| = {}^nC_i$ for each $i \in \{0,1,2,\ldots,n\}$, where ${}^nC_k = \frac{n!}{k!(n-k)!}$ will in general denote the number of ways in which k objects can be selected out of n given objects. Now, consider the mapping $\eta^{\mu^0} : V(R(C_n, \mu^0)) \to \{0,1\}^n$ that assigns to each node $u \in R(C_n, \mu^0)$ the marking vector derived by the sequence of transitions fired starting from the initial marking vector μ^0 as specified by the unique path from the root vertex u_0 whose marking vector is μ^0. Hence, we consider the *refinement* π'_H of π_H defined as follows: For each $i \in \{0,1,2,\ldots,n\}$ and for each $(a_1,a_2,\ldots,a_n) \in V_i$, let $U^i_{(a_1,a_2,\ldots,a_n)} = \{u \in V(R(C_n,\mu^0)) : \eta^{\mu^0}(u) = (a_1,a_2,\ldots,a_n)\}$. Then, clearly, U^i's form a partition of the set V_i for each $i \in \{0,1,2,\ldots,n\}$. It may be easily verified that no two marking vectors in V_i are adjacent in $R(C_n,\mu^0)$, whence π'_H is a homomorphism of $R(C_n,\mu^0)$. Further, the homomorphic image $\pi'_H(R(C_n,\mu^0)) \cong L_n$ because (V_i, V_{i+1}) is an arc in L_n if and only if there is an arc from a marking vector in V_i to a marking vector in V_{i+1} in $R(C_n,\mu^0)$.

This completes the proof. □

In the above theorem, we have shown that by fixing the sequence of transitions in a Petri net for firing tactfully, one can produce the complete Boolean lattice as a homomorphic image of its reachability tree. One can perhaps produce many such interesting results like, for instance, getting the vertices of a regular polyhedron in terms of marking vectors and using them for analysis of Boolean circuits with given properties. This raises another new question, viz., to characterize 1-safe Petri nets whose reachability trees have a given property $\mathcal{P}$.

Note that given any 1-safe Petri net C of order n, its reachability tree $R(C,\mu)$, with an arbitrary binary n-dimensional vector μ as its root, is essentially finite (cf.: [11]) and has all its nodes labeled by the function η^{μ} into the vertex set of the Boolean complete lattice L_n, possibly with repetitions of marking vectors. Consider the *Hamming distance partition* $\pi_H := \pi_H(V(R(C,\mu))$ of the vertex-set of $R(C,\mu)$ defined by letting $V_0 = \{\mu\}$ and

$$V_i = \{(a_1, a_2, \ldots, a_n) : d_H(\mu, (a_1, a_2, \ldots, a_n)) = i\},$$

for each $i \in \{1, 2, \ldots\}$. Then, its refinement $\pi'_H = \{V_0, V_1, V_2, \ldots, V_n\}$ is a homomorphism of $R(C,\mu)$ into a connected sublattice of L_n. Thus, we are lead to the problem of determining 1-safe Petri nets whose reachability trees are homomorphic to a given sublattice of L_n. First of all, we have the question whether for any arbitrarily given connected sublattice L of L_n there exists a 1-safe Petri net whose usual reachability tree is homomorphic to L. We have a conjecture that the answer to this question is in the affirmative.

Next, given a connected sublattice L of L_n, let C_L^n denote the set of all 1-safe Petri nets of order n whose reachability trees are homomorphic to L. Let $\mathcal{L}_n$ denote the set of all pairwise nonisomorphic connected sublattices of L_n. Clearly, $\{C_L^n : L \in \mathcal{L}_n\}$ is a partition of the set $\mathcal{S}_1$ of all 1-safe Petri nets of order n. In other words, 1-safe Petri nets in any one of the sets in C_L^n are all 'equivalent' in the sense that the dynamics of any two of them are in accordance with the given connected sublattice L of L_n; thus, it is enough to pick any one of them so that we have an option to choose the 'required' one as per our practical constraints.

8. Towards characterizing Boolean Petri nets

We discuss here some necessary and sufficiency conditions for a 1-safe Petri net to be Boolean.

Lemma 1. *[9] If a 1-safe Petri net* $C = (P, T, I^-, I^+, \mu^0)$, $|P| = n$ *is Boolean then* $p \in t^{\bullet} \Rightarrow p \in {}^{\bullet}t$.

Proof. Suppose $p \in t^{\bullet}$ and $p \notin {}^{\bullet}t$. Since C is 1-safe, ${}^{\bullet}t \neq \emptyset \; \forall \; t \in T$ (see [2]). This means that there exists at least one place $p_i \in P$ such that $p_i \in {}^{\bullet}t$. Further, since C is Boolean, $\mu^0(p)$=1 $\forall \; p \in P$ (Proposition 1) and, therefore, every transition is enabled. In particular, t is enabled. After firing of t the place p will receive 2 tokens ($\because \mu'(p) = \mu(p) - I^-(p,t) + I^+(p,t)$), which contradicts the fact that the Petri net is 1-safe. Hence, $p \in t^{\bullet} \Rightarrow p \in {}^{\bullet}t$. □

Lemma 2. *[9] If a 1-safe Petri net* $C = (P, T, I^-, I^+, \mu^0)$, $|P| = n$ *is Boolean then* $|P| \leq |T|$.

Proof. Since C generates all the binary n-vectors, it generates the marking vectors of the type $(0,1,\cdots,1), (1,0,1,\cdots,1), \cdots, (1,1,\cdots,0)$, each having the Hamming distance 1 from the initial marking vector μ^0=$(1,1,\cdots,1)$. These n marking vectors can be obtained only in the very first step of firing because the marking vector whose Hamming distance is 1 from the initial marking cannot be obtained from any other marking vector whose Hamming distance is greater than or equal to 2 from the initial marking. These n marking vectors can be generated only if for every place $p_i \in P$, $i = 1, 2, 3, \cdots, n$, there exist n distinct transitions say $t_1, t_2, t_3, \cdots, t_n$ such that $p_i \in^{\bullet} t_i$ and $p_i \notin t_i^{\bullet}$, $\forall \; i = 1, 2, 3, \cdots, n$. Hence, $|P| \leq |T|$. □

Lemma 3. *[9] If a 1-safe Petri net $C = (P, T, I^-, I^+, \mu^0)$, $|P| = n$ is Boolean then the incidence matrix I of C contains $-I_n$, the identity matrix of order n as a submatrix.*

Proof. Since C is Boolean, $\mu^0(p)$=1 $\forall\ p \in P$ (Proposition 1). Again, because of the generation of all the binary n-vectors, the vectors of the type $(0,1,\cdots,1), (1,0,1,\cdots,1),\cdots,(1,1,\cdots,0)$ each at a Hamming distance 1 from the initial marking, have also been generated. These vectors can be obtained only in the first step of firing, as shown in Lemma 2. Therefore, $\forall$ $p_i \in P$, $i = 1,2,3,\cdots,n$, there exist n distinct transitions, say t_1,t_2,t_3,$\cdots$,t_n such that $p_i \in {}^\bullet t_i$ and $p_i \notin t_i^\bullet$ and hence $I^-(p_i,t_j)$=1 if i=j and 0 if $i \neq j$ and also $I^+(p_i,t_i) = 0\ \forall\ i = 1,2,3,\cdots,n$. Since I=I^+-I^-, I contains $-I_n$ as a submatrix. □

Lemma 4. *[9] If a 1-safe Petri net $C = (P, T, I^-, I^+, \mu^0)$, $|P| = n$ is Boolean then there exists at least one transition t such that $t^\bullet = \emptyset$.*

Proof. Suppose, under the hypothesis, there does not exist any $t \in T$ such that $t^\bullet = \emptyset$; i.e., $t^\bullet \neq \emptyset$ for every $t \in T$. Since $t^\bullet \neq \emptyset$, $p \in t^\bullet$ for some $p \in P$. Then, by Lemma 1, $p \in {}^\bullet t$. Then, at p, the number of tokens remains one throughout the dynamic states of C. This implies that the vector $(0,0,\cdots,0)$ would never occur as a marking vector, a contradiction to the hypothesis. Therefore, the lemma follows by contraposition. □

Now, we will study necessary and sufficient conditions for a 1-safe Petri net that generates all the binary n-vectors as its marking vectors.

Theorem 5. *[9] A 1-safe Petri net $C = (P, T, I^-, I^+, \mu^0)$, $|P| = n$ with $t^\bullet = \emptyset\ \forall\ t \in T$ is Boolean if and only if*

1. $\mu^0(p) = 1\ \forall\ p \in P$
2. $|P| \leq |T|$
3. *The incidence matrix I of C contains $-I_n$ as a submatrix.*

Proof. Necessity: This follows from Proposition 1, Lemma 2 and Lemma 3 above.

Sufficiency: Given the hypothesis and conditions (1), (2) and (3), we claim that C is Boolean. Since $I = I^+ - I^-$ and $t^\bullet = \emptyset$, $\forall\ t \in T$, $I^+ = 0$. This implies that $I = -I^-$. Since I contains $-I_n$ as a submatrix, $\forall\ p_i \in P$, $\exists\ t_i \in T$ such that $p_i \in {}^\bullet t_i\ \forall\ i = 1,2,\cdots,n$. Also, $\mu^0(p) = 1\ \forall p \in P$. Therefore, all the n transitions $t_1, t_2, \cdots, t_n$ are enabled and fire. After firing, we get distinct ${}^nC_1 = n$ marking vectors whose Hamming distance is 1 from the initial marking vector. At these n new marking vectors, $n-1$ transitions are enabled and give at least ${}^nC_2$ distinct marking vectors, each of whose Hamming distance is 2 from the initial marking. Therefore this set of new vectors contains at least ${}^nC_2$ new distinct binary $n-$vectors.

In general, at any stage j, $3 \leq j \leq n$, we get a set of at least ${}^nC_j$ new distinct binary n-vectors whose Hamming distance is j from the initial marking, which are also distinct from the sets of ${}^nC_r$ distinct marking vectors for all r, $2 \leq r \leq j-1$. Therefore, at the nth stage we would have obtained at least ${}^nC_1 +^n C_2 + \cdots +^n C_n$=$2^n - 1$ distinct binary n-vectors. Together with the initial marking $(1,1,\cdots,1)$, we thus see that all the 2^n binary n-vectors would have been obtained as markings vectors, possibly with repetitions. □

Theorem 6. *[9] A 1-safe Petri net $C = (P, T, I^-, I^+, \mu^0)$, $|P| = n$ with $I^-(p_i, t_j) = 1 \ \forall\ i, j$ is Boolean if and only if there exist at least ${}^nC_r$, $r = 1, 2, \cdots, n$ distinct transitions $t \in T$ such that $|t^\bullet| = n - r$, where r is the Hamming distance of any binary n-vector from the initial marking $(1, 1, \cdots, 1)$.*

Proof. Necessity: Since C generates all the binary n-vectors, we have binary n-vectors $(0, 1, 1, \cdots, 1)$, $(1, 0, 1, \cdots, 1)$, $(1, 1, 0, \cdots, 1)$, $\cdots$, $(1, 1, 1, \cdots, 0)$, whose Hamming distance is 1 from the initial marking $(1, 1, 1, \cdots 1)$. They are n in number. Since $I^-(p_i, t_j) = 1 \ \forall i, j$, these vectors can be obtained only if $I^+(p_i, t_j) = 0$ for $i = j$ and 1 for $i \neq j$, $1 \leq j \leq n$. This implies that there are at least ${}^nC_1$ distinct transitions say t_1, t_2, $\cdots$, t_n such that $|t^\bullet|$=$n - 1$. After firing, they become dead. Further, we also have the binary n-vectors $(0, 0, 1, \cdots, 1)$, $(1, 0, 0, 1, \cdots, 1)$, $(1, 0, 1, 0, 1, \cdots, 1)$, $\cdots$, $(1, 1, \cdots, 1, 0, 0)$ whose Hamming distance is 2 from $(1, 1, 1, \cdots 1)$, $r = 1, 2, \ldots, n$. These vectors are ${}^nC_2$ in number and can be obtained only if there exist at least ${}^nC_2$ distinct transitions with $|t^\bullet| = n - 2$. In general, there are at least ${}^nC_r$ distinct transitions t such that $|t^\bullet| = n - r$, that yield ${}^nC_r$ binary n-vectors at Hamming distance r from $(1, 1, 1, \cdots 1)$, $r = 1, 2, \ldots, n$.

Sufficiency: Since $\mu^0(p) = 1 \ \forall p$, all the transitions are enabled and fire. After firing they all become dead as $I^-(p_i, t_j) = 1 \ \forall\ i, j$. This implies that the matrix I^- is of order $n \times m$ where $m \geq 2^n - 1$ and the matrix I^+ gets constructed as follows. By hypothesis, there are at least ${}^nC_1 = n$ distinct transition in C say t_1, t_2, $\cdots$, t_n which on firing generate all the binary n-vectors each having exactly one zero because $|t_i^\bullet| = n - 1$ (w.l.o.g., we assume that there is no arc from t_i to p_i i.e., $I^+(p_i, t_i) = 0$ for $i = 1, 2, \cdots, n$). Thus, we place the transpose of these binary n-vectors as the first n-columns in I^+ matrix. Next, by hypothesis, we have ${}^nC_2$ distinct transitions, say t_{n+1}, t_{n+2}, $\cdots$, $t_{{}^nC_2}$, such that $|t_j^\bullet| = n - 2$. Since they all become dead after firing and $|t_j^\bullet| = n - 2$ for all $n + 1 \leq j \leq {}^nC_2$ these must generate all the distinct binary n-vectors each having exactly two zeros. Hence, the transpose of these ${}^nC_2$ vectors are placed as columns in the matrix I^+ immediately after the previous $n = {}^nC_1$ columns. We are thus enabled by the hypothesis to construct the submatrix H of order $n \times (2^n - 1)$ of I^+ which contains all the $2^n - 1$ distinct binary n-vectors, the last column of H being the all zero n-vector. We may augment to H the initial all-one n-vector as a column either on the extreme left or on the extreme right of H in I^+. Let the so augmented submatrix of I^+ have more columns. That means, each one of them is a repetition of some column in H. Thus, we see that the Petri net C generates all the binary n-vectors as its marking vectors. □

Definition 5. *A Petri net C=(P, T, I^-, I^+, μ^0) is said to have a **Strong chain cycle** (SCC) Z if Z is a subnet satisfying $|{}^\bullet t|$=2, $|p^\bullet|$=2 and $|t^\bullet|$=1 $\forall$ p,t$\in$ Z (See Figure 15). Any SCC is said to become a **strong chain** after the removal of the arcs of any one of its self loops.*

Theorem 7. *[9] A 1-safe Petri net $C = (P, T, I^-, I^+, \mu^0)$, $|P| = n$ having an SCC Z, covering all the places, is Boolean if and only if*

1. $\mu^0(p) = 1 \ \forall\ p \in P$
2. *there exists at least one transition t outside Z such that $t^\bullet = \emptyset$.*

Proof. Necessity: Suppose that the 1-safe Petri net C with an SCC covering all the places is Boolean.

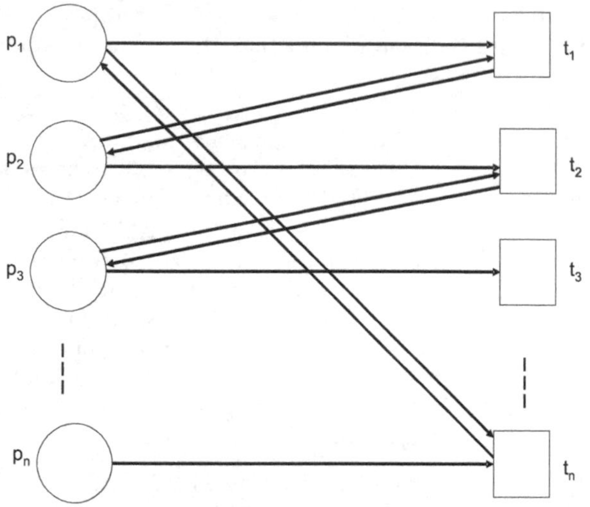

Figure 15. Strong Chain Cycle

In part 1 of the statement of the theorem, let $\mu^0(p_i) \neq 1$ for some $p_i \in P$. Then, $\mu^0(p_i) = 0$. Since C has an SCC, we cannot get one token in the place p_i. So, we cannot get all the binary n-vectors, which is a contradiction to the hypothesis.

In part 2 of the theorem, since C generates all the binary n-vectors, we have $(0, 0, \cdots, 0)$ as a marking vector. This vector can be obtained only if there is a transition t such that $t^\bullet = \emptyset$, by virtue of Lemma 4. We claim that such a transition t does not belong to Z. Suppose $t \in Z = (p_1, t_1, p_2, t_2, p_3, t_3, \cdots, p_{n-1}, t_{n-1}, p_n, t_n, p_1)$ where (p_i, t_i) is a single arc in C and (t_i, p_{i+1}) is a symmetric arc in C. This means, $t = t_i$ for some i, $1 \leq i \leq n$. This implies, $|t^\bullet| = |t_i^\bullet| = 1$, which is a contradiction to our assumption that $t^\bullet = \emptyset$. Therefore, t does not belong to any SCC.

Sufficiency: Since $\mu^0(p) = 1 \ \forall \ p \in P$, all the transitions belonging to Z are enabled and fire. After firing, they give ${}^nC_1$ distinct binary n-vectors $a_1 = (0, 1, 1, \cdots, 1)$, $a_2 = (1, 0, 1, \cdots, 1)$, $\cdots$, $a_i = (1, 1, \cdots, 1, 0, 1, \cdots, 1)$, $\cdots$, $a_n = (1, 1, \cdots, 1, 0)$, whose Hamming distance is 1 from μ^0, since $p_i^\bullet = \{t_{i-1}, t_i\}$ for $i > 1$ and $p_1^\bullet = \{t_1, t_n\}$, at each of these vectors a_i, exactly $(n-2)$ remaining transitions on Z are enabled and fire. After firing them, we get at least ${}^nC_2$ distinct marking vectors each of whose Hamming distance from μ^0 is 2 because in this second stage of firing there are $n(n-2)$ binary n-vectors in each of which there are exactly two zeros. In the third stage, at least ${}^nC_3$ distinct marking vectors are obtained by firing the above n-vectors obtained in the second stage and each of these vectors contains exactly three zeros. Continuing in this manner in the rth stage we get at least ${}^nC_r$ distinct marking vectors, each containing exactly r zeros, by firing all the n-vectors obtained in the $(r-1)$ stage. Since r ranges from $1, 2, \cdots, (n-1)$, we thus obtain at least ${}^nC_1 + {}^nC_2 + {}^nC_3 + \cdots + {}^nC_{n-1}$ which is equal to $2^n - {}^nC_0 - {}^nC_n = 2^n - 2$ distinct n-marking vectors. Since all of them are distinct from μ^0 as well as from the zero vector $(0, 0, \cdots, 0)$, which is obtained due to the hypothesis that there exists a transition t outside Z such that $t^{\bullet} = \emptyset$. Thus, we see that all the 2^n distinct binary n-vectors are generated by C. □

Lemma 5. *Let $C = (P, T, I^-, I^+, \mu^0)$, $|P| = n$ be a 1-safe Petri net with $\mu^0(p) = 1\ \forall\ p \in P$ and let Z be an SCC that passes through all the n places. Then any Petri net C' obtained from C by the deletion of any of the self loops belonging to Z generates all the binary n-vectors.*

Proof. First, we note that the removal of any self-loop from C results in a Petri net C' with $\mu^0(p) = 1\ \forall\ p \in P$ and a transition t such that $t^{\bullet} = \emptyset$. Now, if C' has an SCC Z' then by Theorem 7, C' is Boolean and hence there is nothing to prove. Hence, without loss of generality, we may assume that the given Petri net C has an SCC, say Z. We shall then prove the result by invoking the PMI on $n = |P|$. First, let $n = 1$. Then C does not contain any SCC and, therefore $C' = C$. Further, it is easy to verify that C' generates all the binary 1-vectors, namely (1), (0) as shown in Figure 16. Next, let $n = 2$. Then C' contains the following

Figure 16. Petri net $C' =:\cong C$ for 1 place

structure, shown in Figure 17. Here, $t_2^{\bullet} = \emptyset$. Since $\mu^0(p) = 1\ \forall\ p \in P$, t_2 is enabled and it

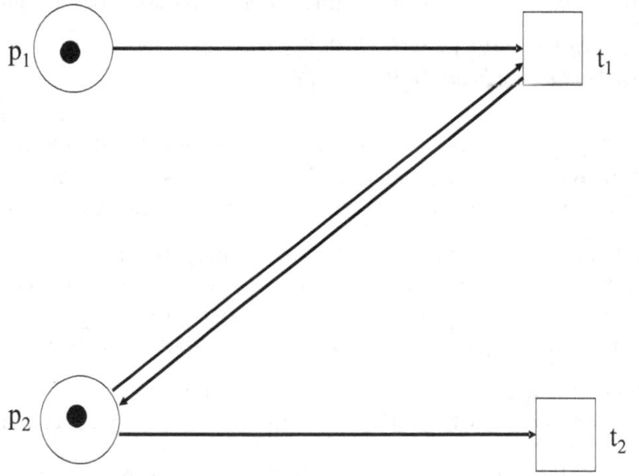

Figure 17. Petri net C' for 2 places

fires. After firing t_2, we get the marking vector $\mu^1 = (1, 0)$. Since t_1 fires simultaneously with t_2, we get the marking vector $\mu^2 = (0, 1)$. At this stage, t_2 is enabled and after firing, it gives the marking vector $\mu^3 = (0, 0)$. Hence we can obtain these marking vectors procedurally by taking two marking vectors obtained in the previous case namely, (1), (0) as follows.

Step-1. Augment 1 in the second position (corresponding to the case $t_2^{\bullet} = \emptyset$) in each of these vectors.

Step-2. In each case, t_2 fires and after firing, we get the marking vectors (1,0) and (0,0), respectively.

Next, take $n = k \geq 3$ and assume the validity by the above procedure to get all the 2^k binary k-vectors.

Let $n = k + 1$. Then, apply the following procedure.

Step-I. Augment 1 to each of the marking vectors $(a_1, a_2, \cdots, a_k)$ at its right most end to get the $(k+1)$-vector $(a_1, a_2, \cdots, a_k, 1)$.

Step-II. In this case, t_{k+1} fires and after firing we get the marking vectors $(a_1, a_2, \cdots, a_k, 0)$.

By the induction hypothesis, we have all the 2^k marking vectors to which Step-I has been applied to obtain the 2^k binary $(k+1)$-vectors as marking vectors (because of firing at each stage), having 1 in the $(k+1)^{th}$ coordinate. Further, each of these 2^k binary $(k+1)$-vectors has been fired using Step-II to obtain the binary $(k+1)$-vectors of the form $(a_1, a_2, \cdots, a_k, 0)$ which are all distinct from those obtained in Step-I. Together, therefore, we have obtained $2^k + 2^k = 2^{k+1}$ binary $(k+1)$-vectors as marking vectors from C'. Thus, the proof follows by PMI. □

9. An embedding theorem and complexity

The following is a "frustration theorem" due to the negative fact it reveals, to the effect that one cannot hope to have a "forbidden subgraph characterization" of a Boolean Petri net.

Theorem 8. *[10]: Every 1-safe Petri net* $C = (P, T, I^-, I^+, \mu^0)$, $|P| = n$ *with* $\mu^0(p) = 1 \ \forall \ p \in P$ *can be embedded as an induced subnet of a Boolean Petri net.*

Proof. Let $C = (P, T, I^-, I^+, \mu^0)$, $|P| = n$ be a 1-safe Petri net. If C is a Boolean Petri net then there is nothing to prove. Hence, assume that C is not a Boolean Petri net. Then, we have the following steps to obtain a Boolean Petri net C' in which C is one of its induced subnets.

Step-1: First of all, find those places in C each of whose postsets has single distinct sink transition (if the postset of a place has more than one distinct sink transitions then choose only one transition giving K_2). Suppose such places are $p_1, p_2, \cdots, p_k$, $1 \leq k < n$. If there is no sink transition in C, then augment one sink transition to each place in C.

Step-2: Augment $n - k$ new transitions and join each of them to the remaining $n - k$ places in C by an arc from a place to a new transition creating $n - k$ new active transitions.

Step-3: Thus, in C' we have n-copies of K_2 as its subgraph. Since $\mu^0(p) = 1 \ \forall p \in P$, all the transitions are enabled. Firing of n transitions forming n 'pendant transitions' will produce ${}^nC_1$ distinct binary n-vectors whose Hamming distance is 1 from the initial marking vector. At these marking vectors, $n - 1$ transitions out of those n transitions are enabled, and after firing give at least ${}^nC_2$ distinct marking vectors, each of whose Hamming distance is 2 from the initial marking.

In general at any stage j, $3 \leq j \leq n$, we get a set of at least ${}^nC_j$ new distinct binary n-vectors whose Hamming distance is j from the initial marking, which are also distinct from the sets of ${}^nC_r$ distinct marking vectors for all r, $2 \leq r \leq j - 1$. Therefore, at the nth stage we would have obtained at least ${}^nC_1 +{}^n C_2 + \cdots +{}^n C_n = 2^n - 1$ distinct binary n-vectors. Together with the initial marking $(1, 1, \cdots, 1)$, we thus see that all the 2^n binary n-vectors would have been obtained as marking vectors, possibly with repetitions. Thus C' is Boolean.

Therefore, every 1-safe Petri net C can be embedded as an induced subgraph of a Boolean Petri net. □

10. Scope for research

Precisely which Petri nets generate all the binary n-vectors as their marking vectors, or the so-called Boolean Petri net? This has been a hotly pursued research problems. We have shown in this chapter some necessary and sufficient conditions to characterize a Boolean Petri net, containing an SCC. However, the general problem of characterizing such a 1-safe Petri net C, when C does not contain an SCC or a strong chain, is still open. A Petri net containing an SCC is strongly connected, in the graph-theoretical sense that any two nodes in it are mutually reachable. However, the converse is not true; that is, if the underlying digraph of a Petri net is strongly connected, it need not contain an SCC. So, even a characterization of strongly connected Boolean Petri net is an open problem. Further, in general, characterizing crisp Boolean Petri nets is open too. If we relax the condition on the depth of the reachability tree in our original definition of minimality of a 'minimal' crisp Boolean Petri net and require instead that the number of enabled transitions be kept at minimum possible, the reachability graphs of such Petri nets may not have their underlying graph structures isomorphic to $K_{1,2^n-1}$, whence they would all be trees of the same order 2^n. Since they would be finite in number, determination of the structures of such Petri nets and their enumeration would be of potential practical interest. It involves orienting trees of order 2^n (in general, for theoretical purposes, trees of any order as such) that admit an orientation of their edges to make them the reachability trees of minimal 1−safe crisp Boolean Petri nets.

11. Concluding remarks

As pointed out, many fundamental issues regarding Boolean Petri nets emerge from the above study. For example, it is found and established that the reachability tree of a 1-safe Petri net can be homomorphically mapped on to the n-dimensional complete Boolean lattice, thereby yielding new techniques to represent the dynamics of these Petri nets. One can expect to bring out in the near future some salient features of 1-safe Petri nets in general as a part of a theory that is likely to emerge even in our work.

Following our first discovery of an infinite class of 1-safe star Petri nets that are Boolean, we came across crisp Boolean Petri nets, viz., that generate every binary n-vector as marking vector exactly once. This motivated us to move towards a characterization of such 1-safe Petri nets in general. Our work towards this end revealed to our surprise that there can be even such disconnected 1-safe Petri nets. We demonstrated the existence of a disconnected 1-safe Petri net which was obtained by removing the central transition from the star Petri net S_n, whose reachability tree can be tactically represented as an n-dimensional complete lattice L_n [7]. In this disconnected Petri net, the firing of transitions in a particular way (which we may regard as a 'tact' or 'strategy'), gives exactly 2^n marking vectors, repetitions occurring possibly only within a level, that can be arranged as a homomorphic image of the reachability tree of the Petri net, forming the n-dimensional complete Boolean lattice L_n.

The results of this chapter can perhaps be used gainfully in many purely theoretical areas like mathematics, computer science, universal algebra and order theory, the extent and effectiveness of its utility in solving the practical problem requiring the design of multi-functional switches for the operation of certain discrete dynamical systems of common use such as washing machines and teleprinters (e.g., see [1]).

Acknowledgement

The authors deeply acknowledge with thanks the valuable suggestions and thought-provoking comments by Dr. B.D. Acharya from time to time while carrying out the work reported in this chapter.

Author details

Sangita Kansal, Mukti Acharya and Gajendra Pratap Singh
Department of Applied Mathematics, Delhi Technological University, Shahbad Daulatpur, Main Bawana Road, Delhi-110042, India

12. References

[1] Acharya, B.D (2001). *Set-Indexers of a Graph and Set-Graceful Graphs,* Bull. Allahabad Math. Soc. 16, pp. 1-23.

[2] Best, E. and Thiagarajan, P.S. (1987). Some Classes of Live and Safe Petri Nets, Concurrency and Nets, Vol. 25, pp. 71-94.

[3] Harary, F. (1969).Graph Theory, Addison-Wesley, Reading, Massachusettes.

[4] Jensen, K. (1986). Coloured Petri nets, Lecture Notes in Computer Science, Vol. 254, Springer-Verlag, Berlin, pp. 248-299.

[5] Kansal, S., Singh, G.P. and Acharya, M. (2010). On Petri Nets Generating all the Binary n-Vectors, Scientiae Mathematicae Japonicae, 71, No. 2, pp. 209-216.

[6] Kansal, S., Singh, G.P. and Acharya, M. (2011). 1-Safe Petri Nets Generating Every Binary $n-$Vectors Exactly Once, Scientiae Mathematicae Japonicae, 74, No. 1, pp. 29-36.

[7] Kansal, S., Singh, G.P. and Acharya, M. (2011). A Disconnected 1-Safe Petri Net Whose Reachability Tree is Homomorphic to a Complete Boolean Lattice, proceeding of PACC-2011, IEEE Xplore, Catalog Number: CFP1166N-PRT ISBN: 978-1-61284-762-7.

[8] Kansal, S., Acharya, M. and Singh, G.P. (2012). Uniqueness of Minimal 1-Safe Petri Net Generating Every Binary n-Vectors as its Marking Vectors Exactly Once, Scientiae Mathematicae Japonicae, pp., e-2012, 75-78.

[9] Kansal, S., Acharya, M. and Singh, G.P. (2012). On the problem of characterizing 1-safe Petri nets that generate all the binary n-vectors as their marking vectors, Preprint.

[10] Singh, G.P., Kansal, S. and Acharya, M. (2012). Embedding an Arbitrary 1-Safe Petri Net in a Boolean Petri Net, Research Report, Deptartment of Applied Mathematics, Delhi Technological University, Delhi, India.

[11] Nauber, W. (2010). *Methods of Petri Net Analysis.* Ch.5 In: Lectures on Design and Analysis With Petri Nets, <http://www.tcs.inf.tu-dresden.de/nauber/dapn.shtml>

[12] Peterson, J.L. (1981). Petri Net Theory and the Modeling of Systems, Prentice-Hall, Inc., Englewood Cliffs, NJ.

[13] Petri, C.A. (1962). Kommunikation Mit Automaten, Schriften des Institutes fur Instrumentelle Mathematik, Bonn.

[14] Reisig, W. (1985). Petri nets, Springer-Verleg, New York.

Chapter 10

Reachability Criterion with Sufficient Test Space for Ordinary Petri Net

Gi Bum Lee, Han Zandong and Jin S. Lee

Additional information is available at the end of the chapter

1. Introduction

Petri nets (PN) are widely recognized as a powerful tool for modelling and analyzing discrete event systems, especially systems are characterized by synchronization, concurrency, parallelism and resource sharing [1, 2]. One of the major advantages of using Petri net models is that the PN model can be used for the analysis of behaviour properties and performance evaluation, as well as for systematic construction of discrete-event simulators and controllers [3, 4]. The reachability from an initial marking to a destination marking is the most important issue for the analysis of Petri nets. Many other problems such as liveness and coverability can be deduced from this reachability problem [5, 6].

Two basic approaches are usually applied to solve the reachability problem. One is the construction of reachability tree [7, 8]. It can obtain all the reachable markings, but the computation complexity is exponentially increased with the size of a PN. The other is to solve the state equation [9]. The solution of the matrix equation provides a firing count vector that describes the relation between initial marking and reachable markings. Its major problem is the lack of information of firing sequences and the existence of spurious solutions.

Many researchers have investigated the reachability problem [10, 11]. Iko Miyazawa *et al.* have utilized the state equation to solve the reachability problem of Petri nets with parallel structures [12]. Tadashi Matsumoto *et al.* have presented a formal necessary and sufficient condition on reachability of general Petri nets with known firing count vectors [13]. Tadao Murata's paper has concentrated on presenting and analyzing Petri nets as discrete time systems. Controllability and reachability are analyzed in terms of the matrix representation of a Petri net [14].

In most cases, it is not necessary to find all reachable markings. One of the most important things is to know whether a given marking is reachable or not. If the destination marking

$\mathbf{M}_d$ is reachable from the initial marking $\mathbf{M}_0$, it is significant to find a firing sequence, which is an ordered sequence of transitions that lead $\mathbf{M}_0$ to $\mathbf{M}_d$. The following method can be utilized to find a reachable marking [15].

i. Solve the equation $\mathbf{AX}=\mathbf{M}_d-\mathbf{M}_0$ to ascertain all the solutions $\mathbf{X}_1$, $\mathbf{X}_2$, … and construct the set X={$\mathbf{X}_1$, $\mathbf{X}_2$, …}.
ii. Test if $\mathbf{X}_i$ in X is an executable solution from $\mathbf{M}_0$, i.e. there is at least one sequence S($\mathbf{X}_i$) that is a firing sequence under $\mathbf{M}_0$.
iii. If an executable solution exists, then $\mathbf{M}_d$ is reachable. On the contrary, if X=Φ or all solutions are spurious, then $\mathbf{M}_d$ is not reachable.

However, this approach is theoretic rather than practical, because there are two problems: One is that the solution of the fundamental equation $\mathbf{AX}=\mathbf{M}_d-\mathbf{M}_0$ is infinite in some cases. In that case, it is impossible to test all solution $\mathbf{X}_i$. The other is that the computation complexity of testing $\mathbf{X}_i$ increases at least exponentially as the length of S($\mathbf{X}_i$) increases.

In this chapter, the above two problems will be solved as follows: First, we construct a sufficient test space to include at least one executable solution within set X. An approach is secondly proposed to test whether there is an executable solution within the sufficient test space or not. A systematic method to search an executable solution in a sufficient test space and to enumerate the associated firing sequence is presented.

The remainder of the chapter is arranged as follows: Definitions and notations required in this chapter are given in Section 2. Section 3 describes how to determine the sufficient test space for the reachability problem. In Section 4, an algorithm is developed to determine if $\mathbf{X}_i$ is a executable solution under $\mathbf{M}_0$ and gives the associated firing sequence S($\mathbf{X}_i$). The illustrative examples are given in Section 3, Section 4, and Section 5.

2. Preliminaries

In this section, we present some definitions and notations to be necessary in the following sections.

Definition 1. Let PN=(P, T, I, O, M_0) be a marked Petri net. P={p_1, p_2, …, p_n} is the finite set of places. T={t_1, t_2, …, t_m} is the finite set of transitions. I is the input function. O is the output function. M_0 is the initial marking.

A PN is an ordinary Petri net iff I(p, t)→{0, 1} and O(t, p)→{0, 1} for any p∈P and t∈T. **A=O-I** is the incidence matrix, where **O** and **I** are the output and input function matrices [16]. Let $\mathbf{X}=[x_1\ x_2\ \dots\ x_m]^T$ be a column vector. If **X** is the firing count vector of S(**X**), the sequence S(**X**) is called the transition sequence associated with **X.** The transition set T(**X**) is called the support of **X** if it is composed of transitions associated with positive elements of **X**, i.e. T(**X**)={t_i | x_i>0}. p° is the set of output transitions of p, °p is the set of input transitions of p, t° is the set of output places of t, and °t is the set of input places of t.

Definition 2. C_i=<p, T_{ci}> is called a conflict structure [17] if it satisfies the following condition: T_{ci}={t | t∈p°} and |T_{ci}|≥2, where |T_{ci}| is the cardinality of T_{ci}. We note that C={C_1, C_2, …} is the set of all C_i and T_c=T_{c1}∪T_{c2}∪…. is the set of all conflict transitions.

Definition 3. For transition t_j and **X**, the sub-vector **H**(t_j|**X**) is defined as: **H**(t_j|**X**)=$e[t_j]\cdot x_j$. $e[t_j]$ is the unit m-vector which is zero everywhere except in the j-th element.

Definition 4. For the conflict structure C_i=<p, T_{ci}> and **X**, the sub-vector **H**(C_i|**X**) is defined as follows:

$$\mathbf{H}(C_i \mid \mathbf{X}) = \sum_{t_j \in T_{ci}} \mathbf{H}(t_j \mid \mathbf{X}) \quad (1)$$

Definition 5. C_i=<p, T_{ci}> is in a spurious conflict state for **X** under **M** if there exists a firing sequence S(**H**(C_i|**X**)) under **M**, i.e. the mathematic criterion is $\mathbf{M} \geq \mathbf{I} \cdot \mathbf{H}(C_i \mid \mathbf{X})$.

Otherwise, C_i is in an effective conflict state for **X** under **M**, and the transition in T_{ci} is called the effective conflict transition for **X** under **M**.

Notation 1. N(t_j|S(**X**))=x_j is the number of occurrence times of t_j in S(**X**).

Notation 2. If q=min{**M**(p_i), $p_i \in {}^\circ t_j$}, we call t_j q-enabled under marking **M**. This q is denoted as E(t_j|**M**).

Definition 6. **F**=$[f_1\ f_2\ \ldots\ f_m]^T$ is called an actual firing vector whose j-th element is f_j=min{N(t_j|S(**X**)), E(t_j|**M**)}. **F** can be partitioned into two parts as follows: $\mathbf{F}=\mathbf{F}_o+\mathbf{F}_c$, where $\mathbf{F}_c=[f_{c1}\ f_{c2}\ \ldots\ f_{cm}]^T$ is associated with effective conflict transitions, $\mathbf{F}_o=[f_{o1}\ f_{o2}\ \ldots\ f_{om}]^T$ is associated with the other transitions. $\mathbf{F}_o$ and $\mathbf{F}_c$ satisfy the following conditions:

a. If t_j is an effective conflict transition for **X** under **M**, then $f_{oj}=0$ and $f_{cj}=f_j$.
b. Otherwise, $f_{cj}=0$ and $f_{oj}=f_j$.

3. Determination of the sufficient test space

If all the solutions of the equation $\mathbf{AX}=\mathbf{M}_d-\mathbf{M}_0$ are tested, It can be found whether M_d is reachable or not. But in some case, the solutions are infinite. Therefore, the tested range is determined in order to keep the method practical. This range must be finite and include at least one executable solution if it exists. This section will discuss how to determine the tested range.

Definition 7. Given the initial marking $\mathbf{M}_0$ and the destination marking $\mathbf{M}_d$ of a PN, **X** is a solution of $\mathbf{AX}=\mathbf{M}_d-\mathbf{M}_0$. If $\mathbf{M}_d$ is reachable from $\mathbf{M}_0$ under **X**, then **X** is called an executable solution. Otherwise, **X** is called a spurious solution.

Definition 8. X={$\mathbf{X}_1$, $\mathbf{X}_2$, … } is the set of a solution **X**, the subset X_e={$\mathbf{X}_{e1}$, $\mathbf{X}_{e2}$, … } of X is called the sufficient test space if it satisfies following conditions:

i. If $\mathbf{M}_d$ is reachable from $\mathbf{M}_0$, there must exist at least one element in X_e which is executable solution; in other words, if all elements in X_e are not executable, then all the elements in X are not executable either.
ii. X_e is a finite set.

Definition 9. The vector **X** which is a solution of **AX**=0 is known as a T-invariant [18]. A solution **X** is called positive if every element of **X** is nonnegative.

Definition 10. The positive T-invariant solution **U** of **AU=0** is minimal if it satisfies the following condition: for any other T-invariant $\mathbf{U}_i$, at least one element of $\mathbf{U}-\mathbf{U}_i$ is negative. The set of minimal T-invariant solutions is $U=\{\mathbf{U}_1, \mathbf{U}_2, \ldots, \mathbf{U}_s\}$.

Definition 11. The positive particular solution **V** of $\mathbf{AV}=\mathbf{M}_d-\mathbf{M}_0$ is minimal if it satisfies the following condition: for any T-invariant **U** of PN, there must be at least one element in **V-U** which is negative, i.e. $\{\mathbf{U} \mid \mathbf{V}-\mathbf{U}\geq 0, \mathbf{U} \text{ is a T-invariant}\}=\Phi$. The set of minimal particular solutions is $V=\{\mathbf{V}_1, \mathbf{V}_2, \ldots, \mathbf{V}_q\}$.

The general solution of $\mathbf{AX}=\mathbf{M}_d-\mathbf{M}_0$ must be expressed by the form of one minimal particular solution and the arbitrary linear combination of the T-invariant solutions as follows:

$$\mathbf{X} = \mathbf{V}_i + \sum_{j=1}^{r} k_j \mathbf{U}_j \tag{2}$$

where $\mathbf{V}_i \in V$, k_j is nonnegative integer.

Algorithm 1. Interpretation of the computation for X_e.

Step 1. Solve the equation **AX=0**, get all the positive integer solutions $U=\{\mathbf{U}_1, \mathbf{U}_2, \ldots, \mathbf{U}_s\}$, where each $\mathbf{U}_j$ ($1\leq j\leq s$) is a minimal T-invariant.

Step 2. Solve the equation $\mathbf{AX}=\mathbf{M}_d-\mathbf{M}_0$, get all the positive integer particular solutions $V=\{\mathbf{V}_1, \mathbf{V}_2, \ldots, \mathbf{V}_q\}$, where each $\mathbf{V}_i$ ($1\leq i\leq q$) is a minimal particular solution. $B=\{\mathbf{B}_1, \mathbf{B}_2, \ldots, \mathbf{B}_n\}$ is a subset of V.

If $V=\Phi$, $\mathbf{M}_d$ is not reachable, then end.

Step 3. Initialization: Let $X_e=V=\{\mathbf{V}_1, \mathbf{V}_2, \ldots, \mathbf{V}_q\}$ and $X_{temp}=\Phi$.

If $U=\Phi$, then end.

Otherwise, for every $\mathbf{V}_i$, if $T(\mathbf{V}_i)\subset T(\mathbf{U}_j)$, then $\mathbf{V}_i\notin B$. If $T(\mathbf{V}_i)\not\subset T(\mathbf{U}_j)$, then $\mathbf{V}_i\in B$.

Go to Step 4.

Step 4. For each pair of $(\mathbf{B}_i, \mathbf{U}_j)$, where $i=1, 2, \ldots |B|$, $j=1, 2, \ldots s$, and $|B|$ is the cardinality of set B, carry out the following operations:

If ${}^\circ T(\mathbf{B}_i)\cap T(\mathbf{U}_j)^\circ = \Phi$, choose the next pair of $(\mathbf{B}_i, \mathbf{U}_j)$.

If ${}^\circ T(\mathbf{B}_i)\cap T(\mathbf{U}_j)^\circ \neq \Phi$ and $T(\mathbf{U}_j)\subset T(\mathbf{B}_i)$, choose the next pair of $(\mathbf{B}_i, \mathbf{U}_j)$.

If ${}^\circ T(\mathbf{B}_i)\cap T(\mathbf{U}_j)^\circ \neq \Phi$ and $T(\mathbf{U}_j)\not\subset T(\mathbf{B}_i)$, then $\mathbf{D}_i=\mathbf{B}_i-\max(\mathbf{B}_i)\cdot\mathbf{U}_j$, where $\max(\mathbf{B}_i)$ is the maximum value of elements in $\mathbf{B}_i$.

Let $\mathbf{D}_i(r)$ be the r-th elememt of $\mathbf{D}_i$.

$\mathbf{W}_i(r)=f(\mathbf{D}_i(r))$, where $f(x)=\begin{cases}\mathbf{D}_i(r), & \text{if } \mathbf{D}_i(r)>0\\ 0, & \text{if } \mathbf{D}_i(r)\leq 0\end{cases}$, $r=1, 2, \ldots m$.

$\sum_{r=1}^{m}(\mathbf{W}_i(r)\cdot\left|\{p\mid p\in {}^\circ t_r \cap T(\mathbf{U}_j)^\circ\}\right|)=\beta$, where $\mathbf{W}_i(r)$ is the r-th element of $\mathbf{W}_i$, $m=|T|$.

Add $\mathbf{B}_i+k\cdot\mathbf{U}_j$, k=1, 2, … β, to X_{temp}

When all pairs of ($\mathbf{B}_i$, $\mathbf{U}_j$) have been tested, go to Step 5.

Step 5. If $X_{temp}=\Phi$, then end.

Otherwise, Let B=X_{temp}, $X_e=X_e\cup B$, $X_{temp}=\Phi$, go to Step 4.

Step 1 and Step 2 are to determine all the positive integer solutions **X** for equation $\mathbf{AX}=\mathbf{M}_d-\mathbf{M}_0$. The firing count vector of any firing sequence from $\mathbf{M}_0$ to $\mathbf{M}_d$ belongs to **X**. In Step 4, if $\mathbf{B}_i$ is not an executable solution, then there must be some transitions in T($\mathbf{B}_i$) which aren't enable it, i.e. some places in °T($\mathbf{B}_i$) are lack of tokens. In this case, if {p | p∈°T($\mathbf{B}_i$)∩T($\mathbf{U}_j$)° and T($\mathbf{U}_j$) ⊄ T($\mathbf{B}_i$)}≠ Φ, then T($\mathbf{U}_j$)° may provide tokens for °t, where t∈T($\mathbf{B}_i$). Consequently, $\mathbf{B}_i+k\cdot\mathbf{U}_j$ may be an executable solution, where k=1, 2, … β. Since the number of places and transitions in PN is finite, Step 4 and Step 5 only add finite elements to X_e. Since the number of minimal T-invariants is finite, the finishing condition $X_{temp}=\Phi$, i.e. |{p | p∈°T($\mathbf{B}_i$)∩T($\mathbf{U}_j$)° and T($\mathbf{U}_j$) ⊄ T($\mathbf{B}_i$)}| = Φ, is satisfied after all the related T-invariants have been considered. As a result of the iterative process of Step 4→Step 5→Step 4, X_e includes at least one executable solution if it exists.

The following examples show how to implement the computation algorithm. These examples illustrate that suppressing any k_i in $\mathbf{B}_i+k\cdot\mathbf{U}_j$, k=1, 2, … β, may eliminate some possible executable solutions.

Example 1. When the initial marking is $\mathbf{M}_0$=(1,0,0,0,0,1,0,0,0) and the destination marking is $\mathbf{M}_d$=(1,0,0,0,0,0,0,0,1) in Figure 1, calculate the sufficient test space X_e. The • and ○ symbols are represented as the initial and destination markings respectively.

Step 1. Solve the equation **AX**=0, get the positive integer minimal T-invariant $\mathbf{U}_1$=(1,1,1,1,0,0,0,0).

Step 2. Solve the equation $\mathbf{AX}=\mathbf{M}_d-\mathbf{M}_0$, get the positive integer minimal particular solution V={**V**}=(0,0,0,0,1,1,1,1)

Step 3. Initialization: Let X_e=V, $X_{temp}=\Phi$, B=X_e

Step 4-1. For (**V**, $\mathbf{U}_1$),

If T($\mathbf{U}_1$) ⊄ T(**V**), then **D**=**V**-max(**V**)·$\mathbf{U}_1$, **W**(r)=f(**D**(r)),

$$\sum_{r=1}^{8}(\mathbf{W}(r)\cdot\left|\{p\,|\,p\in{}^{\circ}t_r\cap T(U_1)^{\circ}\}\right|)=3.$$

Then add $\mathbf{V}+\mathbf{U}_1$, $\mathbf{V}+2\cdot\mathbf{U}_1$, $\mathbf{V}+3\cdot\mathbf{U}_1$ to the set of X_{temp},

Therefore, X_{temp}={$\mathbf{V}+\mathbf{U}_1$, $\mathbf{V}+2\cdot\mathbf{U}_1$, $\mathbf{V}+3\cdot\mathbf{U}_1$}

Step 5-1. If $X_{temp}\neq\Phi$, then let B=X_{temp}={$\mathbf{V}+\mathbf{U}_1$, $\mathbf{V}+2\cdot\mathbf{U}_1$, $\mathbf{V}+3\cdot\mathbf{U}_1$}

$X_e=X_e\cup B$={**V**, $\mathbf{V}+\mathbf{U}_1$, $\mathbf{V}+2\cdot\mathbf{U}_1$, $\mathbf{V}+3\cdot\mathbf{U}_1$}, $X_{temp}=\Phi$.

Go to Step4 in Algorithm 1.

Step 4-2. For any pair of ($\mathbf{B}_i$, $\mathbf{U}_1$), T($\mathbf{U}_1$) $\subset$ T($\mathbf{B}_i$) is satisfied. Therefore, $X_{temp}=\Phi$

Step 5-2. If $X_{temp}=\Phi$, then end.

As a result of above sequence, $\mathbf{M}_d$ is reachable from $\mathbf{M}_0$. The firing sequence is $t_5*t_1*t_2*t_6*t_7*t_3*t_4*t_8$. Its firing count vector corresponds to $\mathbf{V}+\mathbf{U}_1=(1,1,1,1,1,1,1,1)$ in the sufficient test space X_e. This example shows that suppressing $\mathbf{B}_i+k\cdot\mathbf{U}_j$ (k=1) in X_e may eliminate some possible executable solution.

Example 2. Consider the PN of Figure 2, given the initial marking $\mathbf{M}_0=(1,0,0,0,0,0,0,0,1,0)$ and the destination marking $\mathbf{M}_d=(0,0,0,1,0,0,0,0,1,0)$, calculate the sufficient test space X_e.

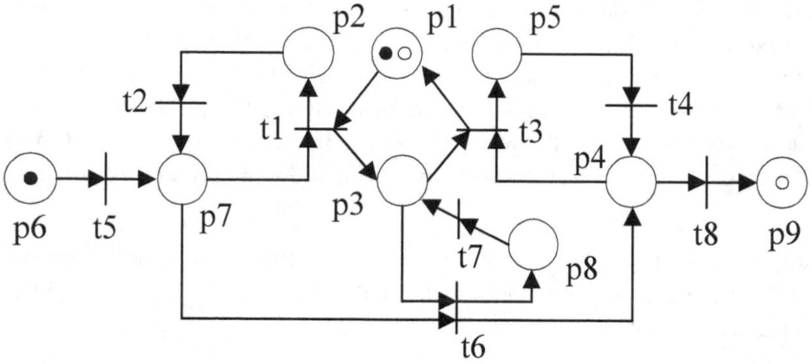

Figure 1. Petri net structure

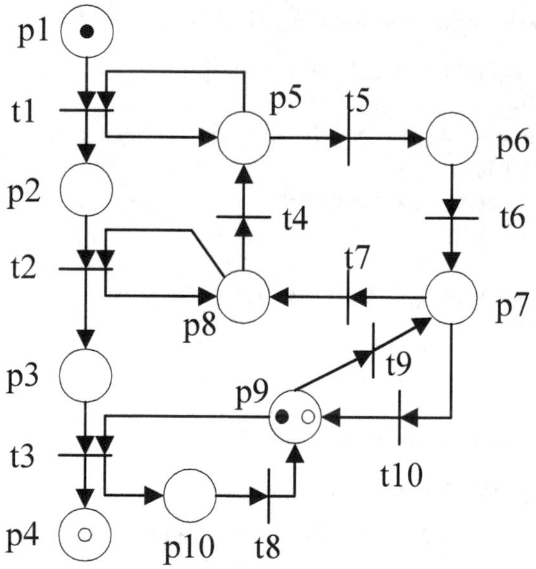

Figure 2. Petri net structure

Step 1. Solve the equation **AX**=0, two positive integer minimal T-invariants are obtained: $\mathbf{U}_1$=(0,0,0,1,1,1,1,0,0,0), $\mathbf{U}_2$=(0,0,0,0,0,0,0,0,1,1)

Step 2. Solve the equation $\mathbf{AX}=\mathbf{M}_d-\mathbf{M}_0$, get the positive integer minimal particular solutions V={**V**}={(1,1,1,0,0,0,0,1,0,0)}

The general solution can be expressed as follows:

$$\mathbf{X} = (1,1,1,0,0,0,0,1,0,0) + k_1 \cdot (0,0,0,1,1,1,1,0,0,0) + k_2 \cdot (0,0,0,0,0,0,0,0,1,1)$$

k_1 and k_2 are nonnegative integer.

Step 3. Initialization: Let X_e=V, $X_{temp}=\Phi$, B=X_e

Step 4-1. For (**V**, $\mathbf{U}_1$),

If $T(\mathbf{U}_1) \not\subset T(\mathbf{V})$, then $\mathbf{D}=\mathbf{V}-\max(\mathbf{V})\cdot\mathbf{U}_1$, $\mathbf{W}(r)=f(\mathbf{D}(r))$,

$$\sum_{r=1}^{10}(\mathbf{W}(r)\cdot\left|\{p\mid p\in {}^{\circ}t_r \cap T(\mathbf{U}_1)^{\circ}\}\right|)=2.$$

Then add $\mathbf{V}+\mathbf{U}_1$, $\mathbf{V}+2\cdot\mathbf{U}_1$ to X_{temp}. So $X_{temp}=\{\mathbf{V}+\mathbf{U}_1, \mathbf{V}+2\mathbf{U}_1\}$

For (**V**, $\mathbf{U}_2$),

If $T(\mathbf{U}_2) \not\subset T(\mathbf{V})$, then $\mathbf{D}=\mathbf{V}-\max(\mathbf{V})\cdot\mathbf{U}_2$, $\mathbf{W}(r)=f(\mathbf{D}(r))$,

$$\sum_{r=1}^{10}(\mathbf{W}(r)\cdot\left|\{p\mid p\in {}^{\circ}t_r \cap T(\mathbf{U}_2)^{\circ}\}\right|)=1.$$

Then add $\mathbf{V}+\mathbf{U}_2$ to X_{temp}. So $X_{temp}=\{\mathbf{V}+\mathbf{U}_1, \mathbf{V}+2\mathbf{U}_1, \mathbf{V}+\mathbf{U}_2\}$

Step 5-1. If $X_{temp}\neq\Phi$, then let $B=X_{temp}=\{\mathbf{V}+\mathbf{U}_1, \mathbf{V}+2\mathbf{U}_1, \mathbf{V}+\mathbf{U}_2\}$,

$X_e=X_e\cup B=\{\mathbf{V}, \mathbf{V}+\mathbf{U}_1, \mathbf{V}+2\mathbf{U}_1, \mathbf{V}+\mathbf{U}_2\}$. Let's put $X_{temp}=\Phi$.

Go to Step 4 in Algorithm 1.

Step 4-2. For ($\mathbf{V}+\mathbf{U}_1$, $\mathbf{U}_1$), because $T(\mathbf{U}_1)\subset T(\mathbf{V}+\mathbf{U}_1)$, choose the next pair.

For ($\mathbf{V}+\mathbf{U}_1$, $\mathbf{U}_2$),

If $T(\mathbf{U}_2) \not\subset T(\mathbf{V}+\mathbf{U}_1)$, then $\mathbf{D}_1=(\mathbf{V}+\mathbf{U}_1)-\max(\mathbf{V}+\mathbf{U}_1)\cdot\mathbf{U}_2$, $\mathbf{W}_1(r)=f(\mathbf{D}_1(r))$,

$$\sum_{r=1}^{10}(\mathbf{W}_1(r)\cdot\left|\{p\mid p\in {}^{\circ}t_r \cap T(\mathbf{U}_2)^{\circ}\}\right|)=2.$$

Then add $\mathbf{V}+\mathbf{U}_1+\mathbf{U}_2$ and $\mathbf{V}+\mathbf{U}_1+2\mathbf{U}_2$ to X_{temp}. So $X_{temp}=\{\mathbf{V}+\mathbf{U}_1+\mathbf{U}_2, \mathbf{V}+\mathbf{U}_1+2\mathbf{U}_2\}$

For ($\mathbf{V}+2\mathbf{U}_1$, $\mathbf{U}_1$), because $T(\mathbf{U}_1)\subset T(\mathbf{V}+2\mathbf{U}_1)$, choose the next pair.

For ($\mathbf{V}+2\mathbf{U}_1$, $\mathbf{U}_2$),

If $T(\mathbf{U}_2) \not\subset T(\mathbf{V}+2\mathbf{U}_1)$, then $\mathbf{D}_2=(\mathbf{V}+2\mathbf{U}_1)-\max(\mathbf{V}+2\mathbf{U}_1)\cdot\mathbf{U}_2$, $\mathbf{W}_2(r)=f(\mathbf{D}_2(r))$,

$$\sum_{r=1}^{10}(W_2)(r)\cdot\left|\{p\,|\,p\in{}^{\circ}t_r\cap T(U_2)^{\circ}\}\right|)=3.$$

Then add $\mathbf{V}+2\mathbf{U}_1+\mathbf{U}_2$, $\mathbf{V}+2\mathbf{U}_1+2\mathbf{U}_2$, and $\mathbf{V}+2\mathbf{U}_1+3\mathbf{U}_2$ to X_{temp}. So $X_{temp}=\{\mathbf{V}+\mathbf{U}_1+\mathbf{U}_2, \mathbf{V}+\mathbf{U}_1+2\mathbf{U}_2, \mathbf{V}+2\mathbf{U}_1+\mathbf{U}_2, \mathbf{V}+2\mathbf{U}_1+2\mathbf{U}_2, \mathbf{V}+2\mathbf{U}_1+3\mathbf{U}_2\}$

For $(\mathbf{V}+\mathbf{U}_2, \mathbf{U}_2)$, because $T(\mathbf{U}_2)\subset T(\mathbf{V}+\mathbf{U}_2)$, choose the next pair.

For $(\mathbf{V}+\mathbf{U}_2, \mathbf{U}_1)$,

If $T(\mathbf{U}_1)\not\subset T(\mathbf{V}+\mathbf{U}_2)$, then $\mathbf{D}_3=(\mathbf{V}+\mathbf{U}_2)-\max(\mathbf{V}+\mathbf{U}_2)\cdot\mathbf{U}_1$, $\mathbf{W}_3(r)=f(\mathbf{D}_3(r))$,

$$\sum_{r=1}^{10}(W_3(r)\cdot\left|\{p\,|\,p\in{}^{\circ}t_r\cap T(U_1)^{\circ}\}\right|)=3.$$

Then add $\mathbf{V}+\mathbf{U}_2+\mathbf{U}_1$, $\mathbf{V}+\mathbf{U}_2+2\mathbf{U}_1$, and $\mathbf{V}+\mathbf{U}_2+3\mathbf{U}_1$ to X_{temp}. So $X_{temp}=\{\mathbf{V}+\mathbf{U}_1+\mathbf{U}_2, \mathbf{V}+\mathbf{U}_1+2\mathbf{U}_2, \mathbf{V}+2\mathbf{U}_1+\mathbf{U}_2, \mathbf{V}+2\mathbf{U}_1+2\mathbf{U}_2, \mathbf{V}+2\mathbf{U}_1+3\mathbf{U}_2, \mathbf{V}+\mathbf{U}_2+3\mathbf{U}_1\}$

Step 5-2. If $X_{temp}\neq\Phi$, then let $B=X_{temp}=\{\mathbf{V}+\mathbf{U}_1+\mathbf{U}_2, \mathbf{V}+\mathbf{U}_1+2\cdot\mathbf{U}_2, \mathbf{V}+2\cdot\mathbf{U}_1+\mathbf{U}_2, \mathbf{V}+2\cdot\mathbf{U}_1+2\cdot\mathbf{U}_2, \mathbf{V}+2\cdot\mathbf{U}_1+3\cdot\mathbf{U}_2, \mathbf{V}+\mathbf{U}_2+3\mathbf{U}_1\}$.

So, $X_e=X_e+B=\{\mathbf{V}, \mathbf{V}+\mathbf{U}_1, \mathbf{V}+2\cdot\mathbf{U}_1, \mathbf{V}+\mathbf{U}_2, \mathbf{V}+\mathbf{U}_1+\mathbf{U}_2, \mathbf{V}+\mathbf{U}_1+2\cdot\mathbf{U}_2, \mathbf{V}+2\cdot\mathbf{U}_1+\mathbf{U}_2, \mathbf{V}+2\cdot\mathbf{U}_1+2\cdot\mathbf{U}_2, \mathbf{V}+2\cdot\mathbf{U}_1+3\cdot\mathbf{U}_2, \mathbf{V}+\mathbf{U}_2+3\mathbf{U}_1\}$. Let's put $X_{temp}=\Phi$.

Go to Step 4 in Algorithm 1.

Step 4-3. For any pair of $(\mathbf{B}_i, \mathbf{U}_j)$, because $T(\mathbf{U}_j)\subset T(\mathbf{B}_i)$, $X_{temp}=\Phi$
Step 5-3. If $X_{temp}=\Phi$, then end

$\mathbf{M}_d$ is reachable from $\mathbf{M}_0$. The firing sequence is $t_9{*}t_7{*}t_4{*}t_1{*}t_5{*}t_6{*}t_7{*}t_2{*}t_4{*}t_5{*}t_6{*}t_{10}{*}t_3{*}t_8$. Its firing count vector corresponds to $\mathbf{V}+2\cdot\mathbf{U}_1+\mathbf{U}_2=(1,1,1,2,2,2,2,1,1,1)$ in the sufficient test space X_e. This example illustrates that suppressing $\mathbf{B}_i+k\cdot\mathbf{U}_j$ $(k=\beta)$ in X_e may eliminate some possible executable solution.

4. Search of a firing sequence

Given the initial marking $\mathbf{M}_0$ and the destination marking $\mathbf{M}_d$ of a PN, a solution $\mathbf{X}_{ei}$ is solved from $\mathbf{AX}=\mathbf{M}_d-\mathbf{M}_0$. Then, an algorithm is developed to determine whether $\mathbf{M}_d$ is reachable from $\mathbf{M}_0$ under $\mathbf{X}_{ei}$ or not. If $\mathbf{M}_d$ is reachable from $\mathbf{M}_0$, the algorithm gives the associated firing sequence $S(\mathbf{X}_{ei})$.

Definition 12. Let $S=t_1t_2\ldots t_r$ be a finite transition sequence. The transitions appearing in S are defined by the set $Z(S)=\{t_1, t_2, \ldots, t_r\}$. The set of transitions Z(S) is called a sequence component. Z(S) is the set of elements that appear in a transition sequence S.

Algorithm 2. Search of a firing sequence $S(\mathbf{X}_{ei})$ under $\mathbf{M}_0$

Step 1. According to **I**, determine all the conflict structure $C_i=\langle p, T_{ci}\rangle$, and construct T_c and C.

Step 2. Initialization: Let M=$\mathbf{M}_0$, X=$\mathbf{X}_{ei}$, S=λ (λ is the sequence of length zero)
Step 3. Under M and X, calculate $\mathbf{F}$=$\mathbf{F}_o$+$\mathbf{F}_c$ from Definition 6.

If $\mathbf{F}_o \neq \mathbf{0}$, go to Step 4.

If $\mathbf{F}_o = \mathbf{0}$ and $\mathbf{F}_c \neq 0$, go to Step 5.

If $\mathbf{F}$=$\mathbf{0}$, go to step 6.

Step 4. If $\mathbf{F}_o \neq 0$, then there exists an S($\mathbf{F}_o$) that has a firing sequence under M. Therefore, S($\mathbf{F}_o$) can be fired. The reachable marking is calculated by $\mathbf{M}'=M-\mathbf{A}\cdot\mathbf{F}_o$,

Let M=$\mathbf{M}'$, X=X–$\mathbf{F}_o$, S=S*S($\mathbf{F}_o$), where * is concatenation operation and S*S($\mathbf{F}_o$) means S followed by S($\mathbf{F}_o$). Go to Step 3.

Step 5. $\mathbf{F}_o$ =0 and $\mathbf{F}_c \neq 0$ means that all transitions in S($\mathbf{F}_c$) are effective conflict transitions. Therefore, branching occurs and the number of branches is |T($\mathbf{F}_c$)|. From here, the computation has to consider all |T($\mathbf{F}_c$)| branches.

After selecting a transition $t_j \in$T($\mathbf{F}_c$), fire it, then the reachable marking is calculated by $\mathbf{M}'=M-\mathbf{A}\cdot e[t_j]$.

Let M=$\mathbf{M}'$, X=X–$e[t_j]$, S=S*t_j.Go to Step 3

Step 6. If X=0, then $\mathbf{M}_d$ is reachable from $\mathbf{M}_0$ and S=S($\mathbf{X}_{ei}$) is one of the firing sequences, end. Otherwise, go to Step 7.
Step 7. If all the branches in Step 5 have been implemented, then $\mathbf{M}_d$ is not reachable, end. Otherwise, go to Step 5 and implement the remaining branches.
The validity of the above algorithm is proved as the following four cases:
Base: Let **X** be a solution of $\mathbf{AX}=\mathbf{M}_d-\mathbf{M}_0$. The actual firing vector $\mathbf{F}$=$\mathbf{F}_o$+$\mathbf{F}_c$ is obtained with **M** and **X**. Let $t_o \in$T($\mathbf{F}_o$) and $t_c \in$T($\mathbf{F}_c$).

Case 1: If $\mathbf{F}_o \neq \mathbf{0}$ and $\mathbf{F}_c = \mathbf{0}$, then multiple firing of S($\mathbf{F}_o$) doesn't affect a firing sequence associated with **X** under $\mathbf{M}_0$, for the input places of T($\mathbf{F}_o$) don't affect the enabling condition of other transitions in T(**X**) except transitions in T($\mathbf{F}_o$).

Case 2: If $\mathbf{F}_o = \mathbf{0}$ and $\mathbf{F}_c \neq \mathbf{0}$, then the firing of each transition in S($\mathbf{F}_c$) is considered as a branch and implemented with respect to all branches. It means that all possibilities are involved. So, Algorithm 2 doesn't eliminate any possible firing sequence.

Case 3: If $\mathbf{F}_o = \mathbf{0}$ and $\mathbf{F}_c = \mathbf{0}$, then no transition is enabled.

Case 4: If $\mathbf{F}_o \neq \mathbf{0}$ and $\mathbf{F}_c \neq \mathbf{0}$, then the multiple firing of S($\mathbf{F}_o$) can be implemented before S($\mathbf{F}_c$). It doesn't eliminate any probability of finding a firing sequence associated with **X** under $\mathbf{M}_0$. It is proven in Proposition 1.

Proposition 1. If $\sigma \in$S(**X**) is a firing sequence under $\mathbf{M}_0$, then (S($\mathbf{F}_o$)*σ')$\in$S(**X**) is a firing sequence under $\mathbf{M}_0$ for any sequence σ'.

Proof:

Step 1. Let $T(\mathbf{F}_o)=\{t_{o1}, t_{o2}, \ldots, t_{on}\}$. For a transition $t_{o1}\in T(\mathbf{F}_o)$, σ can be represented as $\sigma=\sigma_1 * t_o * \sigma_2$, where $t_{o1}\notin Z(\sigma_1)$. Then $\mathbf{M}_0 \xrightarrow{\sigma_1} \mathbf{M}_1 \xrightarrow{t_{o1}} \mathbf{M}_2 \xrightarrow{\sigma_2} \mathbf{M}_d$ is a firing sequence. Since $T(\mathbf{F}_o)$ is the set of transitions possible to be enabled under $\mathbf{M}_0$, $\mathbf{M}_0$ enables t_{o1}. Therefore it is possible to put $\mathbf{M}_0 \xrightarrow{t_{o1}} \mathbf{M}_3$. By the definition of $\mathbf{F}_o$, we have $M_3(p)\geq M_0(p)$ for any $p\in{}^{\circ}Z(\sigma_1)$. So σ_1 is enabled under M_3 because σ_1 is enabled under M_0 (Monotonicity Lemma). After σ_1 firing, $\mathbf{M}_2$ is reachable from $\mathbf{M}_3$. Therefore, we have $\mathbf{M}_0 \xrightarrow{t_{o1}} \mathbf{M}_3 \xrightarrow{\sigma_1} \mathbf{M}_2$. Since σ_2 is enabled under M_2, $t_{o1} * \sigma_1 * \sigma_2$ is a firing sequence under $\mathbf{M}_0$.

Step 2. Under $\mathbf{M}_3$, let's consider the new $T(\mathbf{F}_o)=\{t_{o2}, \ldots, t_{on}\}\cup T(\mathbf{F}_o')$, where $T(\mathbf{F}_o')$ is the set of transition generated after t_{o1} firing and may be empty. For a transition $t_{o2}\in T(\mathbf{F}_o)$, $\sigma_1 * \sigma_2$ can be represented as $\sigma_1 * \sigma_2=\sigma_3 * t_{o2} * \sigma_4$, where $t_{o2}\notin Z(\sigma_3)$. Then $\sigma_3 * t_{o2} * \sigma_4$ is a firing sequence. By the same way described in Step 1, we can prove that $t_{o2} * \sigma_3 * \sigma_4$ is a firing sequence under $\mathbf{M}_3$.

Step 3. By Step 1 and Step 2, $t_{o1} * t_{o2} * \sigma_3 * \sigma_4$ is a firing sequence under $\mathbf{M}_0$.

Step 4. In the same way, it is proven that $t_{o1} * t_{o2} * \ldots * t_{on} * \sigma_i * \sigma_j$ is a firing sequence under $\mathbf{M}_0$. According to the definition of $\mathbf{F}_o$, all transitions in $\{t_{o1}, t_{o2}, \ldots, t_{on}\}$ can fire simultaneously under $\mathbf{M}_0$. Let's put $\sigma'=\sigma_i * \sigma_j$, then $(S(F_o) * \sigma')\in S(\mathbf{X})$ is a firing sequence under $\mathbf{M}_0$.

Example 3. Let us now apply the proposed algorithm to the PN of Figure 3. Given $\mathbf{M}_0=(0,0,0,0,0,0,1,0,0)$, $\mathbf{M}_d=(0,0,0,0,1,0,1,0,0)$ and $\mathbf{X}=(1,2,1,1,1,1,1)$, determine if $\mathbf{M}_d$ is reachable or not under $\mathbf{M}_0$ and $\mathbf{X}$.

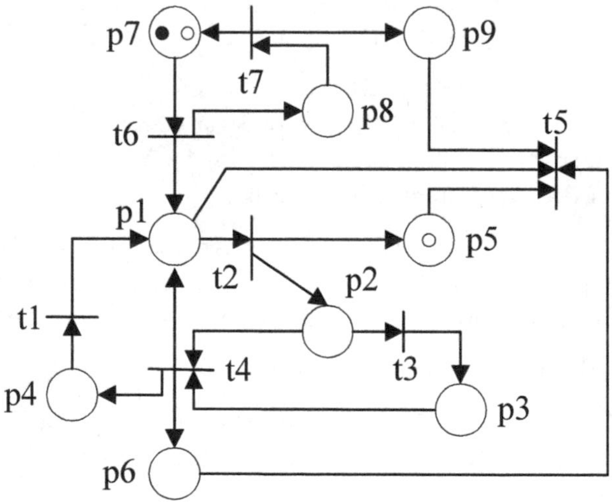

Figure 3. Petri net structure

Step 1. There are two conflict structures, C_1=<p_1, {t_2, t_5}>, C_2=<p_2, {t_3, t_4}>, T_c={t_2, t_3, t_4, t_5}.
Step 2. Initialization: M=$\mathbf{M}_0$= (0,0,0,0,0,0,1,0,0), X=$\mathbf{X}$=(1,2,1,1,1,1,1), S=λ
Step 3. Under M and X, only t_6 is 1-enabled. Then, $\mathbf{F}_o$=(0,0,0,0,0,1,0).
Step 4. Fire S($\mathbf{F}_o$)= t_6. Then the reachable marking $\mathbf{M}'$ becomes (1,0,0,0,0,0,0,1,0)

Let M=$\mathbf{M}'$, $\mathbf{X}$=$\mathbf{X}$-$\mathbf{F}_o$=(1,2,1,1,1,0,1), S=t_6. Go to Step 3 in Algorithm 2.

Step 3-1. Under M and X, $\mathbf{F}_o$=(0,0,0,0,0,0,1).
Step 4-1. Fire S($\mathbf{F}_o$)=t_7. Then, the reachable marking becomes $\mathbf{M}'$=(1,0,0,0,0,0,1,0,1)

Let M=$\mathbf{M}'$, $\mathbf{X}$=$\mathbf{X}$-$\mathbf{F}_o$=(1,2,1,1,1,0,0), S=t_6*t_7. Go to Step 3 in Algorithm 2.

Step 3-2. Under M and X, $\mathbf{F}_o$=(0,1,0,0,0,0,0). Go to Step 4 in Algorithm 2.
Step 4-2. Fire S($\mathbf{F}_o$)=t_2 (t_2 is not an effective conflict transition because t_5 cannot enable),

then the reachable marking becomes $\mathbf{M}'$=(0,1,0,0,1,0,1,0,1)

Let M=$\mathbf{M}'$, $\mathbf{X}$=$\mathbf{X}$-$\mathbf{F}_o$=(1,1,1,1,1,0,0), S= t_6*t_7*t_2. Go to Step 3 in Algorithm 2.

Step 3-3. Under M and X, $\mathbf{F}_o$=(0,0,1,0,0,0,0). Go to Step 4 in Algorithm 2.
Step 4-3. Fire S($\mathbf{F}_o$)=t_3 (t_3 is not an effective conflict transition because t_4 cannot enable),

then the reachable marking becomes $\mathbf{M}'$=(0,0,1,0,1,0,1,0,1)

Let M=$\mathbf{M}'$, $\mathbf{X}$=$\mathbf{X}$-$\mathbf{F}_o$=(1,1,0,1,1,0,0), S= t_6*t_7*t_2*t_3. Go to Step 3 in Algorithm 2.

Step 3-4. Under M and X, **F=0,** go to Step 6 in Algorithm 2.

Step 6. Because X≠**0,** go to Step 7 in Algorithm 2.

Step 7. There is no effective conflict transition i.e., no branch. Consequently, $\mathbf{M}_d$ is not reachable under **X** because X≠**0.**

The above implementing process can be presented by a firing path tree as shown in Figure 4.

5. Application of Reachability Criterion

An example will be given to illustrate how to use the proposed method of Algorithm 1 and Algorithm 2 to solve the reachability problem.

Example 4. When the initial marking is $\mathbf{M}_0$=(1,0,0,0,0,0,0,0,1) in the PN of Figure 5, is the destination marking $\mathbf{M}_d$=(0,0,1,0,1,0,0,0,1) reachable from $\mathbf{M}_0$?

First, calculate sufficient test space using the following steps:

Step 1. Solve the equation **AX**=0, get one positive integer minimal T-invariant **U**=(0,0,0,0,0,0,1,1).
Step 2. Solve the equation **AX**=$\mathbf{M}_d$-$\mathbf{M}_0$, get the positive integer minimal particular solutions $\mathbf{V}_1$=(0,2,1,0,2,2,0,0), $\mathbf{V}_2$=(2,2,1,2,0,0,0,0) and $\mathbf{V}_3$=(1,2,1,1,1,1,0,0)
Step 3. Initialization: Let X_e={$\mathbf{V}_1$, $\mathbf{V}_2$, $\mathbf{V}_3$}, X_{temp}=Φ, B=X_e
Step 4-1. For ($\mathbf{V}_1$, **U**),

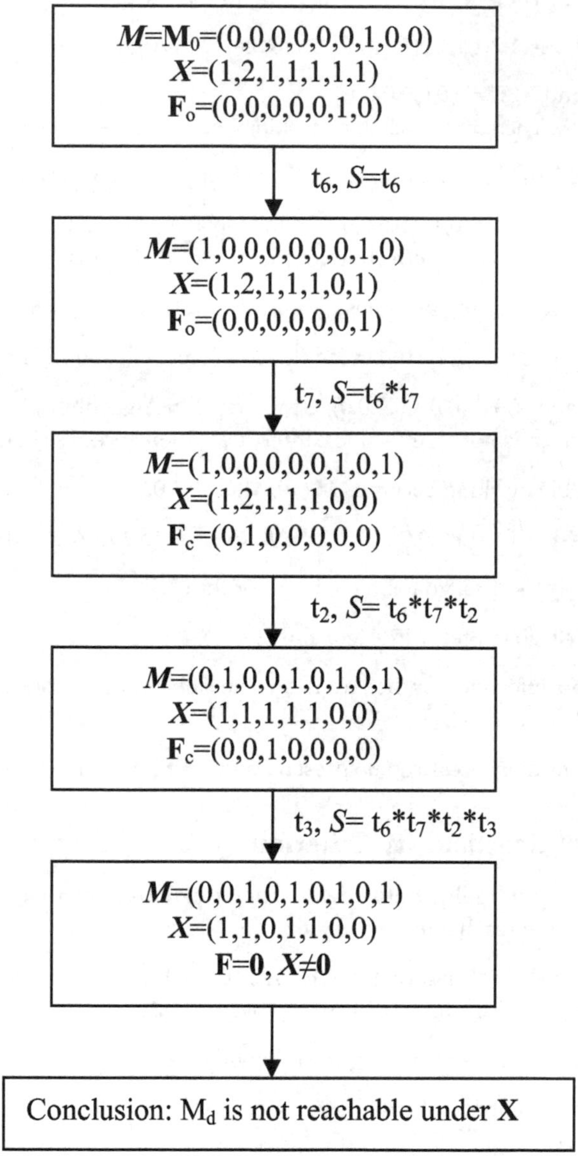

Figure 4. Firing path tree on reachability of Figure 3.

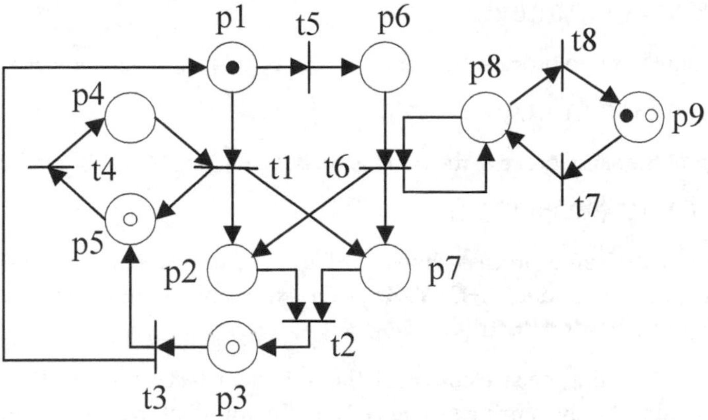

Figure 5. Petri net structure

If $T(\mathbf{U}) \not\subset T(\mathbf{V}_1)$, then $\mathbf{D}_1=\mathbf{V}_1-\max(\mathbf{V}_1)\cdot\mathbf{U}$, $\mathbf{W}_1(r)=f(\mathbf{D}_1(r))$,

$$\sum_{r=1}^{8}(\mathbf{W}_1(r)\cdot\left|\{p \mid p\in {}^{\circ}t_r \cap T(\mathbf{U})^{\circ}\}\right|)=2$$

Then add $\mathbf{V}_1+\mathbf{U}$, $\mathbf{V}_1+2\cdot\mathbf{U}$ to X_{temp}. Then, $X_{temp}=\{\mathbf{V}_1+\mathbf{U}, \mathbf{V}_1+2\cdot\mathbf{U}\}$

For $(\mathbf{V}_2, \mathbf{U})$, because ${}^{\circ}T(\mathbf{V}_2)\cap T(\mathbf{U})^{\circ}=\Phi$, choose the next pair.

For $(\mathbf{V}_3, \mathbf{U})$,

If $T(\mathbf{U}) \not\subset T(\mathbf{V}_3)$, then $\mathbf{D}_3=\mathbf{V}_3-\max(\mathbf{V}_3)\cdot\mathbf{U}$, $\mathbf{W}_3(r)=f(\mathbf{D}_3(r))$,

$$\sum_{r=1}^{8}(\mathbf{W}_3(r)\cdot\left|\{p \mid p\in {}^{\circ}t_r \cap T(\mathbf{U})^{\circ}\}\right|)=1$$

Then add $\mathbf{V}_3+\mathbf{U}$ to X_{temp}, $X_{temp}=\{\mathbf{V}_1+\mathbf{U}, \mathbf{V}_1+2\cdot\mathbf{U}, \mathbf{V}_3+\mathbf{U}\}$

Step 5-1. If $X_{temp}\neq\Phi$, then let $B=X_{temp}=\{\mathbf{V}_1+\mathbf{U}, \mathbf{V}_1+2\cdot\mathbf{U}, \mathbf{V}_3+\mathbf{U}\}$,

$X_e=X_e\cup B=\{\mathbf{V}_1, \mathbf{V}_2, \mathbf{V}_3, \mathbf{V}_1+\mathbf{U}, \mathbf{V}_1+2\cdot\mathbf{U}, \mathbf{V}_3+\mathbf{U}\}$. Let's put $X_{temp}=\Phi$. Go to Step 4 in Algorithm 1.

Step 4. For any pair of $(\mathbf{B}_i, \mathbf{U})$, because $T(\mathbf{U}_j)\subset T(\mathbf{B}_i)$, $X_{temp}=\Phi$.

Step 5. If $X_{temp}=\Phi$, then end.

Consequently, the sufficient test space becomes $X_e=\{\mathbf{V}_1, \mathbf{V}_2, \mathbf{V}_3, \mathbf{V}_1+\mathbf{U}, \mathbf{V}_1+2\cdot\mathbf{U}, \mathbf{V}_3+\mathbf{U}\}$.

Second, calculate a firing sequence in order to test if M(d) is reachable from M(0) under some element in X_e

The elements of the sufficient test space X_e are calculated separately as follows:

Step 1. For $\mathbf{X}=\mathbf{V}_1=(0,2,1,0,2,2,0,0)$

The implementing process is shown in Figure 6.

Step 2. For $\mathbf{X}=\mathbf{V}_2=(2,2,1,2,0,0,0,0)$

Carrying out the same process, the conclusion is as follows: M_d is not reachable under $\mathbf{V}_2$.

Step 3. For $\mathbf{X}=\mathbf{V}_3=(1,2,1,1,1,1,0,0)$

Carrying out the same process, the conclusion is as follows: M_d is not reachable under $\mathbf{V}_2$.

Step 4. For $\mathbf{X}=\mathbf{V}_1+\mathbf{U}=(0,2,1,0,2,2,1,1)$

Carrying out the same process shown in Figure 7, the conclusion is as follows: M_d is reachable from M_0 under $\mathbf{V}_1+\mathbf{U}$. $\mathbf{V}_1+\mathbf{U}$ is an executable solution in X_e, and the firing sequence is $t_5*t_7*t_6*t_2*t_3*t_5*t_6*t_2*t_8$.

As a result of calculating each element of the sufficient test space $X_e=\{\mathbf{V}_1, \mathbf{V}_2, \mathbf{V}_3, \mathbf{V}_1+\mathbf{U}, \mathbf{V}_1+2\cdot\mathbf{U}, \mathbf{V}_3+\mathbf{U}\}$ individually, a firing sequence is finally found at the fourth element ($\mathbf{V}_1+\mathbf{U}$) of X_e. Therefore, the elements $\mathbf{V}_1+2\cdot\mathbf{U}$ and $\mathbf{V}_3+\mathbf{U}$ don't need to be calculated. Consequently, the structure of the Petri net (Figure 5) is shown to possess at least one reachable firing sequence.

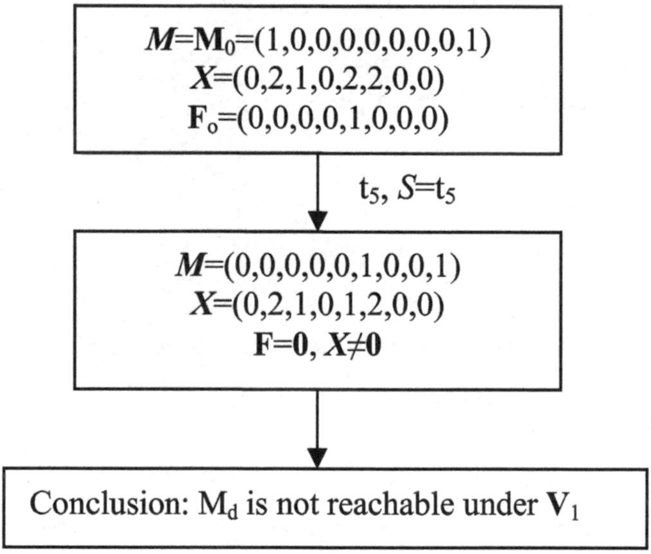

Figure 6. Firing path tree for $\mathbf{V}_1$.

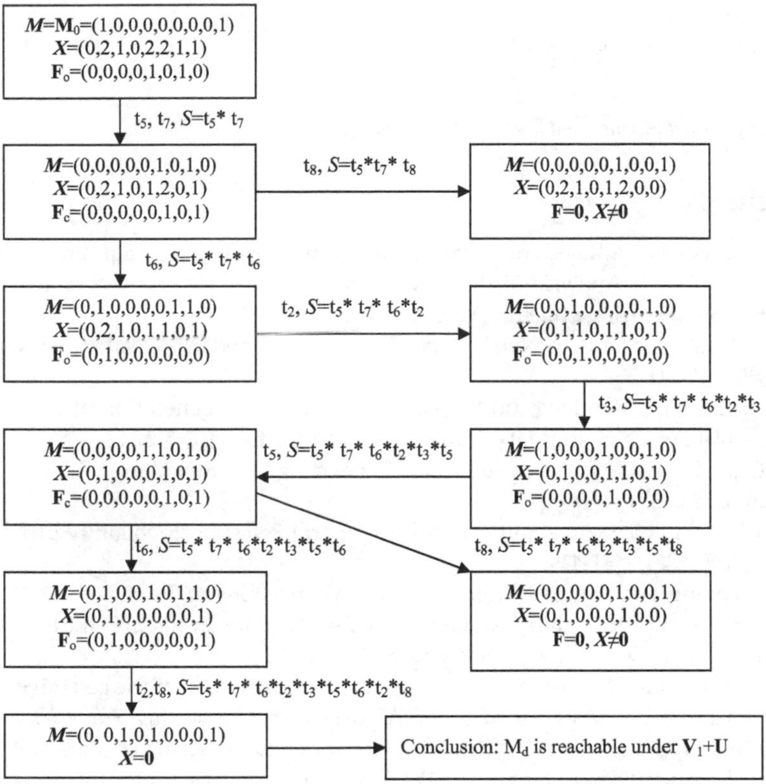

Figure 7. Firing path tree for V_1+F.

6. Conclusions

In this chapter, a new general criterion has been created to solve the reachability problems for ordinary Petri nets. This criterion is based on two processes: (i) Calculating the sufficient test space. (ii) Testing whether or not the destination marking is reachable from the initial marking under the sufficient test space. The sufficient test space significantly reduces the quantity of computation needed to search for an executable solution in X. The firing path tree shows the firing sequence of an executable solution. Consequently, if the destination marking is reachable from the initial marking, this method gives at least one firing sequence that leads from the initial marking to the destination marking. Some examples are given to illustrate how to use this method to solve the reachability problem. This algorithm can be utilized in the following fields: Path searching, auto routing, and reachability between any places in a complicated network.

Author details

Gi Bum Lee
Research Institute of Industrial Science & Technology, Pohang, Korea

Han Zandong
Tsinghua University, Beijing, P.R. China

Jin S. Lee
Pohang University of Science and Technology, Pohang, Korea

7. References

[1] Frank L. Lewis, Ayla Gurel, Stjepan Bogdan, Alper Doganalp and Octavian C. Pastravanu (1998) Analysis of deadlock and circular waits using a matrix model for flexible manufacturing systems. Automatica. 34(9): 1083-1100.
[2] Tadao Murata (1989) Petri Nets: Properties, Analysis and Applications. Proceedings of the IEEE . 77: 541-580.
[3] Gi Bum Lee, Han Zandong, Jin S. Lee (2004) Automatic generation of ladder diagram with control Petri Net. Journal of Intelligent Manufacturing. 15(2): 245-252.
[4] MengChu Zhou (1995) Petri nets in flexible and agile automation [M]. Boston: Kluwer Academic Publishers Group.
[5] Ernst W. Mayr (1984) An algorithm for the general Petri net reachability problem. SIAM J. COMPUT. 13(3): 441-449.
[6] Jeng S. Huang and Tadao Murata (1997) Classifications of Petri Net Transitions and Their Application to Firing Sequence and Reachability Problems. IEEE International Conference on Systems, Man, and Cybernatics. 1: 263-268.
[7] Jorg Desel and Javier Esparza (1995) Free choice Petri nets: Cambridge University Press.
[8] Kunihiko Hiraishi (2000) An Efficient Algorithm for Exploring State Spaces of Petri Nets with Large Capacities. IEICE Trans. Fundamentals. E83-A(11): 2188-2195.
[9] Karsten Schmidt (2001) Narrowing Petri Net State Spaces Using the State Equation. Fundamenta Informaticae. 47: 325-335.
[10] Alexander E. Kostin and Svetlana A. Tchoudaikina (1998) Yet Another Reachability Algorithm for Petri nets. SIGACT News. 29(4): 98-110.
[11] Toshiro ARAKI and Tadao KASAMI (1977) Some Decision Problems Related to the Reachability Problem for Petri nets. Theoretical Computer Science. 3: 85-104.
[12] Iko Miyazawa, Haruki Tanaka, and Takashi Sekiguchi (1996) Classification of solutions of matrix equation related to parallel structure of a Petri Net. IEEE Conference on Emerging Technologies and Factory Automation: 446-452.
[13] Tadashi Matsumoto and Yasushi Miyano (1998) Reachability criterion for Petri Nets with known firing count Vectors. IEICE Trans. Fundamentals. E81-A(4): 628-634.
[14] Jaegeol Yim, Peter C. Nelson, and Tadao Murata (1994) Predicate-Transition Net Reachability Testing Using Heuristic Search. T. IEE Japan. 114-C(9): 907-913.
[15] David (1992) Petri net and Grafcet: Prentice Hall International Ltd.
[16] Gi Bum Lee, Jin S. Lee (2002) Conversion of LD program into augmented PN graph. International Journal of Modelling & Simulation. 22(4): 201-212.
[17] Gi Bum Lee, Han Zandong, Jin S. Lee (2003) Generalized State Equation of Petri nets with Priority. International Journal of Intelligent Systems. 18(11): 1145-1153.
[18] Peterson (1981) Petri net theory and the modeling of systems: London: Prentice Hall international (UK) Ltd.

Chapter 11

Performance Evaluation of Timed Petri Nets in Dioid Algebra

Samir Hamaci, Karim Labadi and A.Moumen Darcherif

Additional information is available at the end of the chapter

1. Introduction

The theory of Discrete Event Dynamic Systems focuses on the analysis and conduct systems. This class essentially contains man-made systems that consist of a finite number of resources (processors or memories, communication channels, machines) shared by several users (jobs, packets, manufactured objects) which all contribute to the achievement of some common goal (a parallel computation, the end-to-end transmission of a set of packets, the assembly of a product in an automated manufacturing line).

Discrete Event Dynamic Systems can be defined as systems in which state variables change under the occurrence of events. They are usually not be described, like the classical continuous systems, by differential equations due to the nature of the phenomenon involved, including the synchronization phenomenon or mutual exclusion. These systems are often represented by state-transition models. For such systems, arise, among others, three problems: Performance evaluation (estimate the production rate of a manufacturing system), resource optimization (minimizing the cost of some resources in order to achieve a given rate of production). To deal with such problems, it is necessary to benefit of models able to take into account all dynamic characteristics of these systems. However, the phenomena involved by Discrete Event Dynamic Systems, and responsible for their dynamics, are much and of diverse natures: sequential or simultaneous, delayed tasks or not, synchronized or rival. From this variety of phenomena results the incapacity to describe all Discrete Event Dynamic Systems by a unique model which is faithful at once to the reality and exploitable mathematically.

The study of Discrete Event Dynamic Systems is made through several theories among which we can remind for example the queuing theory, for the evaluation of performances of timed systems, or the theory of the languages and the automatons, for the control of other systems. The work presented here is in line with theory of linear systems on dioids. This theory involves subclass of Timed Discrete Event Dynamic Systems where the evolution of the state is representable by linear recurrence equations on special algebraic structures called diod algebra. The behavior of systems characterized by delays and synchronization can be described by such recurrences [1]. These systems are modeled by Timed Event Graphs (TEG). This latter constitute a subclasses of Timed Petri Nets with each place admits an upstream transition and downstream transition. When the size of model becomes very significant, the techniques of analysis developed for TEG reach their limits. A possible alternative consists in using Timed Event Graphs with Multipliers denoted TEGM. Indeed, the use of multipliers associated with arcs is natural to model a large number of systems, for example, when the achievement of a specific task requires several units of a same resource, or when an assembly operation requires several units of a same part.

This chapter deals with the performance evaluation of TEGM in dioid algebra. Noting that these models do not admit a linear representation in dioid algebra. This nonlinearity is due to the presence of weights on arcs. To mitigate this problem of nonlinearity and to apply the results used to evaluate the performances of linear systems, we use a linearization method of mathematical model reflecting the behavior of a Timed Event Graphs with Multipliers in order to obtain a linear model.

Few works deal with the performance evaluation of TEGM. Moreover, the calculation of cycle time is an open problem for the scientific community. In the case where the system is modeled by a TEGM, in the most of works the proposed solution is to transform the TEGM into an ordinary TEG, which allows the use of well-known methods of performances evaluation. In [12] the initial TEGM is the object of an operation of expansion. Unfortunately, this expansion can lead to a model of significant size, which does not depend only on the initial structure of TEGM, but also on initial marking. With this method, the system transformation proposed under *single* server semantics hypothesis, or in [14] under *infinite* server semantics hypothesis, leads to a TEG with $|\theta|$ transitions.

Another linearization method was proposed in [17] when each elementary circuit of graph contains at least one *normalized* transition (*i.e.,* a transition for which its corresponding elementary T-invariant component is equal to one). This method increases the number of transitions. Inspired by this work, a linearization method without increasing the number of transition was proposed in [8]. A calculation method of cycle time of a TEGM is proposed in [2] but under restrictive conditions on initial marking. We use a new method of linearization without increasing the number of transition of TEGM [6].

This chapter is organized as follows. After recalling in Section 2 some properties of Petri nets, we present in Section 3, modeling the dynamic behavior of TEGM, which are a class of Petri nets, in dioid algebra, precisely in $(min, +)$ algebra. In this section we will show that TEGM are nonlinear in this algebraic structure, unlike to TEG. This nonlinearity prevents us to use the spectral theory developed in [5] for evaluate the performances of TEG in $(min, +)$ algebra. To mitigate this problem of nonlinearity, we will encode the mathematical equations governing the dynamic evolution of TEGM in a dioid of operators developed in [7], inspired by work presented in [3]. The description of this dioid and the new state model based on operators will be the subject of Section 4. To exploit the mathematical model obtained, a linearization method of this model will be presented in Section 5, in order to obtain a linear model in $(min, +)$ algebra and to apply the theory developed for performance evaluation. This latter will be the subject of Section 6. Before concluding, w e give a short example to illustrate this approach for evaluate the performances of TEGM in dioid algebra.

2. Petri Net

2.1. Definitions and notations

Petri Nets (PN) are a graphical and mathematical tool, introduced in 1962 by Carl Adam Petri [15]. They allow the modeling of a large number of Discrete Event Dynamic Systems. They are particularly adapted to the study of complex processes involving properties of synchronization and resource sharing.

The behavior over time of dynamical systems, including evaluation of their performance (cycle time, ...), led to introduce the notion of time in models Petri Net. Several models Petri Net incorporating time have been proposed. These models can be grouped into two classes: deterministic models and stochastic models. The former consider the deterministic values for durations of activity, whereas the latter consider probabilistic values.Among the existing Timed Petri Net include: the Temporal Petri Net [11] associating a time interval to each transition and each place, the T-Timed Petri Net [4] associating a positive constant (called firing time of transition) at each transition and P-Timed Petri Net ; [4], [9] associating a positive constant (called holding time in the place) at each place of graph. It has been shown that P-Timed Petri Net can be reduced to T-Timed Petri Net and vice versa [13]. In the next, for consistency with the literature produced on the dioid algebra, we consider that P-Timed Petri Net.

A *P-Timed Petri Net* is a valued bipartite graph given by a 5-tuple (P, T, M, m, τ).

1. P is the finite set of places, T is the finite set of transitions.
2. $M \in \mathbb{N}^{P\times T \cup T\times P}$. Given $p \in P$ and $q \in T$, the multiplier $M_{pq'}$ (resp. M_{qp}) specifies the weight of the arc from transition $n_{q'}$ to place p (resp. from place p to transition n_q).
3. $m \in \mathbb{N}^P$: m_p assigns an initial number of tokens to place p.
4. $\tau \in \mathbb{N}^P$: τ_p gives the minimal time a token must spend in place p before it can contribute to the enabling of its downstream transitions.

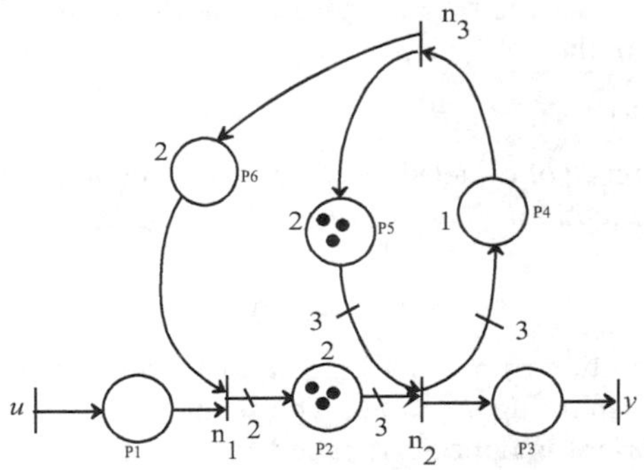

Figure 1. Example of a P-Timed Petri Net.

More generally, for a Petri Net, we denote $W^- = [M_{qp}]$ (input incidence matrix), $W^+ = [M_{pq}]$ (output incidence matrix), $W = W^+ - W^-$ (incidence matrix) and considering S a possible firing sequence from a marking m_i to the marking m_k, then a fundamental equation reflecting the dynamic behavior of Petri Net, is obtained:

$$m_k = m_i + W \times \underline{S}. \tag{1}$$

$\underline{S}$ is the characteristic vector of the firing sequence S. In Figure 1, the firing sequence $S = \{n_2\}$, the characteristic vector is equal to $\underline{S}^t = (0, 1, 0, 0)$, and from marking $m_0^t = (0, 3, 0, 0, 3, 0)$, is reached the marking $m_1^t = (0, 0, 0, 3, 0, 0)$ by firing of the transition n_2, after a stay of 2 time units of tokens in the places P_2 and P_5.

2.2. Invariants of a Petri Net

There are two types of invariants in a Petri Net; *Marking Invariants*, also called P-invariant and *Firing Invariant*, also called T-invariant [4].

Definition 1. (P-invariant)

Marking Invariants illustrate the conservation of the number of tokens in a subset of places of a Petri Net.

A vector, denoted Y, which has a dimension equal to the number of places of a Petri Net is a P-invariant, if and only if it satisfies the following equation:

$$Y^t \times W = \vec{0}, \qquad Y \neq \vec{0}. \tag{2}$$

From Equation 1, we deduce that if Y is a P-invariant, then for a given marking, denoted m_i, obtained from an initial marking m_0, we have:

$$Y^t \times m_i = Y^t \times m_0 = k, \quad k \in \mathbb{N}^*. \tag{3}$$

This equation represents an invariant marking, it means that if Y is a P-invariant of Petri Net then the transpose of the vector Y multiplied by the marking vector m_i of the Petri Net is an integer constant regardless of the m_i marking reachable from the initial marking m_0. All the places for which the associated component in the P-invariant is nonzero, is called the conservative component of the Petri Net.

Definition 2. (T-invariant)

A nonzero vector of integers θ of dimension $\mid T \mid \times 1$ is a T-invariant of Petri Net if and only if it satisfies the following equation:

$$W \times \theta = \vec{0}. \tag{4}$$

From Equation 1, the evolution from a marking m_i to a sequence whose characteristic vector θ back the graph to same marking $m_k = m_i$. The set of transitions for which the associated component in the T-invariant is nonzero is called the support of T-invariant. A T-invariant corresponding to a firing sequence is called feasible repetitive component.

Definition 3. (Consistent Petri Net)

A Petri Net is said *consistent* if it has a T-invariant θ covering all transitions of graph. A Petri Net which has this property is said *repetitive*.

The graph reaches a periodic regime when there is a firing sequence achievable with θ as characteristic vector.

Definition 4. (Conservative Petri Net)

A Petri Net is said conservative if all places in the graph form a conservative component.

The Petri Nets considered here are *consistent* (*i.e.,* there exists a T-invariant θ covering all transitions: $\{q \in T|\theta(q) > 0\} = T$) and *conservative* (*i.e.,* there exists a P-invariant Y covering all places: $\{p \in P|Y(p) > 0\} = P$). Such graphs verify the next properties [13]:

- A PNPetri Net allows a live and bounded initial marking m *iff* it is consistent and conservative.
- A consistent Petri Net is strongly connected *iff* it is conservative.
- A consistent Petri Net has a unique elementary T-invariant.
- The product of multipliers along any circuit of a conservative Petri Net is equal to one.

In the next, we denote by ${}^\bullet q$ (resp. $q^\bullet$) the set of places upstream (resp. downstream) transition q. Similarly, ${}^\bullet p$ (resp. $p^\bullet$) denotes the set of transitions upstream (resp. downstream) place p.

3. Dynamic behavior of Timed Petri Nets in dioid algebra

Definition 5. An ordinary *Timed Event Graph* (TEG) is a Timed Petri Net such that each place has exactly one upstream transition and one downstream transition. Weights of arcs are all unit.

These graphs are well adapted to model synchronization phenomena occurring in Discrete Event Dynamic Systems. They admit a linear representation on a particular algebraic structure called the *dioid* algebra [1].

Definition 6. *A dioid* $(\mathcal{D}, \oplus, \otimes)$ is a semiring in which the addition $\oplus$ is idempotent ($\forall a,\ a \oplus a = a$). Neutral elements of $\oplus$ and $\otimes$ are denoted ε and e respectively.

- A dioid is *commutative* when $\otimes$ is commutative. The symbol $\otimes$ is often omitted. Due to idempotency of $\oplus$, a dioid can be endowed with a natural order relation defined by $a \preceq b \Leftrightarrow b = a \oplus b$ (the least upper bound of {a,b} is equal to $a \oplus b$).
- A dioid $\mathcal{D}$ is *complete* if every subset A of $\mathcal{D}$ admits a least upper bound denoted $\bigoplus_{x \in A} x$, and if $\otimes$ distributes at left and at right over infinite sums. The greatest element denoted T of a complete dioid $\mathcal{D}$ is equal to $\bigoplus_{x \in \mathcal{D}} x$. The greatest lower bound of every subset X of a complete dioid always exists and is denoted $\bigwedge_{x \in X} x$.

Example 1. The set $\mathbb{Z} \cup \{\pm\infty\}$, endowed with (*min*) as $\oplus$ and usual addition as $\otimes$, is a complete dioid denoted $\overline{\mathbb{Z}}_{\min}$ and usually called $(min, +)$ algebra with neutral elements $\varepsilon = +\infty$, $e = 0$ and $T = -\infty$.

Example 2. The set $\mathbb{Z} \cup \{\pm\infty\}$, endowed with (*max*) as $\oplus$ and usual addition as $\otimes$, is a complete dioid denoted $\overline{\mathbb{Z}}_{\max}$ and usually called $(max, +)$ algebra with neutral elements $\varepsilon = -\infty$, $e = 0$ and $T = +\infty$.

Definition 7. A *signal* is an increasing map from $\mathbb{Z}$ to $\mathbb{Z} \cup \{\pm\infty\}$. Denote $S=(\mathbb{Z} \cup \{\pm\infty\})^{\mathbb{Z}}$ the set of signals.

This set is endowed with a kind of module structure, called *min-plus semimodule,* the two associated operations are:

- pointwise minimum of time functions to add signals: $\forall t \in \mathbb{Z}, (x \oplus y)(t) = x(t) \oplus y(t) = \min(x(t), y(t))$;
- addition of a constant to play the role of external product of a signal by a scalar: $\forall t \in \mathbb{Z}, \forall \rho \in \mathbb{Z} \cup \{\pm\infty\}, (\rho.x)(t) = \rho \otimes x(t) = \rho + x(t)$.

Definition 8. An operator Ψ is a mapping defined from $\mathbb{Z} \cup \{\pm\infty\}$ to $\mathbb{Z} \cup \{\pm\infty\}$ is *linear* in $(min, +)$ algebra if it preserves the min-plus semimodule structure, *i.e.*, for all signals x, y and constant ρ,

$$\Psi(x \oplus y) = \Psi(x) \oplus \Psi(y) \quad \text{(additive property)},$$
$$\Psi(\rho \otimes x) = \rho \otimes \Psi(x) \quad \text{(homogeneity property)}.$$

To study a TEG in $(min, +)$ algebra, considered state variable is a *counter* , denoted $x_q(t)$. This latter denotes the cumulated number of firings of transition x_q up to time t ($t \in \mathbb{Z}$). To illustrate the evolution of a counter associated with the transition x_q of a TEG, we consider the following elementary graph:

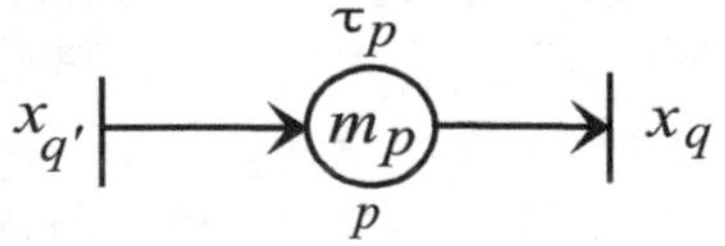

Figure 2. Elementary TEG

$$x_q(t) = \min_{p \in {}^\bullet q, q' \in {}^\bullet p} (m_p + x_{q'}(t - \tau_p)). \tag{5}$$

Note that this equation is nonlinear in usual algebra. This nonlinearity is due to the presence of the (min) which models the synchronization phenomena [1] in the transition x_q. However, it is linear equation in $(min, +)$ algebra:

$$x_q(t) = \bigoplus_{p \in {}^\bullet q, q' \in {}^\bullet p} (m_p \otimes x_{q'}(t - \tau_p)). \tag{6}$$

In the case where weight of an arc is greater than one, TEG becomes weighted. This type of model is called Timed Event Graph with Multipliers, denoted TEGM.

The *earliest* functioning rule of a TEGM is defined as follows. A transition n_q fires as soon as all its upstream places $\{p \in {}^\bullet q\}$ contain enough tokens (M_{qp}) having spent at least τ_p units of time in place p. When transition $n_{q'}$ fires, it produces $M_{pq'}$ tokens in each downstream place $p \in q'^\bullet$.

[1] Synchronization phenomena occurs when multiple arcs converge to the same transition.

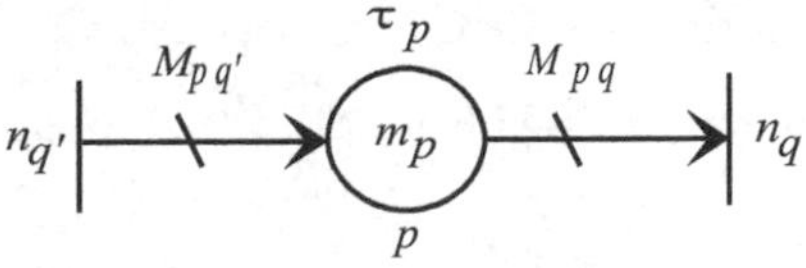

Figure 3. Elementary TEGM.

Assertion 1. The counter variable associated with the transition n_q of an elementary TEGM (under the earliest firing rule) satisfy the following *transition to transition* equation:

$$n_q(t) = \min_{p \in {}^\bullet q, q' \in {}^\bullet p} \lfloor M_{qp}^{-1}(m_p + M_{pq'} n_{q'}(t - \tau_p)) \rfloor. \qquad (7)$$

The inferior integer part is used to preserve the integrity of Equation 7. In general, a transition n_q may have several upstream transitions $\{n_{q'} \in {}^{\bullet\bullet}q\}$ which implies that the associated counter variable is given by the *min* of *transition to transition* equations obtained for each upstream transition.

Example 3. Let us consider TEGM depicted in Figure 4.

$$\begin{cases} n_1(t) &= \lfloor \frac{4+3n_2(t-1)}{2} \rfloor, \\ n_2(t) &= \min(\lfloor \frac{2n_1(t-1)}{3} \rfloor, 2 + 2n_3(t-1)), \\ n_3(t) &= \lfloor \frac{n_2(t-1)}{2} \rfloor. \end{cases}$$

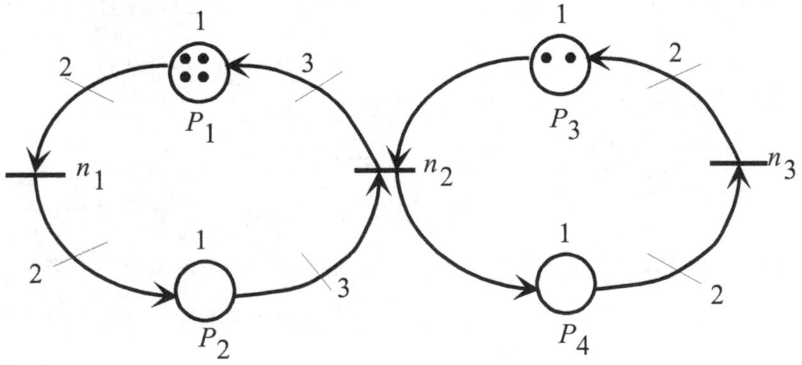

Figure 4. Timed Event Graph with Multipliers.

The mathematical model representing the behavior of this TEGM does not admit a linear representation in $(min, +)$ algebra. This nonlinearity is due to the presence of the integer parts generated by the presence of the weights on the arcs. Consequently, it is difficult to use $(min, +)$ algebra to tackle, for example, problems of control and the analysis of performances. As alternative, we propose another model based on operators which will be linearized in order to obtain a $(min, +)$ linear model.

4. Operatorial representation of TEGM

We now introduce three operators, defined from $\mathbb{Z} \cup \{\pm\infty\}$ to $\mathbb{Z} \cup \{\pm\infty\}$, which are used for the modeling of TEGM.

- **Operator** γ^{ν} to represent a shift of ν units in counting ($\nu \in \mathbb{Z} \cup \{\pm\infty\}$). It is defined as follows:

$$\forall t \in \mathbb{Z}, \quad \forall\, n_{q'} \in \overline{\mathbb{Z}}^{\mathbb{Z}}, \qquad n_q(t) = \gamma^{\nu} n_{q'}(t) = n_{q'}(t) + \nu.$$

Property 1. Operator γ^{ν} satisfies the following rules:

$$(\gamma^{\nu} \oplus \gamma^{\nu'})n'_q(t) = \gamma^{min(\nu,\nu')} n'_q(t).$$

$$(\gamma^{\nu} \otimes \gamma^{\nu'})n'_q(t) = \gamma^{\nu+\nu'} n'_q(t).$$

Indeed, we have

- $(\gamma^{\nu} \oplus \gamma^{\nu'})n'_q(t) = min(n'_q(t) + \nu, n'_q(t) + \nu') = n'_q(t) + min(\nu, \nu') = \gamma^{min(\nu,\nu')} n'_q(t).$
- $(\gamma^{\nu} \otimes \gamma^{\nu'})n'_q(t) = \gamma^{\nu}(n'_q(t) + \nu') = n'_q(t) + \nu' + \nu = \gamma^{\nu+\nu'} n'_q(t).$

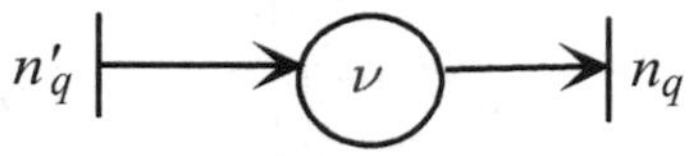

Figure 5. Operator γ^{ν}

- **Operator** δ^{τ} to represent a shift of τ units in dating ($\tau \in \mathbb{Z} \cup \{\pm\infty\}$). It is defined as follows:

$$\forall t \in \mathbb{Z}, \quad \forall\, n_{q'} \in \overline{\mathbb{Z}}^{\mathbb{Z}}, \qquad n_q(t) = \delta^{\tau} n_{q'}(t) = n_{q'}(t - \tau).$$

Property 2. Operator δ^{τ} satisfies the following rules:

$$(\delta^{\tau} \oplus \delta^{\tau'})n'_q(t) = \delta^{max(\tau,\tau')} n'_q(t).$$

$$(\delta^{\tau} \otimes \delta^{\tau'})n'_q(t) = \delta^{\tau+\tau'} n'_q(t).$$

- Knowing that the signal $n_q(t)$ is non decreasing, we have :

$$(\delta^{\tau} \oplus \delta^{\tau'})n'_q(t) = min(n'_q(t-\tau), n'_q(t-\tau')) = n'_q(t - max(\tau, \tau')) = \delta^{max(\tau,\tau')} n'_q(t).$$

$$(\delta^{\tau} \otimes \delta^{\tau'})n'_q(t) = \delta^{\tau} n'_q(t - \tau') = n'_q(t - \tau' - \tau) = \delta^{\tau'+\tau} n'_q(t).$$

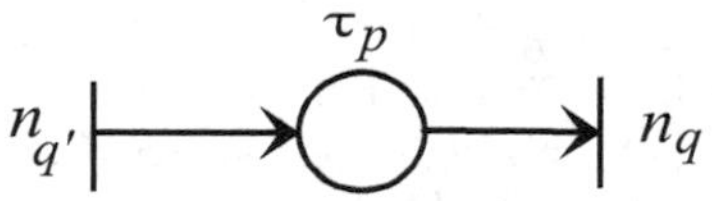

Figure 6. Operator δ^{τ}

- **Operator** μ_r to represent a scaling of factor r ($r \in \mathbb{Q}^+$). It is defined as follows:

$$\forall t \in \mathbb{Z},\ \forall\, n_{q'} \in \overline{\mathbb{Z}}^{\mathbb{Z}}, \qquad n'_q(t) = \mu_r n'_{q'}(t) = \lfloor r \times n'_{q'}(t) \rfloor,$$

with $r \in \mathbb{Q}^+$(r is equal to a ratio of elements in $\mathbb{N}$).

Property 3. Operator μ_r satisfies the following rules when composed with operators δ^τ *and* γ^ν *:*

$$(\mu_r \otimes \delta^\tau) n'(t) = (\delta^\tau \otimes \mu_r) n'(t),$$

$$(\mu_r \otimes \gamma^\nu) n'(t) = (\gamma^{\nu \times r} \otimes \mu_r) n'(t), \text{for } \nu \in r^{-1} \times \mathbb{N}.$$

Indeed, we have:

- $(\mu_r \otimes \delta^\tau) n'(t) = \lfloor r \times n'(t-\tau) \rfloor = (\delta^\tau \otimes \mu_r) n'(t)$.
- $\forall \nu \in r^{-1} \times \mathbb{N}, \quad (\mu_r \otimes \gamma^\nu) n'(t) = \lfloor r \times \nu + r \times n'(t) \rfloor = r \times \nu + \lfloor r \times n'(t) \rfloor = (\gamma^{\nu \times r} \otimes \mu_r) n'(t)$, since $\nu \times r \in \mathbb{N}$.

Figure 7. Operator $\mu_r (r = \frac{a}{b})$

Denote by $\mathcal{D}_{\min}$ the (noncommutative) dioid of finite sums of operators $\{\mu_r, \gamma^\nu\}$ endowed with pointwise *min* ($\oplus$) and composition ($\otimes$) operations, with neutral elements equal to $\varepsilon = \mu_{+\infty} \gamma^{+\infty}$ and $e = \mu_1 \gamma^0$ respectively. Thus, an element in $\mathcal{D}_{\min}$ is a map $p = \bigoplus_{i=1}^{k} \mu_{r_i} \gamma^{\nu_i}$ defined from S to S such that $\forall\, t \in \mathbb{Z}$, $p\,(n(t)) = \min\limits_{1 \le i \le k} (\lfloor r_i(\nu_i + n(t)) \rfloor)$.

Let a map $h : \mathbb{Z} \to \mathcal{D}_{\min}$, $\tau \mapsto h(\tau)$ in which $h(\tau) = \bigoplus\limits_{i=1}^{k_\tau} \mu_{r_i^\tau} \gamma^{\nu_i^\tau}$. We define the power series $H(\delta)$ in the indeterminate δ with coefficients in $\mathcal{D}_{\min}$ by: $H(\delta) = \bigoplus\limits_{\tau \in \mathbb{Z}} h(\tau) \delta^\tau$.

The set of these formal power series endowed with the two following operations:
$F(\delta) \oplus H(\delta)$: $(f \oplus h)(\tau) = f(\tau) \oplus h(\tau) = \min(f(\tau), h(\tau))$,
$F(\delta) \otimes H(\delta) : (f \otimes h)(\tau) = \bigoplus\limits_{i \in \mathbb{Z}} f(i) \otimes h(\tau - i) = \inf\limits_{i \in \mathbb{Z}} (f(i) + h(\tau - i))$,
is a dioid denoted $\mathcal{D}_{\min}[\![\delta]\!]$, with neutral elements $\varepsilon = \mu_{+\infty} \gamma^{+\infty} \delta^{-\infty}$ and $e = \mu_1 \gamma^0 \delta^0$.

Elements of $\mathcal{D}_{\min}[\![\delta]\!]$ allow modeling the transfer between two transitions of a TEGM. A formal series of $\mathcal{D}_{\min}[\![\delta]\!]$ can also represent a signal n as $N(\delta) = \bigoplus\limits_{\tau \in \mathbb{Z}} n(\tau)\, \delta^\tau$, simply due to the fact that it is also equal to $n \otimes e$ (by definition of neutral element e of $\mathcal{D}_{\min}$).

Assertion 2. The counter variables of an elementary TEGM satisfies the following equation in dioid $\mathcal{D}_{\min}[\![\delta]\!]$:

$$N_q(\delta) = \bigoplus_{p \in {}^\bullet q,\, q' \in {}^\bullet p} \mu_{M_{qp}^{-1}} \gamma^{m_p} \delta^{\tau_p} \mu_{M_{pq'}} N_{q'}(\delta). \tag{8}$$

• $N_q(\delta)$ is the counter $n_q(t)$ associated with the transition n_q, encoded in $\mathcal{D}_{\min}[\![\delta]\!]$. It is equal to the counter $N_{q'}(\delta)$ shifted by the composition of operators $\mu_{M_{pq'}}, \delta^{\tau_p}, \gamma^{m_p}$ and $\mu_{M_{qp}^{-1}}$ connected in series. Let us express some properties of operators γ, δ, μ in dioid $\mathcal{D}_{\min}[\![\delta]\!]$.

Proposition 1. Let $a, b \in \mathbb{N}$, we have:

1. $\gamma^a\delta^b = \delta^b\gamma^a$, $\mu_a\delta^b = \delta^b\mu_a$ (commutative properties).
2. $\mu_{a^{-1}}\mu_b = \mu_{(a^{-1}b)}$.
3. Let $N(\delta)$ such that, $\forall t \in \mathbb{Z}$, $n(t)$ *is a multiple of a, then* $\mu_{a^{-1}}\gamma^b N(\delta) = \gamma^{\lfloor a^{-1}b \rfloor}\mu_{a^{-1}}N(\delta)$.
4. $\gamma^b\mu_a = \mu_a\gamma^{a^{-1}b}$, or equivalently, $\mu_a\gamma^b = \gamma^{ab}\mu_a$.

Proof:

- Point 1 is obvious.
- Point 2: $\mu_{a^{-1}}\mu_b N(\delta)$ corresponds to $\lfloor a^{-1}\lfloor b\,n(t)\rfloor\rfloor = \lfloor a^{-1}b\,n(t)\rfloor$ which leads to $\mu_{(a^{-1}b)}N(\delta)$.
- Point 3: $\mu_{a^{-1}}\gamma^b N(\delta)$ correspond to $\lfloor a^{-1}(b + n(t))\rfloor = \lfloor a^{-1}b\rfloor + a^{-1}n(t)$ since $n(t) \in \mathbb{Z} \cup \{\pm\infty\}$ is a multiple of a, which leads to $\gamma^{\lfloor a^{-1}b\rfloor}\mu_{a^{-1}}N(\delta)$.
- Point 4: $\gamma^b\mu_a N(\delta)$ corresponds to $b + \lfloor a\,n(t)\rfloor = \lfloor a(a^{-1}b + n(t))\rfloor$ which leads to $\mu_a\gamma^{a^{-1}b}N(\delta)$.

Example 4. The TEGM depicted in Figure 4 admits the following representation in $\mathcal{D}_{\min}[\![\delta]\!]$:

$$\begin{pmatrix} N_1 \\ N_2 \\ N_3 \end{pmatrix} = \begin{pmatrix} \varepsilon & \mu_{1/2}\gamma^4\delta^1\mu_3 & \varepsilon \\ \mu_{1/3}\delta^1\mu_2 & \varepsilon & \gamma^2\delta^1\mu_2 \\ \varepsilon & \mu_{1/2}\delta^1 & \varepsilon \end{pmatrix} \begin{pmatrix} N_1 \\ N_2 \\ N_3 \end{pmatrix}$$

5. Linearization of TEGM

The presence of integer part modeled by operator μ induces a nonlinearity in Equation 8 used to represent a TEGM. So, as far as possible, we seek to represent a TEGM with linear equations in order to apply standard results of linear system theory developed in the dioid setting, which leads to transform a TEGM into a TEG (represented without operator μ).

5.1. Principle of linearization

A consistent TEGM has a unique elementary T-invariant in which components are in $\mathbb{N}^*$. The used method is based on the use of commutation rules of operators and the impulse inputs (Proposition 1 and 2).

In the next, we suppose that all tokens in a TEGM are "frozen" before time 0 and are available at time 0 which is a classical assumption in Petri Nets theory. Hence, with each counter variable of a TEGM is added a counter variable corresponding to an impulse input e (*i.e.,* $e(t) = 0$ for $t < 0$ and $e(t) = +\infty$ for $t \geq 0$). These initial conditions are weakly compatible. For more details, see [10].

To linearize the expression of counters variables written as Equation 8, one expresses each counter according to an entry impulse. This latter will permit to linearize the mathematical model reflecting the behavior of a TEGM in order to obtain a linear model in (min, +) algebra.

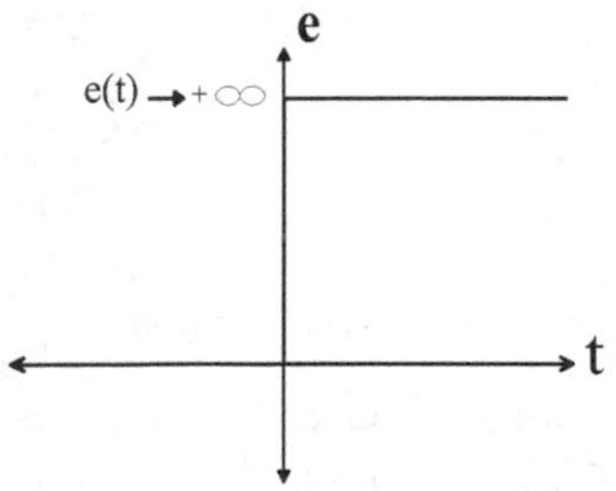

Figure 8. Impulse (Point of view of counter).

Proposition 2. let E an impulse input, we have : $\forall a \in \mathbb{N}, \beta \in Q^+$,

$$\mu_\beta \gamma^a \delta^\tau E(\delta) = \gamma^{\lfloor \beta a \rfloor} \delta^\tau E(\delta). \tag{9}$$

Proof: Thanks to Proposition 1.3, $\mu_\beta \gamma^a \delta^\tau E(\delta)$ corresponds to $\lfloor \beta \times (a + e(t-\tau)) \rfloor = \lfloor \beta \times a \rfloor + e(t-\tau)$ since for $t \geq 0$ $e(t) \mapsto +\infty$, hence $e(t)$ is a multiple of β, which leads to $\gamma^{\lfloor \beta a \rfloor} \delta^\tau E(\delta)$.

We now give the state model associated to the dynamic of counters of a TEGM. Consider the vector N composed of the counter variable. The counter variables corresponding to impulse input e added with each transition n_i:

$$N(\delta) = A \otimes N(\delta) \oplus E(\delta). \tag{10}$$

Knowing that such equation admits the following earliest solution:

$$N(\delta) = A^* \otimes E(\delta), \tag{11}$$

$A^* = e \oplus A \oplus A^2 \oplus \cdots$.

Proposition 3. For initial conditions *weakly compatible*, consistent and conservative TEGM is linearizable without increasing the number of its transitions.

Proof: Consider a consistent and conservative TEGM represented by the equation $A(\delta) = A \otimes N(\delta) \oplus E(\delta)$. Using Equation 11, and then apply the Proposition 2, we obtain a linear equation between transitions of graph (corresponding to a linear TEG). This linearization method may be applied to all transitions of graph, since for any transition, one can involve an impulse input.

Example 5. The TEGM depicted in Figure 9 admits the elementary T-invariant $\theta^t = (3, 2, 1)$.

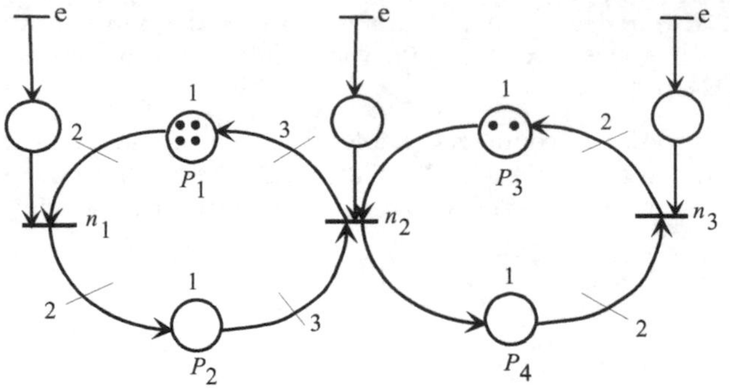

Figure 9. TEGM with impulse inputs added to each transition.

The inputs e correspond to the impulse inputs. They have not influence on the evolution of the model. Indeed, $\forall t \geq 0, \forall n_q \in \mathcal{T}, \min(n_q(t), e(t)) = n_q(t)$, since $e(t) \mapsto +\infty$.

$$\begin{pmatrix} N_1 \\ N_2 \\ N_3 \end{pmatrix} = \begin{pmatrix} \varepsilon & \mu_{1/2}\gamma^4\delta^1\mu_3 & \varepsilon \\ \mu_{1/3}\delta^1\mu_2 & \varepsilon & \gamma^2\delta^1\mu_2 \\ \varepsilon & \mu_{1/2}\delta^1 & \varepsilon \end{pmatrix} \begin{pmatrix} N_1 \\ N_2 \\ N_3 \end{pmatrix} \oplus \begin{pmatrix} E \\ E \\ E \end{pmatrix}.$$

Using Equation 11, $N(\delta) = A^*E(\delta)$. The Proposition 2 allows to calculate $A^*E(\delta)$:

$$\begin{aligned} A^*E(\delta) &= (e \oplus A \oplus A^2 \oplus A^3 \oplus ...)E(\delta) \\ &= (\, E(\delta) \oplus A\,E(\delta) \oplus \underbrace{A \otimes AE(\delta)}_{A^2E(\delta)} \oplus \underbrace{A \otimes A^2E(\delta)}_{A^3E(\delta)} \oplus ...). \end{aligned}$$

$$A^*\,E(\delta) = \begin{pmatrix} (\gamma^2\delta^2)(\gamma^3\delta^4)^* \\ \delta^1(\gamma^1\delta^2)^* \\ \delta^4(\gamma^1\delta^4)^* \end{pmatrix} E(\delta),$$

which is the earliest solution of the following equations:

$$\begin{pmatrix} N_1(\delta) \\ N_2(\delta) \\ N_3(\delta) \end{pmatrix} = \begin{pmatrix} \gamma^3\delta^4 \\ \gamma^1\delta^2 \\ \gamma^1\delta^4 \end{pmatrix} \begin{pmatrix} N_1(\delta) \\ N_2(\delta) \\ N_3(\delta) \end{pmatrix} \oplus \begin{pmatrix} \gamma^2\delta^2 \\ \delta^1 \\ \delta^4 \end{pmatrix} E(\delta).$$

Let us express these equations in usual counter setting (dioid $\overline{\mathbb{Z}}_{\min}$), we have, $\forall t \in \mathbb{Z}$:

$$\begin{cases} n_1(t) = 3 \otimes n_1(t-4) \bigoplus 2 \otimes e(t-2), \\ n_2(t) = 1 \otimes n_2(t-2) \bigoplus e(t-1), \\ n_3(t) = 1 \otimes n_3(t-4) \bigoplus e(t-4). \end{cases}$$

These equations are quite $(min, +)$ linear. It turns out that the TEG depicted in Figure 10, composed of three elementary circuits: (n_1, n_1), (n_2, n_2), (n_3, n_3), is a possible representation of the previous equations.

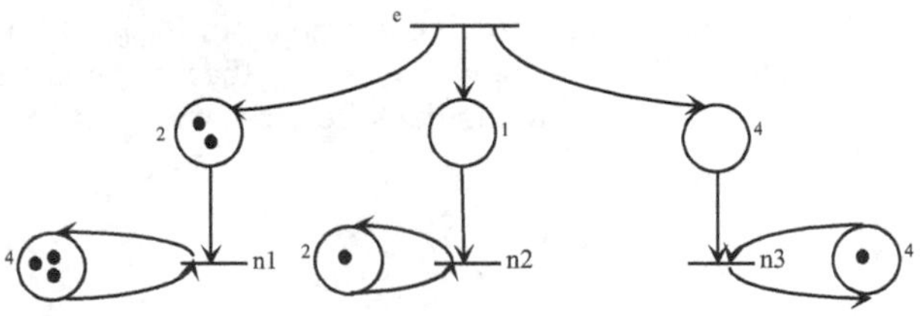

Figure 10. TEG (Linearized TEGM).

6. Performance evaluation of TEGM

• **General case**: To evaluate the performance of a TEGM returns to calculate the cycle time and firing rate associated with each transition of a graph.

Definition 9. [16] The cycle time, TC_m, of a TEGM is the average time to fire once the T-invariant under the earliest firing rule (i.e., transitions are fired as soon as possible) from the initial marking.

This cycle time is equivalent to the average time between two successive firing of a transition. It is calculated by the following relation:

$$TC_m = \frac{\theta_q}{\lambda_{m_q}}. \tag{12}$$

• θ_q is the component of T-invariant associated with transition n_q, and λ_{m_q} is the firing rate associated with transition n_q of TEGM corresponding to the average number of firing of one transition per unit time.

• For an industrial system, the cycle time corresponds to the average manufacturing time of a piece, and the firing rate is the average number of pieces produced per unit of time.

• **Particular case**: Elements of performance evaluation for TEG. We recall main results characterizing an ordinary TEG modeled in the dioid $\mathbb{Z}_{\min}$. Knowing that a TEG is a TEGM with unit weights on the arcs, and their components of T-invariant are all equals 1.

Definition 10. A matrix A is said *irreducible* if for any pair *(i,j)*, there is an integer m such that $(A^m)_{ij} \neq \varepsilon$.

Theorem 1. [5] Let A be a square matrix with coefficient in $\mathbb{Z}_{\min}$. The following assertions are equivalent:

- Matrix A is irreducible,
- The TEG associated with matrix A is strongly connected.

One calls *eigenvalue* and *eigenvector* of a matrix A with coefficients in $\mathbb{Z}_{\min}$, the scalar λ and the vector v such as:

$$A \otimes v = \lambda \otimes v.$$

Theorem 2. [5] Let A be a square matrix with coefficients in $\mathbb{Z}_{\min}$. If A is irreducible, or equivalently, if the associated TEG is strongly connected, then there is a single eigenvalue denoted λ. The eigenvalue can be calculated in the following way:

$$\lambda = \bigoplus_{j=1}^{n}(\bigoplus_{i=1}^{n}(A^j)_{ii})^{\frac{1}{j}}. \tag{13}$$

λ corresponds to the firing rate which is identical for each transition. This eigenvalue λ can be directly deduced from the TEG by:

$$\lambda = \min_{c \in C} \frac{M(c)}{T(c)}, \tag{14}$$

- C is the set of elementary circuits of the TEG.
- T(c) is the sum of holding times in circuit c.
- M(c) is the number of tokens in circuit c.

In the case of Ordinary TEG strongly connected, The inverse of eigenvalue λ is equivalent to cycle time, denoted TC.

$$TC = \frac{1}{\lambda}, \tag{15}$$

Example 6. The TEG depicted in Figure 10, which is not strongly connected, is composed of three circuits : (n_1, n_1), (n_2, n_2) and (n_3, n_3). Each circuit admits a T-invariant composed of one component equals 1.

Using the Definition 9 and Equation 15, one deduce that each circuit, which is an elementary TEG strongly connected, admits the following cycle time:

- Circuit (n_1, n_1), $TC = \frac{4}{3}$.
- Circuit (n_2, n_2), $TC = \frac{2}{1}$.
- Circuit (n_3, n_3), $TC = \frac{4}{1}$.

The cycle time of TEGM depicted in Figure 4, corresponds to the time required to fire each transition a number of times equal its corresponding elementary T-invariant component. Hence

$$TC_1 = 3 \times \frac{4}{3}, \qquad TC_2 = 2 \times \frac{2}{1}, \qquad TC_3 = 1 \times \frac{4}{1}.$$

Note that the cycle time is identical for all transitions of the graph which is equal to 4 time units. This means that each transition is asymptotically fired once every four time units.

About the firing rate associated with each transition of the graph, using the relation (12):

$$\lambda_{m_1} = \frac{3}{4}, \qquad \lambda_{m_2} = \frac{1}{2}, \qquad \lambda_{m_3} = \frac{1}{4}.$$

Confirmation of these results can be deducted directly to the following marking graph of the initial TEGM.

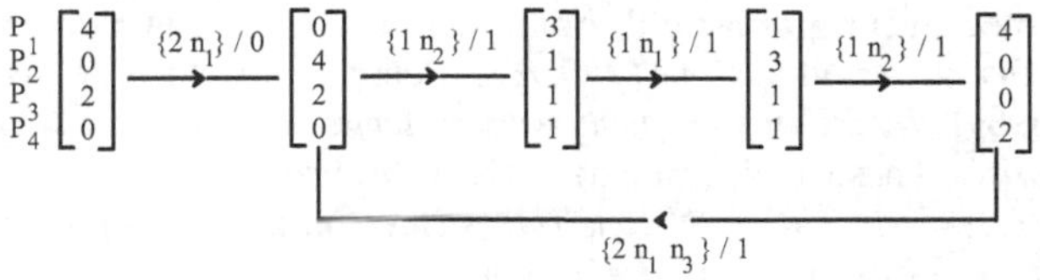

Figure 11. Marking graph of the initial TEGM.

- kn_i/t: after t time units, the transition n_i is firing k time.

7. Conclusion

Performance evaluation of TEGM is the subject of this chapter. These graphs, in contrast to ordinary TEG, do not admit a linear representation in $(min, +)$ algebra. This nonlinearity is due to the presence of weights on the arcs. For that, a modeling of these graphs in an algebraic structure, based on operators, is used. The obtained model is linearized, by using of pulse inputs associated with all transitions of graphs, in order to obtain representation in linear $(min+)$ algebra, and apply some results basic spectral theory, usually used to evaluate the performance of ordinary TEG. The work presented in this chapter paves the way for other development related to evaluation of performance of these models. In particular, the calculation of cycle time for any timed event graph with multipliers is, to our knowledge, an open problem to date.

Author details

Samir Hamaci, Karim Labadi and A.Moumen Darcherif
EPMI, 13 Boulvard de l'Hautil, 95092, Cergy-Pontoise, France

8. References

[1] Baccelli, F., Cohen, G., Olsder, G.-J. & Quadrat, J.-P. [1992]. *Synchronization and Linearity: An Algebra for Discrete Event Systems*, Wiley and Sons.

[2] Chao, D., Zhou, M. & Wang, D. [1993]. Multiple weighted marked graphs, *IFAC 12th Triennial World Congress*, Sydney, Australie, pp. 371–374.

[3] Cohen, G., Gaubert, S. & Quadrat, J.-P. [1998]. Timed-event graphs with multipliers and homogenous min-plus systems, *IEEE Transaction on Automatic Control* Vol.43(No.9): 1296–1302.

[4] David, R. & Alla, H. [1992]. *Du Grafcet au réseaux de Petri*, Editions Hermès, Paris.

[5] Gaubert, S. [1995]. Resource optimization and (min,+) spectral theory, *IEEE Transaction on Automatic Control* 40(11): 1931–1934.

[6] Hamaci, S., Benfekir, A. & Boimond, J.-L. [2011]. Dioid approach for performance evaluation of weighted t-systems, *16th IEEE International Conference on Emerging Technologies and Factory Automation (ETFA)*, Toulouse, France, pp. 1–8.

[7] Hamaci, S., Boimond, J.-L. & Lahaye, S. [2006]. On modeling and control of hybrid timed event graphs with multipiers using (min,+) algebra, *Journal of Discrete Event Dynamic Systems* Vol.16(No.2): 241–256.

[8] Hamaci, S., Boimond, J.-L., Lahaye, S. & Mostefaoui, M. [2004]. On the linearizability of discrete timed event graphs with multipliers using (min,+) algebra, *7th international Workshop on Discrete Event Systems (WODES)*, Reims, France, pp. 367–372.

[9] Hillion, H. [1989]. *Modélisation et analyse des systèmes de production discrets par les réseaux de Petri temporisés*, Thèse, Université de Paris IV, France.

[10] Lahaye, S. [2000]. *Contribution à l'étude des systèmes linéaires non stationnaires dans l'algèbre des dioïdes*, Thèse, LISA - Université d'Angers.

[11] Merlin, P. [1979]. Methodology for the Design and Implementation of Communication Protocole, *IEEE Transaction on Communication* Vol.24(No.6).

[12] Munier, A. [1993]. Régime asymptotique optimal d'un graphe d'événements temporisé généralisé: application à un problème d'assemblage, *APII* Vol.5(No.5): 487–513.

[13] Murata, T. [1989]. Petri nets: Properties, analysis and applications, *IEEE Proceedings* Vol.77(No.4): 541–580.

[14] Nakamura, M. & Silva, M. [1999]. Cycle time computation in deterministically timed weighted marked graphs, *IEEE-International Conference on Emerging Technologies and Factory Automation (ETFA)*, Universitat Politècnica de Catalunya, Barcelona, Spain, pp. 1037–1046.

[15] Petri, C. [1962]. *Kommunikation mit Automaten*, Phd thesis, Institut für Instrumentelle Mathematik, Bonn, Germany.

[16] Sauer, N. [2003]. Marking optimization of weighted marked graphs, *Journal of Discrete Event Dynamic Systems* Vol.13: 245–262.

[17] Trouillet, B., Benasser, A. & Gentina, J.-C. [2001]. Sur la modélisation du comportement dynamique des graphes d'événements pondérés, *in* G. Juanole & R. Valette (eds), *Conférence, Modélisation des Systèmes Réactifs (MSR),*, Hermès, Toulouse, France, pp. 447–462.

Chapter 12

A Forward On-The-Fly Approach in Controller Synthesis of Time Petri Nets

Parisa Heidari and Hanifa Boucheneb

Additional information is available at the end of the chapter

1. Introduction

Controller synthesis refers to finding a controller which is running in parallel with the system under study and preventing any violation from the given properties. Such a controller guarantees satisfaction of the desired properties; a controller makes an open-loop system to be closed-loop.

Controller synthesis can also be explained by game theory as a timed game with two players: environment and the controller. The strategy of the game determines the sequence of actions to be executed. In this context, the objective of controller synthesis is to find a strategy such that no matter what action is executed by the environment, the controller wins absolutely the game. Two main questions arise for the controller: the existence and possibility of implementation. The first question, *Control Problem* says given a system $\mathcal{S}$ and a property φ, does a controller C exist for the system $\mathcal{S}$ such that C running in parallel with $\mathcal{S}$ satisfies the property φ ($\mathcal{S}||C \models \varphi$). And the second one is the *Controller Synthesis Problem*; if the mentioned controller exists, is there a solution to implement it? First, a system should be modeled and then, synthesized regarding the desired property.

Among various models used to describe the behavior of $\mathcal{S}$, Timed Automata (*TA* in short) and Time Petri Nets (*TPN* in short) are the well-known. The properties studied in the TPN and TA for control purposes are classified in two main categories:

1. Safety properties: Whatever path is traveled, for all situations, a given set of forbidden states (or bad states) are never reached.
2. Reachability properties: Whatever path is traveled, for all situations, a state of a given set of states (good states) will eventually be reached.

Some research has been done to find algorithms to control these kinds of properties for timed models (TA and TPN), such as [10, 11, 20]. Two known methods in the literature are the backward *fix point* method and the backward/forward *on-the-fly* method. Both methods are based on computing controllable predecessors of abstract states (state zones). This computation involves some expensive operations such as computing differences between abstract states (state zones).

In this chapter, we discuss an efficient approach to check whether a safety / reachability controller in time Petri nets exists or not [13]. Our approach is a completely forward on-the-fly algorithm based on the state class graph method. Unlike approaches proposed in [10, 11, 20] based on the state zone graph method, our approach does not need to compute controllable predecessors. It consists of exploring the state class graph while extracting sequences leading to undesired states and determining subclasses to be avoided. The state class graph is a suitable choice for the forward on-the-fly exploration. Using the state class graph method, the exploration algorithm converges fast and does not need any over-approximation operation to enforce the convergence.

This chapter is organized as follows: The definition of time Petri nets and its semantics as well as the state graph method come in Section 2. In Section 3, after a short survey on the control theory, previous algorithms and related work are discussed. The algorithm proposed in this chapter is developed in Section 4. Finally, Section 5 presents the conclusion and future work.

2. Time Petri nets

2.1. Definition and behavior

A time Petri net [14] is a Petri net augmented with time intervals associated with transitions. Among the different semantics proposed for time Petri nets [18], here we focus on the classical one, called intermediate semantics in [18], in the context of mono-server and strong-semantics [7].

Formally, a *TPN* is a tuple $(P, T, Pre, Post, M_0, Is)$ where:
- P and T are finite sets of places and transitions such that $(P \cap T = \emptyset)$,
- *Pre* and *Post* are the backward and the forward incidence functions $(Pre, Post : P \times T \to \mathbb{N}$, $\mathbb{N}$ is the set of nonnegative integers),
- M_0 is the initial marking $(M_0 : P \to \mathbb{N})$, and
- Is is the static interval function $(Is : T \to \mathbb{Q}^+ \times (\mathbb{Q}^+ \cup \{\infty\}))$. $\mathbb{Q}^+$ is the set of nonnegative rational numbers. Is associates with each transition t an interval called the static firing interval of t. Bounds $\downarrow Is(t)$ and $\uparrow Is(t)$ of the interval $Is(t)$ are respectively the minimum and maximum firing delays of t.

In a controllable time Petri net, transitions are partitioned into controllable and uncontrollable transitions, denoted T_c and T_u, respectively (with $T_c \cap T_u = \emptyset$ and $T = T_c \cup T_u$). For the sake of simplicity and clarification, in this manuscript the controllable transitions are depicted as white bars, while the uncontrollable ones as black bars.

A *TPN*, is called bounded if for every reachable marking M, there is a bound $b \in \mathbb{N}^p$ where $M \leq b$ holds. In this condition p stands for the number of places in P.

Let M be a marking and t a transition. Transition t is enabled for M iff all required tokens for firing t are present in M, i.e., $\forall p \in P, M(p) \geq Pre(p, t)$. In this case, the firing of t leads to the marking M' defined by: $\forall p \in P, M'(p) = M(p) - Pre(p,t) + Post(p,t)$. We denote $En(M)$ the set of transitions enabled for M:

$$En(M) = t \in T | \forall p \in P, Pre(p,t) \leq M(p). \tag{1}$$

For $t \in En(M)$, we denote $CF(M,t)$ the set of transitions enabled in M but in conflict with t:

$$CF(M,t) = t' \in En(M) | t' = t \vee \exists p \in P, M(p) < Pre(p,t') + Pre(p,t). \tag{2}$$

Let $t \in En(M)$ and M' the successor marking of M by t, a transition t' is said to be newly enabled in M' iff t' is not enabled in the intermediate marking (i.e., $M - Pre(.,t)$) or $t' = t$. We denote $New(M',t)$ the set of transitions newly enabled M', by firing t from M:

$$New(M',t) = \{t' \in En(M') | t = t' \vee \exists p \in P, M'(p) - Post(p,t) < Pre(p,t')\}. \tag{3}$$

There are two known characterizations for the TPN state. The first one, based on clocks, associates with each transition t_i of the model a *clock* to measure the time elapsed since t_i became enabled most recently. The TPN clock state is a couple (M,ν), where M is a marking and ν is a clock valuation function, $\nu : En(M) \rightarrow \mathbb{R}^+$. For a clock state (M,ν) and $t_i \in En(M)$, $\nu(t_i)$ is the value of the clock associated with transition t_i. The initial clock state is $q_0 = (M_0, \nu_0)$ where $\nu_0(t_i) = 0$, for all $t_i \in En(M_0)$. The TPN clock state evolves either by time progression or by firing transitions. When a transition t_i becomes enabled, its clock is initialized to zero. The value of this clock increases synchronously with time until t_i is fired or disabled by the firing of another transition. t_i can fire, if the value of its clock is inside its static firing interval $Is(t_i)$. It must be fired immediately, without any additional delay, when the clock reaches $\uparrow Is(t_i)$. The firing of a transition takes no time, but may lead to another marking (required tokens disappear while produced ones appear).

Let $q = (M,\nu)$ and $q_0 = (M_0,\nu_0)$ be two clock states of the TPN model, $\theta \in \mathbb{R}^+$ and $t_f \in T$. We write $q \xrightarrow{\theta} q'$, also denoted $q + \theta$, iff state q' is reachable from state q after a time progression of θ time units, i.e.:

$$\bigwedge_{t' \in En(M)} \nu(t) + \theta \leq \uparrow Id(t_i), M' = M, and\ \forall t_j \in En(M'), \nu'(t_j) = \nu(t_j) + \theta. \tag{4}$$

We write $q \xrightarrow{t_f} q'$ iff state q' is immediately reachable from state q by firing transition t_f, i.e.: $t_f \in En(M)$, $\nu(t_f) \geq\downarrow Is(t_f)$, $\forall p \in P, M'(p) = M(p) - Pre(p,t_f) + Post(p,t_f)$, and $\forall t_i \in En(M'), \nu'(t_i) = 0$, if $t_i \in New(M',t_f)$, $\nu'(t_i) = \nu(t_i)$ otherwise.

The second characterization, based on intervals, defines the TPN state as a marking and a function which associates with each enabled transition the time interval in which the transition can fire [5].

The TPN state is defined as a pair (M, Id), where M is a marking and Id is a firing interval function ($Id : En(M) \rightarrow \mathbb{Q}^+ \times (\mathbb{Q}^+ \cup \{\infty\})$). The initial state is (M_0, Id_0) where M_0 is the initial marking and $Id_0(t) = Is(t)$, for $t \in En(M_0)$.

Let (M, Id) and (M', Id') be two states of the TPN model, $\theta \in \mathbb{R}^+$ and $t \in T$. The transition relation $\longrightarrow$ over states is defined as follows:

- $(M, Id) \xrightarrow{\theta} (M', Id')$, also denoted $(M, Id) + \theta$, iff from state (M, Id), we will reach the state (M', Id') by a time progression of θ units, i.e., $\bigwedge_{t' \in En(M)} \theta \leq \uparrow Id(t'), M' = M$, and $\forall t'' \in En(M'), Id'(t'') = [Max(\downarrow Id(t'') - \theta, 0), \uparrow Id(t'') - \theta]$.
- $(M, Id) \xrightarrow{t} (M', Id')$ iff the state (M', Id') is reachable from state (M, Id) by firing immediately transition t , i.e., $t \in En(M), \downarrow Id(t) = 0, \forall p \in P, M'(p) = M(p) - Pre(p,t) + Post(p,t)$, and $\forall t' \in En(M'), Id'(t') = Is(t')$, if $t' \in New(M', t), Id'(t') = Id(t')$, otherwise.

The TPN state space is the structure $(\mathcal{Q}, \longrightarrow, q_0)$, where $q_0 = (M_0, Id_0)$ is the initial state of the TPN and $\mathcal{Q} = \{q | q_0 \xrightarrow{*} q\}$ ($\xrightarrow{*}$ being the reflexive and transitive closure of the relation $\longrightarrow$ defined above) is the set of reachable states of the model.

A *run* in the TPN state space $(\mathcal{Q}, \longrightarrow, q_0)$, of a state $q \in \mathcal{Q}$, is a maximal sequence $\rho = q_1 \xrightarrow{\theta_1} q_1 + \theta_1 \xrightarrow{t_1} q_2 \xrightarrow{\theta_2} q_2 + \theta_2 \xrightarrow{t_2} q_3 ...$, such that $q_1 = q$. By convention, for any state q_i, relation $q_i \xrightarrow{0} q_i$ holds. The sequence $\theta_1 t_1 \theta_2 t_2 ...$ is called the timed trace of ρ. The sequence $t_1 t_2 ...$ is called the firing sequence (untimed trace) of ρ. A marking M is reachable iff $\exists q \in \mathcal{Q}$ s.t. its marking is M. Runs (resp. timed / untimed traces) of the TPN are all runs (resp. timed / untimed traces) of the initial state q_0.

To use enumerative analysis techniques with time Petri nets, an extra effort is required to abstract their generally infinite state spaces. Abstraction techniques aim to construct by removing some irrelevant details, a finite contraction of the state space of the model, which preserves properties of interest. For best performances, the contraction should also be the smallest possible and computed with minor resources too (time and space). The preserved properties are usually verified using standard analysis techniques on the abstractions [16].

Several state space abstraction methods have been proposed, in the literature, for time Petri nets like the *state class graph (SCG)* [4], the *zone based graph (ZBG)* [6], and etc. These abstractions may differ mainly in the characterization of states (interval states or clock states), the agglomeration criteria of states, the representation of the agglomerated states (abstract states), the kind of properties they preserve (markings, linear or branching properties) and their size.

These abstractions are finite for all bounded time Petri nets. However, if only linear properties are of interest, abstractions based on clocks are less interesting than the interval based abstractions. Indeed, abstractions based on intervals are finite for bounded TPN with unbounded intervals, while this is not true for abstraction based on clocks. The finiteness is enforced using an approximation operation, which may involve some overhead computation.

2.2. Zone Based Graph

In the Zone Based Graph (ZBG)[6], all clock states reachable by runs supporting the same firing sequence are agglomerated in the same node and considered modulo some over-approximation operation [2, 12]. This operation is used to ensure the finiteness of the ZBG for Bounded TPNs with unbounded firing intervals. An abstract state, called state zone, is defined as a pair $\beta = (M, FZ)$ combining a marking M and a formula FZ which characterizes the clock domains of all states agglomerated in the state zone. In FZ, the clock of each enabled transition for M is represented by a variable with the same name. The domain of FZ is convex and has a unique canonical form represented by the pair (M, Z), where Z is a DBM of order $|En(M) \cup \{o\}$ defined by: $\forall (x,y) \in (En(M) \cup \{o\})^2$, $z_{xy} = Sup_{FZ}(x - y)$, where o represents the value 0. State zones of the ZBG are in relaxed form.

The initial state zone is the pair $\beta_0 = (M_0, FZ_0)$, where M_0 is the initial marking and $FZ_0 = \bigwedge_{t_i,t_j \in En(M_0)} 0 \leq ti = tj \leq \bigwedge_{t_u \in En(M_0)} \uparrow I_s(t_u)$.

As an example, consider the TPN given in [11] and reported at Figure 1, its state zone graph is reported at Figure 2 and its state zones are reported in Table 1.

In this document, we consider the state class method and study the possibility to enforce the behavior of a given TPN so that to satisfy a safety / reachability property. The idea is to construct on-the-fly the reachable state classes of the TPN while collecting progressively firing subintervals to be avoided so that to satisfy the properties of interest.

2.3. The state class graph method

In the state class graph method [4], all states reachable by the same firing sequence from the initial state are agglomerated in the same node and considered modulo the relation of equivalence defined by: Two sets of states are equivalent iff they have the same marking and the same firing domain. The firing domain of a set of states is the union of the firing domains of its states. All equivalent sets are agglomerated in the same node called a *state class* defined as a pair $\alpha = (M, F)$, where M is a marking and F is a formula which characterizes the firing domain of α. For each transition t_i enabled in M, there is a variable $\underline{t_i}$, in F, representing its firing delay. F can be rewritten as a set of atomic constraints of the form[1]: $\underline{t_i} - \underline{t_j} \leq c$, $\underline{t_i} \leq c$ or $-\underline{t_j} \leq c$, where t_i, t_j are transitions, $c \in \mathbb{Q} \cup \{\infty\}$ and $\mathbb{Q}$ is the set of rational numbers.

Though the same domain may be expressed by different conjunctions of atomic constraints (i.e., different formulas), all equivalent formulas have a unique form, called canonical form that is usually encoded by a difference bound matrix (DBM) [3]. The canonical form of F is encoded by the DBM D (a square matrix) of order $|En(M)| + 1$ defined by: $\forall t_i, t_j \in En(M) \cup \{t_0\}, d_{ij} = (\leq, Sup_F(\underline{t_i} - \underline{t_j}))$, where t_0 ($t_0 \notin T$) represents a fictitious transition whose delay is always equal to 0 and $Sup_F(\underline{t_i} - \underline{t_j})$ is the largest value of $\underline{t_i} - \underline{t_j}$ in the domain of F. Its computation is based on the shortest path *Floyd-Warshall*'s algorithm and is considered as the most costly operation (cubic in the number of variables in F). The canonical form of a DBM makes easier some operations over formulas like the test of equivalence. Two formulas are equivalent iff the canonical forms of their DBMs are identical.

The initial state class is $\alpha_0 = (M_0, F_0)$, where $F_0 = \bigwedge_{t_i \in En(M_0)} \downarrow Is(t_i) \leq \underline{t_i} \leq \uparrow Is(t_i)$.

Let $\alpha = (M, F)$ be a state class and t_f a transition and $succ(\alpha, t_f)$ the set of states defined by:

$$succ(\alpha, t_f) = \{q' \in \mathcal{Q} \mid \exists q \in \alpha, \exists \theta \in \mathbb{R}^+ \text{ s.t. } q \xrightarrow{\theta} q + \theta \xrightarrow{t_f} q'\} \quad (5)$$

[1] For economy of notation, we use operator $\leq$ even if $c = \infty$.

$\beta_0 : p_1 + p_2$	$0 \le \underline{t_1} = \underline{t_2} \le 3$
$\beta_1 : p_2 + p_3$	$0 \le \underline{t_2} \le 3 \wedge 0 \le \underline{t_3} \le 3 \wedge 0 \le \underline{t_2} - \underline{t_3} \le 3$
$\beta_2 : p_1 + p_4$	$2 \le \underline{t_1} \le 4$
$\beta_3 : p_3 + p_4$	$0 \le \underline{t_3} \le 3 \wedge 0 \le \underline{t_4} \le 1 \wedge 0 \le \underline{t_3} - \underline{t_4} \le 3$
$\beta_4 : p_2$	$2 \le \underline{t_2} \le 3$
$\beta_5 : p_3 + p_4$	$0 \le \underline{t_3} = \underline{t_4} \le 2$
$\beta_6 : p_4$	

Table 1. State zones of the TPN presented at Figure 2

The state class α has a successor by t_f (i.e. $succ(\alpha, t_f) \neq \emptyset$), iff t_f is enabled in M and can be fired before any other enabled transition, i.e., the following formula is consistent[2]: $F \wedge (\bigwedge_{t_i \in En(M)} \underline{t_f} \le \underline{t_i})$. In this case, the firing of t_f leads to the state class $\alpha' = (M', F') = succ(\alpha, t_f)$ computed as follows [4]:

1. $\forall p \in P, M'(p) = M(p) - Pre(p, t_f) + Post(p, t_f)$.
2. $F' = F \wedge (\bigwedge_{t_i \in En(M)} \underline{t_f} - \underline{t_i} \le 0)$
3. Replace in F' each $\underline{t_i} \neq \underline{t_f}$, by $(\underline{t_i} + \underline{t_f})$.
4. Eliminate by substitution $\underline{t_f}$ and each $\underline{t_i}$ of transition conflicting with t_f in M.
5. Add constraint $\downarrow Is(t_n) \le \underline{t_n} \le \uparrow Is(t_n)$, for each transition $t_n \in New(M', t_f)$.

Formally, the SCG of a TPN model is a structure $(CC, \longrightarrow, \alpha_0)$, where $\alpha_0 = (M_0, F_0)$ is the initial state class, $\forall t_i \in T, \alpha \xrightarrow{t_i} \alpha'$ iff $\alpha' = succ(\alpha, t_i) \neq \emptyset$ and $CC = \{\alpha | \alpha_0 \xrightarrow{*} \alpha\}$.

The SCG is finite for all bounded TPNs and preserves linear properties [5]. As an example, Figure 2 shows the state class graph of the TPN presented at Figure 1. Its state classes are reported in Table 2. For this example, state class graph and state zone based graph of the system are identical while classes and zones are different.

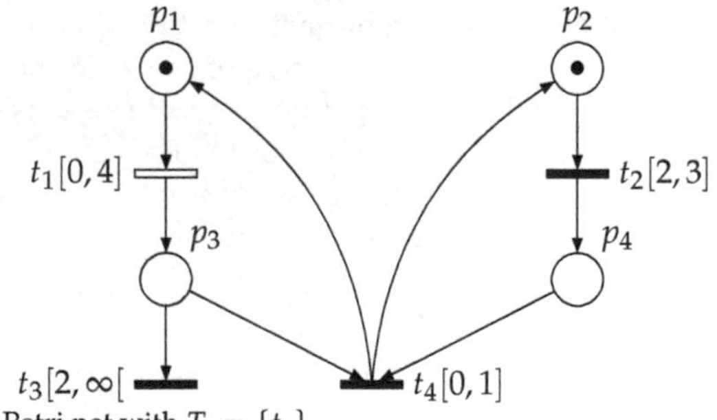

Figure 1. A simple Petri net with $T_c = \{t_1\}$

[2] A formula F is consistent iff there is, at least, one tuple of values that satisfies, at once, all constraints of F.

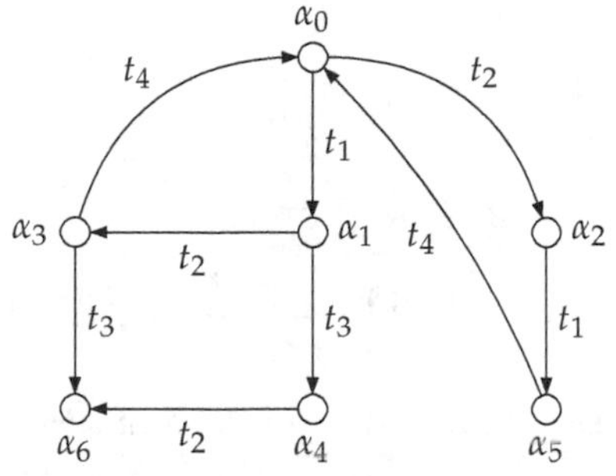

Figure 2. The State Graph of the TPN presented at Figure 1

$\alpha_0 : p_1 + p_2$	$0 \leq \underline{t_1} \leq 4 \wedge 2 \leq \underline{t_2} \leq 3$
$\alpha_1 : p_2 + p_3$	$0 \leq \underline{t_2} \leq 3 \wedge 2 \leq \underline{t_3}$
$\alpha_2 : p_1 + p_4$	$0 \leq \underline{t_1} \leq 2$
$\alpha_3 : p_3 + p_4$	$0 \leq \underline{t_3} \wedge 0 \leq \underline{t_4} \leq 1$
$\alpha_4 : p_2$	$0 \leq \underline{t_2} \leq 1$
$\alpha_5 : p_3 + p_4$	$2 \leq \underline{t_3} < \infty \wedge 0 \leq \underline{t_4} \leq 1$
$\alpha_6 : p_4$	

Table 2. The state classes of the TPN presented at Figure 2

2.4. A forward method for computing predecessors of state classes

Let $\alpha = (M, F)$ be a state class and $\omega \in T^+$ a sequence of transitions firable from α. We denote $succ(\alpha, \omega)$ the state class reachable from α by firing successively transitions of ω. We define inductively this set as follows: $succ(\alpha, \omega) = \alpha$, if $\omega = \epsilon$ and $succ(\alpha, \omega) = succ(succ(\alpha, \omega'), t_i)$, if $\omega = \omega'.t_i$.

During the firing of a sequence of transitions ω from α, the same transition may be newly enabled several times. To distinguish between different enabling of the same transition t_i, we denote t_i^k for $k > 0$ the transition t_i (newly) enabled by the kth transition of the sequence; t_i^0 denotes the transition t_i enabled in M. Let $\omega = t_1^{k_1}....t_m^{k_m} \in T^+$ with $m > 0$ be a sequence of transitions firable from α (i.e., $succ(\alpha, \omega) \neq \emptyset$). We denote $Fire(\alpha, \omega)$ the largest subclass α' of α (i.e., $\alpha' \subseteq \alpha$) s.t. ω is firable from all its states, i.e.,

$$Fire(\alpha, \omega) = \{q_1 \in \alpha \mid \exists \theta_1, ..., \theta_m, q_1 \xrightarrow{\theta_1} q_1 + \theta_1 \xrightarrow{t_1^{k_1}} q_2...q_m + \theta_m \xrightarrow{t_m^{k_m}} q_{m+1}\} \quad (6)$$

Proposition 1. *$Fire(\alpha, \omega)$ is the state class (M', F') where $M' = M$ and F' can be computed as follows*[3]*: Let $M_1 = M$ and M_{f+1}, for $f \in [1, m]$, be the marking reached from M by the subsequence $t_1^{k_1}....t_f^{k_f}$ of ω.*

1. *Initialize F' with the formula obtained from F by renaming all variables $\underline{t_i}$ in $\underline{t_i^0}$.*

[3] We suppose that the truth value of an empty set of constraints is always true.

2. *Add the following constraints:*

$$\bigwedge_{f\in[1,m]} \Big(\bigwedge_{t_i\in(En(M_1)-\bigcup_{j\in[1,f[} CF(M_j,t_j))} \underline{t}_f^{k_f} - \underline{t}_i^0 \leq 0 \wedge \\ \bigwedge_{j\in[1,f[,t_n\in(New(M_{j+1},t_j)-\bigcup_{k\in]j,f[} CF(M_k,t_k))} \underline{t}_f^{k_f} - \underline{t}_n^j \leq 0 \wedge \\ \bigwedge_{t_n\in New(M_{f+1},t_f)} \downarrow Is(t_n) \leq \underline{t}_n^f - \underline{t}_f^{k_f} \leq \uparrow Is(t_n) \Big) \quad (7)$$

3. *Put the resulting formula in canonical form and eliminate all variables $\underline{t}_i^j$ such that $j > 0$, rename all variables $\underline{t}_i^0$ in $\underline{t}_i$.*

Note that $Fire(\alpha,\omega) \neq \emptyset$ (i.e., ω is firable from α) iff ω is feasible in the underlying untimed model and the formula obtained at step 2) above is consistent.

Proof. By step 1) all variables associated with transitions of $En(M)$ are renamed ($\underline{t}_i$ is renamed in $\underline{t}_i^0$). This step allows us to distinguish between delays of transitions enabled in M from those that are newly enabled by the transitions of the firing sequence.

Step 2) adds the firing constraints of transitions of the sequence (for $f \in [1,m]$). For each transition $t_f^{k_f}$ of the sequence, three blocks of constraints are added. The two first blocks mean that the delay of $t_f^{k_f}$ must be less or equal to the delays of all transitions enabled in M_f (i.e., transitions of $En(M)$ and those enabled by t_j $(New(M_{j+1},t_j), 1 \leq j < f)$ that are maintained continuously enabled at least until firing $t_f^{k_f}$). Transitions of $En(M)$ that are maintained continuously enabled at least until firing $t_f^{k_f}$ are transitions of $En(M)$ which are not in conflict with $t_1^{k_1}$ in M_1, and, ..., and not in conflict with $t_{f-1}^{k_{f-1}}$ in M_{f-1}. Similarly, transitions of $New(M_j,t_j)$ (with $1 \leq j < f$) that are maintained continuously enabled at least until firing $t_f^{k_f}$ are transitions of $New(M_{j+1},t_j)$ which are not in conflict with $t_{j+1}^{k_{j+1}}$ in M_{j+1}, and, ..., and not in conflict with $t_{f-1}^{k_{f-1}}$ in M_{f-1}. The third block of constraints specifies the firing delays of transitions that are newly enabled by $t_f^{k_f}$.

Step 3) isolates the largest subclass of α such that ω is firable from all its states. □

As an example, consider the TPN depicted at Figure 1 and its state class graph shown at Figure 2. Let us show how to compute $Fire(\alpha_0, t_1^0 t_2^0 t_3^1)$. We have $En(M_0) = \{t_1,t_2\}$, $CF(M_0,t_1) = \{t_1\}$, $CF(M_1,t_2) = \{t_2\}$, $New(M_0,t_1) = \{t_3\}$ and $New(M_1,t_2) = \{t_4\}$. The subclass $(p_1 + p_2, F') = Fire(\alpha_0, t_1^0 t_2^0 t_3^1)$ is computed as follows:

1. Initialize F' with the formula obtained from $0 \leq \underline{t}_1 \leq 4 \wedge 2 \leq \underline{t}_2 \leq 3$ by renaming all variables $\underline{t}_i$ in $\underline{t}_i^0$: $0 \leq \underline{t}_1^0 \leq 4 \wedge 2 \leq \underline{t}_2^0 \leq 3$

2. Add the firing constraints of t_1 before t_2, t_2 before t_3 and constraints on the firing intervals of transitions enabled by these firings (i.e., t_3 and t_4):

$$\underline{t}_1^0 - \underline{t}_2^0 \leq 0 \wedge \underline{t}_2^0 - \underline{t}_3^1 \leq 0 \wedge 2 \leq \underline{t}_3^1 - \underline{t}_1^0 \wedge 0 \leq \underline{t}_4^2 - \underline{t}_2^0 \leq 1$$

3. Put the resulting formula in canonical form and eliminate all variables $\underline{t}_i^j$ such that $j > 0$, rename all variables $\underline{t}_i^0$ in $\underline{t}_i$: $0 \leq \underline{t}_1 \leq 2 \wedge 2 \leq \underline{t}_2 \leq 3 \wedge 1 \leq \underline{t}_2 - \underline{t}_1 \leq 3$.

The subclass $Fire(\alpha_0, t_1^0 t_2^0 t_3^1)$ consists of all states of α_0 from which the sequence $t_1 t_2 t_3$ is firable. If t_1 is controllable, to avoid reaching the marking p_4 by the sequence $t_1 t_2 t_3$, it suffices to choose the firing interval of t_1 in α_0 outside its firing interval in $Fire(\alpha_0, t_1^0 t_2^0 t_3^1)$ (i.e., $]2, 4]$).

Note that this forward method of computing predecessors can also be adapted and applied to the clock based abstractions. For instance, using the zone based graph, the initial state zone of the TPN shown at Figure 1 is $\beta_0 = (p_1 + p_2, 0 \leq \underline{t}_1 = \underline{t}_2 \leq 3)$. The sub-zone β_0' of β_0, from which the sequence $t_1 t_2 t_3$ is firable, can be computed in a similar way as the previous procedure where delay constraints are replaced by clock constraints:

$\beta_0' = (p_1 + p_2, 0 \leq \underline{t}_1 = \underline{t}_2 \leq 2)$. To avoid reaching by the sequence $t_1 t_2 t_3$ the marking p_4, it suffices to delay the firing of t_1 until when its clocks overpasses 2, which means that its firing interval should be $]2, 4]$.

3. Related work

The theory of control was initially introduced by Ramadge and Wonham in [17]. They have formalized, in terms of formal languages, the notion of control and the existence of a controller that forces a discrete event system (DES) to behave as expected. The concept of control has been afterwards extended to various models such as timed automata [21] and time Petri nets [19], where the control specification is expressed on the model states rather than the model language. Thus, for every system modeled by a controllable language, timed automata or time Petri nets, controller synthesis is used to restrict the behavior of the system making it to satisfy the desired safety or reachability properties. The typical procedure is: a system is modeled, the desired properties are defined, then, the existence and the implementation of the appropriate controller (control problem and controller synthesis problem respectively [1]) are investigated.

Several approaches of controller synthesis have been proposed in the literature. They may differ in the model they are working on (various types of Petri nets or automata), the approach they are based on (analytical as in [22], structural as in [9], semantic as in [10, 11, 20]), and finally the property to be controlled.

In [22], the authors have considered a particular type of capacity timed Petri net, where timing constraints are associated with transitions and some places, and all transitions are controllable. This timed Petri net is used to model a cluster tool with wafer residency time constraints. The wafers and their time constraints are represented by timed places. Using analytical approaches of schedulability and the particular structure of their model (model of the cluster tool), the authors have established an algorithm for finding, if it exists, an optimal periodic schedule which respects residency time constraints of wafers. The control consists

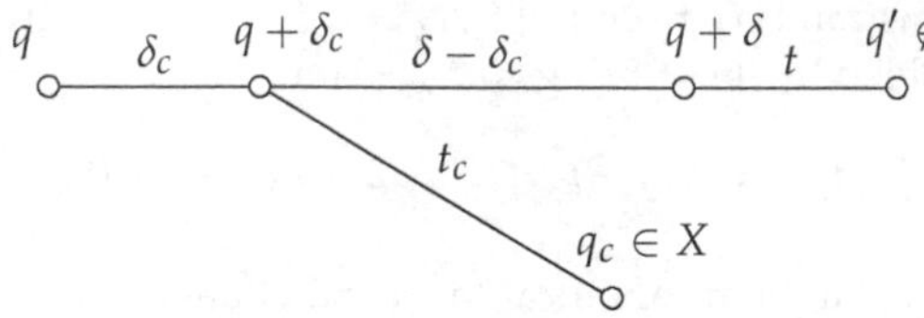

Figure 3. Controllable Predecessors

of limiting timing constraints of transitions and some places so as to respect residency time constraints of wafers.

In [8, 9], the authors have considered safe and live time Petri nets where deadlines can be associated with some transition firings. The control consists of enforcing the model to meet deadlines of transition firings. The controller has the possibility to disable any transition t which prevents to meet the deadline of a transition t_d. A transition t is allowed to fire only if its latency (the maximum delay between firing t and the next firing of t_d) is not greater than the current deadline of t_d. The latencies of transitions are computed by constructing an unfolding Petri net of the underlying untimed Petri net. This approach does not need to explore the state space. However, in general, the resulting controller is not maximally permissive (i.e. meaning that the controller may disable a net behavior that does not violate the properties of interest).

In [10, 11, 20], the authors have considered timed models (TA or TPN) with two kinds of transitions (controllable and uncontrollable) and investigated the control problem for safety or reachability properties. To prevent some undesired states, the controller can act on any firable and controllable transition by delaying or forcing its firing but it cannot disable transitions. The control problem is addressed by computing the winning states of the model, i.e. states which will not lead, by an uncontrollable transition, to an undesired state. The computation of the winning states is based on the concept of controllable predecessors of states. In the literature, the set of controllable predecessors is usually denoted by $\pi(X)$, where X is a set of states satisfying the desired property (safe/goal states). The set $\pi(X)$ is defined by [11]:

$$
\begin{aligned}
&\pi(X) = \{q \in \mathcal{Q} | ((\exists\, \delta \in \mathbb{R}_{\geq 0}, t \in T\; q' \in X\; q \xrightarrow{\delta}\xrightarrow{t} q') \vee \\
&(\exists\, \delta \in \mathbb{R}_{\geq 0}, q' \in X\; q \xrightarrow{\delta} q')) \wedge \\
&\forall\, \delta \in \mathbb{R}_{\geq 0}\; if\; \exists\, t \in T, q' \notin X\; q \xrightarrow{\delta}\xrightarrow{t} q' \\
&then\; \exists\, \delta_c < \delta, t_c \in T_c,\; q_c \in X\; q \xrightarrow{\delta_c}\xrightarrow{t_c} q_c\}
\end{aligned} \tag{8}
$$

Intuitively, $\pi(X)$ is the set of predecessors of X which will not bring the system out of X. Figure 3 clarifies this concept. If the environment can execute an uncontrollable transition after δ time units, leading the system out of X (denoted by $\bar{X}$), then the controller should be able to execute a controllable action to keep the system in X before δ time units. In addition, in the context of timed models with strong semantics (a transition must be fired, without any additional delay, when the upper bound of its firing interval is reached), the controller should not be forced to execute a controllable transition leading the system out of X.

Let $AG\,\phi$ be a safety property and $X_0 = Sat(\phi)$ the set of states which satisfy the property ϕ (safe states). The fix point of $X_{i+1} = h(X_i) = X_i \cap \pi(X_i), i \geq 0$ gives the largest set of safe states whose behaviors can be controlled so as to maintain the system inside this set of states (i.e., winning states). If the largest fix point of h includes the initial state then, it gives a controller which forces the system to stay in safe states (i.e., a winning strategy).

Similarly, the fix point method is also used for reachability properties. Let $AF\ \psi$ be a reachability property and $X_0 = Sat(\psi)$ the set of goal states. The least fix point of $X_{i+1} = h(X_i) = X_i \cup \pi(X_i), i \geq 0$ is the set of states whose behaviors can be controlled so as to reach one of the goal states (i.e., winning states) [10, 20].

In the context of a timed model, this technique is applied on a state space abstraction of the timed model. In this case, X_i is a set of abstract states. If X_i is a finite set of abstract states, then the controllable predecessors of X_i is also a finite set of abstract states. The computation of the fix point of h will converge after a finite number of steps if the state space abstraction is finite [10, 11, 20].

Note that the state space abstractions used in [10, 11, 20] are based on clocks but the state space abstraction used in [11] is not necessarily complete. The fix point method cannot guarantee to give the safety controller when it exists, unless the state space abstraction is both sound and complete. A state space abstraction of a given model is sound and complete iff it captures all firing sequences of the model and each firing sequence in the state space abstraction reflects a firing sequence of the model. Indeed, a synthesis may fail because of some unreachable states, while for the reachable state space the safety controller exists. However, the cost of processing is increased as a sound and complete state space abstraction should be entirely calculated before applying the fix point algorithm.

Let us explain by means of an example how to compute the fix point of h for a safety property. Consider the TPN given in [11] and reported in Figure 1. The state class graph (SCG) and the zone based graph (ZBG) of this TPN are equal, except that nodes are defined differently (state classes or state zones). The state class graph is depicted in Figure 2. Its state zones and state classes are reported in Table 1 and Table 2, respectively.

Consider the state zone graph and suppose that we are interested to force the following safety property: $AG\ \Sigma_{i=1}^{4} p_i = 2$ which means that the number of tokens in the TPN is always 2. The transition t_1 is the only controllable transition and the forbidden markings is determined by $\Sigma_{i=1}^{4} p_i \neq 2$. As the state class graph shows, if t_2 happens before t_1 the right path happens which is safe and the controller has nothing to do. On the other hand, if t_1 happens before t_2, two state classes having forbidden markings may be reached (α_4, α_6).

To verify whether or not there is a controller for such a property, we compute the fix point of $X_{i+1} = h(X_i) = X_i \cap \pi(X_i)$, where $X_0 = \{\beta_0, \beta_1, \beta_2, \beta_3, \beta_5\}$ is the set of state zones which satisfy the property *not* $p_1 + p_3 = 0$. Such a controller exists iff the initial state of the model is a winning state (i.e., belongs to the fix point of h). The fix point is computed, in 3 iterations, as follows:

1) Iteration 1: $X_1 = X_0 \cap \pi(X_0) = \{\beta_0, \beta_1', \beta_2, \beta_3', \beta_5\}$. In this iteration, all states of β_1 and β_3, which are uncontrollable predecessors of bad state classes β_4 and β_6 are eliminated:

$\beta_1' = (p_2 + p_3, 1 < \underline{t}_2 \leq 3 \wedge 0 \leq \underline{t}_3 < 2 \wedge 1 < \underline{t}_2 - \underline{t}_3 \leq 3)$ and

$\beta_3' = (p_3 + p_4, 1 \leq \underline{t}_3 <\leq 3 \wedge 0 < \underline{t}_4 \leq 1 \wedge 1 \leq \underline{t}_3 - \underline{t}_4 \leq 3)$.

2) Iteration 2: $X_2 = X_1 \cap \pi(X_1) = \{\beta_0, \beta_1'', \beta_2, \beta_3', \beta_5\}$. This iteration eliminates from β_1' all states, which are uncontrollable predecessors of bad states of $\beta_3 - \beta_3'$:

$\beta_1'' = \{p_2 + p_3, 2 < \underline{t}_2 \leq 3 \wedge 0 \leq \underline{t}_3 < 1 \wedge 2 \leq \underline{t}_2 - \underline{t}_3 \leq 3\}$.

3) Iteration 3: $X_2 = X_2 \cap \pi(X_2) = \{\beta_0, \beta_1'', \beta_2, \beta_3', \beta_5\}$. The fix point X_2 is then the set of winning states. Since the initial state zone belongs to X_2, there is a controller for forcing the property *AG not* $p_1 + p_3 = 0$. To keep the model in safe states (in states of X_2), the controller must delay, in β_0, the firing of t_1 until its clock overpasses the value 2. Doing so, the successor of β_0 by t_1 will be β_1''.

This approach needs however to construct a state space abstraction before computing the set of winning states. To overcome this limitation, in [10, 20], the authors have investigated the use of on-the-fly algorithms besides the fix point to compute the winning states for timed game automata (timed automata with controllable and uncontrollable transitions). We report, in Fig 4, the on-the-fly algorithm given in [10] for the case of reachability properties and timed game automata. This algorithm uses three lists *Passed* containing all state zones explored so far, *Waiting*, containing the set of edges to be processed and *Depend* indicating, for each state zone S, the set of edges to be reevaluated in case the set of the winning states in S ($Win[S]$) is updated. Using this on-the-fly method, in each step, a part of the state zone graph is constructed and an edge $e = (S, a, S')$ of the *Waiting* list is processed. If the state zone S' is not in *Passed* and there is, in S', some states which satisfy the desired reachability property, then these states are added to the winning states of S' ($Win[S']$). The winning states of S will be recomputed later (the edge e is added to the *Waiting* list). If S' is in *Passed,* the set of the winning states of S ($Win[S]$) is recomputed and possibly those of its predecessors and so on. The set $Win[S]$ is the largest subset of S which is included in the controllable predecessors of the winning states of all its successors.

This on-the-fly algorithm, based on computing controllable predecessors, requires some expensive operations such as the difference between abstract states (state zones). The difference between two state zones is not necessarily a state zone and then may result in several state zones which need to be handled separately.

In this chapter, we propose another on-the-fly approach which does not need this expensive operation. Our approach differs from the previous ones by the fact it computes bad states (i.e.: states which may lead to an undesired state) instead of computing the winning states and it constructs a state class graph instead of a state zone graph. In addition, the bad states are computed, using a forward approach, for only state classes containing at least a controllable transition.

4. An on-the-fly algorithm for investigating the existence of a controller for a TPN

This chapter aims to propose an efficient forward on-the-fly method based on the state class graph for checking the existence of a safety/reachability controller for a TPN. As discussed earlier, the state class graph is a good alternative for the on-the-fly algorithms as the exploration converges fast and does not need any over-approximation operation to enforce the convergence. The method, proposed here, is completely a forward and does not compute

Initialization:

$Passed \leftarrow \{S_0\}$ **where** $S_0 = \{(\ell_0, \vec{0})\}^{\nearrow}$;
$Waiting \leftarrow \{(S_0, \alpha, S') \mid S' = \mathsf{Post}_\alpha(S_0)^{\nearrow}\}$;
$Win[S_0] \leftarrow S_0 \cap (\{\mathsf{Goal}\} \times \mathbb{R}^X_{\geq 0})$;
$Depend[S_0] \leftarrow \emptyset$;

Main:

while $((Waiting \neq \emptyset) \wedge (s_0 \notin Win[S_0]))$ **do**
$e = (S, \alpha, S') \leftarrow pop(Waiting)$;
if $S' \notin Passed$ **then**
$Passed \leftarrow Passed \cup \{S'\}$;
$Depend[S'] \leftarrow \{(S, \alpha, S')\}$;
$Win[S'] \leftarrow S' \cap (\{\mathsf{Goal}\} \times \mathbb{R}^X_{\geq 0})$;
$Waiting \leftarrow Waiting \cup \{(S', \alpha, S'') \mid S'' = \mathsf{Post}_\alpha(S')^{\nearrow}\}$;
if $Win[S'] \neq \emptyset$ **then** $Waiting \leftarrow Waiting \cup \{e\}$;
else (* **reevaluate** *)[a]
$Win^* \leftarrow \mathsf{Pred}_t(Win[S] \cup \bigcup_{S \xrightarrow{c} T} \mathsf{Pred}_c(Win[T]),$
$\bigcup_{S \xrightarrow{u} T} \mathsf{Pred}_u(T \setminus Win[T])) \cap S$;
if $(Win[S] \subsetneq Win^*)$ **then**
$Waiting \leftarrow Waiting \cup Depend[S]$; $Win[S] \leftarrow Win^*$;
$Depend[S'] \leftarrow Depend[S'] \cup \{e\}$;
endif
endwhile

[a] When $T \notin Passed, Win[T] = \emptyset$

Figure 4. On-the-fly algorithm for timed game automata proposed in [10]

controllable predecessors (which is considered as an expensive operation). To explain the method, we start with safety properties.

Let us introduce informally the principle of our approach by means of the previous example. Consider the TPN shown in Figure 1, its state class graph depicted in Figure 2 and its state classes reported in Table 2. Our goal is to avoid to reach bad states (i.e., state classes α_4 and α_6) by choosing appropriately the firing intervals for controllable transitions.

From the initial state class α_0, there are two elementary paths $\alpha_0 t_1 \alpha_1 t_3 \alpha_4$ and $\alpha_0 t_1 \alpha_1 t_2 \alpha_3 t_3 \alpha_6$ that lead to bad states. In both paths, there is only one state class (α_0) where the controllable transition t_1 is firable. To avoid these bad paths, we propose to compute all states of α_0 from which $t_1 t_3$ or $t_1 t_2 t_3$ is firable, i.e., $B(\alpha_0) = Fire(\alpha_0, t_1 t_3) \cup Fire(\alpha_0, t_1 t_2 t_3)$, where:

$Fire(\alpha_0, t_1 t_3) = (p_1 + p_2, 0 \leq \underline{t_1} \leq 1 \wedge 2 \leq \underline{t_2} \leq 3 \wedge 2 \leq \underline{t_2} - \underline{t_1} \leq 3)$ and

$Fire(\alpha_0, t_1 t_2 t_3) = (p_1 + p_2, 0 \leq \underline{t_1} \leq 2 \wedge 2 \leq \underline{t_2} \leq 3 \wedge 1 \leq \underline{t_2} - \underline{t_1} \leq 3)$.

To avoid these bad states, it suffices to replace in α_0, the firing interval of t_1 with $]2, 4]$. This interval is the complement of $[0, 2] \cup [0, 1]$ in the firing interval of t_1 in α_0 ($[0, 4]$).
The approach we propose in the following section, is a combination of this principle with a forward on-the-fly method.

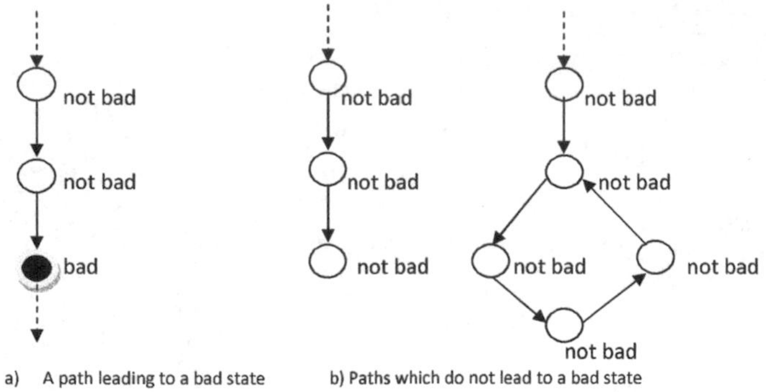

Figure 5. Path satisfying or not a safety property. Black states should be avoided.

4.1. Controller for safety properties

A controller for safety properties running in parallel with the system should satisfy the property '*AG not bad*' where 'bad' stands for the set of states having a forbidden marking and it means that 'bad' states will never happen. We introduce here an algorithm to re-constrain the controllable transitions and reach a safe net.

The idea is to construct, using a forward on-the-fly method, the state class graph of the TPN to determine whether controllable transitions have to be constrained, in order to avoid forbidden markings. This method computes and explores, path by path, the state class graph of a TPN looking for the sequences leading the system to any forbidden marking (bad sequences or bad paths). And using Proposition 1, we get the subclasses causing the bad states happening later through the found sequences (bad subclasses). We restrict the domain of controllable transitions in the state class where they were enabled so as to avoid its bad subclasses. The restriction of the interval of a controllable transition t of a state class α is obtained by subtracting from its interval in α ($INT(\alpha, t)$), intervals of t in its bad subclasses.

Before describing the procedure formally, we define an auxiliary operation over intervals to be used in the algorithm. Let I and I' be two nonempty (real) intervals. We denote $I \oplus I'$ intervals defined by:

$$\forall a \in \mathbb{R}, a \in I \oplus I' iff \exists b \in I, \exists c \in I', a = b + c. \tag{9}$$

As an example, for $I = [1,4]$ and $I' =]2,5]$, $I \oplus I' =]3,9]$. And also

$$LI(\alpha) = \{(t_c, t_s, BI) | t_c \in En_c(M), t_s \in En_c^0(M); BI = \bigcup_{\omega \in \Omega(\alpha)} INT(Fire(\alpha,\omega), \underline{t}_c - \underline{t}_s) \neq INT(\alpha, \underline{t}_c - \underline{t}_s)\} \tag{10}$$

This method is presented in the algorithms 1 and 2. The symbol T_c refers to the set of controllable transitions and all forbidden markings of the net are saved in a set called, *bad*. The list *Passed* is used to retrieve the set of state classes processed so far, their bad sequences, and the bad intervals of controllable transitions (their domains in bad subclasses). Function *main* consists of an initialization step and a calling to the recursive function *explore*. The call $explore(\alpha_0, \emptyset, \{\alpha_0\})$ returns the set of bad sequences that cannot be avoided, from α_0, by restricting firing domains of controllable transitions. If this set is nonempty, it means that such a controller does not exist. Otherwise, it exists and the algorithm guarantees that for each state class α with some bad sequences, there is a possibility to choose appropriately the firing intervals of some controllable transitions so as to avoid all bad subclasses of α. The control of α consists of eliminating, from the firing intervals of such controllable transitions, all parts figuring in its bad subclasses. The restriction of domains is also applied on firing delays between two controllable transitions of α. We get in *Ctrl*, all possibilities of controlling each state class. In case there is only one controllable transition in α, its delay with a fictitious transition whose time variable is fixed at 0 is considered.

Each element of *Passed* is a triplet $(\alpha, \Omega(\alpha), LI(\alpha))$ where $\alpha = (M, F)$ is a state class s.t. $M \notin bad$, $\Omega(\alpha)$ is the set of bad sequences of α, which cannot be avoided, independently of α, from its successors, and $LI(\alpha)$ gives the intervals of controllable transitions in bad subclasses of α (bad intervals). The set $LI(\alpha)$ allows to retrieve the safe intervals of controllable transitions, by computing the complements, in α, of the forbidden intervals (i.e., all possibilities of controlling α, $Ctrl(\alpha)$).

The function *explore* receives parameters α being the class under process, t the transition leading to α and C the set of traveled classes in the current path. It uses functions $succ(\alpha, t)$ and $Fire(\alpha, \omega)$ already explained by equations 5 and 6 (in sections 2.3 and 2.4, respectively). It distinguishes 3 cases:

1) α has been already processed (i.e., α is in *Passed*): In this case, there is no need to explore it again. However, its bad sequences have to be propagated to its predecessor by t, in case the control needs to be started before reaching α in order to avoid bad states of its predecessors. The control of α is independent of its predecessors along the path if all possibilities of control in α are limited to the newly enabled transitions. In case there is, in α, a possibility of control, which limits the firing interval of some controllable transition not newly enabled in α, it means that the predecessor of α by t has some bad states that must be avoided. The condition $Dep(\alpha, t, LI)$, used in Algorithm 2, is to control α independently of its predecessor by t.

2) α has a forbidden marking (i.e., α is a bad state class): In this case, the transition t is returned, which means that this sequence needs to be avoided before reaching α.

3) In other cases, the function *explore* is called for each successor of α, not already encountered in the current path (see Figure 5), to collect, in Ω, the bad sequences of its successors. Once all successors are processed, Ω is checked:

3.1) If $\Omega = \emptyset$, it means that α does not lead to any bad state class or its bad sequences can be avoided later by controlling its successors, then $(\alpha, \emptyset, \emptyset)$ is added to *Passed* and the function returns with $\emptyset$.

3.2) If $\Omega \neq \emptyset$, the function *explore* determines intervals of controllable transitions in bad subclasses, which do not cover their intervals in α. It gets such intervals, identifying states to be avoided, in LI (bad intervals). It adds (α, Ω, LI) to *Passed* and then verifies whether or not α is controllable independently of its predecessor state class in the current path. In such a case, there is no need to start the control before reaching α and then the empty set is returned by the function. Otherwise, it is needed to propagate the control to its predecessor by t. The set of sequences, obtained by prefixing with t sequences of Ω, is then returned by the function.

This algorithm tries to control the system behavior starting from the last to the first state classes of bad paths. If it fails to control a state class of a path, so as to avoid all bad state classes, the algorithm tries to control its previous state classes. If it succeeds to control a state class, there is no need to control its predecessors. The aim is to limit as little as possible the behavior of the system (more permissive controller).

Algorithm 1 On-the-fly algorithm for safety control problem of TPN- Part A

Function $main(TPN\ \mathcal{N},\ Markings\ bad)$
Where $\mathcal{N}$ **is a TPN**
bad **is a set of bad markings.**
Let T_c **be the set of controllable transitions of** $\mathcal{N}$ **and**
α_0 **the initial state class of** $\mathcal{N}$**.**
$Passed = \emptyset$
if $(explore(\alpha_0, \epsilon, \{\alpha_0\}) \neq \emptyset)$ **then**
 {Controller does not exist}
 return
end if
for all $((\alpha, \Omega, LI) \in Passed)$ **do**
 $Ctrl[\alpha] = \bigcup_{(t_c,t_s,BI)\in LI} \{(t_c, t_s, INT(\alpha, \underline{t_c} - \underline{t_s}) - BI)\}$
end for

(*)
$\alpha = (M, F);$
$En_c(M) = En(M) \cap T_c;$
$En_c^0(M) = En_c(M) \cup \{t_0\};$
$New_c(M,t) = New(M,t) \cap T_c;$
$New(M_0, \epsilon) = En(M_0);$
t_0 is a fictitious transition whose time variable is fixed at 0.
$Dep(\alpha, t, LI) \equiv$
$\exists (t_c, t_s, BI) \in LI, t_c \notin New(M,t) \wedge (t_s \notin New(M,t) \vee$
$INT(\alpha, \underline{t_c} - \underline{t_0}) \not\subseteq \bigcap_{I \in BI} (I \oplus INT(\alpha, \underline{t_s} - \underline{t_0})))$

4.2. Example

To explain the procedure, we trace the algorithm on the TPN shown in Figure 1. Its SCG and its state classes are reported in Figure 2 and Table 2, respectively. For this example, we have $T_c = \{t_1\}$, $bad = \{p_2, p_4\}$, $Passed = \emptyset$ and $\alpha_0 = (p_1 + p_2, 0 \leq \underline{t_1} \leq 4 \wedge 2 \leq \underline{t_2} \leq 3)$.

The process starts by calling $explore(\alpha_0, \epsilon, \{\alpha_0\})$ (see Figure 6). Since α_0 is not in $Passed$ and its marking is not forbidden, $explore$ is successively called for the successors of α_0: $explore(\alpha_1, t_1, \{\alpha_0, \alpha_1\})$ and $explore(\alpha_2, t_2, \{\alpha_0, \alpha_2\})$. In $explore$ of α_1, function $explore$ is successively called for α_3 and α_4. In $explore$ of α_3, function $explore$ is called for the successor α_6 of α_3 by t_3: $explore(\alpha_6, t_3, \{\alpha_0, \alpha_1, \alpha_3, \alpha_6\})$. For the successor of α_3 by t_4 (i.e., α_0), there is no need to call $explore$ as it belongs to the current path. Since α_6 has a forbidden marking, $explore$ of α_6 returns to $explore$ of α_3 with $\{t_3\}$, which, in turn, adds $(\alpha_3, \{t_2 t_3\}, \emptyset)$ to $Passed$ and returns to $explore$ of α_1 with $\{t_2 t_3\}$.

Algorithm 2 On-the-fly algorithm for safety control problem of TPN- Part B

Function $Traces\ explore(Class\ \alpha, Trans\ t,\ Classes\ \mathcal{C})$
if $(\exists\Omega, LI$ **s.t.** $(\alpha,\Omega,LI) \in Passed)$ **then**
  if $(\Omega \neq \emptyset \wedge Dep(\alpha,t,LI))$ **then**
    return $\{t.\omega|\omega \in \Omega\}$
  end if
  return $\emptyset$
end if
if $(M \in bad)$ **then**
  return $\{t\}$
end if
$Traces\ \Omega = \emptyset;$
for all $t' \in En(M)$ **s.t** $succ(\alpha,t') \neq \emptyset \wedge succ(\alpha,t') \notin \mathcal{C}$ **do**
  $\Omega = \Omega \cup explore(succ(\alpha,t'),t',\mathcal{C} \cup \{succ(\alpha,t')\})$
end for{Ω **contains all bad sequences of** α.}
if $(\Omega = \emptyset)$ **then**
  $Passed = Passed \cup \{(\alpha,\emptyset,\emptyset)\}$
  return $\emptyset$
end if
$LI = \{(t_c,t_s,BI)|(t_c,t_s) \in En_c(M) \times En_c^0(M) \wedge$

$$BI = \bigcup_{\omega\in\Omega} INT(Fire(\alpha,\omega),\underline{t}_c - \underline{t}_s) \subset INT(\alpha,\underline{t}_c - \underline{t}_s)\}$$

$Passed = Passed \cup \{(\alpha,\Omega,LI)\}$
if $(Dep(\alpha,t,LI))$ **then**
  return $\{t.\omega|\omega \in \Omega\}$
end if
return $\emptyset$

In *explore* of α_1, function *explore* is called for α_4 ($explore(\alpha_4,t_3,\{\alpha_0,\alpha_1,\alpha_4\})$). This call returns, to *explore* of α_1, with $\{t_3\}$, since α_4 has a forbidden marking. In *explore* of α_1, the tuple $(\alpha_1,\{t_2t_3,t_3\},\emptyset)$ is added to *Passed* and $\{t_1t_2t_3,t_1t_3\}$ is returned to *explore* of α_0. Then, *explore* of α_0 calls $explore(\alpha_2,t_2,\{\alpha_0,\alpha_2\})$, which in turn calls $explore(\alpha_5,t_1,\{\alpha_0,\alpha_2,\alpha_5\})$. Since α_5 has only one successor (α_0) and this successor belongs to the current path, the call of *explore* for α_5 adds $(\alpha_5,\emptyset,\emptyset)$ to *Passed* and returns to *explore* of α_2 with $\emptyset$, which, in turn, returns to *explore* of α_0.

After exploring both successors of α_0, in *explore* of α_0, we get in $\Omega = \{t_1t_2t_3,t_1t_3\}$ the set of bad paths of α_0. As the state class α_0 has a controllable transition t_1, its bad subclasses are computed: $Fire(\alpha_0,t_1t_2t_3) = \{(p_1+p_2, 0 \leq \underline{t}_1 \leq 2 \wedge 2 \leq \underline{t}_2 \leq 3 \wedge 1 \leq \underline{t}_2 - \underline{t}_1 \leq 3)$ and $Fire(\alpha_0,t_1t_3) = (p_1+p_2, 0 \leq \underline{t}_1 \leq 1 \wedge 2 \leq \underline{t}_2 \leq 3 \wedge 2 \leq \underline{t}_2 - \underline{t}_1 \leq 3)\}$. The firing interval of t_1 in α_0 ($[0,4]$) is not covered by the union of intervals of t_1 in bad subclasses of α_0 ($[0,2] \cup [0,1] \neq [0,4]$). Then, $(\alpha_0,\{t_1t_2t_3,t_1t_3\},\{(t_1,t_0,\{[0,2]\})\})$ is added to *Passed*. As t_1 is newly enabled, the empty set is returned to the function *main*, which concludes that a controller

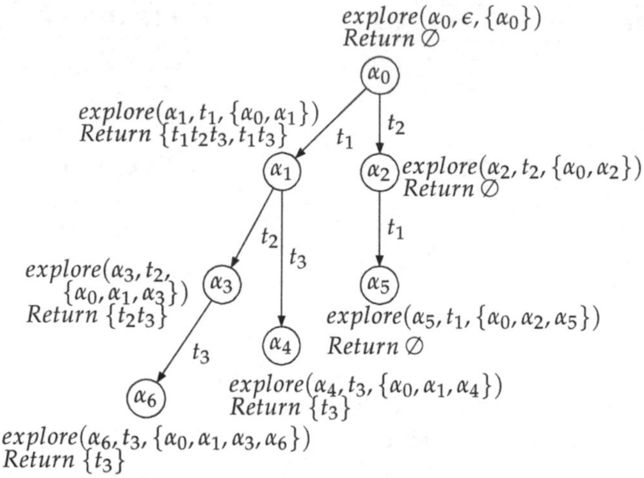

Figure 6. Applying Algorithms 1 & 2 on the TPN at Figure 1 for *AG not* $p_1 + p_3 = 0$

exists. According with the list *Passed*, α_0 needs to be controlled ($Ctrl[\alpha_0] = \{(t_1, t_0, \{[0,4] - [0,2]\})\}$). For all others, there is nothing to do.

Note that for this example, it is possible to carry out a static controller, which is, in this case, a mapping over controllable transitions. Indeed, it suffices to replace the static interval of t_1 with $]2,4]$. Such a controller is in general less permissive than the state dependent controller. However, its implementation is static and very simple as if the model is corrected rather than controlled.

It is also possible to carry out a marking dependent controller (a mapping over markings). Such a controller can be represented by duplicating t_1, each of them being associated with an interval and conditioned to a marking (see Table 3 and Figure 7).

This algorithm is able to determine whether a safety controller exists or not. If the algorithm fails to determine a controller, then the controller does not exist. This failure may have two

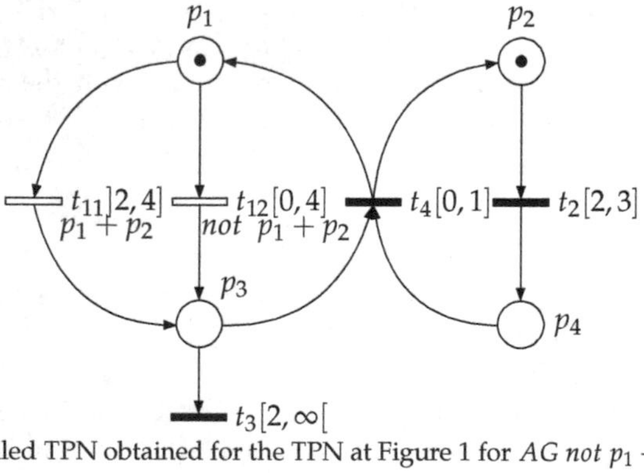

Figure 7. The controlled TPN obtained for the TPN at Figure 1 for *AG not* $p_1 + p_3 = 0$

Marking	Constraint to be applied on t_1
$p_1 + p_2$	$2 < t_1 \leq 4$
Others	$0 \leq t_1 \leq 4$

Table 3. A marking dependent controller for the TPN at Figure 1

reasons: no class having enabled controllable transitions exists in a bad path; or, calculated bad subclasses covers entire domain of controllable transitions. Note that, in a time Petri net[15] it is impossible to cancel a transition. Thus, if the entire domain of a controllable transition leads to bad states, as it cannot be canceled or delayed, the state class cannot be controlled so as to avoid bad states.

In the algorithms presented here, a state class is declared to be uncontrollable if it does not contain controllable transitions or it cannot be controlled so as to avoid all bad state classes. Note that if a state class cannot be controlled to avoid all bad classes, it can be however controlled to avoid some bad classes. To limit as little as possible the behavior of the system, the set of bad sequences of a state class α can be partitioned in two subsets: the set of bad sequences that can be avoided from α and the set of bad sequences that cannot to be avoided from α. The former set is avoided from α while the latter is let to be controlled by the predecessors of α. The function *explore* in this case should return the set of bad sequences that cannot be controlled from α. In this way, we increase the permissiveness of the controller.

The most significant advantage of this algorithm is the possibility of choosing the level of control. Three levels of control can be carried out:

1) Static controller: The control is independent of markings and states of the system. For each controllable transition, the intersection of all safe intervals is considered. Let t_c be a controllable transition whose interval needs to be restricted and $SIr(t_c) = \{Ir | \forall(\alpha, \Omega, L) \in Passed, \exists(t_c, SI) \in Ctrl[\alpha], Ir \subseteq SI \wedge Ir \neq \emptyset\}$. The static firing interval of t_c should be replaced with any interval of $SIr(t_c)$. Note that $SIr(t_c)$ may be empty. In this case, such a controller does not exist. Otherwise, it exists and its implementation is static as if the model is corrected rather than controlled. On the other hand, the permissiveness is sacrificed for the sake of simplicity of implementation. Albeit being simple, the controller has a high impact on performance of the system. For the previous example, such a controller exists and consists of replacing the static interval of t_1 with $[2, 4]$.

2) Marking dependent controller: The controller is a function of marking. The intersection of all safe intervals of controllable state classes with the same marking is considered, causing loss of permissiveness. Let t_c be a controllable transition whose interval needs to be restricted and $SIm(M, t_c) = \{Im | \forall((M, I), \Omega, L) \in Passed, \exists(t_c, SI) \in Ctrl[(M, I)], Im \subseteq SI \wedge Im \neq \emptyset\}$. For each marking M, the firing interval of each controllable transition t_c enabled in M should be any interval of $SIm(M, t_c)$. The set $SIm(M, t_c)$ may be empty and then such a controller does not exist. Otherwise, it exists and can be represented by duplicating some controllable transitions, each of them being associated with an interval and conditioned to a marking. Such a controller exists for the previous example and is given in Table 3 and the controlled TPN is what comes in Figure 7.

3) State dependent controller: The third level is the most permissive. A controllable transition is limited depending on the class the system is. In fact, making decision is delayed as much as possible. When the algorithm is being synthesized, different scenarios are considered. During the execution, the controller decides upon the scenario the system is (the current state class).

4.3. Controller for reachability properties

The algorithm proposed here for the safety properties, is also adaptable to reachability properties. A reachability controller running in parallel with the system should satisfy the property $AFgoal$ meaning that a goal state will certainly be reached, where 'goal' is an atomic proposition specifying the goal states (Figure 8). For reachability properties, the controller should prevent all paths which terminates without reaching a goal state, or contains a loop on none goal states (Figure 8.b). Then, if we define state classes leading to such cases as bad states, a safety controller is able to control this system to satisfy the given reachability property. Thus, the algorithm proposed to safety properties is extensible to reachability properties with some minor modification and is presented in the algorithms 3 and 4. Note that, in this case, the set $goal$ stands for the set of markings of goal states.

Algorithm 3 On-the-fly algorithm for the reachability control of TPN- Part A

Function $main(TPN\ \mathcal{N}, Markings\ goal)$
Where $\mathcal{N}$ **is a TPN and**
$goal$ **is a set of goal markings.**
Let T_c **be the set of controllable transitions of** $\mathcal{N}$ **and**
α_0 **the initial state class of** $\mathcal{N}$**.**

$Passed = \emptyset$
if $(explore(\alpha_0, \epsilon, \{\alpha_0\}) \neq \emptyset)$ **then**
  {Controller does not exist}
  return
end if

for all $((\alpha, \Omega, LI) \in Passed)$ **do**
  $Ctrl[\alpha] = \bigcup_{(t_c,t_s,BI)\in LI} \{(t_c, t_s, INT(\alpha, \underline{t}_c - \underline{t}_s) - BI)\}$
end for
return

(*)
$\alpha = (M, F);$
$En_c(M) = En(M) \cap T_c;$
$En_c^0(M) = En_c(M) \cup \{t_0\};$
$New_c(M,t) = New(M,t) \cap T_c;$
$New(M_0, \epsilon) = En(M_0); New^0(M_0, \epsilon) = En(M_0) \cup \{t_0\};$
t_0 is a fictitious transition whose time variable is fixed at 0.
$Dep(\alpha, t, LI) \equiv$
$\exists (t_c, t_s, BI) \in LI, t_c \notin New(M,t) \wedge (t_s \notin New(M,t) \vee$
$INT(\alpha, \underline{t}_c - \underline{t}_0) \not\subseteq \bigcap_{I\in BI} (I \oplus INT(\alpha, \underline{t}_s - \underline{t}_0)))$

Algorithm 4 On-the-fly algorithm for the reachability control of TPN-Part B

```
Function Traces explore(Class α, Trans t, Classes C)
if (∃Ω, LI s.t. (α, Ω, LI) ∈ Passed) then
   if (Ω ≠ ∅ ∧ Dep(α, t, LI)) then
      return {t.ω | ω ∈ Ω}
   end if
   return ∅
end if
if (M ∈ goal) then
   return ∅
end if
if (En(M) = ∅) then
   return {t}
end if
Traces Ω = ∅
for all t' ∈ En(M) s.t succ(α, t') ≠ ∅ do
   if succ(α, t') ∈ C then
      Ω = Ω ∪ {t'}
   else
      Ω = Ω ∪ explore(succ(α, t'), t', C ∪ {succ(α, t')})
   end if
end for
if (Ω = ∅) then
   Passed = Passed ∪ {(α, Ω, ∅)}
   return ∅
end if
LI = {(t_c, t_s, BI) | (t_c, t_s) ∈ En_c(M) × En_c^0(M) ∧
        BI = ⋃_{ω∈Ω} INT(Fire(α, ω), t̲_c − t̲_s) ⊂ INT(α, t̲_c − t̲_s)}
Passed = Passed ∪ {(α, Ω, LI)}
if (Dep(α, t, LI)) then
   return {t.ω | ω ∈ Ω}
end if
return ∅
```

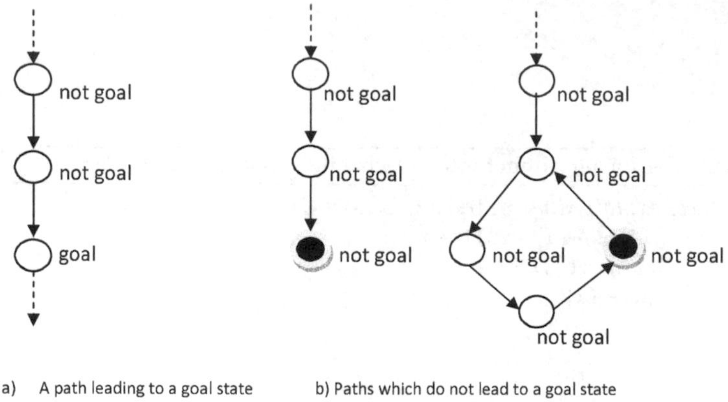

Figure 8. Paths satisfying or not a reachability property. Black states should be avoided.

5. Conclusion

In this chapter, we have proposed a completely forward on-the-fly algorithm for synthesizing safety and reachability controllers for time Petri nets. This approach guarantees to find a controller if it exists as it explores all possible state classes in the state graph and collects paths which do not satisfy the properties (bad paths).

To limit as little as possible the behavior of the system (more permissive controller), this algorithm tries to control the system behavior starting from the last to the first state classes of bad paths. If it fails to control a state class of a path, so as to avoid all bad paths, the algorithm tries to control its previous state classes. If it succeed to control a state class, there is no need to control its predecessors. The control of a state class consists of restricting the firing intervals of controllable transitions and does not need to compute any controllable predecessor.

Computing controllable predecessors involves some expensive operations such as the difference between time domains. Three levels of control can be carried out from the algorithm: the first level being independent from marking and state is static but not permissive. Second and third levels being dependent of marking and state, respectively are more permissive. One can choose to control the system during execution (third level), modify the model and make transitions conditioned to marking (second level), or re-constraining the intervals, correct the system statically before execution(first level). Correcting the system statically before the execution can reduce the impact of controller interference and solve the problem of synchronization between the controller and system.

The algorithm proposed here is decidable for a bounded TPN because the state class graph is finite and the algorithm explores, path by path, the state class graph (the exploration of a path is abandoned as soon as a loop is detected or a bad state class is reached).

One perspective of this work is the investigation of the use of more compact abstraction (abstraction by inclusion, abstraction by convex-combination) and then, extend the devised and optimized algorithm to large scale and modular systems.

Author details

Parisa Heidari and Hanifa Boucheneb
École Polytechnique de Montréal, Canada

6. References

[1] Altisen, K., Bouyer, P., Cachat, T., Cassez, F. & Gardey, G. [2005]. Introduction au contrôle des systèmes temps-réel, *Journal Européen des Systemes Automatises* 39(1-3): 367–380.

[2] Behrmann, G., Bouyer, P., Larsen, K. & Pelanek, R. [2006]. Lower and upper bounds in zone-based abstractions of timed automata, *International Journal on Software Tools for Technology Transfer* 8(3): 204 – 15.

[3] Bengtsson, J. [2002]. *Clocks, DBMs and states in timed systems.*, dissertation, Uppsala Universitet (Sweden).

[4] Berthomieu, B. & Diaz, M. [1991]. Modeling and verification of time dependent systems using time Petri nets, *IEEE Transactions on Software Engineering* 17(3): 259–273.

[5] Berthomieu, B. & Vernadat, F. [2003]. State class constructions for branching analysis of time Petri nets, *9th International Conference on Tools and Algorithms for the Construction and Analysis of Systems (TACAS)*, pp. 442–457.

[6] Boucheneb, H., Gardey, G. & Roux, O. H. [2009]. TCTL model checking of time Petri nets, *Journal of Logic and Computation* 6(19): 1509–1540.

[7] Boyer, M. & Vernadat, F. [2000]. Language and bisimulation relations between subclasses of timed petri nets with strong timing semantic, *Technical report, LAAS* .

[8] Buy, U. & Darabi, H. [2003]. Deadline-enforcing supervisory control for time Petri nets., *IMACS Multiconference on Computational Engineering in Systems Applications (CESA)*.

[9] Buy, U., Darabi, H., Lehene, M. & Venepally, V. [2005]. Supervisory control of time Petri nets using net unfolding, Vol. 2, pp. 97–100.

[10] Cassez, F., David, A., Fleury, E., Larsen, K. G. & Lime, D. [2005]. Efficient on-the-fly algorithms for the analysis of timed games, *16th International Conference on concurrency theory*, pp. 66–80.

[11] Gardey, G., Roux, O. E. & Roux, O. H. [2006a]. Safety control synthesis for time Petri nets, *8th International Workshop on Discrete Event Systems*, pp. 22–28.

[12] Gardey, G., Roux, O. & Roux, O. [2006b]. State space computation and analysis of time petri nets, *Theory and Practice of Logic Programming* 6: 301 – 20.

[13] Heidari, P. & Boucheneb, H. [2010]. Efficient method for checking the existence of a safety/ reachability controller for time Petri nets, *10th International Conference on Application of Concurrency to System Design(ACSD)*, pp. 201–210.

[14] Merlin, P. M. [1974]. *A study of the recoverability of computing systems*, Ph.d. dissertation, University of California, Irvine, United States.

[15] Merlin, P. M. & Farver, D. [1976]. Recoverability of communications protocols-implication of a theoretical study., *IEEE Trans. on Communications* 24(9): 1036–1043.

[16] Penczek, W. & Polrola, A. [2004]. Specification and model checking of temporal properties in time Petri nets and timed automata, *25th International conference on application and theory of Petri nets*, Vol. 3099 of LNCS, pp. 37–76.

[17] Ramadge, P. J. & Wonham, W. M. [1987]. Supervisory control of a class of discrete event processes, *SIAM Journal on Control and Optimization* 25(1): 206–230.

[18] Roux, O.-H., Lime, D., Haddad, S., Cassez, F. & Bérard, B. [2005]. Comparison of different semantics for time Petri nets, *3rd Automated Technology for Verification and Analysis* Volume 3707 of LNCS: 293–307.

[19] Sathaye, A. S. & Krogh, B. H. [1993]. Synthesis of real-time supervisors for controlled time Petri nets, *32nd Conference on Decision and Control*, Vol. 1, pp. 235–236.

[20] Tripakis, S. [1998]. *L'Analyse Formelle des Systèmes Temporisés en Pratique*, PhD thesis, Université Joseph Fourier - Grenoble 1 Sciences et Geographie.

[21] Wong-Toi, H. & Hoffmann, G. [1991]. The control of dense real-time discrete event systems, *30th IEEE Conference on Decision and Control Part 2 (of 3)*, Vol. 2, pp. 1527–1528.

[22] Wu, N., Chu, C., Chu, F. & Zhou, M. [2008]. Modeling and schedulability analysis of single-arm cluster tools with wafer residency time constraints using Petri net, pp. 84–89.

Section 3

Other

Chapter 13

Petri Nets Models for Analysis and Control of Public Bicycle-Sharing Systems

Karim Labadi, Taha Benarbia, Samir Hamaci
and A-Moumen Darcherif

Additional information is available at the end of the chapter

1. Introduction

Public Bicycle-Sharing Systems (PBSS), also known as self-service public bicycle systems, are available in numerous big cities in the world (Vélib' in Paris, Bicing in Barcelona, Call-a-Bicycle in Munich, OyBicycle in London, etc.). Since its inception, Bicycle-sharing programs have grown worldwide. There are now programs in Europe, North America, South America, Asia, and Australia. A still growing list of cities which provides such green public transportation mode can be found at the Bicycle-sharing world map (http://Bike-sharing.blogspot.com) as shown in Figure 1. As a good complementary to other urban transportation modes, bicycle use entails a number of benefits including environmental, mobility and economic benefits. The public bicycle sharing systems are especially useful for short-distance city transport trips and to face many public transport problems, including growing traffic congestion, pollution, greater car dependency, buses caught in city congestion, and ageing transport infrastructure.

A PBS system can be described as a bank of bicycles that can be picked up and dropped off at numerous stations (service points) across an urban area. The bicycle stations are usually located 300 meters apart, consisting of terminals and stands for fastening the bicycles. Every station is equipped with roughly twenty bicycle stands (the number can be estimated depending on the location of the service point and the estimated level of use). A customer uses a bicycle to travel from one station to another. A bicycle can be taken out from any station and returned to the same or any other station, provided that there is an available locking berth. A PBS system requires more than just bicycles and stations; a variety of other equipment is needed to keep the bicycles and stations functioning at adequate level of service. Particularly, this includes a fleet of vehicles for redistribution of bicycles between stations in order to balance the network (see Figures 2 to 4).

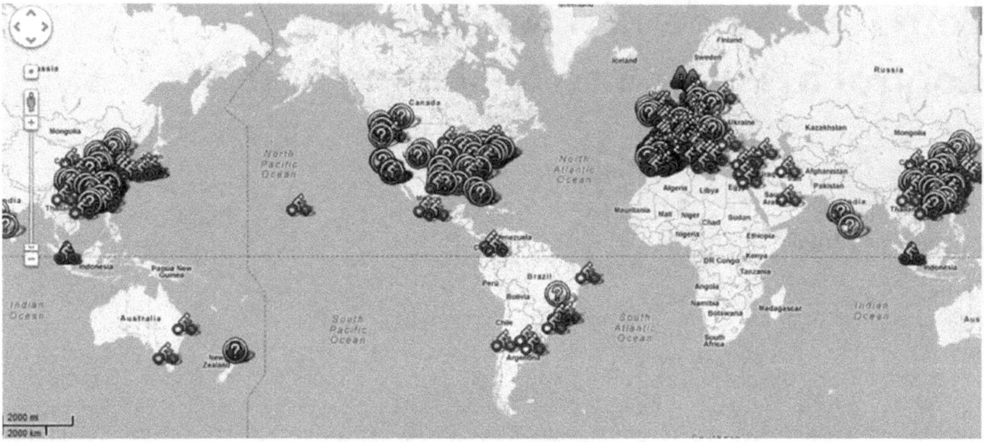

Figure 1. Bike-Sharing world map (source http://Bike-sharing.blogspot.com).

Figure 2. Full station, (http://www.velib.paris.fr/)

Figure 3. Empty station, (http://www.velib.paris.fr/)

Figure 4. Redistribution vehicle (http://www.velib.paris.fr/)

Over the recent years, public bicycle-sharing schemes have developed from being interesting experiments in urban mobility to mainstream public transport options in cities as large and complex as Paris and London (http://www.velib.paris.fr/). PBS schemes have evolved dramatically since their introduction in the 1960s and undergone various changes. These changes can be categorized into three key phases, known as Bicycle sharing generations [9]-[8]. These include the first generation, called white Bicycles (or free Bicycles); the second generation, coin-deposit systems; and the third generation, or information technology based systems. Potential "fourth generation" design innovations are already under development including electric bicycles, movable docking stations, solar-powered docking stations, and mobile phone and iPhone real time availability applications. Of these innovations, the introduction of electric bicycles is likely to be the most significant in terms of attractiveness. The Table 1 gives a survey of some significant public bicycle-sharing programs over the world since the first generation schemes that were introduced in Amsterdam.

A crucial question for the success of a PBS system is its ability to meet the fluctuating demand for bicycles at each station and to provide enough vacant lockers to allow the renters to return the bicycles at their destinations. Indeed, some stations have more demand than others, especially during peak hours. In addition, not surprisingly stations located at the top of hills are chronically empty of bicycles, as the customers ride down the hill but do not wish to make the return trip uphill. Bicycles also tend to collect in stations in the city centres and stay there. In some cases, the *imbalance is temporary*, e.g., high return rate in a suburban train station in the morning and high renting rate in the afternoon. In other cases, the *imbalance is persistent*, e.g., relatively low return rate in stations located on top of hills [30]. If no action is taken by the service provider they rapidly fill or empty, thus preventing other users from collecting or delivering bicycles.

Thus, the system requires constant monitoring to balance the network. The monitoring system dispatches motorized redistribution vehicles (trucks) to rebalance bicycles between stations that are emptying out and those that are filling up. This operation can be carried out in two different modes [30]:

- *Static mode* — The bicycle redistribution operation can be carried out during the night when the usage rate of the PBS system is very low. The bicycle repositioning is performed based on the status of the system at that time and the demand forecast for the next day.

- *Dynamic mode* — The bicycle redistribution operation can be carried out during the day when the usage rate of the PBS system is significant. The bicycle repositioning is performed based on the current state of the station as well as aggregate statistics of the station's usage patterns [16].

Year	City	Bicycle-sharing program
1960	Amsterdam (Netherlands)	The first Bicycle sharing system in the world appeared in Amsterdam, the Netherlands on July 28, 1965. Bicycles were painted white and offered to the public who would like to use them. Due to theft and abuse, unfortunately the program only survived for several days.
1995	Copenhagen (Denmark)	In 1995 in Copenhagen, Bycyklen or City Bicycles was operated as the first large-scale second generation Bicycle sharing program. The system had improved in many aspects. The bicycles are specifically designed for intensive urban use and stations were set up with each equipped with a coin deposit.
1998	Rennes (France)	Rennes launched "Vélo à la Carte" in 1998, which was the first computerized system in the world and the first one in France, and was also operated by ClearChannel, a private company. In 2009, the operator changed to EFFIA and shifted to a new system called "VéloStar".
2005	Lyon (France)	Lyon started its Bicycle sharing system Vélo'V with an unusually large scale in 2005. The city of Lyon and JC Decaux funds the system together through an advertisement contract, which the latter one operates the scheme. Vélo'V is based on stations and has long and short term subscription available with first 30 minutes free.
2007	Paris (France)	Velib' was introduced to Paris in 2007. With the similar operation scheme as Lyon, city of Paris and Cycocity fund the system together and the latter one operates it. Velib' has fixed stations and requires registration beforehand.
2008	Hangzhou (China)	In May, 2008, the first Bicycle sharing program in China started its operation in Hangzhou, a city 180 km southwest of Shanghai, with 4.2 million inhabitants in the metropolitan area, 8 districts included.
2008	Washington (USA)	SmartBicycle DC was a bicycle sharing system implemented in August 2008 with 120 bicycles and 10 automated rental locations in the central business district of Washington, D.C. The network was the first of its kind in North America.
2009	Canada (Quebec)	Bixi is a public bicycle sharing system serving Montreal, Quebec, Canada. The system was launched on May 12 2009, with 3000 bicycles and 300 stations located around Montreal's central core, and it expanded to 5,000 bicycles and 400 stations later that summer.

Table 1. Summary of some PBS systems over the world

Vogel et al., (2011) [38] identify three management and design measures alleviating these imbalances divided into different planning horizons: *(1) Strategic (long-term)* network design comprising decisions about the location, number and size of stations, *(2) Tactical (mid-term)* incentives for customer based distribution of bicycles. For example, the Vélib in Paris grants some extra minutes for returning bicycles at uphill stations, *(3) Operational (short-term)* provider based repositioning of bicycles. The most important issues for the success of a PBS system are summarized in Table 2.

Stage	Questions
Before deployment (Strategic / Tactical)	• *How many bicycles and stations?* • *Where to locate stations?* • *What is the size of each station?* • *How should the bicycles be distributed?* • *How many vehicles (and what sizes) are needed for bicycle redistribution?* • …
After deployment (Operational)	• *How often should the bicycles be redistributed?* • *Is the current number of redistribution vehicles and projections sufficient?* • *Should more bicycles be purchased?* • *More stations needed?* • *Regular or preventative maintenance required?* • …

Table 2. Management and design measures of a PBS system

To help planners and decision makers answer these crucial questions, modelling and performance analysis and optimization methods and tools for PBS systems are needed. A literature review describing some existing works developed in this research area is dressed in the section 2. After, the rest of this chapter deals with an original Petri net approach dedicated for PBS systems modelling for control purposes [2]-[19]-[20]-[21]. The section 3 provides an introduction for Petri nets with the "marking dependent weights" concept [17] as it is used throughout this chapter to model PBS systems for control purposes. In the sections 4 to 6, a modular framework based on Petri nets with marking dependent weights is developed for modelling and performance evaluation of PBS systems. The concluding section 7 gives some remarks and perspectives of this work. Our approach is intended to help planners and decision makers in determining how to implement, and operate successfully these complex dynamical systems.

2. A review of the literature

Public Bicycle-sharing systems have attracted a great deal of attention in recent years. Although the growth of the system has been rapid following the development of better tracking technology, most of the studies related to PBS systems in the literature have focused on their history, development and some practical advises [9]-[31]-[39]. There are, however, relatively few studies addressing strategic and operational issues that arise in such systems.

About strategic issues, Lin and Yang (2011) [22] and Lin et al., (2011) [23] address the strategic problem of finding optimal stations using mathematical programming techniques. The problem is formulated as a hub location inventory model. The key design decisions considered are: the number and locations of bicycle stations in the system, the creation of bicycle lanes between bicycle stations, the selection of paths of users between origins and destinations, and the inventory levels of sharing bicycles to be held at the bicycle stations. The design decisions are made with consideration for both total cost and service levels. Dell'Olio et al. (2011) [7] present a complete methodology for the design and implementing of bicycle sharing systems based on demand estimates considering the stations and the fares. Vogel et al. (2011) [38] develop a methodology for strategic and operational planning using data mining. A case study shows how Data Mining applied to operational data offers insight into typical usage patterns of bike-sharing systems and is used to forecast bike demand with the aim of supporting and improving strategic and operational planning.

Regarding operational issues, besides the work presented in [38], the static balancing problem studying the repositioning of bicycles among bicycle stations where the customer demand is assumed to be negligible is addressed in [5]-[30]. Several mathematical formulations of the problem can be found in [30] and an exact algorithm based on column generation and a suitable pricing algorithm based on dynamic programming are given by Chemla et al.; (2011) [5]. From an OR perspective, the bicycle repositioning problem bears great similarities to some other routing problems which have been largely studied in the literature. As an example from this point of view, Forma et al. (2010) [12] consider the bicycle repositioning problem as a variation of the Pickup and Delivery problem (PDP). Naturally, some similarities between bicycle-sharing and car-sharing systems can be explored in order to adapt some existing results in this field (see, for example [26]-[36]).

Besides OR approaches developed, particularly by using mathematical programming techniques [5]-[12]-[22]-[23]-[30] to support decision making in the design and management of PBS systems, Data Mining techniques receives attention in academia as well as in practice. Data Mining is particularly suitable to analyze and to predict the dynamics of a PBS system. By exploring and analyzing the temporal and geographic human mobility data in an urban area using the amount of available bicycles in the stations of a PBS system [3], statistical and prediction models can be developed [13]-[16] for tactical and operational management of such systems.

As noted in [37], although extensive analysis of bicycle data or customer surveys can be applied to predict future bicycle demand at stations, the demand still has to be considered stochastic and not deterministic. Moreover various points in time have to be incorporated in a suitable mathematical optimization models. Such a stochastic and dynamic model can be computational intractable. In addition, customer behavior cannot be modelled in these mathematical optimization models. According to our knowledge, unlike our work [2]-[19]-[20]-[21], no other studies has been undertaken on the dynamics modelling and performance evaluation of such dynamical systems. In addition to their self-service mode, PBS systems are dynamic, stochastic, and complex systems, this makes their modelling and analysis very complicated. Among the formalisms used to model the dynamic systems, Petri nets are one of the graphical and formal specification techniques for the description of the operational behavior of the systems. They are widely used in a number of different disciplines including engineering, manufacturing, business, chemistry, mathematics, and even within the judicial system [17]-[18]-[40]-[32]-[42]-[41]. They have been accepted as a powerful formal specification tool for a variety of systems including concurrent, distributed, asynchronous, parallel, deterministic and non-deterministic.

However, although Petri nets have been widely used in various domains, they played a relatively minor role in modelling and analysis of urban transportation systems. According to some existing works, the modelling of the systems by using Petri nets formalisms can be considered from either a discrete and/or a continuous point of view. Continuous Petri nets for the macroscopic and microscopic traffic flow control are used in [15]-[34], while hybrid Petri nets are used in [11] to provide a valuable model of urban networks of signalized intersections. Recently, batch Petri nets with controllable batch speed are used [10] to study a portion of the A12 highway in The Netherlands. From a discrete point of view, generalized stochastic Petri nets are used [1]-[4] for modelling and planning of public transportation systems. The two complementary tools, Petri nets and (max, +) algebra, have been used [28]-[29] to deal with the modelling and the performance evaluation of a public transportation system. For the modelling of passenger flows at a transport interchange, as shown in [33] colored Petri nets are able to incorporate some specific parameters and data in the model such as the variation of walking speeds between passengers and the restricted capacity of features of the interchange infrastructure.

These are a few works that demonstrate the high potential of Petri nets as a tool for modelling and performance analysis of urban transportation systems, but also on the other hand, it is shown that the application of Petri nets is still in its early stage and particularly limited to intersection traffic control [11]-[14]-[15]-[25]-[35]-[34] and to some studies dealing with the modelling of urban transportation systems for planning purposes [28]-[29]-[33]. In addition, according to our knowledge, unlike traditional urban transportation systems, no work has been undertaken on PBS systems modelling and performances analysis by using Petri net models. Our contribution in this context is the first one in the literature [18]-[19]-[20]-[21].

3. Petri nets with variable arc weights

In its basic form, a Petri net may be defined as a particular bipartite directed graph consisting of places, transitions, and arcs. Input arcs are ones connecting a place to a transition, whereas output arcs are ones connecting a transition to a place. A positive weight may be assigned to each arc. A place may contain tokens and the current state (the marking) of the modelled system is specified by the number of tokens in each place. Each transition usually models an activity whose occurrence is represented by its firing. A transition can be fired only if it is enabled, which means that all preconditions for the corresponding activity are fulfilled (there are enough tokens available in the input places of the transition). When the transition is fired, tokens will be removed from its input places and added to its output places. The number of tokens removed/added is determined by the weight of the arc connecting the transition with the corresponding place. Graphically, places are represented by circles, transitions by bars or thin rectangles (filled or not filled), tokens by dots. For a comprehensive introduction of Petri nets, see for example [27].

Formally, a Petri net can be defined as $PN = (P, T, Pré, Post, Inhib, M^0)$, where: $P = \{p_1, p_2, \ldots, p_n\}$ is a finite and non-empty set of places; $T = \{t_1, t_2, \ldots, t_m\}$ is a finite and non-empty set of transitions; *Pre*: $(P{\times}T)\rightarrow N$ is an input function that defines directed weighted arcs from places to transitions, where N is a set of nonnegative integers; *Post*: $(P{\times}T)\rightarrow N$ is an output function which defines directed weighted arcs from transitions to places; *Inhib*: $(P{\times}T)\rightarrow N$ is an inhibitor function which defines inhibitor weighted arcs (circle-headed weighted arcs) from places to transitions; and M_0 is called initial marking (initial distribution of the tokens in the places). A place connected with a transition by an arc is referred to as input, output, and inhibitor place, depending on the type of the arc. The set of input places, the set of output places, and the set of inhibitor places of a transition t are denoted by ${}^{\bullet}t$, $t^{\bullet}$, and ${}^{\circ}t$, respectively. The weights of the input arc from a place p to a transition t, of the output arc from t to p, and of the inhibitor arc from p to t are denoted by $Pre(p, t)$, $Post(p, t)$, and $Inhib(p, t)$, respectively.

The behavior of many systems can be described in terms of system states and their changes. In order to simulate the dynamic behavior of a system, a state or marking in a Petri net is changed according to the following transition rules:

- A transition t is said to be enabled if each of its input places contains at least a number of tokens equal to the weight of the corresponding input arc, and each of its inhibitor places contains tokens less than the weight of its corresponding inhibitor arcs.

Formally:

$$\forall p \in {}^{\bullet}t,\ M(p) \geq \mathrm{Pre}(p,t) \tag{1}$$

$$\forall p \in {}^{\circ}t,\ M(p) < Inhib(p,t) \tag{2}$$

- An enabled transition t fires by removing from each of its input places a number of tokens corresponding to the weight of the corresponding input arc, and adding a number of tokens in each of its output places corresponding to the weight of the corresponding output arc.

Formally:

$$\forall p \in P, M'(p) = M(p) - \mathrm{Pre}(p,t) + Post(p,t) \tag{3}$$

The firing of transitions in a Petri net model corresponds to the occurrence of events that changes the state of the modelled system. This change of state can be due to (*i*) the completion of some activity or/and (*ii*) the verification of some logical condition in the system. Since transitions are often used to model activities (production, delivery, order…), transition enabling durations correspond to activity executions and transition firings correspond to activity completions. Hence, deterministic or stochastic temporal specifications can be naturally associated with transitions [24].

In addition of the concept of time and the introduction of inhibitor arcs, which are not given in the original definition of Petri nets, the modelling of the complex dynamic of a PBS system requires the use of Petri nets models with *"variable arc weights depending on its marking"* and possibly on some decision parameters of the system. The same modelling concept is introduced for modelling inventory control systems and supply chains in [17]-[6]. Precisely, the Petri net model of an inventory control system whose inventory replenishment decision is based on the inventory position of the stock and the reorder and order-up-to-level parameters. Similarly, in the case of a PBS system, the redistribution operation of the bicycles between stations depends on the number of the available bicycles in each station when controlled.

By allowing the weights of some arcs of a Petri net to depend on its marking, control policies of the stations can be easily described in the PBS model. Therefore, we consider in this chapter that for any arc (i, j), its weight $w(i, j)$ is now defined as a linear function of the marking M with integer coefficients α and β. The weight $w(i, j)$ is assumed to take a positive value.

$$w(i,j) = \alpha_{ij} + \sum_{p_i \in P} \left(\beta_{ij}\right)_{P_i} \cdot M\left(p_i\right) \tag{4}$$

To understand the mathematical and intuitive meaning of this concept, consider the Petri net shown in Figure 5.

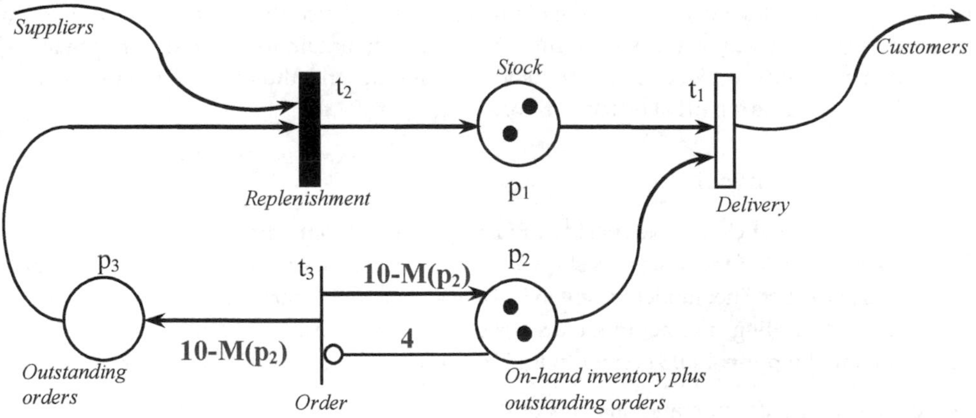

Figure 5. Illustration of a Petri net with variable arc weights depending on its marking

The model represents an inventory control system with continue review (s, S) policy (here $s = 4$ and $S = 10$) [17]. The different operations of the system are modelled by using a set of transitions: generation of replenishment orders (t_3); inventory replenishment (t_2); and order delivery (t_1). In the model, the weights of the arcs (t_3, p_2), (t_3, p_3) are variable and depend on the parameters s and S of the system and on the marking of the model ($S - M(p_2); s$).

- According to the current marking $M_i = (2, 2, 0)$ of the net, the transition t_3 is enabled, since the following condition is satisfied:

$$M(p_2) = 2 < Inhib(p_2, t_3) = 4$$

- After the firing of t_3, $10 - M(p_2) = 10–2 = 8$ tokens are added into the places p_2 and p_3. In other words, the firing of the transition t_3 from the initial marking M_i leads to a new marking $M_f = (2, 10, 8)$ as the following:

$$M_f(p_2) = M_i(p_2) + \left[10 - M_i(p_2)\right] = 2 + \left[10 - 2\right] = 10.$$

$$M_f(p_3) = M_i(p_3) + \left[10 - M_i(p_3)\right] = 0 + \left[10 - 2\right] = 8.$$

4. Modelling of a PBS system

As mentioned in the second section of this chapter, modelling, analysis and performance evaluation of PBS systems is crucial not only for their successful implementation and performance improvement but also for ensuring an effective regulation of bicycle traffic flows. This section deals with our original Petri net approach dedicated for PBS system modelling and analysis for control purposes. We consider a PBS system with N stations noted by $S = \{S_1, S_2, \ldots, S_N\}$. Each station $S_i \in S$ is equipped with C_i bicycle stands (the capacity of a station S_i). In practice, the number C_i depends on the location of the service point and the estimated level of use. The system requires a constant control which consists in transporting bicycles from stations having excess of bicycles to stations that may run out of bicycles soon. In the general way, the main objective of the control system, performed by using redistribution vehicles as shown in Figure 4, is to maintain R_i (reorder point) bicycles per station S_i to ensure bicycles are available for pick up and thus ($C_i - R_i$) vacant berths available for bicycle drop off at every station.

4.1. The Petri net model

Firstly, for the sake of clarity, we consider a PBS system with only three stations and then we design a Petri model of the system as shown in Figure 6. The designation of the elements and parameters of the Petri net model are given in Tables 3, 4 and 5. Thereafter, as will be shown in this section, according to the modular structure of the resulting Petri net model, its generalization to represent PBS systems with N stations will be straightforward and intuitive.

Before a formal description and analysis of the model in the next sub-sections, the Figure 6 and the Tables 3, 4, and 5 allow readers to quickly gain an understanding of the Petri net model of the system. A closer look at the Petri net model shows three subnets (modules) representing three different functions named as follows: (*1*) the "station control" subnet; (*2*) the "bicycle flows" subnet; and (*3*) the "redistribution circuit" subnet. The main function of each subnet is described in the following:

- The "bicycle flows" subnet represents the bicycle traffic flows between the different stations of the network. A customer uses a bicycle to travel from one station to another. In other words, a bicycle can be taken out from any station and returned to the same or any other station, provided that there is an available locking berth.
- The "station control" subnet represents the control function of the stations to ensure bicycles are available for pick up and vacant berths available for bicycle drop off at every station S_i. The purpose of this function is two-fold: First, the control of the state of the station in terms of the number of bicycles available for new users; and second, according to the state of the controlled station, take one decision among three alternatives: (*i*) Add bicycles in the station, or (*ii*) Remove bicycles from the station, or (*iii*) Take no action.
- The "redistribution circuit" subnet represents the path (circuit) to be followed by the redistribution vehicle in order to visit the different stations of the network. Its objective is to rebalance bicycles between stations that are emptying out and those that are filling up.

Place	*Interpretation*
PS_i	Represents a station S_i. Its marking $M(PS_i)$ correspond to the number of bicycles available in the station S_i.
PR_i	Represents a redistribution vehicle used to regulate the stations. Its marking $M(PR_i)$ correspond to the number of bicycles available in this redistribution vehicle when the station S_i is visited in order to be controlled.
PO_i	Specify whether the number of bicycles in a station S_i is greater than the reorder point R_i. It is indicated when $M(PO_i) = 1$.
PC_i	Specify the end of the control of a station S_i by the redistribution vehicle. $M(PC_i) = 1$ means that the control of the station S_i is completed and indicates that the redistribution vehicle is liberated to go to the next station.

Table 3. Interpretation of places of the PN model

Transition	*Interpretation*
TR_i	Test and add (if necessary) bicycles into a station S_i.
TO_i	Test if the number of bicycles available in a station S_i is greater than the reorder point R_i.
TS_i	Remove bicycles from a station S_i if the number of bicycles available in this station is judged less than the reorder point R_i
TE_i	Test if the number of bicycles available in a station S_i is equal to the reorder point R_i

Table 4. Interpretation of transitions of the PN model

Parameter	*Interpretation*
R_i	Reorder point fixed for each station S_i. It is the minimum level of available bicycles in the station S_i when a decision should be made to adding or removing bicycles into (from) the station (redistribution of bicycles between stations)
C_i	Capacity of each station S_i. More precisely, C_i corresponds to the maximal number of bicycle stands in a station S_i.

Table 5. Decision parameters of the PN model

Thanks to the modularity of the developed model, its generalization for a system with N stations is simple to make according to the different functions cited previously. For example, to model N stations S_i ($i = 1, 2, \ldots, N$), we need to N places denoted by PS_i and the control subnet is duplicated for each station similarly to the model represented for three stations (see Figure 6). Finally, by considering all the modules, the Petri net model representing a PBS system with N stations should contain:

$|T| = N^2 + 5 * N$ transitions; $|P| = 4 * N$ places; $|A_d| = 2 * N^2 + 21 * N$ directed arcs, and $|A_i| = N^2 + 7 * N$ inhibitors arcs.

4.2. Description of the Petri net model

4.2.1. The "control stations" subnet

The subnet representing the control function of each station S_i is indicated in Figure 6. As shown in the model, the considered subnet is duplicated for each station S_i. We recall that, the main objective of the control function is to rebalance bicycles between stations that are emptying out and those that are filling. The control function of the system is realized by using three places denoted by PS_i, PC_i, PR_i; for transitions denoted by TE_i TR_i, TS_i, TO_i. As indicated in the tables 3 and 4, the place PS_i represents a station S_i; the place PR_i represents the redistribution vehicle when visiting the station S_i; and the place PC_i means to indicate the end of the control operation of the station S_i. When the redistribution vehicle arrives at a station S_i, the state of this station is controlled. According to the number of bicycles available in the station, the decision to be made is either (*a*) to put bicycles in the station, or (*b*) to take bicycles from the station, or (*c*) take no action. The different operations are described and illustrated as follows.

a. **"Addition of bicycles to a station" operation**: The decision to add bicycles in a station S_i is performed by the transition TR_i connected by the corresponding arcs to the places PR_i and PS_i. Indeed, the transition TR_i means to verify the current number of bicycles in the station and to add (if necessary!) a given number ($R_i - M(PS_i)$) of bicycles to the station S_i. When the transition TR_i is fired, $R_i - M(PS_i)$ tokens (bicycles) will be removed from the place PR_i (the regulation vehicle) and at the same time, $R_i - M(PS_i)$ tokens (bicycles) will be added to the place PS_i (the station S_i). At the same time, one token will be deposited in the place PC_i to indicate the end of the control of the station S_i, and then the redistribution vehicle can travel to the next section S_{i+1}.

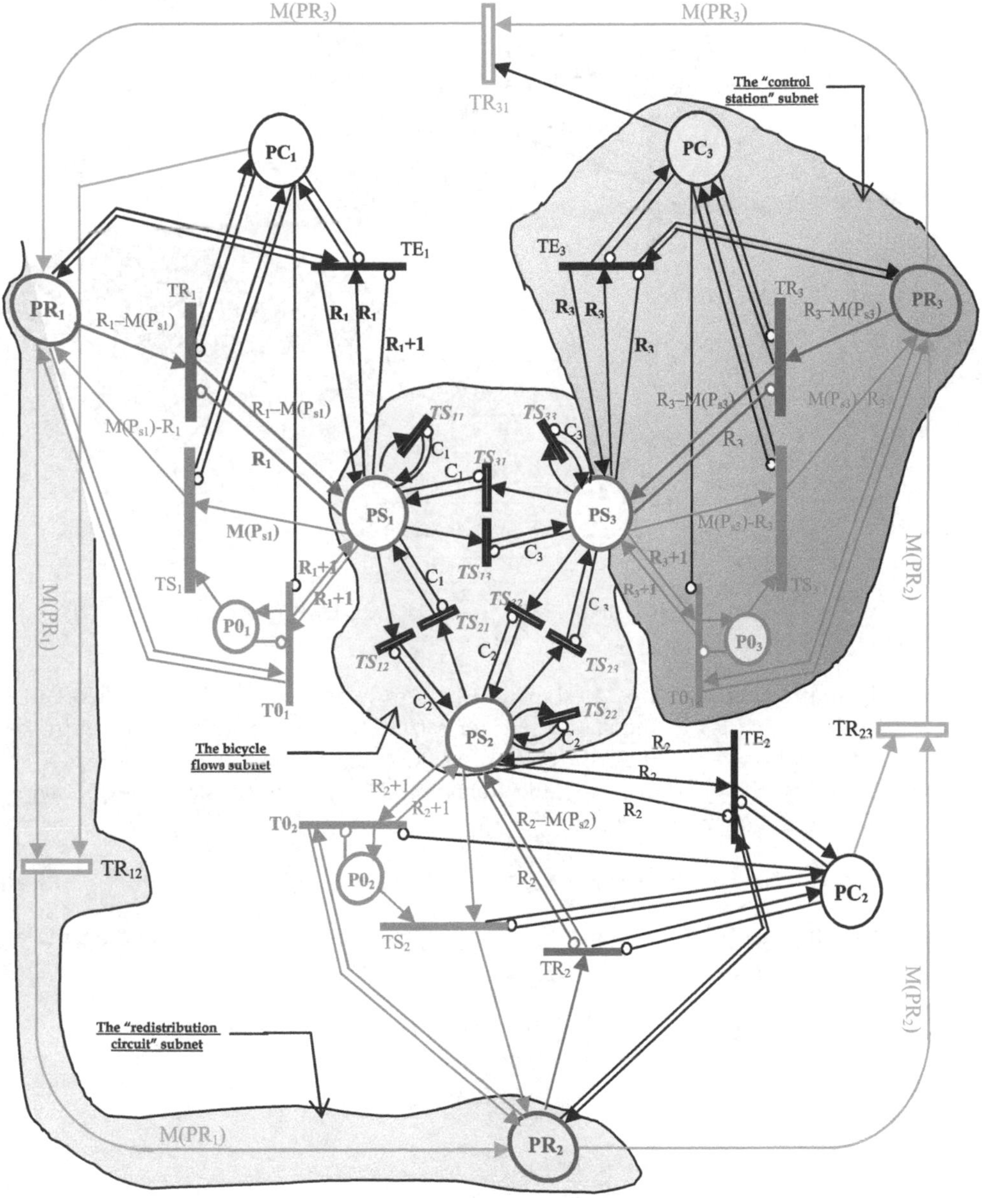

Figure 6. The Petri net model of a self-service public bicycles system (with three stations)

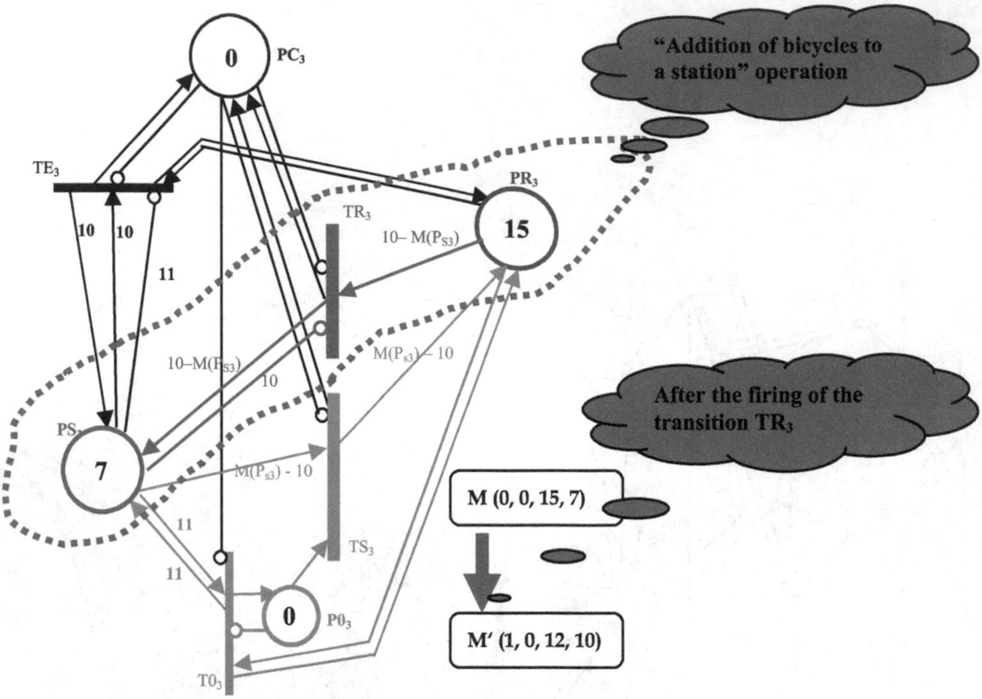

Figure 7. "Control station" subnet illustration: The number of available bicycles in the station S_i is less than R_i *(i.e.,* $M(S_i) < R_i = 10$*)*

- **Illustrative example 1.**— As shown in Figure 7, consider that initially there are 7 available bicycles in the station S_3 (i.e. $M(PS_3) = 7$); 15 available bicycles in the redistribution vehicle (i.e. $M(PR_3) = 15$); $M(PC_3) = 0$; and the reorder point R_3 is fixed to 10. For this marking, only the transition TR_3 is enabled since the following enabling equations are satisfied:

$$M(PS_3) = 7 < 10 \ ; M(PR_3) = 15 \geq 10 - M(PS_i) = 3 \ ; \ M(PC_3) = 0 < 1 \ .$$

After the firing of the transition TR3, the marking of the corresponding places changes in this way:

$$M'(PS_3) = M(PS_3) + \left[10 - M(PS_3)\right] = 7 + \left(10 - 7\right) = 10. ;$$

$$M'(PR_3) = M(PR_3) - \left[10 - M(PS_3)\right] = 15 - \left(10 - 7\right) = 12. ;$$

$$M'(PC_3) = M(PC_3) + 1 = 0 + 1 = 1.$$

b. **"Remove bicycles from a station" operation:** The decision to remove bicycles (superfluous) from a station S_i is made by the two transitions TO_i and TS_i. More precisely, the transition TO_i means to test if the current number of bicycles in the station

S_i is greater than the reorder point R_i and the transition TS_i allows us to remove bicycles (if necessary!) from the station S_i and put them in the regulation vehicle. When the transition TO_i is enabled, its firing will add a token into the place PO_i to indicate that the current number of bicycles in the station S_i is greater than the reorder point R_i fixed for the station S_i. This indication (i.e. $M(PO_i) = 1$) is one of the enabling conditions of the transition TS_i. When the transition TS_i is enabled, its firing leads to remove $M(PS_i)-R_i$ bicycles (superfluous) will be removed from the station S_i and, at the same time, they are deposited in the place PR_i which represents the redistribution vehicle.

- **Illustrative example 2.**— Now, as illustrated in Figure 8, consider that initially there are *15* available bicycles in the station S_3 (*i.e.* $M(PS_3) = 15$); *22* available bicycles in the redistribution vehicle (i.e. $M(PR_3) = 15$); $M(PC_3) = 0$; and the reorder point R_3 is fixed to *10*. For the current marking of the subnet, the transition TO_3 is enabled, since:

$$M(PS_3) = 15 \geq 11 \ ; \ M(PO_3) = 0 < 1 \ ; \ M(PC_3) = 0 < 1 \ .$$

After the firing of the immediate transition TO_3, a token will be placed in PO_3 indicating that the current number of bicycles in the station S_3 is greater than $R_3 = 10$ ($M(PS_3)>10$). That is: $M'(PO_3) = M(PO_3) + 1 = 1$. With this indication, the transition TS_3 is systematically enabled, according to the following satisfied enabling equations:

$$M(PS_3) = 15 \geq 15 \ ; M(PO_3) = 1 \geq 1 \ M(PC_3) = 0 < 1 \ ; M(PR_3) = 22 \geq 10 \ .$$

Then, after the firing of the transition TR_3, the state of the subnet will change as follows:

$$M'(PS_3) = M(PS_3) + \left[10 - M(PS_3)\right] = 10 \ ;$$

$$M'(PR_3) = M(PR_3) - 10 + M(PS_3) = 22 - 10 + 15 = 27 \ ;$$

$$M'(PC_3) = M(PC_3) + 1 = 1 \ ; M'(PO_3) = M(PO_3) - 1 = 0.$$

c. **"No action" operation:** Contrarily to the two previous actions corresponding "to remove" or "to add" bicycles from (resp. into) the station S_i, the "not action" function will be performed when the current number of bicycles in the controlled station S_i is equal to the reorder point R_i. Testing that $M(PS_i) = R_i$ is made by the transition TE_i with its corresponding arcs connecting the places PS_i and PC_i with the transition. The firing of TE_i will not change the marking of the place PS_i which represents the number of bicycles in the controlled station S_i. Similarly to the two previous functions, after the firing of TE_i one token will be deposited in the place PC_i. This is to indicate the end of the control of the station S_i and then the redistribution vehicle can travel at the next section by the firing a transition TR_{ij} in the Petri net model. This case is illustrated in Figure 9 where we consider $M(PS_3) = 10$.

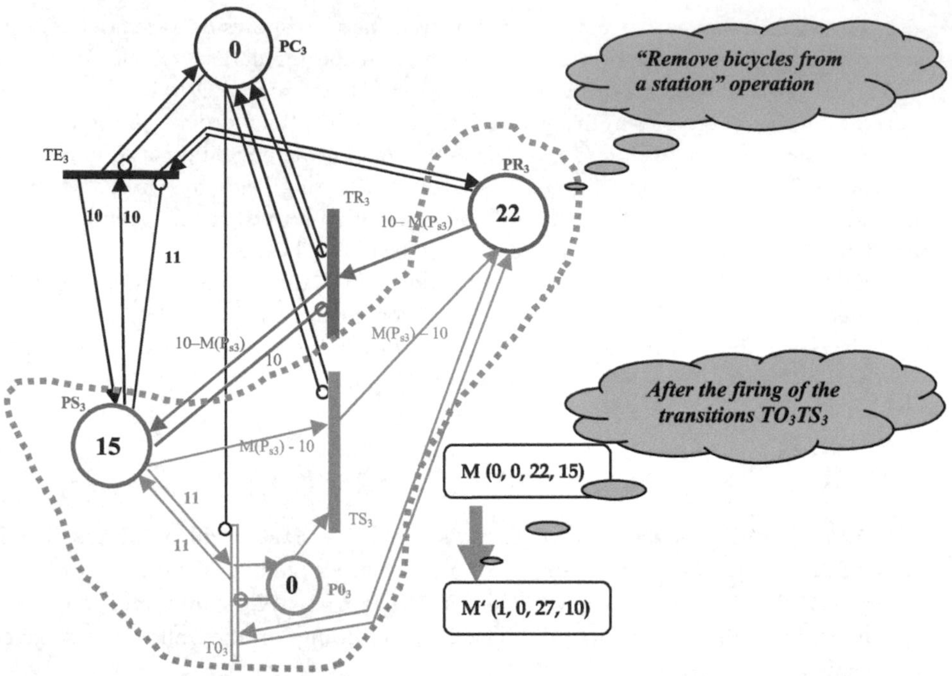

Figure 8. "Control station" subnet illustration: The number of available bicycles in the station S_i is greater than R_i (i.e., $M(S_i) > R_i = 10$)

4.2.2. The "bicycle flows" subnet

A public bicycle system is a bank of bicycles which are continuously used by users to travel from one station to another. Thus, each bicycle of the system can be taken out from any station and returned to the same or any other station, provided that there is an available locking berth. The subnet representing the displacements of the bicycles between the different stations of the system is represented in Figure 10 and indicated in Figure 2. Each station S_i of the system is modelled by using a place denoted by PS_i. The bicycle flows is represented by the multiple token displacements from any place to the same or any other place by firing transitions denoted by TS_{ij} (possibly TS_{ii}) connecting the different places of the subnet. Each station S_i is equipped with C_i bicycle stands. It is the capacity of each place PS_i in the subnet. The parameter C_i represents the weight of the inhibitor arcs connecting the places PS_i with the transition TS_{ij}. The inhibitor arcs are used in order to respect the capacity C_i of each station. According to the stochastic behavior of the bicycle flows between the different stations, the transitions of the subnet must be stochastic transitions.

4.2.3. The "redistribution circuit" subnet

As noted previously, the PBS system requires constant control which consists in transporting bicycles from stations having excess of bicycles to stations that may run out of bicycles soon. In our model, we consider that the vehicle(s) used to rebalance bicycles between stations visits successively stations $S_1, S_2, \ldots, S_N$.

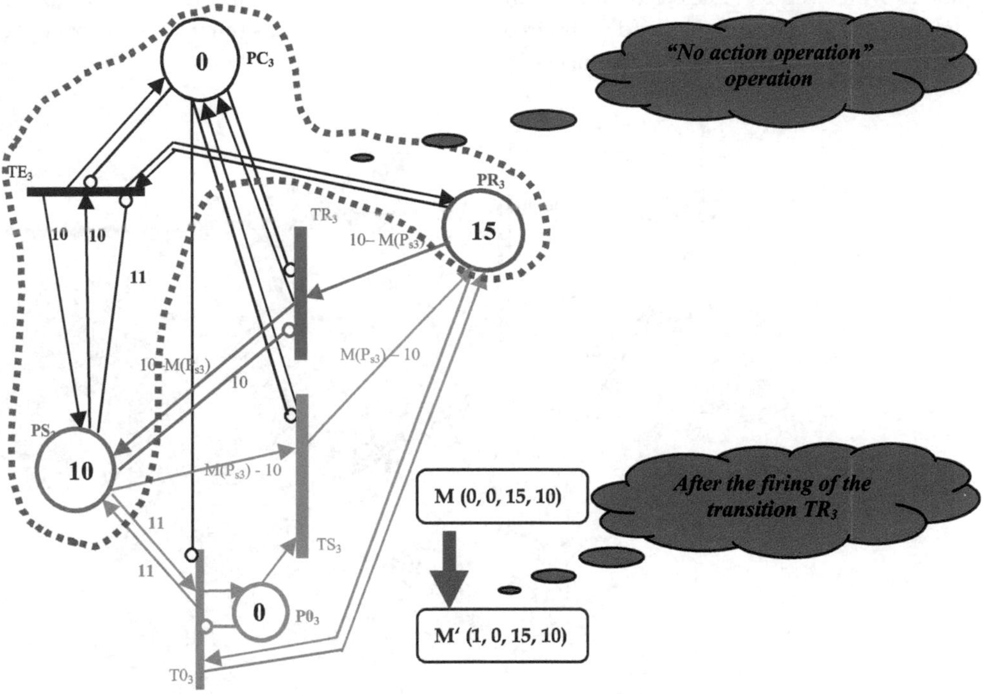

Figure 9. "Control station" subnet illustration: The number of available bicycles in the station S_i is equal to R_i (i.e., $M(S_i) = R_i = 10$)

As can be seen in the Figure 6, the places denoted by PR_i ($i = 1, 2, \ldots, N$), the transitions denoted by TR_{ij} ($i \neq j$ and $i, j = 1, 2, \ldots, N$) and all of the corresponding arcs form a closed path. The resulting subnet represents a circuit which the redistribution vehicle follows in order to visit and to control successively the different stations of the network. When the redistribution vehicle arrives at a given station S_i, the marking of the place PR_i (i.e., $M(PR_i)$) indicates the current available bicycles in the vehicle. The displacement of the vehicle from a station S_i to another station S_j is modelled by the transition TR_{ij}. Obviously, the circuit is connected to the control subnet of the system. Indeed, each place PR_i is connected to the three transitions TS_i, TE_i, and TR_i in order to execute the control function of the station S_i. The connection is made by the corresponding arcs.

Now, suppose that the control of a given station S_i is finished. Then, the redistribution vehicle leaves the station S_i and goes to the next section S_j. The firing of the enabled transition TR_{ij} leads to a new marking the place PC_i, $M'(PC_i) = 0$, indicating that the redistribution vehicle is arrived at the next station S_j with $M(PR_i)$ bicycles in its trailer. $M(PR_i)$ corresponds to the rest of bicycles just after the control of the previous station S_i.

In the presented Petri net model (for three stations), we used a single redistribution vehicle for the control of the stations. Obviously, in practice, for a system with N stations implemented in a given city, the regulation can be performed by several redistribution vehicles which can be affected to different districts of the city. Thus, in the Petri net model, several redistribution vehicles and their circuits can be represented similarly to the example presented with one redistribution vehicle.

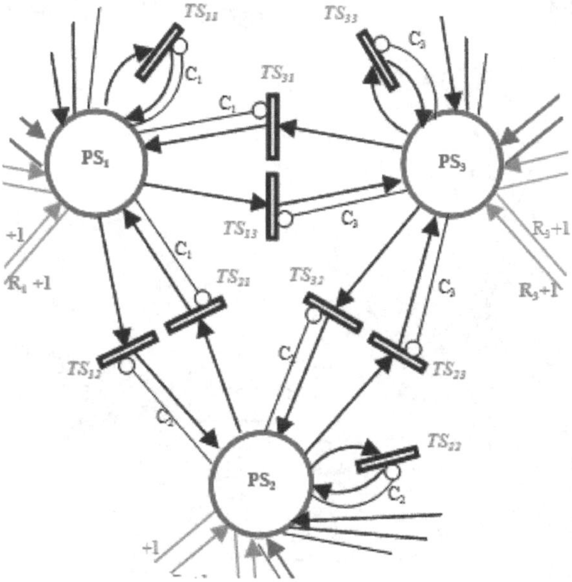

Figure 10. The "bicycle flows" subnet.

5. Performance evaluation with simulation

Real systems are large and complex and so are the Petri nets used for their modelling and analysis. As the model complexity increases, the use of analytical techniques for analysis and performance evaluation becomes harder for many real-life applications or case studies. Despite the many free software tools available for Petri nets simulation and analysis, we had to develop our specific simulation tool in order to validate and analyze the performance of the models presented in this chapter. In fact, the "marking dependent weights" concept, which is an important feature to model self-service public bicycle systems, does not exist anywhere in the existing Petri nets simulation tools.

Our simulation tool has been developed by exploiting the *BDSPN* simulator recently realized by us [17]-[6] for the simulation of *BDSPN* models developed for the modelling and performance evaluation of inventory control systems and logistic systems where we also used the "marking dependent weights" concept. The developed simulation tool provides functions for calculating some important perfomance indices of the Petri net model. These indices can then be mapped to the system's performance indices by the modeler. At the end of the simulation, some performance indices for places and transitions can be obtained. Some of them are formulated and interpreted for the performance evaluation of PBS systems as follows:

a. Average number of tokens in a place P ($M_{avr}(P)$):

$$M_{avr}(P) = \frac{\sum M(P) * \tau}{T_s} \tag{5}$$

where $M(P)$ is the number of tokens at the beginning of the cycle; T_s is the total simulation time and τ is the duration of the cycle. This performance indice can be used particulary to get the mean number of bicycles in each station S_i and in the regulation vehicle(s) by computing the average marking of the corresponding places PS_i and PR_i.

b. Mean sojourn time of tokens in a place (Savr(P)):

$$S_{avr}(P) = \frac{\sum M(P) * \tau}{N_t} \tag{6}$$

where N_t is the number of different tokens that have passed through the place until the current cycle. The value of N_t can be obtained by incrementing a counter each time an input transition fires and put tokens in the place. $M(P)$ is the number of tokens in the place P and τ is the duration of the cycle. By calculating the mean sejourn times of the places PS_i, we get important informations about the the turnover (rotation) of bicycles between the different stations of the transport network.

c. Effective firing rate of a transition T (Favr(T)):

$$F_{avr}(T) = \frac{NF(T)}{T_s} \tag{7}$$

where T_s is the total simulation time; $NF(T)$ is the number of firings of the transition. The firing rates of some transitions of the Petri net model, such as the transitions TR_i, TS_i, and TR_{ij}, measure some operations rates of the regulation function in order to quantify the dynamics of the system or some rates of specific activities.

d. Rates of empty and full places (REmpty(P); RFull(P)):

$$R_{empty\%}(P) = 100 \cdot \frac{T_s - \sum(\tau_k - \tau_{k+1})_{M(P)=0}}{T_s} \tag{8}$$

$$R_{full(\%)}(P) = 100 \cdot \frac{T_s - \sum(\tau_k - \tau_{k+1})_{M(P)=C_p}}{T_s} \tag{9}$$

where T_s is the simulation time ($T_s \rightarrow \infty$); (τ_k - τ_{k+1}) represente the the duration of the cycle where the place P is empty (resp. full) (i.e., $M(P) = 0$ resp. $M(P) = C_p$ where C_p is the capacity of the place P). The performance indices are particularly interesting to measure the rates of two uncomfortable situations that can occur in the system. That is the case of empty and full stations which have necessary to be avoided.

6. Simulation and validation of the model

Now, the relevance of the Petri net model represented in Figure 6 and described in the previous sections is demonstrated through several simulations made for different interesting configurations of the system. They are defined according to the functions to be activated (or not) in the Petri net model of the PBS system.

1. *Configuration (a).— The dynamic model with the regulation system:* In this case, we consider the general functioning of the system. That is, stations are available for users and the system is under control to rebalance bicycles between stations that are emptying out and those that are filling up. The Petri net model represented in Figure 6 reproduces this case when all of its subnets are not disabled as it is the case in the following configurations (case *b* and case *c*).
2. *Configuration (b).— The dynamic model without the regulation system*: Unlike the first case, here, we consider that the regulation system is unavailable. So, the stations remain operational for users but without any control of the bicycle flows. According to the Petri net model, this configuration is obtained when the initial marking of all the places PR_i is equal to zero. This configuration deactivates the redistribution vehicle path and the whole control function of each station.
3. *Configuration (c).— The static model:* This case represents the behavior of the system when the frequentation of the stations is very low (functioning of the system during night, for example). In terms of the Petri net model, this situation can be simulated by increasing considerably the transition firing delays of the transitions TS_{ij} which represent the displacements of bicycles between different stations. Similarly to the case B, the stations remain operational for users but without any control because (for the case *c*) of the limited bicycle flows.

6.1. Simulation of the PBS model under the configuration (a)

Let us consider the configuration (a) with the parameters given in the Table 6. The first part of the Table 6 gives the initial marking of the Petri net where we consider that initially there are 15 bicycles available in each station S_i. In the second part of the table, we read the parameters R_i and C_i of the control function of the system. It is assumed that the reorder point R_i (resp. the capacity C_i) of each station is the same and fixed to 10 (resp. 20) bicycles. Finally, the table gives the parameters of the transitions of the Petri net model. For each transition, are indicated its nature which can be an immediate transition (I); a deterministic transition (D); or an exponential transition (E); its rule policy namely continue process (C) or restart process (R); and also its firing delay given in minutes (constant firing delay for deterministic transitions; zero firing delay for immediate transitions, and mean firing delay for stochastic transitions).

Configuration Of The Initial Marking Of The Model					
$M_0(PS_1)$	$M_0(PS_2)$	$M_0(PS_3)$	$M_0(PR_1)$	$M_0(PR_2)$	$M_0(PR_3)$
15	15	15	10	0	0
$M_0(PS_1)$	$M_0(PS_2)$	$M_0(PS_3)$	$M_0(PR_1)$	$M_0(PR_2)$	$M_0(PR_3)$
0	0	0	0	0	0
Configuration Of The Parameters R_i And C_i Of The Petri Net Model					
R^1	R^2	R^3	C^1	C^2	C^3
10	10	10	20	20	20
Configuration Of The Transitions Of The Model					
TS_{11}	TS_{12}	TS_{13}	TS_{21}	TS_{22}	TS_{23}
E, C, 20	E, C, 5	E, C, 10	E, C, 5	E, C, 20	E, C, 5
TS_{31}	TS_{32}	TS_{33}	TR_1	TO_1	TS_1
E, C, 10	E, C, 5	E, C, 20	E, C, 3	I, 0	E, C, 3
TR_2	TO_2	TS_2	TR_3	TO_3	TS_3
E, C, 3	I, 0	E, C, 3	E, C, 3	I, 0	E, C, 3
TR_{12}	TR_{23}	TR_{31}	TE_1	TE_2	TE_3
E, C, 15	E, C, 15	E, C, 15	I, 0	I, 0	I, 0

Table 6. Configuration data of the Petri net model

Considering all the parameters of this configuration, evolution graphs and some performances of the system can be established thanks to our simulation tool. We focus our attention on the behavior of the time evolution of the number of available bicycles in the stations which can be observed in Figure 11. According to the control function integrated in the model, it can be observed that the number of bicycles (marking the places PS_i) in the three stations "oscillates" around the reorder point R_i (=10) and the capacity C_i (= 20) of each station is respected. Obviously, the dynamic behavior of this part of the system is similar to the one of inventory control systems [17].

As shown in Figure 12, the dynamic behavior of the redistribution vehicle can also be observed through the time evolution of the marking of the places PR_i together. For the chosen parameters of the system, we see that there are always enough bicycles in the redistribution vehicle.

6.2. Simulation of the PBS model under the configuration (b)

As defined previously, in this configuration, we consider the dynamic model without the regulation system. Here, the initial markings of all the places $M(PR_i)$ are equal to zero. That is the only modification to be made in the Table 6 to obtain this situation. Thanks to this change, the redistribution vehicle path and all of the control function of each station are not available in the Petri net model (see Figure 6). Formally, for $M(PR_i) = 0$ and $M(PC_i) = 0$, the transitions TE_i, TS_i, TO_i, TR_i (control function) and TR_{ij} (displacement of the redistribution vehicle) are never enabled for this configuration. Consequently, the stations remain operationnal for users but whitout any control.

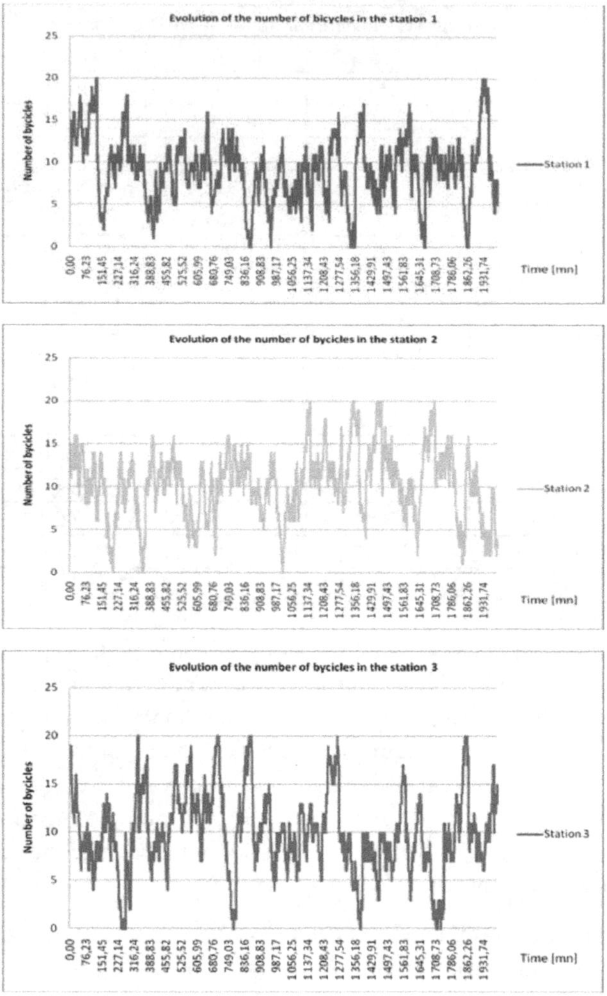

Figure 11. Evolution of the number of available bicycles in the stations (configuration a)

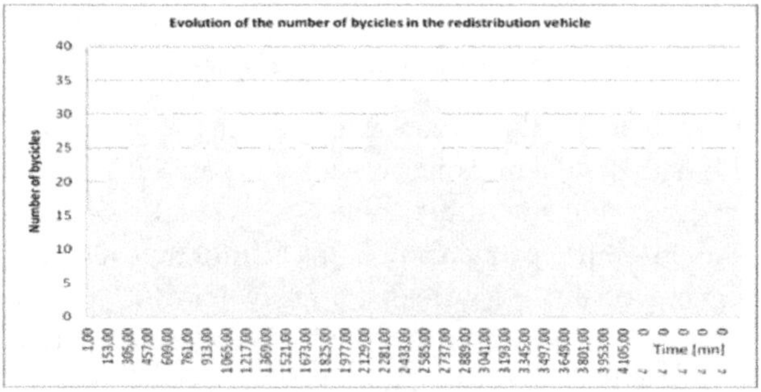

Figure 12. Evolution of the number of bicycles in the redistribution vehicle (configuration a).

Thanks to our simulator, the evolution time of the number of bicycles in the different stations is given in Figure 13. With regard to the first configuration (a), here, we see clearly the absence of the control functions of the system. It is observed that the stations are very frequently full. In contrast, empty stations are not observed in this configuration. This is only due to the parameters chosen for this case. Indeed, recall that we have 15 bicycles in each station (there are a total of 45 bicycles in the system) and the capacity of each station is fixed to 20. Thus, the minimal number of bicycles which can be found in a given station is 5 bicycles (Indeed, 45 - 20*2 (two full stations) = 5) which can be observed in the graphs.

Finally, the Table 7 gives some performances of the system for the two configurations obtained by computing the equations (5-9). The average number of available bicycles in each station is represented by the average marking of the places PS_i. For the configuration A, $M_{avr}(PS_i)$ is approximately equal to 10 which is coherent with the reorder point R_i fixed to 10 for this configuration. In contrast, for the configuration B where the system is without the regulation function, the average number of bicycles in the stations is over 15. The rates of empty and full stations are also given in the table. The rate of empty and full stations (together), $R_{F/F}(PS_i)=R_{Full}(PS_i)+R_{Empty}(PS_i)$, is estimated to 6.80% in the case of the configuration (a), and 51% in the case of the configuration (b) for each station.

Perf. evaluation of the configuration (a)		
$M_{avr}(PS_1)$	$M_{avr}(PS_2)$	$M_{avr}(PS_3)$
10,18	10,14	10,21
$R_{Empty}(PS_1)$	$R_{Empty}(PS_2)$	$R_{Empty}(PS_3)$
3.33%	3.30%	3.31%
$R_{Full}(PS_1)$	$R_{Full}(PS_1)$	$R_{Full}(PS_1)$
3.52%	3.50%	3.51%
$R_{E/F}(PS_1)$	$R_{F/E}(PS_1)$	$R_{F/E}(PS_1)$
6.85%	6.80%	6.82%
Perf. evaluation of the configuration (b)		
$M_{avr}(PS_1)$	$M_{avr}(PS_2)$	$M_{avr}(PS_3)$
15,72	15,57	15,53
$R_{Empty}(PS_1)$	$R_{Empty}(PS_2)$	$R_{Empty}(PS_3)$
0%	0%	0%
$R_{Full}(PS_1)$	$R_{Full}(PS_1)$	$R_{Full}(PS_1)$
51.0%	51.1%	50.8%
$R_{F/E}(PS_1)$	$R_{F/E}(PS_1)$	$R_{F/E}(PS_1)$
51.0%	51.1%	50.8%

Table 7. Some performances indices of the model (for the considered parameters)

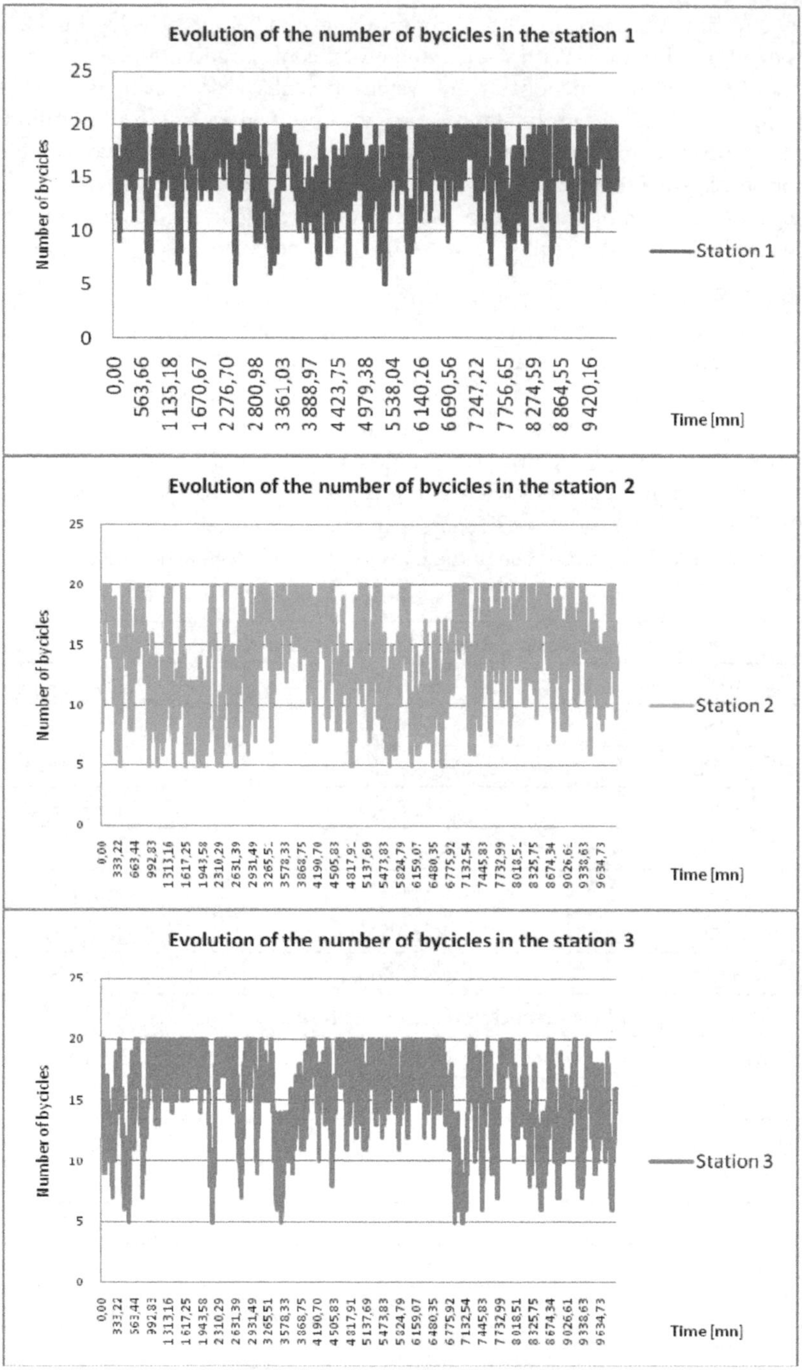

Figure 13. Evolution of the number of available bicycles in the station 3 (configuration b)

As noted previously, to obtain the configuration c, the Petri net model shown in Figure 6 must be parameterized as in the configuration b but by increasing considerably the transition firing delays of the transitions TS_{ij}. Contrary to the behavior of the system shown in Figure 13, in this situation, we obtain a static model with very low (negligible) evolution of the distribution of the bicycles in the network.

7. Conclusion

In this chapter, we have presented an original Petri net approach for public bicycle sharing systems modelling and performance evaluation for control purposes. A modular dynamic model based on Petri nets with marking dependent weights is proposed and a simulation approach is developed and used to simulate and validate models described in this chapter. Very likely, this approach is the first one in the literature dedicated to this urban transportation mode by using Petri nets. The authors believe that this new area of research has significant promise for the future to help planners and decision makers in determining how to implement, and operate successfully these complex dynamical systems. Now, we are working in the following directions: (1) Development of some natural extensions of the models including more complex modelling features such as the application of other control strategies used for the latest systems which operate with smart technologies and provide users and controllers with real-time bike availability information; (2) Development of optimization methods for optimal control purposes. For example, the objective is how to search optimal values of the decision parameters R_i, C_i of the model in order to minimize the two uncomfortable situations $M(PS_i) = 0$ (empty station) and $M(PS_i) = C_i$ (full station) that may occur in the different stations of the system.

Author details

Karim Labadi, Taha Benarbia, Samir Hamaci and A-Moumen Darcherif
EPMI, Ecole d'Electricité, de Production et Management Industriel, France

8. References

[1] Abbas-Turki A.; Bouyekhf R.; Grunder O.; El Moudni A.; (2004) "On the line planning problems of the hub public-transportation networks", *International journal of systems science,* Vol. 35, No. 12, pp. 693-706.

[2] Benarbia, T., Labadi, K., and Darcherif, M., (2011) "A Petri Net Approach for Modelling, Performance Evaluation and Control of Self-Service Public Bicycle Systems", *16th International IEEE conference on Emerging Technologies on Factory Automation,* ETFA'2011, September 5-9 2011, Toulouse, France.

[3] Borgnat, P., Abry, P., Flandrin, P., Robardet, C., Rouquier, J-B., Fleury, E., (2011), "Shared Bicycles in a City: a Signal Processing and Data Analysis Perspective", *Advances in Complex Systems,* Vol. 14, No. 3, pp. 415-438.

[4] Bouyekhf R., Abbas-Turki A., Grunder O., El Moudni A., (2003) "Modelling, performance evaluation and planning of public transport systems using generalized stochastic Petri nets", *Transport reviews*, Vol. 23, No. 1, pp.51-69.

[5] Chemla, D., Meunier, F., Wolfler-Calvo, R., "Balancing the stations of a self-service bike scharing system", *Working paper, 2011.*

[6] Chen H., Amodeo L., Chu F., and Labadi K., (2005)"Performance evaluation and optimization of supply chains modelled by Batch deterministic and stochastic Petri net", *IEEE transactions on Automation Science and Engineering*, Vol. 2, No. 2, pp. 132-144.

[7] Dell'Olio, L., Ibeas, A., Moura, J.-L, (2011) *"Implementing bike-sharing systems"*, Proceedings of the ICE-Municipal Engineer, Volume 164, Issue 2, pp. 89 –101

[8] DeMaio, P., (2003). "Smart Bicycles: Public transportation for the 21st century", *Transportation Quarterly*, Vol. 57, No.1, pp. 9–11.

[9] DeMaio, P., (2009) "Bicycle-sharing: History, Impacts, Model of Provision, and Future", *Journal of Public Transportation*, Vol. 12, No.4, pp. 41-56.

[10] Demongodin I., (2009) "Modelling and Analysis of Transportation Networks using Batches Petri Nets with controllable Batch Speed", *in Proc. 30th Int. Conf. Applications and Theory of Petri Nets, Giuliana Franceschinis, Karsten Wolf, Ed. Paris, France.*

[11] Di Febrarro, A., Giglio, D., Sacco, N., (2004) "Urban traffic control structure based on hybrid Petri nets", *IEEE Transactions on Intelligent Transportation systems*, Vol. 5, No. 4, pp. 224-237.

[12] Forma, I.; Raviv, T.; Tzur, M., (2010), "The Static Repositioning Problem in a Bike-Sharing System", *In the proceeding of the 7th Treinnial Symposium on Transportation Analysis* (TRISTAN 2010), Tromso, Norway, pp. 279-282.

[13] Froehlich, J., Neumann, J. & Oliver, N. (2009), "Sensing and Predicting the Pulse of the City through Shared Bicycling", *Proceedings of the International Workshop on Urban", Community and Social Applications of Networked Sensing Systems.*

[14] Gallego J.L., Farges J.L., Henry J.J., (1996) "Design by Petri nets of an intersection signal controller" *Transportation Research, part. C*, Vol. 4, No. 4, pp. 231–248.

[15] Júlvez J., Boel R.K., (2010) "A continuous Petri net approach for model predictive control of traffic systems" *IEEE Transactions on Systems, Man, and Cybernetics, Part A: Systems and Humans*, Vol. 40, No. 4, pp. 686 – 697.

[16] Kaltenbrunner, A., Meza, R., Grivolla, J., Condina, J. & Banchs, R. (2010), "Urban cycles and mobility patterns: Exploring and predicting trends in a bicycle-based public transport system", *Pervasive and Mobile Computing*, Vol.6, No.4, pp. 455–466.

[17] Labadi K., Chen H., Amodeo L., (2007) "Modelling and Performance Evaluation of Inventory Systems using Batch deterministic and stochastic Petri nets", *IEEE Transactions on Systems, man and Cybernetics, Part C: Applications and review*, Vol. 37, No. 6, pp. 1287-1302.

[18] Labadi, K. and Chen, H., (2010) "Modelling, analysis, and optimisation of supply chains by using Petri net models: the state-of-the-art", *Int. J. Business Performance and Supply Chain Modelling*, Vol. 2, No. ¾, pp.188-215.

[19] Labadi, K., Benarbia, T., Darcherif, M., (2010) « Sur la régulation des systèmes de vélos en libre-service : approche basée sur les réseaux de Petri (avec des arcs a poids

variables) », *8th ENIM IFAC International Conference of Modeling and Simulation,* MOSIM'10, 10 au 12 mai 2010 - Hammamet – Tunisie.

[20] Labadi, K., Benarbia, T., Darcherif, M., and Chayet, M., (2012) "Modelling and Control of Self-Service Public Bicycle Systems by Using Petri Nets", *International Journal of Modelling, Identification and Control,* Vol. x, No. x, xxxx Vol. x, No. x, 2012 (accepted, to appear)

[21] Labadi, K., Hamaci, S., Benarbia, T., (2010) "Un modèle dynamique pour la régulation des systèmes de vélos en libre-service", *ROADEF 2010, 11e Congrès annuel de la société française de Recherche Opérationnelle et d'Aide à la Décision,* 24-26 février 2010, Toulouse.

[22] Lin, J.-R., Yang, T.-H. (2011), "Strategic design of public bicycle sharing systems with service level constraints", *In Transportation Research Part E: Logistics and Transportation Review,* Vol. 47, No.2, pp. 284–294.

[23] Lin, J.-R., Yang, T-H., Chang, Y-C., (2011) "A hub location inventory model for bicycle sharing system design: Formulation and solution", *Article in Press, Computers & Industrial Engineering xxx (2011) xxx–xxx.*

[24] Lindemann C., (1998) "Performance modelling with deterministic and stochastic Petri nets", *John Wiley and Sons Edition.*

[25] List, G.F.; Cetin, M.; (2004) *"Modeling traffic signal control using Petri nets"*, IEEE Transactions on Intelligent Transportation Systems, Vol. 5, No. 3, pp. 177–187.

[26] Mukai, N., Watanabe T., (2005) "Dynamic location management for on-demand car sharing system", *KES'05 Proceedings of the 9th international conference on Knowledge-Based Intelligent Information and Engineering Systems,* Melbourne, Australia, pp. 768-774.

[27] Murata T., (1989) "Petri nets: Properties, analysis, and applications," *in Proc. of the IEEE,* Vol. 77, No. 4, pp. 541-580.

[28] Nait-Sidi-Moh A., Manier M-A., El Moudni A., (2005) "max-plus algebra Modeling for a Public Transport System", *Journal of Cybernetics and Systems, Vol. 36/2, pp.165-180.*

[29] Nait-Sidi-Moh A., Manier M-A., El Moudni A., Manier H., (2003) *"Performance Analysis of a Bus Network Based on Petri Nets and (max, +) Algebra"*, International Journal of Systems Science (ex. SAMS: Systems Analysis Modelling Simulation), Vol. 43, No 5. pp. 639-669.

[30] Raviv T., Tzur M., Forma I., (2011), *"Static Repositioning in a Bike-Sharing System: Models and Solution Approaches"*, Working paper.

[31] Shaheen, S., Guzman, S., & Zhang, H. (2010). *"Bikesharing in Europe, the Americas, and Asia: Past, Present, and Future"*, Journal of the Transportation Research Board, 2143, pp. 159–167.

[32] Silva M., Teruel E., (1997) "Petri nets for the design and operation of manufacturing systems", *European Journal of Control,* Vol. 3, No. 3, pp. 182-199.

[33] Takagi R., Goodman C.J., Roberts C., (2003) *"Modelling passenger flows at a transport interchange using Petri nets"*, Proceedings of the Institution of Mechanical Engineers, Part F: Journal of Rail and Rapid Transit, Vol. 217, No. 2, pp. 125-134.

[34] Tolba C., D. Lefebvre, Thomas P., El Moudni A., (2005) "Continuous and timed Petri nets for the macroscopic and microscopic traffic flow control", *Simulation Modelling Practice and Theory,* Vol. 13, No. 5, pp. 407-436.

[35] Tzes A., Seongho K., and McShane W. R., (1996) "Application of Petri networks to transportation network modeling" *IEEE Transactions on Vehicular Technology*, Vol. 45, pp. 391–400.

[36] Uesugi K., Mukai, N., and Watanabe T., (2007) "Optimization of Vehicle Assignment for Car Sharing System", *Lecture Notes in Computer Science, Knowledge-Based Intelligent Information and Engineering Systems*, Vol. 4693/2007, pp. 1105-1111.

[37] Vogel, P., & Mattfeld, D. (2010). *"Modeling of repositioning activities in bike-sharing systems"*. Proceedings of 12th WCTR.

[38] Vogel, P., Greisera, T., Mattfelda, D., (2011) "Understanding Bicycle-Sharing Systems using Data Mining: Exploring Activity Patterns", *Procedia Social and Behavioral Sciences*, Vol. 20, pp. 514–523.

[39] Wang Shang, Zhang Jiangman; Liu Liang, Duan Zheng-yu (2010),"Bike-Sharing-A new public transportation mode: State of the practice & prospects", *IEEE International Conference on Emergency Management and Management Sciences*, (ICEMMS 2010), pp. 222-225

[40] Zhou Mengchu and Kurapati Venkatesh., (1999) "Modeling, simulation, and control of flexible manufacturing systems: A Petri net approach", Vol. 6 of Series in Intelligent Control and Intelligent Automation, World Scientific.

[41] Zhou MengChu, and DiCesare Frank., (1993) "Petri net synthesis for discrete control of manufacturing systems", *Kluwer Academic Publishers*.

[42] Zurawski, R., and Zhou Mengchu., (1994) "Petri nets and industrial applications: A tutorial", *IEEE Transactions on Industrial Electronics*, Vol. 41, No. 6, pp. 567-583.

Permissions

The contributors of this book come from diverse backgrounds, making this book a truly international effort. This book will bring forth new frontiers with its revolutionizing research information and detailed analysis of the nascent developments around the world.

We would like to thank Pawel Pawlewski, for lending his expertise to make the book truly unique. He has played a crucial role in the development of this book. Without his invaluable contribution this book wouldn't have been possible. He has made vital efforts to compile up to date information on the varied aspects of this subject to make this book a valuable addition to the collection of many professionals and students.

This book was conceptualized with the vision of imparting up-to-date information and advanced data in this field. To ensure the same, a matchless editorial board was set up. Every individual on the board went through rigorous rounds of assessment to prove their worth. After which they invested a large part of their time researching and compiling the most relevant data for our readers. Conferences and sessions were held from time to time between the editorial board and the contributing authors to present the data in the most comprehensible form. The editorial team has worked tirelessly to provide valuable and valid information to help people across the globe.

Every chapter published in this book has been scrutinized by our experts. Their significance has been extensively debated. The topics covered herein carry significant findings which will fuel the growth of the discipline. They may even be implemented as practical applications or may be referred to as a beginning point for another development. Chapters in this book were first published by InTech; hereby published with permission under the Creative Commons Attribution License or equivalent.

The editorial board has been involved in producing this book since its inception. They have spent rigorous hours researching and exploring the diverse topics which have resulted in the successful publishing of this book. They have passed on their knowledge of decades through this book. To expedite this challenging task, the publisher supported the team at every step. A small team of assistant editors was also appointed to further simplify the editing procedure and attain best results for the readers.

Our editorial team has been hand-picked from every corner of the world. Their multi-ethnicity adds dynamic inputs to the discussions which result in innovative outcomes. These outcomes are then further discussed with the researchers and contributors who give their valuable feedback and opinion regarding the same. The feedback is then collaborated with the researches and they are edited in a comprehensive manner to aid the understanding of the subject.

Apart from the editorial board, the designing team has also invested a significant amount of their time in understanding the subject and creating the most relevant covers. They scrutinized every image to scout for the most suitable representation of the subject and create an appropriate cover for the book.

The publishing team has been involved in this book since its early stages. They were actively engaged in every process, be it collecting the data, connecting with the contributors or procuring relevant information. The team has been an ardent support to the editorial, designing and production team. Their endless efforts to recruit the best for this project, has resulted in the accomplishment of this book. They are a veteran in the field of academics and their pool of knowledge is as vast as their experience in printing. Their expertise and guidance has proved useful at every step. Their uncompromising quality standards have made this book an exceptional effort. Their encouragement from time to time has been an inspiration for everyone.

The publisher and the editorial board hope that this book will prove to be a valuable piece of knowledge for researchers, students, practitioners and scholars across the globe.

List of Contributors

Ivo Martiník
VŠB-Technical University of Ostrava, Czech Republic

Razib Hayat Khan and Poul E. Heegaard
Norwegian University of Science & Technology, Trondheim, Norway

Kazi Wali Ullah
Aalto University, Helsinki, Finland

Pece Mitrevski and Zoran Kotevski
Faculty of Technical Sciences, University of St. Clement Ohridski, Bitola, Republic of Macedonia

Hussein Karam Hussein Abd El-Sattar
Ain Shams University, Faculty of Science, Mathematics & Computer Science Dept., Abbassia, Cairo, Egypt
Al-Yamamah University, CCIS, Riyadh, KSA

Wlodek M. Zuberek
Memorial University, St.John's, Canada,
University of Life Sciences, Warsaw, Poland

G. Mavlankulov, M. Othman, S. Turaev and M.H. Selamat
Faculty of Computer Science and Information Technology, Universiti Putra Malaysia, UPM Serdang, Selangor, Malaysia

J. Dassow and R. Stiebe
Fakultät für Informatik, Otto-von-Guericke-Universität Magdeburg, Magdeburg, Germany

Gustavo Callou, Paulo Maciel, Julian Araújo, João Ferreira and Rafael Souza
Informatics Center, Federal University of Pernambuco - Recife, Brazil

Dietmar Tutsch
Automation/Computer Science, University of Wuppertal, Wuppertal, Germany

José Reinaldo and Silva
University of São Paulo, Mechatronics Department, Escola Politécnica, São Paulo, Brazil

Pedro M. G. and del Foyo
Federal University of Pernambuco, Department of Mechanical Engineering, Recife, Brazil

Sangita Kansal, Mukti Acharya and Gajendra Pratap Singh
Department of Applied Mathematics, Delhi Technological University, Shahbad Daulatpur, Main Bawana Road, Delhi-110042, India

Gi Bum Lee
Research Institute of Industrial Science & Technology, Pohang, Korea

Han Zandong
Tsinghua University, Beijing, P.R. China

Jin S. Lee
Pohang University of Science and Technology, Pohang, Korea

Samir Hamaci, Karim Labadi and A. Moumen Darcherif
EPMI, 13 Boulvard de l'Hautil, 95092, Cergy-Pontoise, France

Parisa Heidari and Hanifa Boucheneb
École Polytechnique de Montréal, Canada

Karim Labadi, Taha Benarbia, Samir Hamaci and A-Moumen Darcherif
EPMI, Ecole d'Electricité, de Production et Management Industriel, France

Printed in the USA
CPSIA information can be obtained
at www.ICGtesting.com
JSHW011503221024
72173JS00005B/1190

9 781632 402288